THE MACKENZIE KING RECORD

Volume 2

The Rt. Hon. W. L. Mackenzie King signs the
charter of the United Nations at San Francisco, June 26, 1945
Photograph by Nick Morant

THE

MACKENZIE KING

RECORD

VOLUME 2
1944-1945

J. W. Pickersgill
and
D. F. Forster

UNIVERSITY OF TORONTO PRESS

© University of Toronto Press 1968
Printed in Canada

SBN 8020 1525 5

To

L. B. PEARSON

prospective successor

and

the late NORMAN ROBERTSON

trusted counsellor

Preface

AS IS INDICATED in the Preface to Volume 1 of the Mackenzie King Record, this book is not a biography, though it is an integral part of the biographical project undertaken by the Literary Executors of the late W. L. Mackenzie King, shortly after his death in 1950.

Eight years have passed since the first volume of the Mackenzie King Record appeared, and while readers are advised to read the Preface to Volume 1, I make no apology for repeating in this Preface, for those who do not have the first volume, some of the statements made there.

The original objective of the Literary Executors was to have an official biography written by a single author. The late Professor R. MacGregor Dawson was chosen and he completed a first volume which brought Mackenzie King's life up to 1923 and which, regrettably, was not published until just after his death in 1958. After Professor Dawson's death, Professor Blair Neatby, then of the University of British Columbia and now of Carleton University, undertook to continue the official biography up to the beginning of the Second World War. When Professor Neatby first undertook that task, he expected to produce only one volume. He found, however, that it was difficult to condense the material and he decided, with the approval of the Literary Executors and the University of Toronto Press, to divide the period, concluding his first volume with 1932. That volume appeared in 1963. He is now engaged on his second volume, the third of the official biography, which will bring the life of Mackenzie King up to the beginning of the War.

My own association with the biographical project arose early in 1958, several months after I had ceased to be a member of the St. Laurent government, at a time when I found that my duties as a Member of Parliament in Opposition did not occupy my full time and that I must find some means of supplementing my income. My fellow Literary Executors were good enough to concur in my suggestion that I should prepare a rough narrative from Mackenzie King's wartime and postwar diaries as a basis for MacGregor Dawson's biography. I had not got very far before Dawson's death. By then, it was already becoming clear to me that so much had happened in the war and postwar years that a narrative of the war and postwar years could be compressed into one volume only by condensation on such a scale that the result would have been very unsatisfying. Equally unsatisfactory would be the selection of a few highlights to the exclusion of other events which, while less dramatic, were equally important.

The Literary Executors agreed that I should complete my narrative as a finished work, and that it should serve in place of an official biography from the outbreak of war to Mackenzie King's death. I told the Literary Executors I would prefer to do two volumes instead of one. They concurred in that suggestion. As the work proceeded I realized, more and more, that Mackenzie King's own unrevised record of events would have far greater interest to the public and far greater historical validity than anything I could write, and that I should let him tell the story, adding only what continuity was necessary to make the context clear. Insensibly, as I indicated in the Preface to Volume 1, the character of the book changed and I found myself presenting Mackenzie King's own record of events.

Mackenzie King's diary was kept largely to serve as a record from which he could recount and explain his conduct of public affairs and he had indicated to the Literary Executors that it was to be used for this purpose. In Volume 1, I sought to let his own words recount and explain his conduct and his view of the events of the period from September 1939 to May 1944. It was my hope then, and it is still my hope, that some day it may be possible to publish, in several volumes, the consecutive day-to-day record of those momentous years. Meanwhile, I tried in Volume 1 to select what seemed to Mackenzie King most important and, as far as possible, to preserve his own sense of relative importance. But that task was not easy. The whole record was so voluminous and most of it so interesting that the selection of extracts became a major problem. I set certain standards for myself. The first was that my purpose was to present Mackenzie King's public life, not his private life, and the references to his private life were therefore confined to extracts from the diaries which seemed to have an essential bearing on his public life.

The second was that I was seeking to present Mackenzie King, not to write the history of his times or to present the views of his contemporaries. The diaries for the wartime and postwar period were dictated and typewritten and rarely revised. For that reason, in quoting them, I did not hesitate to correct obvious mistakes in names and in spelling and even in sense, where it was perfectly clear that what was dictated by Mackenzie King had not been correctly transcribed. The relatively rare extracts from the handwritten diary were not changed. Omissions from sentences and paragraphs were indicated by ellipses. Apart from rare cases where references of a character which precluded publication because the persons concerned were still living or because Mackenzie King himself would not have wished them to be published, the omissions consisted of irrelevancies, repetitions or trivia and were made almost entirely to save precious space.

Mackenzie King himself referred to his diaries as the "record." Hence the title of this book.

After the publication of Volume 1 in 1960, I began the selection from the diaries of the extracts which I felt should be considered for publication in what I planned would be a second volume. I had virtually completed this task and had arranged the selected material in a rough first draft to which I had added very little in the way of continuity, at the time the government changed and I became once more a Minister of the Crown in April 1963. I soon discovered that I would have no further time to devote to the revision and completion of Volume 2 of the Mackenzie King Record.

Late in 1963, I approached Professor D. F. Forster of the University of Toronto and asked him if he would be willing to collaborate with me in completing the second volume. I told him I had extracted from the diaries all the material that was needed, but that it had been arranged only in a very rough fashion and would need a great deal of editing and paraphrasing to avoid unnecessary repetition, as well as the preparation of a continuity of the narrative. He was good enough to agree to undertake this task on the understanding, of course, that when he had completed his revised draft, I would have a final look at it in order to make sure that I concurred fully in the publication of the extracts ultimately selected and was satisfied with the continuity.

For a variety of reasons Professor Forster, because of his many preoccupations at the University of Toronto and elsewhere, has taken a good deal longer to complete his share of the task than he had originally expected to. Like me, and like Professor Neatby, he found the volume of material so great and of such great interest that, with the concurrence of the University of Toronto Press and the Literary Executors, he decided it would be preferable to bring out two more volumes instead of one. The present volume therefore will carry the record from Mackenzie King's return to Canada from the Conference of Commonwealth Prime Ministers in London in May of 1944 to the close of the war with Japan, and the third volume will deal with the period from the end of the war with Japan to the close of Mackenzie King's life.

In order, as I indicated in the Preface to Volume 1, to avoid as far as possible the irritation of footnotes, all the quotations in the text, unless otherwise specified, are from the diaries. In referring to other persons, the same practice is followed in Volume 2 as was followed in Volume 1 of abandoning the conventional distinctions between the living and the dead, and omitting Mr. and other titles, except where they may be needed for identification, though in the quotations the actual form used by Mackenzie King in the diary is retained.

In the Preface to Volume 1, I said something about my own connection with Mackenzie King which does not need to be repeated in detail in this Preface. At the time this volume begins, I had been in the Prime Minister's office for something more than six years. From the beginning of the war, I had had a relatively close and frequent association with Mackenzie King personally. It is no exaggeration to say that there were very few prepared speeches or statements made by him in Parliament or elsewhere in public in which I did not have some part. In the preparation of speeches, correspondence, and memoranda and in their subsequent revision with him, I gradually developed a familiarity with his attitude, with his modes of expression, and with what might be expected to be his reaction to various situations. From the first Conscription Crisis of 1942 onward, our association was much closer than it was before that year. I should, however, emphasize, as was done in Volume 1, that I was not Mackenzie King's principal adviser at any time during the war, and that I was not the head of the Prime Minister's office until just after the election of 1945. However, I think it is fair to say that my personal knowledge of the events recorded in Volume 2 is greater than it was of those recorded in Volume 1.

As the person who selected the material to be included, and as a co-author, I take full responsibility for everything included in this volume but I am indebted to my fellow Literary Executors, and especially to Dr. W. Kaye Lamb, the head of the Public Archives of Canada, for advice and assistance, as I was for Volume 1.

In concluding this Preface, I should like to renew my expression of gratitude for the understanding help of the University of Toronto Press, and particularly of Miss Francess Halpenny.

I wish also to express my gratitude to Miss Florence Moore, Miss Shirley Tink, and my wife for the hours they spent typewriting the first draft of this volume. My wife has also shared, to some degree, in the final revision and checking, as has my secretary, Miss Audrey McQuarrie.

Finally, I should like to say how happy I have been with the collaboration of Professor Forster who is, in the true sense of the word, a co-author of this volume. In a way, what I did was to assemble the building materials and to draw the rough plans for the structure. Out of these raw materials and rough plans he has fashioned a structure with shape and form. In doing so, he has retained to a greater degree than I did in Volume 1 the actual words of Mackenzie King himself. I believe this is a sound decision. In the intervening eight years since Volume 1 appeared, many things recorded by Mackenzie King can now be published which could not have been published eight years ago without causing embarrassment to many persons still living and some still active in public affairs. Time has added these records to history. Three chapters of the ten in Volume 2 deal with the Conscription Crisis of 1944. The late MacGregor Dawson, before his death, had completed his own chapters on this crisis which were published posthumously by the University of Toronto Press in 1961, with the approval of the Literary Executors. For that reason, Professor Forster has allowed Mackenzie King's own record, with a bare minimum of continuity, to tell the story of that crisis. The two accounts are complementary and serious students will wish to read both. The continuity in other chapters, provided by Professor Forster, is obviously more objective than mine could have been and for that all students will be grateful.

J.W.P.

Ottawa, March 1968

I can add little to the comments made by Mr. Pickersgill but I can repeat his appreciation of the assistance rendered by the University of Toronto Press and its Managing Editor. My association with the senior author of this volume and with the Literary Executors has been a pleasant and productive experience and I am grateful for my colleague's courtesy, kindness, and, above all, his forebearance. At the University of Toronto, both Claude Bissell and John Sword tolerated and understood occasional excursions into the intricacies of Canadian politics in the mid 1940's.

On behalf of my colleague, myself, and our publisher, I should like to express appreciation to H. V. Nelles for the Index.

D.F.F.

Toronto, March 1968

Contents

Illustrations

THE MACKENZIE KING RECORD

Volume 2

CHAPTER ONE

Introduction

THIS VOLUME is a record made largely by Mackenzie King himself of his leadership of the Government of Canada from the end of May, 1944, until the end of the war against Japan at the beginning of September, 1945.

Volume 1 ended with Mackenzie King's return, in triumph, from his visit to Britain for the meeting of Commonwealth Prime Ministers in May of 1944. At that moment, Mackenzie King, then in his seventieth year, had reached the very peak of his career. The great problems of the war had been met. Preparations for the post-war period were well in hand and there seemed to be smooth sailing ahead. Despite the strain of nearly five years of war, Mackenzie King was still in excellent health and there seemed to have been no deterioration of his mental or physical powers. This was in part because he had, except when there was an occasional crisis, taken great care not to become over-tired. He continued to get at least a little exercise nearly every day and to take a good deal of rest. During the war he spent even more time than he had before the war on the record, the diaries, which he had kept throughout the greater part of his life. As was indicated in the Introduction to Volume 1, these diaries are an amazing combination of intimate, personal details with the most careful and painstakingly accurate reporting of the events in which he had a part.

Even more than was the case before the war, Mackenzie King found most of his recreation in his work at which he continued to be almost as unsystematic as he was in the earlier years. The increasing demands of war, of course, forced him to spend even more time at his desk, dealing with the problems which came up from day to day.

Throughout the war, his passion for detail and accuracy continued to be as great as ever and his fear of making even the most minor error of fact or of form grew greater as he grew older. The result was that everything he wrote or had written for publication was revised and re-revised. Most of his speeches were delivered before he had completed their revision to his satisfaction. As was pointed out in the Introduction to

Volume 1, speeches and public statements were almost never completed on time, deadlines were constantly being missed, and publicity sacrificed in his quest for the perfection never in his eyes quite attained.

Even more than before the war, his diaries are filled with references to the lack of time to complete the record. During the war, as before the war, Mackenzie King spent most of his working time in the Library at Laurier House or, when circumstances would permit it, in the farm house at Kingsmere.

It is true, of course, that he had to spend more time in his offices because there were more frequent and more crucial meetings. He also spent a good deal of time in the House of Commons, though increasingly he shrank from attending the evening sessions unless some urgent question requiring his own personal attention was under consideration. Outside meetings of the Cabinet and the War Committee, most of his work came to him in the form of memoranda or letters to which he gave written replies. Communications and draft speeches and statements, together with a vast quantity of private correspondence and an increasing number of despatches regarding the war, reached a volume that made it more difficult than ever for him to cope with it from day to day. Throughout the latter years of the war, and the years that followed, he developed the practice of having clean-up sessions in the Library at Laurier House nearly every Saturday afternoon, though sometimes, if the weather was good, particularly in the summer time, these sessions were held at Kingsmere.

But there always remained a back-log which, as indicated in the Introduction to Volume 1, at once oppressed Mackenzie King and unconsciously provided him with an excuse for putting off the beginning of urgent tasks, particularly the preparation of speeches which he always found distasteful to begin, though once a beginning had been made, he often became, particularly during the latter years of the war, increasingly absorbed in their preparation.

He continued, during the period covered in this volume, to feel that he had never been able to find adequate staff to relieve him of routine work, though the truth was, of course, that nothing was routine which was done in his name and even the most unimportant letters and messages were given meticulous care, even at the very height of the war. Because he spent so much of his time and did so much of his work at home, the secretaries at Laurier House continued to have a place of critical importance in his life and in his work. The key figure in Mackenzie King's personal secretarial staff, throughout the war and afterwards, was J. E.

Handy. The other members of the staff at Laurier House changed from time to time but basically the same group of devoted women, Miss Zavitske, Miss Moore, and Miss Conniffe, remained at the core of this staff. He continued to have the aid of James Gibson, now President of Brock University at St. Catharines, who had been seconded from External Affairs to the Prime Minister's office and who served at Laurier House throughout this period.

During the period covered by Volume 2, the Under-Secretary of State for External Affairs, Norman Robertson, remained Mackenzie King's closest adviser, though Norman Robertson never quite took the place of his predecessor, O. D. Skelton, in the domestic field, nor did he exercise any degree of supervision over the Prime Minister's office or the Privy Council Office.

From the time Arnold Heeney became Clerk of the Privy Council and Secretary to the Cabinet, just before the 1940 election, there was a steady improvement in the efficiency of that office, and in the quality and the comprehensiveness of the work done there. Shortly after Mackenzie King returned from England in May of 1944, Major General Maurice Pope, who had been in the Canadian Military Mission in Washington, returned to Ottawa to become associated with the Privy Council Office as the Prime Minister's Military Adviser and Military Secretary of the War Committee of the Cabinet. Pope was invaluable as an adviser during the very critical period of the reinforcement crisis which began quite soon after he took up his post.

In the Prime Minister's office there was little change in the senior staff. Walter Turnbull continued as the principal secretary to the Prime Minister, chief executive in the Prime Minister's office, and the chief contact between the Prime Minister and Members of Parliament and the public. J. W. Pickersgill continued to perform the function of number two in the Prime Minister's office. Pickersgill was primarily concerned with policy questions, with following the deliberations of Parliament, with the supervision of official correspondence, and, above all, with the preparation of public statements and speeches. He was, during the reinforcement crisis, almost constantly occupied in dealing with the documentation prepared for the Prime Minister in connection with that crisis.

One other person should be particularly mentioned in connection with the Prime Minister's staff and his work. That person was Brooke Claxton, M.P., who had become Mackenzie King's Parliamentary Assistant in May 1943. From the time the National Liberal Federation was revived in September of 1943, Brooke Claxton became more and more the link between Mackenzie King and the political organization of the Liberal party. Above all, he had a growing concern and a growing responsibility for the development of the post-war programme forecast by the Liberal Federation and set out in detail in the Speech from the Throne which opened the Session of 1944.

The Session of Parliament, of course, was still continuing when Mackenzie King returned from London and continued well into August. It was as productive of as much important legislation as any Session in the history of the Canadian Parliament up to that time, but the legislation was mainly concerned not with the war but with the preparations for the post-war period.

In nearly five years of war the Cabinet had changed a good deal in its composition. At the middle of 1944, the most prominent members of the government were Ralston, the Minister of National Defence; Power, the Associate Minister of National Defence and Minister of National Defence for Air; Ilsley, the Minister of Finance; Howe, the Minister of Munitions and Supply; and St. Laurent, the Minister of Justice. A full list of the Cabinet and of Cabinet changes will be found as an Appendix to this volume. Though they did not have quite the same prestige as the Ministers already mentioned, there were certain other of Mackenzie King's colleagues who were very influential with him personally. The long association with his only contemporary, T. A. Crerar, gave him a special place, though the relations between them became strained when the reinforcement crisis developed.

After the death of Senator Dandurand, he had been replaced as Government Leader in the Senate by Dr. James H. King, who had been a Minister from British Columbia in the Mackenzie King government in the twenties and had retired to the Senate in 1930. Dr. King, because of his long association with Mackenzie King, because they belonged to the same generation, because he had no administrative responsibilities and no personal ambitions, was often looked to by Mackenzie King for disinterested advice.

Ian Mackenzie continued to have an intimate, personal relationship with the Prime Minister, notwithstanding Mackenzie King's feeling that he was not capable of discharging any very heavy responsibilities.

The Minister of Agriculture, J. G. Gardiner, remained, as always, a force in the Cabinet, but the relations between him and Mackenzie King were never particularly close.

Norman McLarty, who had been Minister of Labour in the early stages of the war and who had been replaced by Humphrey Mitchell, had certain responsibilities in the field of political organization and in the organization of official functions of one kind and another and, though his prestige was not great, his personal relations with Mackenzie King were friendly. The same was true of J. A. MacKinnon, the Minister of Trade and Commerce.

Angus Macdonald, the former Premier of Nova Scotia, who was Minister of National Defence for Naval Services and who had entered the government almost a favourite of the Prime Minister, had become in many ways the Minister with whom Mackenzie King felt the least sympathy, and there was to develop between them in the next few months a growing antagonism.

Humphrey Mitchell, the Minister of Labour, was a man for whom Mackenzie King had a good deal of affection but, because of his portfolio, which Mackenzie King never lost the feeling he could administer himself better than anyone else, and because of Mackenzie King's feeling that Mitchell did not really enjoy the confidence of organized labour, he had less influence than he otherwise might have had.

The other members of the government had, relatively speaking, a great deal less influence and much less close personal relations with Mackenzie King.

The Prime Minister had returned from England with the conviction that success in the war in Europe was absolutely assured, and this feeling was greatly strengthened after D-Day by the speed and success of the advance of the Allied troops through France, the success of the campaign in Italy, and the growing successes of the Soviet forces in eastern Europe.

He shared the general view that the Canadian forces were adequate to fill any role required of them, both in the immediate campaign in Europe and in the war with Japan, where the Canadian role was expected to be a relatively minor one. This conviction about the Canadian part in the war with Japan was strengthened at the second Quebec Conference. The two Allied leaders with whom Mackenzie King had developed steadily closer relations, Roosevelt and Churchill, were still in control of their governments. It was clear, however, that the strain of war was beginning to tell on them, particularly on Roosevelt, much more than it seemed to on Mackenzie King. During his visit to England, the Prime Minister had had meetings with Eisenhower and Montgomery, and a visit to the headquarters of General Crerar who had succeeded General McNaughton as Commander of the Canadian Army. These meetings and discussions had greatly reassured him about the prospective invasion, even though he continued to have some concern about the division of the Canadian

Army between the Corps in Italy and the Corps which was to invade France, misgivings which had in part developed at the time of the retirement of General McNaughton as commander of the Canadian Army at the end of 1943.

In the summer of 1944, McNaughton was still on leave and the question of his future employment was one of the unresolved questions which was to give Mackenzie King and Ralston a good deal of concern in the next few months.

One of the latent problems that many realized might arise, once the invasion took place, was the question of what should be done about the 60,000 men who had been conscripted under the National Resources Mobilization Act for service in Canada, and who had not volunteered for service overseas. Apart altogether from any question as to whether they would really be needed to reinforce the Army, there was a good deal of feeling in Canada that these highly trained soldiers were no longer needed for the local defence of Canada and that they should either be disbanded or used for some useful military purpose. In fact, there was a steady stream, though a stream growing steadily smaller, of volunteers from these N.R.M.A. troops, but their existence did constitute a potential political problem which, before many months passed, was to create the greatest crisis Mackenzie King faced in his whole political career. The fact that the army in Canada also contained some 120,000 troops enlisted for General Service anywhere gave rise to much misunderstanding and controversy when the reinforcement crisis came.

When General McNaughton had retired as commander of the Army, he had been succeeded on a temporary basis by General Stuart, who had been Chief of the General Staff. Later when General Crerar became commander of the Army, General Stuart became Chief of Staff at Canadian Military Headquarters in London and General Murchie succeeded Stuart as Chief of the General Staff in Ottawa. These officers were the leading military figures in the reinforcement crisis.

The situation in Parliament in May 1944 was the same as it had been since the time of the Conservative Convention in 1942. John Bracken, who had been elected leader of the Conservative party and who had insisted that its name be changed to Progressive Conservative, had made no attempt to find a seat in Parliament and was concentrating largely on organizing the party in the country for an election which many felt might come before the end of 1944 and which would certainly come as soon as the war in Europe was over.

Gordon Graydon, who had been chosen as Leader of the Opposition by

Bracken in 1942, still occupied that position and he continued to maintain very close and friendly relations with Mackenzie King.

R. B. Hanson, who had served as Leader of the Opposition in the early years of the war and who was less friendly to Mackenzie King, was still prominent in the Conservative Opposition in Parliament.

There was a development beginning in the Conservative party, which Mackenzie King found very distasteful, and that was the retirement from posts in the public service of a few prominent Conservatives, particularly Mr. Justice McTague and Henry Borden who associated themselves very quickly with the political organization of the Conservative party. There was also a growing hostility developing between George Drew, the Conservative Premier of Ontario, and the federal government.

The other two parties, the C.C.F. and Social Credit, continued to be led by M. J. Coldwell and John Blackmore respectively.

The Parliamentary strength of the C.C.F. was somewhat weakened by the withdrawal of T. C. Douglas to lead the C.C.F. party in Saskatchewan, where shortly after the middle of the year 1944 his party won a political victory and he became Premier.

In Parliament there was, speaking generally, a good deal less concern with the prosecution of the war than with the legislation looking to the post-war period. The great controversies about the war which had characterized previous sessions were largely absent during the regular Session of 1944. Indeed, the questions of reconstruction, of demobilization, of the re-settlement and re-employment of the veterans, and of the development of social welfare were the great concerns of the parliamentary Session.

In summary, it might fairly be said that, until mid-summer 1944 had passed, there was little feeling in Canada that any further crisis would develop over the prosecution of the war and an almost universal preoccupation with the prospects for the post-war period.

Apart from a few British Columbians, there was little interest in Canada in the prosecution of the war against Japan and a widespread feeling that the Canadian part in this war would be a very small one indeed. One of the most striking differences, of course, between the attitude in Canada and in the United States was that, from the beginning, the war in the Pacific seemed to be the prime concern of the Americans, whereas the Canadians were preoccupied almost exclusively with the war in Europe.

THE MACKENZIE KING MINISTRY, MAY 1944

Prime Minister, President of the Privy Council and Secretary of State for External Affairs	W. L. Mackenzie King
Minister of Mines and Resources	T. A. Crerar
Minister without Portfolio and Leader of the Government in the Senate	J. H. King
Minister of National Defence	J. L. Ralston
Minister of Pensions and National Health	Ian A. Mackenzie
Minister of National Defence for Air and Associate Minister of National Defence	Charles G. Power
Minister of Finance and Receiver General	J. L. Ilsley
Minister of Transport	J. E. Michaud
Minister of Munitions and Supply	C. D. Howe
Minister of Agriculture	James G. Gardiner
Secretary of State of Canada	Norman A. McLarty
Minister of Trade and Commerce	James A. MacKinnon
Postmaster General	W. P. Mulock
Minister of National Revenue	Colin W. G. Gibson
Minister of National Defence for Naval Services	Angus L. Macdonald
Minister of Justice and Attorney General	Louis S. St. Laurent
Minister of Labour	Humphrey Mitchell
Minister of Public Works	Alphonse Fournier
Minister of Fisheries	Ernest Bertrand
Minister of National War Services	L. R. La Flèche

CHAPTER TWO

A Domestic Interlude

WHEN MACKENZIE KING returned from London and the meeting of Commonwealth prime ministers on May 21, he no longer doubted that victory in Europe would come late in 1944 or early in 1945. Reviews of the military situation during the Conference had been optimistic and encouraging. In Ottawa there were two immediate preoccupations, one to conclude the work of the session which had begun on January 27, and the second to get the Liberal party organized to face an election as soon as victory was won in Europe. The Canadian government had no real share in the strategic direction of the war and its main concern was merely to maintain the nation's war effort to the end of hostilities. No one in May 1944 even suspected that the task of maintaining this effort would, within six months, create the gravest political crisis of the war.

On the day after Mackenzie King returned to Ottawa, the first message he received was from Gordon Graydon, the Progressive Conservative house leader, "who rang up to say that he was sorry not to have been at the airport last night but had made arrangements to see his own leader Bracken and one or two others with him. He extended very warm good wishes and mentioned that he intended to extend a welcome in the House this afternoon. He was in every way most friendly. Also said he would seek to have my wishes met in regard to the time of taking up External Affairs estimates."

That afternoon, when the Prime Minister entered the House, "the Members generally began to applaud quite vigorously. Graydon crossed the floor to extend a welcome. We shook hands at my desk. When he returned to his seat he immediately extended a welcome very solicitously expressed. I noticed, however, he was careful to have it appear that all that took place in Britain was intended for Canada and in no way personal. In that respect, Coldwell was more generous in bringing in a personal note, also Blackmore. The remarks of the three leaders were loudly applauded. I was given a real ovation in getting up to reply. I did not have any notes in my hand, just a typed extract from Churchill's speech, at the conclusion of the Conference, which I brought with me to read as a message from him epitomizing the significance of the Conference [see vol. 1, pp. 672–3]. I found it easy to speak, though feeling somewhat tired, and with that subconscious feeling that there is always a critical attitude on the opposite side lest one speak too long. Hanson came in while I was speaking. He always brings that sort of feeling with him. However, the House was as one in its welcome and, indeed, I can think of no triumph in my whole political career that could have been greater than that of having succeeded in winning the unanimous approval of the House of Commons, not only to what I said, on speaking on behalf of Canada in Britain, but with reference to the entire mission abroad. To have represented Canada to the satisfaction of Members of all Parties and the people as a whole at a time such as this is something for which, in my heart, I cannot be too grateful to God. I concluded my address with words, which had also come to me in the course of the morning, that I was never more proud to be a Canadian —never more proud to be a citizen of the British Commonwealth, both of which statements are wholly true. Both Crerar and Ralston, who were on either side of me, commented on what I had said in eulogistic terms."

The next day Mackenzie King again recorded his delight at the universal approval of his speech to the two Houses of Parliament in London, convinced that it had increased his prestige in the country and the prospects for victory in the next election.

On May 25, the Prime Minister attended the party caucus and greeted the members at the door as they came in. "I doubt," he wrote, "if any man has ever received a greater welcome than I received from all who were present. They stood and cheered and cheered and later began a series of speeches, the tributes of which could not have been more generous or more sincere. . . . I then gave Caucus outstanding impressions gained in England. Gave a little outline of proceedings at the Conference and of some of the impressions gained in England. Spoke of how impressed I was by the seriousness of the war, of the terrible cost in human lives that it would involve and the assurance that those highest up were certain of ultimate victory, but that the best estimate was that the war might last until November or that it might go on for another year or two. I spoke of the terrific risks involved in invasion, etc. I then spoke along the lines I did in the House [at Westminster], about Britain's significance as the keeper of the gates of freedom. Of what would have become of our country if the Dominions had not assisted Britain and of the necessity of ending all talk of isolation, of the need for keeping closely associated with Britain and other nations of the Commonwealth and of furthering a new world order by good-will, etc. I spoke of the terrible period which would follow the war, and of a war worse than all we had known coming within another generation, unless we succeeded in getting many forces of evil destroyed and good-will established between nations, etc.

"I, of course, told the Members that I was presenting their point of view and that as we held our views so strongly in common I was able to find it easy to give them expression. . . . Member after Member spoke after I concluded. They were representatives of every province, each in turn spoke spontaneously, then Crerar, Ralston and St. Laurent all emphasized how the feeling toward myself was more favourable throughout the country than it had ever been. They said that the Party's stock had gone up 100%. That I had no conception of the impression the speech had made, etc. That my leadership had proven itself correct on all occasions, even where others had differed. That I must have had great courage to speak as I did, etc., and even political opponents were loud in their praise. Ralston in speaking said he regretted I had not a wife to share the joys of hearing what others were saying. When I closed I made a reference to the fact that in coming home I had not felt any sense of loneliness. It had been a joy to me to see the faces of the men with whom I had been associated so long and that I believed in the survival of human personality. I felt that my parents, to whom so largely I owed whatever of good there was in me, were sharing with me the rejoicing and the home-coming.

"A reference had been made to the reception I had received in the House of Commons. There never has been anything equal to it. I said that while that reception was on, my thoughts were of my grandfather's struggle for responsible government, of his going to England at his own expense to try and get reforms, of his period of exile, of my mother being born in exile and also debating whether they had food or whether her life was worth saving, as they had so little in the way of food wherewith to supply the needs of the children. I drew the inference that there was an eternal justice which helped to work out things in the long run, one generation reaped what another sowed, etc. As a matter of fact, the tributes paid were so from the heart, and my own feelings so intense that I more or less made a confession of my inner convictions and belief to a degree I have never done in public before. I felt it was a chance to say something to the men which they would remember."

At the War Committee on May 24, Mackenzie King had given a report on the war situation based on his experiences in the United Kingdom, and some revisions were made in a directive Ralston had prepared to send to General Crerar outlining his authority regarding the disposition of Canadian troops. During a talk with General Montgomery on May 18 [see vol. 1, pp. 691–2], Mackenzie King had agreed that, when battlefield conditions warranted it, Canadian units could be dispersed and placed under

British command. The directive was drafted "taking care to see that nothing was inserted which would make it appear that national reasons used in the sense of government pressure should be allowed to limit in any way Montgomery's power to see that nothing should be allowed to interfere with the highest military needs. In other words, the winning of the battle and the saving of life were to be supreme considerations and Montgomery to be the judge of this where any question might arise as to whether a certain action was to be taken in the way of keeping Canadian forces together rather than dispersed with others as a military necessity. The direction made plain that the wish of the Government was to keep our forces as much together as one as possible."

During the session there had been a good deal of discussion about the government's position on old age pensions, a subject J. L. Ilsley, the Minister of Finance, raised with the Prime Minister after the meeting of the War Committee on May 24. The issue, Mackenzie King reported, was "whether the provinces should be encouraged to have them granted at the age of 65 or whether to stand firm on not lowering the age unless a contributory system was brought into being. Cabinet is much divided. It is a very difficult question to decide. I shall be thinking it over during the night."

In the morning (May 25), he examined the material on old age pensions the Minister of Finance proposed to include in his budget speech. "I was to decide between a paragraph that omitted any reference to reducing the age and one to be included which would undertake to reduce the age from 70 to 65 immediately, provided the majority of provinces urged the Government so to do. This would mean lessening the leverage which the Government could place on the provinces to come quickly into a contributory system which would be more generous in its treatment of old people, both as to absence of means test, amount of pension and age at which pension could be received. . . . Felt early this morning that first of all the opportunity to introduce a contributory system might never come to the present administration if we waited until after an election or for agreement with the provinces to reduce the pensionable age. Already more has been made of that reduction than aught else. Moreover, I felt that the entire Opposition would be for reduction of age. All interested in soldiers and their families would be, and that it would be difficult, if not impossible, to hold our men to support us in the House. When it came to an election in the country it would be fought largely on the issue of Old Age Pensions. Much else that we have done would not be so much as debated. . . .

"On the merits, I feel that the problems after the war will be such that older people will have to be largely looked after and that those who have fought the country's battles would demand that they should not be saddled with the burden of helping to meet the living of those whose day's work is done through no fault of their own, but because of conditions of society as they will have developed at that time. Also that the example of other countries would tell greatly. I was quite clear in my own mind that we should reduce the age and the reading of the Speech from the Throne made clear that in this particular we had left the door open.

"During the afternoon, I told Clark of my view. He spoke of the leverage position but said he saw the other aspect. Ilsley had told me that the finding of the money was not a real difficulty."

On May 29 Mackenzie King spoke in the Cabinet "on the desirability of having Old Age Pensions age reduced from 70 to 65. I gave reasons very fully. They were accepted without comment by Ilsley and, indeed, by members of the Council as a whole." Thus the government's policy was established of agreeing to pay a pension without a means test to everyone 70 years of age and over and to contribute 50 per cent of the cost of provincially administered old age assistance programmes under a means test for people from 65 to 69. These proposals became part of the federal government's proposals at the Dominion-Provincial Conference in August 1945.

During his stay in London, Mackenzie King had been informed of the approximate date fixed for the invasion of the Continent but neither he nor anyone else in Canada knew the precise date. On June 6 he was wakened about half past four in the morning by the constable on duty knocking on his bedroom door and "coming in and saying: Mr. King the invasion has begun. Mr. Robertson wants you on the phone. I questioned him as to what information he had. Rang up Robertson immediately. Asked him if he were sure the report was correct. He said he was; that official communiqués had come in. That the Germans had been broadcasting that Europe had been invaded from early in the morning but that he had not called me until he had verified the facts. Eisenhower had issued a statement from his headquarters; his headquarters had also stated that the Canadians were in along with the Americans and the British. He then told me that the press wanted a statement from me. That Pickersgill had drafted something which he read to me over the 'phone. I took it down in pencil. Did not like one or two of the expressions as, for example, that the word would be received with sober satisfaction. Also that the operation marked the climax of the war. I thought something should be added that we must not expect early results and approved cordially of concluding with a sentence that the hearts of all in Canada would be filled with silent prayer for the success of our own and Allied forces and for a speedy liberation of Europe. I substituted the latter for something regarding Nazi oppression."

After talking again with Norman Robertson, Mackenzie King continued with his revision of the statement "making it clear that the Government had received official information that the invasion of Europe had begun, leaving out the receiving with satisfaction. Fortunately Pickersgill had got the further information that our troops were being supported by the Canadian navy. Nelles had got over word to Macdonald. We added also the R.C.A.F. Still later, Macdonald, Minister of Navy, rang me to say the press were after him. Ralston is away in the Maritimes and Power is not here. I read him what I had in mind saying. Said I thought the one statement would be sufficient for the present. I then got Dunton [A. Davidson Dunton, General Manager, Wartime Information Board] on the 'phone and read him at 25 to 5 what I had written as revised. I arranged also through Pickersgill to make a brief broadcast between 7.45 and 8.00 A.M., just before the morning news. Arranged for the constable to call me at 7; to get Handy [J. E. Handy, Mackenzie King's personal secretary] here, and Pickersgill had promised to come along to Laurier House at 7. I woke exactly at 7. Did not sleep very well but rested; finally decided to get up. When I looked at the clock, it was exactly 7.00 o'clock. Had a bath.

"Came upstairs. Made revision of material Pickersgill had, practically what was already written out. Felt it was inadequate. Went through morning paper and picked out a statement from Crerar which I included. Pickersgill was anxious to put in something about Eisenhower's command of the gallant forces of France. I did not think it desirable to do this in the first broadcast. He had been asked to see that something was prepared for Europe, and I agreed to include this statement. He said word had come specially requesting that something should be sent back emphasizing Canada's satisfaction at the French being in the fight. I then went up to the Chateau. Made the broadcast at 8.00 A.M., then a further broadcast to Europe. Returned to Laurier House."

Later in his diary entry for the day, he noted that he had "been puzzled in my mind this morning by what was said to me by Churchill in last morning's conversation we had together in which he indicated that it might be as late as the 21st of this month before the invasion would take place; also by the statements made repeatedly by himself at the Conference of Prime Ministers that an invasion movement would be started from Russia in the Balkans following upon the movement north of the forces in Italy. In other words, the impression left at the time of the Conference was that the invasion would be in three stages; that the surrounding of Germany would come in three stages—the first of which would be the movement north of the forces in Italy; 2nd, the movement from the forces in Russia westward, and 3rd, the British to Western Europe. Also Churchill told me that he would see that I got a special word from him just a day or two in advance, sufficient to let me know just what to expect within the next day or two."

"Another thing," Mackenzie King added, "that causes me to feel that some change of plans has been made and that the present move has been made more quickly than was anticipated when I left England, is that Churchill himself had spoken of having no mention made of other than allied forces when the invasion itself was to take place. Eisenhower had stressed and requested this and yet today from Eisenhower's own headquarters came mention of British, Canadian and American troops [see vol. 1, pp. 695–6]. No word coming in the interval of any change in this particular has thrown me a little off my guard. Had I not been looking to a later moment, I would, at the week-end, have had something carefully prepared and in readiness for the press."

After his broadcast, Mackenzie King had an hour's sleep and then gathered together some bulletins and other notes to use in the House in the afternoon. Arriving late at the Cabinet meeting, around noon, he reported that he had "seldom seen the Ministers more silent than they were as I indicated to them the nature of the word that had been received. Referred again to what had been said to me in Britain about what we should expect at the time of the invasion and read to them the background material. Ralston had not got back. Power is away. Macdonald had just a little information which the Defence Department had got together." The Prime Minister suggested that the House should not open until after the King's broadcast at 3.00 P.M.

The members of the House and Senate had assembled in Room 16 in the Centre Block and the King had just begun speaking when the Prime Minister came in. "There was applause in the room. Members began immediately to applaud but I shook my head indicating that anything of the kind was inappropriate and seated myself on the sofa with some of the Members of the House. I was somewhat disappointed in the King's speech both in delivery and in the substance of it. Particularly I did not like a reference which seemed to indicate that the British peoples as included in the Empire were to be the ones that were chosen of the Almighty as the instrument to save the world. It seemed to me extraordinary that this should come in the King's speech when the susceptibilities of Americans would be keener than ever with their two or three million men waiting to go on to the Continent of Europe. It seems impossible for the British people ever to recognize that others as well as themselves can have a place in history on these occasions. It seems necessary to them to assert their pre-eminence which must be disliked by other peoples; also it did seem to me that there was still too much of the old futile note in what was said as though words from the Throne were by grace and a form of reward to those who were sacrificing their lives. There is something fundamentally wrong in this accepted attitude. As Arnold Toynbee has said, the mass of people are right at heart in believing that God does not dwell here or dwell there but in the whole people. I was distinctly disappointed; also while I think it is right that emphasis should be placed upon prayer, it does seem to me that relating it primarily to the success of arms at a particular time rather than to a constant attitude to save situations is other than what it should be. I wish that there could be less pomp and ceremony and feasting, and that a word of prayer should come as I have experienced it at the little service in the synagogue where one felt it represented the life's endeavour and soul of a man rather than a part of the trappings of privileged position."

On Sunday, June 4, Mackenzie King had been distressed to learn that A. J. Freiman, a prominent Ottawa merchant and friend, had died that afternoon while unveiling a tablet in the synagogue. "He was a very fine citizen and a good friend," the Prime Minister wrote in his diary. Despite all the preoccupations of D–day, Mackenzie King took time on June 6 to attend Freiman's funeral, which he found "deeply moving and in every way worthy of his fine, unselfish life."

To Mackenzie King, the proceedings in the House of Commons that afternoon were "very dignified." His own statement was "all things considered, most suitable. No effort at exhortation and making of the moment an occasion for eloquence, personal prominence or glorification of the country, etc., but simply direction of attention of the House to essential points. The House was very responsive and what was said by different leaders was most appropriate. I took advantage of the moment to make an appeal for expedition of the business of Parliament which I think will be effective. Later in the day, got through External Affairs estimates without any discussion. Left the Privy Council estimates, those related to War Information Board to Claxton. Did not go back in the evening."

In some quarters in Canada, the invasion of the Continent revived speculation about the necessity of conscription for overseas service and, in the Cabinet on June 9, Mackenzie King read a telegram from the Canadian Legion suggesting this policy. He asked for discussion. "Invited Ralston to discuss the matter. He spoke of the means he was taking to take all men possible voluntarily. I pointed out that certain suggestions had been based on a certain estimate of losses. That nothing like that number had been incurred. Ralston also mentioned that we had the numbers needed for the next four months without doubt. I said little but made it clear that it would be impossible to consider any matter of conscription between now and the end of the war in the light of all that Canada had done. That it would undo all our war effort. Power was not present, nor was Macdonald, but other Members of the Cabinet all seemed to be of my mind though nothing was said openly."

On June 10, Mackenzie King completed seventeen years of service as Prime Minister and on August 7, 1944, he would complete twenty-five years as leader of the Liberal party. Not only was he anxious to have these occasions recognized for their own sake, but he was also conscious of the necessity for good personal publicity in advance of a general election. On June 5 the sculptor, Avard Fairbanks, had brought the completed bust of Mackenzie King to Ottawa and the Prime Minister saw it the following day in one of the rooms of the House of Commons [see vol. I, p. 587]. He "was delighted. . . . When I saw it, it was exactly as it was when it left Kingsmere—only a different colour, a sort of old ivory colour. I was tremendously relieved and so was Fairbanks who naturally had felt dejected about my impressions of the other photographs," seen on an earlier visit by the sculptor. On June 10 Mackenzie King met Emil Ludwig to go over the manuscript of the biographical study Ludwig had begun the previous November [see vol. I, p. 588].

In his diary for June 14, Mackenzie King considered tentative plans for celebrating the twenty-fifth anniversary of his leadership. "On reflection I am inclined to make of the occasion one for furthering Party organization in each province; suggested a meeting on that day with messages to be sent to Ottawa and to be read at a dinner to be given at the Chateau here. This largely to avoid cost of delegates coming to Ottawa and using railways in wartime. It would also bring out better than anything else the expression of confidence over the country as a whole in a manner which would be helpful in the general campaign. Also the period of my leadership has been continuously in Ottawa. It will avoid, too, uncertainties as to the war situation that might develop and also the uncertainty of Parliament being still in session."

Work on the Ludwig manuscript, on another biographical sketch by Ray Lawson, and on a volume of his own speeches continued to receive a good deal of Mackenzie King's personal attention during the summer. On June 21 he received the last of the page proofs of *Canada and the Fight for Freedom*, a volume of his wartime speeches. "The chapters on Selective Service and Conscription which I would not have selected myself for publication seem now to appear almost providentially. McTague in a nomination speech at Guelph came out as the National Chairman of the Conservative Party for compulsory conscription for overseas of the mobilized forces in Canada. Drew has endorsed him. It is clear, however, that there is an effort to raise a cry as Borden did near the end of the last war for conscription. These last fighters will fight till the last ditch. I am glad to have the position of the plebiscite stated where the public will be able to read the true facts concerning it" [see vol. I, pp. 657–8].

Although the political situation seemed generally favourable, Liberal party prospects suffered one set-back in June 1944, the defeat of the Patterson (Liberal) government in Saskatchewan. The Prime Minister noted in his diary on June 16 that "last night had brought word that the C.C.F. had carried Saskatchewan, which was no surprise. Hepburn can be blamed for this. He gave the C.C.F. their big chance in Ontario. Also Patterson and the Government of Saskatchewan to blame for having prolonged their term of office unduly. Douglas as a man of high ideals is a better leader in the minds of the rural people, I am sure, than Patterson, who is heavy, lethargic and less idealistic. The Province has lost the kind of active leadership Tommy Davis and others have given it. The Liberals have gone a little to seed there. I think, too, Gardiner has lost a certain hold, and is looked upon too much as a machine politician. The Tories running candidates ensured the election of the C.C.F. They did not elect a member, but the C.C.F. got only 52 percent of the entire vote, though the numbers elected constitute almost a complete sweep. The result does not cause me much concern for federal politics except that it shows what organization can do and we have not the organization we should have. Of course, federal restrictions in war time have counted for much."

The Prime Minister returned to this theme after the meeting of the War Committee on June 28, deploring the lack of organization in the federal party. With the defeat of the provincial Liberals in Saskatchewan, prospects for Mackenzie King's re-election in Prince Albert constituency had become particularly cloudy. "Howe said he hoped on no consideration would I run in Prince Albert again," Mackenzie King noted. "He said I should run in Ottawa where Laurier House was situated. I told him that no matter what the consequences were, I would certainly run in Prince Albert defeat or no defeat. That I had represented the constituency for a long time. If the Party were not interested in having me win there, I should welcome a chance to get out of public life if it had to come in that way. I have never seen a look of greater concern on the faces of all of my colleagues. For a moment, they seemed to be struck dumb. They were face to face with the future of the Party without myself as its leader. Howe spoke out quite emphatically on this as did one or two of the others. That there would be no one who could save the after-war situation if I were defeated. I told them that regardless of all else, defeat meant nothing to me as long as it was honourable. I was going to stay with the ship and go down with colours flying at the mast if we had to go down. I told them further that my conviction was we could win if we could only get some organization meanwhile.

"Last night I had stressed to McLarty the need of having every constituency organized for August the 7th. He had spoken about one hundred meetings instead of a few in the Capitals. I had said there should be meetings in every constituency and word from every constituency, and if possible the presence of every candidate that was in the field. That that was the only kind of expression of confidence or good-will that I wished."

Three of the ministers most concerned with federal organization, Ian Mackenzie, Norman McLarty, and J. G. Gardiner, met with Mackenzie King on July 13. He pointed out that nothing had been done to prepare for a campaign "which might easily come in October. That I thought it was a great pity as we were throwing away chances of winning and explained my own helplessness if Ministers would not take on the responsibilities which they had been asked to assume. Gardiner began talking about organization being useless if the Wartime Prices and Trade Board continued by regulations, etc., to appoint Tories who have made our position next to impossible. I felt very worried with this discussion." At Howe's urging, Gardiner re-opened the question of the Prince Albert constituency. The Prime Minister was firm. "I let him know definitely that I would not consider another constituency. I said if I were defeated, I believed the day would not be far distant when both the constituency and the country would regret it."

Enjoying the peace and quiet of Kingsmere on Saturday, July 15, Mackenzie King reflected on his political hopes and ambitions. He felt he "would like to take a trip through Canada, to speak to the people before actually entering on a political campaign, and making the trip the occasion of explaining the policies in regard to the new order for which nations must work from now on. I know that personal contact with the people will mean more than anything else. I could, too, perhaps visit my own constituency and arouse the feeling of interest and enthusiasm there, which might even possibly lead to the winning of the seat. I have really in my thoughts been wholly indifferent to what the consequences of a political election may be. Indeed I felt I would welcome honourable defeat and that I would be glad to be out of the next Parliament with the problems that have to be faced, not because of the problems but because of my own feeling of inadequacy through fatigue I experience on account of my years.

However, something seemed to say to me this morning that I should instead of being indifferent, do all possible to win and that I should not, if it can be avoided, drop out of public life for a time at least. That the thing to do was to get the new program under way, see a new Parliament started and a beginning made in the larger work of industrial and international peace and furtherance of social welfare, etc. In other words, I should make this coming election centre around myself as a man with a mission—the mission being that which is set out in 'Industry and Humanity', to do today what the public were not prepared to have me do at the end of the last war but what large numbers of them will welcome today. Such a campaign might save the country from falling into the hands of inexperienced men who might head its affairs in the direction of a socialistic state with consequences which might prove more disastrous than can be foreseen at the moment. I might make the campaign such that from all sides forces would rally toward the Liberal banner. This will mean taking a trip West in September and October if the war is still on, and not calling an election but preparing the way for one on the issue of the future in the light of the Government's efficiency and regard in the past. Such a trip would avoid the necessity of a similar campaign when the election itself comes off.

"McGeer [G. G. McGeer, Liberal M.P. for Vancouver-Burrard] yesterday suggested planning a careful program of work of construction, calling Parliament in the new year to vote the money necessary for it and then go to the country on the strength of it. There may be something in that. What would give me much satisfaction would be to tire out Bracken, McTague and others who have been expecting an early campaign and make them wait until the spring of the year. Against that, I do not want to leave everything to the last. However, the decision lies beyond my control. I have made the decision depend on the continuance or cessation of the war in Europe."

These thoughts obviously coloured the Prime Minister's position at a Cabinet meeting on August 1 during a difficult discussion of the adequacy of the indemnity paid to Members of Parliament. He reported that "Ilsley was agreeable to allowing about half the indemnity exempt from taxation. I told him quite frankly that I intended to come out for complete freedom from taxation of the indemnity. That the principle was one of independence of the Members of Parliament and Parliament itself, which is the supreme court of the realm. Ilsley was very insistent on wanting to know if this was government policy rather intimating that he would have to oppose it if it were. All the Members of Council present were strongly on my side. Some of them quite outspoken. Ilsley persisted in his attitude. I finally told him that regardless of Government policy or not I intended to make clear the position I had stated as being the position I would take if I were in the next Parliament. That I felt the most serious thing this country was facing was having a Parliament composed only of men who were wealthy or were the creatures of the bank interests, or whose earning capacity was so low that an indemnity of itself would be all they could hope for in the way of a livelihood. I wanted to see Parliament be more representative of different classes in the country—Labour, farmers, men from the armed forces, people of moderate incomes, women and others. I did not see how this could be without seeing that they were given an allowance large enough to make them independent of influence. Ilsley has got extremely autocratic and is very narrow. As a matter of fact his narrowness has cost the Party heavily already. He was arguing that Members would be quite satisfied with what he was proposing. In speaking I mentioned that as Prime Minister, if it had not been for the gift of Laurier House to myself and the assistance I had received from Mr. Larkin and one or two others to help to maintain it, I would have had to resign as Prime Minister and could not have afforded to continue in public life and this because of the policies of the Finance Department. It could never have been meant that the Prime Minister would have to leave office because his own Government had made it impossible for him to continue in the public service and I spoke of other of the Ministers being more or less similarly faced. I made it clear that I would speak if necessary at the same time of the independence of the judiciary, etc. This led me to speak of my attitude whether I was returned or not. Bertrand had been favouring only a part being allowed but as one Minister said, that was all right for him in the position he was in. It was not for others. Bertrand did not want me to say anything at present. I replied that I had now reached 70 years of age, had stood for certain principles all my life and intended to assert them. I felt more strongly on the independence of Parliament than on almost anything else; whether I was defeated, as I probably would be, or not, I intended to make my position clear. He then said I should not think of being defeated but of having another seat. I said on no consideration, would I consider another seat."

Another serious political problem the Prime Minister faced during the summer of 1944 was the situation of the Liberal government in Quebec, under attack by both the Bloc Populaire and the resurgent Union Nationale Party under Maurice Duplessis. The Quebec problem had been the subject of a conversation with St. Laurent and Power on June 13. Mackenzie King noted that a provincial election was likely to be announced in Quebec that week and that the two ministers both had the impression that Godbout, the Liberal Premier, felt sure of victory. "He intends taking the line that I have saved the province from conscription overseas, but in order to carry on a Liberal Government I had to take some Conservatives into the Administration. Point out to the electorate the action of McTague, Borden [Mr. Justice McTague and Henry Borden had served voluntarily in wartime tasks and, after resigning, became active in the Conservative party] and others—of these men in positions in the Service, who had been responsible in part for restrictions, [and] were now seeking to defeat the Government on some of the restrictions, which were of their own making, which is true."

A few days later it was announced that the Quebec election would be held on August 8. During the provincial campaign several problems connected with it arose in the federal field. On June 22 Mr. King was called out of the House during the afternoon to see Premier Godbout and the chief Quebec organizer, Arthur Fontaine, who had come to Ottawa "to speak about serious situation which they believed would be created if Houde were let out of internment just at the moment the Quebec elections were announced." Camilien Houde, the Mayor of Montreal and a former leader of the provincial Conservative party, had been interned in August 1940 for urging non-compliance with the national registration undertaken under the Mobilization Act [see vol. 1, pp. 104–5]. Godbout and Fontaine argued "very strongly that his mere appearance would be the occasion for demonstrations in Montreal. That while the leaders of the Bloc Populaire would not want him as their leader, they would nevertheless be happy to have him create all the unrest possible. That the breaking up of Tim Buck's meeting by young people, students and the like, was evidence of the organization from other sources to stir up trouble. There had been these disputes between the members of the services and civilians. There was real danger of serious breaches of the peace . . . just at this time when fighting was taking place in France, there would almost certainly be a serious situation develop. . . . St. Laurent who was present took the position that as Minister, he was bound to follow the regulations, and if left to himself, he would have no alternative but to free Houde, or be put in the position of favouring the Communists as against Houde—of having done for the Communists what he was not prepared to do for Houde now that the latter had signed a document admitting his errors in the past and undertaking not to repeat them in the future. It was clear, however, St. Laurent said that he had designedly waited months, if not years, to make the admission he had and to give the undertaking he had, and this that he might play a certain part at the moment of the Quebec elections."

The Prime Minister's position was that the whole Cabinet would have to consider the situation. "There were reasons of high policy related to the war which they could not afford to ignore at this moment with McTague and others coming along raising the conscription issue at this moment, and possibility of the Tory Party in the House adopting it as theirs in an amendment to the budget. We could not be too careful in the matter of saving what might develop into a species of civil war at this time. I told Godbout in the presence of St. Laurent without making any promise as to what would be done, that I would see that all aspects of the situation were considered in the Cabinet. Personally I feel it would be a great mistake to free him of internment until the elections are over. If I were thinking of the federal government's position politically apart from any national aspect related to the war I would say the sooner he was out the better. That to keep him in internment during the Quebec elections and letting him out after would be much harder on the federal party, our own Party when it comes to a campaign. On the other hand I feel we can only take one step at a time and that our duty now is to prevent a crisis developing in Canada when there is such a terrible situation in Europe. Our duty is to see the war through in the best way possible regardless of what the consequences may be to the Party."

In the Cabinet on July 13, St. Laurent raised the Houde problem and "also mentioned some articles, drew attention to speeches and articles recently published by one or two other extremists which clearly were contrary to the Defence of Canada Regulations. While technically Houde might have to be released, the report made to the Minister indicated that there were grounds for considering the time it was wisest to make the release and the unwisdom at a time of tension of adding to what might take place through demonstrations if Houde were released at once. I took the position that we were responsible for peace, order and good government; also for a policy of total war effort and that just now with our men giving their lives in France, we could not possibly risk anything which might lead to further clashes between civilians and members of the armed forces in the province. That as Houde had had two years to make the statement he has made only at the moment of provincial elections, all considered, it would be best to wait until this period of excitement was over.

"Council was unanimous in advising that his release be deferred for the present and that action should be taken against others who are going too far."

In Parliament itself, a great deal of controversial legislation had been pending when Mackenzie King returned from London. The Minister of Finance was experiencing difficulty with the decennial revision of the Bank Act, not from the Opposition parties but from the so-called monetary reformers, particularly McGeer and Arthur Slaght, in the Liberal party. At the Cabinet meeting on June 9, Mackenzie King had brought up the question of hidden reserves in commercial banks which had been debated in caucus the day before. "I strongly recommended that in addition to the

Minister of Finance being advised of reserves, that the Minister of National Revenue should also be advised but in addition the Governor of the Bank of Canada, stating that the public had begun to look on the Bank of Canada as their bank and that it was advisable in the event of a change of Government, that it seemed wrong that only one man should have this information. Anything might happen to him. He might change; that especially in the case of a change of Government, we might have some faddist like Douglas or other person become Minister of Finance; one who might take action in any way he liked. I thought it was preferable to have at least three different persons and the Governor of the Bank one of them, who would have this information. Ilsley mentioned that the Governor did not want to take this responsibility. St. Laurent gave the reasons for this; that it might embarrass the Governor in relation with individual banks, if he knew their condition. I pointed out that I thought if there was occasion for embarrassment, it was the more reason why he should know their condition, and he was paid a large salary for the responsibility that he had. The Minister of Finance should not hesitate to have the Governor take some of the responsibilities off his shoulders. Ilsley agreed to this being done provided that suggestion for this came from some other. I think it will help to relieve the situation somewhat. It has become very tense in the banking committee; also to relieve us of some political embarrassment."

Many other hard economic and political questions had still to be settled before the annual budget could be presented. On June 13 the Cabinet approved the release of a part of the compulsory savings collected since 1942, an action "which will enable persons of lower incomes to have larger amounts to meet existing obligations. It will also relieve immensely the National Revenue Department of much difficult bookkeeping and put more money in circulation, which may be hard on keeping the price level. On the other hand, it may provide the means for increased purchase of certificates and war bonds. The exemptions today are greater than the United States or Britain or, indeed, Australia and New Zealand. To increase them might look as though the Government thought the war was nearing conclusion. Ilsley stressed the need of as much in the way of production for war as possible. He claims that working men just won't work when they are at the point that increased wages means getting into a higher category of taxation. He feels using up compulsory income will help to overcome this. I had first thought that it would be well to increase the exemptions. Politically, it probably would be, and certainly the majority of Members will so believe and will press for it. On the other hand, after listening to the discussion of the last two days, and talking with Clark, I have come to the conclusion that a much larger number of people will be helped in a way that will give them more money at once, albeit their own money, and that in relieving burdens on those of the lower class and making for a better feeling over a larger number, the yielding up of income may prove to be a preferable course. In any event, Council was unanimous on the matter. At one time I counted nineteen members of the Cabinet present at the table. The only one absent was Gardiner, who is at present in Saskatchewan."

At the same meeting, the Cabinet approved an immediate start on the drafting of legislation to establish the Department of National Health and Welfare [see vol. 1, pp. 633–5]. "Claxton to take on the responsibility of drafting the measure and assisting in piloting it through the House. An effort will be made to get the right man for Deputy Minister at once, and plan to have family allowances go into effect by July 1st next year. It will take all of six months to get everything in readiness. I spoke to Claxton this afternoon, also to Ilsley. Clark was present at the discussion. Spoke also to Heeney and Robertson about lending a hand in getting the Bill drafted, and instructed Pickersgill to see Clark this afternoon and clear up debatable point as to not having the amounts due under pensions affected one way or the other by family allowances."

The Prime Minister returned on June 15 "to the question of family allowances and the Department of Social Welfare. Discussed the latter matters with Pickersgill who as well as Claxton shared my views and when I went into the Cabinet shortly before one, I told the Ministers I had in the light of the different discussions in Council thought carefully over the whole matter of family allowances and had come to the conclusion that they should be made from July 1st, 1945. This would make certain they would not come into force until after the elections were over, whether the elections were held in the fall of this year or the spring of next. When they actually would be held would depend on the progress of the war. I certainly would not go to the country while the war in Europe was on. I did not like the idea of spending public money immediately before an election. Also plenty of time was needed to get the new Department ready and people were likely to be more grateful for what they were about to receive than anything they might have been given in advance. I believe that politically they will be more likely to support our administration by having the Act on the Statutes with the understanding we were committed to carry it out than they would be had the provisions gone into effect with possible delays and comments upon the amounts and their varying effects on different families.

"I also expressed the view that we could not afford to take back with one hand what we were giving with another, in amounts to be paid those receiving dependents' allowances and pensions. By fixing July 1, 1945, the outlay on those getting dependents' allowances would not likely be very great.

"The Cabinet accepted what I said practically unanimously. Macdonald, Crerar and Ilsley continued to register their objections to the scheme at all and particularly to allowing pensioners' families to have allowances in addition, but it was recognized that the opposition in our own Party in the House would oblige us to come to this in the end. Apart from that I maintained and Ralston with me that what pensioners have lost in many ways which cause their families extra hardship and handicaps was something which should be remembered, also we were assuming that the soldier should not be forgotten, and that this should be remembered. I was glad to get this contentious matter finally agreed to. I went around the table and made each Minister express his views. I suggested changing the name of Social Welfare Department to the Department of National Health and Welfare. [I had] spent part of the morning reading the chapter on Health in my Industry and Humanity and [I concluded] that all forms of social welfare were in the nature of things a matter of preserving health, physical, mental or moral and that there being already a Department of National Health we could not eliminate the name without creating the impression that we were trying to do away with that branch of public service. . . . I also went through the provisions of the Bill which has been drafted and received approval of them. Felt much relieved at these decisions."

On June 20 Mackenzie King spoke in the House on the Bill to establish the Department of Reconstruction. "When I rose to speak," he wrote, "I was very uncertain how I would get along having had three or four days in which my brain seems to have been over-wearied and my body over-tired. However, to my own amazement, I found once I began to speak without reference to notes that I could sail ahead without any difficulty and indeed with a feeling of confidence that I would be able to bring out pretty clearly what I wished to say. I did not follow the order of my notes but spoke in the sequence that came to my mind. The House gave me very close attention and I found it very easy to speak. When I had finished Graydon sent over a note reading 'You were in rare form today.' I could see our men were well pleased. As a matter of fact, I kept regretting that I had not gone ahead as I had definitely thought of doing on Sunday with a speech on Reconstruction in a broad sense in the first instance, and then narrowing down to the Bill as the latest measure toward that end."

The budget was discussed again in the Cabinet on June 22. According to Mackenzie King, there was "a long discussion on the advisability of increasing exemptions on lower classes, versus giving relief of taxation by yielding up compulsory savings feature, with advantages this will give to keeping men at work in industries. Today they are quitting work the moment that extra wages means getting into a higher category of taxation. They would rather get less in the way of earnings than turn over additional earnings in the form of taxation for war purposes. I stated to Ilsley I thought he should be able to say that the budget brought relief of taxation for those experiencing hardship in lower levels of income. He flatly said that this would not be the effect of the budget. I then said that I and others must have been under a wholly erroneous impression when we had previously expressed our willingness to agree to the second alternative, namely yielding up a portion of compulsory savings, even though this was a man's own money which he was retaining instead of allowing the state to retain it. I felt that any budget on the eve of an election which did not show some consideration for those who were suffering a certain injustice through the narrow margins their present earnings afforded, in the matter of their living due to increase in cost of living which there certainly had been in the years of war, would be just fatal to the Government and play into the hands of the C.C.F. for their return to power. Ilsley came back by saying that he did not want to create the impression that we could afford any relief of taxation at this stage of the war and kept arguing on comparisons with the United States and Britain. However, the whole business seemed so complicated that even he could not explain the comparisons except by a statement so involved that anyone listening to it would become impatient. I tried to have him see that anything that was not easily and quickly explained would be worse than nothing. I told him it was absolutely necessary to keep the human side before the public. The mere statements of statistics, by economists, etc., would be almost worse than useless. On reflection he came back to the fact that there was relief afforded for cases of hardship, but he did not like to admit this. Practically all members of Council agreed with me that that was a wrong position to take, that what he should do, as I suggested, was to make clear wherein relief was being given but in a way which would not mean that there was less need for savings, work, etc. That what it did serve to do was to remove certain elements of injustice. He argued that to make any admission was equivalent to saying we were wrong at the start. His whole mind is in the direction of being consistent ad infinitum. I pointed out that as conditions changed, a consistent course might become a wrong course. That everyone had assumed in planning at the start that the war would be three or four years. They did not dream of a war of five or six years. Hardships had developed in consequence on those least able to bear them. . . . This argument finally came to carry some weight. Ilsley took the position that if it was necessary for him to base his budget on yielding up taxation, heightening exemptions, he would have to resign and let someone else handle the finances. He could not, he felt, continue as Finance Minister and say anything which would admit that the course he had pursued thus far was not a wholly correct one. He stressed the resignation feature very strongly. He kept saying that he would be blamed for whatever was done. I told him he was mistaken there. I was the one that would get blamed for everything that the Government could be criticized for. That there was no need to even talk of resignations. The Government could not consider such a thing, but he would realize that as a Minister we all had to bend to a consensus of view of the Cabinet and must try to bring our views as closely together as we could. I said that much depended on the way in which matters were presented in the statement and suggested the best way to do was to bring tomorrow to Council the presentation he intended to make and let us see what the reaction would likely be to it."

Conscious of western Canada's interest in freedom of trade, the Prime Minister insisted that the budget speech should contain some reference to freer trade. "I said I thought it was absolutely imperative that we should nail our colours to the mast in the budget, in reference first of all to greater freedom of trade as essential to new world order and in the budget itself make some changes that would make it clear that we intended to help the farmer in preparing for meeting post-war situations. I spoke of something being done on agricultural implements, cream separators, etc. I pointed out that if we did not do something the C.C.F. would move an amendment which . . . many of our Members would support or at all events would not vote against. We might in the end be obliged to accept it and the C.C.F. would get the whole credit of being the Party that was really giving relief to the primary producers. There seemed to be reason to believe that relief could be given at the present time without really harming anyone at the same time giving possible benefits to consumers as well as producers. Ilsley promised to have this looked into and bring up the matter tomorrow."

Later in the day the Prime Minister had a talk with Gardiner who, he reported, "admitted to me that if we could get agricultural implements put on the free list, get something done in that way, he thought the budget in respect to what was being done by yielding up a part of the compulsory savings would meet the situation. This was a great relief to my mind, as he and one or two others had determined to fight until the last ditch for higher exemptions, and I know Ilsley will absolutely resist this to the point of resignation."

The budget was considered again at the Cabinet meeting the next day, June 23. Mackenzie King noted: "I took the proceedings in hand myself. I asked Ilsley first to read his presentation. What he had in the way of presentation regarding taxation and compulsory savings. When he read it through I said that to my mind it gave no clear statement of the desire to effect relief to those who were experiencing hardships. That there was no phrase in it that could be used as headlines in the press or which M.P.s or public could take as the purpose in view, that most of it was an effort at explanation so long in detail as to be confusing and irritating. I was not asking that what was there set forth as what would actually be done should be changed, but that I felt an entirely different emphasis should be given to the material. I then gave my own view of how I thought it should be presented which was something as follows: It has come about in the years of war that some persons are experiencing real hardship, the long duration of the war, also the fact that we are still at war has made necessary some changes. Relief to those in hardship could be given in two ways. One, heightening exemptions from income tax or two, yielding up part of the compulsory savings. The former might create wrong impressions of the Government's view as to what was needed for the winning of the war, namely that all must contribute as largely as possible and that there could be no relaxation in that regard. The latter method however had the advantage of making money immediately available to persons of low income and at the same time it would assist further continuous employment by removing what is happening today through men quitting their work because of additional earnings which bring them into higher brackets where their incomes are more largely taxed. I suggested that emphasis should be put on what is being done at keeping the cost of living down and meeting war problems through the battle against inflation and by bringing in a system of family allowances showing that there was real relief in taxation though without yielding any principles. . . . It was clear that Members of Council generally consented to this and Ilsley said he thought this could be recast."

Later, when the Deputy Minister of Finance joined the meeting, Mackenzie King revived the discussion. "At first I could see he was resisting very strongly what I was suggesting. In other words the secret came out when it was stated that Towers of the Bank felt he had such a time keeping his finance committee on war loans together and continuing their work that he could not allow anything to be said or done which might indicate a lessening of monies from taxation. I pointed out that Towers was thinking like all of us about the ideal thing. What he did not see was that, in seeking to do this one individual thing, which was relatively small in regard to consequences as a whole, he might be helping to lose the country a Liberal administration and get in instead a C.C.F. administration, which would soon clean up the whole financial position. They would deal with the financial situation in a way which would make all efforts at saving, etc., pretty much at naught. It was necessary to emphasize this strongly to show the need for some very reasonable interpretation. I think I made an impression on Clark speaking in the presence of all ministers and also by getting Robertson to see him again.

"Then there came the question of trade and relief from indirect taxation. Ilsley read what he had said last year. I said at once that he should repeat that only adding that we have moved a step further and that we are now in the stage of negotiation or leading up to that. Gardiner and others said to use that alone without anything else, would be better to have nothing. We needed to give evidence really of what we were intending to do. I immediately spoke of the question of farm implements and cream separators. Two arguments were raised against this after sending for McKinnon [Hector McKinnon, the expert on tariff policy in the Department of Finance] to explain the position. The first was that it was desirable to hold these items for purposes of trading when it came to trying to make an agreement with the States. My answer to that was that if we held the item for that purpose we might find that we ourselves would not be here to do the trading. The other was that the immediate decline in prices might not follow the change in tariff because of other circumstances. My answer to that is that it would show there were at least some other circumstances and that the circumstance was not that the Liberal Party would not carry out its program of free implements. Gardiner pointed out that the West were saying that for twenty-five years we have promised implements, that if we were sincere we would grant them. People would then find out what the other circumstances were. As the explanations were proceeded with it became evident that manufacturers themselves had applied for removal of duties on parts, also that their position would not likely be prejudiced, the duty being very small down to five percent now from twenty-five percent to which Bennett had raised it. Council finally agreed to the farm implement reduction—to the freeing of farm implements. I then spoke further about cream separators. We were told by the experts they were supposed to hang together for implements doing for the dairy industry what was being done for farming, so that was agreed to. This at least was a nailing of the colours to the mast. I think the argument that carried most was that if we did not do this the C.C.F. would move an amendment and we would be obliged either to accept their amendment, letting them get the lead or find our own people deserting us and ourselves being put into a secondary position which is true. In this and some other particulars the results in Saskatchewan have not been without their advantages as well as disadvantages. Ilsley keeps raising the question of how far we are to go. It appears impossible to do certain things unless pressure comes from some other direction. The answer to that is sufficient to the day is the evil thereof. Even if it did cause the manufacturers to vote against us, it would save them voting for the C.C.F. as they apparently did in Saskatchewan."

The Prime Minister was "immensely relieved and pleased at the outcome of the morning's work. Members had recognized at the beginning it might be a very difficult meeting but by letting Ilsley hold to his first part on direct taxation, we were able to get a readier concession on the indirect; also there was the obvious argument for it that it was part of the necessary reconstruction for post-war work, helping agriculturists to meet demands that would come upon them in the post-war period."

The budget speech was delivered on June 26. In Mackenzie King's opinion, Ilsley's presentation "was very good. I did see, however, in his presentation of it, how important it was that he had been led to emphasize the need of meeting cases of hardship and so presenting matters as to make clear he was seeking to meet this as well as other objectives. He did not yield up any of his ground on the importance of all in the home front doing their part and continuing to make the necessary financial sacrifices to that end.

"What pleased me particularly was the provision of the Budget for free implements including cream separators. That makes good in its entirety one more plank of Liberal policy with respect to greater freedom of trade. That portion of the speech received the loudest applause. Indeed it was one of the few parts in which there was real applause. There was not much to relieve the feelings of Members in the other clauses. On the whole, however, I felt the statement was an exceptionally fine one, very statesmanlike, sound, far-reaching and in many respects exemplary. When he concluded, I made it a point of going to his seat and warmly congratulating him before the House. He has fought a very big battle."

Immediately after budget day, the House began debate on the bill to establish the Department of National Health and Welfare, and the Prime Minister observed on June 27 that "the last two speakers Diefenbaker and Castleden had annoyed me very much by cynical references and questionings of the former regarding jurisdiction in the new measures to be carried out, the possible usefulness of the Department, etc., and the word of the latter that the measure was a paper gesture. I had not intended to say anything in reply more than a word, hoping to get through the committee stage of the Bill before eleven as I believed I might have, had I not felt an impulse to take issue at once with what had been said in that critical way by making comparisons between what was said when the Department of Labour was established over forty years ago—I should have said forty-four—and what was being said today. This, however, I can repeat on another occasion. Though very tired my mind was quite clear and I managed to get on the record a pretty telling story of the significance of creating a new Department of the Government. I was able to link my convictions with experiences and associations I have had with different measures and what I have lived to see making good what Ludwig has pointed out as to a man creating his program and living to see it carried out in the course of his life. Our men were immensely pleased and applauded me loudly."

At the Liberal caucus on June 29, a division of opinion on family allowances gave Mackenzie King an opportunity to deliver a lecture on his social philosophy. George Fulford, the member for Leeds and an old friend, "brought up family allowances. He said that wherever he had gone in Brockville, there was the strongest opposition to this and made clear, in a careful way, that the whole business was based on racial feeling. That this was an effort to help the French-Canadians at the expense of others. I let myself go very strongly in Caucus. First of all, told the Members that political battles were not won or lost during a campaign. It was before the campaign itself started. The Government of Ontario had been dead long before the time set and also the Government of Saskatchewan. Both had made the mistake of prolonging their term of office. That where people saw a government did not trust them, they would take the first opportunity and withdraw their trust from the government. Also I spoke of the organization the C.C.F. had and then came out strongly about what we had done for agriculture. Pointed out that in the campaign, I would go to Saskatchewan myself and ask the people whether anyone had done more for agriculture than I had in getting the reciprocal agreements with the United States, reducing to 7½% duties Bennett had put up to 25%. Did they think anyone else would be in a better position to negotiate with Roosevelt than myself. If they did, by all means to choose him. That kind of talk would very soon show where the people in the Prairies stood. I stressed that I would have gone to the country last fall after the defeat in Ontario feeling sure of winning but held back because the Party was so far behind in its organization. I then spoke about not wanting to delay unduly the life of the present Parliament. They were beginning to talk about Parliament running until the first of July, 1945. I said I would not do what Tupper had done and keep Parliament on till the clock struck midnight of the last day. That the 17th of April was the expiration of the present Parliament according to the Electoral Officer, and they could be sure an election would come some time before then. I had wanted to warn them for preparation of an election this autumn but omitted that and left the impression it might be yet some time. Of course, this I will correct later.

"It was on the family allowances matter that I let out strongly. I told Caucus that this thing went down to the very roots of one's convictions and beliefs. That my Liberalism was based on the belief that, in the sight of God, every soul was precious. My Liberalism was based on getting for men equality of opportunity. I had written Industry and Humanity during the last war to help reconstruction in the period after the war. They would find that I had therein set out the doctrine of a national minimum of living, and that everything that had been done since by the Government, family allowances, too, were set out therein, evidencing my belief as to what was needed. That my belief in public life had been to help all I could for the improvement of the lot of the people in my day and generation. That perhaps because I saw the days were getting shorter and time more limited, I may have felt more strongly on hurrying some measures than I otherwise would. That I would gladly get out of public life tomorrow as far as my personal wishes were concerned except for what there was still to be done in the way of social reform. I would give my entire strength to that battle in coming months.

"I then spoke to George Fulford and pointed out to him the people that he had been talking with would naturally speak to him in that way. He had been a generous contributor to everything in the constituency; helped cases of suffering; was large-hearted, etc., and particularly they would take a view that they thought he might himself hold. He said he had not expressed any view. I then pointed out quite frankly to him: George, you were blessed with a father and mother who gave you every advantage, from the moment of your birth. Had the best of nourishment, the best of education and care. All advantages, where his father had been distinguished as a Senator, and all of these things combined brought you here as a member of Parliament carrying on their work. I said what would have been your chances had the positions been reversed, and you had been one of the men, bringing up a poor family, that was struggling for its existence but doing honourable work. Unable, however, to provide the children with what they should receive. Would not you today have been in the position of some of these people you have been talking to, and might not some of their sons be in your position. I said if equality of opportunity meant anything, it meant that every man, every child, should have his chance. . . .

"Also spoke about how George himself was being exempted for the children he had, and that all this measure meant was that those who had not enough income to entitle them to exemption would be placed in equality with him in that particular. That light was somewhat new to the Caucus, and I could see it was making a profound impression. They gave me a great ovation when I finished. They told me that if I would get out in the campaign and say to the people what I had said to Caucus, we would sweep the country. I told them if they would organize properly, they would see what could be done.

"I came away from Caucus feeling that what I had just made known was the fruition of my life work, and that it is all contained in my Industry and Humanity, and that I should preach that gospel across this country, which I will do."

At the Cabinet meeting on July 18, the legislative programme for the rest of the session was discussed. "Had both Ilsley and Clark present. Was deeply sorry for both, especially Clark. They have kept far too much in their own hands and have a staff only about one-tenth of what they should have. I had as tactfully as possible to take up measure after measure still to be introduced.

"Had Council give final decision on no further legislation on health at this session until Cabinet were agreed; that we had gone as far as we should on public expenditures and on social security matters, and that to announce further large new expenditure in view of outlay for family allowances, would only alarm one side of the electorate in the matter of taxation, and no further thanks from the other. The programme, if anything, is already quite heavy enough though not beyond what I feel is desirable if the changing conditions of the times are to be adequately met.

"It was after 3 before I got away from the office. Told Ralston before leaving that I had in mind the possibility of adjourning Parliament at the end of July, if we were still more in arrears and Finance Department unable to cope with the situation. The order paper is now clear of further legislation except family allowances."

On July 24 the Prime Minister had a pleasant talk with T. C. Douglas, the new Premier of Saskatchewan, and his Provincial Treasurer, C. M. Fines. "Said he had come to say Saskatchewan would co-operate in any way it could with us on Dominion-Provincial matters. I confess I was very pleased to see Douglas looking so young and enthusiastic about his work, and a young man with him as Minister of Finance. It recalled my early days in Government and I spent some little time talking to the two of them about their opportunities, the pleasure it gave me to see them taking on new responsibilities, wishing them well, though regretting the defeat of the Liberals. Told them I expected them to win; the previous government had made a mistake in extending its time, etc. They both spoke to me very appreciatively of my work on social problems as a young man, and particularly on External Affairs and the status Canada has won. Referred to it as a fine conclusion of my life's work. It is clear that the public is beginning to recognize as I am that that period is rapidly approaching so far as Parliament is concerned. There will be other work to do and writing."

Debate on the family allowances legislation occupied the House until the end of July. The bill provided for the monthly payment of tax-exempt allowances to mothers ranging from $5.00 for a child under 6 years of age to $8.00 for a child between 13 and 15 years of age. Allowances, to be spent exclusively on a child's maintenance, care, training and education, ceased at the age of sixteen. Mackenzie King entered the debate on July 25. The day was very hot and he "found my throat giving me trouble and my mind seemed tired. Indeed it was with the greatest difficulty that I found it possible to get individual words as, for example, urban and rural —trying to find the word 'rural' after having pronounced the word 'urban.' I could see that the whole speech was going to be difficult for this reason. I had just to face it out as best I could. One serious mistake I made which was the result of insufficient consideration and in not following my own judgment from the start was in bringing in references at some length to the bearing of the Family Allowances Bill on those receiving dependents' allowances and veterans' pensions. Pickersgill had suggested yesterday dealing with the matter in this way, and I had two statements which he had carefully prepared but which we had not time to look at together. The reading of them spoiled the effect of what I was saying at the start. I should have gone at once into the material about the proportion of the population gainfully employed and the numbers of children they had to support; the numbers that were married and the numbers of children the latter had to support. It is an amazing statement and one which suggests a destruction from within the life of the nation. I have seen nothing so startling in reference to the citizenry of the Dominion. I shrink so strongly inwardly from anything that savours of a demagogic appeal that I find it difficult to say much about the poor and the masses of the people lest it be thought that this is being done for political reasons. What, however, distresses me most is that I had all the material I needed for a really powerful and telling speech, had the full knowledge of it through my own mind and could easily have expressed it but found myself weighed down with fatigue and even the thoughts that I wished to utter were buried beneath the weight of fatigue. Indeed I felt a sort of complete exhaustion of both body and mind. I found, too, great difficulty in expressing in a manner I was most anxious to, what related to the contention of some labour leaders that family allowances may be a substitute for wages and help to keep wages down, and to refer to what I wanted to say about my own lifework in reply to Bracken and his talk of bribery. While I was speaking, I felt discouraged at the way in which I seemed to feel I was touching on different topics. However, there was the largest attendance we have had in the House for a long time past and our men seemed to be exceedingly interested and at the close of my remarks, gave me a really great ovation. One of the most continuous I have received in Parliament. What distresses and depresses me is that this whole subject is so completely my own and I understand it so well but find myself at the time of greatest need of exposition, completely tired out and unable to deal with the different criticisms as they arise and to expound the merits of the measure as they should be expounded. However, it may well be that a political campaign will afford ample opportunity for this, and that I will get time meanwhile to prepare in a series of speeches what needs to be said. I am sorry, however, not to leave this on the records of Hansard as I would like it to have been there for future years. I feel too tired to attempt another speech in reply in closing the debate on the second reading. Most of the points will already have been adequately covered.

"Graydon's performance was exceedingly poor. The reading of an essay written for him by Charlotte Whitton or someone else, and moving an amendment which he must have known was out of order. Worst of all was the appealing from the decision of the Speaker who was obviously right. That was done, I noticed, at Hanson's suggestion. Certainly put Graydon and his Party in a very untenable position. As a matter of fact, it served to line up every other individual in the House against the solid Tory group."

The next day (July 26) Mackenzie King noted that there were no Conservative speakers. "They really are," he wrote, "getting a strong whipping. They had put themselves pretty well out of business." Later in the day he added: "The great decision we had to make in Council this year was on family allowances. I am more persuaded than ever as I listen to the debate and continue to think over the present day problems and what they require by way of solution that the decision made was the right one."

The debate was closed by the Prime Minister on July 28. "When I rose to speak," he wrote, "I was anything but composed. However, my mind fortunately was clear and I seemed to have regained the power of more ready expression. I had decided not to attack the Opposition in any hard way but rather to poke fun at them and be as persuasive as possible with a view of bringing them all into line when the vote came. To my delight, I found it was very easy to speak until toward the very last when I found it difficult to compress what I wanted to say on the justice of the measure. My mind became a little clouded at that point, I think in part due to the heat and humidity of the day. I concluded what I had to say by referring to Max [his brother] having drawn my attention to Pasteur's writing and to the words of Pasteur having been the inspiration of my book 'Industry and Humanity'. It was one of the very few occasions in which I have ventured to speak of our family or of myself or of my book in Parliament, but instinctively I felt I was paying what I owed to both Pasteur and my brother in the way of credit, for the good that is going to come out of the children's allowance measure. It links their lives with this great social reform and shows how God selects the weak of the earth to confound the strong. I did not hesitate to say that my brother was writing his book on the battle of tuberculosis at the time that he sent me the life of Pasteur. All of this, to my mind, is evidence of the forces that are working together to help to bring into being this great reform which I feel perfectly certain is going to have its influence on the outlook of coming generations; that it is revolutionary in its way; that it really is in accord with the law of peace, work and health, and will help to show the way out of possible actual revolution and, at the same time, a way to a very necessary development of the life of our nation. The official opposition had evidently had an understanding not to interrupt me. They know that I can answer them quickly. I was given the best of hearings by the House. I think they felt that being in my 70th year, and nearing the 25th anniversary of my leadership, something was owing to me in speaking on a measure that related to the well-being of the children of our country.

"Our own men gave me another magnificent ovation when I had concluded. They were visibly delighted. I felt sorry that the last part of my address had not been clearer than it was. When the speech was over, we compelled a vote on the second reading. It was one I shall never forget; one that will not be forgotten in the records of Canada's Parliament. Every member in the House, of all parties, supported the measure—139 to nil was the vote recorded. Dr. Bruce by previous arrangement of a pair was left the one Member of Parliament against the principle of the Bill, he a former Lieutenant-Governor and noted medical practitioner. What a reflection!

"But for the excerpts which were helpful in expressing concisely certain definitions, etc., I spoke without notes and in the course of speaking, said many things I had not contemplated mentioning when I rose to my feet: references to the coming elections, and without mentioning their names, denunciation of McTague and Borden and of Tories and C.C.F.; their effort to destroy the Government while we are prosecuting the war. I think I laid a good foundation for the campaign itself. Indeed the campaign of 1944–45 is already upon us. This debate has been the opening round. It is a campaign that will be long remembered in Canadian history, and it runs back to the conditions surrounding my mother's birth in New York City when her father was in exile."

Mackenzie King's diary entry for July 29 reflected his personal satisfaction. "Though very tired, I feel a great peace at heart and an assurance that I am carrying out the purpose of my life in the social reforms in which we have at last entered. I believe earlier reading of this diary will make it clear that I foresaw when we were preparing the Speech from the Throne, what the sequence was likely to be, the struggle in the Cabinet, this particular legislation being held to the very end of the session and marking the beginning of a real campaign. It will be part of a memorable period in the life of the Dominion. How far reaching it all may be, God alone knows. I am sure that the 100% of the House of Commons in support of the Family Allowances Bill will have an enormous effect in other parts of the world, particularly in Britain. The whole campaign that follows will arouse the peoples in all the countries to the new conception of industry being in the nature of social service and the right of all the people to their share of the transformed natural resources which God has given the people as a whole and not to individuals for their use. It is truly a conception that will help to bring in a new order, and which will help to give to the lives of the humble the world over something of the dignity which God has meant those who have been made in His image, to possess. I should not forget that at this time much is owing in my thoughts to Robert Burns and his noble independence and humanitarian teachings, but more than all else are the beautiful teachings of Christ, and none more beautiful than the one which begins: 'Suffer the little children to come unto Me.' "

During the Committee stage on the Family Allowances Bill on July 31, the Prime Minister reported that "it was apparent during the afternoon that the Conservatives had decided to delay matters and at six it was apparent that Dr. Bruce intended to stage a scene by restating in Parliament that the Bill was political bribery and would not withdraw his words. It was clear that not having gone on with the Bill on Saturday had given time to the Globe and Mail and Bracken to have this performance put on to try to square Bracken's followers with him and his statements regarding political bribery. The scene began just as we were about to adjourn. It recommenced in earnest at eight when Bruce openly defied the Speaker and I was obliged to move that he be suspended for the remainder of the sitting. I purposely made the period brief so as not to give the Globe and Mail an opportunity to make a martyr of him. The whole business was an effort on the part of the Tories to get out of the mess they were in from voting for the measure notwithstanding Bracken's statement and having to square themselves later, with the Globe, etc. They have now made the situation worse themselves and helped it immensely by making clear to the people how little they can be trusted to administer the measure sympathetically." The Bill was finally approved on August 1.

The provincial election in Quebec, set for August 8, was now imminent. The day before, the date of his anniversary festivities, Mackenzie King noted that "Godbout had telephoned through his Minister of Labour to ask that our Government should do something toward helping to end the strike of taxi drivers and, if possible, the one in Montreal as both likely to be prejudicial on the following day, if continued, when the votes were to be polled.

"The Cabinet were absolutely one with me that a regulation of the War-time Prices and Trade Board which really created an unfair condition toward the underpaid taxi drivers in Quebec should not be allowed to pre-judice the possible results in that City. It was admitted that taxi drivers had justice on their side but had not followed the right procedure to get it duly considered. When Ilsley came in the matter was further gone over but he took his customary obstinate stand of not permitting anything to be done likely to lead to other demands, etc. I pointed out that the elections in all probability would be very close; that it was unreasonable to think that we should not seek to help our strongest ally to hold his own in a contest where obviously we were in a position to do at least something for him. That the issue was not taxi drivers; it was if the Godbout Government was to be returned to power or whether our own Government was to incur the hos-tility of our best friends by refusing to be of some degree of assistance to them. When Ilsley continued to be unyielding, I felt I would have to speak out very plainly. I finally said that general strategy was as important in political warfare as in actual war. I could not imagine General Eisenhower refusing to lend assistance to Montgomery or Crerar where their position was in peril simply because some rule of war had to be recognized rather than the situation itself. That I felt the interests of Canada demanded that we should, at this stage, leave no stone unturned to help to secure God-bout's return. That the winning or losing of a single seat or two might well determine which Government could hold office. I then went on to say that as Prime Minister, I asked that this Cabinet find a way to meet the situa-tion, and to have that strike settled before election day.

"I felt so incensed at Ilsley's inconsiderate attitude particularly on this day toward myself that having said this, I left the meeting of Council. It grieved me very much to have had this kind of attitude on the part of any colleague and I think all the others present felt exactly as I did. It was agreed after I left that steps would be taken which would meet what I had suggested. I really feel, however, that a man who acts like Ilsley does in these matters, no matter how conscientious he may be, has not the poli-tical judgment which would justify one recommending him for the position of leadership. His attitude has been the same from the day we began to dis-cuss apples as they might affect his constituency in Nova Scotia. I shall ever recall how he would not go to the League of Nations and get a wider outlook on world problems until I had assured him that the question of apples in his own riding would not be settled until after his return. He is like a horse with blinders. I felt the situation the more keenly as it helped to unfit me from quietly thinking out what I wished to say in the evening [at the dinner] and being in the mood for the occasion."

The first returns from Quebec were brought into the Cabinet between 6 and 8.00 P.M. on August 8. They indicated that the Liberals were leading but by a narrow margin and Mackenzie King took as "ominous" the defeat of the Liberal candidate in Hull. He "believed Godbout would nevertheless win. However, by 10 o'clock, he and Duplessis were running neck and neck and Bloc Populaire did not appear to be getting more than a few seats. C.C.F. only 1; Independent, 1, Labour 1. The Montreal seats seemed to be going Liberal and the two Quebec seats, but the rural parts of Quebec were going Union Nationale.

"I got the latest returns at Laurier House before going to bed. They indicated that Godbout might be beaten. This was a great surprise. I had expected he might lose some seats but not very many to a man like Duplessis. However, I felt no concern about the outcome as I realized there would be some decided advantages, strange as it may seem, in having an Opposition Government in office at Quebec. I think a mistake all through the campaign was in the Liberals of Quebec not standing up for the Liberal Government at Ottawa but allowing the campaign to be fought on the record of the Godbout Government and sharing with their opponents in their attacks on Ottawa. I confess Godbout is in a very trying position, having the kind of Opposition he had from combined Union Nationale and Bloc Populaire."

The following morning, news broadcasts confirmed the Liberals' defeat. The Prime Minister "did not communicate with Godbout so as to be free to say I had made no suggestions about what he should do. . . .

"Returns from Alberta [the election was on August 8] indicated Social Credit had practically swept the province. There were no Liberals running or Conservatives, just so-called Independents and C.C.F.s—everywhere practically all defeated." Somewhat surprisingly, the results of the two provincial elections encouraged Mackenzie King to think that "if our Party will organize on effective lines, we are in a splendid position to win. The elections have made plain first that the Tories can hope for nothing in either Saskatchewan or Alberta and I assume also very little in Quebec. Duplessis had to openly dissociate himself from Bracken in the elections. So far as the C.C.F. is concerned, elections have shown that they cannot win in Alberta and that they cannot win in Quebec. That means that their chance of a party able to govern from coast to coast is questionable. What perhaps is best of all in Quebec is that it is apparent the Bloc Populaire can get nowhere as a Party. Their following will probably recognize this and their influence will gradually disappear. They have taken three or four seats from the Liberals in Quebec and are responsible through the votes they have taken in from Liberal candidates in other constituencies for having defeated the Liberal Government in Quebec. They were aiming at our Government. Now that Duplessis will come into office in Quebec, they will not be so keen on allowing the Tory Party or the C.C.F. to get into power at Ottawa. I think the situation has made clearer than ever that I am in a better position to keep our country united and to form an administration than any of the other leaders. One thing has given me great satisfaction. I was right in not allowing Houde to be released. Had he not been kept in during the campaign, Godbout would have felt that our action in releasing him had been responsible for the defeat of his Government. Also as in Saskatchewan in the last election, if we had taken away the seats in redistribution, the Government there would have claimed that their defeat was owing to our action. Also I was pretty nearly right in the Cabinet on Monday when I stated that the election might be very close and our action in Quebec City might make the difference of one seat and that one seat might help to turn the tide. I am glad we got the word there in time to let Godbout see our willingness to help. One of the best things is that from now on, the other provinces cannot say that what we are doing is being done for Quebec. It certainly won't be done for the Duplessis Government and that will make clearer than ever that we are not doing anything for any province in particular, which, of course, is the truth. Some of our Federal members who left the Federal House to run provincially have been defeated. Foolish men to take that chance.

"Were one to go into the causes of the defeat they would all be traced back to Hepburn's defeat in Ontario, giving the C.C.F. their chance there, all of which has had the effect of helping to influence the present elections. It is apparent, however, there is strong feeling against federal Government for the restrictions that have helped to keep down the prices and the recruiting of men for the forces, taking them off the land. No Government that conducts the war can hope except by a miracle to long withstand the resentment that comes from inevitable restrictions. I am very happy that on Monday night I made clear our intention to have no election while the war is on and not to stay beyond the constitutional term. That was repeating what I had said before but the statement could not be credited in Quebec. When I attended Council today I saw Members looking rather glum. I outlined my views very much as recorded here which seemed to cheer them up a bit. St. Laurent was very much put out at the way the rural seats had gone. The damage that the Bloc Populaire had done without doing any good but was very pleased that his own seat had been carried by Drouin which will make more or less secure his own chances of winning. I told him by himself of my idea to have another session, and put through the redistribution, transferable vote, compulsory voting and possibly proportional representation. He saw very much to commend it. He is a real Liberal. Howe was for any excuse to get to the country fairly soon. He is fearful of what the change from wartime to peacetime industry may cause in the way of temporary unemployment or other embarrassments."

No amount of concern about the Quebec election could dim Mackenzie King's anticipation of the 25th anniversary of his leadership. When the day came on August 7, he expected some reference would be made to it in the House of Commons. In his diary he noted that, in the morning, he "tried to think of what to say at the opening of the House. I have been unable to bring my thoughts to what I could appropriately say. During the past week, the Tories have been particularly unpleasant and the feeling is anything but kindly between the two sides at the moment. Graydon's mention of the attitude of some of his own followers in the House and that of those who are really controlling the Party in Toronto made me feel that nothing should be expected from them in the way of concession in the matter of sitting tonight." He added that he "had learned from Mackenzie that Graydon himself had decided, regardless of what his Party felt or said, to extend a cordial welcome. I had no doubt that the others, Coldwell and Blackmore, would join in it."

When the Prime Minister entered the House he was given a great ovation. "Graydon rose almost immediately and made quite extended remarks which he had written out in advance. Coldwell and Blackmore followed with appropriate words. I followed without any notes but I had thought out on the way in what it might be appropriate to say, taking care particularly to mention my hope that Canada would continue to be a part of the British Commonwealth of Nations, and, referring to the latter, that it might endure as it is an instrument for good throughout the world. This, of course, in addition to a reference to Canada's future itself and to our friendship with the United States. Naturally I have had in mind that this may well be one of my last utterances in the Parliament of Canada and anything said on this twenty-fifth anniversary would perhaps carry with it added significance through years to come. I had the feeling that whatever comes about would be wholly for the best. I should be happy beyond words if my Party should be returned to power and I should be returned in Prince Albert. It would be a magnificent conclusion to the different chapters of my public life. On the other hand, if the Party should be defeated, I would certainly prefer to be defeated than to go into Opposition. If the Party is defeated and I am defeated, I shall welcome retirement and opportunity to attend a little to my own affairs and to enjoy something of the quiet in the sunset of life before its close. If the Party were returned and I should be defeated, as might well be the case, there would be no difficulty in securing a vacancy for such time as I might wish to remain in public life and participate in post-war matters."

All was not sunshine in the House, however. Dr. Bruce attempted to introduce a motion to discuss inadequate hospital accommodation for the wounded. Mackenzie King commented that "this was based on a letter sent me by Drew, special delivery, on Saturday. The whole thing makes perfectly clear the Toronto Tories had decided to spoil as far as possible in the public mind, the possible effects of any mention or celebration of my twenty-fifth anniversary as Leader of the Party. The whole thing clearly is deliberate, having as its objective not the matter of hospitalization, etc., which could have been brought up months ago or a week or days hence, but all carefully related to just come on the 25th anniversary. That is typical Tory method. No sense of decency or chivalry."

The anniversary dinner was held in the Chateau Laurier Hotel. Mackenzie King arrived at 7.00 P.M. "Crerar was waiting at the Mackenzie Street entrance. The guests were all seated in the large ball-room; also in the adjoining dining-rooms—all told about 1,000 present. There was no wait from the moment of arrival.

"Crerar, Jennie [the Prime Minister's sister, Mrs. H. M. Lay of Barrie] and I walked in together being preceded by a piper. The entire audience rose and gave us a great ovation. I was seated between Crerar and Mrs. Crerar; Jennie was given a seat next to Mr. McLarty and beside Speaker Vien of the Senate. . . . The bust of myself [by Fairbanks] was immediately in front of the head table and the little silver statuette placed later on the table in near proximity to it.

"The evening's proceedings passed off in splendid fashion. There were no delays. All of the speeches were exceptionally fine. As tributes nothing could have surpassed them. All had been prepared with evident care. What I had feared might be most embarrassing gradually solved itself for thoughts came to me as different presentations were being made, and remarks made by those who spoke suggested what it might be best to say. Happily before my turn came to speak, I felt how true it was that what was being a tribute to myself was in reality a tribute to the entire Party as an organization and its work over a quarter of century. I was able to express my acknowledgement in that way; also in a little story of Lincoln. As a matter of fact, when my time came to speak, I simply took the programme of the speakers and gave expression to a few thoughts in regard to each item as they came into my mind rejecting, for the most part, the plan that I had in mind, using, however, some of the thoughts, expressing them in reference to particular items.

"I had the thought of making some reference to Mulock and Aylesworth as well as to Sir Wilfrid but found that I had spoken much longer than it was intended. I had asked to be allowed to speak for fifteen minutes and spoke for about an hour.

"At the conclusion of the proceedings, the different guests were presented and I shook hands with most of those who were present. It pleased me very much to see how most members had their wives with them, and there was a chance to renew an expression of friendship. In speaking, I debated a little as to how far I should go in revealing my inner beliefs and outlook on life but concluded that I owed this to the Party and did not hesitate to express quite publicly my firm belief in the survival of human personality and to make at the close a reference to the influences of childhood and home, what I owe to my parents and also to my grandfather and others.

"I concluded with a message which has meant more to me than any other during life, of his love for the poor. Managed during the evening to make it clear there would be no election until after the war unless we ran our time limit of the Constitution thereby making clear our position before results of tomorrow's elections appear. Also stated I would run in Prince Albert but worded this in a way that I would give the electors there the opportunity to support me; words that may become significant in time. Should I be defeated, for generations to come, the constituency will regret it. It was a bold challenge but one which naturally our people liked. I made clear too that the issue would be the new order of things which the social programme based on 'Industry and Humanity' contains.

"There was a fine spirit of enthusiasm throughout the entire evening. I felt the right persons had been chosen to take different parts in the evening's program; chosen appropriately in reference to their different positions. What pleased me most was the tone of all the addresses. Their obvious sincerity. I should not forget that during the afternoon, I received from Mr. Churchill a telegram as fine in its wording as was his introduction of me before the two Houses of Parliament in Britain. A really magnificent tribute and one than which there could not have been anything finer. It of itself would have meant all that I could have most wished for on this 25th anniversary."

CHAPTER THREE

Waiting for Victory

BECAUSE MACKENZIE KING was so preoccupied by domestic issues after his return from the Commonwealth Conference, the remarkable success of the invasion of Europe is only occasionally reflected in the diaries for this period. On June 15 he received an interesting report from Malcolm Macdonald, the British High Commissioner in Canada, who had just returned from England. Among other things, "Malcolm said the situation with de Gaulle was very difficult. Churchill had spoken in front of Eden and a representative of the Free French so strongly against de Gaulle that the latter said he would have to withdraw. Malcolm said that neither Churchill, de Gaulle nor the President or any two of them could see eye to eye on the French situation. I expressed my sympathy with de Gaulle though he is very troublesome, as being entitled to every consideration in the light of fighting from the first for France."

In mid-July, General de Gaulle himself visited Ottawa after talks with President Roosevelt in Washington. He arrived at Rockcliffe airport on July 11 and was met by the Prime Minister. From the airport de Gaulle went to Government House and then, with the Governor-General and Princess Alice, went to Parliament Hill, where he spoke from an outdoor platform to a huge crowd. Mackenzie King observed that all the speeches "were given a fine reception on the Hill and I am told that they came over the radio very well, though at the time of speaking, there was a terrible echo from the buildings immediately opposite." During a luncheon at Government House Mackenzie King had a talk of some length with de Gaulle and, in the afternoon, the General came to the Prime Minister's office at the House of Commons for a conversation at which Mr. St. Laurent was also present. Mackenzie King reported that "the conversation with de Gaulle was most interesting. St. Laurent acted as interpreter. Robertson was present. Also Bonneau [the Representative of the Free French Movement in Ottawa]. I asked the General if there was anything he would like to speak on in particular. He had spoken previously of the recognition of the provisional Government of France but had said to me that this did not matter at the present time, and that in the long run, it might be just as well if no recognition were given, or if recognition were not given until a Government was formally established in France. The United States would then find it necessary to have its Ambassador in France and the moment they had an Ambassador there, that would be recognition. The same thing would be true of Britain. Meanwhile no group would have been said to have been recognized to the advantage of the other.

"He had much enjoyed his talks with the President who had shown a very open mind. Also his talks with Mr. Cordell Hull whom he liked. They had discussed arrangements respecting the administration of affairs in France. It was agreed that administration should be carried on, where possible, by the French but that it was also necessary that Eisenhower should be the judge as military leader, of when the territory should be turned over to the French. He felt sure the talks he had had with the President would be helpful. What he seemed most concerned about was that France would be duly recognized in regard to matters of world organization, international relations in which he would be interested. Small powers as well as great powers would have to have their voice. He felt that France standing for democratic ideals, it was all important that she should be of the group that would have mostly to do with the shaping of the new order.

"In conversation, I took a bit of paper and pointed out there were different stages at which different nations might participate to a greater or lesser degree in these matters. I spoke of how we had managed while the war is on, in allowing the United States, Britain and Russia and, for certain purposes, China, to be regarded as the directing powers. Asked whether to bring out of a nebulous condition into concrete forms of beginning, it would not be advisable perhaps to continue these groups. This would come after the signing of the Armistice and before the conclusion of peace. In that period, a sort of constitution could be worked out, and then there would come the part which each could play in peace negotiations, and following that, there would be the parts which all would take in the administration of the world organization.

"De Gaulle was non-committal beyond emphasizing that France should be recognized at as early a date as possible, where her interests immediate or in the future were likely to be affected. I mentioned having, in England, spoken of the distinction between the U.K. and the Commonwealth, and our readiness to have the U.K. act as one of the great Three or Four to bring an organization into being, though as a nation of the Commonwealth, we would wish to be consulted and have our views heard in reference to whatever pertains to ourselves. Robertson pointed out that in that connection, there was a parallel with the position of France at present and her position once she becomes a free nation with her regularly established government. Robertson added that that would be based on the functional idea as expressed by myself last year and that it was perhaps the way of having the situation met. De Gaulle pointed out that some questions would come up at once, for example, the matter of the establishment of bases for world protection, and there the question of the islands in the Pacific would immediately come to the fore. France would not allow their islands to be disposed of by other powers. I mentioned the Dutch had large possessions also which they would wish to have considered. He said these problems would certainly have to be watched very carefully. . . ."

After the interview, the Prime Minister and General de Gaulle met the press and Mackenzie King reported that he "introduced the press to the General rather than the General to the press. He made a little speech seated to my right. Referred to his visit to the States and Canada and then asked for questions, to all of which he made remarkably skilful replies."

"At dinner," Mackenzie King wrote later, "I had an exceedingly interesting talk with de Gaulle. He spoke English remarkably well. . . . During the dinner, I tried to decide what I should do and say. I had told St. Laurent to be prepared to speak for the Government. When the moment of speaking came, I had the happy thought of referring to our having two official languages and began what I had to say in proposing the General's toast by mentioning this country being one of two official languages, and tonight I thought we should honour the one we had most in our thoughts. Before calling on St. Laurent, I welcomed the visitors de Gaulle had with him. Thanked him for his visit to Canada and what he had said on Parliament Hill. Spoke of the composition of those at the table: Foreign Ministers representing allied nations; our own Ministers, Chiefs of Staff, chief officials of State, Chief Justice, etc., all being present to do him honour. I then spoke of his visit as opening another chapter in the interesting history of Canada; looking out on the river, recalled how Champlain had come up the St. Lawrence and then the Ottawa, past where we were, 310 years ago, then founding settlement of government and planting the emblem of his faith, spreading the tenets of Christianity, etc., laying the foundation of New France in this new world. How this later had become British North America and was now Canada—one country, and that today to Canada, he had come again from France to express to us his appreciation of what Canada was doing toward the restoration of old France. (This is the second time in a quarter of a century that Canada has been performing this role.) There was room and material for a speech but I did not wish to take the time and was too tired to work out my thoughts. However, I concluded with a few references from the heart saying that I hoped God would bless him, continue to give him strength and vision for his great task, and ended up by saying that I hoped he might live long to see the France he loved and served so well, and to which he had been so faithful, enshrined again not only in the hearts of all her own people, but enshrined in the hearts of the free nations of the world. It was a spontaneous utterance, but it evoked an immediate and very marked response.

"When I sat down, de Gaulle turned to me and said: Your words are deeply moving. Later in the evening, many who were present came up and some of them said it was one of the best speeches I had made at any time.

"St. Laurent made an impassioned and fine speech, the effect of which was spoiled just a little in his having to look to his notes to get his thought, and to read part of what he was saying. French Members present told me it was an extremely fine utterance. De Gaulle himself spoke in French, very quietly, very effectively and exceedingly well. Gave one the impression of a man with a very clear mission; high and noble purpose."

The Prime Minister later recorded his dinner conversation with de Gaulle: "Combining what he said then with what he said at other times, the following were points I should wish to remember: I asked him to explain to me the reason for the difference between the feeling that there seemed to be at times between Churchill and himself and the unwillingness of the President and Mr. Hull to recognize himself as the head of a provisional government and kindred matters.

"In a very quiet way, he told me that this went back to June, 1940, when France collapsed. That Churchill was at Paris along with Halifax and Beaverbrook and another man; that he, de Gaulle, had been a member of Reynaud's Government. They were discussing the situation, and the question came up as to help from America. When they found they could get no help from America, some of the French Members of the Government began to feel there was no hope whatever for France. That they had better come to terms at once with the Germans. De Gaulle at once said: we have our Empire. The British will help. They have their Dominions. We can fight. Pétain, Weygand and some others took the view that it was hopeless. One of them said—I think it was Pétain—that we have no Empire that can fight. (These were not the exact words.) The British will be beaten in six days. Their Dominions will not fight if she is beaten. He then said something to the effect that Churchill and others had said: Oh, this was a terrible situation; if America would not help, he could not see what could be done. De Gaulle evidently got the impression that Churchill at the time was ready to give up so far as France was concerned. He did not say this and I am not sure that I am right in the impression I gathered but what was left on my mind was something to the effect that that was what he felt. I think it must have been over the question of supplies where Churchill refused to give up the last lot of planes which Britain had to keep and which saved the day so far as Britain was concerned. It was, however, at that time that de Gaulle had formed the impression that Britain was ready to let France go if the necessity arose to save herself. (Of this, I am not too sure.) It was a little difficult to follow what he was telling me but the following is perfectly clear: It relates to the United States. They were planning to have the Government moved to Bordeaux. He said the Cabinet had been meeting and planning this when Bullitt, the United States Ambassador, arrived and said he was instructed by President Roosevelt not to leave Paris—that his instructions were not to go to Bordeaux and not to leave Paris. That meant that he would not be accredited representative of the United States to a portion of government that was prepared to fight, but would be the accredited representative to the government that was yielding to the Germans. From that time on, the United States representative was to Vichy and Vichy of course became increasingly the creature of Germany. De Gaulle thought that the President and the Secretary of State had made a mistake at that time. It was a mistake they did not like to admit, and it was difficult for them to admit it now. They had continued to recognize Pétain and they had refused to recognize de Gaulle in any of their important negotiations regarding North Africa, etc. He said no doubt he himself had been difficult and said sharp things at times but he had to maintain his position as representing what he believed to be France. He said the more they attacked him and dealt with Vichy and the like, the more they were rallying the true Frenchmen to his side and helping to make him the recognized head of the French nation. He spoke of this not in any egoistic way but of this being the effect of their action though they had intended to have their attacks on him have the very opposite effect. The French people came to look on him as standing for the freedom of France. He said to me he thought the Government of Britain was not too united in their own views and it was hard for those who were in Paris to reach decisions that they could be sure would be supported. He went on to say that this of course was all past. The main thing was friendship for France. He was satisfied to allow everything to be subordinated to that.

"I spoke to him about the Maginot line and other matters of defence. He told me that the Belgians would not work out the Maginot line with the French and had severed their agreement just before the war. Mentioned other circumstances which he said accounted for France having got a very much worse result than she was really entitled to get. That she deserved better than had come of what she actually had done and was prepared to do.

"When I spoke about Pétain, he said that he was all right for appearances and occasions and the like but that really at heart, he had no feeling. That he was a showman on the surface but hard at heart. That today he slept nearly all the time though for two or three hours he might understand matters quite well. The rest of the time he was almost stupid. He said there were different reasons why different men took the course they did, but the main reason that most of them acted as they did was their belief that the Germans would destroy Britain and all would be gone in a very short time."

De Gaulle, according to Mackenzie King, thought the war "is pretty sure to be over this autumn. Spoke of superiority of the allies in planes, in gun power, the way the Russians are advancing and the advances made from the South and North. While the Germans would fight determinedly, he believed they could not last very well beyond October and might give up sooner.

"After dinner, he spoke to me quite earnestly about coming over to France. He said he wished I would take occasion to come before long; come on to the French soil, see our troops there and be there. I told him about just having returned from England, and about possibility of elections here. He continued to press saying that I could be of great help to the situation and to having it properly interpreted if I would spend some time in France at any time from now on. I told him Ralston would be going but doubted if I could. He, however, continued to press that and at night, when he said good-bye at the door, he said we would meet in Paris he hoped before long. He is quite confident of victory."

Later Mackenzie King added: "More and more, I keep seeing in de Gaulle and his stand the kind of purpose and stand which my grandfather had taken in his day. I felt as though he and other forces were working to help to a true understanding of de Gaulle's position and the position generally."

The Prime Minister said farewell to de Gaulle at the airport at 7.30 the next morning (July 12). "When de Gaulle arrived at the airport," Mackenzie King wrote, "he greeted me very warmly as he got out of the Governor General's car. In a few minutes, he had in his hands a wrapped paper parcel which he placed in mine saying it was only a picture of himself. I had thought several times last night of asking one of his staff if he could secure a photo for me. It touched me deeply that he should have handed me a framed photo of himself. I did not upwrap the picture until coming back to the library at Laurier House. We had a little talk together and I walked with him to his plane. Shook hands with him, three times holding his hand in mine and looking into his eyes and wishing him well. I told him that his visit had been a great inspiration and would do great good. The latter I had said last night probably. I feel it has been a very important episode in his career and that his coming to Canada has been extremely fortunate at this time. I feel, too, that our meeting together has been remarkably fortunate.

"When I came to the library, I unwrapped the parcel and found to my delight that the picture was one evidently taken quite recently and exquisitely framed, black leather with gold. Had been inscribed in the morning: 'A Monsieur Mackenzie King, Premier Ministre du Canada—En témoignage d'amitié française.' It is dated July 12, 1944, and is signed 'C. de Gaulle.' As I unwrapped the frame, I placed it on my desk and turned it involuntarily towards the picture of my grandfather. I thought how strange it was that the photographs of these two men who had played similar roles, true patriots, should be on my table at this hour."

At this same time, Mackenzie King was concerned with aspects of the war situation that affected the timing of an election in Canada. He was greatly upset to learn on July 10 that as a result of a bill to amend the Election Act which had passed the House of Commons while he was absent in England, it would require four months to complete the overseas voting in the next general election. "Apparently," he wrote, "no one has paid much attention to this measure which went through while I was away. Also am definite that provision must be changed which takes away the right to vote in all parts of Canada from Japanese who are Canadian citizens. This will make much unpleasantness, but I cannot see my way to being a party to depriving any Canadian citizens of the first right of a citizen regardless of his origin. The reason I am doing it is that it represents all I have stood for in fighting against Borden's legislation at the time of the last war."

On July 12 he took up in Cabinet "the necessity of appointing immediately Registrars to take the vote of soldiers overseas in preparation of possible election before the date of the Presidential elections. Colleagues I think seemed a bit surprised this might come so soon. It was necessary, however, in view of provisions of Statute re taking of soldiers' votes to have this matter attended to at once."

The next day in Cabinet the Prime Minister "brought up the question of the amendment to the War Services Election Act which would preclude the Canadian citizens of Japanese origin from voting in provinces other than British Columbia. I said quite openly in Council that a Bill had been approved in Cabinet the day after I had arrived in London. Nothing had been said to me about it; that this was quite wrong; that all Members must have known that I was very strongly opposed to the War-time Elections

Act passed by Borden and had fought throughout my life for the protection of minorities. That the question of the rights of a British subject was a fundamental question and that for my part, I would not countenance the taking away of those rights under a Liberal Government and particularly my own administration. That I had said in Council that I thought the matter should be remedied in the Senate but was told that a plan had been reached which would satisfy everyone and occasion no comments. However, instead of that, there had been prolonged debate in the Senate which was now being carried on in the country and which had to be ended one way or another. I pointed out that to accept the Bill as it is was to have Canadian franchise for the Federal House determined for all the provinces by what was law in only one. That this was a position that the Dominion could not countenance.

"I spoke of the clause, by rights, not having any place at all in the War Services Bill. That it related to the Elections Act generally and that the War Services Bill applied to the services alone. I then said I had taken up the matter with Clerk of the House [Arthur Beauchesne] and had a report from him on what could be done to meet the situation by amending the Senate amendment. . . . I then mentioned that while I was quite agreeable to not allowing the Japanese to vote in British Columbia, as was already the case, I was opposed to allowing the Japanese who were Canadian citizens and who had been Canadian citizens in the other provinces prior to the war having this right taken away from them. I added that I did not think it was right to extend the franchise to Japanese who had left or been taken away from British Columbia to other provinces, if they could not have had the right, had they remained in British Columbia itself. As soon as I made this statement, I saw at once I had eased the situation for everybody. I said that Dr. King [government leader in the Senate] had thought it was best to have the clause struck out altogether. That perhaps I had embarrassed him by letting matters go the length they had. Dr. King said at once that what I had suggested would be acceptable in the Senate, he was sure, and McLarty who, as Secretary of State, was responsible along with Mackenzie for what has been done said he thought what I had stated was right in principle. There was some discussion as to whether Beauchesne's interpretation of the law was correct, but it was agreed that if it was not, an amendment should be made along the lines that I had indicated. McLarty was to bring in the amendment on Monday and we were to get the Bill over as quickly as possible to the Senate. That clears up for the time being at least, and will do so ultimately, a very difficult question."

For some time, George Drew, the Conservative Premier of Ontario, had been deluging other provincial premiers, the press, and the federal government with letters urging the calling of a Dominion-Provincial Conference. On Saturday, July 22, Mackenzie King was told that Drew had said on the radio the previous evening that "what he was living most for was to get the Government at Ottawa out of office. I secured a copy of what he had said. It gave me just what I needed for not having a Dominion-Provincial Conference before the elections. When the Prime Minister of one Government attacks another, tries to put it out of office, instead of co-operating at a time of war, one has a pretty good reason for not attempting any negotiations in the nature of a joint conference before an election. I had decided not to have the Conference for the reason that I knew this would be his attitude. I had not expected him to say so in the open, but it is like Drew."

Conservative pressure on the government continued and Mr. King was especially conscious of it as his 25th anniversary as leader approached. On August 4, the External Affairs estimates were before Parliament and the Prime Minister discovered that the Opposition "intended to carry on a considerable debate. This became more apparent in the evening. Fortunately I was able to have a little rest at the dinner hour and to keep fairly fresh throughout the evening. Green, of Vancouver South, Hazen of Saint John, and Adamson, of Toronto, all reverted back to an Imperial Council for war; centralized secretariat and one voice for the Empire. Effort also to have it appear that I was not loyal. I did not use enough expressions of loyalty; also that I was against centralization of the Empire, etc. Before the day was over, I was able to put the entire party into a humiliating position by reading questions which Maclean's Magazine had put to Bracken and his answers. Pickersgill had picked up this material before we went to England. I never saw a party look more chagrined as I read this material to them, all the time pointing out that their criticisms had been really criticisms of their own Leader's position. When 11 o'clock came, the debate was not concluded. I announced other business for tomorrow. Graydon could not help asking when the debate on External Affairs would conclude. I gave him no satisfaction stating we would get through with our other legislation first. A few weeks ago, he had asked if when Friday of this week came, I would not review the question of sitting on Saturday and possibility of having a brief intermission over the week-end presumably including Monday which is a Civic Holiday. The Tories hoped that I would try to have the House not sit on Monday and then would make a strong plea of my having held up Parliament in order to glorify myself on the 25th anniversary. Mackenzie told me he had spoken to Graydon about the House not sitting on Monday evening. Graydon had said he had real affection for me but some of his party were very bitter and also there was the group from Toronto; they would not like it, would attack him, and make trouble. He suggested nothing be said on Saturday night, hoping to move adjournment for Monday night. I told Mackenzie on no account to accept any favours. Mackenzie said he could get enough men to keep the business going Monday night. They could take turns in squads from the dinner. I told him by all means to do this but I confess I did feel that our public life is at a pretty low level; that among public men serving in Parliament, it was evidence of pretty mean natures where after 25 years and considering the circumstances of Monday night's dinner, the Opposition would not of its own motion propose an adjournment to enable all Members to attend. It shows the bitter hatred of the Tory Party toward myself. It has become violent over the social legislation and a mounting praise that has come from London and the prestige I am gaining because of the 25th anniversary of leadership contrasted with what the Tories are experiencing in the leadership of their Party today. I think what worries them most is my not fixing a definite time for an election. They look upon the uncertainty as a war of nerves which undoubtedly it is to them."

The External Affairs debate was resumed on August 11. Mackenzie King reported he "allowed Diefenbaker to make a speech at some length to which I made an immediate reply. Graydon later made a brief speech to which I also replied. As he brought in Lord Halifax's name [see vol. I, pp. 636–41], I sought to straighten out the record in that particular. Also took advantage of the occasion to place on record my own feelings about the iniquity of stirring up racial prejudice, making a drive, without naming him, at Drew; also spoke on the need of a national flag and national anthem thinking it well to get this on record before the session ended.

"Pickersgill, who was in the gallery, and Robertson, who was on the floor, both were quite elated at the way the debate ended. Also Claxton. Either Claxton or Pickersgill said it had ended in a blaze of glory."

On August 12, a lengthy meeting of the Cabinet considered "communications from Drew regarding . . . Dominion-Provincial Conference. . . . I indicated to the Cabinet the line I intended to take—to have Conference postponed until after elections. Drew has brought himself into a very awkward position."

August 14 was the closing day of the session. After the Supply Bill had passed, the Prime Minister read a statement he had prepared about the Dominion-Provincial Conference, which he noted "immensely pleased our men. It was the right moment at which to have brought in the statement. Drew today had telegraphed that there had been a misunderstanding of previous telegrams, had his officers coming down tomorrow, etc. Nothing could have been more opportune than the chance to make the statement when I did and nothing could have been more conclusive than the quotations from Drew's own speech as to why no Conference could be a success before an election than was contained therein. Graydon tried to say something to cover the situation and in the course of remarks said that I could not have said more about Drew. I replied, no, he had said all that was necessary, which is about as effective a reply as I have made to anything in my years in the House of Commons."

The same day, the Prime Minister also made a statement about Members' indemnities. Hansell, a Social Credit Member, had been speaking about the expenses of Members and Mackenzie King recorded that he "at once sent out for the English Hansard of 1911 with quotations from Lloyd George on payment of Members and rose and made a strong plea for the indemnity not being taxed in subsequent sessions. Ilsley was at my right. I was conscious of the discussion we had had and of his attitude but spoke out emphatically as I had said I would, about the position I would take at another session. . . .

"I could see that the Members of the House generally greatly appreciated what I said and I am sure it will be helpful in securing as candidates some of those who otherwise would have failed us altogether, and above all I am sure that it is in the national interest that the independence of Members of Parliament be maintained and that the best type shall be brought into the House. I was glad that this opportunity came before the session ended."

As the Prime Minister rose to leave the House to go to the Senate for the Royal Assent, the Members gave him an ovation. "I was very happy," he wrote. "Went out feeling like a young man and rejoicing that a tremendous programme had been carried through with complete success. Virtually nothing left undone that was planned at the time the Speech from the Throne was framed.

"I had had meanwhile to arrange about the Senate and the Deputy of the Governor being on hand at the right time. Went myself to the Speaker's Apartments of the Senate just after midnight and at a quarter past 12, Dr. King and I were on either side of Rinfret [the Chief Justice acting as Deputy Governor-General] in the Senate Chamber. The Commons were sent for. A goodly number attended at the Bar. By half past twelve, Royal Assent had been given to the Bills and the long adjournment till January 31st had begun. As I sat in the Senate Chamber, I ran over in my mind the names of those with whom I have been most closely associated in my personal and political life. I felt exceedingly peaceful and happy and completely unconcerned as to the future. It may well be the last time that I shall be in either the House of Commons or the Senate though I rather imagine what I have in mind as to another session for electoral reform will actually come in the course of events. On the other hand, pressure may have come from the Party itself which, in the light of events, actual happenings may occasion and before the 31st of January. Be all this as it may and be the outcome what it may, I shall sincerely feel that it is all for the best. To me it has been amazing the way in which I have in the last few days been able to leave of record and round out my views on such matters as the national flag, national anthem, attitude toward foreign nations, relations with the provinces, independence of Parliament, etc., etc. All things seem to have come to a complete fruition and I have had the certain knowledge that the Party is more loyal towards me today than if possible it has been at any time. Also that I have in greater measure than at any time the respect of Members of all Parties in the Commons and of the press and people of the country. It certainly has been a fulfillment for the Government of God's promises however little deserved they may have been."

One of the Prime Minister's preoccupations in the weeks following the adjournment was the supervision of arrangements for the second Roosevelt–Churchill conference at Quebec. On August 12 he had received through Sir Patrick Duff, the Deputy High Commissioner for the United Kingdom, "a communication from the Secretary of State for the Dominions to ask if I would be agreeable to having Churchill and the President meet at Quebec on September 10 or 11. That, if so, the King would ask the Governor General to allow them the use of the Citadel. I said at once that the Government would be only too pleased to make all the necessary arrangements. Churchill, at the moment, is in Italy and the President, at the Pacific Coast. They have concluded they should meet in Quebec as Quebec affords the ideal location. Duff did not know how many arrangements would have to be made but thought the delegations might be only half the size of last year. I said I supposed they would expect me to act as host as I did before. If so, I shall be very happy so to act.

"It was rather amusing when Redfern [Sir Shuldham Redfern, Secretary to the Governor-General] came in. His mission was to tell me of a message received from the King that the Governor General had asked him to communicate to me, asking the Governor to allow the Citadel to be used by Churchill and the President if the Conference were definitely settled for the 10th or the 11th. He had not known of what mission Duff had been on.

"I told Redfern of my talk with Sir Patrick and the undertaking given. Sir Shuldham then asked what I thought the Governor should do, whether he should change his dates for the Maritimes tour or keep them as they were and go out on a little trip for the time the Conference might be held. I said that was entirely for the Governor to decide himself. Sir Shuldham thought it would be best not to change the arrangements, for Their Excellencies to go on a little fishing or other trip. I said I thought it would be best as it would not raise any suspicion about the Conference. He asked about the time to get things in readiness. I told him I thought three days would be ample so far as the preparations of the Citadel were concerned.

"I must say that this word on the whole was very welcome to me. It, of course, gives a further reason why there should be no immediate haste with an election. It does, of course, cut into possibilities of a trip to Western Canada but, this year, being free of Parliament, not having another heavy session ahead of us, and time to breathe, I shall really enjoy I think being at Quebec with the President and Churchill. Besides nothing could be more interesting than the questions which will be discussed and to be so completely on the inside in relation to all of them would mean a great deal. Moreover the close relationship of Churchill, the President and myself cannot fail to be of help to me politically. Altogether I greatly welcome the prospect. September, too, will be a pleasant month to be at the side of the St. Lawrence."

The Prime Minister had a discussion about the arrangements for the Conference with E. H. Coleman, the Undersecretary of State, on August 18. The visitors were expected to be about half the number attending in 1943, but Mackenzie King indicated there should be nothing essentially different in the arrangements though he "emphasized the importance of my taking more completely the position of host in the matter of entertaining distinguished guests." Characteristically, he added that "it will be helpful to myself and the Party to be again so intimately associated with Churchill and the President at Quebec."

The arrangements for the Quebec Conference gave Mackenzie King much less concern than they had in 1943. He did, however, note in his diary on September 3 that "during the afternoon a telegram came from Churchill saying he was looking forward to seeing me but also mentioning as most secret that he had had a touch of his old complaint but 'barring accidents, felt he would be able to keep his engagements.' If it means bronchitis that is not so bad, if it means pneumonia it might be very serious.

"I felt I should send him a message which would reassure him in the matter of any delays. This I did before the night was over. Already there has been a postponement of a day or two of the time originally fixed for arrival at Halifax.

"Robertson and I also had some communicating back and forth on the matter of press arrangements and accommodation at Quebec. The President seems to be concerned about both and I am afraid much is being done without his knowledge. . . . I feel a real concern as regards both Churchill and himself and I am glad to be with them both in the near future provided that in the interval all goes well."

Mackenzie King went to Quebec on August 21 to stay with the Governor-General and Princess Alice at the Citadel. He arrived just before lunch after a wretched night on the train and was very weary. The Lieutenant-Governor of Quebec, Sir Eugene Fiset, was at tea that afternoon and the Prime Minister reported that he "enjoyed very much the talk with Fiset, both at this time and later when we drove together around the National Battlefields Park. He says Godbout's organization was exceedingly poor. Nothing done in an effective way in the rural constituencies where Union Nationale had been busy with organization. Godbout was fearful of cities, Montreal and Quebec, which were really the ones that supported him. He felt Godbout had made a terrible mistake in not defending the Federal Government in its stand against conscription and inflation, or having Federal Ministers assist in the campaign. He thinks the fight will be a hard one federally. Duplessis is good at organizing. He said I should insist on Power taking hold at once" along with Senator Lesage (Liberal organizer), and "get to work constituency by constituency. He believes if they do we should be able to count on at least 40 seats in Quebec but unless there is effective organization work, we will certainly lose. Feels it will be a good deal of a miracle if we win throughout Canada after, as a government, going through four or five years of war."

Unfortunately, this talk with Fiset was the only thing Mackenzie King did enjoy during his two-day visit. After going to the train on the evening of August 22 he wrote in his diary, "I do not know why I should have felt so completely ill at ease throughout the whole of the visit. I do not recall in my life having experienced more in the way of restraint and this wholly due to some curious subjective force within myself. It was in no way the fault of His Excellency and Her Royal Highness. They did their utmost to make me feel happy and comfortable. Had I been in prison, I could not have felt more constrained or more ill at ease. It cannot be helped but here it is."

The next evening (August 23) he returned to the theme in his diary. "The experience of the Citadel," he wrote, "continues to haunt me like a nightmare. I feel so sorry to have not been able to measure up in any sort of way to what would have been expected of me." And he added: "Today there was a sense of freedom and a sense of equality. Instinctively I revolt at anyone from the Old Country exercising even outwardly any semblance of control over Canada."

On the way back from Quebec Mackenzie King bought an Ottawa evening paper "which told of Paris and Marseilles both having been freed. This means the rapid freedom of the whole of France. There will be heavy fighting when it comes to the invasion of Germany itself. However, the liberation of France has been in every way much more rapid and less costly than was ever contemplated. It is a tremendous relief to see the skies clearing and the end drawing near. . . .

"Robertson met us on our arrival at Ottawa. Was tremendously pleased at the news from France. Wanted to have celebrations throughout Canada. I said I would phone him of this in the morning. Lay [the Prime Minister's chauffeur] was waiting with the car. We drove out to Kingsmere. I was never more grateful to be getting back to the quiet of my little home." The next morning (August 24) the Prime Minister advised "against any celebration at the instance of the Government. Mentioned among other things that the announcement of a previous celebration had been premature. Also that I felt there were domestic reasons and international ones why we should wait until France itself had been liberated before becoming over-enthusiastic about Paris. Before evening word came that Paris was by no means freed as yet." After his return from Quebec, the Prime Minister spent most of his time at Kingsmere until he went to Quebec again to meet Roosevelt and Churchill.

The last of a series of provincial elections during 1944 took place in New Brunswick on August 28. That evening Mackenzie King "received a fairly conclusive report . . . which would indicate a substantial Liberal victory. It was a welcome piece of news but I thought it best to await the morning before sending any message." The next morning he "wrote out a message to McNair, Premier of New Brunswick, congratulating him on yesterday's victory. It is a splendid victory, the Liberals having been returned by a considerably increased majority. It will have a profound effect throughout the whole Dominion. It is now apparent that the Conservatives have nothing to hope for in the Maritime Provinces or Quebec or the Prairie Provinces, that the C.C.F. have nothing to hope for in the Maritime Provinces, Quebec or Alberta, and that the Liberal Party is the only one which can hope to have a following in all the provinces of Canada. Altogether, if our people were organized, and have a properly organized campaign, it would seem to me that we are certain of victory, particularly with the feeling as it is as to the importance of Canada being represented by myself at the Peace Conferences. I felt a considerable weight off my mind as a result of the victory in New Brunswick. It was the best tonic the Party has had in the last two years."

In preparation for the Quebec Conference, the War Committee gave consideration at this period to Canada's part in the war against Japan. On

August 31, Mackenzie King "spent the morning going over papers relating to strategy and Canada's possible contribution to the war against Japan. I have been over much of this material before. Sought to get a pretty complete picture. We discussed the matter at considerable length in the War Committee during the afternoon. I took the position strongly at the outset that Canada's contribution should be one made north of the Equator as had been the case with our contribution to Europe. Also that we should have the all-over plans before deciding upon our contribution and should consider together the contributions proposed by the different defence services. Also decide on what was to be done in the way of contributions toward forces for occupation in Europe and demobilization. As I expected the defence Ministers were pretty much set to make a very large contribution. Ralston was very quiet. Had his proposals on the lines of the recommendations of the British Chiefs of Staff for one division to operate from Canada but had had also their proposals for what amounts to two divisions for occupation in Europe. I refused to have any decision made till we knew the proposed contributions from the Navy and Air Force. It was apparent from confidential despatch from Churchill that the British were counting on the co-operation of Australia and New Zealand in the Bay of Bengal, the taking of Rangoon. Were anxious to get out of certain Burma commitments but in the memo no mention was made of any suggested co-operation from Canada. However, in the aide memoire of the Chiefs of Staff, Canada was down for a very large air force and for a very large naval force. Power pointed out that what was set out as a British air force really included what they were expecting in the way of some 50 squadrons from Canada. He took strongly the position that there was no commitment that these forces should be used in the south east. He felt they should be used in the north along with American forces. I can see, however, there is going to be a real struggle to maintain that position. There will be the same struggle over the naval forces, the British seeking to use pretty much our whole naval service.

"Before War Committee I had a talk with General Pope who has come from Washington to take on a new post here. He told me that we were neither being asked nor were we wanted to take part in the fight against Japan so far as any existing need was concerned. It is apparent that the Americans want to make that fight themselves. It is also apparent that the British are having difficulty in getting a look in with them, but are most anxious to do so. Apparently they feel they must retake Singapore themselves to redeem face in the Far East. The whole aide-memoire of the British looked to our helping initially with the air force and the navy and then being 'shifted' to the north later should there be large operations there. I drew attention to the fact that the aide-memoire pointed out that large operations would probably be necessary to conquer the main island of Japan and that we should keep that in mind. I agreed that it was desirable we should have some forces with the Americans in fighting against Japan itself. I took particular care to point out that a general election was immediately ahead. Said that I would have to state frankly to the public what our contribution was to be. That I was perfectly sure the Canadian people would not agree to any contribution south of the equator. It was to be remembered that though we had fought for five years that America had fought for two years less and Russia also for two years less. There is a possibility, indeed a probability of Russia coming in against Japan. It is going to be hard to control the situation vis-a-vis the defence departments, but I have stated that the matter is so important it must be decided by the Cabinet as a whole and I am planning accordingly. The Ministers have lost a sense of proportion in the matter of expenditures. I learned that Power and others take the attitude that it is desirable to keep our forces employed rather than have them come home from now on. I feel we must seek now to save both life and money. I have been taking this position right along. Indeed I believe there can be only an anti-climax in our effort if we string it out over another couple of years, except to operate from our own coast in what we do against Japan.

"Ralston had suggested bringing Pope to Ottawa and letting Letson go to Washington [General Letson was Adjutant General at Army Headquarters; he was later Secretary to Governor-General Alexander]. He is bringing over someone from England, an officer he regards as exceptionally good to help on the work of demobilization. He and I both agreed that Pope should be associated with myself as Prime Minister as a Military Staff Officer. He would also be associated with the War Committee as a Military Secretary and with the Chiefs of Staff as an associate either with or without the use of that name. This contact . . . would give us the benefit of his wide and general knowledge and be helpful to keep under review the work of all departments that should be related. I had a pleasant talk with Pope. He was most cordial about his readiness to take on whatever was required of him in the way of service. I explained that I wanted someone to whom I would not have to tell what to do but who would tell me what was required, why and how it should be done, and who would keep me fully informed on everything I should know. I explained the relationship of Robertson, Heeney and others, of confidence and mutual trust, etc. I emphasized what I was most concerned in was making sure that Canada's contribution was what was right and just, but not anything that was unnecessary, something simply for keeping on men, etc. I can see that the work of demobilization is going to be very heavy."

Participation in the Japanese war was discussed in the full Cabinet on September 6. Apparently "all were agreed Canada should participate. Seemed to be a consensus of view of having one division prepared to go to Japan; one to remain as army of occupation in Europe. Navy to be cut down 50%. The contribution of the Air Force to be made smaller than contemplated.

"St. Laurent was the most outspoken and I thought the most sensible in his view of justice of what Canada has done and has been doing."

Mackenzie King left for the conference in Quebec on Sunday, September 10, and arrived late that evening. He was surprised to find the station filled with cameramen and reporters. "Learned from Coleman that all the arrivals had been materially advanced. That the President's train was arriving at 9, and Churchill's at 10. It had been arranged that the President's train would wait till after Churchill had arrived. I would meet Churchill and his party. The Governor General and Princess Alice would meet the President and Mrs. Roosevelt, and Churchill and myself, and then the procession would take place to the Citadel. This would all be at Wolfe's Cove. The procession to the Citadel would be: the Governor General and the President; then Princess Alice, Mrs. Roosevelt and Mrs. Churchill, and in the last car, Mr. Churchill and myself. We would leave at 10, arriving at the Citadel immediately after.

"The Chiefs of Staff were at the station; also Brigadier Blais, Commanding Officer of the district. After more photographs had been taken, I drove to the Citadel with Coleman. Was given the Commanding Officer's apartment, all very beautifully and comfortably arranged."

In closing the day's entry in the diary, he reflected: "Remarkable indeed is the fact that today is the fifth anniversary of the day on which Canada entered the war and that I should be in Quebec receiving both Churchill and Roosevelt on their second visit to the Citadel for conference, and that during this week, we should have meeting at Montreal the representatives of some forty of the United Nations. It all shows how in the period of the war, Canada has emerged in every sense of the word into a world power."

Mackenzie King, with General Pope, left the Citadel at 9.40 the next morning (September 11) to go to Wolfe's Cove station to meet Churchill. On arriving, the Prime Minister was informed that President Roosevelt was waiting to see him. "I looked about for the Governor General. He had not arrived. I mentioned that I thought the arrangements were somewhat different but he [a member of the President's staff] explained that the car was there and the President was anxious to see me. I went in. He was seated to the right, Mrs. Roosevelt was standing in front of the sofa. I shook hands first with the President and then with Mrs. Roosevelt telling them how delighted I was to see them both again and particularly to welcome them in Quebec.

"The President said at once: I wanted to see you first; also to be ahead of Winston, so I gave orders to have the car moved in. It seemed to me that the President was rather assuming that he was in his own country. It seemed to me, looking at the President, that he had failed very much since I last saw him. He is very much thinner in body and also is much thinner in his face. He looks distinctly older and worn. I confess I was just a little bit shocked at his appearance. He asked me if we were going to have an election. I told him I was not going to have an election till the war was over. That I had made that clear some time ago. Also that I thought it would be more helpful to him if our elections were delayed till his were over. He said at once that he agreed with that. I pointed out that if by any chance we were defeated, it might react and that there was a greater possibility of our being defeated than of him. He said to me he was far from sure of the results. I asked why that was. He said: we cannot get our people to register; cannot get the vote out. I then spoke on the possibility of having a special session to put through electoral reform, compulsory voting and transferable vote. Mrs. Roosevelt said she thought compulsory voting was a very good thing, would be very helpful. . . .

"His Excellency was just arriving as I came out of the President's car. I went over to his motor and then took him and Princess Alice to the President's car as far as the door and left him there, while I went to meet Mr. and Mrs. Churchill. Their train was just drawing in at that moment. I boarded the car and greeted Churchill by saying: I am so delighted to see you again, also Mrs. Churchill. I added that I was glad to see them both looking so well. He spoke of not having been too well but feeling much better today. He then spoke about the President. I told him that the President's car had come in, and I took him and Mrs. Churchill over to the platform. To my surprise, the President had already moved out of his own car into his automobile and he was coming down the plank way as we arrived at the foot of it.

"Churchill went to the door of the car and he and the President had a little talk together. I introduced Mrs. Churchill and Mrs. Roosevelt and Princess Alice. Later Mrs. Churchill came and had a word with the President. I conducted the three ladies to the car which they were to take to the Citadel and then later had Churchill come with me to the car in which we were to drive together. His first remark was that they had given us a closed car. I said I thought that was because it was the Governor's own car, and said I was sorry that it was closed.

"A procession was formed with the Governor General and the President in the President's car followed by a closed car with Her Royal Highness and Mrs. Roosevelt and Mrs. Churchill, and then a car with Mr. Churchill and myself."

During the drive to the Citadel, Mackenzie King had a pleasant talk with the British Prime Minister. "I asked him if he expected the war to be over this year. He said the military authorities believed it will, 'I don't.' 'I think it will be longer.' About his own health, he told me that he had had a chill after coming back from Italy and they discovered a small patch on one of his lungs but that had cleared away. He had not felt well. While crossing the Atlantic, he had stayed in bed most of the time. In fact it was not until yesterday that he really felt better. He then spoke of the welcome received at Halifax about leading in the singing of songs and said how much that had cheered him up. He said he had enjoyed his visit to Italy. He then spoke of seeing our troops in Normandy and of having been to the front as far as the firing line. He thought they were fighting exceedingly well. Regretted the losses. Said they had been given the places that had been a real opportunity which was as it should be, Dieppe, the Channel ports, etc. Said it was really wonderful what Canada was doing in the war. Spoke particularly of the latest financial assistance we had given Britain and in order to give what we had, we had really had to cover up in a way. I told him we were anxious to do everything that could be done. That as far as I was aware, we had left nothing undone which we could have done. He spoke about the political situation in Canada. He said: your Party looks a little in a better position. Spoke of the results in Quebec. Of what they demonstrated of the difficulty we had. Talked of the President's chances. He could not see that the President would not win. Said that it would be ingratitude itself. . . .

"When we reached the Citadel, he asked if there was a Guard of Honour for the President to inspect. I told him yes.

"When we drove into the grounds, we got out of our car and walked forward to the President's car while the United States national anthem was being played, and then, on returning to the Citadel, he suggested our walking which led to the ladies also walking.

"As we were reaching the main entrance, the President's car drove to the ramp and the President himself was seated in the sunroom when the party walked upstairs."

The Governor-General presided at a small luncheon party. "The Governor General," Mackenzie King noted "was at one end of the table with Mrs. Roosevelt to his right. Winston and Princess Alice were next. The President was at the other end of the table. I was to the right of the President and had Mrs. Churchill to my right. She to the left of the Governor General.

"The conversation at the table turned largely on discussion of personalities. It was clear that Churchill feels as strong as ever against de Gaulle. The President mentioned that he and de Gaulle were now friends. Princess Alice and I also stood up for de Gaulle and spoke of the favourable impression he made here. Finally Mrs. Churchill, I think it was, said we are all against you. It was mentioned that de Gaulle had two strains in him and he was quite a different man at times. The President having in mind the uncertainties of the times felt he would either be President or in the Bastille a year from now.

"Similarly with regard to Madame Chiang Kai-Shek. There was criticism of her pretentions and extravagances. Churchill not anxious to have her in England. Mrs. Roosevelt felt she found it difficult to distinguish between being at one time the head of the State, and at another, just a natural person. They all seemed to feel she had theoretically democratic ideas but really was unpractical. Churchill remarked to the President that he was the head of the strongest military power today, speaking of air, sea and land. The President said it was hard for him to realize that, as he did not like it himself. He could not feel that way. Asked me if I could feel that I was the head of a strong military power. I told him no. It did not enter into my feelings. Churchill said quite frankly he was sure if Britain had not fought as she did at the start, while others were getting under way, that America would have had to fight for her existence. If Hitler had got into Britain and some Quisling government had given them possession of the British navy, along with what they had of the French fleet, nothing would have saved this continent and with Japan ready to strike, the President was inclined to agree with him they could not have got ready in time.

"The President again spoke about his chances of re-election. Said there was nothing they did not stop at. Referred to the story about Falla [his dog] having been left at Kiska and sending a destroyer back a thousand miles for him. All pure fabrication. What is most serious is that the vote regarding the army depends on the action of individual states. Several states will not allow their soldiers to vote. They are favourable to the President.

"I can see that he is really concerned; also that he is genuinely tired and weary. He has lost much weight—30 pounds. I should think he looks much thinner in the face and is quite drawn and his eyes quite weary. Churchill, on the other hand, who was sitting opposite to me looked as fresh as a baby."

Mackenzie King also noted that while they were driving to the Citadel "Churchill said he would like to have one or two meetings with our Cabinet and myself as was done the last time. He noticed that the press had said that there was some uncertainty as to where Canada would figure in the present conference. I told him I had been careful to say nothing until I had had a chance to see him. He said we will arrange for a couple of meetings."

After the luncheon Mackenzie King called on Cardinal Villeneuve whom he found "exceedingly friendly." With respect to a general election, he told the Cardinal "I would not have any until after the war was over unless we got to the end of the constitutional period." Cardinal Villeneuve was on the point of flying overseas but had delayed his flight one day to attend the Governor-General's dinner that evening.

After the dinner, Mackenzie King reported that he "had a very pleasant talk with the Cardinal. He said to me of his own accord: 'I need not tell you how much I am with you. How completely I agree with your views and understand them.' There is a great sympathy between us. It was all to indicate that he was very friendly in relation to the Government and myself. Later, when we were talking he told me he had had a good deal of trouble with his own clergy. He had been speaking at a meeting yesterday and had told them in some of their own views they were making a great mistake. He also said that the lesser clergy were not as amenable as they should be. He said he did not like the extremists like the Bloc Populaire. Thought they were quite wrong. Believed part of it was impulse and ignorance of youth. That it would all straighten out by degrees."

At the dinner, which Mackenzie King described in some detail, he noted that "the Governor General extended a greeting on behalf of Princess Alice and himself. Also made a reference to myself as Prime Minister. Said he was extending a welcome on behalf of myself and the Government. He had a few carefully prepared sentences with nice references to Churchill and Roosevelt and to their wives and of Quebec and Canada as the place of meeting, and the hopes of the Conference leading to victory. He proposed the health of the President. The Governor was seated while he spoke and the President's health was drunk all seated as in the Navy. . . .

"The President made an offhand reply, referring particularly to his friendship with the Athlones. His delight at being back in Quebec. In fact there were parts in what he said in which he referred to feeling he was again at home. This seemed to imply a feeling of belonging to all that which he had in common before any separation from Britain. He referred to the pleasure of Mrs. Roosevelt being with him and made the kindest of references to Mr. and Mrs. Churchill. Of myself he spoke in the friendliest way, calling me Mackenzie and spoke of our friendship antedating all other of the present relationships. He made one reference which indicates a good deal of how he is feeling. He referred to the abuse and the attacks on himself as 'a senile old man.'

"At luncheon he reminded Churchill that another year had to be added to the years of Churchill, myself and himself, which made us the oldest of the living statesmen. Churchill said, referring to myself, that I had them all beaten. He spoke about the 25 years of leadership. Asked if it was not 20 years of Prime Ministership. I told him no, I was in my 18th year. He said that was a record. He said we might add Stalin as one who had been a long time leader. (He said he liked Stalin despite all his rudeness. Said there was something about him that he really liked.)

"The President spoke of the possibility of both himself and myself being out of office and referred to the freedom that would be gained thereby in having a chance to enjoy friendships. After he had finished I noticed that Churchill leaned over to him before Princess Alice and reminded him about proposing the King. He had a candy in his mouth at the time and had to wait until he had finished it. He then made a reference to the fact that it was known he and Churchill had promised to meet in the north of Scotland, but said that had to be foregone at this time. He went on from that to speak of a great gentleman he was very fond of, one who had visited them at Washington and Hyde Park. Referred to the close friends that they were and how close their friendship would always be. He then proposed the health of the King. It seemed to me as Roosevelt was speaking that language was very loosely used. There was the closest friendship with everyone—the same for the King, the same for the Athlones, the same for Churchill, etc. Rather a lack of discrimination. I felt as the President spoke that more than ever he had lost his old hearty self and his laugh. Conceded he has suffered a good deal and really is a man who is gradually losing his strength."

The next day (September 12) Mackenzie King had lunch with the Athlones, the Roosevelts, and the Churchills. "Today is the 36th anniversery of Mr. and Mrs. Churchill's wedding. She told me she had forgotten about it but that Winston came in with a bowl of roses to present to her. I congratulated both of them wishing them many happy returns.

"We had a very interesting conversation at luncheon. Quite different from yesterday which was largely on personalities. Today it was more on matters connected with the war. Some very interesting bits of information were disclosed. One was the position that Russia is likely to take or will take vis-a-vis Japan once the war in Europe is over. Churchill said that what he was saying in that connection was in the nature of a promise given to the President and himself, I presume at Teheran. This was a statement made by Stalin in the presence of the President and himself.

"Churchill was greatly pleased at the word which had come about 11 this morning that Le Havre had been taken by the Canadians.

"The conversation touched on relations with India and Japan. Churchill spoke of the very small numbers of persons in India keeping order. Small forces there. He said it was a fact that nowhere else in the world had there been less loss of life by steel and lead between the peoples than in India. In regard to starvation he said that in part has been due to the hoarding of food by the people themselves for speculative purposes. He also spoke of the early years at which marriage took place. Many children marrying at 13 and their lives extending to only about 30 years. He was making clear in the presence of the President and Mrs. Roosevelt that there were two sides to the story of conditions there. . . .

"The President spoke of the time when he had negotiations with three different Prime Ministers in France in the same week. Both were very strong on the dangers of many parties in government. The President had some discussion of the American constitution. Churchill said that he believed that despite all their faults, there was no people on earth where there was as much freedom and happiness as had been secured in America. The President agreed.

"There was discussion of the problem of the negroes, and of how great that problem was in Africa. It was one Smuts always declined to discuss. Churchill said that while Smuts was a great Liberal, when it came to the negro question, he just would cut it off from all the rest of his Liberal views.

"I asked Churchill if he had decided, as between the Russians and Stalin, and the other armies, which would enter Berlin first. No one would venture an opinion on that. Churchill was particularly concerned about the British, if possible, getting into Vienna before the Russians worked their way into that part.

"Speaking of France, he said, if he were de Gaulle, he would keep widening his bases of election of a tentative government; bringing in at one stage those who had helped in the resistance movement, to run on for three months, and at another stage, bring in men who were returned prisoners, and those from internment camps, and not try to get a final government until about a year had gone by. He thought if that were done, it might be possible to establish a firm government but he greatly feared and the

President agreed, there would be civil war in France, and that of a very terrible kind.

"Churchill seemed more reconciled to de Gaulle's position in conversation today than yesterday. At one stage when there was talk of the problem of India and China, Churchill said to the President that they had agreed if the President would leave his Indians alone, he would leave the President's Chinese alone. . . ."

After lunch, Churchill took Mackenzie King into the map room and went over the different battle areas. "What he is particularly interested in is the movement of British and other troops across the Adriatic over to the mainland and up the route that Napoleon took with a view to making a drive in through the Balkan States during the winter months and the spring, should the war continue beyond the end of the year. He said, of course, if the war should end in a couple of months, all of this would go up in smoke but we have to be prepared with our plans in advance in case the war should run through the winter on into next year.

"He was greatly pleased about Le Havre, and France now is pretty well cleared. Once Calais is captured, it will mean very much; also we saw on the map where the American armies of the North and South had today met together.

"Churchill mentioned that he would have to have an election before long. When asked if he would wait until after the Japanese war, he said: by no means. He added that the Labour Members of his Government might have to leave it in October. Their Party would demand their getting out and preparing for the campaign."

Earlier President Roosevelt had referred to the Kiska expedition "making fun of the Canadian brigade—of the whole business but poking fun at me for Canada being determined to have a brigade. We should never have forced our way into that position."

Mackenzie King had Field Marshal Sir John Dill, head of the British Joint Staff Mission in Washington, to dine alone with him that evening. He found Dill "particularly concerned about the future. He spoke to me of the very secret matter that we know of and said he wishes that could be buried in the centre of the earth. He feared it had in it the possibilities of total destruction. He used the expression 'The Bible says we shall have forty years of peace.' He thought wars would come every forty years. He seemed to feel it was inevitable that another war would follow the present one, particularly with this secret weapon. He was sure the Russians were working on the same matter. He doubted if the Germans had made the same advance that we had. In all the supplies they had asked for, the Russians had never requested 'uranium.' They had great supplies of it."

Later in the evening the Prime Minister had a long talk with Field Marshal Sir Alan Brooke (Chief of the Imperial General Staff). "He spoke particularly of the contrast of the early years and gave me a hurried outline of the problems they had to meet, first in France and then the Middle East. He felt it was miraculous that they had gone through that period at all. At the present time, victory was wholly certain and he felt it was coming rapidly. I spoke of our desire to have Canadian forces reunited. He said he knew Crerar's wish in that regard and hoped he might be able to meet it but there were difficulties ahead. He spoke in the highest terms of fighting of the Canadians and of Crerar's leadership. I told him of my recent letter to McNaughton. He seemed deeply interested in that and revealed clearly he felt deeply concerned about McNaughton. Asked if he was better in health, and said he had thought of writing him but was not sure that he should. I told him by all means to do so. That I thought he had been in very poor health but was much better now. That he might view things quite differently."

After breakfast on September 13, Mackenzie King examined models of the equipment used in the invasion which Churchill had brought and received a full explanation from the officer on duty. "All intensely interesting. The most interesting fact was that the planning on this had begun at the last conference here at Quebec. All the structures, etc., had been planned and carried out since that time. Until last summer when they received one important message from Churchill on the constructing of a pier, there had been no intention of doing other than to seek to cross the channel and bombard their way in. By the plan devised, they were able to bridge their way in. Apparently at Dieppe, what cost the lives there was that they had not figured on the tanks sinking in the sand. That much had come out of Dieppe. Out of Dieppe also, they learned the necessity of finding means of getting the heavy vehicles ashore other than by running them right on the beaches. Clearly the martyrdom of the men at Dieppe has helped to save Britain and the countries of Europe. Has made possible the quick invasion and the sweep that has since taken place."

During the afternoon Mackenzie King attended a meeting of the War Committee of the Canadian Cabinet at the Chateau Frontenac Hotel. There was another long discussion about Canada's participation in the war against Japan. "I held very strongly to the view that no government in Canada once the European war was over would send its men to India, Burma and Singapore to fight with any forces and hope to get through a general election successfully. That to permit this would be to raise at a general election, a nation-wide cry of Imperial wars versus Canada as a nation. Ilsley as usual was very difficult. Macdonald too, both from Nova Scotia, strongly advocating fighting anywhere and making no distinction between the North Pacific and the South Pacific. Macdonald anxious to have the navy part of the British navy, and to be worked in with the British navy, and Ilsley figuring to have the air force serve with the Americans would mean an expenditure of more millions for equipment.

"There was also some discussion on latest request from Britain for additional expenditures to permit of orders for further munitions, agricultural products, etc. In this Ilsley pointed out that what was requested would mean an additional billion dollars spent for mutual aid which would mean a budget of four billion dollars. I agreed with him that we could never get a budget of that kind through Parliament."

Later the Canadian Chiefs of Staff joined the meeting. "There was little difficulty about the army," the Prime Minister wrote. "As to the navy, I could see that Jones [Chief of Naval Staff] was seeking to work in an extra aircraft carrier, maintaining that having our own ships fight in the South Pacific would involve, in the way of expense, reconditioning which he said would be essential if in use there. The other day it was explained that our ships would have to be done over for the Southern Seas if they were used there.

"In the Air Force, Power is coming around very strongly against having our men fight in India because of our possible relation with the Indian Government and as a result of a letter from Stevenson speaking of the wretched conditions which men will have to work under. However there appears to have been enormous amount of commitments for a large number of air force to the South Pacific, though the British have carefully avoided making any mention of our forces in what they have provided for in the way of what may be necessary. I had to do most of the fighting myself to maintain what I would call the only tenable position which means keeping our forces for North or Central Pacific areas.

"The British in their own memo make it clear that the final fighting will have to be done there. They talk of shifting Canadian forces to the North in a year or two, fighting in the meantime in the South Pacific. I took the position we would have to have a private meeting with Churchill first and then the Chiefs of Staff in order that I could explain to him the political situation and what would be involved in raising an issue in Canada on the question of fighting what would be termed Imperial wars. Our people, I know, would never agree to paying out taxes for Canadian troops fighting whether in the air or at sea or on land for the protection of India, the recovery of Burma and Singapore. I understand the Americans feel Singapore, Burma and all is a side-show to save the British prestige, and that there is a possibility of American troops actually conquering Japan before the conquest of Singapore might be effected.

"Word came while we were in session that the British and Americans had agreed today to have their navies fight together in the Pacific. That opens the way to our making some contribution but it should be held to the North. It was stated that if we fought with the Americans, we would have to change our equipment, etc. If the Americans will fight in the North and Britain in the South, I asked how it was that over Europe, the two forces had fought together, and why that order need be changed. Leckie [Chief of Air Staff] had to admit this was true. They had worked together over Europe and some arrangement might be made to have them work together over the Pacific.

"Between demands that are being made for additional grants of money from Canada to carry on the war and the mixing of our troops with British troops and fighting what would certainly be construed as Imperial wars, I feel so strongly the consequences of acts of the kind that I said to St. Laurent after the meeting that I would have to consider whether I could allow my name to be associated with a Canadian Ministry that would go that far. I thought we had reached a crisis and that if it was decided our forces had to fight in southern Asia, I would have to say as Prime Minister, I could not agree to such a policy and would have to leave it to other Members of the Government to carry it out. He said to me he agreed entirely. He thought it was impossible to meet demands of the kind. He added that he thought the entire Cabinet were with me though they would not speak out with the possible exception of Ilsley, and I added Macdonald.

"The unhappy part is that, excepting Ralston, the others hang back and leave me to do all the fighting. Ralston is silent in regard to the other services but helps in relation to the Army simply because the British have said that to send the Army to the South Pacific would be a mistake. Already we have men there at the instance of the Defence Department preparing for the training of others in jungle warfare, etc."

Mackenzie King expected a "very difficult day" if the British Prime Minister pressed his demands. "Today's [Montreal] Gazette has an article about the British Empire and Commonwealth acting as a unit in defence instead of preserving the individual parts—all framed up to fit into the discussion at this moment for an Imperial point of view. I said dozens of times today if we take it by individual provinces or in any other way, we would find that the majority of the people all through Canada would be opposed to other than the policy I announced at Westminster."

The following afternoon (September 14) Churchill met with the Canadian War Committee without the Chiefs of Staff present. "When we were assembled," Mackenzie King reported, "I said to Churchill the reason I had asked for this meeting was that we were contemplating a general election and that he would understand that all our policies would have to be

considered in the light of the issues that might be fought out on the platform and we wanted to be perfectly sure of our position. I then said the
main question is that of extent of participation in the war with Japan and
read to him the statement which Heeney had prepared as embodying the
decision reached both yesterday and at a meeting of the full Cabinet as to
our preference for fighting in the North Pacific rather than in the South
Pacific. Churchill instantly said that the problem really was one of whether
the Americans were going to take over the whole business themselves. He
said that has been their attitude. That so far as the British were concerned
they had said to the Americans that they had to regain some of the territories which they themselves had lost in Burma, Singapore, etc. That they
could not do other than insist on taking this in hand themselves. He said
that only this morning the British had agreed to place their navy under the
command of an American commander. They had agreed to fight along
with the American navy as one. How far agreement could be reached and
what part Canada could play he said he would have to speak with the
President about. He asked me to let him have the memo which I had read
and which he would take up with the President at once.

"He then made quite clear that he did not expect the Canadians to fight
in any tropical region. In fact he used those very words either at that time
or later when the Chiefs of Staff were present that our men should not be
expected to go into the South Pacific."

The Chiefs of Staff of the United Kingdom and Canada were then
brought into the meeting. Mackenzie King reported that "When the Chiefs
of Staff came in the question was reopened without mention of a general
election. Churchill stated what our preference was and repeated he had
said that the Americans would have to be consulted.

"We then took up what was contemplated in regard to the Army, the
Navy and Air. Churchill made it quite clear there was no need for our
Army at all in the South Pacific and, indeed, he rather indicated that they
were not counting on the Army to take any real part. He thought it was
right we should have a token force and made it clear that more than that
was not needed.

"With regard to the Navy there again he spoke of the British and American navies working together and having preponderating strength but that
if we wished to have some of our ships participate as a subsidiary part of
the British Navy, well and good. One of the British Chiefs mentioned that
there would be only a few ships required, referring to one or two cruisers,
one or two destroyers and one carrier. I noted particularly the mention of
one carrier—Jones yesterday had spoken of two—and that these ships
would fight in the North Pacific.

"Churchill said something to the effect that he thought there would be place for us along the Aleutian Islands and the Kuriles and I at once said that when we spoke of North Pacific we were not referring simply to that area but to the area that could extend as far south as Formosa and the Philippines. He repeated words about our readiness to participate in, say, an attack on Formosa and I made it clear that we looked upon the defence of the Pacific in the same way as the defence of the Atlantic. We had Europe on one side, on the far side of the Atlantic and that we had corresponding areas on the Pacific. I did not wish to have our men assigned to any second Kiska role."

With regard to the Air Force, "when Sir Charles Portal stated what was being planned, he showed wherein the whole British contribution was to be less than they had been planning on originally but it left us with a very large number. Churchill himself without any discussion in advance or suggestion, turned to Portal and said: why do you put such a heavy burden on the Canadians. Portal replied that our mission in Britain said we wished it. Power felt it necessary to speak at once and to say that nothing had been decided. It was simply for purposes of planning; that we had made no commitments. I said we wished to make no decision until we knew what the relative contributions were to be between the different services. Churchill thought the word 'relative' meant British, Canadian, etc. He went on to say something about it and I said I meant 'relative' as between our different services in Canada—the Army, the Navy and Air Force and that it was not correct to say that we wished to have the number of squadrons mentioned. That, as a matter of fact, the Cabinet were of the view that the number was too large.

"Sir Charles Portal stated that they had succeeded in getting from the Americans certain bases which they could use for long range bombing and this would permit of the Canadians working with the British without having to change the types of planes, supplies, etc. He mentioned two classes of bombing planes which would be used. Said others would be ruled out which did away altogether with the item with which we were faced yesterday by Leckie and which seemed to make it imperative that we would have to fight in South Asia with the British or involve the enormous expense of many millions for getting new classes of planes that could be serviced by the Americans which were operating with them. The discussion made it clear that there would be no need for any change in that respect. Indeed every argument that was put forth yesterday about fighting the enemy wherever he might be, etc., was completely knocked out by Churchill and his own Chiefs of Staff. Ilsley who had argued so strongly on that score, also Macdonald, must have felt a little bit embarrassed. Every argument that I had put forth and fought for both in Council and in War Committee was sustained in the light of the discussion which we had. It was clear from what Churchill said that we could do much in the way of service that would be recognized, that all that would be expected in the light of our past contributions would be assisting in the policing of Europe for a time. He said that there would not be any attempt to have Germany controlled immediately by our forces. What would be done would be to have the Germans do the policing themselves of their own people. That they were a race that loved that sort of thing. Once they were beaten to be given any little authority they would wield it over others. What we would do would be to have, as it were, centralized stations on towers around the different cities. If there was any difficulty they could be threatened with a local bombardment. If the difficulty kept up they could be given a very effective one from the skies. He did not contemplate continued active fighting.

"When we were speaking of the strategy of the Pacific, I said that my recollection of the aide-memoire was that there were likely to be major operations required in the North in the war against Japan before it was over. If that were so I could see no reason why our forces might not be held in reserve to meet that situation when it came. That our Army had been kept waiting for four years in Britain but was now helping to win the essential battles for ultimate victory. That it seemed to me Canada might well keep all her forces in that position. I said I urged this as I was perfectly sure if that were not done and we used up our strength meanwhile that when an appeal might be made at the time of need in the North the Canadian people would not find it possible to respond to it. I thought we had already got out of our depth in the extent to which we had gone with the additional commitments in our own social problems and the like and we had to look ahead if others were not to be disappointed later on. Churchill himself used the expression 'not using up all your strength.' That is right, he said. In fact, there was not a point in the whole conversation in which he did not acquiesce with what I said, not merely acquiescing, but in the way of supporting my view on the ground of wisdom and strategy."

Then Mackenzie King asked about the duration of the war and "Churchill said that the view of the military man in Europe was that it would be over before the end of the present year. That he himself felt, however, there were reasons which might preclude that. That they might continue to fight on in the Alps and elsewhere. Just now they were making a very strong fight in Italy. He was sorry that we were incurring such heavy losses. Fighting might have to go on through the winter. He then added that it was quite conceivable the war might not have any real ending, that it would drag on with resistance in different places. That Hitler and his crowd knew that their lives were at stake and that they would fight to the bitter end. This might mean that we would have at some time to take the position that the war was really won and that what was going on anew was just mopping up groups here and there.

"About the war in Japan, he said that the Chiefs of Staff estimated it might last eighteen months. That would bring us until March 1946. It was after this had been mentioned that I referred again to the possibility of our holding our forces for the first year and being in a position to come in in the last 6 months, which would be when the final Northern fighting would take place. Ralston asked a question or two about the army to make sure that he had got a correct impression. Churchill made it quite clear that none of them would be expected to serve in the South. Indeed he rather took the view that they would hardly be needed at all. Certainly he pressed for nothing and asked for nothing."

After the Chiefs of Staff left the meeting, Mackenzie King reported that Churchill "spoke very feelingly of what Canada had done in the war and wished on behalf of Britain to thank us for all that we had done, the Government, the Ministers and he mentioned myself particularly by name. He referred to what the Army had done and how we had built a navy and an air force. Spoke of the Air Training Plan and went on to say how above everything else we had helped them financially. Really they were the one debtor nation that would come out of the war. He said they needed to expand their trade to hold their place in the future and build up their industries. He referred to the financial part as meaning more than anything else. He said he understood it was to be kept secret for the present. But that he would like to know as soon as what we had done could be made public in order that we might make reference to it.

"He spoke of the place that Canada will hold in centuries to come for the part that she played in this war. He again referred to myself as his old friend and what my part had meant and spoke of the part of the Ministers in the Government, and in his closing words he reached quite a climax of deeply felt gratitude. In thanking him I expressed the pleasure it had given us all to see him here again; wished we might have his power of eloquence to express what we really felt for that part which he himself had played in the war. That, as for Canada, what we had done as Ministers was really simply an expression of the spirit of the people. That we had a trust which we were carrying out but that it was the people themselves who felt strongly about the war and the preservation of freedom. I expressed the hope that he might be spared long in health and strength to enjoy the fruits of victory and referred to our appreciation of his never failing to express in public and in no uncertain terms as to the part that Canada had really played.

"When I had finished he reached his hand across the table and shook hands with me using some such expression as 'My dear old friend.' "

Later in the afternoon of the 14th Mackenzie King and Churchill drove in the President's open car to the Quebec Legislative Buildings to call on the Premier of Quebec. Churchill was given "a fine reception as he reached and came away from the Legislative Buildings. Duplessis conducted Mr. Churchill to the Legislative Council. . . . The members of the Cabinet, about 20 in number, were seated on either side of the Council table and Mr. Churchill to the right of Mr. Duplessis and I to his left. Numerous photographs were taken. Duplessis made a short speech in which he welcomed Mr. Churchill and assured him that nowhere was there greater loyalty than in Quebec. He gave his words the slant of the hatred against Hitler by a people who were against oppression of the minorities. He expressed pleasure at Churchill being in Quebec and of the recovery of his health.

"Churchill responded sitting at the table referring to governments under British institutions whereby different shades of opinion were given opportunity of carrying on. He referred to his previous visit and now to his visit to another government but all carrying on in a similar way the problems of government. He spoke about the changes that had come in the interval. France had been freed from oppression and referred to the approaching victory.

"Duplessis then said they were sure they would all like to have me say a word referring to me as the Prime Minister of Canada and saying that though we did not agree with your views, all felt that I was sincere.

"In a few words I mentioned that when Mr. Duplessis had taken office it was my pleasure to write to him of the intended arrival of Mr. Churchill and to convey good wishes to him for the discharge of his responsibilities. I said that I was pleased to have this opportunity to extend the same wishes to all who were present. I said that did not mean I hoped they would be there for any length of time. I then said to Mr. Churchill that it was a pleasure to me to be able to tell him that in the discharge of my duties during this period of war I had felt that all the provinces of Canada were united in their determination to see the Nazis destroyed, but while inevitable differences existed here and there, we were all one in our determination to see victory. I then said it was not often that I got a chance to seek to convert the heathen. I added that perhaps I'd better not continue speaking too long lest I might succeed, and therefore impose upon Mr.

Duplessis by taking advantage of his hospitality. They took this very well. Both going into the building and coming out I was given a fine reception by the people in the corridors."

On the way to and from the Citadel Mackenzie King had a good chance for a more personal and intimate talk with Churchill. "I asked him when he expected to have a general election. Said not to answer if it would embarrass him. He said he would tell me what was in his mind though he had not said a word of it to his own colleagues. He did not think that it was in accordance with democratic principles of government that he should try to carry on with a Parliament that was ten years old. Some of them would like to justify continuing for another year, but he did not feel that would be right. He said of course something depended on what might happen with the Labour Members in the present administration. Their Party might call them out. He would be just as glad if that were the case, as it would be easier to line up and have a straight election. He thought the people should have freedom to express their views. He said of course, the election would come after the war. It might be that the war would string out. For instance, there might have to be fighting in the Alps with no real end. In that event he would come out and say frankly he thought the real war was over, that this was only mopping up and that he thought the time for an election had come. This would be three months before the election itself. He spoke as if it might be February when he would make that statement, which would bring an election about in May. I asked him did they not need to have a re-distribution. He said that was being arranged at the present time. He believed that the people would return him again. He would then seek to form a new kind of coalition—one to deal with the domestic problems, the need for food, housing, etc. That what he would like to do would be to stay on in office until at least the troops had all returned to their homes and were demobilized. That would take at least a year. He said of course, there is the Japanese war. That he would like to see that through. He believed the people would give him the chance to see the Army demobilized and a start made on these problems.

"I said I hoped he would not try to carry on long after the war. He had knowledge of so many things it was important the world should have the record from himself. He replied that all of this was practically in his papers already except to give it a certain turn, there was nothing he could tell that would not be known in that way. I could see that his feeling at present is more than it was some time ago for a continuance in Parliament. He said to me he thought our position was better than it was a year ago when he was here last. Also that he thought Bracken was through. He regarded it as extraordinary that a certain leader had not had his place in the House of

Commons in this Parliament. I told him I would probably guide my actions by what he might himself say as to a general election in England. He told me he would keep me informed.

"He said he thought the President would be returned. Said it would be ingratitude itself were he not, so far as he was concerned. He said he would be prepared to come and help by making speeches on my behalf to ensure my election if I thought that would help. I said he had already said things which were more helpful than speeches. That the tributes he had paid me were greater I believed than any man could have received from another. He said they were all meant. He also said they wanted me in public life for all that it meant to the British Empire for the problems that lie ahead."

Mackenzie King added that, "in talking with Churchill, this afternoon, he stressed the wisdom of changes of government, feeling that democratic principles demanded letting different parties have to do with government and particular advantage being that men were never the same in their criticisms and views after they had once had the responsibilities of office. He told me, too, that his idea would be after an election to form another coalition, not perhaps with the Labour group who might have left him or opposed him but with those who would be interested in getting troops re-established and carrying out a program of simple needs such as proper housing, proper food, proper education, etc.

"I shall be surprised if he will be able to carry out his wishes for reasons of health if for no other, but to look at him today one would think he was a boy. I was particularly pleased when we met him in conference to see how very well he looked."

On the evening of September 14 Mackenzie King dined with Roosevelt and Churchill. Since the other guests were late in arriving, he "had a first-rate chance for a good talk" with the American President. "I told him something of the meeting we had had this afternoon and that Churchill would be speaking to him about our desire to have our Chiefs of Staff confer with his Chiefs of Staff. He said: By all means. We were allies. That would be expected. I then said to him that as he knew we were prepared to participate in the war in the Pacific against Japan but that we felt it must be in the Northern or Central regions. The President said he thought we should have a token representation but indicated that nothing might be needed for some time. He spoke of some extremely Northern region and indicated that toward the end, the Japanese might have to be driven out of the northern end of China. There was a hint that our men might be useful there. The President said I think Canada should have a token force to march into Berlin. I said I thought they would appreciate that and that it would be expected; that part of our army would be associated with the

American and British armies. It was in this connection that the President referred to token forces in the other connection. The President made some reference to Russia and I asked him direct what part Russia would likely play. He repeated to me what had been said the other night and added that he could only say that Stalin had given that word himself.

"I must confess that I feel immensely relieved in my mind as a result of this afternoon's conference, talks with Churchill and the talk this evening with the President. I can now see the road pretty clear ahead, first of all as to our contribution to the Pacific; there is no reason why it should be made one that would be costly in life. The question of the South Pacific, etc., has been completely cleared up. We shall now get back the men that the Army sent out to prepare for possible jungle warfare. It should be possible to get the relative contributions of the defence forces speedily determined. Ilsley asked a question about that at the meeting. He said he had no knowledge at present what that should be. I said we would have to settle that immediately.

"What I had most dreaded in regard to Imperial forces, etc., can be entirely explained away by having whatever we do, done on a token basis with forces that are wholly and exclusively Canadian, fighting as such but under American command in the same way as . . . the British navy, as Churchill had expressed it but as a Canadian unit if that can be effected."

The domestic political implications of these decisions were not far from the Prime Minister's mind. "As to elections we can either decide to bring them on the moment surrender comes in November or December if that should be the way the war will end, or it can wait until Churchill makes a formal declaration himself that he regards the war in Europe as over and gives public notice of three months that an election will take place at the end of that time. That would bring us, if we so desired, into an election in the Spring. We could bring Parliament together and prorogue in January; give three months' notice and have our election in April. It looks to me, however, as if there will not be a formal ending of the war in November and that we might find it necessary to go on with the winter campaign. Anyway it is our own fault if we don't get properly organized and get our literature into shape forthwith. Also the Presidential elections will be over before ours, and Churchill taking the stand that the war is over, that he must have an election before completing the war with Japan, will remove any question that might be raised as to obligating the Government to stay on after the war in Europe is over, to see the end of the Japanese war. It is interesting to get the impression from outside visitors that Bracken is through, and that our chances have improved since last year, and the impression that we will probably carry on. This reminds me that Churchill in speaking to our War Committee yesterday said that the Canadian Cabinet impresses him more and more as a very stable institution. He enlarged on that by saying that we knew what we were doing and were doing it in an efficient and helpful manner. He went on to say that the heirs and future generations would stand out more and more as Canada had done one of the finest things in the history of the world."

In the context of the discussions about the progress of the war in Europe and Canada's role in the Pacific conflict, Mackenzie King's speech during a luncheon at the Quebec Reform Club on September 14 was significant. All the federal ministers then in Quebec, except Ralston, were present and the guests included Godbout and some of his former colleagues. At the luncheon, Mackenzie King reported, "Godbout told me it had been a mistake not fighting the issues on federal lines and trying to hold to purely provincial questions. He said that he himself would have been defeated in his own riding if he had not explained the federal issues. He also admitted the poor organization. He thought that Cardin was much more friendly. There seems to be quite a move to have me bring him back into the Cabinet and I am sure it emanates wholly from the Simard influence.

"After the luncheon Power made a first rate introductory speech. I was given a very warm welcome, spoke freely and out from the shoulder. It was the first strictly political meeting I have addressed since the war. I told the gathering that it made me very happy to be again in the atmosphere of the Party surrounded by friends, etc. Referring to Godbout's defeat told them that there were worse experiences and cited my own of 1925–26 and 1930–35, of how much stronger we were as a consequence of moving out at those two periods. I stressed, however, the need for unity and the need for the Liberal Party fighting as one. I urged strongly the forgetting of differences and also the need of organization . . . and the need to reach individual homes. I spoke of the record of the Government in the war, how Canada stood as a foremost nation of the world, for the part she had played. The absence of graft in the administration and dwelt on the fact that this was a task we had been given to perform. That we must now look forward to the future and that the campaign should be on policies that are going to be helpful to the people. Referred to the returned soldiers and what our anti-inflation policies had meant in helping to keep the dollar at the dollar value. I told them of my interests in boyhood and manhood in seeking to better the conditions of the people. I said that this would be my last election if the Party were defeated and that I did not intend to continue on but that if we were elected nothing would give me more satisfaction than to devote another five years if Providence gave me the strength to complete the great social reforms that I had been above all else interested in.

"Earlier I spoke about conscription and how I had maintained the position that there would be no conscription unless it were absolutely necessary. That I never believed it was necessary. Now men saw for themselves those who had served had done so voluntarily. I also mentioned that it was clear that had Canada not done her part with Britain, in all probability the United States with Japan ready to attack would have had to fight much earlier and Canada might well have been the plain by which the attack would have been launched and we could all have been fighting for our existence. I concluded by speaking of the need of the Party working as one in support of great Liberal principles. Told them to forget the past and unite as never before. . . . If we got back into power it would not be long before Duplessis would be out.

"I also spoke of Senator Lesage and the help that he would give the Party in organization. This he quite enthusiastically responded to in words with me afterwards. I spoke of Power and the place his name and he himself will hold in the history of Quebec and of our country and the help he had been, and then spoke of St. Laurent and of how I had wondered if I could go on after Lapointe's death. That I prayed that I might be given someone who was worthy of succeeding him and Laurier. The country had certainly found that one in the person of Mr. St. Laurent. Power tells me that St. Laurent has proven the best politician in the lot and is making a wonderful place for himself here. Godbout made a very warm reply. The meeting broke up with great enthusiasm."

The following evening (September 15) Ralston came to see Mackenzie King, and after a few brief generalities the Prime Minister reported that Ralston said: "I have something I want to speak of which unfortunately is disagreeable. He then said that he had understood that I had said yesterday at the Reform Club that I would not stand for conscription or be at the head of a Government that would. He said he had been one of the team and had wondered whether I was changing our policy. That it made a pretty hard time with him dealing with his staff and others in trying to squeeze out the numbers that they need for reserves. That there might be a holocaust when they try to get into Germany which we would have to be in a position to meet. I told him I had made no statement of the kind. That what I had said was that I had mentioned that conscription would not be resorted to unless it was necessary. That now it was apparent the war was going to end soon and that it would be to the glory of the men overseas to be able to say they had enlisted voluntarily. What I had said about there being no conscription to be feared was that we would certainly not have conscription for any participation with Japan. I reminded Ralston we had agreed to that in Council. I would not certainly be head of any government that sought conscription against Japan. He said he had not thought of that difference. I told him that Power had asked me to make clear that there would be no conscription; that if I would say that to them, it would do more than anything else to solidify our people here. Ralston asked me whether I thought it would be arranged to have the N.R.M.A. men [troops conscripted for service in Canada only] go for service, to do army of occupation work in Europe.

"I told him I did not think that could be done; that they were an army purely for service within Canada. However, what they might do is to give them a chance to volunteer for that kind of service—as Churchill had said, to see something of the world—the point being that if ships bringing men were used to take back the others for the army of occupation, it would let the fellows overseas get the first jobs that were opening. It was necessary to keep the N.R.M.A. men here in the army to prevent them getting the positions that fellows overseas felt they would be first entitled to."

That morning Mackenzie King had received a telephone message from J. W. McConnell of Montreal, asking if he could make it possible for the President and Churchill to accept honorary degrees from McGill University. The Chancellor and Board of Governors were prepared to come to the Citadel for the purpose. "I did not hold out much hope but promised to do my best; as soon as the President and Churchill had finished their lunch, I went to them and told them of the message I had received, of Morris Wilson being Chancellor, and of their having only a word to say in acknowledgment of a degree. Churchill seemed to favour the idea and turned to the President saying he thought it would be a nice little ceremony. The President said he had no clothes. I told him I would have gowns and hoods brought along. I also mentioned that the Governor General was the official visitor of the University. Something was said of the possibility of his being here. Finally I got their consent and later 'phoned McConnell."

While Mackenzie King was talking to the President and Churchill about the McGill Convocation, "Churchill said to wait a moment and he then spoke to the President about our participation in the war in the Pacific; of our desire to be in the Northern part and have our forces to serve in North Pacific; also our wish to have our Chiefs of Staff have a talk with his. The President replied: Mackenzie and I had a talk together on that, last night. That is all understood.

"The President then said something about the Kuriles needing a good deal of patrolling, also Northern China, probably requiring Japs to be driven out later. When he stressed that he would have his divisions leave Seattle, and that Canadian forces could leave Vancouver, Churchill referred again to naval forces coming through the Panama Canal into the

Pacific. Told me he was putting his former aide, McCready, whom I know, in command. I did not want to leave matters to just the North and indicated that we were prepared to operate in the central area as well. Churchill also indicated that we were prepared to go as far South as Burma.

"Churchill said it would not do to have our Canadians fighting in the Tropics. . . ."

The McGill ceremony took place on September 16 after lunch. At the luncheon Mackenzie King had spoken about "the U.S. proposal to have an international conference on world organization on the 30th of October, just 7 days before the Presidential elections. I took advantage of a moment when only the President and Churchill and Eden and myself were at the table to say to the President that I had been concerned on learning that it was proposed to hold this international conference at the time suggested. That I was afraid it might operate very strongly against him in his campaign. That once it was learned that the four great powers—Churchill expected me to say 3—were to have the main authority of the Council to tell other nations what other contributions they might have to make in carrying out the decisions of the Council, there would almost certainly be a strong objection on the part certainly of the small nations to have it appear that Great Powers were seeking to control the world in the organization of its affairs. I pointed out that in Canada the nationalist feeling would be aroused in opposition to the proposals and the internationalists and C.C.F. would certainly raise strong objection. That what I feared was that with so many persons in the States of foreign descent, they would all likely side in with anyone who became champions of the smaller nations. That I thought Dewey in his speeches would certainly find objection to the scheme. I said it was clear in the minds of those who had been working on the problems, that they understood what the ultimate objective was, but the American public would not be expected to grasp it inside of a week especially with the campaign on. I pointed out that there was need to make clear that it was only to bring the organization into being to meet transitional period, and Churchill chimed in and said: just for the transitional period. When I had begun what I had to say, Eden beckoned Churchill to listen. Churchill joined and said he did feel very strongly the truth of what I was saying. Eden similarly. Both said they would do whatever they could to help the President in his election but agreed with me that this might really injure him.

"The President said that the conference was only on official level. That the objection had been that after the last war, they were so long in bringing into being any new organization. This was to show that no time was being lost. I said I thought it would be much more helpful to him to hold the

conference in abeyance and promise that if returned, he would see to it
that it was called forthwith. It was much better to have the people feel that
he was the man that was needed for the conference than to have his opponents pick holes in it. I also said that when I ran first for Parliament, I was
strong on getting out a manifesto and old Sir William Mulock had advised
me that to attempt anything of the kind would mean that my opponents
would find fault with whatever was there; pick some holes in what was
there and anything that was not there they would claim had been omitted
intentionally. Churchill then said that they had not come to an agreement
with Stalin on the duties and powers of the Council in settling disputes.
Stalin wants, as a member of the Council, the right to veto even in regard
to disputes in which the U.S.S.R. was a party which means of course that
Russia would prevent any action taken against herself. If they cannot reach
an agreement with Stalin on that point, of course the conference would
not be held.

"While I had not been in on any of these discussions with either
Churchill or Eden, nor had I had a word with them, I felt that the matter
might become so injurious to the President and also raise such embarrassing questions in our elections here, that it was better to speak out at
once if there was still a chance to save the situation. I think both Churchill
and Eden were very grateful that I spoke as I did."

With the departure of President Roosevelt that afternoon the Confer-
ence was officially over. Churchill and his party and Mackenzie King
remained at the Citadel over Sunday. On Sunday morning Mackenzie
King accompanied Mrs. Churchill to the morning service at the Anglican
Cathedral and was surprised to find the Governor-General and Princess
Alice waiting at the door with the Dean on their arrival at the Cathedral.
Bishop Carrington preached a sermon which "surprised and pleased" the
Prime Minister. "After the service," he reported, "the Bishop stood on the
steps to receive the Governor General and Mrs. Churchill, came forward
and shook hands with myself. Some of the others seemed to regard the
Vice-regal party as the one element to be noticed and did not come forward even to shake hands. When the Governor General and Princess Alice
said good-bye at the church steps, in doing so, His Excellency said he
was glad that I 'had come along.' I assumed from this that there might
have been some understanding on their part that Mrs. Churchill would be
attending the service but there had been no thought of myself. Personally
I care nothing about this aspect of things but I do not like to appear to be
butting in. I am determined not to allow the position of Prime Minister of
Canada to be blotted out in my own country by those who come from
another land. I cannot get rid of the feeling of resentment at Englishmen

coming here and holding in the eyes of any body of Canadians a place more honourable or worthy than that of those who have been born in Canada itself and are their chosen representatives. I have felt right through this Conference though nothing had been said that so far as the Governor General and Princess Alice are concerned, there has been since the last Conference, a sort of carefully planned arrangement to be in evidence in relation to the Conference in a way much more conspicuous than they were at the time of the last Conference, or in relation to the Prime Minister of the country, emphasizing in this way before the Americans and people of England and others the place which privileged position and the Crown continues to hold in Canada.

"I was surprised at the dinner which they gave when the President was speaking that he should have used the expression that it was right that Churchill should come out and see something of 'his' Dominions. This from the President was very surprising."

Mackenzie King lunched with the British Prime Minister. Lord Cherwell and Anthony Eden were also present. "At the table, I mentioned having 'butted in' yesterday on the subject of the world Conference to be called for October 31. I said to Churchill I had not been sure whether I should have, but felt it was something I should say. Churchill at once said you butted in in a magnificent manner, it could not have been better. He made some comparison in his own characteristic effective way to doing what was effective at the right moment. Eden joined him and said I should say it was fortunate you did. Churchill went on to say he thought the President was wholly wrong. He could not understand what was planned. Said he would do anything to help the President in an election but that this thing he felt would really hurt him. I told Churchill and Eden about having had a further word with the President in his car as he was leaving. They both said they were so glad that I had. That it was so important. Churchill added it was such a mistake to have arranged these things before matters were properly concluded. Stalin might not come in and the whole thing might be upset if it were dealt with in a premature way. I mentioned having stressed to the President the wisdom of holding the conference over as something which he would see would be brought about immediately if returned."

Dinner with the Churchills that evening was a family affair and Mackenzie King enjoyed it thoroughly. "Churchill sat and talked like one who was father of a family. I have seldom seen him more placid, quiet and in a thoroughly contented mood. Most of the conversation was across the table between us. He spoke about the war and a good deal about de Gaulle toward whom he still entertains feelings of great distrust. He spoke of the difficulties of getting de Gaulle to allow some of his people to cross over into France at the time of the invasion, of his being at heart an enemy of Britain, of his being ungrateful and that at any moment he might show a different side of his nature. He admitted quite frankly that he was much abler in every way than Giraud. He did not like Giraud who was a gentleman of the old school, not one suited for these times. He also said that de Gaulle had a popular appeal. He did not think he would escape very serious situations in France in the course of a year. He spoke with deep feeling of the way the paratroops were landing in the Netherlands, of the amusing manner in which tanks, guns, munitions, as well as men were transported by air. All were speaking with equally deep feeling of the losses that some of our Canadians had sustained. Of their magnificent fighting. He spoke particularly of Canada's part in the war, of how exceptional in every way it was. He raised his glass to me and reached across the table to touch mine, and then was quite eloquent on the relief from bondage, regaining full freedom, etc. It was really quite a little ceremony, all related to the close friendship which we had enjoyed. I recalled that it was 44 years since we had first met. He placed his emphasis not on the meeting in Canada, but on the meeting later when I went to England to get legislation through the British Parliament.

"As it got on to train time Mrs. Churchill said she would go and get ready but he told her not to go but stay, that she must stay. He seemed to be feeling that it was the moment that he had been longing for of real peace and quiet contentment. He had a great sense of accomplishment.

"When finally, to make sure of getting off on time, Mrs. Churchill rose, he said you may go dear, but I am going to stay here. He stayed on for another ten minutes, somewhat quiet but every now and then saying some words of appreciation. Finally when he was about to rise I lifted my glass, looked across at him and said God bless, guide and guard you. His eyes filled with tears, he rose and when he came across to my side of the table he put my arm in his and spoke about the years we have had together; how faithful a friend I have been; of the little dance we had together at Chequers. I told him if spared we would yet have another in the days of Victory.

"At the luncheon table he had stated that when the war was really won he would treat the situation as the Germans were in the habit of treating similar situations by stating that the war was over and that he refused to recognize the skirmishing that was going on any longer and would give an official date for the end of the war. He said he did not intend to recognize any mopping up in the Alps, etc. We had a story or two, comparing the walls of the Citadel with those of Chester, which caused much merriment.

"We went together arm in arm from the sunroom where we had had dinner to the map room and had a last look at events of the last few days and of today. Churchill each time drew my attention to the little bridge-head from which they had spread out to make a sweep in France and advance into the Netherlands, etc. We came downstairs together. At the door Mrs. Churchill was waiting and the servants were lined up on both sides of the entrance. The car to go to the station was rather small. He and Mrs. Churchill said to get in and I was seated in the centre between them. We had a very happy talk together as we drove from the Citadel along the sides of the Plains of Abraham to Wolfe's Cove. Churchill began speaking of the historical significance of the two Conferences and said he hoped that we might have a tablet made recording the events and the tablet to be placed somewhere appropriately at the Citadel. I told him that that would certainly be done. I repeated what I had said at the table in the evening that I had felt this war had brought the different parts of the British Empire closer together than they had been at any time, but that this was owing to the fact that we all felt a special pride in having gone into the war, volun-tarily from the very beginning. Churchill had spoken eloquently of that at the table, of our not desiring an acre of land, of not wishing anything in the way of additional power, but fighting simply for the maintenance of our honour and the preservation of freedom.

"As we were driving through the narrow gateway of the Citadel, be-tween the guardrooms and the gate, I said to him that while this was true, I believed it had been due to the recognition of the complete position of each of the Dominions acting on its own; the absence of any centralization. Said that any attempts at centralization would do great harm. Churchill to my great surprise said I agree 100 percent with you, you are perfectly right. Each part of the Empire must direct completely its own affairs. The rela-tionship must be one of co-operation not centralization. What Churchill said was not expressed just in those words but that was the meaning. What came to me as a surprise was the emphatic way in which he spoke and say-ing he agreed with my point of view in the method of maintaining Com-monwealth relations 100 percent. We then spoke of the mistake it would have been to have tried to form an Empire Cabinet to run the affairs dur-ing the war. He said, you remember Menzies, he wanted to put me out; he wanted to have the war run by himself and others. Mrs. Churchill ex-pressed some surprise at this. I said I remembered very well what Menzies had said to me on his arrival in Canada from Britain. That he wanted to speak to me very seriously about the need of having myself, himself and others control the policy of the war. I said that my last words to him at Ottawa had been that he would find when he got back to Australia that he had lost . . . the leadership of his country, also that the place of all of us as leaders of the Dominions was in our own Dominions and not in London. Churchill said you were perfectly right. He then went on to say you have been so fine about letting England lead, not making it difficult for us by insisting always on several having direction. I said it had been difficult to maintain my position at times but that as long as I knew we were being consulted and getting informed on new policies and were able to speak about them before they were settled, I thought it was much better before the world to leave the matter of leadership in the hands of the President and himself. He said that had meant everything in the effecting of needed co-operation. I then told him that a fine thing about our war effort was that there had never been throughout the years of war a single difference between the civil and military power in Canada on anything. I mentioned the difficulty at the time of McNaughton's retirement. Churchill said he of course would not have done as Commander of the forces on the continent. He was a fine fellow, a good engineer, etc. I replied he was a broken man in health and of course his life's ambition had been frustrated. I spoke of the position I was in with Ralston and himself and having a terrible week there. I said there had not been as far as I could recall it a single difference between any of us throughout the whole war. He said that was perfectly true. He then went on to say that what he marvelled about above all was how on top of everything we had done we had been able to give the further financial assistance which meant so much to England particularly at this moment. He said I want to speak about that in Parliament the first chance I have. I replied we have a Victory Loan on at present and it is just as well to get that over. He said very well but let me know when I can make some public recognition of it. . . .

"At the table we had had a talk about security. Also about the secret service men who were with the President, etc. He spoke of abhorring that side of things but that in their movements such as the time of getting off plane or cars it was really necessary to use devices of deception to conceal movements. He used the expression 'truth is indeed a very precious thing. It has to be surrounded as we are in a world of lies, and has to be kept concealed very closely in moments such as those relating to critical times.' I said I regretted we could not have let the people know to be at the station for a farewell. There was a fine number present notwithstanding. Both Churchill and Mrs. Churchill were very pleased at the reception given there. They asked me to come into the car with them. When I did so he thanked me again and I expressed what a joy it had been having them both here. Mrs. Churchill turned to me and said with her eyes glistening 'Dear Mr. King,' emphasizing the word 'Dear' in a very expressive way and with real emotion, as much as to say you have meant so very much to Winston and myself in what you have done for us and what Canada has done through the war. It said much more than words themselves could have begun to express. Each of them shook hands with me and then went to the door to wave good-bye to the people as their car was being joined to others to have the train moved out. When they came back they shook hands once more. The little gathering outside around the car started the singing of Auld Lang Syne, and just as the train began to move off children again appeared on the platform and Churchill reached over the little iron gate and shook hands with me as the train started. I felt the contrast in my mind of this little farewell where . . . both Churchill and Mrs. Churchill were looking so well and so greatly benefited by the trip and what I felt in saying my last good-bye to the President, leaving him for a moment quite alone at the end of his car looking so frail, his face and body so visibly reduced in size and his legs so infirm—his right leg falling away from the other making almost a right angle at the knee. I am sorry to have had a last word with him about the anxious problem of the world security conference but I felt the greatest service I could render him was to stress again the importance of not letting an issue arise on that score in the last week of the U.S. elections."

When Churchill's train left shortly after 10.00 P.M. the Prime Minister drove with General Pope to the Palais station and there boarded his own railway car.

CHAPTER FOUR

Cabinet Reorganization

ON HIS WAY BACK TO OTTAWA from the Quebec Conference, Mackenzie King stopped in Montreal on September 18 to speak at a conference of the United Nations Relief and Rehabilitation Administration which was being held at the Windsor Hotel. Lehman [former Governor of New York State], the American head of UNRRA, Pearson and Claxton met the Prime Minister at noon "to take me to the conference hall to address the assembled gathering. I had, of course, no difficulty in reading over the radio the speech as written but had a sort of feeling as I was reading that my voice was showing evidence of fatigue and that I was not giving to the whole the inflections it should have. As a matter of fact, I am experiencing a fatigue which does not allow me to really notice what is going on in the way of applause or appreciating the effects of what I am saying. The address was evidently shorter by three minutes of what was expected. There was a hiatus before Governor Lehman came on. While not sure how I would get through, I felt I should add another word with a little more warmth and feeling.

"I then got up and spoke for exactly two and a half minutes and made a much more telling speech in those few minutes than in the address itself. I was able to speak from the heart and fortunately made the point that all along I had hoped I might get to making. I was able to make the most significant point of all which was that what nations like ours which were so fortunate were doing now in the way of relief and rehabilitation was not by way of charity but by way of paying of a debt to the nations which had resisted in a manner which had helped to maintain our freedom and our liberty. I really did express in a manner and phrasing which surprised myself, a great thought in a truly eloquent way. I was given a great reception and it pleased me particularly that it was wholly apparent that what I said was spontaneous and not part of anything which had been previously prepared. As a matter of fact the thought was one to which I had given expression at some of the Country Club dinners to Queen Wilhelmina and others regarding countries that have been overrun.

"After Governor Lehman had spoken—he really made a fine statement of UNRRA—I asked him and Pearson to join me in welcoming the delegates at the reception, which had been arranged by the Government. This was really a very pleasing affair. It gave me a chance to shake hands and have a personal word with all the delegates and a personal word as well with some of our own Members of Parliament who had been invited to be present. It delighted me to be able to have a chance to say the right word to representatives of different European and Asiatic countries that have suffered through years and to renew friendships with many of those whom I have met either in conferences here, in the States, in England or in Geneva. I felt that this reception was just the right thing and came just at the right moment. The opportunity it afforded for personal contact was just what was needed. Also I must confess to being at my best and again entirely on my own."

Mackenzie King drove that afternoon to Dorval and had tea with Mr. and Mrs. J. W. McConnell. "One very fine thing about McConnell and his wife," he wrote, "is that I have never heard them make a single complaint about the very heavy taxation. He has been hit harder than perhaps almost any one else. When I spoke to him about family allowances and what they meant about letting the country see the determination of the Government to redistribute wealth, he strongly approved the policy. I pointed out to him that unless we were going to allow the C.C.F. to sweep the country and take measures that would be extreme, how necessary it was that we should keep Liberal principles continually to the fore. He agreed with me entirely on this."

That evening when he reached Ottawa the Prime Minister was surprised to be met by several of the ministers including Ilsley, the latter obviously somewhat agitated. "Ilsley's words to me at the station were that the sooner we could have the elections, the better. The pressures were getting very heavy. I noticed when he walked away from the station, he was waiting to catch a street car to ride home."

On September 23 the Minister of National Defence was scheduled to go overseas and, until his departure, the Cabinet was mainly concerned with further discussion of questions relating to Canada's participation in the war with Japan and demobilization (to be described in the next chapter). After Ralston's departure, Mackenzie King's attention turned back to domestic problems.

The afternoon of September 26 was devoted to consideration of party organization. Mackenzie King "had an interview with Howe, Gardiner, Power and Mackenzie. Howe represented that the Ontario organization were getting nowhere effectively, was most anxious to have Roebuck appointed to the Senate and let him devote his time to organization work meanwhile. I somewhat shocked Howe, as I thought I would, by saying that I was thinking of Roebuck for Minister of Labour. That I did not think Mitchell had the confidence of Labour as Roebuck had and doubted if Mitchell could carry his own city. Roebuck certainly would. Howe reacted as I expected he would by mentioning the antagonisms there were against Roebuck and the harm there might come from taking him into the Ministry. I subsequently told Howe, in the presence of the others, that he could represent to Roebuck that I was prepared to appoint him to the Senate or give him something better. I did not tell the others that I had an understanding with Roebuck, at the time of the Ontario election, that I would have him in mind for the Senate if he helped in that campaign, as he did.

"The next situation was in regard to Cardin, and the desire that I should get in touch with him and talk over the Quebec situation. I made clear that I would not take him back into the Cabinet. To do so would work great injury in other provinces. That I would certainly see him and would authorize Howe to tell him I would be glad to see him very soon. Howe is to be in Sorel next week."

Discussion then turned to a possible election date, "all of them very strong for having it brought on just as soon as possible. I made it clear that I would not change my position of waiting until the war in Europe was over, but said I would be prepared to go to the country immediately thereafter, provided that the work of organization was in proper shape. That until I was satisfied that we had the right candidates in the field generally and Members of the Party speaking the same language in the campaign and material ready, I would not bring on an election. That I did not propose to sacrifice the Party by any risks that could be avoided and would not send men into political battle without having them properly organized. Did not intend to have it a matter of hit or miss.

"Later in the Cabinet I took up the question of organization, having set apart today for that discussion. Read to my colleagues (there were 19 of us present) the report from Fogo of the Liberal Information Office. Pointed out wherein what had been done, up to the present, would amount to nothing in a campaign, but indicated wherein the right beginning was under way. Emphasized need for following up in these matters further as rapidly as possible. Also had Ministers express their views on the situation as they have found it in the last fortnight. Everyone who spoke gave evidence of the improved position of the Party. All were most optimistic."

On September 27 the Prime Minister resumed active consideration of the reorganization of the Cabinet. Three weeks earlier, at a Cabinet meeting on September 7, arrangements for the establishment of the three new departments created during the session (Reconstruction, National Health and Welfare, and Veterans Affairs) had been first discussed. Mackenzie King had "suggested to Howe he take the Reconstruction but he openly objected saying he had all he could do with the present Department. Did not think he was the one to meet delegations and deputations. The reconversion of industries was all he could manage. I referred to the nature of the duties but he spoke pretty feelingly against taking the Department.

"I spoke of Mackenzie taking War Veterans and Acting for National Health and Welfare. I was very tired in Council all afternoon. Discussed at some length with Council the possible programme in the event of elections not coming this year. Suggested they consider the wisdom of a special session for electoral reform, introducing transferable vote, compulsory voting and also redistribution. I found a mixed reception. Gardiner, to my surprise, was strongly against transferable vote. Crerar and MacKinnon, quite the opposite. I could see Council generally did not like the idea of another session or waiting that long. However, they all saw that with another Victory Loan coming, it was a question of whether we could manage a campaign before the snow was on the ground. The Presidential campaign comes on the 7th. The general view was that the President would be returned. I tried to get Ilsley to move forward his loan so as to come before the election but apparently things have been so far advanced as to make that difficult."

The next day (September 28) the Prime Minister "had a talk with Ian Mackenzie about his health and the creation of the Departments of Veterans Affairs and Health and Welfare. I said I would let him start them but said I thought he should be only Acting Minister of one. He was quite ready to do anything.

"I spoke to him seriously about attempting another campaign but he said he thought unless he and Gerry McGeer ran in Vancouver, the seats would be lost and that they needed him in the Province. I said he must consider his health first. He said he was going out for a convention and would certainly wish to run. I said if there was anything else he wanted, to let me know. I also said: Remember, we might not win and he had better think of his future. He said he had thought sometimes he might like a diplomatic post."

The next talk was with C. G. Power to test his interest in the Department of Reconstruction. "When I talked to him," the Prime Minister wrote, "he volunteered the view that he could be more useful to the Government in Veterans Affairs than anything else. I had really never thought of this but as soon as he mentioned it, I saw what an effect it would have on the troops to have him in that department.

"He was not keen about Reconstruction saying not because I had offered it to Howe first but he felt he could do so much more in the other portfolio. He did not want to hurt Ian's feelings. I told him what I had said to Ian but agreed we would not settle matters definitely at once."

On September 27, Mackenzie King discussed the question of the Minister of Reconstruction with St. Laurent. He felt that Howe would take the Department "under certain considerations. Howe had suggested bringing in the National Research Bureau in connection with the Department. St. Laurent felt that with the Committee of the Cabinet they could help. I spoke of bringing Claxton into the Ministry somewhere, that he would be helpful in that work, as well as others. Also that he had important offers from other sources. St. Laurent said he would be glad to take Claxton on as Solicitor General, the position was there and he could carry out the Report on Penitentiaries and criminal reform and deal with other matters. He thought Power would be excellent for War Veterans. He had thought of Claxton for National Health and Welfare. I explained the problem with regard to Mackenzie, if Power were to take War Veterans. St. Laurent felt, as I did, about the splendid work Mackenzie has done in both these fields. I agreed to continue the discussion later."

The next day the Prime Minister was closer to making up his mind. "The more I think of it the more I feel it would be a very cruel thing to deprive Mackenzie, notwithstanding the risk to his health of taking one or other of the Departments which he, more than anyone else, has been responsible for bringing into being. His wish is for the War Veterans and I think he deserves that, though there is no doubt that Power in that position would make a tremendous appeal to the soldiers. However, Power wishes to hang on to the Air Ministry as well, and is erratic. . . . Then I feel that I really need a Minister for National Health and Welfare who is deeply interested in the whole work of that Department. Mackenzie could do it up to a point, but on the side where it is weak, e.g., the handling of the hospital situation, that aspect has got ahead of him. Claxton is an excellent organizer, has great business capacity and drive, would be helpful in the reconstruction work and certainly better than anyone else in the supervision of literature, etc. I need a Minister beside me who can follow up the things that I suggest and see that they are done. My mind, subject to further discussion with the Ministers, is now practically made up to bring Claxton into the Ministry at once, though it increases the number of Ministers, and leave to subsequent arrangement the changes that may be necessary to balance representation by provinces, race, religion, etc. Claxton would be able to organize the Department of Health and Welfare quickly and thoroughly and a new Minister can do what Ministers that have had relationships that already embarrass them could not begin to do. While it will be embarrassing in some ways to him, to me and to my colleagues, to bring Claxton into the Government at once, I feel that the advantages will outrun the difficulties and it will be an evidence to the younger men that I propose to see that they get their chance in government and that we are not tied only to those who already hold office."

Mackenzie King told St. Laurent of his decision and found that he believed Howe could be persuaded to take Reconstruction. The next day (September 29) the Prime Minister "had an important interview with Power and Mackenzie who came together to see me about a somewhat embarrassing and critical situation which had arisen through the medical officers of the Defence Departments seeking to gain control over the hospitals. It was a battle that was fought out after the last war. They had been given control at the start but in nine months the plans had to be changed and returned to civilian control. [Power and Mackenzie] felt most of the difficulty had arisen through the conflict between the doctors and Wodehouse, the Deputy Minister of Pensions and Health. They both strongly recommended getting rid of Wodehouse.... They suggested the immediate establishment of the two new Departments. This gives me just the opportunity I had wanted without bringing it up myself. I mentioned that all three Departments would have to be established at once and I think the first should be Reconstruction, and that we must insist on Howe taking that work in hand, that I believed this could be arranged through certain ideas that Howe himself had and that I intended to clear up the three this week but Howe had left on Tuesday. He would be back on Tuesday and I shall arrange an interview with him then. I said we would seek to get the new Departments established on Tuesday. Power was to be absent that day and gave other reasons why Wednesday might be better. I agreed to this."

Ian Mackenzie then left and Mackenzie King continued his talk with Power. "Told him I thought Mackenzie would be broken hearted if he did not get a chance to be first Minister of War Veterans Department. That I doubted whether he would be able to continue long in that position on account of his health but he felt that he had really created the Department and would like to have that association. Power said at once that he knew that that was so and it was right to have him appointed as Minister of the Department of Veterans Affairs. I then discussed with Power the matters we have been taking up in Council. He said he thought I was wrong in seeking to have a parity as between the contribution of the three defence forces to the Pacific war. That he did not see any necessity for the army participating at all. He doubted if the situation would ever go that far. I questioned him about the size of his squadrons and the number he was contributing. He said that he had cut down to as small a figure as he thought could make a useful contribution. Anything under that would not be of real help. He was letting out large numbers now and believed there would be difficulties arising therefrom. Also he was quite prepared to see all of his men come back by way of Canada and leave granted to those who had been serving for some time before they would have to take on more duties in the Orient. I spoke of the size of the proposed naval contribution and urged that it should be kept to a reasonable token force.

"On concluding our interview I had Mackenzie come in and told him that my decision would be to have him take on Veterans Affairs and that I would probably bring Claxton in as Minister of National Health and Welfare. We discussed what to do with Wodehouse and agreed he would have to be dropped out when the new Department was created and some arrangement come to with him by way of supplement of the years he has still to serve as Deputy. Mackenzie said everything was ready for getting the new Departments set up instantly, excepting the appointments of the deputies. I expressed my agreement to having him go overseas to personally see that the soldiers were being fully informed of what we have done and propose to do for them on their return. He assured me that the literature had gone but was not sure whether it would get through some of the higher army officials. He said to me that he would like me to know he would be quite prepared to give up the portfolio within a month or two if I wished to put a younger man in charge of the Veterans Affairs, as he had mentioned to me in the House of Commons. He felt it was important that the Minister should have the entire confidence of the men and we should have the best possible appointment. He realizes the condition of his own health. It was, as I thought, a matter of his Scotch pride which makes him anxious to stay on for a time. He strongly approves of Claxton as the best man. I was immensely relieved at the talk with Mackenzie."

Despite these preoccupations, Mackenzie King continued to be concerned about the government's position in the Province of Quebec. On the afternoon of September 27, the same day he was reaching conclusions about changes in the Cabinet, he had had an interview with ex-Premier Godbout and Arthur Fontaine which he described as "very important." "Godbout told me that there was no doubt he had lost Quebec through the feeling there was against the Federal Government because of the recruiting for the war and the way it had been gone about. Said it was largely the women's vote; that the men, he thought, had understood the situation but the women seemed to feel that since it was their brothers, or fathers or sweethearts that were taken to war, by voting against his Government they would be helping to prevent that step. Godbout claimed that there had been very poor judgment used on the part of officials of the War Departments and Selective Service in the way of farm help. Had been told that men had been kept waiting for days, moved from place to place. . . . What Godbout wanted to impress on me was that the same thing was being started anew now, new regulations being made, men of the National Selective Service and the Army interfering in a way that was again rousing the fears and prejudices of the people. He said in the case of his own farm and his special herds, if they sent him an ordinary man instead of a skilled man, he would have to sell the whole herd. He told me that on a previous occasion Mounted Police had come into his own house at night, gone to the bedroom where he and his wife were sleeping, flashed a light around and claimed they were looking for certain of the men that he had on the farm. He said there would be no doubt I would be defeated in Quebec if this underground method by those who were determined to have the last word on conscription was to be continued.

"I at once sent for St. Laurent, Power and Mitchell. Had Godbout repeat what he had said to me, adding about other regulations respecting University students, etc. I said to both Power and Mitchell that I looked to them to see that if officials were carrying out orders in a manner deliberately to injure the party politically that they should take drastic measures to see that that kind of thing was stopped. Power said we might have to change the policy that was agreed upon. Godbout pointed out that it was not a question of our changing the policy, it was a question of changing the methods now being adopted in seeking to bring up fresh recruits. Power and I both asserted that for anything necessary to win the war we would agree to but we would never agree to conscriptionists having the last word —and that one of vengeance—when the war was practically won, so far as Europe was concerned.

"Mitchell was, as usual, very talkative and evasive, disclaiming having responsibility, etc. I became rather impatient with the indifference of Power and Mitchell and spoke out very plainly to both of them, more plainly than I have ever done in the presence of others. I made it perfectly clear that I did not intend to have our Party submarined in Quebec and that before I would allow this to take place I would turn over the Government to someone else and not contest the next election as leader. They made it clear that if I did not stay as Leader we might as well give up everything."

According to Mackenzie King, both Godbout and Fontaine urged him to have a talk with Cardin who had resigned from the Cabinet in 1942.

"That all his friends were advising him to support me strongly. That they felt, as Power and others had indicated, that the danger was Cardin making an alliance with Duplessis which would be to get independent candidates who would, after elected, support me, in that way holding the balance of power. I told Godbout and Fontaine that I would never be at the mercy of any group holding the balance of power. That I had had one parliament with a majority of one and a short parliament in a minority and that unless I had a straight majority I could rely upon, I would not continue even in the office of Prime Minister after an election. That they would then see where the Province of Quebec would be under any other leadership that might be formed. That I would tell Cardin that quite plainly. That I had stood by Quebec in what I thought was right and that I would expect that Province to stand by me, but I would not be held up by any group. They told me that in the provincial campaign when my name was mentioned it received more applause than that of any other name. They did feel that if Cardin could be brought into line there would be no difficulty in carrying the Province. I said I would not bring Cardin back into the Ministry. That he and I had never had any difficulty, that I had tried to have him stay on in the Government and I would be surprised if he did not recognize some obligation to me by the way I had stood by him during the year of his illness. They seemed to feel that a talk would be all that was necessary."

On October 6, Cardin did come to see the Prime Minister. He arrived at one o'clock and they talked until 2.30. "When he came in I said it was like old times to see him again in the office and thanked him for coming up to have a talk. The conversation opened about the death of his wife and he spoke at some length of the sorrow it had been to him to lose her. . . . I then said I was anxious to talk to him about the situation in Quebec. That I was anxious to go over it all with him and to do all that was possible to ensure the return of the Liberals in the Province. I then said to him that as far as he and I were concerned, there had never been any difference between us. He would recall my having been anxious to have him stay on in the Ministry [see vol. I, chap. 14]. Also that I had sought in Parliament to say nothing which could occasion an estrangement later. Cardin then said it was true I had held with him in everything up to the last few minutes of the last Caucus he attended, when he thought that I had in the concluding words taken a different position. I told him that I could recall nothing of the kind. That anything I had said in Caucus was in accordance with what I had said in the Cabinet before. He would remember that I had always been careful to not go in Caucus beyond what had been agreed upon in the Cabinet. He then said that was so and began to speak of he himself perhaps having spoken out in Parliament more strongly than he realized or meant to, and referred to what he had told me of how at the beginning of his practice of law, he had had to be bold before his opponents and more particularly before the Court and jury to impress them. Perhaps he had gone too far in what he had said in the House of Commons. But that all of that was now of the past and was buried. I told him I had no feeling about anything that he had said, rather I had always felt that some of our colleagues had not been fair with him and I had said so quite frankly. I then told him that in accepting his resignation I had been influenced by what his Secretary had told me which was that the doctor had advised him to let me know that Cardin was a very sick man. That if he offered his resignation not to try to persuade him to stay on but to accept it as the means of saving his life.

"I said, notwithstanding that, I had tried to have him not present his letter of resignation at Kingsmere. He then spoke at some length about his health being now so much better. Credited it to what he had inherited from his family. Says he has one consolation today. His mother who is in her nineties is still living and he keeps in touch with her."

Discussion then turned to the recent election in Quebec. Mackenzie King "pointed out how the election had been lost by enabling the others to get in by a minority of votes; also the bad organization in the constituencies etc. In reply to that he said he thought it was really that Godbout had allowed himself to get in with different groups and had forgotten those who had helped put him in office. He said if Lapointe had lived that mistake would never have been made. That Godbout had said to him (Cardin) in my presence, that he (Cardin) had got the wrong associates, speaking of Letellier, the organizer. I said I thought Godbout's reference was to the organizer and not to Cardin himself. Cardin felt particularly bitter towards Brais, who, he said, had very poor political judgment. He spoke also of Fontaine as being an enemy of his. Raymond was another enemy and Brais. . . . He said he did not think the Bloc Populaire had any influence left and also spoke of Dorion and Roy as possibly trying to form a separate party, but he did not think they were likely to go far. Duplessis would not show his hand at all. Wanted really to become a Provincial Prime Minister and doubted, except by trying to get a few candidates in, that he would take any part openly. As for Houde, Duplessis would not link up with him and Houde would likely take an independent role, unless he could be leader of a group. He doubted if Houde knew his own mind as yet, but that he would be a real factor in Montreal. I told Cardin that all his friends I thought wanted him to be back with me and the Liberals. He seemed to approve that view. I said to him I was very anxious for him and me to be working together. Cardin said something about the situation being very obscure and it looked as though no party would have a majority. I then said that I believed that would be the case if Quebec were divided, but that if Quebec stood solidly behind me I thought our party would be returned to power by a good majority. If, however, after the elections, there were groups in the House and we had not a majority over all I would not continue in leadership of the party. I would never be dependent on the support of particular groups. We must either have a majority over all or I would not attempt to carry on. I wanted to make this very clear, so that Cardin would see that any thought of my continuing at the mercy of a number of independents would not be realized.

"I then spoke of how I had stood by Quebec but felt that in so doing I was standing by Canada. If Quebec lost me as Leader I thought they would rue the day no matter what group got in, Tories or C.C.F. I believed he had been told that even in the Province of Quebec, my name was cheered more than any other. He said he thought that was true. He said it was true that the Tory party counted for nothing in Quebec. They were gone. Drew and Bracken had no influence there. I pointed out it would be impossible to say what position the Province might be in if we did not keep united. That he and I were interested in the larger questions of Canadian unity, advancing democratic ideas and social reforms, as the family allowance, and the like. I thought we should work together. He said he did not know what his influence or position or power would be were he to take an active part. I do not know whether he was seeking to have me mention what position I would give him, or whether he was just thinking in terms of what his prestige would be today. I replied by saying that I thought his influence at Quebec would be very real and would be what it had always been. He was not sure of that."

Mackenzie King continued: "I then reminded him of the year that he was here and said that I had been a true friend to him when he needed a friend, especially when he was in such a bad state of health. I had kept the Public Works and the other Department running during an absence of about a year, when really it was not in the public interest to have matters held so long in that condition. That I felt it was not right to let anything influence his health and that it should be restored. I indicated that I felt I would now appreciate his help in keeping the party in office and its principles the governing ones. I told him that but for the latter reasons I would not myself wish to go into the present campaign but that I felt Canada needed me at this juncture. I also said that in relation to the post-war period, in connection with the peace, I thought I could do more to preserve Canada's full rights as a nation than anyone else. I also told him of my thought of putting the Canadian flag on the Parliament Buildings the minute surrender came.

"I told him if he had any thoughts or suggestions he would like to make not to hesitate to make them, but he did not follow up in any concrete way.

"When he was leaving, I again repeated to him that I looked on him as an old friend and colleague and hoped that in considering matters he would find his way to have us working closely together in the next campaign. He thanked me for entertaining the kindly sentiment toward him, but did not go further. He looked to me very frail, though as he says, he has not seen his doctor for some time. I imagine his health is far from being what he thinks it is."

A political difficulty also existed in Nova Scotia. On September 29, Mackenzie King and Ilsley discussed a judicial vacancy to which Pottier, the M.P. for Shelburne-Yarmouth-Clare might be appointed. "Ilsley spoke of not knowing what Macdonald had in mind. He feels sure that Macdonald wants to run in Nova Scotia and he feels that the people of Pottier's constituency would take him and elect him, but he realizes the embarrassment of two Ministers from Nova Scotia. I said I thought we could take a chance on that, that I imagined Macdonald did not want to stay on long after the war, really wanted to go on the Bench. We could give him a post there later. I undertook, however, to discuss the whole matter with Macdonald on Tuesday."

Oddly enough there is no record of this interview in the diary, but it is clear that it took place because the Prime Minister, in his diary for October 6, reported that he "told Ilsley of my conversation with Angus Macdonald which he seemed to regard as all for the best. (It would, of course, relieve him by getting Angus out of the picture here and insuring Ilsley the one position in Nova Scotia.) I gathered that Ilsley would not recommend Pottier for a judgeship but would advise him to run again. He said he thought Nova Scotia politics would get a bad breakup if anything happened to Macmillan [Premier of Nova Scotia]. That he was now getting very old, is blind in one eye, had had paralysis. Angus taking over the Premiership would secure things there."

Sir William Mulock died on October 1 and on October 4 Mackenzie King was in Toronto for the funeral, which he described in the minutest detail.

That evening in Toronto, the Prime Minister went to see Joseph Atkinson, the publisher of the *Toronto Star*, who, he felt, "was very pleased with the Government's programme, specially the family allowances. He would like to see the excess profits tax become a regular thing. He told me that his own experience in the money the Star had made showed him that very much was going as profits to capital which should have been divided among the people." He added that they "were laughing about Hepburn's attitude. He thinks Hepburn will be effective against the Tories. That the Party may gain by his action. He would not be surprised to see him become Leader of the Liberals in Ontario at Tuesday's Caucus. What has happened is that he was resentful against me for not taking him into the Cabinet, or letting him determine Federal policies as well as giving him my confidence in everything. That confidence has now turned against Drew for the same reason. Atkinson says it is likely to fade out as against myself and intensify toward Drew—the same hatred but vented in a new direction. Atkinson feels that our chances are, on the whole, very good. That we will certainly be the largest party, but in all probability will have a majority over all."

On October 6, after the Cabinet meeting, Mackenzie King discussed the political situation in Ontario with Senator Bench. "It was on Wednesday in talking with Howe, that he [Howe] told me we were getting new additions to the party from strange quarters. That that afternoon Hepburn would be out with an article attacking Drew and saying he was out for the Liberal party both provincially and federally to fight reactionary Toryism. Later when the article appeared, it was certainly a real blast and makes any allegiance on Hepburn's part, from now on, with the Tories, impossible. It probably means a breach between Hepburn and the Globe.

"Bench said he had come in to tell me what he knew of circumstances which occasioned Hepburn's actions. He began by saying as Howe had mentioned to me that when he, Bench, was with Howe, at Fort William at the time of Howe's Convention, Hepburn had been in those parts and he and Bench had had a talk together in which Bench had said to him he thought he, Hepburn, ought to be in the fight with the Liberals. Hepburn in leaving said he would like to have a talk with him some time in the near future. There had been a meeting of Liberals in Hamilton, last week, at which some things were discussed but he did not go into what they were. He then said that Hepburn had 'phoned him to come and spend the weekend with him at his farm. He said he has known Hepburn well. Has been friendly to him though he would not want to be too intimate with him or get into any harness with him. He had gone over in the afternoon and had started the conversation by stating that he thought Hepburn was making a mistake in not joining at once with the Liberals. That he would get nowhere keeping up the kind of attitude he had. That Hepburn had then begun to talk about his resentment toward myself. That he, Bench, had said that had got him nowhere. He had lost ground everywhere on that account and that he ought to see it. Hepburn then spoke of not liking Drew saying he hated the man and his methods and was prepared to attack him. . . . They continued the discussion about Hepburn's future if he wished to continue in politics and the wisdom of his losing no time in regaining the ground that he had lost through his attacks, etc.

"Hepburn had then said the question was how he should go about taking a new attitude. This was on Saturday afternoon. He then said: I see the opening that I need. The Liberals of Elgin are having a meeting on Monday to nominate a candidate. They want me to accept the nomination but I won't do that. We can get a man who can carry the constituency though Mills won't run again but I can make an address which will declare my position. I can make an attack on Drew and his reactionary Toryism. He spoke of Drew wanting to make a little republic of Ontario, to be a dictator there himself. Also spoke about the trouble he was making with Quebec. If he kept on as he was doing, there would be civil war. . . ."

Mackenzie King's account continued: "Bench then said that on Sunday, he had helped Hepburn to work out the statement which he made at the Convention in his riding the next day. They had discussed what the attitude of the Liberals at Ottawa would be. Bench had said that he thought everything depended on how Hepburn went ahead with his advocacy of Liberal principles and the stand he took publicly. That the question of the possible future leadership of the party in Ontario was discussed, was plain enough to me from what Bench said. He frankly stated that Harry Nixon while a nice fellow was most ineffective and the party would get nowhere with him. He thought the men who were there now would rally around Hepburn but the question was how it was best to bring this about, whether it would be wise for Hepburn to act quickly. There is to be a caucus of Ontario Liberals on Tuesday and it is possible that there the question might come up of his again becoming the Leader, but he, Bench, had advised against any hasty step. He thought it would be better for him to speak out his mind, etc., or take his stand publicly for some little time before anything finally was arranged. Bench did not say that his mission was to find out how I would feel about it or what my attitude would be but in reference to the matter, he said he had indicated that I had never been other than openminded about Liberal party affairs and had not sought to exclude anyone. I said to Bench that I had been very careful all through my public life not to say anything that would cause a breach with anyone. I told him I had never had a breach with Hepburn except over export of power business and had been careful except when he had destroyed the party in Ontario, in references to the results of his actions. That I did not claim a monopoly of control of the party. That I was anxious to have everything done that would make for unity and strength of the party. Those who were fighting its battles sincerely were welcome to make this known and take what part they might wish.

"I was careful not to extend any welcome and equally careful not to say anything which would imply exclusion or animus or anything of that kind which, so far as I am concerned, I have not, though I do not trust Hepburn.

"I gave Bench no messages to take back. No advice. Except to agree with him that Hepburn could do us good if he served to bring the party together in the Province and to end feuds but that I had nothing to say about future developments. Bench repeated again he did not want to be arm in arm with Hepburn and on the other hand, did not want to let him drift. Asked me if he was right in keeping in touch. I said: certainly.

"During our conversation, I said I thought Hepburn was annoyed at me for not taking him into the Government or taking his own men in. Also that his feeling against Drew was doubtless due to the same reason that Drew had not taken him into the Government. His reply was that that was not so. That Drew had offered four portfolios to the Liberals. That Hepburn and St. Clair Gordon were to be two of the number. He said St. Clair Gordon was a true Liberal. I said nothing but listened to all that was being said. When he was leaving, Bench said if Harry Nixon were to drop out for any reason, they would wish to have the matter done gracefully, and that they might ask me to consider what could be done for Harry which, of course, meant his appointment to the Senate. I said I was very friendly with Nixon. Had always been ready to be of service to him and to help him in any way I could. It was unfortunate that he had become so ineffective as a Leader. Another thing Bench said was that he thought this action of Hepburn's would spike Drew's guns against bringing on an election in Ontario at present; when he returned from Europe he wanted the Cabinet to agree with him to bring on an election but his colleagues were opposed to that and while Drew might still be considering it, this would effectively prevent that which he thought would be wise. I agree. He thought it wise to let Hepburn fight Drew over the military matters.

"I have been carefully thinking over the whole matter. The conclusion I have come to is that Howe and other of the Ontario Liberals have felt the Liberals would get nowhere with Nixon at the head. That they could see no other person in sight who had dynamic powers or powers of leadership than Hepburn and that it might be well to try and get him back into line. That this undoubtedly was discussed between Howe and Bench at Howe's convention, and that they might both have talked to Hepburn about it. How far matters have been secretly arranged by other Ontario Ministers in having the conference they had at Hamilton, I cannot say but it in a way was related to the meeting which the Ontario Liberals were to have on Tuesday. It would look as though there were a relationship between the Elgin Convention last week and the meeting of Ontario Liberals this week, and that there had been more planning than sudden action and decision in regard to these meetings. It is clear now that there is an effort on foot to have Hepburn again brought into the leadership of the Ontario Liberals.

Whether they are seeking to convince him that if he plays the game with the Liberals for the balance of the term of this Parliament, and that I should be defeated at Prince Albert, or not wish to continue in the leadership, then Hepburn might be brought forward as Leader in the federal arena, I do not know. I am quite convinced in my own mind that whatever may be thought of in that way today will never be countenanced by the Party as a whole. On the other hand, I am quite prepared silently to acquiesce in having Hepburn used in any way possible by my colleagues in helping to win the election and I have no fears whatever as to the consequences. He will never have the confidence of the people of Canada as a whole and only the confidence of the worst elements in the Province. Unfortunately, all men have votes and for that reason all methods that are honourable can be used. It is all right in carrying on the fight to bring into line as many as possible so long as this is done by honourable means."

Returning to the problem of Cabinet reorganization on October 5, the Prime Minister spoke to C. D. Howe again about taking on the new Department of Reconstruction. He reported that Howe said "that St. Laurent had pressed him very hard to accept. That he had great respect for St. Laurent and was prepared to undertake the work if he could be sure of getting results but there were some matters that he wished to have understood. He then read from a memo which he had prepared which suggested the appointment of Alex Skelton as Secretary, the transfer of the National Research Council from Trade and Commerce to the new Department with [C. J.] Mackenzie made Director General of Research. This to link the research work of industry, forestry, mining, etc., with reconstruction. Another Director General to take up some of the work of the Transport part connected with civil aviation, which would give him R. A. C. Henry to assist. Then a Director General of industrial reconversion—Mr. Carmichael and Mr. Berry in charge. We then discussed the appropriations being made to the Department of Reconstruction, for all reconstruction work and monies allotted to the different departments of the government. He was strong on stating he would not undertake it without my backing. I told him I naturally was anxious to have the work done in a large way and while I would not become an automaton and back anything that the Minister would suggest I certainly believed my judgment and where the Minister should be backed up would do so strongly. I spoke of having a committee of the Cabinet to work with him. He was not too keen on this, but when I pointed out they could be helpful in matters of reallocation and mentioned who the Ministers would be: St. Laurent, Ilsley, and MacKinnon, he readily acquiesced in this aspect. He had a strange sort of final paragraph which was that he could only accept the position with a promise from myself that if he presented his resignation from the post it would be accepted; that he would do all he could to make the ministry effective but if it became ineffective, without full support of colleagues, etc., he would insist on retiring. What Howe feels is that he has achieved a reputation and is taking on something that he is risking his reputation on. He knows of the conflict in the Cabinet and has foreseen how impossible it would be to make headway without the fullest co-operation. I told him I would do everything possible to have co-operation given in largest measure."

It was not until October 13 that the new Departments were finally established. The Prime Minister called in Brooke Claxton on the 13th and told him that he would become Minister of National Health and Welfare. "Told him it gave me great pleasure to be able to offer him this portfolio at last and he had been a great help to me as Parliamentary Assistant and in the work he had done for the Government. That I felt sure he would make a real success of the new Department and that he had a great future before him and wished him well. I mentioned that there were one or two matters connected with his appointment which I should mention; one was the possible embarrassment it would be to Abbott where only one English-speaking Minister in Montreal is possible; also there were difficulties in adding another English-speaking Minister to Montreal without corresponding French Minister, especially if we should remove LaFleche as it was practically understood with him I would be doing later on. Also I spoke of other men who had been longer in Parliament. Cited the attitude of Guthrie and others toward myself in Sir Wilfrid's day. Said I felt he would be recognized as the right person for the Department of Health and Welfare. He spoke most appreciatively emphasizing his loyalty towards myself and his desire to help me all he possibly could. I mentioned I would look to him to keep an eye on the political situation in the National Liberal Office, and to assist in any way possible.

"He then spoke of a Deputy. I gave him authority to sound out Davidson [Dr. G. Davidson, now President of the C.B.C.] further and to talk with me about other appointments, (1) of a Doctor and (2) someone from Quebec. Also spoke of the possibility of having Mrs. C. T. Casselman [M.P. for Edmonton East] as a Parliamentary Assistant. I thought some woman should be identified with the work of the Department. Spoke, too, of his keeping an eye on Reconstruction matters."

The Prime Minister then sent for Ian Mackenzie and told him "in Claxton's presence of my intention of appointing Claxton this afternoon," and of his appointment as Minister of Veterans Affairs.

"What I want to record particularly," he added, "is the talk I had with

Ian in which I said to him yesterday, and repeated in part today, that I had discussed his appointment with some of the Ministers. They felt that the new Department would require more in the way of direct administration than he had given Pensions and Health. That I hoped he would give matters his personal attention. That I knew he had left the running of his Department to his officials,—that that would not do. Also I asked him just what he had in mind when he spoke to me about being ready to turn over the position to anyone later on. He said it was a matter of Scotch pride with him to be made the Minister of the Department he had helped to create, but that he would be quite ready to give it up at any time I thought best. He volunteered the thought that I would probably want to make the change when I was getting ready to go to the country and reorganize the Government at that time. That perhaps some returned soldier would be best. He still spoke about running in the elections. I spoke again of his health, but it was clearly understood that he would give up whenever I wished. He had a plane ready to leave for England tomorrow, but I told him I would like him to wait until after Ralston was here. I did not think it well for both to be on the other side at the same time. Also better for him to be on hand until the new Department got a little under way and matters connected therewith definitely settled. I think he realizes it is the last opportunity to get overseas."

The Cabinet met in the afternoon to confirm the changes and approve the recommendations to the Governor-General. The new Ministers were sworn in at Government House later in the afternoon. "Claxton was the first one to be sworn as a Privy Councillor. Then Mackenzie, Howe and Claxton in turn to their new offices. I congratulated all three and extended all good wishes. Did not wait because of the press conference. Howe was leaving by plane for Nova Scotia, so Mackenzie, Claxton and I returned to my office where we met the press. Shortly after 7 I announced that the Ministers had been sworn in, and the new Departments proclaimed. This came as a complete surprise. We had a pleasant interview."

CHAPTER FIVE

The Reinforcement Crisis, 1944
Phase I

THE REINFORCEMENT and conscription crisis burst on the Cabinet and the country in mid-October of 1944. Until that time, the general assumption had been that the European phase of the war was virtually over; the government's main military preoccupations in the late summer and early fall of 1944 were with Canada's part in the war against Japan and with the problem of demobilization and re-employment of the armed forces. Closely connected with this latter problem was the question of what further service General McNaughton could render.

The impression that all was well in Europe had been confirmed by General Stuart, the Chief of Staff (Canadian Military Headquarters Overseas), when he returned to Canada at the beginning of August to report to the government on the progress of the war on the Continent. The Prime Minister wrote that at the War Committee on August 3 Stuart "gave an exceedingly interesting account of the invasion and progress of the war; of his own intervention to retain Burns in command for the Corps in Italy against the desire of the British Commanding Officer Lees to have a British officer put in his place. Burns is not popular but Stuart was convinced that more would be accomplished under him than by a change. He showed great tact and skill in the manner he had worked out his investigation of the case. In referring to what had been accomplished in Normandy, he made clear the plan of campaign whereby Montgomery sought to keep the German troops engaged against the British and the Canadians, to enable the Americans to advance on the Western flank. All had worked out splendidly. Stuart felt that the British and Canadians would now make further rapid advances. He was most emphatic about there being no doubt of ultimate success and the possibility of war being over sooner than we expected. He made clear that we had plenty of reserves. Presented a request for some additional men for use in Italy but emphasized that this would not lead to any pressure for further men. I asked him the question pointedly. His reply was equally definite to the effect that the war would likely be over before any further numbers would be required beyond those already available. His whole report was intensely interesting. . . ."

At the Quebec Conference, too, the discussion, so far as Canada was concerned, had largely turned on the nature and extent of participation in the war against Japan. Discussion of this matter was continued by the War Committee in Ottawa on September 20. Mackenzie King spoke out very frankly "to make my position wholly clear. That I thought our duty was to save lives. That we were trustees of the people of Canada in the matter of saving lives of our young men and also the money of the people; that we were not justified in making vast expenditures which were only for the purposes of show but which could not help but lead to probable considerable loss of life and certainly to great and unnecessary expenditure. I pointed out that the Defence Ministers and their staffs had fought me on everything that I had said about it being not necessary for us to serve in the South Pacific, India, Burma, etc. That we were not expected to do more at most than have a token force, etc. That in all of this, I had been shown at Quebec to be right; that they had heard the Prime Minister of England ask Sir Charles Portal why he had put such a burden on Canada so far as the Air Force was concerned. I also mentioned that the President and Churchill together had mentioned our doing patrol duty in the North of the Aleutians and spending time to drive the Japanese out of China. That it would be quite wrong in the light of these circumstances for us to push our way in where we had nothing to gain but everything to lose. I pointed out that the British had their possessions and interests in the Orient which they wished to recover; that the Americans had their possessions and interests; that Canada had not an acre of land or property in the Orient. That it was only because of our undertaking to be at the side of the United States and Britain that we were going in to the extent that we could really be of some help.

"I spent some time going over the estimates and a very substantial reduction was made. I am not sure that the reduction in ships was not 50%. As regards the air force, it was also very considerable. Power had been talking about 3 squadrons to Australia as a token. He has come to think that even as a token, they are hardly welcome there and agreed to strike them off.

"After speaking very plainly and pointing out what I felt, giving the reasons why I thought we should reduce it to just a token force, at least for the present, I made each Member of the Council present express his views. Crerar a little wobbly, general in talk. Said he agreed with me. St. Laurent very strongly of my view, according very much with what he had himself said before. Mitchell, this time, equally strong. Howe pointing out need of men in industry today and emphatically of my opinion. Ilsley finally saying outright that he thought what I had said was right. There were only the 3 Defence Ministers who said nothing but realized that they were put on the spot. I said it was painful to have to disagree with colleagues but I knew they felt an obligation to support their officials, but it was the duty of all of us to tell the officials what they could and should do.

"I came back again saying that my conscience would not allow waste of a single life for the sake of appearance. I did not think we were justified in trying to make a show on top of all that had been done. It was different if we had not been in the war a couple of years before the United States."

On September 22, just before Ralston left on his inspection trip overseas, procedures for demobilization were discussed. According to the Prime Minister, the Minister of Defence argued that none of the N.R.M.A. men should be re-employed until the General Service men in Canada and overseas were placed. "I pointed out that the whole basis on which he was arguing was wrong which was that the quantity of work would be limited, and that we should seek to get men in individual jobs. I pointed out and was supported in this view by both Clark and Robertson speaking out that we have got work and that we should state frankly that our policies had been to create work, to have a large national economy and that we would have work for all.

"St. Laurent was quite outspoken about an effort to penalize the N.R.M.A. men by keeping them on for an indefinite period saying that the Government would probably find out if they did, there were constitutional objections to that and would get into difficulty with provinces, etc. I said we had no right to penalize anyone, that all were doing duties required of them by the State and that this should be recognized. I agree we should carry out our policy of seeing that General Service men did not have their places taken by men who had remained at home but felt we should demobilize just as rapidly as we could all the N.R.M.A. men guarding at the same time to see that the General Service men got employment and making regulations necessary to see that the places were not taken which belonged to those who had gone overseas.

"Howe was very outspoken about the need for men in industry today and said we were holding back industries by keeping a standing army that was useless, that was doing nothing in the way of real military service. He thought the sooner they were disbanded and the whole business forgotten, the better. I think his view was entirely right and sensible. It was necessary, however, to consider the views of the men fighting in the forces and how they might feel if they suddenly saw all posts going to N.R.M.A. men.

Besides Ralston is quite determined to keep these men until he is sure we do not have to have conscription which means, in his mind, practically until the war is over. We went back and forth over the ground, Ralston anxious to get away tonight by 'plane but finally saying he was going to stay on tomorrow and asking if a further meeting of the Cabinet would be possible. I told him I would be on hand while St. Laurent had to leave, and Power was away. Decided it best, however, to call a meeting for a quarter to eleven."

To Mackenzie King this meeting on September 22 "was the most interesting one I have been at at any time. It developed into a sort of test of endurance between Ralston and myself to see which one would hold out the longest in our respective points of view. I think I was supported pretty strongly by Crerar, and Howe, Mitchell and St. Laurent and, to some extent, by Ilsley and Macdonald. Ralston was holding out in an extreme way against all though he had Ilsley and Macdonald ready to join with him at any point at which agreement could be reached. There was slight possibility of others coming to his point of view."

In the Cabinet the next morning, with only Ralston, Ilsley, Macdonald, Michaud, and Mackenzie King present, the Prime Minister reported that "there was further discussion and study of the wisdom of having N.R.M.A. men demobilized just as soon as possible; not keeping them any length of time in the army. I think all present, even Macdonald, were against keeping a standing army of N.R.M.A. men, but were in favour of demobilizing them at once. Ralston insisted that if that were done men would conclude there was no possible need of further reinforcements and it might make that task impossible." Ralston left for the United Kingdom later that day.

It was this discussion which led Mackenzie King on September 28 to talk to St. Laurent "very openly about my feelings of the determination of the conscriptionists still seeking to undermine the Government, and the possibility even of Ralston returning with a demand for conscription, as Borden had done in 1917, though I do not believe this will happen."

In Ralston's absence, the debate about participation in the Japanese war was continued in the Cabinet on September 28 when the Prime Minister read "to the entire Cabinet the Minutes of the meetings at Quebec with Churchill and told the Members exactly what had been said there. I spoke too about the air force being kept at much too great strength. I had opened the discussion by saying the real question before us was to decide whether Canada from now on was to seek to return to an industrial country, eager to further the arts of peace, or to regard itself as the countries of Europe had for so many years, under steady preparation for war with large armed forces." The discussion grew out of proposals for further large expenditures under the mutual aid program. Mackenzie King argued that the government had no right to limit its freedom by giving future contracts now which were not absolutely necessary, or undertaking obligations which "involved further taxation where provision had not been made out of the estimate this year. The Cabinet were very solidly with me, Ilsley among the number, though he said he believed we would come to reverse this policy to avoid dislocation and some unemployment just at the moment of elections. The final word was to be given when Howe was present. I argued that our whole campaign should be the expansion of our own industry for our own purposes to meet civil needs rather than supplies for further war.

"I also took up the statement which had appeared on the arrival of certain of the army technical personnel in Australia and the unfortunate interview given there by Davis [T. C. Davis, Canadian High Commissioner in Australia] which seemed to emphasize using large forces in the Pacific and even in Australia. I asked Power to see that it was made clear that we were not intending to send forces to Australia. I pointed out how strongly I had objected to even the advance party, who had arrived there at a very inopportune moment. It is strange that one should have to fight in a Liberal administration for limitation of expenditures on war, when told by both Britain and the United States that they can manage the situation themselves and that we are really not wanted, excepting where it is necessary for Canada to keep her position, vis-a-vis Japan in evidence in the way of token participation. I took very strong exception to the attitude of the three Defence Departments in seeking to retain so many men under arms and with heavy cost to the taxpayers. I told the Cabinet that I had the responsibility of leading the country into the war and it was the heaviest responsibility any man could have and that I did not intend to allow a single life to be sacrificed unnecessarily, or the taxpayers burdened any further than was absolutely necessary on war account. What was needed to win the war I would help to further, but I would not agree to anything that was expended merely that the services might qualify themselves or extend their activities." "The discussion," he added, "I know will make the Defence Ministers more antagonistic towards myself, but I feel certain I have again helped to clear the air on the real position."

The discussion on the naval contribution was resumed at the War Committee on October 5 and the Prime Minister "found Angus Macdonald extremely difficult," so difficult that he left the meeting early. "I found myself getting a little incensed, and for that reason did not wish to wait and get into a bitter argument with my colleagues."

The differences with Angus Macdonald continued at the next meeting of the War Committee on October 11. Macdonald had submitted a written memorandum and the Prime Minister "pointed out where the memo had a new turn to it, for example, that it read the British requested certain ships. Also mentioned that others were indispensable and the like. I said this was a new attitude toward Canada on the part of the British Government. They had no business to request anything or to state that our ships were indispensable for purposes of protecting their colonial possessions in South Pacific, India, Burma, etc. Macdonald withdrew the word 'requested.' It was apparent the memo had been prepared in the Department which is really saturated with the Imperial Navy idea.

"I was amazed at Macdonald's crudeness and indifference to decent amenities toward his colleagues in repeating statements that have been gone over time and again. I kept very quiet but finally said that I thought there was not much use discussing the matter further in War Committee but we would take it to the Cabinet as a whole which had already given its decision. I agreed to what had been suggested as to ships that should proceed via the Panama Canal into the Pacific but stated that I had said my last word with respect to ships serving in South Pacific. Macdonald then said they could, of course, inform the Admiralty that Canada could not provide these ships. Later he said they would so inform the Admiralty.

"The point I kept urging was that the Canadian people could not countenance our men serving in India, Burma or elsewhere to enable Britain to reconquer her colonial possessions. While the request might be a small one and desirable on some grounds, it would raise a political issue in Canada out of all proportions to the good that could be rendered. With this removed, Council next discussed the wisdom of having two carriers included in the balance of the ships to contribute to the Pacific. I thought Macdonald made out a strong case for these ships as being the ones that are most useful. While I feel that the Department has not been straightforward in dealing with the Cabinet in the way it has gone about securing these ships as a gift from England, the real object being to make a fleet unit for post-war purposes rather than for the war, I nevertheless see the wisdom of making effective whatever we do; also as the contribution in war against Japan has been cut down from 25,000 men afloat to 13,500 and equals only ⅓ of the total strength of the navy as it now is, I have felt that this was a contribution which was appreciable and to which exception could not be taken by the people whereas anything smaller might not be really effective. It was a hard battle to fight but I won after struggling alone —after having fought over and over again."

There can be little doubt that this bitter confrontation with Macdonald was, for Mackenzie King, an unfortunate prelude to the reinforcement crisis. On the other hand, Mackenzie King's relations with Ralston at this time were better than they had been since 1942. Just before Ralston left for overseas, he and the Prime Minister had shared a common concern over McNaughton's future. On September 22 Mackenzie King noted that Ralston had told him "in the last day or two that the time had come for McNaughton's leave to expire, and that he would either have to continue in the army or resign. We agreed it would be right to have him made a General and we discussed what might be possible in the way of an appointment for him. Some position in External Affairs or in connection with movement of population overseas was what we had in mind. Ralston had a talk of two hours with him yesterday. He told me of the conversation which he said was kept up in a natural way but with nothing very much decided and without letting Ralston feel there was something still between them. Ralston had felt [McNaughton] was not committing himself in any way but was trying to find out where we really wanted him, and whether he would be really needed in the service of Canada. He wanted me to have a talk with him re possible appointment. I said I thought it might be best for Robertson to have a word with him. He could indicate more clearly the scope of External Affairs, the opportunities, etc., and [McNaughton] would perhaps speak more freely to Robertson on some things that he wanted me to know about."

Later that day Norman Robertson did have a talk with McNaughton and reported its substance to the Prime Minister immediately. Robertson had the impression that McNaughton "was very friendly to me," Mackenzie King wrote, "but was not friendly to Ralston and two other Ministers. I think he means the Ministers of Defence. Robertson gathered he evidently could not work with them in the Cabinet or otherwise, pressing also that overtures had been made to him more or less by certain parties, among others organized labour, to actively interest himself in their affairs. He told Robertson he was anxious to do constructive work for the country where it would tell with most effect." That evening Mackenzie King reported these developments to Ralston and indicated that he proposed to see McNaughton the next day.

Before going to the Cabinet meeting the following morning (September 23), the Prime Minister saw McNaughton who, he felt, was "quite happy and friendly in his attitude toward myself. I told him I had rebuked myself for not having seen something of him in the months he had been here, but it had been due to pressure from day to day. He said he understood it. . . . " After a few more social preliminaries, the Prime Minister came to the point of the conversation.

"I said to him that when we last talked I had spoken to him about possible appointments. Had thought it well to have Robertson talk with him before I saw him. He would remember we had carefully avoided even discussing certain appointments when we last talked so that it could not be said any kind of a bargain was made. Now I wished to say to him that what I had in mind was some appointment in External Affairs. Some of the Legations or High Commissionerships, or assisting in moving of peoples on the continent; work in connection with UNRRA. Also the post of Governor General. But I gathered from Robertson that he was not anxious to leave Canada but to stay and work in this country and for this country.

"I then spoke of the Research work. Said I had no doubt that for him a great interest existed there but there again I gathered he felt Mackenzie had taken a hold and that it would be unwise in any way. He then said he did not think it would be either right or in the public interest. He had induced Mackenzie to give up his post at the University and take on this work. He had done it exceedingly well. Scientists were sensitive people. Were he, McNaughton, to go in and tackle the job anew, he would find that four years had made a difference. They might feel there was a sort of 'dead hand' of the past controlling their endeavours. He thought Mackenzie had been able to bring about a close relationship between industry and the Research Council. That in every way, it would be better for Mackenzie to keep on. In fact, he thought he ought to be definitely confirmed in the position of President.

"I asked if there was any way the work could be shared. He said: no, that would be a mistake. Better be controlled by one head. I told him his attitude would be very noble as well as right, and that I declined to make any appointment as President until I had talked over the matter with him but that it might be well now to have Mackenzie confirmed.

"He then spoke to me of having been approached to interest himself in affairs. He said he could not mention any names for obvious reasons. I said I fully understand. I would be surprised if there were not tremendous pressure put on him by political parties to enter the arena of politics, and that certainly they would wish to secure him. I wondered about his being interested in social questions, and if he would be at all interested in an appointment to the Senate. That I had thought when Currie returned from England he should have been appointed to the Senate because of the knowledge of conditions in which soldiers were interested. I thought soldiers would feel their interests would have a voice in Parliament if he were in the Senate himself. He could be going on with his other work at the same time. He said that to enter the Senate would look as if he were on the shelf and had given up other things. I said on the contrary; while I did think that the Senate had gone down, it ought to be a place in which men could be selected for service which they could render the country. As we were discussing it further, he said no, that would not interest him, and volunteered the statement that the one high executive office I had spoken of was something in which he might interest himself and he would be glad to have that considered. I said to him that I was glad to hear him say that, that I felt he could fill that position. I would feel every confidence in his appointment to that position. He then said something about being interested in constitutional questions and relationships between the different parts of the Empire. I said to him I thought no two men shared more in common than he and I did in the constitutional position and relationship. He said he agreed with that. I confess I was surprised at his even mentioning he would be interested, but I was relieved when he spoke of it as it would be impossible, because of Ralston, to give him any of the Cabinet positions, though I should like to have him for one, either as Minister of Reconstruction or as Minister of War Veterans Affairs, or deputy head of any of these. But the Governor Generalship fits in with my feeling I have come to have about the desirability of standing for a true nation, getting away from this subsidiary position and to have a Canadian Governor General. To my mind I have been thinking over Massey and his wife, Vanier and his wife, and last night quite a bit of McNaughton and his wife. Of the three I really believe McNaughton would be the best and it would be a fine recognition of his services as a General at the beginning of the war. Churchill has said to me he would be prepared, if he were in England, to offer him a Peerage.

"I told McNaughton I was right in what I had said to him as to Ralston not being one who had in any way conspired against him but that he was simply repeating what had been said to him at Washington [see vol. I, chap. 20]. The statement Stuart had made was wholly true, as I knew from my own experience that Ralston and Stuart both felt that if things were being said as to his not being the one to lead the armies overseas that that should be made known to him at once. He accepted all this very nicely and said that all that was past. He seemed on the whole to appreciate what I had said to him there.

"When we had finished talking about the Governor Generalship and I felt it was time to get back to Council, I spoke to him about his being made a General. Said Ralston had spoken of that himself and made the suggestion. . . . He then said to me that he felt he should no longer take advantage of the leave; that he must decide to sever his connections with the army, as he did not see there was any place he would fit in or any place overseas, or that he was needed. He thought he ought to do that right away. I said to him that raises a question in my mind as to the procedure of a step of the kind. That what I was anxious to avoid was to have it taken in such a way as to let anyone think the Government had been responsible for the decision that had been imposed on him. He said at once I have already told Ralston that I want to resign. I feel I should not continue leave any longer and I will be glad to write him to that effect. I said if you will write him to that effect, I think that would in every way relieve Ralston's mind and mine and would be the best. I said to him may I say to Ralston that you would be prepared to write him saying you would like to retire, and let him then proceed accordingly. He said: certainly, to do that. This as he was leaving the door. He spoke again of the position of Governor General. He then said: I will have to make a decision pretty soon, either settle on this or throw my hat into the ring. While he did not say it, I saw clearly he would have to take his part in politics and it would probably mean taking it certainly in opposition, not to myself, but in some form which would mean controversy.

"Before anything had been said of the Governor Generalship, I mentioned there were some other positions which he might wish but to which it would not be possible to make an appointment for some little time. As to the position of Governor General, for example, the appointment was not up until the spring. We had also discussed the question of what he might do in the way of writing. He told me that all his records were clear. He intended to turn them over to the State and had no desire to begin any controversy. I mentioned what Churchill had said to me that he was prepared to leave his records and not to attempt writing his memoirs. All he would do would be to put the framework on what was already there. [McNaughton] used the expression that the best course as to the division of the army is something which would be fought over and over again through years to come but that was something that could look after itself."

As soon as McNaughton left the office, Mackenzie King "sent to Council for Ralston and told him what had taken place. When I began to speak, not knowing what was coming, his face was ashen pale and motionless, like that of a man who . . . was having his own fate decided. As I went on with the discussion, his calmness came back a little, and when I mentioned about the Governor Generalship he was at once immensely relieved. When I told him about McNaughton having agreed to write him himself, his countenance completely changed, he stood up and said that there again I had shown my remarkable skill in doing a splendid bit of work. He was so immensely relieved and pleased. . . . "

Later that day, according to Mackenzie King, Ralston telephoned McNaughton. "Ralston told me the talk had been very pleasant; that McNaughton was writing at once to him and he was writing a reply and that both letters would be given to Robertson with authority to alter the language to make it suitable. Both would be dated today. He had arranged for his appointment as General. Ralston had spoken to McNaughton about the government giving him a dinner. At first McNaughton had paused a moment, but later he had said he would be pleased to accept that. He, McNaughton, had talked to him about the post of Governor General and Ralston had told him I had discussed that with him. Ralston made clear he would like to be at the dinner himself and he might therefore have to postpone it until after his return. Ralston said that McNaughton had spoken to him about past relations and said we had all been working in our directions but all of that was now past and they apparently parted the best of good friends. I said to Ralston I was always a believer in Providence and hoped He will protect you in your journey and safe return. I then extended good wishes to him for his birthday, which comes in a couple of days from now, and he left with the lightest heart that I think he has had for many a day."

After a very full day, Mackenzie King closed his diary entry for September 23 by recording his impressions of a broadcast address to a labour meeting by President Roosevelt, adding: "I personally long to get into a straight fight, not so much along lines of the divisions of the past between parties as enabling me to complete the work of constructive reform in which I have been interested all my life and which I should like to see made as complete as possible but also standing for a real Canadian programme.

"If between now and that time it should be possible to have the Canadian flag made the flag of Canada; a Canadian like McNaughton announced as the next Governor General, and then go to the country on a straight social reform programme, and the importance of my being the one to serve in the making of peace, I believe it would be possible to carry the country."

On September 28, the Prime Minister decided to publish the correspondence between McNaughton and Ralston, and the following day he arranged an appointment with General McNaughton for Tuesday, October 3. The interview took place as scheduled before the Prime Minister left for Toronto to attend Sir William Mulock's funeral, but there is no record of it in the diary. In a conversation on October 13, the Prime Minister informed Dr. C. J. Mackenzie that he would be confirmed as President of the National Research Council.

Even before the Minister of Defence had left on his overseas inspection trip, Canadian newspapers had begun to carry reports of poorly trained reinforcements, of convalescent soldiers returned to duty before they had made a complete recovery, and other charges that a lack of adequately trained reinforcements was hampering the effectiveness of the infantry. The Premier of Ontario, George Drew, renewed his attacks on the government and again demanded conscription for overseas service. Just before he went into the Cabinet meeting on October 13 to announce the Cabinet changes, Mackenzie King received a telegram from Ralston which caused him great concern. "It was in part a reply to my long message to him regarding Drew's statement. In part, an intimation that he was coming back with the intention of making proposals which may involve the whole question of conscription. He spoke of arranging to leave on Sunday and to bring Stuart with him. He asked if I would have an early meeting of the Cabinet. Also that he would be seeing Crerar in the interval. All of this I can see means that he is coming back prepared to urge that the situation has become so much more serious than contemplated and that drastic steps will have to be taken to secure the necessary number of trained men. It will not be so much the question of numbers of reinforcements as the training. All of this of course will be an effort to have the N.R.M.A. men serve overseas. This is not altogether unexpected. Ilsley had said in Council . . . that he might be returning with some suggestion of the kind. I feel that the conscriptionists in the Government are still working together, particularly Macdonald and Ralston; possibly Ilsley who, however, is pretty certain to support anything Ralston suggests."

Mackenzie King read the telegram to St. Laurent that afternoon. The Minister of Justice agreed "that it gave occasion for concern, but he I think will agree that considering all aspects of the situation more harm than good would be done with any attempt to force conscription at this time. I could not bring myself to being the head of a Government which would take that course—a course which might, after five years of war in Europe, and preparation for a year and a half of another war in the Pacific—lead to spurts of civil war in our own country. It would be a criminal thing, and would destroy the entire war record, as well as help to dismember the Empire, for I am certain that its after effects would be all in the direction of demand for complete independence, if not annexation with the United States. Anything to be separated from being involved in wars because of Britain's connection with them. I want to see the Empire endure. It can only endure by there being complete national unity in Canada. This is going to be a trying experience for me. Indeed, Ralston has been a thorn in my flesh right along. However, I have stood firm before and shall do so again. The situation is very different today than it has been heretofore. But these are the heavy loads to carry. It is a repetition of the kind of thing that led to the creation of the Union Government after Borden's return from England. That will not take place under me."

In this context, the Prime Minister felt that the most important event for his record on October 14 was "McNaughton's letter saying he was now convinced that his best contribution could be made by holding himself 'available to undertake the office you have suggested.' Also stating that he had told those who wanted him to enter the political arena, of his decision, though giving no information as to the office contemplated—only that it is a task strictly non-political in character which is under consideration. He adds: 'May I say it is only the observations which you, yourself, made to me which have given me confidence even to think of undertaking this work and to feel that through it I might do something which would be of value to Canada.'

"This means that Canada will have as her Governor General or rather as the representative of the King, one of her own citizens and he, one of the most distinguished in Canada's history. The appointment will create something of a sensation in Britain and in Canada but I am sure will be overwhelmingly approved in Canada. It will help to remove a certain badge of colonialism but will have to be accompanied by a change in the title—from Governor General to King's representative. I am certain that the time has long since gone by when we should continue to have as the King's representative in Canada members of the nobility from England as if from among our own citizens, men of equal distinction and ability could not be found and trusted. To McNaughton is owing the highest honour which Canada can confer. He is a great man and has already served Canada and the Empire and the world in a great way through his contribution to the work of research and in the formation and training of the Canadian army overseas. His resignation for the reasons given, as President of the National Research Council, was a mark of his noble character. He is a true Canadian. In visiting in other parts, his name, record and appearance will be an inspiration along the right lines to the younger generation who will begin to look up to their own citizens, instead of being taught to worship as of a superior breed those who come to Canada from the privileged positions in the Old Land. His appointment will be in accord with the spirit of the times and of the Canadian people, which aims at a true democracy. I can understand all the feelings of the Pilgrim Fathers and others who left Britain to get away from class and privilege and who decided on a presidency instead of a monarchy in shaping the constitution of the United States.

"I have come increasingly to feel that while the institution of monarchy has much to commend it, I do not wish to see it abolished so long as it serves to maintain highest standards of honour and integrity in public life. Nevertheless, it serves to foster a false idea of what is to be aimed at in life, in what it begets of a worship of social position. Government House in Canada and in the provinces has come more and more to stand for a certain Grand Hotel and first class inns at which members of the aristocracy and others in places of privilege from the Old Land are to be entertained on their visits to Canada.

" . . . It is ridiculous that a whole staff of young Englishmen should surround the Governor in Canada, including ladies-in-waiting, secretaries, etc., instead of having a household of young Canadians who can be truly representative of our own country. All these things were well in early colonial days but they are not suited to a country which has played the part that Canada has in two great world wars, and whose citizens in several walks of life are the equals [of any] to be found in any land.

"When I 'phoned to McNaughton tonight I told him I was greatly pleased to receive his letter and to learn of the decision. Said I would have a talk with him shortly. . . . I told him I thought his decision had been a wise one. He repeated what he says in the letter about my own talk with him and said that he had also talked the matter over with his wife who was of the view that they should accept. In speaking to him about his having built up the Research Council and then the Army and that he would now be helping to build up a new order in which Canada would increasingly stand as a nation on her own, he remarked that he had, strangely enough, seemed to have gone on from one place to another in the most unexpected ways, but not going back. I said to him I believed there was a Providence in all this.

"Singularly enough, I have in my bag for reading which I received yesterday, the draft of orders in council re use of Canadian flag on Houses of Parliament and public buildings and to be declared the national flag of Canada. This step too will create a commotion but it is one which will help to draw the line in a clear-cut fashion between reactionary Toryism and Liberalism—Tory Imperialism and Liberal Nationalism in the shaping of the future of Canada in the new order of things which we pray will make for more in the way of peace and good-will throughout the world. It is singular how without my seeking, it seems to have fallen to me to complete in a fine way the aim and purpose of my grandfather in seeking to have Canada a nation within the community of British nations—a nation in every sense of the word, within the community of free British nations and so recognized by all other nations."

On October 16, Mackenzie King went to tea at Government House to tell the Governor-General about McNaughton. In their conversation, the Governor referred to the question of demobilization and this gave the Prime Minister an opening to mention "the Connie Smythe–Drew controversy with Ralston re training, etc. His Excellency said that sort of thing always was said in connection with the war. I told him Ralston would be returning tomorrow and from what I gathered from his telegram, might be raising some question of conscription which I said would be madness at this stage of the war. His Excellency agreed that it was late for anything of the kind. He did say something about reinforcements becoming possibly a question and also the position of the N.R.M.A. men being a problem. I pointed out care was being taken to see that General Service men would have their preferences preserved."

Then, in his characteristically abstruse way, Mackenzie King broached the subject of McNaughton's possible succession as Governor-General. "I was interested to see how His Excellency would receive this word. While it seemed to occasion a moment's surprise in his mind, his reaction seemed to me to be distinctly favourable rather than otherwise. He raised no question but supplemented what I had said about McNaughton possessing a fine character and being well suited for the position. He said nothing about it being any break in the tradition. He added that his wife was a fine woman. I said to him that the question of having an outstanding Canadian as Governor General had been much discussed as he would know over many years. That the choice would lie between having someone like Mc-Naughton or having to find someone in the Old Country who could succeed His Excellency and Her Royal Highness. That having gone as high as we could, our choice would necessarily be limited to someone of lesser rank overseas and that it was increasingly difficult to secure the right persons for the office."

On the morning of October 18, Ralston returned from overseas. Mackenzie King arranged to see him at his parliamentary office at 5 o'clock that afternoon but, as he was about to leave for the office, Ralston arrived at Laurier House. They drove together to the East Block.

"After reaching the office, we talked in general terms for a while. I asked him the impressions he got about the duration of the war. He said it was now felt it would go on into the spring. Montgomery had changed his view and believed that the fighting would be longer than he had anticipated. General Eisenhower had said to him that he thought it would be the spring before it was over but that there would be no cessation of operations, no digging in for the winter, and that the fighting would go right on regardless.

"After a pause, Ralston said: Mr. King I want to speak of the question of reinforcements, which is a serious one. He went on to say that the fighting had been more intense than had been anticipated. Spoke of the numbers in the reserve being considerably less than had been anticipated when the estimate was made. This both in Italy and in Belgium and Holland; that the intensity of fighting had been greater and men had been kept longer in active conflict. He spoke particularly of some of the men who had been in Italy who had been away for five years and said that they would have to be allowed to come home. He then went on to say that he thought some of the men felt keenly about a standing army in Canada doing nothing while they were so short of reinforcements; that their morale for fighting would be increased if the reinforcements were larger. He spoke of visiting men in hospitals; seeing them go up to the front and others returning again to the fighting line. He did not wish to be emotional, but this had affected his feelings as to the necessity of easing the situation."

The Prime Minister then asked Ralston "if he had not been told at War Committee, when we received the request for additional men for another brigade in Italy, that this would not mean any more difficulty in raising the required numbers without conscription [see vol. 1, pp. 607, 610]. Ralston gave some explanation about the nature of the brigade but I could not follow him. I also asked if it were not a fact that as the army was enlarged at different stages that each time we had received assurances that conscription would not be necessary. He said at no time had he given such assurance. I said nothing more on that point, but said to him that that was one side. The other side was the effect upon the whole war situation, and the domestic situation in particular, of attempting to introduce [conscription] at this stage of the war and in the light of information which I had received and which was more or less public knowledge as to the probable early termination of the war and, in particular, Germany's present position and the rapidity with which it was worsening. I asked Ralston if he had read the despatch which came within the last three days. It was dated October 14, giving a summary of appreciation dated Sept. 27th by British military advisers on weaknesses in Germany's capacity to resist. He said he had not seen the despatch. I read it through aloud. Said to him the report of the Intelligence Department in Britain contained a similar statement. I also had [seen] intercepted telegrams bearing out the probable early defeat of Germany. That it must be apparent with one country after another being liberated, Germany losing, and the Allies gaining the support of these countries, resources, manpower, etc., and the ring being drawn steadily tighter around Germany itself; with the Russian invasion against Prussia beginning on the scale it was, and also the break through there had been at different places into Germany; that the people of Canada would hardly understand why we should resort to conscription at this time. To do so would create confusion, which would undo much of the good which our war effort up to the present had effected. That we would have a repetition of what occurred after the last war when Borden returned and demanded conscription, only that the situation will be worse; that we have to think of the future of Canada as well as the present; that conscription after the last war had left a scar which had not been healed and was responsible for most of the trouble we had had in the present war. That all of this would have to be considered very carefully. We would have to weigh the probable moral advantage it might serve to send some of the N.R.M.A. men overseas against the very grave situation to which that would give rise. That I thought it would be much better if the necessity demanded to reduce the size of our army overseas. We had been in the war for five years. The Americans for less than three. That our war effort had been larger in proportion than that of any other country. I did not think any country would expect us at this stage to attempt to increase that effort through conscription. I said we would have to think also of the political consequences of an act of the kind. That while, as he knew, I was perfectly indifferent myself to power or a continuation in office, I did not think it would be to Canada's interests to hand the country over to the C.C.F., which would certainly be the result of any move by the Government in the direction of conscription.

"Ralston's reply to this was that there would be a realignment; that soldiers' families were scattered throughout the country and they would all support sending N.R.M.A. men across. I indicated I did not see just how one could justify any action of the kind in the light of what I had read as to the weakness of Germany's position. It was clear the Allies did not need to look to us to win the war. That I personally felt that if it was the saving of lives that had to be considered it would be much better to have the war last a little longer and Germany brought to her knees in that way than to sacrifice more lives through haste. The greatest thing Churchill had done had been to hold back the invasion of Europe for a couple of years. That I thought the leaders overseas would be wise in taking a little longer and not making any undue sacrifice of lives. That with the ring tightening around Germany it was now only a matter of months at the most that she would be able longer to resist. Finally I said to Ralston that it seemed to me that what we had to consider was whether it was possible at this stage to meet the situation to attempt conscription after five years of war in Europe, preparation for a year and a half of war in Asia, and the probability, if not the certainty of civil war added to both in consequence of any attempt at conscription. That I could understand, for reasons of pride, the desire of the army to be kept up to full strength to the last. It was admitted that the reserves for the artillery and other branches are above what is necessary. It is only the infantry that it is difficult to keep up. He mentioned particularly the French-Canadian regiments which were considered below standard. I said we would have to consider whether a better plan was to reduce the size of the army in one way or the other. He intercepted at one point a sort of defence at having separated the army; also as to sending part of it to Italy, saying we had done honour to our country in giving it a place in world affairs by doing this or some such expression. I imagine he begins to see that McNaughton and Churchill were not unwise in wishing to keep the Canadian army intact for final operations in Germany. When I spoke of reducing the size of the army he stated that that would give rise to very serious complications in the army itself. He spoke of the difficulty there was in breaking up units and how strongly that would be resented. He said he agreed with me as to the political difficulties but that the situation in other respects presented a real problem. I thought I saw in that remark that he was seeking to draw a line between military necessity and what might be regarded as political considerations. I note in that connection that a despatch which I referred to was one prepared by the military advisers.

"I did not go further in the discussion but said we would of course have to have a full Cabinet to consider the matter, and asked if he would prefer to have a full Cabinet to follow or have War Committee first. He replied perhaps it would be best to have War Committee first. I said: yes, very well. That will be arranged for tomorrow. I told him this morning, as he had already been informed, that I had intended to have War Committee today but that Macdonald was away, would not be back till Thursday. He told me also that Power left from the airport today for Montreal so that he was quite prepared to have the meeting on Thursday. He asked me if I would have Stuart stand by. Earlier he had said that Stuart felt he had painted too rosy a picture when talking to the War Committee in the summer.

'We did not try to pursue the subject further. Thought it best to show no feeling in the matter but to hold the discussion wholly on its merits. Talked briefly on other things. Ralston left in a happy mood. In the conversation he remarked that at no time had he said there might not be conscription, to which I replied on each occasion I had given my consent on the score that what was being done would not, in the opinion of military experts or advisers, involve that necessity. He said to me that he was sorry to add these burdens to others I have. I told him I was deeply sorry he had the load which he had to carry, that we must seek to find the right way out. I thought in looking at Ralston that he looked much older and not too well."

After his talk with Ralston, Mackenzie King began to sort out the political implications and the possibly explosive repercussions in the Cabinet. "What I am concerned about is not [so] much the question of working out something which in the light of conditions would avoid any need of conscription which I believe can be done, but that Ralston himself may again take it into his mind to tender his resignation because of what he feels the reinforcement situation demands, and that Angus Macdonald may decide to leave the Government to go to Nova Scotia. Ilsley taking the view that he must stand by Ralston and Macdonald. Power might do the same, as he did in Parliament, though I don't see how he could very well do this at present in the light of what is being done to make enormous reduction in the Air Force in Canada as well as what is being done overseas. If there is need for more military aid we could give it in the form of increased air power, but that is not what the army wants. It is the desire of the army to keep its numbers intact. That is at the bottom of everything else. It is tragic that this situation should arise at this time, when the party's fortunes are steadily rising and the country in a mood to see the war through in a noble way. To me it is about as heavy a task as could be given to a man to bear; for whatever decision is made I shall be the one that will be pilloried on the one side by the Army and its friends, if I do not yield to what in the long run would not be in its interests and certainly at no time in the interests of Canada, and on the other hand by the great majority of the people of Canada itself if, after the stand I have taken right along and with such success, I should permit a situation to develop that will help to destroy the unity of Canada for years to come and that to no avail so far as the winning of the war is concerned. Ralston did say it was not the winning of the war that was at stake. To my mind that is the only stake on which we are justified in sacrificing more lives than may be absolutely necessary. I do feel that the position of the war at the moment is such that the certainty of defeat of Germany is possible in a short time and that it will not be possible for Ralston to carry the Cabinet with him and that he certainly would not carry Parliament if called as it would have to be before such a step were taken unless the issue were made one for a general election. The shame is that there should have to be any issue at this time. I believe that we shall get through without conscription and that the same power which has guided me in the past will continue to guide me through another very difficult period."

The following morning, October 19, Mackenzie King had a conference at his office with Norman Robertson, General Pope, and Arnold Heeney. He "gave them the bare outlines of my conversation with Ralston last night. Pope and Heeney had been going over the minutes of the War Committee and stated there was no doubt in the world about the understanding having been all along that there would be no need for conscription in any step that had been taken. Also the minutes made perfectly clear that General Stuart had given a definite assurance at the time the brigade in Italy was formed, that it would not mean any additional tax on manpower. That is, they were sure of having all the reinforcements that were needed."

With this information in hand, the Prime Minister called on the Minister of Defence to make his report at the meeting of the War Committee in the afternoon. He reported that Ralston gave a brief review of what he had seen overseas and "then came to what he said would be the hardest thing that the Cabinet had to face, or words to that effect. He then repeated pretty much what he had said to me last night about there being need to have the trained men in the N.R.M.A. sent overseas in numbers sufficient to make up the reinforcements needed to keep the Canadian army up to strength. I need not repeat what I recorded last night.

"He did not mention Eisenhower's name today but did say that Montgomery would not say that the war would not be over by the end of the year though he was less prepared to make the statement he did earlier. He said however that Montgomery had stated that the war could not be won by what was equivalent to digging in. That the armies must fight straight ahead, whether winter or not. Not let up. He also said that Montgomery had spoken about bringing units together and had stated that he had spoken to me of that. I told the Cabinet that Montgomery had told me distinctly that he felt no concern about units being joined together [see vol. 1, pp. 690–2].... That what he would do would be to call the men together, ask them what they were most concerned about; was it winning the war, if possible, without losing their lives, or taking greater chances on their lives through not joining together. That I had discussed the conscription issue with him [Montgomery] and he had agreed there was not likely to be any need of conscription but that he must have a free hand in the matter of arranging disposition of units; apparently he and Crerar differ on this.

"Ralston did say that Crerar had not declined to consider reducing the size of the units; that was one of the things suggested. Ralston ended up his statement by reading a report which Stuart had prepared and which stated that reinforcements were insufficient and that unless they could be secured in sufficient numbers voluntarily, it would be necessary to send the N.R.M.A. men overseas. . . .

"There was great silence after he [Ralston] had spoken," Mackenzie King wrote. "I waited some little time and then said quite quietly that the question that had been raised was the most serious one that had come before the Cabinet since Confederation. That we could not weight it too carefully. That I hoped the Cabinet would realize exactly what was involved;

that it meant the calling together of Parliament. A bitter debate in Parliament, and then almost certainly taking the issue from Parliament to the people. That our elections act required at least 60 days to take the vote. That it would, therefore, be on into the new year before we would know what the result of the vote might be. In the meantime, however, it was certain that the most bitter kind of a campaign would be waged from one end of Canada to the other. We would have province set against province in the central part of the Dominion. Other parts of Canada also divided. That would not be the worst feature. We would have after it all a situation very much worse than was left by the tactics of the last war in seeking conscription near the end of the war. That I visualized the effect of all this in relation to Canada's position vis-a-vis the other nations of the Commonwealth toward Britain in particular and the effect upon the United Nations and their work. Also upon the whole of our war effort up to the present which had been without exception, in proportion, the finest of that of any country in the world and so admitted by all the countries. I pointed out that clearly what was being asked for was not needed to win the war. If it were essential to win the war, I would not have another word to say but no one living could say that in the light of the statements made by the Prime Minister of Britain, the Chiefs of Staff of different countries and others. Victory was certain. It was only a matter of time. I pointed out that in the last war, conscription had been based on the fact that the enemy was likely to win. That progress had not been made in France as had been expected but that the cry was that conscription was needed not merely for purposes of reinforcements but to win the war. That it was not so at this time. I then spoke of the entirely changed situation since D-day. Said that had men been slaughtered in numbers seeking to establish a bridgehead, there might have been need to look for reinforcements but that instead of that, unexpected gains had been made all along the way; instead of the enemy now controlling France, we had new allies in France and France was free. The same was true of Belgium. The same would be true of Holland. It was true of Greece. Roumania and Bulgaria had become enemies of Germany instead of allies. That the Allies are defeating the Germans. The Russians had within the last day gained control of the Carpathian passes which would cut off and help to destroy large numbers of German armies. That Germans were losing their strength in Norway. That in Italy, they were in a more precarious position and that even now the Russian armies were on German soil and advancing in a formidable way. In the face of all this and much else, the Canadian people would be staggered to understand why as the area of fighting was contracting, we were gaining new allies and all the resources which formerly belonged to the enemy, and our might was increasing—

why, at this stage, Canada had to be the one country to change its policy and adopt conscription. That Australia, New Zealand and South Africa had lessened the numbers of their troops; that we were well along the way of demobilization; plans already made; reducing our navy and air strength because we had a surplus there; that it was not total conscription that was being asked for but simply the one matter of keeping reinforcements of an army which had been made the size it was in view of assurances that had been given that conscription would not be necessary to that end. I mentioned that at every stage since the beginning of the war, I had raised that question and had been assured that the additions would not involve conscription in the end. Spoke particularly of assurances given by Stuart only a couple of months ago [see p. 111 above]. I said that I had talked the matter over with McNaughton who had told me that there would be no necessity for conscription; also that he knew what anything of the kind would mean to Canadian unity, and how unfair it would be to the province of Quebec. That I had not talked with Crerar except as we drove together [see vol. 1, p. 689] but had talked with Montgomery."

The Prime Minister then read the communication of October 14, to which he had referred in his conversation with Ralston the day before, pointing out "it was part of what had been sent by military advisers of the British Commonwealth to the Prime Minister of Canada for his information. I felt we would be bound in considering military advice, to take that also into account; as well as other documents which had been received. I then spoke of how the people of Canada would view the introduction of conscription at the end of five years of war on top of all that we have done; while we were preparing for another year and a half of war in the Pacific, when the introduction of this issue was likely to create civil war in Canada. I said I would like the Cabinet to consider what would become of our policies, first of all, the programme of social legislation. The post-war plans. Rehabilitation, etc. The effect later on demobilization. That I would like the Cabinet to realize that the years immediately following the war were going to be very difficult years; there would be a welter of unrest in all countries which our own would not escape.

"I did not wish to add to all this the appalling bitterness which would be developed by an issue of conscription meanwhile. . . . I then told the Cabinet I thought we should do our utmost, realizing this, [to find] means to meet the situation. I spoke of what the British had done. While I would not suggest lessening the number of divisions, I would suggest lessening the size of the units; also that Ralston had told us Montgomery had said it was not certain the Canadians would be in the big fight that was being built up at the moment. That I thought our men having been kept [fighting] so strenuously, it was altogether probable that the high command had taken that fact into account and would not expect them to participate to the same extent from now on. That attention might well be drawn to what they had done and to the issue that would be raised in Canada if we had, in order to meet any situation, to, at this stage, introduce conscription. I said I thought a smaller area could be given for fighting purposes. I made a final appeal to the Cabinet to weigh very carefully everything that had been said but of course the whole matter would have to be discussed with the full Cabinet. Ralston then wanted to have Stuart brought in."

Mackenzie King then left the Council Chamber for a few minutes and met General Stuart in the antechamber. "Shook hands with Stuart. Told him I was pleased to see him back and looking so well. He said he was glad to be back but sorry to have to bring the report he had brought with him. I had done everything that a man could do to support the army; had given them everything they had asked for and it was pretty hard to have to bring the report he had. I said that he had left the door open for a way of meeting the situation and I hoped it would be met short of any action that could make for complete disunity throughout the whole of Canada."

With General Stuart and General J. C. Murchie, the Chief of the General Staff, Mackenzie King then returned to the meeting. "I asked Stuart if there was anything he wished to say. He mentioned having regretted he had to bring the report he did but that [it] was his duty to state the situation as he saw it, etc. I mentioned that in considering it, he and his staff would remember that the whole question would have to come before Parliament which might debate it at great length. There might then have to be a general election and that it would be on into the new year before decision could be reached. It would be best to consider if there was not some way that the situation could be met without all this turmoil and strife before the end of the year. I asked Stuart about his statement, his assurance two months ago as to there being plenty of reinforcements, and also about the additional brigade in Italy not making any additional drain on manpower. He gave some sort of an explanation about the latter, that it simply meant changing over certain units; did not touch the question of extra men involved. As to the former, he said he had made a mistake. Later I said to him that having given us the wrong information and having made a mistake, I hoped he would, as I know he would, do all he could to help the Government out of the present situation. When it came to discussing methods of reducing the numbers, he said he thought they were building up to a big decisive round which might end the war at any time. I had been saying I thought our men would be entitled to a rest but he came back with a statement they would want to be in that and play a big part, and said something about ending up in glory. When he used the word 'glory,' I found it difficult to contain my feelings. I said pretty strongly that I did not think *glory* ought to be entered into where it was a question of saving human lives. Another thing he said was that the strategy of the war was to go right on with the war in the winter regardless of all the extra difficulties involved. He painted a frightful picture of men having to stay out in the rain and drenched; more or less freezing and the like, in order to carry on through the winter but that was the strategy to press on. I asked if we had ever been consulted about strategy. He said something about Crerar and others keeping in touch. I asked had the Government of Canada approved strategy of the kind? I said this was the first time the Cabinet had heard strategy involved action of the kind. That where lives of Canadians were concerned, we were entitled to know what was involved in the strategy. That I for one felt better strategy would be that which Churchill had followed in regard to premature invasion of the Continent. Take a little longer but have matters so arranged that lives would be saved and not sacrificed unnecessarily. This point had never been apparently thought of either by Stuart or any members of the Cabinet or Ralston, though Ralston in previous years has been very strong on our knowing what disposition was of all our forces, when, etc. I then again counselled very careful study of the whole situation, to remember what it would involve in matter of time, etc. and then said to the Cabinet I thought we could not settle a matter of this kind in a day or two. It would require mature consideration.

"When I had finished, Ralston said that I had made a very powerful statement and then took up one or two of the points I had raised as to methods of meeting the situation, but I said I did not wish to argue at this stage. I then asked each of the members present if he had anything to say. . . . I was only speaking as one member of the Cabinet giving my firm convictions which I believed were held in large part by others."

Louis St. Laurent then entered the discussion. "He . . . spoke about the bitter feeling there was between men at the front and those who were not fighting; of that bitterness likely to continue whether nothing was done until after the war or not. That the men who were fighting overseas were the young men who would govern Canada hereafter and that the N.R.M.A. men would be marked men through their lives. He thought, however, it was unfair that the assumption should be that wherever N.R.M.A. men were concerned, it meant Quebec. He understood there was only about ⅓ so far as Quebec was concerned. He then said nothing had been said about conscientious objectors. None of whom fought. They are all Protestants. While the Catholic Church admits the right to kill in war, there are no conscientious objectors in their number. It is not a matter of conscience.

Consequently conscientious objectors have to be set off. I could not tell what he was leading to but he ended up rather strongly about certainty of division that would be made in Canada for a long time to come if this measure had to be taken. Howe said he had not had time to consider the matter. This was the first he had heard of it. Michaud felt like Howe but added that he believed the adoption of conscription would work very great harm. Angus Macdonald said he would like time. He had his views on it but would like to think them over as to whether he had been right or wrong. This remark was to me significant. It means that men who were conscriptionist at the start are all trying now to find something which would justify their previous position. Power said that he had not had much chance to think of matters. He thought it was the duty of Stuart to make the report he did. That it had to be considered very carefully. He felt, however, if it became necessary to have conscription, the serious effect of such a step would be felt in Canada for 20 years or more. Ralston had nothing further to add."

General Stuart and his colleague withdrew at this point, but before the meeting of the War Committee broke up, Mackenzie King suggested that "it would not be well to try to settle this matter at once nor to take it before the whole Cabinet tomorrow. That indeed I wanted every member of the Cabinet present when the matter was to be discussed and settled, and that each member would have to show exactly where he stood. . . . The responsibility would have to rest on each one individually; each one would have to take their full share of responsibility. It was then that Power said something about Mackenzie leaving on Friday or Saturday. I said Mackenzie will stay here and every member of the Cabinet will have to be present. I spoke of Crerar and Gardiner and one or two others being absent. Said I would see they returned. When I spoke of Monday [the October 19th meeting which Mackenzie King is reporting was on a Thursday], Power said he had to be away on Monday which caused Ralston to say that we should not delay long but that he himself would suggest Tuesday which seemed to me to signify he counts on Power's support of his attitude. Ilsley, I am quite sure, will support Ralston in the report. I then arranged for War Committee tomorrow to take up remaining matters which is air force contribution to the war with Japan, and to leave over further discussion of this matter until next week."

The next morning (Friday, October 20) Mackenzie King discussed the question of conscripting N.R.M.A. soldiers with St. Laurent who stated "quite frankly that there could be no doubt about [his] position from the start. When he ran in Quebec East, he said he believed that if it were necessary to have men conscripted I [Mackenzie King] would not hesitate to take that stand and he would follow me. He was equally sure that if I did not think it was necessary I would not, and he wished to be elected as my follower. He had always understood and the people had understood that by necessary was meant necessary to win the war." St. Laurent thought Ralston had used the word necessary to mean necessary to provide reinforcements. But St. Laurent "was sure that in the House I had made my position quite clear. He said if there were an election on the issue that, of course, everyone from Quebec on the Liberal side would be against conscription. Those that stood with Ralston in his point of view would be wiped out. He agreed that it was calamitous. He agreed of course that there was no necessity from the point of view of winning the war. I told him that I had about come to the conclusion that if Ralston persisted in his attitude and tendered his resignation, I would accept it and would invite McNaughton to come into the Cabinet. That I felt pretty sure McNaughton would accept with Ralston out. And that if Ralston knew in advance that that was likely to be the case, he and Stuart would quickly find some way of preventing this happening, for they would know that the first thing McNaughton would do would be to make a very rapid change in officials at Headquarters. St. Laurent said he was not sure but that it would be a good idea to have that change made. That the people had great confidence in McNaughton and would accept his statement on what was necessary and what was not. I said I hoped he would speak out in the Cabinet."

At the War Committee in the afternoon there was a brief discussion about the air force contribution to the war against Japan. After that question had been settled tentatively, the Prime Minister noted that "there was a sort of unreality about our even talking about the things we had been discussing in the light of questions that Ralston had brought up yesterday, that none of us would have to do with these problems further if we had to face a general election on a conscription issue at this stage of the war. I suggested that while Tuesday had been fixed for the meeting of the Cabinet as a whole, it would be well I thought if we just talked over the situation quietly ourselves and looked at what was really involved in the decisions. I spoke then first of all of whether it would be necessary to call the House. Said that that could not be done before the first week of November. That the House debate would take a week or two. We would then dissolve and our Election Act made it necessary to take two months at least for the elections. That would be the middle of January, no decision being reached until after the election. There was every reason to believe that the war might end while we were in the middle of a conflict asking people to conscript soldiers for overseas. All that we would do would be to ensure the election of the C.C.F., divide the Party completely without helping the situation at all in the war. That we would be helping Germany's cause by allowing them to point to Canada's controversy. It would be said of the British, they had to conscript their subjects in the Dominions to help them save being defeated.

"Ralston said that he did not think a general election would be necessary. That I had said if it was necessary to adopt conscription I would go into the House and say so. There would be no debate. It would be put through by closure, I said if there was any closure, he would be the one to apply it, I certainly would not at this stage. However, I did not think the question was one we could leave to Parliament alone at this stage. That there would be a demand that the people should pronounce upon it whether we wished it or not. That certainly conscription would become the issue at the general election. Ralston then said I had given that pledge. I said that I had said if I thought it was necessary to win the war I would tell them so. If I were to take an oath as to whether I believed it were necessary or not, I said I would have to say I was sure it was not. Ralston contended it was necessary and that necessary meant necessary to keep up reinforcements. Said that that was what he had made very plain. St. Laurent said he thought there was no doubt Ralston had had that in his mind, may have said it, but he was equally certain what I had in mind was the necessity to win the war, that was what the people understood in Quebec and that was what he understood when he ran as a candidate supporting me. I said to Ralston I certainly would not go into Parliament and say there was any necessity of conscription to win the war. I then pointed out that there would be no conscripting of N.R.M.A. men. It would have to be a Conscription Act applying to everyone. He agreed to this, but he said of course they would take the men that were specially trained. I did not say at the time, but I might have added that this of itself would raise a very terrible situation, where men who had served their country for three or four years under compulsion would now be compelled to go abroad under compulsion as though they had been guilty of an offence and men who had not been conscripted would remain free. That was an issue which should not be allowed to arise. I could see that it would lead to bloodshed immediately.

"I then said I thought we ought to consider very carefully what still might be done to get the reinforcements that might be necessary without conscription; that, for example, I did not see why further inducement might not be offered the men who have been in training to take up general service by agreeing to allow the time they had spent in training to count in connection with gratuities to be paid. That, after all, it was training that they were contributing to the war effort, and it should be paid for. Those that did not volunteer for general service could remain as they are. That I had further thought the others should be put in labour battalions, work in lumber camps or elsewhere. Many of them would prefer soldier's life to the work in industries. St. Laurent joined strongly in this. Angus Macdonald, much to my surprise, took up this idea, though he kept supporting Ralston in a general way, but I could see that he had begun to realize that there were real difficulties. Again I spoke about not wishing to be alone in debating the subject with Ralston. St. Laurent came out in a way which indicated he would certainly oppose attempting conscription for service overseas. Power indicated that it would mean that everyone in Quebec would be gone, and it would leave a situation in Canada that would not be cured in a quarter of a century. Fortunately, Ilsley has been away for a week. It was agreed to leave matters over until Tuesday."

"One just cannot imagine how serious a break in the ranks of the Government at this time would be to the whole future of Canada," Mackenzie King reflected in his diary the next day (October 21). "I feel more and more, as McNaughton does, about Ralston; that there is something inhumanly determined about his getting his own way, regardless of what the effects may be on all others. In this thing I believe there is a desire to justify in his own mind his earlier convictions for conscription. He was quick to point out in Council yesterday what he had said in the House which made apparent he would expect to act in regard to reinforcement to keep up the size of the army. Has evidently had this in view all along."

For the Prime Minister, there was a welcome comic interlude that Saturday afternoon. The child prodigy film actress Shirley Temple had come to Ottawa to help in the Victory Loan campaign. He reported that he "arrived at the Parliament Buildings at noon and had a really interesting afternoon as a consequence. In the Railway Committee room met Shirley Temple, her mother and father, and some of the repatriated boys. Also Miss Coyne of the Air Force, who is the granddaughter of Coyne of St. Thomas. I was greatly attracted by Shirley Temple—a young girl of great charm, very pretty, very natural; I liked her father and mother, both of whom were quiet, pleasant people. Her father a man of business; her mother most unassuming. I have seldom found anyone more natural than Shirley Temple was, or quicker to adapt herself to every situation. We walked out together to the platform facing Parliament Hill and I sat to her right, and St. Laurent to her left. It was quite interesting to watch her methods to rouse the boys to cheer. Very self-possessed, full of joyous freedom and expression in every way. It was a little cold on the Hill, there being no sun. Proceedings a little long on that account, but all went very well.

"After the proceedings we had a very exciting time. I walked with her to the car, allowed her father and mother to get in, and sat on a small seat myself. We were not more than started when crowds gathered in front of the car and on all sides. It was such that it was impossible for us to move. This kept up all the way to the Hotel. Police arrangements not good. I was afraid children would get crushed under the car. But the worst situation came in front of the Chateau and inside. There the crowd was such that to move the car at all would have meant someone would have been killed or crushed to pieces. We got out on the platform and with the help of huge powerful policemen got across the station platform into the Hotel. I expected to find it easy once in the Hotel, but there the situation was worse than ever. There was no police, except a big man, who had gone in first and another who joined in later. The Chateau was crowded with children. Young people squeezed in around us. Shirley's father and I tried to protect her but Mrs. Temple got lost in the crowd to one side. To my amazement we had to crash through all the way, to one of the elevator doors, leaving Mrs. Temple behind. She, by the way, had left her furs on the platform in front of the Parliament Buildings. I told her I was sure they would turn up all right. When we got to their floor, they invited me to come in to their suite, but I said no I would go back and get Mrs. Temple, which I did. Fortunately, she had been able to get to the door with the aid of others.

"When we came up together everyone was pretty well fatigued. I found my heart beating very fast, and [I was] finding it a little difficult to get my breath. I had not realized how considerable the strain had been. I was really fearful at one stage that the little girl would be crushed. Certainly if anyone had slipped, there would have been a terrible situation. It was quite shocking, having no police, and to have let the crowds indoors. I literally had to carry her along from the front door through the gathering to the elevator. I was much impressed with the quiet manner of all concerned and how nicely they managed everything in the suite. Later, we all went down to the lunch given by Mr. Ilsley in the Tudor Room. Ilsley sat at the far end of the table. I was given a seat next to Shirley Temple who was to my right. . . . We had a very interesting talk at luncheon. I found . . . Shirley Temple delightfully informed and quick in her perceptions. . . ."

Relief was brief and that afternoon Mackenzie King saw Malcolm MacDonald and told him about the conscription crisis. He reported that "Malcolm at once said something to the effect that this is the most absurd thing he had ever heard of, to talk of conscription at the eleventh hour. I added: practically the twelfth hour, and at a time when it was known that the war was being won. He said there was only one thing to do, which was to communicate with Churchill himself. Ask him frankly what he knew of the strategy of the war and its probable duration; whether he thought it was necessary or desirable that we should resort to conscription; also whether matters could not be so arranged as to keep the Canadian army intact. In the light of all we had done, having matters arranged so that the situation could be met without any question of conscription being raised at this time. He saw at once that it would have a bearing on all parts of the Commonwealth and for years to come. I then said to him that I had come down really to say that I had talked the matter over with Robertson last night. That we had both agreed it would be wise to cable Churchill, but it would be better to do so through Malcolm, than by a cable from Prime Minister to Prime Minister direct, which is what Malcolm had suggested to me. Malcolm agreed it would be better to have a message sent through him. Said he would cable at once to Cranborne, to ask when Churchill would be back, and to let him know that an important private message would be coming from me to him. Malcolm said what a pity it was that this had not all come up at Quebec when we were there and I could have talked over the whole situation with Churchill there. I told him that two months ago we were told that there were plenty of reinforcements. I then told him I would send him a message later to send to Churchill. I had decided to stay in town instead of going to Kingsmere because of the weather; also intended to see McNaughton if he were in town. I tried him tonight, but he was not in."

From Ian Mackenzie, the Prime Minister learned "that Power had let him know that I was entirely in the right; that Ralston was wrong, and to suggest that I ask Angus Macdonald and Ilsley to use what influence they could on Ralston. I phoned Robertson tonight and ascertained he had seen Clark, who was to see Ilsley, and he had arranged to see Stuart in his house in the morning along with Arnold Heeney. Robertson takes the position that it is the Cabinet's decision to do what they think the national situation demands and the army's business to fall in line with whatever is put forward. He says that he had a talk with Murchie, who is in a difficult position, as he regards himself as subordinate to the officials overseas, but he [Murchie] says, [the Department of National Defence] had not even considered trying the suggestion of giving to N.R.M.A. men who would serve overseas the gratuities which overseas men were getting. The idea had not even been broached to them. He [Robertson] told me Murchie had asked if they put on another campaign did he think St. Laurent and others would help from the platform to get N.R.M.A. men to enlist. He said he had thought the whole Cabinet would. I had told Robertson last night I was prepared as a last trump card to take the platform myself; to call the men together and ask them to enlist. I was sure I could carry the whole lot. I said to him however, not to make the suggestion of this to anyone. I am afraid he has let the cat out of the bag a bit and lessened thereby the power I would have with the Cabinet, which would have been to take the matter out of their hands altogether, and to tell the Defence Department I would want to meet the men myself. That is what I intend to do if it comes to a point where that should be done. Mackenzie, in 'phoning me tonight, said to look at the late edition of the Journal; that when McNaughton had been speaking at Queen's he had said there was no excuse for the use of compulsion in Canada. This is out of the blue and without a word having been said to him. It makes pretty clear where he would stand if we got into an issue of conscription at this stage. I am beginning to think that McNaughton is right about what he said about the kind of tyranny that Ralston exercises over men and seeking to have his own way regardless. It is nothing short of a crime that, as Prime Minister, who has saved him from some pretty bad situations, to say nothing of giving him the chances he has had as Minister, that he should allow me to be worried, as I have been, and the whole party to be brought to the verge of destruction just at the moment we are getting ready for a general election. However, I believe the clouds are lifting somewhat, though the situation is by no means other than very critical as it still stands.

"On the question of going to the people, Ralston has not reckoned at all, nor had he seen what two months election campaign is likely to mean. British parliamentary practice is very sound in giving to the Prime Minister the right to appeal at any time. It brings home to Ministers where their authority and power really come from."

On Sunday, Mackenzie King noted that Norman Robertson suggested a change or two in the proposed message to Churchill. Robertson "found I was mistaken in believing legislation would be necessary to extend the N.R.M.A. That instead I had stated it would be extended by Order in Council with the Government asking for a vote of confidence in Parliament. Robertson was very fine in looking up the matter himself. With the exception of Skelton, he has the finest sense of duty of any man I have known. He will not accept the word of another, but verifies everything by himself, if there is the slightest possibility of error. He took the draft as revised to Malcolm MacDonald, who made one or two suggestions, which I thought were good, in the nature of simply asking Churchill for information as to the probable length of the war, and nature of operations in which Canadians would be engaged. Malcolm said that I would find Churchill would send me his own opinions quite independently of [my] asking for them and thereby avoiding any appearance of holding him in part responsible for a decision, though I have made it clear that this was not the intention." The message was sent that night, October 22. Mackenzie King felt "very sure that once Churchill has read it he will be helpful in seeing, from the European end, that nothing in the way of conscription becomes necessary at this end."

"Meanwhile, Robertson and Heeney spent a good part of the forenoon with Stuart, discussing ways and means whereby necessary number of men to make up the required reinforcements could be secured at this end. Robertson told me that the Department of Defence had not even considered the matter of allowing the N.R.M.A. men pay covering the period of their training in Canada should they ultimately decide to enlist for general service. I believe this alone, properly presented, will help to get the required numbers. Robertson is right in stressing the importance of trying to find ways of getting the men rather than of dwelling as yet too strongly on the political issue of conscription as it relates to Parliament and the country. That can come later if need be."

On the morning of Tuesday, October 24, there was a meeting of the War Committee as a prelude to the full Cabinet in the afternoon. Robertson and Heeney were present. "Ralston re-read a report from Stuart, also a memo or aide-memoire he had prepared on the same and statement from General Murchie who had been considering different means of finding necessary numbers of men short of extension of N.R.M.A. to General Service. The latter showed a desire to have something worked out; at least is an indication of a readiness to that end. There were, however, significant omissions to all of which I drew attention. First, nothing was said about paying those of the N.R.M.A. men for their entire training period or part of it in the event of their becoming General Service. There seemed to be a reluctance on Ralston's part to have this done and Ilsley as was expected seemed opposed to the idea. It was alleged that they would all wait to the last minute and then go 'General.' It was suggested in the Cabinet that this might be met by fixing a time limit to enlist, for example, within the next month. There was no mention in the statement of endeavour by the Government to assist in recruiting.

"When I saw this, I came out boldly with the statement that if necessary and before going to Parliament for any matter, I would myself ask to be allowed to address the N.R.M.A. men and would appeal in the name of Canada and the men overseas, etc., to volunteer for General Service but I would wish to have inducement to offer them in the nature of recognition of the time they had spent for training and also might wish my colleagues to join in a regular appeal.

"Power who was distinctly helpful this morning pointed out that there was a precedent for that. Cited the case of Turkey voluntarily recruiting before resorting to conscription in the last war. However the matter was not discussed at any length.

"Robertson and Arnold Heeney had put forward the idea of some extra pay to infantry G.S. men who did the dirty work in the fighting. Ralston had said at previous meetings if he had to do with another war, he would pay the infantry more. I asked if this might not be considered in helping to meet the problem of leave which Ralston had stressed. I did not hear what Ilsley said as we were just breaking up but it was satirical; something quite absurd in talking of paying men more at this stage. (In other words, he would take all the risks of a divided Canada, effect of division on the war itself rather than spend a few more dollars from the Treasury to find means for increasing the size of our forces—but for Air and the Navy, go to lengths that are wholly unnecessary as he has been doing right along.)

"I noticed that Murchie's memo while it put forward as one means, reduction in the size of the regiments and units, argued against it as likely to affect the morale of the troops, etc. Australia, New Zealand, Britain and other countries have done the same but their morale does not seem to have been affected.

"Angus Macdonald had the list of casualties Australia has suffered. Argued very strongly we were not yet up to their figure in casualties. I pointed out that there were other directions in which we had helped in a way that had saved casualties; also what we had spent on latest equipment, etc., was accountable for our not having had so many.

"I was very careful, throughout the morning, to be as conciliatory as possible, to make it clear that the thing we were to concentrate on was to find ways and means of getting the men, not consider other matters until later. At the conclusion of the morning sitting, Ralston suggested that we should first settle on the size of the man pool that we felt we should get, which was a military question, and discuss the political question later. I pointed out that, while I would like to do that, it could not be done, as the two were inseparable. Whether we could get a man pool of any size depended on our ability to get the necessary support for what we might set as a total.

"Robertson sent me a note to the effect that by giving special inducements to the N.R.M.A. men we were killing two birds with one stone— getting men needed for overseas, and reducing the size of the standing army. The truth of the matter is that the Defence people want the N.R.M.A. men forced to go overseas without further consideration. Both Robertson and Heeney felt that the morning had been well worth while and had indicated an easing up of the situation so far as Ralston and the Defence Departments were concerned."

At the Cabinet meeting in the afternoon, all members were present. The Prime Minister opened the discussion by speaking of Ralston's trip with General Stuart and their report, which was presented. "I then called on Ralston to present his statement. He proceeded much as he had at the morning meeting, briefly reviewing his trip, adding a few significant remarks. I thought rather saying more than he had before that the view of the man on the street and the general feeling now seemed to be that the war would run into the spring. He also said, in speaking with Eisenhower, that he, Ralston, himself had said there appeared to be three possibilities: (1) the war ending before the year was out; (2) a stalemate, i.e., dig in for the winter; or (3) go ahead regardless, and asked which it was to be. Eisenhower had said they would go straight ahead; there would be no let up no matter what came. He said as to the time that Eisenhower had once said he believed the war would be over this year, but had since kept his mouth shut. Montgomery had given him nothing definite as to the length of time. (The other day he said Montgomery had indicated the war might still be over before Christmas.) He read the statement, his aide memoire and Murchie's statement, and spoke for quite a long time."

"When Ralston had concluded, there was intense silence," Mackenzie King reported. "I was interested in noticing the faces of the Members. Power and Angus Macdonald were sleeping most of the time, or had their eyes shut and hands over their faces. The men who had not heard anything before looked intensely surprised, amazed and concerned.

"When I started to speak I pointed out that I did not want the discussion to be regarded as a debate between Ralston and myself. It was his duty to give the military point of view. It was mine to raise points of national significance which would have to be considered in connection with the question in all its bearings. Ralston had said he would like to take up the purely military aspect first. I said while I would like to meet his wishes I felt it was not possible to consider that without considering how the end proposed could be attained.

"I then took up Stuart's statement, read the last part of it, drew attention to the fact that what he was asking for was the men necessary for this war against Germany. He did not say to win the war or to keep the army at full strength—just necessary for the war with Germany. Also he did not make any final recommendation but indicated what the recommendation would be in the event of certain contingencies not being fulfilled. I pointed out it was for us to see if we could not have done what was necessary. In reading, Ralston had referred to a telegram which Crerar had sent to Stuart and which he, Ralston, said he had there and had seen only for the first time. It was a telegram dated August 4th in which Crerar said he was concerned about reinforcements. Ralston said there was another telegram in September along the same lines but he did not give the date.

"When I came to speak, I pointed out it was a strange thing that the Cabinet had not had that telegram of Crerar's read to us. That early in August, we were told by Stuart, the Chief of Staff, there was no need to be concerned about reinforcements. Indeed it was only now after the middle of October that we were told for the first time there was such a need and yet this telegram had been in Stuart's hands all the time. It was strange too the Minister should not have known of it until today. I pointed out that the telegrams were probably in the hands of the Chief of Staff when the meeting between Churchill and Roosevelt took place at Quebec and when all the Chiefs of Staff were present at which time we were given the assurance that we had the necessary reinforcements. I pointed out too that this assurance had been given in August when we were asked to supply some 600 or 700 extra men in Italy. I rather stressed the point that this was a fairly serious matter. That it was no fault of the Cabinet we were faced with the problems we were now faced with, according to the latest report.

"I then said that while Ralston had the view that the war would run on until next year, I did not find in the reports I had received, any such conclusion. Indeed the position was stated very much the other way. I then read a long telegram of October 14 which I pointed out I had received while Ralston was on his way to Canada. I also read the intercepted message of September 15 . . . which made clear that from the point of view of the enemy themselves, there was no longer any hope for Germany. I did not enlarge upon the changed position in Europe but drew attention to the fact that the difference between Ralston and myself was that he claimed that the undertaking had been given to keep the army up to strength, whereas I claimed that what I had said in Parliament was what was necessary and desirable; we would always have in mind the time and condition, etc., in reference to the winning of the war, not keeping armed forces up to strength. However, I pointed out I did not want to debate that at present."

The Prime Minister then outlined what would be involved in sending the N.R.M.A. overseas. "That it meant first Cabinet agreeing it was necessary and desirable to extend the N.R.M.A.; secondly, passing an order-in-council to that effect; and thirdly, calling Parliament together and asking for a vote of confidence. This would certainly mean that regardless of anything that might be said of dissolution and discussion on the question of conscription which would run on until the middle of January, this would not secure the men that were needed between now and then or for the period after. I was for doing the best we could to get for the army all the reinforcements that were needed, short of taking a course that would fail altogether to achieve that end but would have very serious consequences in other ways. I then spoke of some of the other consequences, first of the bitter controversy in Parliament and throughout the country, of the divided Canada that would be created. Mentioned Durham having spoken in the '40's a century ago regarding Quebec, two nations warring in the bosom of a single State, that we would now find out we had the same condition only on a much larger and more dangerous scale. We would have the provinces warring with each other and that my fear was that civil strife could not be avoided. Any attempt to enforce conscription now would be certain to lead to bloodshed in many parts of the country. That this would not be helpful to the cause. I then drew attention to what it would mean to our unity. That it was doing for Germany just what she would wish to see, to have her people hold on for a longer time. They would point to the fact that Britain was enforcing conscription on the Dominions. That Canada was divided. If they could hold on longer, they could get a negotiated peace. I spoke too of how serious the whole effect would be on the problem of organization for world peace in which at last apparently Churchill and the President and Stalin were agreed. That that was a policy of maintaining peace by applying force through requiring the different nations to make this contribution. If before that question came before the public and Parliament for discussion, the conscription issue were to arise in Canada, we would have to say good-bye to these many future efforts at peace which involved the application of force. That that would be very serious for years to come."

"There was complete silence for some time," Mackenzie King reported. "I then re-opened the matter by saying in the morning we had been considering possible methods of meeting the situation short of extreme steps. I added that up to this moment I had said nothing about party political considerations . . . but that as Ministers of the Crown, we all had an obligation to those who had sent us to Cabinet Council, to those whom we were representing as Ministers and that as the Leader of the Party and of the Government, I had to consider what was owing to the Party. That all I would say was that if we were driven to the extreme indicated, the Liberal Party would be completely destroyed and not only immediately but for indefinite time to come. That the only party that would gain would be the C.C.F. who would be handed, in an easy fashion, complete control of government. I doubted if even extreme Tories would like to see that particular result. I felt that aspect was one which would have to be considered before final decisions are reached. I drew attention to the fact that Ralston had said as he saw things now, he felt there was no alternative but extension of the N.R.M.A. men for General Service. This, of course, left him a way to see the things differently as time goes by. I was particularly struck by the use of the word "now" and as it occurred the other evening in another connection.

"Discussion became a little general after I had finished. It became a bit acrimonious between Gardiner and Angus Macdonald. Gardiner contended that worse than civil war would result from a step of the kind, by occasioning the debate it did, repeating what had been said in the presence of himself and others that Canada had done more than her share of fighting, that she had fought one-seventh of the war of the British Empire. She should be furnishing food and supplies, etc., and not be expected to do more fighting. Angus Macdonald was wrathy, had laughed at the reference to not being expected to do more fighting. I mentioned of course [Gardiner] was referring to fighting in three or four places on land. I might have said that Gardiner was entitled to say that there had been more than fighting on land and concluded by saying that he had lost a son fighting in the air in the early stages of the war.

"St. Laurent read something from Hansard to bring out what I had said three years ago as to what I regarded as circumstances which would decide the need. At first it sounded as though he was referring to something I would be confronted with adversely, but it really was quite the opposite. I also spoke of the strange position we would be in having to demobilize thousands of the men—some ten thousand of Power's men—at a time when we were conscripting 15,000 for overseas infantry. Also when our navy had reached the proportions it had and we were cutting down on what was needed for war on the Pacific. I pointed out that our whole war policy would be severely criticized on the score of not having been properly planned as between the different services. (For that Ralston himself as Minister of Defence would be primarily responsible.) I of course drew attention to the fact that at every stage we had been assured that the size and addition to the army would not involve conscription. I tried to point out that the N.R.M.A. men had really been doing their duty to the country, that many of them had obligations, that no one could judge but themselves. That as a matter of fact they had served in the country from the point of view of qualifying for service overseas, etc., better than those of their own age who had not been conscripted. When I saw that the discussion was not likely to get anywhere, I suggested we should adjourn until tomorrow afternoon at three giving Members time to think over all aspects of the situation. I counselled the utmost secrecy, but shall be amazed if it is maintained. I expect at any moment to see the whole matter become one of public controversy.

"Before taking up other matters this morning [at the War Committee] Angus Macdonald read a telegram from his Department to say that the British Government wanted to know if they could have some of our ships if we did not need them. They could man them themselves. I said I thought certainly any we were not using they could have. Angus came back with what I expected—that did we think we should, when we were able to man them, let them have these. This for use in South Pacific. I replied that with the manpower problem we were now facing I did not think we should take on anything more in the way of manning ships. St. Laurent pointed out that ships were frequently exchanged."

To the Prime Minister, "Crerar was anything but helpful [at the Cabinet]. Kept talking about his trip across Canada and the talk there was against the Zombie army. He thought the people of Canada would not stand for our men overseas not being kept up to strength as long as there was a Zombie army in Canada to draw from. This was ignoring all the other national considerations and limiting the whole thing to what is really in the minds of some of them. A sort of vengeance at the N.R.M.A. men. Crerar said he had opposed increase in the army at every stage, but now felt that the Zombies ought to be sent overseas. Bertrand asked an important question, which was, what our commitments were and whether they might not be lessened. I pointed out again that I felt sure that in planning the present campaign, Canada had been given her obligations at channel ports, but that others would be expected to take on Antwerp the next large offensive, and our men given a rest which would help very much.

"This morning [at War Committee] Power had asked if Sir Robert Borden had not refused to increase the number of troops after Passchendaele. Had said our men should never have been sent there. Speaking to me alone outside, he referred to some of the army taking matters into their own hands and having a sort of 'Curragh' incident. That Burns in Italy was a good sort of fellow. I said I had no concern on that score but I did feel what might arise from a controversy into which McNaughton and Ralston could be drawn in public, McNaughton taking the ground that this would never have arisen if army had not been divided."

In a conversation with the Prime Minister that evening, C. D. Howe "said Ralston had indicated he would resign on this question if he did not get his way. He counselled me to have Gardiner go easy so as not to antagonize him. Said we would have to try to bring him [Ralston] into line."

Mackenzie King's thoughts at the end of this difficult day turned to the situation which would be created if Ralston tendered his resignation. "First, Council would have to decide whether the majority were with him or with me. If they were with him I would go to the Governor General and tender my resignation, and ask him to call on Ralston to form a Ministry, and leave to Ralston the dealing with Parliament. This, of course, Ralston will never consider doing. He will try to resign himself, thereby placing the Government in a position which would be very false before the public, but would help to destroy it and leave him with the army as his friends and myself as their enemy. However, I cannot believe things will come to this point. The weight of the argument is so strong against attempting to meet Parliament at all, that I feel perfectly sure that other means will be found of meeting the situation. It is, however, a great shame that our opponents should be given the chance to go ahead and organize for an election while we are forced to contend with these problems, and that I should get no chance to even organize matters with the office or to visit my own constituency, speak to the Labour Congress, or to assist the Party in any way through the country. It is all most inconsiderate and quite wrong. However, one can only do the best one can in the circumstances. We have really in the Cabinet come to the point where not only the future of the Government, but the whole future of Liberalism in Canada depends upon the use that will be made by Ralston of one single word—that word 'now' as he may interpret it. This sort of thing should never happen in matters of Government.

"It is rather remarkable that on Saturday at Queen's McNaughton made a speech in which he said: 'When you come, as you will, to places of authority and influence, and you face the acute issues which may divide our country part from part, may I commend this principle of action to your best thought and interest—compulsion is ruled out; we proceed by agreement, or for a time we rest content to not proceed at all.'

"If McNaughton had been looking into the Council Chamber and hearing all that is taking place there, he could not have given wiser counsel. My job has been to try and proceed on that principle and try to have that principle prevail. Up to the moment, I have not had any reply from Churchill to a telegram sent on Sunday. He has had his own problems to deal with. It is almost certain he will consult with Brooke and Brooke with Montgomery before communicating a reply to me. I feel very strongly that the reply will relieve my mind very largely, if not entirely."

The next morning (Wednesday, October 25) when he reached his office, the Prime Minister telephoned Ralston to say that he wished to have a talk with General Stuart. He asked Robertson to be present. The conversation lasted for over an hour and a half. "After mentioning to the General that what he was interested in from the military point of view was getting a certain number of men as reinforcements, I said that I thought we should seek out every possible means to that end short of the adoption of a course which would not only fail to secure the men but would create issues in the country that would leave a legacy of difficulty for a generation or more to come; also create situations which might be injurious to the war effort of the United Nations as well as our own and prejudicial to the solution of some world problems, mentioning in particular the organization for world peace.

"I went over pretty much all the ground that I have gone over in Council. It was a side of the situation of which the General had taken no account whatever and with which he said, as a military man, he of course was not concerned. I pointed out that it was impossible to separate the political or national or international aspects of the problem from a purely military one, and that it was for that reason I felt I should go very carefully into all sides of the question that might be created by an attempt to introduce conscription at this stage of the war. I shall not record here what was said, as it was along lines already taken up in the Cabinet.

"I spoke to him of complications that would arise through McNaughton coming into a campaign that involved a question of conscription at this stage. Said he would be sure to point out the situation created by sending part of the army to Italy. The General said that that would be easily answered. It was that it would have been hard to put men on the continent of Europe without any previous battle experience. I said the country, in controversy, would never stop to consider that aspect or any other if McNaughton took part in a campaign. It would raise many issues that we were trying to bury as much as we could, at least until the war was over. It would certainly be of no help to our army overseas and to our war effort. But that was only one aspect. I pointed out that the Defence Department had not apparently attached importance to giving to N.R.M.A. men pay for the period of their training [basic pay is not meant, but certain financial advantages in relation to service available only to volunteers for general service] nor had they taken up particularly the question of another campaign for inducing the men of the N.R.M.A. to enlist for general service. That I felt he realized there really was not a possibility of getting the men through the application of conscription for the reason that I did not believe conscription could carry in Parliament or in the country and could not be enforced. We should all set more earnestly than ever to the work of setting out means of finding the requisite numbers. I did not speak to Stuart about his telegrams nor about the situation in August, or the situation in September, when we were at Quebec, not wishing to be appearing to be finding any fault with him. Also I felt he had sincerely tried to work through under the voluntary system and believed he would be able to accomplish results in that way.

The Reinforcement Crisis, Phase I, 1944

"He thanked me for having spoken to him frankly. I told him it was not only a duty but a pleasure to talk over the whole situation with him. What I was anxious to do was to help to get the men and not to destroy the effect of Canada's war effort at the present time. I told him I thought efforts should be made overseas in the matter, if need be, of combining units. One thing I suggested was that the French . . . might be willing to let one or two of their units fight with one of our French units. He said he did not think France would do that, that they were anxious to get their own forces as strong as they possibly could. My reply to that was I thought a wire from me to General de Gaulle making the request was all that was necessary; that de Gaulle realized he owed the freedom of France in large part to Canadians. We had supplied them with munitions; our men had delivered their cities, etc., I knew him personally, knew the type he was, and felt we had only to communicate with Vanier for Vanier to get the consent of the General to what we wanted in a day. What annoys me about the Defence Department is that any proposal made, short of conscription of N.R.M.A. men, meets with instant rejection. There is not an attitude of trying to work out the situation. Stuart, I know, is genuinely worried, as he may well be, for if the Government falls it will be due to the Army and the way they have overdone things and also misled the Government."

The Cabinet resumed consideration of the crisis on the afternoon of Wednesday, October 25. This was a very important meeting, because the position of the various Ministers became considerably clearer. Mackenzie King reported that, in opening the discussion, "for once I hardly knew where to begin or what to say. It seemed to me it might be best for the discussion to be general in a way. I said that I felt the situation was very serious. We should avoid anything in the way of unnecessary discussion and concentrate on the question of getting the men that were needed; that that was the problem we ought to work on. I thought, after discussion, perhaps the War Committee could have another meeting and if need be we could have a meeting of the full Cabinet again. Meanwhile we might keep moving along, a step at a time; that time might help to solve the situation.

"Dr. King then said he had thought of leaving for B.C. tomorrow; that he would like to say what he had in mind first. He had gone into the situation very carefully and made really an excellent and impressive speech, ending up by saying . . . it would be political suicide to think of conscription and national suicide as well. He had tried earlier to point out how through having regard to the statement Ralston had made in the House, it should be possible still to get the required numbers by a personal appeal, etc. McLarty was next. His contribution was wobbly and to the effect it was easier to state a problem than to find a solution but agreed conscription would mean the defeat of the administration. Was not sure we could secure it. Gardiner was next. Spoke very clearly and emphatically. Drew attention to Douglas's statement in the press this morning. The C.C.F. would not support conscription without conscription of wealth, which meant they would not support any measure of conscription and, as he said, would sweep the province of Saskatchewan on a conscription issue. The feeling was not against conscription in Quebec only. It was equally strong in the West. Mulock was next and made a splendid contribution. He felt that conscription would destroy the Government, destroy the country. Pointed out that the people generally were beginning to feel that we had done if anything too much, and would certainly be incensed at anything which meant division in Canada at this stage of the war.

"MacKinnon was also emphatic on what conscription would mean by way of defeating the administration. Gibson thought that if we had to have conscription, we would be defeated on that issue; on the other hand, if we did not have conscription to get reinforcements, we would be defeated. We could prevent being defeated if we could find the numbers that were required for supporting the men at the front."

The next speaker, Alphonse Fournier, the Minister of Public Works, was very strongly against conscription. "Felt that General Stuart had no business to make recommendation in the form that he did. That he should have confined himself to stating the problems without indicating what he would recommend. I agreed that Fournier was right in this. It is not the business of the army to tell the Government what its policy should be. Bertrand was strongly opposed to conscription. LaFlèche also thought conscription was unnecessary but if we had to get the reinforcements, we might have to use it at the end. He did not think it was needed now; men could be secured without that. Claxton spoke I thought exceedingly well. Dealt among other things with the question of numbers and brought out, as a result of his remarks, the astonishing statement from Ralston that there were 120,000 General Service men already enlisted in Canada. A big percentage of these were not up to standard; others were being used in particular stations, etc. Ralston's statement caused Power to say: My God, if that is the case, what are you talking about getting more men under conscription? Ralston made out some sort of reply on figures which it was difficult to understand.

"I had then gone around the table and had a word from all present excepting those who were members of the War Committee. Fortunately Dr. King's statement at the outset had caused me to go on from the left and from Members of the Government who were not in the War Committee.

I then left it to Members of the War Committee themselves to interject what they might wish to. I noticed that Ralston said nothing throughout the discussion. Power nothing. Ilsley brought up the question of whether we would have conscription or not, and announce the policy. The Minister of Defence had to reply to questions and he would have to say whether we were for conscription or not. If he announced we would not have conscription, then the alternative would be that, if we did not raise the men necessary, the size of the army would have to be reduced. Ilsley himself was for keeping the army at the size that it is.

"Howe made some interjection to show that he was not sympathetic with attempting conscription and to make clear that there were plenty of jobs. It was not a job but jobs that were available for everyone.

"After discussion had run a certain length, I then said to the Cabinet I had something important which I felt I should say to them. Colonel Gibson's remark that we would be defeated if we sought to get the men by conscription, and defeated if we did not use conscription to get the men, caused me to feel more strongly than I had before on the necessity of making known as soon as possible to the British Government and through them to the United States and possibly others, the present situation in Canada and what the outcome might signify to the war effort and to the Allies generally. That I knew the present Government—not any government, but the continuance in office of the present Government—meant very much to Mr. Churchill and the President and never more than at the present moment as they were facing the problems of peace and post-war. I would mention only two instances which made it, I thought, imperative for me to have our Allies know what might happen if what was threatening could not be averted. The first was: what it meant to the enemy to be able to point to the division of Canada and the application of conscription in Canada at this stage of the war by way of persuading their people to resist longer in the hopes of getting a negotiated peace. In the second place: that I knew there was nothing closer to the hearts of Churchill and the President than the effecting of a world organization for peace to be secured by force if necessary. That I had been at the conference of Prime Ministers and there, after listening to what Mr. Churchill had said of the very serious consequences that might come at any time if such a world organization was not effected (I had in mind what he said of Russia and of her power), [and] much as I did not like the use of force in any form, I was nevertheless prepared to support a world organization that might have force as its ultimate means of maintaining peace. That if conscription came in Canada before this world organization was settled, I felt sure that other parts of the Empire, other self-governing Dominions, and some of the smaller nations, would follow Canada's example in not agreeing to an application of force by what they would call 'The Great Powers,' that the whole plan of world organization might well go to pieces at this stage. That for five years we had been a steadying force between the British and the Americans and they were counting on us to help in the problems that remained; but that if our Government were defeated, as it certainly would [be] once conscription became the issue at this stage, that influence for good could no longer be relied upon. I said they all knew that I was not the one who wished to take another flying trip to Britain at this time but that I felt so strongly what I, as Prime Minister, owed to the other leaders, what the Government of Canada owed to her Allies, I was prepared if need be to leave at once to present these aspects of the situation to Mr. Churchill."

Mackenzie King was asked if he would suggest taking the army out of the line for a month. "I said I would suggest nothing. I would let the situation be known and ask that it be known to the Americans as well; leave it to the British to decide whether it was worth while to interest themselves in the situation or not. I said I would leave no stone unturned to help win the war and make secure the peace, and that this step I felt had come to be necessary in the interests of both unless, in the meantime, we could work out the situation in some way ourselves."

According to Mackenzie King, there was "a great silence" after he had finished. "I then added I had come to feel that my voice had ceased to have much influence so far as the Cabinet was concerned. I did not know what the reason was other than perhaps I had felt obliged to battle so strongly through months seeking to keep the war effort within the limits of our country's power. Some of my colleagues had come to feel I was not sympathetic with them; that I had, as a matter of fact, taken the stand that I had, only to avoid situations such as the present from arising, and I had never made distinction between colleagues, had never in the years I had been Prime Minister, invited any colleague to my room to ask him to take a particular stand in the Cabinet. I felt I had now said [all] that it was possible for me to say.

"Ralston evidently felt it was necessary to reply in regard to his own position. He did so in a quiet way, pointing out what the responsibility was on him. He had said that he would see the army was maintained at strength and he had seen, in visiting hospitals, men being returned to the front too quickly, and if we did not get the reinforcements that were needed his integrity would be attacked. That what he disliked most of all was the fact that McCullagh, Drew and Connie Smythe—that group, would have the satisfaction in the end of saying 'I told you so,' if we were to run short of reinforcements. He did not see how he could remain in the Government unless we could be sure of the reinforcements. I immediately interrupted him to say 'Let me ask you a question, Ralston. Would your resignation from the Government help to get the men that you say are so greatly needed? Unless it would, you should not even think of talking of resignation. Everyone of us has the same motive and we must work together to see that the end is accomplished that we are after in some way short of a step of that kind.

"Macdonald brought up the question as to why there should be an election. He spoke of what had been said at the time, two years ago, of passing an order-in-council, and then going to the House for a vote of confidence, and in a rather, I thought, insulting way, nothing had been said at that time about world questions having to be considered, of the possibility of a general election. My reply to that was that he knew as well as I did that all actions of the Government had to be decided in the light of developments, of conditions as they were in the country and elsewhere. That it was quite a different situation today, when we were nearing the end of the war, and all believed it would end victoriously, to what the situation might have become and what it was two years ago. I emphasized what would be my readiness to go to Parliament had our men begun to be destroyed on seeking to land at the time of the invasion. Now it was quite different. France had been cleared, and Belgium, and part of Holland, etc. Finally, at about 20 to 6, Ralston asked did I think we should have War Committee or Council tomorrow. I said I thought we should follow the course of having War Committee first and Council after, and decided not to continue the discussion any further. I noticed Members were very glad to rise and let matters stop there."

After the Cabinet meeting, Mackenzie King reported, C. G. Power came to his office "and said he thought the only thing to do was for me to have personal talks with Ralston, Ilsley and Macdonald. He said that Ilsley and Macdonald had the greatest influence on Ralston; that it might be hard on me, but to have them together, or separately, to talk the situation over, would be best. Not to try to discuss it in War Committee. The implication was that they would only back up each other and resist opposition. He then said he had thought if I would suggest to Ralston that we would take different courses, I might say that, if in the end we were not successful, we would have conscription. He thought they could get things moved along well enough to get over the time. I said to him how could I say we would resort to conscription at this time, when he knew I and the majority of the Cabinet were against it. He knew how strongly the feeling was expressed today. He then said, yes I know that, I told Ralston that the day he arrived back in Canada, and he said to me that he would resign unless we took that step. I then said to Power that we could not be expected to take that step, to ask for conscription. Power then said why not send some word to Churchill, let him know what the situation is, and have the matter arranged at that end. There was no need of telling the army of what was being done. That anything that was being done in that way would all be fixed up in no time. I said I had spoken today in Council about the wisdom of seeing Churchill. He replied it would not be wise to fly to England; it would be said at once I had gone over to pull the Canadians out of the line. Ralston, by the way, had taken that up at once, about my going to England, I thought he would, but it marks another step that the Government is unwilling to have me take, and yet expect me to go into the House and advocate the use of conscription.

"Power pointed out that while there had been large casualties a few days ago, there were only two or three yesterday. That once the Scheldt business was cleared up, the probability is that our men would be taken out altogether for a time. That will give plenty of opportunity to get others together. I told him I would be prepared to talk to Ralston, Ilsley and Macdonald in the morning, but I felt both Ilsley and Macdonald had a dislike for me; that I had opposed increases to the Navy and use of our navy in the southern seas and Macdonald resented that. To this Power said, Macdonald may have felt a little hurt about that, but he was a politician and a Liberal. He would not wish to see the Party destroyed. He thought both he and Ralston were weakening a little on their first position."

Late that evening (October 25) Mackenzie King surveyed his tactics. He was now convinced that Ralston would resign unless conscription was introduced. "Power said I would have to consider who I could get as Minister. He said he supposed I would ask him, but he would not take the position. Little does he know that he would be the last person I would ask today in this crisis. However, I want to avoid if possible a step of the kind. I think the only way to bring everyone to his senses is for me to make perfectly clear that if the Cabinet wishes conscription then I must feel that I no longer have the support of my colleagues and must tender my resignation to the Governor General, in which event I would ask him to call on Ralston to form a Ministry, he being the only one who could possibly state to the House of Commons that the understanding was that the army was to be kept up to strength and ask for a vote of confidence on that score.

"Ralston would not, I know, for a minute undertake a task of the kind, nor would any other Member of the Government. I think I can make clear to my colleagues that while I can contend with forces opposed to the Government, I cannot contend with my own colleagues. If we cannot get unanimity in the Cabinet, my influence has gone. I have succeeded for nearly 18 years in that task. It is apparent I have got to the time of life where belief in my political wisdom is not what it was some years ago in the minds of some of my colleagues. I do not want to take this course unless it is absolutely necessary, but I believe that mention of it would have more effect on others and prevent Ralston from tendering his resignation than anything else. It is something that I have to weigh very carefully and will seek out every means before resorting to it, but it is a possibility and one which may come before the week is out."

The next morning (October 26), Mackenzie King took the position that Ralston's attitude "was neither that of a soldier nor a Minister of the Crown. Not that of a soldier in that resigning at this time would not gain the men that were needed, and would render the lot of the fighting men more distressing than it is. Not befitting a Minister of the Crown in that he had sworn to serve the King and interests of the State and was giving no thought to his obligation to the State. Was prepared to precipitate the most appalling domestic situation and also to help to destroy the possibility of furtherance of a world order, and actually assisting the enemy by showing divisions in the Dominion."

During the same morning he saw the Minister of National Defence. "When Ralston came in," Mackenzie King wrote, "he seated himself opposite me at the table. I said that one remark he had made yesterday in the Cabinet came as a great surprise and shock to me, namely that he might find it necessary to tender his resignation. I said to him I did not think that thought should be entertained at all by any of us. That we all must seek to keep as united as possible and find ways which will prevent any need of any resignations. The point, however, I wished to put to him was this: was his object not that of finding the necessary number of men to support the troops overseas, that being so, how would his resignation help to further that end? It could only serve in a wholly opposite direction. The situation that might arise out of it would unquestionably lessen the possibility of getting the help that might be sent. I said he himself had heard in Council yesterday Member after Member say it would be suicide for the Government to permit the conscription issue to arise either in Parliament or in the country at this stage of the war. That I had not had a word with one of the Members who had spoken. They, like myself, had been stunned at the report which had been brought in and after a day's reflection, had spoken their minds quite honestly. That he saw that by far the largest number of the Cabinet did not think that we should even consider going to Parliament. That I thought they had made pretty clear what would be the effect. That I questioned if we could get a vote of confidence if we went. He said, of course the whole of Quebec would be against us. I said yes, but that Gardiner had also made it plain that the whole of Saskatchewan would be against us. Douglas's statement had made clear all the C.C.F. would be against us. That I was certain there were large numbers of Ontario Members that would not support us. Ralston said he assumed the Conservatives would. I said: yes, but that I questioned . . . if that would give us the numbers required. I said quite apart from this, I doubted if the matter would ever reach the stage of decision in Parliament as a result of debate, that before Parliament assembled at all, there would be from all sides a demand that this Government should go to the country. That that demand would be irresistible in Parliament and if [we were] forced to the country on the issue, the men would not be secured; that all that would happen would be that the Government would be defeated. A C.C.F. administration come into office and I doubted very much whether the C.C.F. would not immediately begin to reduce the war expenditures in every possible direction. What the consequences to Canada might be, I could not begin to say. However, there was another aspect to consider which was this: that while a government might be able to bring in conscription as a result of an order-in-council, and closure if need be, it would not be possible to enforce conscription unless the opinion of Parliament was so overwhelming as to represent a general sentiment throughout Canada backing the Government. That he would find that if conscription was attempted there would be violent outbursts in different parts of the Dominion, and that the time of the army here would be taken in attempting to suppress these riots. There was also, though I did not mention it, the possibility that the whole army that it was proposed to conscript, might turn against the Government. One could not say to what length things might go. In any event, it would not be finding the men required.

"Ralston said he had thought the whole matter through but could not see how after what he had said in Parliament, that he could do other out of self respect than to resign. He could live in retirement and obscurity but at least would feel that he had carried out what he said he would do, the inference was that he would do this if he did not keep the army up to strength.

"I then said to him: Ralston, you have more than a personal obligation to yourself and I know you will think carefully of this aspect. You have an obligation as a soldier. What you owe to the war effort, and you have an obligation as a Minister of the Crown. As a soldier, I ask you: would you be right in taking any step which might make it more difficult to further the war effort, which would not help to get additional men but would make the lot of the soldiers overseas more distressing than it is. And as a Minister of the Crown, knowing what the consequences of your resignation from the Cabinet might be, occasioning division in the Cabinet, and an appeal to the people, election issue, etc., would you be serving the State as you have sworn to do, as a Minister, in letting situations arise which would be helpful to the enemy by destroying altogether the progress that has been made in bringing about a world organization which would maintain peace by force, if necessary. Also creating situations within the Empire which would run through an indefinite time working havoc to the country's future.

"To all this he came back simply saying that he had thought the matter out and owed it to what he had talked over with himself. I then said to him up to the present, we do not know that we cannot get the men. His reply was the time was short. He was satisfied we could not get them. He had tried recruiting; others had tried, etc. I said we have not yet tried the recruiting by the Government. We have not yet attempted to see what we can do by extra inducements to the men and besides, I said, is not the whole question dependent on how long the war may last and what the casualties are likely to be from this time on. He said, yes, those were the two questions, how long the war would last and what the casualties would be. I then said Well that being the case, am I not right in feeling that I should let this whole situation be known to Mr. Churchill? That I should leave at once to cross by plane and let our allies know what is likely to develop so that they may consider what steps should be taken first. I said there has been mention of having our men in Italy brought to reinforce the men in the north along the Channel. That Crerar had told me there was nothing he was more anxious for than for [the army] to be altogether at the end of the war. I could not see why this might not be arranged rather than create the situation described. That other arrangements could be made in Italy at this time. I did not mention about asking de Gaulle for Frenchmen to help to make up our French units, nor did I discuss what Montgomery had said about uniting units. Ralston won't allow any thought of reduction in size of units or reduction in commitments to enter his mind. I spoke of it being pretty clear that when our men had completed the task at the Scheldt, they would be taken out for a time and that would make a big difference. I said I recognized the difficulty of going overseas through the publicity it would occasion. The alternative was to have someone come here from there, or for me to communicate by telegram with Mr. Churchill. I said I thought we should do all we could at this end and settle nothing until we see what circumstances are at the other end. He spoke about the time that would be taken in crossing, arrangements in the meantime, and not deciding matters at once, and also that these men were needed before the year was out."

The talk was interrupted at this point because Mackenzie King was late for an appointment with the Earl of Athlone at Government House. After a few preliminaries were exchanged there, Mackenzie King reported that the Governor-General said: "How are things going? And I said that I had a real problem on my hands. His Excellency said: I gather you have. I then added I had not wished to trouble him until I knew how matters stood, and felt it necessary to speak to him about the situation. I then referred to Ralston as I had done before on his return from England, of his bringing Stuart with him and of the report that Stuart had presented, etc. I outlined the nature of the discussion that had arisen and told His Excellency something of the Cabinet discussion yesterday, dwelling particularly on the point of view that the overwhelming majority of the Cabinet felt it would be suicide, as far as the Government was concerned, to seek to get reinforcements under conscription at this stage. I also said I thought Stuart had exceeded his authority in recommending a policy to the Government, that it was all right for him to explain the situation and tell us there was need for reinforcements but it was not for him to say what action the Government should take in meeting that situation as he had in recommending that the N.R.M.A. should be extended to General Service. I said a word or two about the situation that would be created if we had to call Parliament together. That we would certainly be forced to the country on it; that certainly the issue of conscription would be the one on which election would have to be fought. I then went on to say that I felt there were very important considerations that affected the whole war effort and the future of the Empire, apart from Canada.

"I then said the reason for my coming this morning was that at Council Ralston had stated that he would find it necessary to resign if we could not agree on getting the reinforcements to keep the army up to its present strength. I said there was a difference between us as to what was meant by what had been said as to consulting Parliament. My view had been regarding the necessity to win the war and Ralston's with the necessity of keeping the army up to strength. Stuart's report spoke of [reinforcements] being necessary for the war against Germany. I had drawn attention to this yesterday, but Ralston had brushed the matter aside. Said it meant of course keeping the army up to strength. I said that it would not be so construed by Parliament. Parliament would look to the real issue which was the necessity and advisability of resorting to conscription at this time. I then told His Excellency of the conversation I had with Ralston this morning, what I had said about his resignation in no way helping to get the number of men and what I had said in addition, regarding the obligation which he owed to himself in respect to what he might feel his own position demanded. That he was both a soldier and a Minister of the Crown and had obligations as such to the army and to the State. I then outlined what I had said in that connection. I told him of Ralston's reply and then mentioned about my having told Council that it might be necessary for me to go over to England by 'plane to see Churchill and others. I did not wish to do this in a public way. I thought every step should be taken before the power and existence of the Government had gone.

"When I had finished, His Excellency said: Will you tell me how many men there are in Canada today available? I said, Your Excellency I cannot tell you that because I cannot find it out. I can get no definite statement from the Minister. Some things have been considered, others have not. The different proposals that we put forward, such as beginning a recruiting campaign, paying the N.R.M.A. men for the time they have been training, etc., are just pushed to one side. I then referred also to the de Gaulle suggestion, to what I suggested regarding Frenchmen to serve with our other Canadian regiments. I said there were in September, I believed, 120,000 G.S. men. I gave him the breakdown as Pickersgill had given me the figures, and then mentioned what in a general way was the position of the N.R.M.A. men. His Excellency at that moment became quite positive. He said something to the effect about that being the wretched part of the whole situation. He went on to say: Yesterday I had Stuart here. (I had noticed in the press he had been there.) He said: I tried to pin him down to numbers, etc., but he could give me nothing that was definite. It was all very inconclusive. He further said: I can make nothing out of him in what he presents. I also told His Excellency about the telegram of August 4th and also said Your Excellency will remember in Quebec in September we were all satisfied there were no questions of numbers of reinforcements, etc., while Churchill and the Chiefs of Staff were present. Now, Ralston reads to the Cabinet a telegram which came from Crerar to Stuart on August 4th stating that there was a concern about the question of reinforcements. Ralston told the Cabinet he had not seen or known of the existence of that telegram until the morning of that day. He was speaking to the Cabinet on the day before yesterday.

"I said, the truth of the matter is the men on whom we have had to rely have not given us the facts or told us what was to be considered. Rather, they have given us assurances in the opposite direction and now they expect us to clear up the whole situation. It is past the middle of October before we know of the word sent by the Commander-in-Chief of the Army to the Chief of Staff in August. I said if we get into discussion in Parliament, all these things will be brought out and we will have a nice situation." This interview was interrupted by Princess Alice coming in to take the Governor-General to lunch.

In the afternoon the Prime Minister had a talk with Angus Macdonald to whom he reported his conversation with Ralston. "I gave him my own view that even if we could agree to go to Parliament and ask for a vote of confidence and secure it, unless it were a vote which represented a large majority right across the country, it would be impossible to enforce conscription under it. Any attempt to do so would certainly give rise to civil strife. Angus said he saw the difficulties. Was very much concerned about everything himself, but Ralston was hard to deal with. That if he really came to the conclusion that men could not be raised, he thought he would resign. I pointed out that that would not get the men, but would make more difficult than ever the bringing of the war to a successful close. I asked him if he and Power would join with Ralston in going over the figures which the Departmental officials had presented. I thought there might be found both here and overseas, ways of still getting more men. He said he would be glad to do that. He impressed me as realizing more than heretofore the seriousness of the situation. I think he still holds to the desirability of attempting conscription."

The War Committee on the afternoon of October 26 considered various expedients for getting more volunteers from the N.R.M.A. As they discussed the suggestions, Mackenzie King noted, "Ralston did not seem too helpful or favourable," and said that he felt there was no use attempting them "unless they were part of a general appeal." And, "when it came to the question of a public appeal, Ralston took up considerable time in reading reports of his officers who had tried to recruit from the N.R.M.A. men. One could see that the officers had been very strongly biased in favour of conscription. For example, one used the phrase: that we had been planting lilies and trying to raise men. The men said they would be ready to go if the Government would order them, but they wanted to be ordered. There were other excuses as to families holding on to them, not liking what had been said against them, etc. In speaking of a general appeal I indicated that I thought the members of the Cabinet as a whole should join in the appeal. Ralston I thought was seeking to have it limited to myself, either giving a radio broadcast, or going to the West and speaking to the men at one of the camps there, including the men who had come back from the Kiska expedition [see vol. 1, p. 552]. That expedition should never have taken place. Somebody said something about a statement to be given to the public. I said the public would require the fullest information. The statement should indicate we had 120,000 G.S. men in Canada now and reasons would have to be given why out of that number we could not raise 15,000. Also full explanation will have to be given of the numbers of men who have gone into General Service from National Mobilization, and how many of the numbers at present in Canada would be available to draw from, assuming they were conscripted. Macdonald did not like the idea of having figures given. He thought a general statement would be enough. Power thought the figures should be given. I again spoke of the need of getting information from the highest authorities as to the probable duration of the war and the plans as to further use of the Canadian army. Ralston wanted to know if we could not regard the question of reinforcements as a purely domestic question. I told him it was anything but purely domestic. That it would have its effect on the future of the war and on the whole post-war problem. That we could not take a step that was going to adversely affect our allies without letting them know in advance. This is going to be the factor that will, if any at all does, save the situation. We cannot even settle the domestic question of numbers without having from the highest authorities the information as to the probable duration of the war and the role of the Canadian army."

To the Prime Minister, the whole discussion was "very disheartening. It left very much to me to bring up everything and discuss everything. Crerar wisely said nothing at all. St. Laurent said nothing, but took up Ralston in a very sharp way on one point which was that it was only too evident that it was to get satisfaction with the zombies that a certain course was being taken. Michaud spoke once or twice but took little part. Howe was present and said nothing. He has said nothing all along. It was left with me to talk with Ilsley, Macdonald, Power and Ralston. Power was most helpful. I suggested that Ralston, Power and Macdonald might go over the figures of the Department and see whether the officials had not left too large a safety margin both here and overseas. Angus Macdonald asked if it was desired they should as well consider the shortening of Canada's line. He meant reduction of the size of Canada's army. I said, by all means, take up anything that would help."

After the meeting, the Prime Minister called in the Minister of Mines and Resources, T. A. Crerar, "and tried to impress him with the seriousness of the situation in the light of what he had said yesterday. I pointed out the three things I had mentioned to Ralston which every minister will have to consider. The first point was how men could best be got. Then the next course that could obviously not get the men but would make conditions worse and why it should not be attempted. Then, the duty to the army, to the country and the oath of office as a Privy Councillor to advise the King of any matters prejudicial to the State and to make the interests of the State uppermost. I stressed to Crerar the effect on the war of assisting the enemy if we allowed a step to be taken that would divide Canada, also the post-war problems including world security and told him the importance Churchill attached to getting this in order as soon as possible. I let Crerar know that he held the view that unless he succeeded in getting such an organization we might have to face another war in the years to come and that war would probably be against Russia. Crerar says he is giving the matter his best consideration. He never wanted to have a large army. He thought all the defence departments were no good and said so right along."

Later the Prime Minister saw Malcolm MacDonald and urged him to expedite a reply from Churchill to his earlier message, a message which Mackenzie King's colleagues did not know had been sent. That evening he wrote: "I have now to consider the best course that may have to be taken, should Ralston tender his resignation or offer to. I shall do my utmost to hold the situation till word comes from England and to be governed by it for the next step. The papers, however, have got a hold of what we are discussing, as I expected they would. I fear unless the word which comes is so definitely helpful as to enable us to get ahead, that I shall have to consider calling Parliament together again even if we do not go to Parliament for a vote of confidence. If Ralston tendered his resignation, and it were accepted, I would have to call Parliament to give the explanation and then state in Parliament whether we would continue to try to carry on till the end of the war or have a general election at once. I certainly shall never ask for adoption of conscription at this stage whether defeated on the floor of Parliament or not. It is an appalling shame just at the moment that we are at the highest point we have been, we should be thus thrust down by one of our own number. This is what I have always told Caucus. That we cannot be defeated by our opponents, but it will only be ourselves who will defeat us, if we are defeated.

"I have got a letter from Godbout tonight that even the Tories of Quebec were counting on voting for me, but the Selective Service are putting in new regulations which are creating terrible disturbance and may cost us the province yet. It was a matter we spoke of some time ago. Really the more I see of it all, the more I am convinced that the Department of Defence has made a terrible mess of our whole war effort. The army has been far too large; the planning has been anything but sound. The judgment, far from good."

In Mackenzie King's opinion, the meeting of the War Committee on Friday, October 27, was highly unsatisfactory. "Power, Macdonald and Ralston had gone over figures with Stuart last night. The result was it was apparent that the army could be kept up to strength and with all necessary reinforcements up to the end of the year. In the new year, the reinforcements would be short, only some 700 could be raised in January and 3,000 by the first of February. This is without any conscription and from men now in training or overseas. And assuming that the rate of infantry casualties would be as high as it has been, but it seemed to me that none of the Defence Ministers were too sure of the figures they were dealing with. Indeed they were questioning each other concerning what was really meant. Power was helpful in raising the question of some possible reduction in the size of the army as a way of meeting the situation. This he had evidently done with Ralston's consent. Ralston raised the question, however, that if as I thought the majority of Council were to be against passing an order for conscription if necessary, that that more or less would settle the matter. I did not quite catch the significance of what he meant.

"The question, however, came up about what would happen if the Cabinet were divided. I said as long as they remained as one and faced the course that was to be taken and agreed upon, I thought we could carry on without any election or calling Parliament together. If an order-in-council were desired for conscription, we would, of course, have to call Parliament together with a general election certainly ensuing. I also felt if we did not keep together as one and there should be any resignation, that it would be necessary to bring Parliament together and explain the situation. This met with instant questioning on the part of the three Defence Ministers: Why would Parliament have to be brought together? Why could we not have a general election at once? In this I felt immediately they had given away their hand completely. What they would like would be a general election on the conscription issue without having the issue properly presented to Parliament first, thereby making clear how the whole thing had come about. That, of course, is the last thing that Ralston or the others wished. I said that the Government was a committee of Parliament and responsible to Parliament. That Parliament was merely adjourned, had been kept adjourned to be advised if any crisis arose so long as the war was on. That I had said I did not want an election in war-time but I felt if there was any resignation, we would certainly be obliged to tell Parliament the reasons for it and let the whole situation be known. They did not seem to like this at all but they realized the power for that is in my hands. There is nothing that men who love power hate more than to have to account for their use of it to those from whom it is derived.

"The discussion then came to information from overseas as to the probable length of the war and the extent of operations. The Ministers said they had had Stuart's wire last night on these matters. Ralston asked me if the question could not be dealt with as a purely domestic one. I said I could not see how it could possibly be such. That the British Government ought to know anything that affected the Allies. They were questioning as to whether a decision should be taken by the Cabinet this afternoon. I said by no means would there be a final decision until we knew all we could possibly know about the duration of the war and the operations in which our men were to participate. When they were pressing for getting a decision today, I said well, I would wish to go across, would be ready to leave on Monday. Ralston said he did not want to oppose that course but the getting of reinforcements was pressing and that each day's delay increased the difficulty. To this I replied well, if that is the case, I will communicate by telegram and I will do so this afternoon. This is my duty. I added nothing further and left the Council to decide whether they wanted to have a decision reached this afternoon. I found later that none of them were very keen on that. I called in Pope and Robertson and Heeney, all three of whom had been at War Committee, and told them to draft up for me a telegram which I could send to Churchill which would enquire for the information desired. They were to work out one this afternoon and did so. Meanwhile I went down to see the Governor General. Ralston had greeted me as I went in to Council, this morning, with the words that he had been sent for by His Excellency. I think he felt it was because of my talk with His Excellency yesterday and that the Governor might try to persuade him not to resign.

"I felt nothing about this but felt I should talk with His Excellency again to make sure that he did not try to say anything to Ralston on the possibility of his resignation or what had taken place in the Cabinet. His Excellency said he had been trying to get in touch with Ralston since he came back. Had only had a word with him when he arrived. He had not seen him since. I said to him he would recall having asked me yesterday about the figures and that I had been unable to give them to him. Ralston knew His Excellency had seen Stuart. He might well ask Ralston to explain the figures to him. He said that was exactly what he wanted to do. He then spoke about not being able to make anything out of the figures that Stuart had talked over with him. That he had had the same trouble with figures that were sent down by Letson [General H. F. G. Letson, Adjutant General]. He had to call in Redfern and ask him to try and make something out of them. . . .

"His Excellency expressed himself very strongly and firmly about the inability or seeming unwillingness of the Defence Departments to make clear statements which would comprehend the situation. He spoke too about the unreasonableness of expecting conscription at this time. Said he personally would have been in favour of conscription at the beginning of the war but he saw no reasons for it after 5 years of war. I told His Excellency of the discussion this morning and of my intention to send a telegram to Churchill at once. He thought I was entirely right in seeking to obtain from Churchill as much information as I could, and also let him know of the situation here.

"Just as I was leaving, an A.D.C.—Clayton—came to the door to say there was an urgent message for me from Malcolm MacDonald. His Excellency then said this might be something that will be helpful. I said I had talked with Malcolm and had asked him to send a message on his own account outlining the situation which was developing. This was probably a reply. I said I had not wished to send any official message which would be open to the Cabinet and did not wish to have His Excellency involved in it. The Governor General thought that was the wisest thing to have done."

Mackenzie King immediately went to the British Commissioner's residence, Earnscliffe, and, after a short wait, Malcolm MacDonald arrived. "He showed me the message," the Prime Minister reported, "saying that ... in some ways it was not so good. When I read it through, I saw that it did not answer the questions which I had asked. At least in an authoritative way. It evaded the question of the part that our troops would be taking between now and the end of the year by stating that the plans were not yet prepared, but indicated that the Canadians would have an intense part in the fighting at the finish though not participating in the next operation. It also stated that Churchill had talked very confidentially with the Chiefs of Staff who indicated that the war might well run on—there again not doing more than indicating what might happen. The message made clear it had no reference to numbers where it referred to the extent of future operations. . . . It does not give the particulars that I wanted.

"I was greatly surprised that Churchill had not indicated his desire to meet the situation; merely indicated he was concerned about the difficulties, the seriousness of which he appreciated but that the British Government and himself would be everlastingly thankful for the help that Canada had given them in the war. All of [this], on examination, making clear they looked upon the war as theirs and that we were giving them help, not that it was a war which was of concern to freedom everywhere. Malcolm said to me he did not see why we could not still meet the situation by other methods than conscription. I told him I felt that way very strongly myself. That I would write a short telegram for him to send thanking Churchill for his message and indicating that I might be sending a further open message which could be answered independently altogether of this message."

Leaving Earnscliffe, Mackenzie King had every reason to feel depressed and upset. A possible trump card in the crisis had been denied him and he now had to rely on his own reserves of political skill and resilience.

CHAPTER SIX

The Reinforcement Crisis, 1944
Phase II

BITTERLY DISAPPOINTED, the Prime Minister went to a Cabinet meeting late in the afternoon on October 27 with the thoroughly unsatisfactory, but diplomatically correct, telegram from Churchill in his pocket. He "told the Ministers that in the morning we had discussed matters but felt it would be better not to try to reach a decision today. That we had to get further information which would come from the Officers Commanding in Europe. That I had said in the morning, I would telegraph Churchill today but had concluded it would be better to wait until we heard from those overseas, our own men. It might look as though I had no confidence in Ministers or our own Commanding Officers but that I still felt the responsibility there was to see that the British Government knew of the situation. Meanwhile Robertson and others had worked out a telegram which I have kept and will probably not use."

Later that evening, the Prime Minister telephoned Malcolm MacDonald and "told him that I had decided to send only one message of acknowledgement which was to the effect that I thanked Churchill for his message and that I was relieved to know that he was aware of the seriousness of the situation in all its possible bearings and consequences. I explained to Malcolm that Churchill's message did not give me the information I really needed. My message to him had fulfilled what I was concerned about, namely that he should understand the situation and its bearings. I have now communicated with him giving him all the facts and feel that I cannot be reproached for not having made him fully acquainted with everything. If I had failed to do this, and consequences were serious, I would have been held responsible for not letting him know."

A new theme appeared in the day's record. "Dr. King, in talking with me this afternoon," the Prime Minister wrote, "said that he would like to tell Ralston and Stuart in my presence that he regarded the whole situation that had arisen as a determined plot on the part of the Defence Department to destroy me for not having agreed to conscription. That he felt sure of that. As a matter of fact, Ralston's position, he thought, was terrible. To think that we had the numbers of men that we had in the Army altogether; there were only a very small number in the fighting line, and that out of 130,000 General Service men in Canada alone, we could not find 15,000. He thought that Ralston, who as Minister of Defence, should have supervised the Navy and the Air Force, had simply allowed Angus Macdonald and Power to run away with everything. Had not controlled them but had allowed them to take men that he should have been free to take in the infantry. That he thought when the facts came out that Ralston would be the first victim and in a terrible position. When I told him that I had mentioned having Parliament meet and they had wanted to have a general election without any word to Parliament first, merely on top of Ralston's resignation, he said: Do not let them put you in that position. While he himself [Dr. King] had not wanted Parliament to meet, on reflection he felt I was right in seeing that the issue was properly stated there.

"In talking with Gardiner [later in the day] . . . he said to me he hoped I would stand firm against conscription. That he would not stay in any government that favoured conscription; that he would join the C.C.F. first. I asked him if the majority in the Cabinet were for conscription, did he think I should go to the Governor General and ask him to call on Ralston to form a government to put through conscription. He said, I might have to consider that but he hoped I would remain the leader of the Liberal Government; that he himself would have to cross the floor if Ralston were leader. I said I would have to do the same myself. He then spoke of the shameful way in which we had all been deceived by being told nothing of the need for reinforcements until the last day or two. Dr. King promised me he would have a talk with Ralston himself. He repeated his position would really be a terrible one."

At the close of the day, Mackenzie King noted: "I came back in my thoughts tonight to the position as I saw it the moment the matter first came to my attention, namely, that at this stage of the war we could not possibly think of imposing conscription. One of the evening papers carries the headline 'War at last lap—Churchill.' That is the statement made to the British House of Commons. It is the one on which I shall base my argument for not supporting conscription at this time. It is better to take the word that he has made public to the House of Commons than anything that might come in an exchange of messages."

There was no meeting of the Cabinet on Saturday, October 28, and Mackenzie King took Malcolm MacDonald with him to Kingsmere for a wide-ranging discussion of the crisis. He noted that "Dr. King had said yesterday afternoon that on no account should I allow a dissolution following Ralston's resignation without having Parliament meet and given an opportunity to discuss the whole situation. This had been my own view as stated to him but he [Dr. King] saw more clearly than I did how Ralston would be seeking to get his own statement before the public before an election, placing me in the position where I would have to give out facts against the Government myself, thereby making it unnecessary for me to explain anything about the general situation other than that reinforcements were inadequate and I would be in a position of having to explain matters for which the Government rather than the Department of Defence were responsible. King said: Don't let them get you into that position. My mind was quite clear that if the Cabinet were divided, I should say it would be impossible to ask Parliament to approve any order-in-council for conscription and then if a way were not found to meet the situation otherwise, and Ralston were to resign, I would then call Parliament and have the position stated and ask for a vote of confidence.

"I spoke to Malcolm in the evening about the form such a resolution ought to take. He said he thought in England, they would have the Prime Minister make his statement first, then some member of the party other than the Government would move that having heard a statement from the Prime Minister, the House was of the opinion that—he was not sure of the remainder. It would either be that the House were to express its confidence in the administration, or some alternative. This would be a straight confidence motion.

"If it carried, the Government would carry on till the time that it wished to dissolve making such changes in the Ministry as would be necessary. If defeated, I would of course resign, tender my resignation and ask the Governor General to call on the leader of whichever party had given the largest number of votes for conscription to form a Government and enforce conscription. I venture to say if it comes to that, whoever takes that task in hand will not be supported at a general election. Malcolm Mac-Donald said that he thought my stand was fully right. It might be 10, 20 years before the country saw this clearly but that it would be recognized that I had taken a statesmanlike position and that had I taken any other, I would have been wrong and the country suffer increasingly. He felt sure history would completely vindicate my course in not allowing conscription in Canada at this stage of the war. He thought it might even be that I would come back in a very short time. He again stressed the fact that there was really no one else that could handle the situation at this time." Mackenzie King added: "If we can escape conscription, I am not afraid of the future."

On Sunday, October 29, Mackenzie King was quite depressed. "When I was in bed this morning," he wrote, "I felt then that perhaps I had reached the point that I could not go any further. That Council might have to carry on tomorrow without my being present. I can see what the shock might mean to them if they discover that at this stage, the Defence Department had succeeded not only in putting Ralston out of the Government but myself also. As long as I am ready to lead, they are ready to let me suffer. They will take every course they can to keep me in that position rather than have one of themselves take responsibility. To me, however, the course is perfectly clear. I cannot take responsibility for a course of action that is against my judgment, as to what is best for the nation and for the war and the future of the world."

On Monday morning Mackenzie King talked to St. Laurent about the position of the government. He had barely started before Ralston, for whom he had also sent, joined them. By his account, he spoke to Ralston "very earnestly about the effort we should all make to avoid having to go to Parliament which would open up a discussion on the whole situation and this could only be avoided by keeping the Cabinet united. I pointed out that whether we went to Parliament to get approval of conscription or to explain the situation and ask for a vote of confidence, the result would be the same, that the Government's war effort would, in large part, be impaired. The main point was to get the men and that would not be helped by a discussion through the country on conscription—of the pros and cons of conscription, at this time. I said I had stated there should be no election in war-time. I thought the people wanted our Government to remain in at least until the war was over. There was no alternative government to it that could carry on. I said if defeated in the House, I, of course, would have to resign and ask the Governor General to call for someone else. If our side gave the largest majority against me, he would be the one that would have to take that responsibility of applying and enforcing conscription and all the other policies of the Government. I thought he or anyone else would find that a very difficult task. I then said to him I thought I ought to let him know that yesterday I had had a considerable fright through finding during part of the morning that it was impossible for me to walk through one leg indicating a return of the old trouble. That except for treatment received in the morning, I could not have gone to the funeral of Gardiner's wife and accompany the family as I did. I felt bound to say in the light of medical advice I had received that while I was prepared to go up to the point where my physical strength enabled me to continue to carry on, I could not go beyond that. That while I had fight in me to oppose political opponents, I could not keep on with divisions in my own ranks; that if I found in Parliament the strain was too great, I would have to give up the leadership of the Party itself and leave it to others to form what Government they could.

"Ralston kept saying he was anxious not to impose, heaven knows he did not want to impose any additional burdens on me but he had said this and he had said that and he did not see how he could possibly stay on unless his words could be implemented. He kept coming back to feeling sure the House would carry on conscription and told me that he relied on me to see that this was done as I had promised it would in short order. I said to him the House of Commons would never consent to closure of debate at this time on the subject of conscription regardless of what one might have said in the past. Also to remember unless the House was over-whelmingly for conscription, the policy could not be applied. That a division of 97 to 106 or the like would not be sufficient to enable any policy of the kind or force to be used. That required an overwhelming public opinion back of it. St. Laurent was helpful by pointing out while Ralston's view was one thing, mine was another. The public he believed would accept the interpretation I placed, namely, winning the war. He and many others could not possibly support introduction of conscription at this time. That as Ralston knew, he, St. Laurent, would at one time have been pre-pared to support conscription but he could not think of it at this time.

"I ended up by speaking again of 'a house divided against itself' and let Ralston realize that as far as words could do so, his resignation would not only mean the defeat of the Government but might necessarily mean as well the end of my leadership, of the Liberal party and the serious conse-quences which would flow through no other groups being able to form a government which would be able to carry on the war effort."

After this interview, the Cabinet met again. Mackenzie King noted that when he went into the Cabinet "there was complete silence. I said that I had, as they all had, been giving further thought over the week-end to the situation we were faced with. That I wanted to avoid an election in war-time. Had said so right along. Wanted to avoid the summoning of Parlia-ment. The only way these possibilities could be avoided was by our finding some way to meet the situation with which we were faced. That to help to that end, I had prepared a constructive draft of what I thought might be issued as a statement by myself which would also be an appeal to the N.R.M.A. men to enlist for General Service. That it had been drafted in a way to avoid any reference to our having done enough in the war but was rather drafted on lines of how we could make the utmost effort and con-tinue the greatest possible contribution. I said it was only a draft but I should like to read it to all present. I also said I was sure in the case of a Cabinet crisis, that all would agree, including the Ministers of Defence, that a Prime Minister should make a statement of the situation to the nation. That something had been said of Ralston giving out a statement to the press in a conference but I thought this was an occasion when the Prime Minister himself should speak to the country. (Ralston all along has been urging the need of his making a statement to the press; also I think had been expecting he would and may have had some statement already prepared which he intends to make.)

"I could see that all Members present accepted that. I then read the statement which Pickersgill had prepared and which I had slightly revised. When I was finished, I pointed out that this was just the basis, that if we agreed to proceed in that way, I would have it further revised; also allow Council to hear everything that was to go into it and that what I said would be followed by an appeal to the men as citizens, etc.

"I then pointed out that if the Cabinet were divided either way we would have to have Parliament summoned and I indicated the line I would have to take in asking for a vote of confidence. That if, for example, the Ministers of Defence thought it necessary to drop out, I would have to explain the situation in Parliament and ask for a vote of confidence and allow full discussion on the motion. If I did not get the vote I would then resign.

"I also mentioned to the Cabinet the experience I had yesterday and repeated what I had said to Ralston about not wishing to continue the leadership of the party if I found that through its divisions I would not have the strength to assume that responsibility any longer. I think what I said had really a sobering effect as things were not pressed to an immediate decision before the meeting was over. Ralston seemed to ease up a little, but very little.

"The time was mostly taken up in discussing facts and figures which Angus Macdonald had been working over the last couple of days. It was to show the necessity for conscription if the numbers required to keep the army up to strength were to be obtained. The statement I had made was received, on the whole, favourably. Suggestions were made as to some modifications which might be needed, additional figures, etc. I said, of course, I would want all the information possible. My handicap would be not to disclose figures to the enemy. LaFlèche in speaking drew attention to one thing which he said was not pleasant to mention which had to be faced and that was a possible en masse refusal on the part of the N.R.M.A. men to go overseas. That, I think, is a wholly possible and probable situation. It might develop if coercion were attempted and might result in a very serious loss of life. Macdonald appeared to be doing his best to help, but Arnold Heeney made the remark [after the meeting] that if Ralston went Macdonald would also go. I was not surprised at this but expressed surprise to Arnold that he should have gathered that impression from Macdonald. He immediately indicated that that was just his own impression. I pointed out [in Cabinet] the serious effect which a division on this matter might have on the Presidential election. It was generally admitted the elections in the United States were very close. Were we to get out and seek to urge men to cross the seas, we would be helping Roosevelt who was stating the need and seriousness of the war to his own people. Were the issue on conscription we would be playing into the hands of all the isolationist elements in the United States who would support Dewey. They would point out the way men in this manner were being coerced to fight in European wars. I think this made some impression."

Tallying up the score at this point, Mackenzie King felt that Ralston, Crerar, Howe, Macdonald, Gibson, and Ilsley would support conscription. He was sure of neither McLarty nor Mitchell. Power, he was convinced, "would find some way of not opposing Ralston and Macdonald." Against conscription, and with him, would be St. Laurent, Michaud, Bertrand, MacKinnon, Claxton, Fournier, Mackenzie, Mulock, LaFlèche, King, and Gardiner.

The Cabinet meeting continued until 7.00 P.M. "Angus Macdonald suggested we should not sit longer. It would be better to adjourn until tomorrow and it was agreed that the afternoon would be better than the morning because of the press. I showed Council the evening paper which mentioned about the King Government being divided and the Chiefs of Staff standing for conscription. Arnold Heeney seemed to think the situation was a little better. I think Council was impressed by some of the larger considerations, but I am not at all sure that there has been any real change of either intention or view on the part of the men mentioned. When I saw Howe present today I felt pretty certain that he had joined with Ralston and the others or he would not have stayed over from going to Chicago as he had indicated to me last week he would have to do, and be absent from Council today. Evidently the tactics had been to bring matters to a decision on the initiative of the Defence Department, but by taking the initiative myself I think I staved that off at least for another day."

That evening Mackenzie King wrote that he was beginning to feel there was a conspiracy against him; that it was "not merely a question of conscription." It was "perfectly plain" to him that "in pretty much all particulars my position is becoming identical to that of Sir Wilfrid Laurier's where his supposedly strongest colleagues left him, one by one, and joined their political enemies and became a party for conscription. They will find that at this time they have not the Wartimes Election Act to assist them in a campaign. That manipulation of the votes of the soldiers, the disfranchisement of persons of foreign extraction, confining the women's votes to those who have relatives overseas. What would probably happen would be that we would have a real Tory party composed of conscriptionists of the different parties who also were seeking to preserve their wealth and perhaps a combination of Liberals and Progressives and Labour who will make up a real Liberal party. For my part I shall certainly become a member of the latter, rather than the former and do what I can to save Liberalism and the lives of the many whether in war or in peace.

"It would be a terrible tragedy, however, if this is the outcome of the years which I have given, and the latitude I have given to the men who are around me. I told Caucus a couple of years ago that it would probably come to this. I have not wholly despaired but the personnel of supporters being who they are and remembering their attitude on other social matters, it is hard to believe that this is not almost certain to come." And he concluded his reflections with these significant words: "If it comes to opposing Ralston and his conscriptionist friends, McNaughton will soon find himself at my side strongly fighting for the peoples' rights in this country."

The following morning (October 31), as he began work in the library of Laurier House, Mackenzie King found waiting for him "a memo—a very helpful one—from Mackenzie as to the present situation. I had rung him up last night to get his impression of the meeting of Council and the probable outcome. He told me he found it all he could do to control himself in the Cabinet. He felt perfectly sure there was a conspiracy from the Defence Departments to get me out. I said to him it was rather noticeable however that the men who wanted conscription were those who opposed our social legislation. He said that was quite clear. There was no doubt that that part might lie back of the raising of the conscription issue. He thought Angus Macdonald tonight was very worried; also Ilsley. He thought I ought to take a bold stand in the statement I would read, say nothing about letting the people judge, but maintain the position we had taken strongly. Also he thought I ought to take McNaughton into the Government. Thought I should communicate with Churchill and that we should demand that our men return from Italy and have one Canadian army. I said nothing but listened to what he was saying. This morning he sent me a letter outlining the situation as he sees it."

Immediately after this entry, Mackenzie King added that he had been "thinking very carefully about seeing McNaughton. I have put that off, not wishing to go behind the back of the Members of Council in approaching anyone. However, as Mackenzie says, it will be necessary to act very quickly and at a stroke, if Cabinet should not follow my suggestion of launching an appeal for men and Ralston should resign. If he goes, I am pretty sure that Angus Macdonald will do the same, and while Power might not, he is liable to find himself in such a shape that he would have to go anyway. There is, of course, the question as to whether McNaughton will come in. He has said to me that he could not enter a Cabinet that Ralston was a Member of and mentioned there were one or two other Ministers he could not very well work with. These are probably the other Defence Ministers. On the other hand it seems to me that we have focussed up to the point which now raises above all other questions whether Mc-Naughton or Ralston is right in the way in which our armed forces were disposed of. I feel that, if I offer McNaughton the position of Minister of Defence, he will see in this crisis two things particularly: one, the appalling situation which would be created in Canada if conscription were made an issue at this time, that his aim is like mine to preserve the unity of Canada above all else; and, two, that he will see a complete vindication of his own judgment and an opportunity of making that clear to all concerned. What I feel more important than all else is that he does not wish needless destruction of human life for the purpose of fame and glory. He will be able to take the position that too much is being asked of our men at the present time and also to give the assurance that the infantry line will never be left thin but neither will it be left too long drawn out, to use the words that Mackenzie had used.

"I had about made up my mind to get in touch with McNaughton before Council today so that I will know whether I can count on him if we are forced to a decision which Ralston is unwilling to accept. After reading Mackenzie's memo, I felt he was right in the advice he had tendered. Howe, some time ago, spoke to me about getting McNaughton. Gardiner said on Sunday night he thought I ought to send for McNaughton. Mackenzie now suggests McNaughton. My own thought was of him at the outset. I spoke of it to St. Laurent. He thought it might all be for the best. McNaughton has none of the enmity towards French Canadians which so many conscriptionists entertain. If he can be brought into the Government it will give confidence and I can repeat my determination not to have an election until the war is over, and will give confidence regarding the defence end. It will enable McNaughton to straighten out all that needs to be straightened out in the arrangements among the three services. Also I cannot see how it is going to be possible for me to carry on with winter planning for the war against the Japanese, with the three Defence Ministers working together and aided by Ilsley, against my judgment, as to what is wisest there. I might add that of the rest of the Cabinet."

The Prime Minister then telephoned General McNaughton. "I said to him I would like to have a confidential talk with him if that were convenient. He said, yes, Mr. King, at what time and place? I suggested 12.15 either at his house or at Laurier House. He thought Laurier House would be best. We then arranged for Laurier House but I changed the hour to 12.20 as I had to go to the osteopath."

When Mackenzie King returned from the osteopath, McNaughton was waiting for him. The Prime Minister recorded the interview in the following words: "I outlined to him in strict confidence the present situation. I began by saying to him I felt the need of his counsel and advice. What I was telling him was in absolute confidence and that I needed guidance with respect to some of the matters that had to be considered. Said I knew no one who could give it to me as well as himself.

"Without following the sequence he indicated to me that in his belief the kind of warfare was changing. That what was required now were guns and heavy ammunition. It was not so much fighting in the line as siege warfare which meant blasting out different cities and infantry falling in. He spoke of having always felt it was a mistake to divide the army and to have some of our men fighting in Italy as well as in northern Europe. That it was nonsense to talk about sending battalions there for training. That he felt officers should be sent and that they could give the men on their return all the training that was needed. That a great many men were used up in maintaining lengthy communications. What he thought should be done was to end the Italian campaign, so far as our men were concerned, and have them brought back and the army made one in Northern France. He agreed that the Canadian Army was not needed for the winning of the war. Also that it was questionable whether it was necessary to resort to conscription at this stage. That could not be decided without going very carefully into numbers of men, disposition, etc. He thought that Canada was perfectly free to make her own decisions as to what disposition should be made of her troops. She could take out divisions, or lessen their strength and certainly she should not allow her men to be too long in the line and fight too continuously and have too large commitments. They had cleared the Caen-Falaise areas. The Scheldt part would soon be cleared up. Time might then offer for resting some of the troops. He of course disagrees cordially with Ralston on some of the things he has done and he says he does not trust Stuart's judgment at all. It was mostly Stuart, he said, who was responsible for sending our men to Italy. He asked me if I knew they were months in Italy doing nothing. That they had not had what was required to fight with, etc.

"He also told me that Gen. Keller [commander until August 1944 of the 3rd Canadian Infantry Division] had told him in confidence that he did not like the way some of our troops had been disposed. Also that today there was not ammunition enough for continuous fighting. That the whole army was rationed in the matter of ammunition which meant they could only use so many rounds a day. That was a bad position in which to put large numbers of men. He said he hoped I would not let them stop the production of big guns as well as the explosives for them, that this had been stopped for a time. He hoped on every account it would be resumed. He did not favour paying the men extra time for their training, except as an act of grace. He thought the idea of a public appeal for enlistment was a wise one and should accomplish results."

Mackenzie King then told McNaughton about his opinion of Ralston's recommendation and something of General Stuart's report. "He said to me Stuart was quite wrong in making a recommendation as to policy. He agreed that reinforcements were not necessary for the winning of the war, and I spoke of our having been told in August that all was well and that we were under that impression throughout the Quebec Conference. . . . I then mentioned to him that I thought Ralston would resign and that I did not see any other person in sight but himself to take the position of Minister of Defence. That I believed if he were Minister he would be able to get things worked out in such a way that we would not need to resort to conscription for overseas service. He was strongly of the belief that the conscription issue in Canada would work irreparable harm. He believed that it might affect the Presidential elections in a real way and also that the Germans would, of course, construe a conscription election as evidence of the breaking up of the Empire and use it with their people for prolonged resistance. He thought it would work great harm in the years to come but he had great faith in the common sense of the Canadian people and believed that one had only to tell them the truth to get them to support any policy that was necessary.

". . . When I spoke about his coming into the Ministry, he immediately rose up off the sofa and stretched himself full length in front of the fireplace. Said there were one or two matters he would have to speak of in very great confidence. That he had told me very strong approaches had been made to him to go into one of the other parties. That McTague and Borden had pressed him very hard, and also Bracken."

McNaughton went on to say that "he had told Bracken that he had made up his mind to take on work other than that of a political nature. He would have to go and tell them quite frankly that an emergency had arisen and explain to them that if he came in, he was coming in only to help meet the emergency. That it was not a matter of Party with him but of service to the country at the time of great need. I told him, of course, that would be the right thing to do. He said that in all his conversations with them and with others, he had made clear he had only the highest opinion of myself and that we were very similar in our views. He added to me that he thought we were agreed on all the fundamentals and saw alike on them."

McNaughton then agreed that, if Ralston did resign, he would be at the Prime Minister's "disposition and prepared to take on the task. He said he would get rid of Stuart and Murchie. That Murchie had never taken part in any operations. He did not trust their judgment. He mentioned one or two other new men who had come over who he thought might be helpful. I told him I would be glad to be out altogether for a while. He said to me but you will have to stay at all costs. He said that I should not get out at this time. I said I would not so long as other situations would be saved. I then asked him about other members of the Cabinet; how he got along with Power and Angus Macdonald. He said very well with both; never had any differences with them and would get on well. I asked about Howe. He said he had been lunching with Howe yesterday. That they were very friendly. I told him that Howe had suggested to me at one stage to bring him in. That Mackenzie had said the same; Gardiner, the same. St. Laurent agreed it would be wise.

"He said at the elevator that if he came in, it would be a major sensation, a matter of world significance. He agreed any change in the Ministry would prove to be such so far as Defence was concerned.

"I asked who were the men he did not care for. He said he did not think much of Mackenzie's judgment but thought he was all right where he was. I told him that Mackenzie had told me when the Bill [to establish the Department of Veterans Affairs] was going through the House that if I wanted the position for McNaughton, he would be glad to let me have it. Also that he had himself suggested McNaughton's coming in as Minister of Defence. . . .

"McNaughton agreed nothing would be said about the matter until I saw him again but left with the understanding that I could definitely count on him."

Mackenzie King reported that, when he went into the Cabinet in the afternoon, he broke the silence by saying "I had said all I thought I should say and it would be better to leave it to Members of Council to speak. Again there was a long hesitation. Finally Mackenzie came out very forcibly about the whole thing being perfectly outrageous; our getting no information about the need for reinforcements until October 16." There was a good deal of discussion which led the Prime Minister to revise his estimate, now eight Ministers for conscription and thirteen against. "Ralston finally told the Cabinet what he thought his recommendation to Council must be. Started in that, after all he had heard in War Committee and

Council at the table, he felt that the N.R.M.A. men should be sent overseas. That to make up what was needed for providing reasonable reinforcements for the army. I thought that the motion he was putting was one that he intended to quote in Parliament or elsewhere. I drew his attention to the fact that no Member of the Cabinet had a right to reveal either directly or indirectly or by implication or otherwise, what had taken place in the Cabinet or War Committee. He expressed some surprise at this. This is illuminating.

"After he had said he would find it necessary to put that motion, he raised the question again about whether at the end of an appeal, we would say if an appeal were not successful, that conscription would be applied. I felt very strongly that it would be wrong to change our policy; that in the end, it would all come to the same kind of a fight. I said I thought what we should do in declaring policy was to simply say it was a policy that had carried us through 5 years successfully and which we believed could be carried through, namely, no conscription for overseas service unless necessary to win the war.

"I then spoke of the situation as I saw it. That I wanted to avoid an election in a time of war, in the interests of the men overseas and their families here. Above all, I wished to avoid an election on conscription. That I would not be a party to bringing on such an election if it could be avoided. For that reason, if Ralston found it necessary to resign or other colleagues, I would have to call Parliament together and ask for a vote of confidence. If that were carried, the Government would go on until the war was over provided it did not last beyond the termination of the life of Parliament. If it did not carry, I would resign but I hoped that a new government would be thereupon formed and that they would not find it necessary to go to the country while the war was on, but would carry on until the war was over. Of course, what they will want will be an election while the war is on to get the soldiers' votes and the votes of their relatives, etc.

"Angus Macdonald said if Ralston resigned he would have to consider his situation very carefully. Later in the discussion, he made it quite clear he could not face his people at Kingston or elsewhere after what he had said in the House on the plebiscite. It was quite apparent that he had intended to do this from the start.

"During the day, he talked about shortening of the line as an alternative to conscription but this was not followed up. It was clear it was not put forward to be pursued.

"Ilsley then said he could not do other than support getting reinforcements. Mulock had made his position the same in a word. Gibson did not say much but what he did say made clear what he intended to do.

"I then asked Ralston whether tonight, because of the division of the Cabinet, I should go to the Governor General and ask for him to send for Ralston. Would he take the responsibility of forming a government and carrying on. He said he would not. I asked Macdonald. He said he would not. I asked Ilsley. He said he would want time to decide. He could not decide in a minute. It is pretty clear he has it in mind he may be the one to be asked to form a Government. If he does, heaven help him and help the Government for he will go all to pieces in no time.

"Ralston said I could hardly go and resign while I had a majority of the Cabinet with me. I said to the Cabinet I hoped that as many of my colleagues as possible would continue to help me carry on if these other gentlemen resigned; that we must remember the King's Government had to be carried on. That it was important to remember that the war was on and that there would be further decisions to be made.

"I then thanked them all for their support in the years we had been together. I was rather hoping and expecting a decision might be finally made tonight. Michaud raised some point he wished to consider further and as it was half past eight or thereabouts, it was suggested we leave matters over until tomorrow. Have another meeting and definitely decide tomorrow afternoon what was to be done. I spoke about the date of calling Parliament together; suggested the 8th as sufficiently early date to meet Parliament. That it would not be wise to have the meeting on the 7th which was the day of the Presidential elections and that to take longer, might delay matters unduly. I think I mentioned that being asked what my intentions were about the election, I said we could carry on till the time of Parliament would be up. Ilsley asked would we have another, new session. I said I did not think of that. I thought we would wait for a week or so before announcing the date of the election. It could be put on just about the time of the expiration of the House. That meant we could stay on till the 17th of April if we wished and have an election during May or June, by which time there would likely be victory overseas and our chances of return would be good.

"My feeling at the moment and it was expressed in the Cabinet when Macdonald said he knew what Nova Scotia would do, if that was correct, that was one of the reasons we should avoid an election. We knew what Quebec would do. We knew what Ontario would do. We knew what the West would do. Nothing could be worse for Canada than have it broken up into blocks. Represented by opposing groups in Parliament.

"My feeling is that the gentlemen who think conscription will carry, will get a real surprise. It may carry in the House because some of our Members have since left and been appointed to office, but the majority will not be large and I question if under it, it would be possible to have conscription properly enforced or to carry on Government satisfactorily for long. The question I have had to ask myself tonight would be whether it would be wise to tender my resignation tomorrow on the score that practically all the Ministers of the War Committee and some of the others were deciding against me, and that I did not feel in these circumstances I could carry on the Government and ask that one of the conscriptionist Ministers be called upon. The first objection to that is that I owe it to those who stand by me to stand by them and for us to continue in office until Parliament votes lack of confidence in the position we are taking. The other thing is that I do not think I should hand over the Government to any conscriptionist until Parliament expresses want of confidence in me—hand over the opportunity of forming a Government and holding power, which can be used to further their ends in all respects. I think the right procedure would be to carry on, not accept some of the resignations of the Ministers until Parliament assembles and if that cannot be done, to fill up the positions with new Ministers. That I may have to do just before Parliament meets.

"In the event of conscription carrying, the responsibility would then be on the conscriptionists to go to the country. That is a responsibility I should not like. If they were to continue Government until the war was over and then brought on an election, I believe they would be defeated, and my position fully vindicated. What I shall do meanwhile remains to be seen."

The following morning (November 1) the Prime Minister telephoned General McNaughton, asking him to come at once to Laurier House. Mc-Naughton was shown in to the library when he arrived. "I moved the circular arm chair over to where his back would be to the light and not have it in his face. Took my usual position at the table. While waiting for him to come, I had written out what the procedure for the day should be and the policy of the Government as it would be referred to this afternoon in Council. I said to the General: well, we are I think now at the final stage. Matters now have narrowed down to this. That all are agreed on an appeal as a possible means of getting the necessary men; some, as probable. Ralston, not sure at all. However, he is prepared to have an appeal made but asks what is the Government's policy should it fail. Will we be prepared to add that if it fails, we will then pass an order-in-council extending the N.R.M.A., call Parliament together and pass it if need be by closure. My purpose is first to avoid an election in war-time, to avoid, above all else, an election which involves the issue of conscription at a time of war. The General interjected: you are perfectly right. I said further to avoid the necessity of having Parliament meet unless that was imperative. It would become imperative if Ralston were to resign and there was no one I could find to take his place. I do not think it would be necessary were you to take over the Department of Defence. I added that the object was to get the men necessary. I stated that I wanted to avoid the issue of conscription altogether. The General said: that is right. I am sure that is sound. I said my appeal is we should continue the policy that we now have and which is the mandate we received at the last election to carry on the war by voluntary enlistment for overseas. That legislation since enacted has made provision for possibility of using conscription. I thought that should all be left as it is because I was not yet persuaded that conscription was necessary.

"The General then said: what Ralston suggests is psychologically unsound. One should not cross a bridge until one comes to it. If an appeal is made and it does not succeed, the time to decide whether conscription is necessary or not, will be then. My view is that if the 'attendant circumstances' at the time and all matters related to the war and our armies in reference thereto should make it necessary, then conscription would have to be adopted. I said: General, let me make perfectly clear what I mean about the need for conscription. I have always used it in reference to the winning of the war, not in reference to keeping the army formations up to strength. I would not want to be understood as considering conscription as necessary in any other sense but if it were necessary to win the war, I would not hesitate to put it into force. The General replied: That is correct. I mean if the situation were such that we were in real danger, danger of the enemy getting the better of us. He did not use those words but something to that effect. It was equivalent to if there were a supreme necessity, that is what I mean. He had said earlier: this must be considered in relation to the unity of Canada and what conscription would mean for or against maintaining that unity. I made it clear [so] that there could be no mistake, that I would not consider conscription in any relationship other than that of the winning of the war. That was the interpretation that I had always given to it. The General said I would not regard the keeping of formations up to strength as a necessary thing.

"He went on to say for example our men had intensive fighting for some 58 days. I think that is wrong. I do not think our army is being used rightly. I think that the mistake which has been made is that there was a let-down in production of cannon, of big guns and ammunition for them. They are rationed on the ammunition and it looks to me as though men were being used in the infantry line to make up for the lack of ammunition and guns which was something I had pointed out as wholly necessary. There should be a week in and a week off. It is wrong that our men should be used at the pace they have been used, and that I think has been due to this cause. That they have not had the necessary artillery ammunition. I then said to him that he might like to read the communication of October the 14th which was in the nature of an appreciation dated September 27, by the military advisers in Britain on Germany's capacity to resist. When he read it through, he said that was pretty much the situation as he surmised it but mentioned some additional feature which he thought should have been taken into account.

"I then let him read the intercepted message [which indicated that the Japanese had learned the Germans considered the war had been lost]. McNaughton said he thought it described the situation well. I must not forget to mention that he stressed the fact that between now and a month hence when we would be committing ourselves to introduce conscription, the whole thing might greatly change, and the need be met in other ways or be entirely removed. That he felt was the strongest of reasons for not committing oneself to any course in the intervening time.

"I gave him Stuart's report. He went over to the window to stand and read it there. Asked if he might smoke. Found he could read better while smoking. At different places in the report, he pointed out there was evidence that the right judgment had not been used. He said it was clear there had been a let-down on some things because of over-optimism. He had sought to impress strongly against anything of the kind. He also referred again to the way our men were being unfairly used. Also where he [Stuart] said he would like to have sent so many infantry men to Italy. His comment was that this report has a good deal of 'I' in it. He thought it was not Stuart's business to recommend, but to let the situation be known to the administration.

"On remustering, he said there he thought a mistake had been made; that remustering was all right in certain circumstances but he felt that to take men out of the artillery and put them into the infantry because of their being short of artillery was evidence that there had been wrong planning. That really the artillery men would be more needed from now on. That they had departed from a sound procedure when they permitted that.

"He also asked what right Stuart had to indicate the form in which anticipated reinforcements would have to be secured. I drew McNaughton's attention to the words that 'anticipated reinforcements would be adequate to meet future requirements of this war against Germany.' I said that was a strange and pretty large order. It indicated lack of thought in preparation and if it was to be taken literally, it ruled out altogether doing anything to meet that end as it was not the end we had in view. McNaughton agreed strongly with this. He went on to say that what it seemed to him was needed was a thorough housecleaning. That one would have to make a careful study before taking any particular steps."

At this point, the Prime Minister said: "General, the time has come, I think, for me to ask you to become Minister of National Defence, having the supervision over all the Defence Departments as well as the army side. I said I think this should be done immediately. Every hour is important. Ralston will probably tender his resignation this afternoon. I will take it to the Governor General. Ask him to accept it and will return to the Cabinet letting them know of the action taken. I will at the same time tell the Governor General I propose to recommend your appointment. . . . I would then pass an order-in-council appointing you and would then ask you to come with me to Government House to be sworn in. After the swearing in, we might return to my office and I will have the press meet us there. We need not say more than that Ralston has resigned and that you are taking over the position of Minister of Defence. They will probably ask some questions. You can deal with them as you think best. The General said: along the line that we have been talking this morning.

"Before I had spoken of meeting the press together, the General had said: yes, I should say that the situation was a very serious one. He believed it could be met I think he added 'without conscription' but I would not refer to conscription in what I have to say.

"When I had finished that statement, the General said: very well, I will be at your disposal. I said to him that it would probably be between 4 and 6 when I would call for him.

"Other things mentioned in conversation were, first, that he would want to go into everything very thoroughly himself. That he did not trust Stuart. That some of the recommendations Stuart had made had been contrary to his views and he thought mistakes had arisen from them. I said to him I hoped he would be considerate of Murchie. I thought Murchie was really trying to be helpful. He said Murchie had had no experience. He had given him a chance to take over a brigade, to get practical experience, but Stuart had immediately snapped him up and brought him to Ottawa so that he would have his man here. That he did not think Murchie was the right person. The Minister must have confidence in those he is working with. He said: fortunately there are two men who have just come out and who are both very good men. He thought they were persons he had confidence in. He spoke of the Ordnance Department and said there might have to be a change but he would see.

"We talked of the numbers. He said it was ridiculous there should be such a large number of G.S. men; that headquarters here was full of people that were doing nothing. The same was true throughout Canada; on the so-called 'Zombie' situation, he said that is a problem. It will have to be dealt with but the thing to do is to get them at work somewhere. In England, he said, I kept my men working at building aerodromes and the like. There is important work to be done here which they could be employed on but these problems have to be broken up into their component parts and dealt with one by one. Other things may have been said that I will think of later.

"As we were going downstairs, I drew the General's attention to the statement which appeared in the press this morning in which Bracken had said there was no difference between Drew and himself. They were a united party. The General expressed amazement at it. Said he could not understand what Bracken meant. The General had told me yesterday he regarded Drew as the most dangerous man in Canada.

"He then said to me he would speak to McTague and Borden after he had been sworn in telling them why he had gone in as the situation was an emergency."

As soon as General McNaughton left, Mackenzie King went to Government House to see the Governor-General. After some preliminaries he told the Governor-General that "we were having a pretty trying time, that we had had steady meetings of the Cabinet, carried on till pretty late on in the evenings. We were now to the point where all were agreed upon an appeal. Ralston was asking that we should declare that if the appeal were not successful within a certain time we would resort to passing an order-in-council extending N.R.M.A. Others were taking the same position. I was taking the position that we should follow just as we have right along the effort to get men. Make the appeal and if at the end of it we were not successful, then would be the time to decide what the next step would be. I thought Ralston would not accept this and that being so I would come down this afternoon to ask His Excellency to accept his resignation. I said Macdonald had said if Ralston left he would have to consider resigning, and Ilsley said he would also have to resign. He gave a strange reason, that he could not face the people of Nova Scotia with both Angus Macdonald and Ralston out, without joining with them.

"I said that if these Ministers did resign, I would ask His Excellency not to accept their resignations, at least until Parliament had been called and the matter discussed there. I repeated that what I wanted was to avoid an election in wartime and, above all, an election on conscription, and that I must take every possible means to do that."

Then Mackenzie King dropped his bombshell. "When I ask you to accept Ralston's resignation, I will also recommend for appointment General McNaughton as Minister of Defence. His Excellency's face coloured up and explained that I had said something that filled him for the moment with consternation, though he kept quite silent. He then asked me: What made you think of McNaughton? I said I had not talked with him about military matters when I had discussed the other post with him, which I have told His Excellency about, but it seemed to me he was the one person who possessed the knowledge that was required to meet the situation successfully.

"His Excellency asked me whether McNaughton had a following in Quebec. I told him I thought McNaughton had always been a friend of Quebec, and speaking of that, LaFlèche had said yesterday in Council that he would gamble his seat he would be able to get the men that were needed in Quebec. I then went on to say that I had spoken to McNaughton for the first time yesterday, when I saw that I was faced with the necessity of getting a new Minister of Defence. That we could not get along further and that, unless I was successful, it would create a desperate situation in the country. I then told His Excellency something of the talk I had had with McNaughton, only mentioning a few points but stressing that he was quite positive he would be able to meet the situation short of conscription by methods that he would propose, and what he felt about the changing nature of the war, etc. His Excellency agreed that he would approve of McNaughton as a Minister and I then said I expected to be down around 4 and would have to come down first with Ralston and his resignation, then would return and pass the order appointing McNaughton and then would bring McNaughton to be sworn in. When I was saying good-bye His Excellency said: I will see you then this afternoon."

When the Prime Minister returned to Laurier House, he began to rally support, first telephoning Mulock "telling him to think carefully about not committing himself too much in Council today. To wait and see what I had in mind which I thought would meet the situation. He said he was quite agreeable. He told me he had given Turnbull [Walter Turnbull, Principal Secretary to the Prime Minister] a note which he thought perhaps might help the situation.

"I then spoke to Claxton who was not too sure that the other Ministers could not walk out on a constitutional position, if they wished to. I told him I was positive that accepting an office under the Crown one was obliged to serve the King. That they would have to consider a request and remain long enough, at least, to help to meet the situation. Claxton sent me a note later urging pressing matters further."

Crerar was asked, also by telephone, "to please be considerate in his attitude and not say anything committing himself as to what he will do if certain people did certain things. His reply was wholly evasive. He did not want to disturb the ship. Certainly would consider very seriously any representations that might be made. Would be interested in seeing them, etc."

When the Prime Minister arrived at the East Block that afternoon he went "almost immediately into Council without a word with anyone. At Council, I found most of the Ministers but not Ralston, Macdonald or Ilsley. I went back to my room and sent for Mr. St. Laurent. Told him I had at last found a way out. Then mentioned that McNaughton had consented to come into the Government and believed that he will be able to secure the necessary reinforcements without any resort to conscription. I mentioned his statement about our troops being given far too much heavy fighting. That he believed casualties were due in part to infantry being obliged to make up in fighting for what the artillery was short in the way of shells and guns. St. Laurent's piercing eyes looked straight ahead and [he] said he wondered what Macdonald and Ilsley might do. He asked me if I had had a talk with Ilsley. I said no. I thought it was best not to say anything to anyone until we were in Council. Word came that all the Ministers were present and I then went into the Cabinet.

"After taking my seat, I asked if they had been discussing any matter. Ralston said he had something he would like to have approved. He then read a message from headquarters overseas regarding paying tradesmen's rate to some petty officers who were reverting to the rank of privates. Apparently that step has already been taken but the authority has not been approved by the Cabinet. It was given without any discussion by Ilsley or others.

"I then asked if there was anything further which related to where we left off last night. I was going to sum up the position at once, expecting that matters would be brought quickly to a head. Ralston said he did not know why he should begin, but he did begin, in an extremely moderate and mild way. He said he and Macdonald and Stuart had been going over figures again to see what further men could be secured. What was being done with regard to the officers was mentioned as one thing. There was then the question of what might be secured by an appeal. Ralston suggested that Angus Macdonald might give the particulars. Angus Macdonald then said he had phoned General Pearkes at noon, to B.C., regarding an appeal. Pearkes thought that it would not be wise for the Prime Minister himself to address the camps, in case numbers were not secured, it might reflect on him. That the Minister of Defence might speak, and some others. They had not been addressed by civilians. Both the chaplains and others had spoken. He said that the Prime Minister might make a broadcast from Ottawa. His estimate was that some 2,500 might be secured. He gave the reasons why men not likely to respond. First: some thought war nearly over and were not needed. Others, thought they had already been badly treated and were snubbed. Some said they might be ready to go if ordered. Pearkes said that they would not likely enlist in a large body but would get into groups. Groups would decide. These were the men who had done so well at Kiska and had shown a readiness to fight there. He had not thought that it would be advisable to state that conscription would follow if they did not respond. Thought it might take two or three weeks to get the numbers he had spoken of.

"This was all a surprise to me. What I commented on particularly was the fact that apparently this information had not been sought until today and that we had been led to believe days ago that the situation had been combed over and that we had the last word. I could not understand how we should have been given the earlier figures as the last figures and yet, apparently, it was not until today that the Commander of the largest camp had been asked what he thought could be done. However, I did not press that unduly.

"There was mention of one or two other things we had already discussed. Little was said of that. Macdonald was as conciliatory as possible and put forward, while Ralston was out of the room, what he thought Ralston was prepared to consider in further ways. I asked a couple of times what would be expected by way of policy. Ralston wanted to know last night if we did not get the men so many weeks hence would we not then agree among ourselves or state that we would resort to conscription. I said that I thought our statement of policy should be that we would continue to carry out the mandate given us by the people—no conscription for overseas. That, as to it being necessary, there still remained the question of whether necessary to keep the army up to strength or necessary to win the war. Ilsley read from a speech of mine in which I had used the word 'maintain.' It is the one that Ralston has had his finger on right along. I said I agreed that the necessary reinforcements should be found but I still believed they could be found voluntarily to the extent of 'maintaining' the army. That meant doing what was necessary in the way of supplying reinforcements, having relation to all phases of the situation, I was prepared to agree to that. That I had never thought of anything else, as reference to other parts of my speech would show. They kept pressing for what was being asked for in that way. I noticed that Ralston was particularly careful not to finally say that we would have to undertake to resort to conscription. They asked me what we would do. I said as to resorting to conscription I did not rule that out if the necessity were there in the terms in which I had described necessity in my speech, but that I did not think we should cross that bridge until we reached it. We could consider it when that time came; the argument about the urgency of the troops starting at once was then touched on but not pressed."

After some further discussion, Mackenzie King noted that one of his colleagues had "spoken of his foreseeing a situation and being right in the end." He added that he then said: "I think I can call to mind of Council where I proved that I had that power to a certain degree. You will recall how in our caucuses, when I was speaking about waiting for the last term of Parliament, there would be endless kinds of demands which it would be very hard to meet. That in regard to conscription I felt that I must be prepared to face what Sir Wilfrid had to face over conscription. After what was said by certain of my colleagues last night of what would follow I realized that I had to face being crucified by some of my own Party because I would not yield to conscription. I came back to what I said about no election during the war. That I wanted to avoid particularly an election on conscription and in that connection to avoid even having to call Parliament. I kept reiterating that I believed we could still get the men if we were prepared to take the most effective means."

At about 6.00 P.M. the discussion had narrowed down "pretty much to the one point of an agreement on the question of conscription in certain circumstances among ourselves. I said that still leaves open what we mean by the necessity for conscription and I thought we should clear that up. Ralston said there was a fundamental difference between us. He thought the decision on that was already made by Council. It was apparent that most of them were against conscription at any time.

"I had been quite frank in stating the position I took. However, different things had to be mentioned, particularly the question of adopting the course of an appeal, which he was prepared to consider further. He spoke of taking tonight to think it over. This was so different from his previous attitude as to the necessity of not losing a day that I said to myself at once: here is a scheme to make the situation still more difficult for me. We will be met tomorrow by some condition of things which will mean going over the same ground again to no effect. At the time I was too much concentrated on what I was about to say to think of what was really being planned, but I am convinced now that what was intended was that, in the morning, all these things would be united together, including my appeal, Ralston's readiness to speak, etc., and then everything limited down to the smallest point, which would go to show that I was not willing even secretly among ourselves to give an undertaking. That if there was a failure to secure the necessary reinforcements I would not then allow a reference to Parliament. The moment I sensed this I felt the time had come for me to speak out. I kept waiting, expecting Ralston would repeat what he had said, that he would have to resign unless so and so were done. When I saw that, I felt that the situation would be worse tomorrow if I did not speak.

"I then said I thought we ought to, if possible, reach a conclusion without further delay; that I had been told each day that an hour's delay would prejudice the securing of men; I did not see we would get any further by not getting an understanding at once. After what was said last night I realized that some way would have to be found, if it could be found, to save the government and to save a terrible division at this time, and at the same time make sure of getting reinforcements if that was possible at all. That I had been asking myself was there anyone who could do this; who believed that our policy, which had worked successfully for five years, would now work for the remaining weeks or months of the war. If there was, I thought it was owing to the country that such a person's services should be secured. I said I believed I had the man who could undertake that task and carry it out. I then mentioned General McNaughton's name and said that there was no man [about] whom the troops overseas would feel their interests were being more taken care of than McNaughton. That there was no man toward whom the mothers and fathers throughout this country would have the same feeling more strongly; that there was no man in whom the citizens of Canada as a whole would have greater confidence for a task of the kind. McNaughton had taken no part in politics; was not a Liberal, a Conservative, or C.C.F., though he was very liberal-minded and very liberal in his policies. There was a difference between a campaign being started by a man who had little faith in what could be accomplished and by one who believed if he put his heart into it he could secure results. Ralston had said that while he was prepared to speak he did not think it would be of much effect. That I knew McNaughton felt otherwise; that he believed that [if it were] tackled in the right way he himself could find the men necessary for reinforcements by the voluntary method.

"I then said I knew this because I had felt I must, as soon as possible, find someone who would undertake this task; that I should find out as soon as possible whether McNaughton would be willing to undertake it. I said I had talked with him this morning and I had an assurance from him that he thought we could get the reinforcements without resorting to conscription; that he thought conscription would be disastrous for Canada; that he knew the French-Canadians. Crerar had referred to the whole campaign centring on the hatred of French-Canadians, because of the so-called Zombie army and spoke about the whole situation being a flame across the country. I said McNaughton knew the French-Canadians and knew the prejudice that was being worked up. It would be a terrible thing for Canada if this was being permitted and if we had one province against the other. He was a strong believer in Canadian unity and believed the unity of Canada could be maintained, but not with conscription as an issue. That an attempt at this stage to do anything of the kind would have an appalling effect through years to come. I said that he believed he could get the reinforcements that were necessary. I pointed out that he believed our men were being given an undue share of fighting, being pressed too hard; indeed, their lives were being unnecessarily sacrificed because of the extent of infantry fighting, resulting from the inadequate munitions and shells for guns, and guns themselves. I had spoken of this yesterday and Ralston had made some statement in regard to it to the effect that the infantry had never been without plenty of ammunition. I said further that McNaughton thought that Drew was the greatest menace to Canada of any man in the country; that linking up with him on conscription would be a terrible thing. I said this whole business had come up since Drew had started his agitation.

"I then said that the people of Canada would say that McNaughton was the right man for the task, and since Ralston had clearly said that he himself did not believe we could get the men without conscription, while McNaughton believed we could, and that he, Ralston, would have to tender his resignation, as he had said at different times he would do if we pressed eliminating the conscription part; that I thought if Ralston felt in that way, he should make it possible for us to bring McNaughton into the Cabinet at once—the man who was prepared to see this situation through. I said that in regard to a resignation from Ralston, he had tendered his resignation to me some two years ago and had never withdrawn it; that that had been a very trying thing for me to go on day in and day out for this period with this resignation not withdrawn, but simply held. I then drew attention to the fact that no one could say that McNaughton was not the best person who could be secured. I drew from my pockets the exchange of letters, as printed, in September last, in which there is a statement that they have not seen eye to eye on some matters, but each shared the belief in the other's sincerity of conviction. I read the passage in which Ralston had made plain what McNaughton had done in training, etc.; his great skill, and certainty of his desire to serve Canada. I said there could be no misunderstanding as to McNaughton's qualifications.

"I then pointed out that the hardest thing for any man to do was to part with a colleague, especially one who had been as close as Ralston had been, and of whom one had such high respect and, indeed, affection; but that these were times of war, the worst war the world had ever known. The situation particularly dangerous and that when it came to a government going under at this time, with all the consequences that that would produce in Canada and other parts of the world, I said I felt no man could allow satisfying his own conscience in carrying out what he had said to outweigh what his conscience must tell him would be the consequences for ill, of what he owed to the army and to the country and to the war effort. Ralston had taken up the words Canada's war effort as used by Crerar. He said that that was what he wanted to further. I pointed out that instead of furthering it [conscription] would destroy the total effort, destroy it in reference to finance and other things. I concluded by saying that I thought we ought not to allow this situation to drag on at all. The strongest of reasons had been given repeatedly why it should not, and that I thought we should decide at once what was to be done. There was intense silence.

"Then Ralston spoke very quietly. He said that he would of course give me his resignation at once. He wished to thank me for the opportunity given him to serve. I had referred to having asked Ralston long ago to come into the Cabinet; that he had made great sacrifices. I had asked him before the war. He had said he could not, but if the war came, he would, and he did immediately. That I did not think any man had served the country more faithfully in every way or given the best of everything he had. Ralston went on to say that he had done the best he possibly could. He knew he was limited in some things, but he had done his best. He spoke of the companionship we had enjoyed and what it meant to share in the work with his colleagues; that he sincerely hoped the new Minister—I forgot how he referred to him—I think he said the new move—might be successful. He was not sure that it would be but he certainly hoped it would. He ended by saying that he would retire to private life.

"I replied that no words could express what we felt of his integrity, service, and the like; that it would be mere heroics to use any words regarding what we all knew so well. This was not a personal matter; it was what the situation at the moment seemed to demand. I thanked him for all he had done, and again expressed how hard it was for me to say what I felt I had to say in the interests of Canada's war effort.

"Ralston then gathered up his papers and turned to me and shook hands. I have forgotten what he said. I think it was: he thanked me for the opportunity he had had. All the Cabinet rose, formed a complete circle around the table, and shook hands with him. As he was going out of the door I called to him that I wanted to have just a further word. I had spoken of the desirability of having the new appointment made at the same time as Ralston's resignation was accepted. I hoped that might be done this evening and have the matter cleared up today. At the door, I asked him whether it would be possible to let me have his resignation tonight. He had said he would write out his resignation. He looked very anxious and strained and said could he have until the morning. I said by all means but to please say nothing about it to anyone; to keep the matter wholly secret and confidential, until the other appointment was made. This he said he would do."

With Ralston gone, the Prime Minister returned to his seat "and repeated to Council that it was one of the hardest things I had to do in my life, but that it was the only course I could see for me which would serve to meet the war situation. I then repeated that I felt every confidence that McNaughton would be able to get the reinforcements. I repeated then what I had said earlier that I had spoken to him about the Cabinet personnel and had asked if there was any man in the Cabinet he could not work with. I said I thought he knew practically all the Members of the Cabinet and he replied he was close friends with most of them. He had spoken particularly of knowing so well both Macdonald, of the Navy, and Power, of the Air. Power, by the way, was not there. Howe also was not there, he is at Chicago. McNaughton told me he had been lunching a day or two ago with Howe and they were great friends. He had tremendous admiration for his work. Howe was really consulting him on aspects of it. I said he had already referred to Ilsley and his tremendous work in finance and said that if he could help in any way all together that was what he wanted to do. I mentioned he was not coming in in any political relationship or capacity but simply to do a job. This, when he felt it was a time of emergency and in the national interests to perform it if he were asked. There was again no comment at all.

"I mentioned what I had said to Ralston about his resignation and said in Council I thought it would be better if we adjourned until eleven tomorrow morning. I swore the Council to absolute secrecy on what had been said. It was a scene I shall never forget, nor will those who were present."

Mackenzie King had had a telephone call made to Government House to say he would not be there before six o'clock but about 5.00 P.M. he telephoned McNaughton to say there would probably be no decision until late in the evening. "Later, after six, I 'phoned to let him know the first step had been taken, and Council would meet tomorrow, and that I would be coming down for him between eleven and twelve. I said I had spoken of him and the Ministers all knew whom I was going to recommend.

"I then went to Government House. Told His Excellency of the afternoon's proceedings and why I had taken so long, by allowing previous discussion to proceed, but finally feeling it necessary to bring matters to a conclusion and the steps I had taken in that connection. It was apparent from His Excellency's face and manner that while he was saying nothing he was greatly concerned. I think his mind related all the time to the trouble there had been with McNaughton in Britain and the effect this might have on the High Command there. In this connection I am glad I let Churchill know in advance that there might be very serious repercussions. His reply to my wire fully justified me in going ahead as he said he would prefer me to act without any reference to himself and do what I could to meet the situation. There would have been a terrible row if I had not got some word to him before taking the present step.

"Whatever His Excellency said of McNaughton was very nice but it was not enthusiastic. He asked me if he might send word to the King; said he would like to get the word over as soon as possible. I said certainly, but I hoped great care would be taken to make sure nothing came from any source in London about it; that the danger was with secretaries, stenographers, etc., newspapers had their friends, and there might be some leakage. If the message came to Canada via Britain it would do great harm and I did not want any leakage on any account. He spoke of the press being terribly troublesome. Said they picked up little words and put on their own construction. I said it was most important this should be held until McNaughton was in office.

"As I dictate, I shall be amazed if the morning papers do not have something of what has taken place. Even if they do, however, it cannot alter the situation as it now exists. My greatest concern has been over the attitude that Macdonald and Ilsley may take. They will wish to resign on Ralston's account and yet I do not see how they can possibly take that ground with McNaughton coming in. It would be a declaration of want of confidence in McNaughton, which would put them in a terrible position. The fact that McNaughton is coming in to protect Canada's army and to get reinforcements will make it impossible for any member of the Government not to seek to work with him at this time, though they will probably continue to watch for an opportunity to get even with me. While I acquit Ralston of any deliberate attempt to destroy the Government, I know that behind him there have been forces that have brought this situation about—deliberately planned it to destroy myself and the Government. There is plenty of circumstantial evidence to make that as clear as day. They are the same forces that do not want social legislation. They are going to have a hard time attacking McNaughton's appointment, because they have been lauding him to the sky and seeking to have it appear that our Government have not treated him fairly. In military circles McNaughton has many friends. I am afraid Ralston does not begin to have anything like the following McNaughton has in that relationship. There will be consternation overseas, for McNaughton has his views about the whole planning of the campaign. Of course it is a terrific blow to Ralston. He has been more afraid of McNaughton than anyone. At times, when I have been trying to keep the peace between them, he has been ashen pale in his fear, lest I might be siding with McNaughton. This will give McNaughton the chance to get the Canadian army together as one. It will give him a chance for much else. He will be a fine Minister of Defence to welcome back the men and will get tremendous ovation from them wherever he appears. While I am deeply sorry to offend Ralston in any way, I cannot forget that he was prepared to have me and the Government destroyed politically.

"Last night, while unable to sleep, I was thinking of a possible new alignment of parties that might follow what seemed to be an inevitable cleavage—some Liberals and Tories coming into a new Tory party; other Liberals joining with the C.C.F. I came to the conclusion that I would not [form a] coalition with any party but would continue to hold the Liberal party as one to save Canada. I think this step will greatly strengthen my position; it will be a knock-out blow to Bracken and his Tory friends in their endeavour to secure McNaughton. The C.C.F. and Labour have been after him as well.

"Altogether I think, in truth, only Providence could have brought all things together to work as one at this moment. There has never been an appointment made in a very difficult situation which so completely . . . destroyed the plans of those who were seeking to destroy the Government or determined to have things their own way. . . . I am tremendously relieved tonight at the thought of not having to have Parliament for the present at least. I am not by any means certain what Ilsley or Macdonald may do. They are the only two that I am concerned about. Gibson, Mulock, Crerar and one or two others cannot take exception. If Macdonald and Ilsley should resign, which I cannot believe they will, I think Ilsley will realize the position he would be in for taking that step, with McNaughton coming in—I will at once find the best men I can for their posts. It is necessary at a time like the present to let the Members of the Cabinet know that a Prime Minister's voice counts for something. It has been providential that Howe has been away. Had he been here he would have joined with those who were saying that we must find reinforcements though only a few weeks ago, he was the one who said to me: why do you not get rid of Ralston and get McNaughton to take his place. He is the man to save the situation. I was well pleased too that Power was not there. He would have been in a very difficult position in trying to square himself with the other Ministers of Defence."

He added that "Angus Macdonald had given the impression of trying to go very far to help all he can and has done well but I realize that behind it there has always been the laying of the ground for his leaving the Government on the score of conscription along with Ralston and embarrassing the Government as a consequence—not in desire, but in effect."

The next morning (Thursday, November 2) Mackenzie King was not surprised when he saw the headline on the Ottawa *Citizen* that Colonel Ralston had resigned and beneath it speculation that General McNaughton would succeed him. "I immediately began to rebuke myself for not having passed the order-in-council accepting Colonel Ralston's resignation without at the same time having recommended the appointment of General McNaughton as his successor so that announcements would be made simultaneously. My reason was first that I did not wish to act so summarily in parting with an old colleague. The second was that I felt it was necessary that to appearances as well as in reality the Governor General as the King's representative should be consulted first and his approval given of the appointment of one of his Ministers. I had also in mind the desirability of having Colonel Ralston's letter of resignation and that I might have the letter and the reply before taking any action.

"On seeing the headlines in the press, particularly on the radio, which stated that Colonel Ralston had resigned but when McNaughton was questioned he said he knew nothing of the matter or some words to that effect (he was right in not allowing any statement to be made as to Ralston's resignation or his appointment until matters had been officially settled), I felt that it put emphasis in the wrong place. This, of course, I had asked all members of Council to be perfectly silent about but I should have realized in one way or another the matter was bound to get out. I blame myself considerably for this. One thing that surprised me very much was that it was clear someone in the Cabinet had been talking as there was reference to my having said that I had had Colonel Ralston's resignation in my hands for two years. That is something that was said only in the Cabinet and would not otherwise be known. It is appalling how Ministers pay so little attention to their oaths of office."

That morning Mackenzie King arrived at the East Block about 10.40. He had already had a message from Ralston that his letter of resignation would be coming very shortly. "The letter," he wrote, "did not arrive until after I was in Council and was brought by the Council messenger and placed before me after I had signed the order-in-council and was about to leave for Government House. In fact, I had without noticing it, left the letter at my place at the Council table. Sent Arnold Heeney back to secure it for me. He gave it to me in the ante-room unopened.

"After reaching the office, I sent for Robertson. Gave him a bare outline of what had taken place both as regards Ralston's resignation and McNaughton's appointment. When I saw it was 11 on my clock, I said I must go at once to the Cabinet. As I was going in, the clock had begun to strike the quarter hours. The Ministers had not all assembled but among those present were Dr. King, Mitchell, Mackenzie, Claxton, St. Laurent and I think Michaud. Possibly one or two others. They kept coming in while I was speaking and I met some in the corridor after I was on my way out.

"As I took my seat with the 3 orders before me, one accepting Ralston's resignation, one making McNaughton a Privy Councillor, and the other appointing him a Minister of the Crown, I heard the clock begin to strike 11. I decided to say nothing until after the strokes of the clock had ceased. I waited for a few seconds longer and said to my colleagues that when we adjourned last night it was understood that nothing would be said about what had taken place yesterday but I see the morning papers have the announcement of Ralston's resignation and a surmise of McNaughton's appointment. I was most anxious that both announcements should be made simultaneously. I had intended as I stated to have the Cabinet come back a little later in the evening so that the whole matter could be cleared up in the one day but did not carry this out first as I did not like, immediately after parting with an old colleague, to make the appointment of a new one in great haste. Also in the case of the appointment of a Minister of the Crown, the Prime Minister must obtain the approval of the sovereign or his representative. . . . That I wished therefore to go to Government House and to learn of His Excellency's approval of the recommendation to appoint General McNaughton before the recommendation itself was made. This I have done. His Excellency is prepared to approve of the recommendation of General McNaughton and I feel therefore that no time should be lost in having the appointment made. I propose therefore now to sign the 3 recommendations. Having signed them, I said I assume that these recommendations meet with the approval of the Cabinet. There was no dissent but rather a nodding of assent on the part of those that I could see, and I put them formally in the right hand box for the Clerk to gather up."

Angus Macdonald came in while the Prime Minister was speaking. "I paused when he did and then repeated what I was saying about the necessity of the Governor General giving approval of the appointment of a Minister before presenting the recommendation. That I was letting my colleagues know that I had obtained this approval. Macdonald nodded his assent. Ilsley was not present. I did not attach any significance to that. As a rule, I, myself, am late for Council.

"I then said that I thought I should go immediately to Government House and have McNaughton sworn in at once. Suggested that the Ministers should remain taking up any business meanwhile and that as soon as he was sworn, I would bring him back to the Cabinet so that we could all meet him."

Mackenzie King then picked up McNaughton at his house and drove him to Government House to be sworn in. On the way back to the East Block Mackenzie King said to McNaughton "I hoped he would make it a point of speaking particularly to Angus Macdonald and Ilsley. That I knew they felt a great loyalty for Ralston and might feel some concern on that account but I thought his coming into the Cabinet would make all the difference and would help to remove the concern that they otherwise would have had. Of not being sure as to adequate reinforcements being secured. I also spoke of Power unfortunately having found the strain too great and of himself being in a very difficult position in regard to Ralston. . . .

"When we reached the East Block, many reporters were gathered there. As we had come out of Government House door, two reporters were there. They stopped and asked me if I had any statement to give out. I said: no. In fact, they had met me as I was leaving to drive to Government House and asked the same question. I said there was no statement at present. The direct question was asked: had General McNaughton been sworn. I said I had nothing further to say.

"At the East Block, reporters were gathering in numbers. I said: we will just go in—without any other word. However someone went ahead and took a flash. I said to the men that I was taking General McNaughton to meet my colleagues and that I would be pleased if they would come to my room later. They could then meet the General. They asked how long it would be. I said: about 10 minutes.

"The General left his hat and coat in my room and we went into the Council Chamber. On the way, I looked at the little room and saw some of them there so went in by the other door. At that moment it struck me that I should have sent word in advance so that all would be seated when we came in. On reflection it was just as well there were no formalities observed at that moment. McNaughton at once shook hands with those in the room and gradually Council assembled. I asked McNaughton to sit to my left without mentioning it was the place that Ralston had. I then spoke briefly to the Cabinet saying that McNaughton had been sworn in at Government House and extended a great welcome to him to the Cabinet. That I wanted to say how grateful we were to him for assuming the great responsibility of Defence Minister at this time and how grateful I felt to him for so doing. I said he would meet many old friends here. I then spoke of the meeting of Council which we had had last night and of it being a painful act for me to have to accept the resignation of a colleague who was a close and intimate friend and as helpful in all ways as Colonel Ralston had been. That the difference had arisen as he knew over what was necessary at this time and I thought it was entirely due to his feeling that there should be no inconsistency in his attitude. That I need not say that everything that had been done, had been done from conviction. I said I want you to know, General, how deeply we all feel at having had to part with Ralston. That every member of the Cabinet had a deep affection for him and that we all knew his action was based on the highest integrity and principle. I have forgotten some other things I said but when I had concluded, others present waited to hear what McNaughton might say."

The Prime Minister was delighted by McNaughton's speech. "He could not possibly have said words more completely satisfying and convincing. He referred to the pleasure it was to him to meet so many old friends and thanked me for the honour that had been given him of joining with all of us at this time. He said he was perfectly sure in his own mind that he understood the situation completely and that it could be met satisfactorily. That of course his purpose was above everything else to see that the war effort was kept up to full strength. That the needs of the army were fully met. That he believed this could be done without any resort to compulsion. From the beginning he had recognized that the manpower problem was an important one and that the entire army had been fashioned in the light of studies which he had made over a period of 20 years, of the manpower problem, so as to avoid any necessity of compulsion arising. He spoke as a man with authority and knowledge, wisdom and understanding. I think he made a profound impression on everyone, and I am sure gave both Macdonald and Ilsley a feeling of confidence, and I could see joy and relief in the faces of all the Ministers.

"We then spoke about the next meeting of Council which I had said might come tomorrow afternoon but would depend on what the General felt. I am inclined to leave it until next week if all goes well. I left it to tomorrow to see whether any other words might come.

"The General and I then went on to my room. I had the press come in. Before speaking, said I would not allow any photographs or questioning to take place. I then said a few words which are to appear in the press, beginning by saying that what had appeared this morning as to Ralston's resignation was correct. Told them of securing McNaughton that morning and of being grateful to him for assuming the responsibilities of Minister at this time. I was asked if there was any statement to be issued. I said: Not at present. I was then asked about Ralston's resignation. I told them it had been made in Cabinet in the presence of members and accepted there. They wanted to know about a letter of resignation. I said it was not necessary to have a letter of resignation but that a Minister, of course, was free to make a statement in writing. That I had received a letter from Colonel Ralston but not until after Council had met and I was on my way to Government House. I had not, as a matter of fact, had time to read the letter and drew the envelope from my pocket. They wanted to know if Parliament would meet. I said I saw no necessity for that. I was asked about what the differences were. I declined to be drawn into anything beyond saying that the facts spoke for themselves."

The Prime Minister and McNaughton then walked down to the Defence Department and to Ralston's office. "Ralston," he wrote, "was there alone at the time. He had just been arranging to have a meeting with his officers to explain to them the situation and to say good-bye to them. I shook his hand quite warmly when I went in and McNaughton came in and they both shook hands in a very friendly way. I explained to the Colonel that McNaughton had been sworn at Government House. We had since been up to the Cabinet. That Angus had been there when I had spoken in the morning. Then I referred to the press having made the statement they had. . . . He said he had not seen the papers. They had been trying to get to him. He refused to see anyone. . . .

"I explained to him about his letter not having been received until after I had signed the order just as I was leaving to go to Government House but pointed out that the letter was not necessary at all. That the resignation had taken place yesterday and been accepted in the presence of the Cabinet. I would, however, send him an answer later.

"We talked a little longer and I asked at once if they could send for my car. When I thought it had come, . . . I said I would leave the General with Ralston. In the meantime, Ralston and I had a little talk in which I said to him I felt so sorry that we were not to be together. That I hoped it was only temporary. He replied he had 'phoned to his law firm in Montreal and was going back to practice. He had also 'phoned his constituency to say he would go down to explain to them the position. That his wife had said she did not want him to be back in Parliament. I said: Oh no. He must stay in Parliament. (It just occurs to me he may be glad to be out of the House when discussion comes up and may resign his membership of the constituency. This would render it impossible for him to be in the House.)

"I am not sure what the constitutional practice is on matters of resignation in that way but I assume he could, if he wished, resign at once though I would prefer to have him stay on though foregoing nomination for the next Parliament. I was thinking that I could not but envy him the freedom that he now has. In fact I think I said that to him. He then came with me to the front door."

During the afternoon, Mackenzie King received word that C. G. Power had been taken to the Hôtel Dieu Hospital in Quebec that morning and had undergone an operation for appendicitis.

The next day (November 3) McNaughton saw the Prime Minister to report on what he had learned in the Defence Department. Mackenzie King wrote that "when he came in, he said that he had been going over the figures and found that those which had been prepared were substantially correct. That it would be necessary to get N.R.M.A. men to help make up the required reinforcements. He believed, however, that it should be possible to secure them as the result of an appeal but that there would have to be an immediate drastic change in what was being done concerning some of them. . . . He had found some were working but were receiving as much as 6 and 7 dollars a day and others were being paid a premium to do extra work while the army pay was only $1.25; that simply meant that men would not think of enlisting for service overseas. He thought they should be put at the necessary army work of one kind or another at army rates of pay. That these men should be brought in at once.

"When we talked together I reminded him of our conversations at Laurier House and in particular what he had said about it not being psychologically wise to cross any bridge until we came to it and that for this reason there should not be any attempt to answer at this time the question of what then? if the required numbers were not secured as a result of a voluntary appeal. I explained to him anew the difficulties of going to Parliament to secure conscription. The uncertainty, even if a recommendation were made, of it passing the House of Commons. Referred to Coldwell's statement through the C.C.F. and also the position of other parties of Canada, the impossibility of forcing conscription unless there was an overwhelming opinion and the inevitability of a complete division of the country once there were an election on conscription."

The two men then went into the Cabinet and the Prime Minister asked General McNaughton to make a report. "He did so in a manner which he might have had had he been sitting with the Cabinet for months past. In other words, there was no restraint or hesitation in his manner. He spoke of the situation being serious and did not question the figures that had been previously discussed in Council. He brought up at once the position of the N.R.M.A. men getting large amounts of money for employment and what he was proposing to do. If they were to be an army they should be an army of soldiers doing work as soldiers and not as wage earners. There was, I think, universal surprise which I shared at the word of what some of them had been receiving. I noticed that Mitchell's face coloured up very much and he looked very embarrassed, but he said this had been done to save the tobacco crop, also that men were working on construction work for the two railways. I did not notice anyone in the Cabinet who had said that he had knowledge of men receiving extra money. They had understood employers were to pay for the labour at the price that other labour would receive, but that whatever was in excess of the pay which the N.R.M.A. men were receiving would go to the state, to be divided up for war purposes in one way or the other. Mitchell said there had not been such an agreement. Ilsley and others thought there had been.

"McNaughton then put forward the proposal that we should begin at once to organize an appeal. Council became for a moment dumb as to what steps should be taken to that end. I suggested that we should seek to bring together as many agencies as possible. Someone else suggested using the War Information Board. Another suggestion was made of having an organization similar to the one which was handling the Victory loan. McNaughton himself suggested getting the preachers and the churches, those who have to do with shaping opinion to interest themselves personally in an appeal. I suggested having representatives of the press called in and their good offices secured and if possible an indirect appeal from McNaughton or myself or the two of us combined. Also a similar course on McNaughton's part with respect to the War Veterans organizations to have them adopt a sympathetic attitude. LaFlèche said he would guarantee to get all the men we required to meet the difficulty with respect to the French regiments. He repeated that a couple of times, that he could do it and would do it. Arnold Heeney passed on to me a suggestion that it might be well to appoint a Committee of Council to work with the General in arranging an organization to effect the appeal. I put this forward at once and named Claxton, Mackenzie, LaFlèche—I had previously suggested St. Laurent, but he pointed out that LaFlèche had already interested himself—Mulock, and when Gardiner returns, Gardiner, also Gibson. Asked Arnold Heeney to act as Secretary. McNaughton to be Chairman. Suggested that Pope should also work with the Committee. It was later planned that Claxton would meet with Dunton and one or two others this evening to get something ready for the General in the morning. First it had been thought to have a meeting of the Cabinet in the morning, but later it was thought advisable to have the report to Council come on Monday. The General had suggested Armistice Day as a good day on which to begin the appeal. I pointed out this was quite a way off. I suggested the Defence Department might make an effort in different directions. That material might begin to be prepared for the use of speakers and statements on the situation should be got ready at once. McNaughton mentioned he was giving a Poppy Day address on Monday night and would bring in something there. He later told me over the 'phone that he was speaking in Arnprior on Sunday and would have something to say there. He had addresses to the War Veterans next week which will give him a chance to speak with them.

"I pointed out that it would not in any event be wise to attempt beginning any campaign before the 7th instant which is the day of the Presidential election. Also that the Victory Loan will be over on Saturday the 11th. We could then go ahead.

"We had all this nicely arranged and were about to pass on to something else when Macdonald raised the question as to the certainty of being asked in any appeal what was to follow if the campaign did not succeed. McNaughton had himself earlier pointed out that no reference should be made to compulsion in the campaign. Macdonald kept pressing his question, saying he would like to know the answer to that. That it was a very important consideration to him in view of what he had said in Parliament. He then began to go over all the ground that we had gone over in previous discussions. There was a look of dismay, almost disgust, on the faces of all the Members of the Cabinet that I could see. However, I kept very quiet and answered each point anew as he brought it up and pointed out that I thought it was well he had raised all the questions so that General McNaughton would hear for himself just what had been discussed in Council when he was not there and could see for himself what the position of the Ministers was. We had got over the ground pretty well, and I was about to suggest that we did not continue the discussion further when LaFlèche began to raise some question with Macdonald. I saw that that would set the heather afire anew and asked LaFlèche not to press matters further for today. That once the organization had been started we could continue as rapidly as possible."

The Prime Minister spent most of the rest of the day drafting a reply to Ralston's letter of resignation which was finally delivered at about 10 o'clock that evening. He was greatly annoyed by a letter from T. A. Crerar going over the same ground. Mackenzie King was "not surprised at the letter but it reveals there is quite clearly going to be, in all probability, further resignations beginning with Crerar, then Macdonald and I am not sure just what others. I do not know what Howe's actions will be when he returns though I think the friendship he has for McNaughton will cause him to hesitate to resign until at least we have had the appeal." He added that he "said nothing to the Cabinet about the letters between Ralston and myself. My own feeling is they should not be made public until Parliament meets and then tabled. There are two special reasons for this course. One is that they disclose highly confidential information which would seriously affect the war effort. The second is the custom which is to reserve the letters until Parliament meets, this being based upon the need of avoiding discussion in the press before there is opportunity for the Ministry to deal with the questions in a responsible way in Parliament. I doubt, however, if this rule will be respected.

"Altogether, then, today has been another very trying and difficult day with the promise of more ahead. I nevertheless still believe that we shall work out of this situation short of conscription, but I can see that it is going to be very hard on myself, and more particularly on my strength."

Mackenzie King saw his doctor on November 4 and received a good report on his physical condition. Another thing that brought him a sense of added security was a message from Malcolm MacDonald that he was flying to England during the coming week and would like an opportunity for a chat before leaving. To the Prime Minister, the message meant that "the British Government want to get first-hand information on the situation here. He [MacDonald] is a true friend and understands the situation, and will be able to get Churchill to understand it. They will not want McNaughton criticizing what is being done in the army if they can possibly avoid it. McNaughton is pretty certain to go and this time, to see the men in the field. As Minister, he has authority over command. It is a complete change from the situation of a year ago. It makes me feel pretty confident that a way will be found short of resort to conscription."

Mackenzie King lunched with MacDonald and brought him up to date. He told him that he "felt immensely relieved having sent the first word I did to Churchill letting him see how serious the situation was. That I felt relieved he had had this knowledge in advance. Also that in the light of his reply, I could in no way be blamed for not sending further information to him before taking the step I had with respect to McNaughton. I said to tell the truth, I had been at first a little hurt by Churchill's reply; that in the light of all I had done to help him in terrific situations and was doing to prevent others arising, I had really felt that something a little more reassuring would have come from him to me. However on reflection, I had clearly seen his difficulties and how difficult it would have been for him to make any kind of commitment. I said to Malcolm that I had nothing to ask at all but I would be pleased if when he was in England, he would arrange to see Churchill and tell him that I would be particularly grateful for any help he could give me in meeting the situation. That I was not asking this in any personal way but for what a little help, at this time, might mean in the interests of all concerned, both in relation to the present and the future."

Later in the day McNaughton came to Laurier House to show Mackenzie King the speech he was proposing to make at Arnprior the following day. "I was glad he came," the Prime Minister wrote, "for there was one phrase in particular to the implication of which I had felt he had not given sufficient thought. It had been written out in pencil in his own hand. He had been writing it out in the office until 6. It was the phrase which now reads—referring to matters of special interest: 'And the 3rd, and certainly at this time the most vitally important is the question of the provision of reinforcements for those forces to the fullest extent that will be required.' This he had previously worded in a way which might have been interpreted as meaning that the army would have to be reinforced to full strength. I pointed out to him that we had agreed the circumstances existing at the time would have to be taken into account and what related to the winning of the war. I said the second phrase he had used was quite in accord with our understanding. He at once said that was right. That as he had worded it, the phrase should be changed and he put it in words 'the fullest extent that will be required.' I made it plain that what would be required was in relation to our bearing, as he had said, our just share of the load in the winning of the war.

"The following words he already had in what he had written: 'And now I would say a few words to you about our men and units in the field and the vital need that must be met that our forces are maintained as is required in the last phase in which we seek to finally destroy the Nazi.' This I mentioned was quite satisfactory. It meant the maintenance of the forces as is required in the last phase. I said that of course meant what is required along with what all the other countries are doing. McNaughton also had the following: 'I believe that they and we are fully determined that we will maintain our just part in the great Allied effort that is still required.' I said that is in accordance with the formula that we have agreed to 'our just part in bearing the burden of the winning of the war' as a part of the great Allied effort.

"This seemed a true statement of the position and the rest was not open to any uncertainty as to policy."

On Sunday, November 5, the Governor-General and Princess Alice had tea at Kingsmere with the Prime Minister. He noted they were both "very discreet in what they said. It was more what was not said which made me realize that they felt concern about the consequences of McNaughton's appointment as related more particularly to overseas. Princess Alice seemed concerned about the hard fighting the Canadians are doing in trenches, mud and water and of the need of their being supported at all costs. I mentioned the political aspects of the situation, and pointed out that to expect me to get reinforcements by conscription, I would best illustrate what it would mean for me to attempt it by saying they would appreciate what such a request would mean to Smuts if he had attempted it or to Curtin, of Australia, after the people there had voted against it and particularly at this stage of the war.

"The Governor spoke of his visit to some of the camps and feeling that there were plenty of men there who, if taken in the right way, would volunteer. I gathered that what was in His Excellency's mind was to see the correspondence that had passed between Ralston and myself. This of course I should have taken down to him at once. He asked me just as he was leaving about it. I told him I would show it to him tomorrow. However, as soon as he left, I 'phoned Gibson to get the originals and take them down to him.

"Her Royal Highness spoke of Ralston being a fine man. That we owed very much to him. I replied that I could not say too much of what we owed to him. That it was a terrible loss to me as I had relied on him more than on anyone else."

On Monday, November 6, Mackenzie King had General Pope go to Washington to represent him at Sir John Dill's funeral. It was agreed that Pope should bring Dill's successor up to date and, if possible, see President Roosevelt and explain the situation to him.

The same day Mackenzie King began working on a broadcast to explain Ralston's resignation to the country. He also saw McNaughton and looked over the text of a speech he was to deliver to the Legion that evening. The press were informed that the Prime Minister would broadcast himself on Wednesday evening, the day after the United States presidential election. Mackenzie King noted that M. J. Coldwell was "asking for bringing of Parliament together. That would be a trying ordeal . . . , particularly for me as I would have no Minister of Defence in the House and Ralston would be there to defend his position. It will make the load very heavy indeed. . . . Despite the fact I had a good sleep last night, I feel a little more depressed today, largely I think because of seeing the frightful attacks on myself and realizing that the whole is to create the prejudice of the Army against me. However I pray for the faith to keep on." The reasons for the Prime Minister's depression were real enough. Although the initial reaction to McNaughton's appointment had been favourable, the press soon became disenchanted, suspicious, and critical. Response to the General's pleas for voluntary enlistments at the Arnprior and Legion meetings was not encouraging and McNaughton's reception by the veterans in Ottawa was definitely hostile.

The next day (November 7) much of his time was taken up with another letter from Ralston and a press statement by the former Minister urging that the correspondence between them should be published. Mackenzie King noted that he "thought I should first of all draft a letter to him drawing attention to the oath of a P.C. as to disclosing what is debated and treated of in the Cabinet, and then draft a reply to his letter. These two communications took me practically all the morning.

"Just about one, I received from the Governor General the return of the correspondence between Ralston and myself which I had had Gibson give him on Sunday evening. It was returned with a letter in which His Excellency said: 'There is actually nothing in the letters which could not be published with the exception of references to certain meetings of the Cabinet. I read in the press, however, that you will make a statement on the whole subject and I hope this will satisfy the general public.'

"This is the first time since his appointment as Governor General, that His Excellency has ventured to advise me even indirectly of the course to be followed in a matter for which I have full responsibility. I confess I felt some annoyance on the receipt of this letter for the reason that I am as sure as I am dictating that it has not been written by His Excellency without His Excellency having sought and acted upon advice from some other source. Redfern, of course, has been an instrument in the matter, but it looks very much to me as if the communications I have shown His Excellency had been communicated to London and that something had come back from that source. The purpose obviously is to assist Ralston in the immediate disclosure of what he has written and thereby to help his aim and make the situation more difficult and embarrassing for General McNaughton and myself. It is something new. I read the communication to both McNaughton and St. Laurent. I had asked the latter, in the morning, over the 'phone, to advise me on parliamentary and constitutional practice as I had asked Malcolm MacDonald a few days ago. I shall say very little to His Excellency about the matter as I do not intend to permit any difference to develop in that quarter but I shall let him know that I had drafted the letter which I did this morning in reference to Ralston's statement in the press before his own letter was received."

At the Cabinet meeting the same day, Mackenzie King reviewed "what I proposed to say on the radio. When I completed the part on Ralston's resignation, there was some question raised by Macdonald as to whether what I had said about Ralston was adequate. Exception was taken to my not having mentioned his readiness to stay on with the Administration and that he had not resigned. I then had to go over the ground again about his saying repeatedly that he would have to resign and would resign if his recommendation was not accepted; that he had put it always on the ground that he would have to resign in virtue of what he had said in Parliament. I referred to what I had said about the larger responsibilities as a Minister of Defence and as a P.C. I reminded Council about what I had said regarding having to look for another Minister when he said he would resign unless we could agree on the recommendation and how he had repeatedly stated that the Cabinet would not agree to the recommendation.

"I then took advantage of McNaughton's presence to tell the Cabinet just when it was I approached McNaughton and what had been said between us, letting them know that it was as late as the day before his [Ralston's] resignation. I reminded Council, too, of Ralston having said at the table that he would then tender his resignation and of my acceptance of it in the presence of others and of his leaving the Council thereafter. It was clear, as I had seen at the time, that they were going to have it appear that he was pursuing things to the ultra limit without resigning. Something gave me the opportunity to bring up the question of making the correspondence public. I spoke of my responsibility in that regard and read to the Cabinet the Oath of the P.C. not to disclose in writing or by words or by any other way anything that had been treated of or discussed in the Cabinet. This arose [out] of some mention of my having referred to Ralston having resigned two years before. I explained that what I was referring to in that connection was being pained that I should have to carry for two years a resignation which was not being pressed but which Ralston had never withdrawn; also which I had been asked to retain. It was not that resignation that I was referring to at all. I said it was strange that reference had appeared to that in the press the next day as I had made no reference to it to anyone save in the Council Chamber that day. I added however it was true that walls seemed to have ears. I asked for suggestions as to what I should put in the letter that would better describe the true position, but none could be made. Angus Macdonald said that Ralston might take exception to what I said if the matter was left as it is. I said I would try to see that nothing could possibly be misrepresented and that I would seek to make a reference to Ralston's sincerity, etc. I then got on to the remainder of the broadcast, and at the end, there was general acceptance of what had been said with some helpful suggestions as to points to be further emphasized or slightly altered or omitted. I was really afraid that the reading of this might open up the whole discussion anew and was immensely relieved when I felt I had reached a point where I could suggest we take up another subject."

At the close of his diary for the day, and after hearing the results of the American election, Mackenzie King wrote that "Before going to bed I got off a wire to the President in the following words: 'My dear friend: I am delighted.' "

The next day (November 8), the Prime Minister delivered his broadcast, which he thought went "very well." In it, he made the first official statement on the Cabinet crisis and the reinforcement situation. Reassuring in tone, the speech committed the government to the voluntary system of recruiting and contained an appeal to the N.R.M.A. men to volunteer for overseas service.

Next morning, the Prime Minister had a talk with St. Laurent, in the course of which he told him that in the event of other resignations he would probably have to resign and ask the Governor-General to call on one of the supporters of conscription to form a government. "Ilsley, I imagine, would accept. If he ever did, he would not last any time with the problem of enforcing conscription and all that would arise out of it but he would, I fear, succeed in helping still further to destroy the Liberal party, for a long time to come. However we shall wait; not cross that bridge until we come to it, and as a cartoonist in the Journal says tonight, we may never come to it. I pray that may be so. Crerar's manner continued to be very churlish and bitter toward myself. He would, of course, join any of the others. Might leave. Of course, if there should be any real response by the men in the camps, that would change everything and be a complete triumph. But what I fear is that now that both McNaughton and I have spoken, very little else will be done. I don't know what further progress there has been in carrying out what the Committee recommended as to individual appeals. No one person seems to have that in hand. General McNaughton cannot be expected to follow it up."

In the afternoon, the Prime Minister received a Legion delegation which advocated immediate conscription. During the discussion, when he made two or three appeals to them to co-operate with the government and General McNaughton in seeking to get N.R.M.A. men to enlist, he noted that, instead of responding, Walker, the President, and one or two others "spoke of the uselessness of it" and Mackenzie King felt their attitude indicated they did not want to co-operate because it might look like helping McNaughton against Ralston. He added: "They will want to prove Ralston was right."

At the War Committee meeting on November 9, in Mackenzie King's view, "McNaughton showed his real effectiveness as a Minister. It is a thousand pities that he and Ralston could not have been in the Cabinet together." He added that "in talking with McNaughton tonight, he mentioned that he was the most hated man of Canada today. Said his desk was showered with anonymous letters of protest, etc. I told him I still thought I could do him one better on that score." He also noted in his diary for November 9 how he had "been horrified and indeed deeply saddened by the pictures" which revealed Roosevelt's failing health. Mackenzie King was referring to press photographs of President Roosevelt casting his ballot and greeting the people on the night of his victory. "Trying as my present situation is, and triumphant as his is, I would not exchange places with him for anything." An incident the next morning, Friday, November 10, might have changed Mackenzie King's view. "When I was getting into the car to go to the office today," he wrote, "two of the C.W.A.C. young women were crossing the street as I came out. Others had gone ahead and some were following behind. One of the young women crossing the road called back: Oh, girls, there is that god-damned. . . . [*sic*] They all stood and waited and as I drove past the corner of Chapel St. a small group of them began to shout. This is an indication of the feeling. I shall be surprised if tomorrow at the National Memorial some demonstration is not made against myself and probably in favour of Ralston who is returning tonight to be in Ottawa tomorrow. It being a war veterans affair there is every possibility of that." But on November 11, a very cold day in Ottawa, there were not as many people at the ceremony as usual and there was "not the slightest disturbance."

On Sunday afternoon, November 12, the Prime Minister received word at Kingsmere that Ralston had issued a statement giving his version of why he had resigned. The former Minister stressed the urgent need for reinforcements and pointed out that only the N.R.M.A. units provided an immediate pool of trained infantry. He also disclosed that the "Government as a whole" did not consider that it was bound to introduce overseas conscription for supplying reinforcements. The Prime Minister felt "a bit dumbfounded." When he received the complete text of Ralston's statement, however, he felt that "it was not quite as bad as I had expected, but it was not wholly true. It disclosed military secrets; also the use of the word 'concur' and other passages, matters that had been discussed in the Cabinet. Repeated the error that I had asked him to resign, etc. I could see at once that it was part of a plot to keep up this controversy and to get me out on the conscription issue. I remarked I fully expected it would be followed by something further that would be embarrassing from Macdonald and Ilsley, possibly their resignations. I felt quite distressed." Mackenzie King consulted McNaughton by telephone and they agreed to meet in the morning and, in the meantime, to say nothing.

In his diary for Monday, November 13, Mackenzie King recorded that before getting up in the morning he had been "thinking of calling Members of Parliament together. Felt very strongly it was necessary to avoid other Ministers tendering any resignations before Parliament met. I felt sure there was a design along that line and that now that the Victory Loan was over, I would be confronted with resignations of Macdonald and of Ilsley, in which event I would then have to call Parliament but matters would have reached a crisis by that time. Ralston's letter required either an answer to the press on the part of McNaughton and myself which would provoke controversy, and with no good effect, or the calling of Parliament to give a statement there and to ask for a vote of confidence, to settle matters one way or the other. The Government is the servant, not the master."

Later he read the newspapers in bed and observed that "the newspapers featured I had asked Ralston to resign and later I wrote out these words by pencil: 'Colonel Ralston either made or did not make a recommendation to Council. His recommendation was either accepted or it was not. He, himself, says he made a recommendation and it was not accepted, and accordingly, he resigned. This scarcely squared with the statement that Colonel Ralston's resignation was at my request. On the contrary, I did my utmost for days not to have Colonel Ralston resign.' "

When McNaughton arrived at 10.30 a.m. the Prime Minister went over with him "the course I thought should be taken; outlined first wherein I thought Ralston was in error and stating that I felt the House of Commons should be reassembled and that I should make a statement in the House and demand a vote of confidence. That I could not go on in this way. That was the only alternative to public controversy.

"While I was talking, a letter from Macdonald was placed in my hands. This was about 11. I was told he had left word to make sure I received it. Before I opened it, I had put in a call for Glen [J. A. Glen, the Speaker of the House of Commons] in Winnipeg to ask him to come down and to tell him I thought Parliament should be called. When I got him a few minutes later, he said he agreed entirely. Would leave by 'plane tonight. We discussed the date. He thought 8 days at least. I at first thought if the announcement were made tonight, of the 21st. He rather favoured the 22nd. When I opened Macdonald's letter, it was another long communication not marked confidential but trying to put on record more material which related to Cabinet discussions, saying he thought the Government ought to decide at once how long the appeal for volunteers was to last. In discussion with Ralston, the latest day had been fixed at November 30. Also asked what was the significance to be attached to the word 'necessary' quoting from my speeches in the House. He also had a reference to what I had said at Quebec at the Reform Club. To what he had taken down as part of what I had said on that occasion. I had really expected to find a reference to his resignation; in that respect, I was agreeably surprised. The letter confirmed me the more strongly on the necessity of re-summoning the House of Commons."

The Prime Minister then called St. Laurent in Quebec. "He told me he had been talking with Power this morning and they had thought if there were any further resignations, I would have to call Parliament. He agreed that it would be wise to call Parliament anyway at this time in the light of Ralston's statement. He was coming from Quebec by train today but I asked him if he could come by 'plane. Later I got word that he was coming by 'plane. Would arrive around 5.00 P.M. He either was with Power at the time or Power had 'phoned to ask me whether I was really decided to call

Parliament at once. He said that Angus had 'phoned him this morning and he had learned from him that he did not intend to take any action for some time, which confirms my view that the Defence Ministers are all working together. Power did his utmost to persuade me not to call Parliament at once but to wait. He offered to come by 'plane to talk matters over, today if need be, or tomorrow. I told him I could not go on this way any longer. That I did not want to get into the position where I would be blamed for having let matters run too long without consulting Parliament and up to a time which made [it] impossible to get the necessary aid to the soldiers overseas. I said I was seeking a vote of confidence. He seemed surprised when I said I thought the House would give that. He was particularly anxious to have some say about the course to be pursued when Parliament met. Did I mean to let the Tories have the Government. . . . I told him that if I took that line, Quebec people would feel that we had intended that from the start. Just now things were 100% satisfactory. It was the old conscriptionist issue over again as in 1917. I told him I had no thought of handing over anything unless I found myself without a party. When we had put the 'phone down, I concluded I perhaps had made a mistake in even 'phoning to St. Laurent. Power will get word and there will doubtless be opposition to my summoning the Members when Council meets. On this, however, I am determined. Macdonald and Ilsley can hardly resign on that issue."

According to the Prime Minister, McNaughton expressed the view that "the only thing to do was to go before Parliament and tell them quite frankly that our policy was that of voluntary enlistment for overseas. That we held to that policy. We had adopted the policy believing it to be the most effective means of getting men for the army and preserving national unity. We still held that view. It would be impossible to get the men that were needed any other way; that unless the N.R.M.A. men could be got in that way, it was almost certain they could not be secured at all." He added that "McNaughton made the interesting and I thought very helpful suggestion that there was no reason why a secret session should not be held and many things told there which it would not be wise to tell publicly for reasons of military secrecy. In this connection, I had been speaking of regretting he could not be in the House with me but I saw no reason why he could not come to a secret session and speak there. He said: the House controls its own procedure. He thought that should be done. He was quite prepared to come and to make clear the position as he saw it. He then told me that he had another good bit of news. He thought one of the bombers that was coming across was bringing details of figures prepared in England, which would show they were a thousand and more better off in available men in England at this time. That the figures which the Department had been using were all placed on the extremes of everything. Making allowance for everything that might happen. It was hardly conceivable that everything would happen at the same time."

Later in the morning, Mackenzie King talked with Gardiner who agreed that it would be wise to have Parliament summoned. "He was in favour, if the Government was defeated, of having a general election on the subject. Personally I feel if the Government is defeated, it would be better to allow the others to take on the conscription business. They would probably not succeed. Would have to have a general election themselves and we would then defeat them in a general election."

Later in the day (November 13) the Cabinet formally approved the summoning of Parliament. After the meeting the Prime Minister learned from McNaughton that sufficient reinforcements were available to meet the expected needs to the end of the year, information "that relieved my mind tremendously as Ralston has been representing that men would have to be conscripted before the end of the month so as to be put aboard ships by November the 30th at the latest."

The Prime Minister had St. Laurent to dinner that evening to discuss strategy in Parliament. Of their conversation, he noted "my own feeling is that if I were not to get a vote of confidence on voluntary system, it would be best if I went to the Governor General and asked for the others to be called on. They would have difficulty first in forming a government, next in carrying out conscription and 3rdly, while they might extend the term of Parliament, they could not extend it for long and would then have to go to the country and they would be defeated in the country. This I feel pretty sure is right. St. Laurent thinks Power feels if I did not go to the people, Quebec would think that the whole thing had been pre-arranged; that we wanted the soldiers to be sent anyway and had just taken this way of meeting the situation. I shall have to look at the project as I have all others, not from the point of view of Quebec alone but from the point of view of Canada as a whole. St. Laurent feels strongly that we have taken the right course."

The next day (November 14) Mackenzie King seemed more confident about the decision. "I am perfectly sure I did the right thing yesterday in having Parliament summoned. Ralston has once again, by his ill-judged action, his insufficient thought or determination to have his own will or none, made it necessary for me to take the action that will, I believe, help to save the day. Where would Canada have been today without McNaughton's appointment? Ralston has himself to thank for that. The country and I have to thank Ralston. Where would we have been if the country had been left without a Minister of Defence or had any other person than McNaughton. Equally but for Ralston's statement to the press on Sunday night, we should probably have gone on for some days longer without re-assembling of the Commons and other resignations could have followed in the Ministry which would have necessitated later the re-assembling of the Commons but under conditions infinitely worse both for the Government and for the country and particularly the men overseas and obtaining for them necessary reinforcements. Ralston has himself to thank for Parliament being called and I and the country have again to thank him for this step being taken at this time.

"I will have to think most carefully of the procedure to be followed when the House meets. More and more it seems to me this morning that the suggestion made by St. Laurent in conversation last night [and by McNaughton earlier] that a secret session might be held before the debate would be the right course to pursue. I felt opposed to it at first as something the country would not like. What the press of course would rejoice in would be a sensational debate but that would not serve the end which is the only one which should be kept in view, namely securing the necessary reinforcements. Also it would be difficult to debate first without Members having all the information that could be given to them. This is a military matter primarily. Much of the information can only be given in secret. That procedure would also allow McNaughton to be heard by all Members of the House. How to bring that about will have to be studied. If, after the secret session, a public session were then held, I could make my speech and conclude with a resolution somewhat along the lines that St. Laurent and I discussed last night; not a resolution of confidence in myself or the administration, following the lines by Churchill a couple of years ago, but something on the following lines: 'That the House approve the decision of His Majesty's Government that the time has not yet arrived to depart from the method of securing by voluntary enlistment men for overseas service in the Army.' This is on the right lines. I am sure I have acted wisely in suggesting to the Cabinet that we do not attempt to discuss any final line of action, until immediately before the House of Commons assembles."

Mackenzie King also felt "pretty strongly" that, if defeated on such a motion, he should call on the Governor-General to ask those who opposed to form a ministry. "See what they can do in enforcing conscription, even should they extend the term of Parliament. They would be bound to go to the country at the time of the termination of the war in Europe and I am certain that any government that has supported conscription would be defeated. I do not see how after my consistent stand in refusing to have

an election during wartime if that could be avoided I could ask for a dissolution of Parliament and bring on a general election while the war is on.
My whole position should continue to be that of seeking to avoid an election during wartime. Another thing which occurs to me is that if any conscriptionist government came in they would either have to adopt our social
legislation policy or repudiate it. If they repudiated it, we would certainly
win. Even if they adopted it, the country would have more faith in myself
to carry it out than they would in any other leader.

"Bracken is demanding in the name of the people of Canada and the
men overseas that conscription should be adopted at once. It is a ludicrous
position for a man who has not even a seat in Parliament, let alone a leader
who had never been in the Federal Parliament. I observe that he made no
comment on the fact that the House of Commons has been reconvened.
What a position for a leader of a political party to be in at a time like this!
From now on, I must concentrate on what is to be said and done in Parliament."

During the morning the Prime Minister had a telephone call from Power
who was still in hospital in Quebec. He suggested the possibility of appointing McNaughton to the Senate and arranging a joint sitting of both Houses.
Power, Mackenzie King reported, "said he supposed he would have to take
up some of the material that McNaughton would not be able to use in the
House. I said I thought he should prepare all he could for a debate. He said
he would do so. It was quite clear from the way he spoke that he will be
prepared to assist in every way and do whatever he can. He will be a real
strength. It is clear that he at least of the Ministers of Defence would not
join in any attempt to add to the number of resignations."

At the Cabinet meeting that same day (November 14), McNaughton
reported on the reinforcement situation and, also, on the conference he
had had through most of the day with the Officers Commanding the Military Districts. Gardiner also reported for his committee on the appeal for
volunteers which, in Mackenzie King's judgment, "was not as satisfactory
as I should have liked." The Prime Minister later spoke to McNaughton
about a Senatorship but discovered no enthusiasm for the idea.

Shortly after 6.00 P.M., two letters arrived from Ralston: "one asking
that I should request the Governor General to allow his letters to me to be
tabled; the other a somewhat short answer seeking to answer the points in
my last letter to him. I do not think I will carry on further correspondence
with him. He loves nothing better than building up a record and having
the last word. It is the technique he has adopted with McNaughton in the
past, in the Cabinet with myself and in relation to every argument that
came up."

The Prime Minister noted on November 15 that he told St. Laurent "that the situation was different than it had been at the time I asked Lord Byng for a dissolution. At that time I had never been defeated in the House. He had been told I had been and it was partly because of this that he refused to accept my advice. The present Governor General would in all probability decline to give me a dissolution if I asked for it after being defeated in the House. It may be that on constitutional grounds I might be entitled to appeal from Parliament to the people but I have taken the position I did not wish to have an election at a time of war least of all an election on the conscription issue. That responsibility would have to be assumed by someone else if I do not get the support of the House. One thing I am sure of, were I to say for a moment that I would follow up the defeat in the House by a dissolution, many of my followers would be inclined to welcome that step. I would have a harder time to keep the party together. The entire House is much more likely to give me its support and incidentally McNaughton, further opportunity, if they know that both of us will necessarily leave the administration if our policy is not sustained."

At the Cabinet meeting on the afternoon of Thursday, November 16, McNaughton reviewed his discussions with the Officers Commanding the Military Districts and reported they "did not hold out much hope of additions from the 'hard core' now in the camps but did report on a gain of some 3,000 in the figures of those trained men available in Britain. Also made clear that up to the end of December, all ships were already booked. That the acute situation might not arise until the latter part of January. Speaking toward the end of the Cabinet meeting, he made a very impressive statement. He drew attention to the fact that he had received a telegram pointing out how much shells were needed for the troops. That word had come to increase the order 5 times. He drew attention of the Government to the fact that these shells would mean much more for ultimate success than increased numbers of men. The papers are advertising for an addition of some 10,000 women and men for the factories. . . . He said for example, amplifying his statement, that if he were Commander of a German army, he would give orders to concentrate on the Canadian Infantry in the light of information already given to the enemy, not paying much attention to those with larger guns in the rear. This concentration of fighting might prove very serious. He seemed to feel this deeply.

"The statement grew out of a discussion which arose from Macdonald's question as to what procedure it was proposed to adopt in Parliament. I said that as Power would be here Monday I thought we had better wait till he came before finally settling procedure. I mentioned that my thought was on the first day to table the exchange of correspondence re Ralston's resignation and then adjourn till the next day to meet in secret session before making any further statement so that the Members would know the facts which could not be publicly disclosed. McNaughton said he was glad to hear this as there was so much material that could not be made public because of what it would mean to the enemy. I said that I hoped it might be possible in the light of the seriousness of the situation to get parties to agree to a discussion without a division. Ilsley laughed at this and was perhaps quite right in doing so. I repeated that I hoped everyone in the House would realize that the question was much larger than that of reinforcements for the Infantry. It would involve the future of Canada's part in the war and the future of Canada for better or worse. I purposely refrained from saying anything about the motion that might be moved at this time. When that comes up we will have the old debate over again and the resignation of Macdonald and Ilsley as a consequence. It is difficult to see how if on a vote they go against the Government they can be kept in office. Macdonald would not be a loss but Ilsley would. There was no disapproval of the course I suggested."

The consensus of advice was "that practically the whole of the correspondence between Ralston and myself should be tabled particularly in view of the fact that Ralston himself has made public the parts that are most dangerous. I should rather hold to the old British tradition of preventing disclosure of Cabinet discussion but I can see that to withhold anything would create a problem in itself, and make the last stage worse than the first without any good and without preventing in the end the disclosure."

On November 17 Mackenzie King recorded a conversation with Ian Mackenzie who had been talking to Power on the telephone. Power indicated that the Quebec members wished the Prime Minister to dissolve Parliament and go to the country on the conscription issue. "I said to Mackenzie nothing would move me to that end. Power had suggested to him I should have an alternative course in my pocket which would be an understanding from the Governor that he would grant a dissolution if the Government were defeated. I am not sure that he would give that understanding. At any rate, I do not intend to embarrass him by asking him. It is the same old story. I have never taken the right course thus far that I have not had to take it against the views of a very strong element in my own Party. This time it might be described as against the whole body of opinion of Quebec which the country accuses me of seeking to oblige on all occasions."

Mackenzie King spent most of Saturday reading over the 1942 debates and preparing notes for Parliament. That evening he had Mackenzie and

Gardiner come to Laurier House. They had been preparing a procedure for the House "on the basis of escaping a possible division altogether, thinking I was anxious to have that done. I told them I thought it would not be well accepted by the public. We had better have a division and I gave them suggestions as to the motion strongly urging to leave out any reference to reinforcements specially or to voluntary or compulsory methods and to have just a general statement of support to the Government in carrying on the war effort. What I had particularly in mind was making it possible for Ilsley and Crerar, indeed every Member of the Government, to vote for the motion though they might have reservations as to what course they will adopt later if they felt impelled to do this. A motion might bring a couple of the extreme Quebec men against us which Pickersgill in some ways thinks might be all to the good though I question whether votes for are not more important than those against. But the important thing is to get a motion that won't link all parties against us on the score that they have not confidence in the administration and give them something that they can unite upon at least for the present. They both agreed that what I was now suggesting was the preferable course; that the two amendments I had suggested were the best of all. One was on lines I had previously written out, and the other, on lines that Pickersgill drafted in the afternoon. Both had the same central idea."

At the meeting of the general officers and district commanders which had been held in Ottawa on November 14, no hope was held out for obtaining the 15,000 men required by the end of December through the voluntary system. Perhaps influenced by excessive optimism, General McNaughton told the press a few days later that "the information given me by the O.C.'s confirmed my belief more than ever that continuation of the voluntary policy will provide the reinforcements." On November 19 four of the district commanders who had been present at the meeting, Pearkes, Riley, Harvey, and Potts, telegraphed Murchie protesting McNaughton's misrepresentation of their position. They repeated that the drive for volunteers had no chance of success. McNaughton showed the telegrams to the Prime Minister that afternoon. According to Mackenzie King, the Minister explained "that his confidence lay in the fact that while they [the district commanders] had spoken frankly of their doubts, they had nevertheless given the assurance they would make another try and that he, himself, felt with that attitude and all the forces that were at work and would be now coming to work, for example the individual efforts from men's families, the Parliament meeting, public opinion shaping up, etc., etc. that everything would come through all right. He said to me that he had to handle these officers very carefully. That if he began to oppose them, he might have a revolt on his hands and a situation which would be very difficult to manage. The one thing to do was to avoid any quarrel; to explain quite clearly what he meant and express the hope that they would, with that understanding, do their best to further the new policy. After showing me their wires, he showed me the reply he had drafted and what he proposed to give to the press, all of which I thought were exceedingly good. As we talked over the situation, he told me he thought Pearkes was probably at the bottom of it. Pearkes was a friend of Stuart and while in England, he had to allow Pearkes to come back to Canada because of situations which developed and that Pearkes no doubt was ready now to blame him for that. I reminded him that in speaking after Council the other day, I had said that our men were suspicious of Pearkes. They felt he had never tried to make the voluntary system go; that he, McNaughton, had replied he was sure he would be loyal and helpful. That he was one of the men that he, McNaughton, had very close to him in England; who had grown up under him and whom he felt he knew thoroughly and trusted absolutely. One soon finds out how little one can trust men when a popular tide is running in an opposite direction. He told me that Macdonald had been pressing him for figures about the men overseas, numbers of available men, etc. He felt he ought to retain these for the Cabinet. I said to remember whatever Macdonald asked, it was for use of Ralston and his friends. He said he had come to see that."

Mackenzie King spent most of the next morning (November 20) working on his speech for Parliament when it met two days later. About noon he had several of his colleagues, including Power, at Laurier House to discuss procedure and strategy. Power was "obviously quite frail, weak from his recent illness and operation, but was very cheerful and in every way most helpful." He again urged a dissolution in case of defeat but the Prime Minister repeated that, under no circumstances, would he ask the Governor-General for a dissolution. "That I did not think he would give it to me and that not enjoying the confidence of the Commons I would not be entitled to ask. Power said he was for appointing McNaughton to the Senate but McNaughton himself would not agree to that. Most of us doubted the wisdom of it. There was some discussion of who should be called upon to form a government. Power did not think it should go to any conscriptionist from our own Government but to Bracken. That if Bracken could not form a government, then I would be justified in appealing to the people. It was suggested that Bracken would be entitled to advise the Governor as to who would be the next to call on but I disagreed with that in that he would not be an adviser. Power left me a memo in which he said formation of a new government before an election might mean a Tory or coalition government and the Liberal party would entirely disappear at the next election. I felt a little humiliated at not having invited these gentlemen to luncheon, but I did not think they would be staying beyond 1.15. I did not like the servants to hear the discussion.

"While we were here another letter came in from Crerar which was in the nature of my keeping with the English speaking Liberals and leaving the Quebec Liberals to look after themselves. Power's memo and Crerar's revealed a kind of cleft stick in which I am being placed at this time."

At the Cabinet meeting on the afternoon of this same day, "the question of men available for overseas" was discussed. "McNaughton gave figures which made a somewhat better showing, but still leaves the lack of reinforcements for January an acute serious problem. There was a considerable discussion on the poor showing of French regiments and the considerable need for additional reinforcements. LaFlèche made clear that the Department had not given him exact figures. He had thought there were 728 instead of there being 728 in addition to other figures. This as McNaughton described was a problem within a problem.

"The main feature of the discussion developed around a possible extension of the time for an appeal. Strong emphasis was placed on the pressing nature of the need. McNaughton thought in a fortnight's time we would know better how the appeal was going. His reference to a fortnight caused the discussion to turn on what, if anything, would be agreed to at that time. That aspect might be considered. I mentioned what I had said in my address about reviewing the situation later on if reinforcements were not forthcoming.

"I went in to have a cup of tea in my room. Turnbull spoke to me about a quota being arranged from the N.R.M.A. I had been thinking on those lines just before for purposes of looking at all sides and when I returned, had the discussion continue on the policy of our waiting a fortnight and then seeing what, in the light of all circumstances, would be best at that time. Macdonald began to say something about it being apparent that the Government was still going to put off and off. That every day's delay made things more difficult and indicated he would have to consider what he was going to do. Ilsley spoke of gambling with human lives and at another stage said he was prepared to think for the night over whether it might not be worth while for him to agree to wait for a fortnight, but that at the end of that time he felt he would stand for the enactment of an order in council sending N.R.M.A. men overseas without any reassembling of Parliament. Crerar said that unless the men are found by the 30th he felt he would have to resign from the Government if we tried to go on with the voluntary enlistments. Howe said he was prepared to do one thing or the other, if the

Government agreed to continue the voluntary system, say so, and he was prepared to stand by that; on the other hand if they approved conscription then he would stand by that, but he thought we would have to have a definite policy one way or the other. It was apparent that Mulock thought that nothing would satisfy the people but to send the Zombies over if they would not enlist voluntarily. While Gibson did not say much I imagine he would take a similar position.

"When McNaughton saw the situation he stopped and addressed the Council very emphatically, saying that members must realize what was involved in attempting to enforce conscription, apart altogether from what its effect upon Canadian unity might be. That he had given the matter a lot of thought, and he had to tell them the position of the army which was that the men who would have to maintain law and order in Canada should any opposition arise when conscription was attempted were for the most part N.R.M.A. men. That they would be the men who would have to be responsible for seeing that trained N.R.M.A. men were sent overseas. He feared situations that might arise with the possibility of bloodshed. Once that sort of thing started it might spread like a prairie fire throughout the country. When he had finished speaking I said what he had told us was an additional reason why there should be a secret session where these things could be said. They could not be said publicly but they could be told the Members privately. I said every Member of the Cabinet should talk with ex-Chief Justice Duff about what he felt about enforcing conscription in the last war and what he thought it might lead to in this. I recalled to their attention the situation where one young man Guenette was shot when he was trying to escape. Ilsley later on said that unless the men were found inside of another fortnight he intended to say in the House he would be for passing an order in council to send the draftees overseas without any further going to Parliament, and he added for the benefit of his colleagues whether there was bloodshed or not that this would be done."

After the Cabinet, the Prime Minister had St. Laurent, Gardiner, Mackenzie, and McNaughton come to his office. "I asked them what they thought of the discussion in Council. Whether there was any possibility of working out an undertaking as to what would be done to the effect that if the appeal was not successful by a certain date, the men would be sent. As to whether there was anything that could be done which would limit those to be sent to those specially trained and to limit the number. St. Laurent said he did not think it was possible to pick out a particular class, that conscription would have to apply generally. I am quite sure that that is right. Mackenzie seemed to think that something of the kind was the only thing that could be done. However, Gardiner was quite strong in opposition to anything other than the present policy. As we discussed matters it was apparent that St. Laurent felt that we would make a fatal mistake if we departed from our policy right along. McNaughton said that he felt there was a real conspiracy right in the Department itself, not to have this voluntary system work. If given a fair chance he believes it would succeed, but instead of helping, everything possible was being done from different sources to enforce conscription. I pointed out what the veterans were doing from all sides. He mentioned other things and said he was fully convinced that the policy would work if given a chance. He then went on to say that we should stand by what he had stated he believed in and had come into the Government to help try to carry out. That we should not yield on the matter of our convictions. It was no use discussing little details, it was a matter of principle and we should stand on principle. I told him I agreed with him. As he was going out of the door he shook hands with me and said, . . . I will stand by you in this.

"I had thought a little earlier about just what my own position should be. That if most of the Ministers who were Members of the War Cabinet were going to withdraw I did not see I would be of any further use. That I was against an election in wartime. That I did not believe I had the strength in me to go through an election while the war was on. Besides I would be accused if I brought on an election through a dissolution of having made it impossible for reinforcements to be supplied and that I would be blamed for the lives that would be lost in the war whether due to that cause or not. That nothing could be gained. Replying to the remark of Gardiner about how elections might go in the West, etc., I said we were far beyond discussing any questions of election. That we were faced with an appalling situation in the country which involved the possibility of civil war. I certainly would not take any course which might lead to anything of the kind or to the accusation that I had not done all that was in my power to help get the men for overseas. That I believed they could be got by voluntary methods properly administered. But that they could not be got in any other way. We left over until tomorrow to talk of what course it might be best for me to take if other Members were to leave the Government, before Parliament meets, as there is every possibility of their doing in the event of my not agreeing tomorrow on fixing a time limit beyond which the public appeal is not to extend."

Earlier that day, McNaughton had issued another press statement, which the Prime Minister had approved the previous afternoon, in response to the district commanders' protests. It indicated that while the difficulties with the voluntary system had been frankly stated by the officers, their "assurance of full support" had convinced the Minister that "the problem will be solved." Before this statement was issued, McNaughton telephoned General Pearkes, General Officer Commanding-in-Chief, Pacific Command, read the draft and secured his approval. However, to the officers in British Columbia, the statement was just another sign of the government's weakness and, prior to a meeting of the unit and command leaders in Vancouver that day, five brigadiers and lieutenant-colonels gave interviews to the press critical of the government's policy. Mr. King heard the statements on the national news broadcast at 10.00 P.M. "It is quite apparent," he wrote, "that there is a conspiracy there [Vancouver]. One after the other has been coming out and saying that the N.R.M.A. men were just waiting for the Government to do its duty and send them overseas. That looks like the Army defying the civil power. These men in uniform have no right to speak in ways which will turn the people against the civil power."

In concluding the day's entry, Mackenzie King reflected that "More and more I come back to my firm convictions that the thoughts I had when the matter first came up were the right ones and that I should stand firmly against agreeing to conscription and not following the voluntary enlistment, because I doubt if it would help to get the men, and secondly the great possibility of making the situation worse for the present and for all time to come in Canada. There is another reason. It is that I should not myself take any step which will prevent the men overseas getting reinforcements they need by becoming responsible for a dissolution before all methods had been tried. I am sure that those who have been responsible for this plot when they begin to administer the carrying out of conscription will find they have made a fatal error and that instead of helping the men overseas they will help to prejudice Canada's entire war effort and ere long it will be shown that this is so."

On Tuesday, November 21, when he woke in the morning, Mackenzie King "felt very depressed at the thought of the appalling situation into which I was being drawn and fearful lest my physical strength and nervous strength might not stand the strain. Also, I could not see how I could possibly carry on the Government if Ilsley were to join Ralston. Macdonald and Crerar do not mean so much. We would be better off without Crerar. Macdonald has ability and knows his own Department, but is contentious and difficult. He has been very trying over the last two months."

During the morning, the Prime Minister had Graydon and Coldwell in to confer with Mackenzie, Power, and himself about procedure to be followed in the House when it assembled the following day. To him "it was apparent from what Graydon told us that his party are out to make all the trouble they can, to insist on the House sitting mornings, Saturdays, and on rushing things through; also objecting to a secret session, and not too sure about whether Members would be prepared to have McNaughton appear. The upshot of our conversation was a tentative arrangement for the tabling of exchange of correspondence tomorrow; McNaughton appearing on the day following, and the debate to start on a motion on Friday. I indicated that such was our intention. I think they have the idea we were going to seek to evade a motion. Graydon asked me if I was introducing a motion of confidence. I told him I could not give him the exact nature of the motion but that there would be one which would permit of their moving the amendments they wished. Power said, jokingly, he could give them an amendment they could certainly use.

"I found Coldwell distinctly helpful, both in regard to the secret session and in not pressing unduly for sittings in the mornings and on Saturdays. I pointed out that the tremendous issues involved were much greater and graver than they could realize. I thought the House ought to deliberate with care on these matters. We were two hours in conferring.

"As the conference broke up, Power came back to me and sympathized with me in the matter. He thought I was right in saying I would resign, as I had told Mackenzie I would, if the conscriptionist group in the Cabinet pressed me unduly. That they ought to be prepared to take office and administer conscription if they pressed for it; that he could not see wherein I could possibly support conscription in the light of existing circumstances. What he said caused me to think carefully over the whole situation, and after coming back for lunch I wrote out the following:

'I would ask the public appeal for the trained men for service overseas be continued until——(three weeks as a minimum). If at the end of that time, the requisite number of men are not available, I will then make way for some other member of the Administration to take over, which will leave the Administration free to pass immediately an order in council under an amendment to the N.R.M.A. Act making its provisions applicable to men called up under the provisions of the Act.'

(By this means there will be no necessity of the Government going back to Parliament for a vote of confidence as the stipulation in that regard related to myself and it was based on the need for a vote of confidence because of it being assumed that I would not have my heart in the enforcement of the Act.)

"In the morning, I had written out that 'I shall not take any step which will prevent the men who are fighting overseas from obtaining needed reinforcements by any method that is feasible. I have taken the only method I believe possible. It is for those who believe in a different method to be given the opportunity of carrying it out.'

"I was so weary that I had Council put off for half an hour. Took the extra time for a rest. Was at Council shortly after 4. McNaughton told Council of certain changes he wished for closing up establishments in British Columbia, at Niagara, and at certain other headquarters, thereby saving considerable numbers of men. When he had finished, I spoke very quietly. I told the Cabinet I had been thinking matters over very carefully. Realized there was a difference which apparently was irreconcilable. Both sides equally sincere in their position. That I wanted to keep the party united for its service to Canada and to the world at this time. I recognized there was a voluntary enlistment wing and a conscriptionist wing. That, except in that, we did not differ. That difference would go when the war was over. In the meantime we must try and not let bitterness make the cleavage too wide so that we could come back naturally together later on. I thought we were all agreed the appeal should be continued for a certain length of time. Definite time should be fixed when appeal should end, and if at that time we had not the adequate number of men I would then make it possible for conscription to be enforced without going back to Parliament for any vote of confidence. That I would myself resign and ask His Excellency to call on some one member of the Cabinet to form a government to carry through conscription. I then told Council of my determination not to have a dissolution in war time and made some mention of the other thoughts I had in the morning. When I spoke of my own intention to drop [out] and let those who believed in conscription carry on, there was a period of intense silence in the Cabinet. No one said a word. All were silent so long that I myself had to break the silence by an observation or two.

"When they began to speak, one after the other spoke of standing with me. Ilsley said that were I to resign it would make the carrying out of conscription much more difficult. I told him I could not see why. He at once realized what the job would be. Even Crerar was nonplussed. Angus Macdonald was quiet for a time; Ilsley not saying too much.

"Power was very helpful by saying he thought Mr. King had a perfect right to expect those who were opposing voluntary enlistment to assume the obligation of carrying out conscription; that they were not fair to me. Dr. King was very outspoken. Mackenzie was solidly with me. Howe said he wanted a straight statement either for voluntary enlistment or for conscription. He would support either as Government policy, but wanted to be definite. He himself did not think there was need for conscription, but spoke of the great storm that had arisen. Gardiner said if I went out, he would go out. McLarty, I do not know how he went. Mulock and Gibson were very set at the start. Toward the end seemed to feel they would go with the conscriptionists. St. Laurent said of course he would go with me. Fournier, Bertrand and LaFlèche said they would do the same. It looked as though the entire Cabinet were pretty well agreed. I said I would want to tell Caucus what my attitude would be and would also want later to tell the House. The effect of so many of the men coming instantly to my side caused Angus Macdonald to say that it was apparent the Government was not for conscription; that there would be no conscription under it; that he thought he might perhaps resign at once. Then we were back to where we had been with Ralston. That he had intended to go out with him but had yielded to persuasion of others to stay along to save a crisis at the time but thought he should go home and write a short letter to me of resignation.

"Ilsley said he felt that he too would not be able to stay in a Government that had not a policy for conscription. I told Macdonald he ought to wait and come to Caucus tomorrow, not to think of resigning until at least he had heard the discussion in Caucus. He had said at one time he thought Caucus would support me strongly. I asked him if there could be better evidence that I was in the right. I thought he had said that the House would, but he said no, he meant only Caucus. He meant in the House we would be defeated. The Conservatives and Social Credit would join with many of our own people. In other words, it means that Macdonald is really prepared to go in with the Conservatives and Social Credit to help defeat the Liberal administration of which he is a Member. Ilsley was more reasonable a little later on. He said he would be prepared to stick out the two weeks to see how the public appeal went but he would have to tell Parliament what he felt about what he would have to do if it was not successful. I told him he would be quite free to do that and that Members would discuss the question fully. I did not want to control anyone. I would not be surprised if Macdonald should send me a note in the morning. He certainly will not stay. I made a very special appeal to Ilsley. I said I thought I should tell the Cabinet that if the men who were in the War Committee and half the others were to leave, that I would not be honest if I did not say I doubted if my own strength would last. That I would not be able to continue as the Leader of the Party under so great responsibilities. I said to Ilsley that he had charge of the finances of the country and was the only one in the Cabinet who knew the whole financial situation at this time and all that was involved. I asked him what would become of the country's war effort if he were out. I hoped he would stay at least until we saw how the next couple of weeks went. McNaughton made the interesting contribution that he had been able to find an additional three or four thousand men all told from the various sources to which he had gone for information. Mc-Naughton stressed very strongly to the Cabinet that the voluntary system had not failed; that he rather indicated the situation now was secure up to the end of January (I think he said this, although I am not quite sure of it). He emphasized there was still a serious problem regarding the French recruits.

"We did not get down to the exact number of days as the discussion became more general and old arguments began to be repeated. There was one thing, however, I was gratified about, namely getting agreement on the resolution which I have to place on the order paper tomorrow and which will read: 'That this House will aid His Majesty's Government in its policy of maintaining a vigorous war effort.' On Howe's suggestion, the word balanced after vigorous was left out. I had substituted aid for uphold as suggested a day or two ago by Power. Also used His Majesty's Government as was done with Churchill's resolution. It would be His Majesty's Canadian Government."

To the Prime Minister, the meeting was, in some ways, "the most solemn" so far held. "I noticed an expression of what I thought seemed real dismay or regret on the faces of some of the Ministers when I spoke of intended resignation as Leader. What strikes me as so cruel on the part of some of the Ministers is that they are quite prepared to gain all the strength that comes to them through my leadership but they are not prepared to help me maintain that position; rather are doing everything in their power to undermine me. Mulock swings back and forth depending on what seems to be the prevailing wind. Howe is uncertain. Gibson more or less to be counted with conscriptionists all the time.

"I talked over with St. Laurent the appalling situation that I was being placed in of thinking of carrying on the Government without Ministers like Ilsley, Howe and practically all the Ontario Ministers. I feel that McNaughton is worth more than Ralston, knows more about the whole business of the Department. I cannot see how I could carry on without Ilsley and Howe in particular. Howe looks very tired and weary.

"Among other things I mentioned to the Cabinet was that if left without the Ministers that had been on the War Committee and who had done such great work, I ought to say that at my age of 70, I did not see how I really could carry on and it would probably mean I would have to go in any event. Would have to ask the Governor-General to let someone else carry on. That it was owing to the country not to assume responsibility greater than one could carry. I mentioned to St. Laurent later in the evening how very difficult it was for me all alone at Laurier House with no one to talk to and by myself to face over too long a period the kind of situation I am faced with today. He was very helpful."

CHAPTER SEVEN

The Switch to Conscription

ON THE MORNING of Wednesday, November 22, the Prime Minister was just beginning to prepare for the day's programme when General McNaughton telephoned with "quite serious news." "That the Headquarters Staff here had all advised him that the voluntary system would not get the men. He had emphasized it was the most serious advice that could be tendered and he wished to have it in writing. Said he would come and see me as soon as he had the written statement. He expressed the opinion that it was like a blow in the stomach. He also said that he had the resignation of the Commander in Winnipeg. That if the Commanders, one after the other, began to resign, the whole military machine would run down, begin to disintegrate and there would be no controlling the situation."

To this news, Mackenzie King reacted quickly. "Instantly there came to my mind the statement I had made to Parliament in June as to the action the Government would necessarily take if we were agreed that the time had come when conscription was necessary. It is apparent to me that to whatever bad management this may have been due, we are faced with a real situation which has to be met and now there is no longer thought as to the nature of the military advice tendered, particularly by General McNaughton. And if so tendered by General McNaughton who has come into the Government to try to save the situation, it will be my clear duty to agree to the passing of the order in council and go to Parliament and ask for a vote of confidence, instead of putting before the House the motion that I have drafted and intended to hand the Clerk. This really lifts an enormous burden from my mind as after yesterday's Council it was apparent to me that it was only a matter of days before there would be no Government in Canada and this in the middle of war with our men giving their lives at the front. A situation of civil war in Canada would be more likely to arise than would even be the case were we to attempt to enforce conscription."

After this momentous decision, Mackenzie King's mind turned to possible procedures. "There might be a brief Caucus this afternoon. We should then have a meeting of the Cabinet. Have McNaughton present his recommendation and put through the order. Will say nothing of it tonight, but have the House meet tomorrow and hear McNaughton's statement which will review the situation in a way which will show why it is only now at this moment, that we have become convinced of the necessity. After McNaughton's statement tomorrow and he withdraws, I shall then read to the House what I have said of the matter of going to Parliament for approval, not having a second debate on conscription, and then ask for a vote of confidence."

Events moved rapidly during the day. "Before General McNaughton came in," Mackenzie King wrote, "went over parts of Hansard relating to what was said in 1942.

"General McNaughton read over memorandum from Chiefs of Staffs stating belief that voluntary enlistments would not find men needed.

"Mentioned resignation of Commanding Officer in Winnipeg [Brigadier R. A. Macfarlane]; thought there was a danger of the whole military machine disintegrating; appalling situation might arise therefrom; would have to cope with carefully.

"Re officers who have spoken at Vancouver; sending out Sansom [Lt.-General E. W. Sansom] to investigate; will deal with later.

"After McNaughton left, prepared material for statement to be made in House this afternoon. . . . Began my introduction with references to cause of assembling of Parliament; references to Ralston and McNaughton; statement re confidential nature of correspondence, etc.

"Also revised Order of Business from what arranged with Beauchesne just before and after lunch."

In view of Mackenzie King's decision earlier in the day, the proceedings in Parliament that afternoon were rather unreal. After prayers, the Prime Minister "rose to speak of death of Poirier [M.P. for Bonaventure]; spoke extemporaneously; was given long and continuous ovation by Members." The correspondence between the Prime Minister and Ralston was tabled and a Progressive Conservative motion advocating conscription was ruled out of order. As the Prime Minister put it, "Tories rather overplayed their part in emphasizing the haste with which things should be done. Also in their general behaviour pretty rowdy."

"Coldwell and Blackmore distinctly helpful.

"Most absurd part of Tory performance was a motion without notice; also Members standing to overrule the Speaker when there was no question of Order.

"No interruptions through the reading except by Hanson, of no importance. Some applause from Tories to statements in Ralston's letter.

"On the motion to adjourn announced the next day's business."

"Was successful in getting permission for McNaughton to speak to House tomorrow.

"Members also very pleased at day's proceedings; shaking hands."

Just before going into Caucus, the Prime Minister asked Angus Macdonald to come in and "told him not to take any action, but to come to meeting of Cabinet tonight. He said he would." At the party Caucus, Mackenzie King "was given a great reception by the Members." He began by speaking of the "presence of Colonel Ralston; of the separation; of missing him from my side. Explained difference of view. Hoped there would be no recriminations. Explained how the situation had arisen from large number of casualties in Canadian Infantry. How men in Government had had their souls tried in this experience. Suggested that they take time to read correspondence and have further Caucus in the morning, having in mind attitude of Tories in House.

"Because of other information reaching me then, that I thought Cabinet should meet tonight. Suggested other Members say their prayers tonight and hope all would be well in the morning.

"After going to my rooms, sent for St. Laurent. Told him of talk with McNaughton. He spoke of it as raising serious question of relations of Army with Government. Very serious if there was anything in the nature of a Palace revolution. I spoke of how impossible the whole matter of Government, law and order might become. He was very much perturbed. Felt that what was suggested might mean the loss of all the seats in Quebec. Mentioned he proposed to give up public life. Before going away he said he would promise to follow my judgment and leadership, but realized how very serious the situation might become."

Mackenzie King then returned to Laurier House, had a light dinner, and rested for a few minutes before going back to his office. "Day more or less first day of winter out of doors—cold, snow falling, melting. Tonight ground covered with snow.

"At office had quiet talk with Power. He thought I was taking the right step—the only step that could be taken to save the existence of the Government, but felt that he would himself have to drop out. He was not going to run anyway; he had done his job, etc. He looks pretty pale and frail. I spoke to him about friendship for him; what a friend I had been through the years. He said no man could have been more so; promised he would not speak out in Council, but would have to take a stand or quietly drop out.

"There was a very full meeting of Council; all present I think—21 [Power was not present until later]. Fournier, Bertrand and LaFlèche on sofa and others around table.

"Began by speaking a word about the proceedings in the afternoon in Caucus. Felt that about 80% of our men are behind me in the voluntary effort and policy.

"Said I had had a conversation this morning with General McNaughton which made it necessary for me to bring them together. That he had now got full data. Felt that while the voluntary system might have succeeded, it now looked as though it could not be counted upon to succeed. What he felt was needed was some way for securing a margin of security against possible failure. That he had a thought in mind on a proposal to take a limited number of men and train them to meet the situation. That I myself had come to feel that his suggestion would have to be most carefully considered.

"McNaughton then reviewed the situation. I was rather surprised that what he said was received so quietly. It was evident that the afternoon meeting of the House and the Caucus had been impressive.

"Gardiner came along with suggestion he had made yesterday about taking a limited number of men. Rather a lengthy discussion about resorting to the old suggestion of calling up limited numbers, not for the duration, but for four months.

"Claxton brought out his quota system, which seemed all right, excepting a little too involved again, and going too far into detail.

"Macdonald asked, if we had agreed on the general principles could we not leave the details to be worked out.

"Ilsley was completely silent throughout the night, though asked a question or two. Seemed to be relieved.

"French Ministers very quiet. LaFlèche succeeded in getting a number of volunteers from Petawawa Camp today.

"Discussion ready to break at a suggestion that McNaughton had to prepare his statement; trust him with working out details later. Members for most part agreed."

According to the Prime Minister, agreement was virtually reached "when Power suddenly came in and said he thought that he would not be able to follow. I had been too kind to him, etc. But he thought that, as he was not running again, it would be better for him to drop out. . . . I made a very strong appeal to him.

"Gardiner then said if others wanted to drop out he would have to drop out too. I then made a very strong appeal again, stating that all would have to be prepared to try to come and meet on as much common ground as we could. That if men were going to drop out I would have to drop out myself. That they could not realize what the responsibility had been, and the danger of a new Government for Canada in a time of war. They must help.

Begged them not to raise that question any further. Later on would see how things would develop.

"I got past this then spoke about proceedings in the morning. Speaking of press getting information. Made the unfortunate suggestion that it might be well to leave Caucus until after McNaughton's statement had been made.

"This brought forth a passionate volley from St. Laurent, who said we would have to do something to help them in Quebec; that if this were sprung on them in the afternoon a terrible situation might develop. I would have to go to Caucus and explain the position; that the whole thing would be like a bolt from the blue to the Members. I at once said how necessary this was and that he was right, etc.

"It was after this that the question arose with Power and Gardiner. I had then to speak as I did about how impossible it would be for me to hope to lead the party any longer unless I could get the support of Members who had been around me for years. That I could fight enemies without but not from within our own household. I then begged them to stay the night. Told them how I saw such a course necessary to save the country from disaster which would come with the collapse of Government in wartime. And much more particularly, that I did not intend to have on my conscience the thought that I had not done everything possible to ensure the lives of the men overseas; of wishing to do everything possible for these men while they were fighting to save our lives and make it possible for us to sit in Council and discuss the situation.

"I then said I would make one last appeal to them to stay united and pray with me to help to save the situation. We all then rose and I went out of Council.

"Dr. King followed me to the ante room. His voice trembled and almost broke down, saying that I had done the right thing. That I had literally saved Canada."

The Prime Minister did not wait to talk to the Ministers but went immediately to his office and sent for St. Laurent, Bertrand, and Fournier. "Had a word or two with them. Thanked them for staying as they did, but begged them to hold together. If we were united we could get the country to stay united and the war would be over. We could then get on with our social programs, etc.

"Later I had a few words with McNaughton about his address. Left when I looked at the clock at 5 to 11. After returning to Laurier House dictated this diary. . . .

"Today has gone well. Tomorrow will be very difficult and the following day possibly most difficult of all. But I believe the right decision has been reached. The only decision that could save our country from chaos while our men are sacrificing their lives for freedom overseas. We must above all keep them first in our thoughts.

"I have left nothing undone up to the present which could lessen their security. What has been done today will bring fresh courage to them and strengthen the hearts of their loved ones at home."

The next morning (November 23) Arnold Heeney sent to Laurier House the draft order in council, which he and others had worked on during the night, authorizing the drafting of 16,000 N.R.M.A. men for overseas service. "I made what I think were one or two important changes, which were accepted, and which Arnold said did improve matters considerably. The order began: 'Whereas it is necessary in order to ensure provision of adequate reserves'; I had it read: 'Whereas it has now become necessary, etc.' I substituted after the words 'dispatched to' for 'The United Kingdom of Great Britain and Northern Ireland and/or, etc.' the words: 'The United Kingdom and/or to European and/or Mediterranean operational theatres.'

"I had at first thought of having Council meet after McNaughton's statement, for a discussion, thinking it would be wiser not to sign the order until the Members had known our policy, when I recognized it was all-important I should make the announcement before McNaughton spoke, while a chance would be given to explain the policy in Caucus, I decided to have the Cabinet meet immediately after Caucus to put through the order.

"I then received from Pickersgill the statement which McNaughton proposed to make. Read it over carefully and made some slight but important changes. I then got McNaughton on the 'phone and went over the suggested changes with him and one or two other points that he himself brought up. We were able to agree on them all.

"I then spent some little time telephoning. It took me however until 11.30 before I could get to Caucus. In the meantime I had been told by Turnbull that he had a letter from Power which contained his resignation, and there was also a communication from Gardiner, which he thought meant difficulty from that source. I told him to hold them at the House of Commons office."

As soon as he reached the Hill, Mackenzie King went directly to the party caucus. "I had not had time, excepting while driving to the office, to think of what I would say. When I went in I was given a tremendous reception by the Members.

"A very remarkable instance of guidance occurred immediately after breakfast. I went in to the back secretary's office to inquire as to when

McNaughton's statement would be ready. While there I saw a letter among the mail, which I picked up, without knowing who it was from or what the contents were, I carried it away to the exclusion of other communications. When I opened it, I found it was from McConnell of 'The Star,' a kindly, understanding and sympathetic letter, but making clear at the end that The Star would have to come out for the sending of the men overseas—against the Government unless we decided to send the N.R.M.A. reinforcements overseas. . . . I immediately rang up McConnell, thanked him for his letter; told him he need have no concern; to hold his horses; not to let anything be printed until this afternoon was over; to keep this entirely to himself. He expressed great relief. There was a happy change in his voice. Said that that was splendid, which steadied the situation at once so far as the Montreal Star was concerned. I then thought of the other press that has helped us very much. I rang up Atkinson. He was very deaf. He kept mentioning they were greatly concerned what to do and were having their own struggle. He felt they would have to say that we should fix a day when public appeal would end, after which they would have to ask the Government to send N.R.M.A. men as reinforcements or they could not support us in our policy further. I told Atkinson he need not be concerned. It was hard to get him to understand but, finally, I did get through to him that steps will be taken today which will satisfy him. I could give him that assurance. He said, very well, that is good, and thanked me for letting him know. He said he was not well. I told him this news ought to help to cheer him. He then said the policy of our paper, once this matter is settled, will be to go after the Globe and other papers that have been fighting the Administration on this matter, and point out that the whole business has been engineered by financial interests; that they want to destroy our social legislation programme and get me out of the way for that reason, which I know is a fact, which I, as well as Atkinson, know for certain."

Continuing to rally support, the Prime Minister then telephoned Cardinal Villeneuve. "I had a little talk with him about his trip. Spoke of how well he had done and that I thought what he had done in England had been of great service and that he had stood out as a great figure in this world-war period. His reply was what I did was owing to you. He meant, of course, my example in crossing by 'plane and getting passage for him was my part. He said he had been wondering whether he should telephone me or come to Ottawa to see me. I told him I hoped to see him soon. He said he was going to make an address on the trip and would say some things that might be helpful.

"I then told him what had been decided last night. Said we would have to take a measure of conscription. I said: Your Eminence, I hope you will do what you can to interpret the situation. He said he understood our problem; saw the difficulties; while he hoped to see no conscription, he nevertheless realized that there were political sides to the matter which necessitated a certain action. He would be glad to see what he could do in a helpful way. It was an extremely pleasant talk. His Eminence mentioned at the close that he would as always continue to remember me in his prayers.

"Later, I got Godbout on the 'phone and explained the situation to him so that he would not be taken by surprise. Explained to him that it was a question of either the whole Government crashing or meeting the situation thus far, but that only in a partial way, keeping control in our own hands; that I hoped he would do what he could to steady the situation. He thanked me for letting him know and said he would wait and see. He made no definite promise but I felt he would seek to be helpful as far as he could.

"I then got Grant Dexter [Winnipeg Free Press] on the 'phone. Just gave him a word which would help to steady the Free Press at the moment. He was very pleased and spoke of wishing to come to see me later."

All the Ministers, except McNaughton, were present at Caucus and the Railway Committee Room was filled to the doors with Members and Senators. "I began by telling them of the attitude of the Opposition yesterday and other information, which had caused me to have a meeting of the Cabinet last night instead of a further Caucus. That they would see from the motion which Graydon had read that the Tory party were out for total conscription. I mentioned that I had come there in the morning without having had a chance to give a moment's thought to what I would say and would just let them know the chain of events as I recalled them. I then went through, in the presence of all the Ministers, and Ralston in the audience, what had taken place since the moment I got Ralston's cable, stressing the shock that the whole business was to my colleagues and myself and my being able to appreciate how stunned they would be. I then referred to their having had a chance to read the correspondence, but gave them more of an inside picture leading up to where, at the moment of Ralston's resignation, I had sought McNaughton's advice and pointed out what the situation would have been had he not agreed to come in. I pictured then the Government being left without a Minister of Defence; spoke of Power being away and ill; no Minister of Defence for Air and the possibility of other Ministers resigning, without mentioning it was apparent there would have been no Minister of Naval Affairs, no Finance Minister, no Minister of Munitions and Supply, and others. I told them to imagine the position I was in, and the party was in, at this time of war, and the consternation to the men giving their lives overseas. That it was like being in some great temple and having pillars pulled out from beneath and the whole thing crashing on my head. The Government laid in ruins at a time of war, and asked them how would that have helped the men abroad and what chaos we would have in the country. That I had to take every measure possible. I then expressed thanks to colleagues that had remained, and went on to detail further happenings much as is set forth in the diary. Coming then to the later situation and the efforts made for a public appeal, of the apparent failure of the public appeal, drawing nearer to the time when the security to men overseas was getting less and less. I then came to the part which had to do with last night's meeting and dwelt on the fact that unless each of us had been prepared to surrender to a certain extent the position we were holding firmly to and seek complete unity, that we might have to be facing this afternoon many resignations and in all probability resignation of the Government itself. I stressed how impossible it was for me to deal with some things and that I could not do it in time of war if colleagues were deserting. I said, happily, we are all together here; all of us are here this morning, united together. This caused Power to rise in his seat and say I had not stated the facts quite correctly; that he had said last night he could not stay in the Government with what, he termed, a change of policy in the light of the decision reached. Gardiner then rose later and said that he had not been satisfied with the conclusion of matters and he too had written me a letter this morning.

"I then pointed out I had not received either Power's letter or Gardiner's. That I had been working on his statement with McNaughton but I took advantage of the moment to say they would then see for themselves if one colleague after the other was going to leave me that I would be in a position where I would have to at once resign. That I had borne all I could; all that any human being could bear and with the responsibilities of the war and all, it was becoming too great unless I was sure of supporters at my side. I then told them of the conclusion we had arrived at and the necessity of taking from these camps a certain limited number to send overseas. Again referred to what was owing to the men who had been fighting, some of them away from home 4 or 5 years. Now on the eve of decisive battles, we could not possibly leave them without every assurance of support. We hoped the war would be over soon. They might not need any more men. We could not leave any uncertainty in their minds.

"I then told them it caused me no concern to say what I was saying to them as I felt I was right and a man who felt he was right had nothing to be concerned about. At an earlier time, speaking of possible break-up last night, I spoke of the faith which I had and which was strong and which was still sustaining me. That all would come well. I then told the party that they would have to at once face the question of finding a new Leader. That was all bound up in the situation which was before us and that they must not expect me, if I did not get real support from my own following, to seek to continue longer. I then stressed what the situation would be. Some kind of a Government would be formed which would demand complete conscription and which would be related not only to this war but possibly also the Japanese war as well. Spoke of the whole of our social legislation being destroyed. The party probably being destroyed and heaven only knows what might happen to the country in all this situation. I made it clear to them that on no condition would I consider dissolution myself. That responsibility would have to come on someone else. When I spoke of finding some new Leader, there were shouts on every side: no, no, but I brought them back to the reality. I said no matter how earnest I was to carry on in the situation, it was impossible, and I could not meet impossibilities. I referred again and again to how trying the situation was for them as well as for me but that we all had to meet these situations. I thought I ought to let them know in a general way the contents of the order pointing out I would have to announce it in the House. It would be followed by McNaughton's statement, etc.

"I made one last appeal that I hoped we could all keep together but for them to realize all the implications. Pointed out too that I would not misjudge anyone's actions. They must take them in the light of what was likely to follow. That on the heads of each one would rest measure of responsibility for what happened to our country at this time."

Ralston spoke next. "Was not difficult. Explained his position. Thought I perhaps had not told as much of what he had said of the need for compulsion at earlier times. I felt his speech was helpful to my position rather than otherwise. Gardiner spoke. Made it clear he had not tendered his resignation. Spoke at some length of being a Liberal and what Liberalism stood for, etc. He then went on to speak of some of the things that he thought should be done. Spoke of his affection for myself as a Leader; his speech was only partly helpful.

"As we were getting on to two o'clock, I told the Chairman not to let the discussion go further when Ralston had concluded. Got the Ministers and said the Cabinet had to meet, and went out.

"I thought the Caucus broke up in an amazingly good way considering what they had to go through. I counselled strongly secrecy. When speaking, I never saw faces so earnest. I watched in particular the faces of many of the French Members. Some of them carried an expression with them of a people that seemed to feel that others had their hand out against them. Very determined look with the jaw drawn forward; eyes partially closed, on the looks of some of them. It is a thousand pities that the educational standards are not higher in Quebec and that prejudices are so strong.

"In speaking either this morning or yesterday, I dwelt on how Quebec had saved Canada for the Empire in 1776; again in 1812. Spoke of the position of Quebec, of men in minority in race and religion, and apologized to them on behalf of the Protestants in Ontario for the way in which they were being insulted by Orangemen and others in some of the parts of Ontario. Tried to let them see I really understood their position."

The Ministers assembled in Mackenzie King's office in the House. "I was seated at the table, looking in the direction of the bust of my grandfather. There was complete silence for a while as we were assembling. I dreaded another discussion on the order in council; was not sure when it was actually before the Ministers, someone would not take exception to what had been drafted, though it was completely in accord with what was agreed to last night. Gardiner did not get the call to come but I sent for him particularly just before the Caucus broke up.

"When all were together, I read the order through very quietly and carefully and when I had finished it, I said I would read it again and did so. St. Laurent raised the question about our power to send the men overseas. On looking up the Statute which we had to search to get, we found that that aspect was all right. Then came the question of striking out the 16,000, lest the question should be raised that it would conflict with my statement that we would put the Act into force which would mean the entire lot were liable. After some careful consideration, we left the broad statement giving full powers but inserted as well 16,000 which the Minister could dispose of but added a clause that additional numbers would have to be secured under the order in council. This over, I took a pen and signed the order with certain changes which I had made pencilled on it. When I found we had got that far without any break, it was then nearly 2.45, I broke up the meeting at once but got Gardiner in time to show him what had been done in the order. McNaughton came in much distressed to say that the Speaker was not going to let him have his officers on the floor with him. I had difficulty in reaching the Speaker. Finally found it was one of Beauchesne's troublesome matters. Told the Speaker they must be allowed to come in. That was arranged.

"The bells were already ringing for prayers when Heeney brought me a freshly typed certified copy, holding my other as the original. I had to miss prayers in order to have this material in shape to table.

"This morning, before going to Caucus, word came from Turnbull that at 10.45, a letter had come from Mr. Power; also that there was possible trouble over Gardiner. I thought he said a letter had come from him as well. I told Turnbull to hold the letter. I could get it from him when I got to the House of Commons. I had to keep on with going over McNaughton's speech with him which delayed me. Doing this, I made use of the words 'effective support of the Army' instead of referring to 'full strength' as this is certain to lead to questions in the House. . . .

"After the Caucus, I explained to Power how it was I had not received his letter. I had made mention of that in Caucus when he took exception to my saying we were all there together. Also explained the same point to Gardiner.

"After the Caucus, Power came to the Cabinet meeting with the others. Said to me at the door as we were going in: Don't on any account let McNaughton announce Government policy. Be sure and do that yourself. There will be a terrible storm if he does. It might indicate the military directing everything. He asked if I would not speak first. I told him I could not possibly make my speech at this stage. That I would, before McNaughton came into the House at all, state the Government's policy and read the order in council. McNaughton would then follow with his explanations.

"I noticed that the papers later gave almost exclusive space to what McNaughton had said and some of them rather indicated directly that he had made the announcement at the end of his speech. They had had so little time to get out the statement by myself in the interval. One thing that pleased me very much was that for once Members of Caucus had maintained a marvellous secrecy about its proceedings. Norman MacLeod [of B.U.P. in press gallery] did get a tip from someone. He has some pipeline and was able to get out a 'scoop.' I understand word got over to the Rideau Club before the House opened. A person with whom Hanson spoke said that was quite impossible. That I would not dare to do that. However up to the time the House met, the secret had been kept so far as the general public and Opposition groups in the House were concerned. Something really quite marvellous.

"Power stayed in my room while other Ministers were there and we were discussing the order. He did not stay for the full discussion but before it was signed, he came over and handed me the envelope containing his resignation. He shook hands with me and thanked me in a warm and friendly way. He was sorry that he had to take the step but did not see how he could possibly do otherwise.

"None of the Members rose as he left my desk to walk out of the door nor did he attempt to shake hands with others. I do not recall anything being said. We went ahead in a regular way as though nothing of significance had happened, though for a moment there was some real concern feeling that on Power's part, perhaps, this action might have been postponed. If he had said nothing at the Cabinet, nothing at Caucus this morning, his resignation might well have been left until today and some way might have been found of meeting the situation so far as he is concerned though I doubt it. Perhaps the order in which things happened is all for the best."

When Mackenzie King went into the House he had "not had time to think out what I would say by way of announcing the policy so I simply read the order in council with a prefatory word." He added that "in the House, there was very marked applause from our side when I had read the order. The Tories looked greatly disconcerted; no applause from them. Some of our men did not applaud. Hanson called out 'Surrender.' I thought the order seemed favourably received in the other groups but not markedly so. There was an element of real surprise on the other side of the House."

The House gave unanimous consent to the Minister of National Defence coming in and sitting at the Clerk's table. McNaughton was accompanied by certain officials. "From that moment on, after McNaughton came in," Mackenzie King wrote, "the Tory party were in a very nasty mood. Graydon called on Ralston as though he were to be the prosecuting attorney and McNaughton in the witness box. Lawyer after lawyer of the official Opposition monopolized the time questioning and really browbeating McNaughton. I had had him move his chair near my side with officers on either side: Major General Gibson and Brigadier DeLalande, with their tables and records. McNaughton was visibly very tired having been up till about 5 in the morning on his speech. His first appearance in the House; and the badgering tactics of the Opposition; I could see he got very flushed around the temples at times but he maintained a sweet calm. Once or twice, he gave a retort which was well deserved. When adjournment came at 6, I think it was felt throughout the House that he had made a very good impression and the sympathy was wholly with him. His manner was in contrast with Ralston's though both maintained a quiet dignity and avoided anything like an open conflict."

In the evening the examination of McNaughton in the House continued. To Mackenzie King, the General "was still obviously very tired but handled himself well. There was less badgering than there had been in the afternoon. The galleries were jammed with people. Press galleries in particular. Reporters piled on the backs of each other. It was curious how little one even was conscious of the presence of another soul. I felt it perfectly natural to be in the House. Indeed felt in better shape than I have felt at almost any time. Quite happy in fact."

The next day (Friday, November 24) Mackenzie King saw Alphonse Fournier who felt he would have to resign and who stayed away from the House for several days. He also saw C. G. Power at noon. Mackenzie King still had Power's "letter of yesterday in my pocket. I had not thus far drafted an answer. I could see he looked pretty weak and flabby. I spoke to him about resting up. He said that he would go down to St. Pacôme, but he said he thought he ought to appear in the House first if only to speak for five minutes. I then spoke to him about reconsidering his whole position. He spoke about having said good-bye to the staff; that Leckie [Chief of the Air Staff] was a good man. He had said there was no politics in their office." The Prime Minister and Power had some discussion about possible successors and about the political situation in Quebec. Then Mackenzie King "finally asked him if he would not reconsider his resignation and reminded him that he was still a Minister. This seemed to cheer him very much. Mackenzie had changed his seat in the House. Fortunately I 'phoned Mackenzie earlier not to change it, but reminded him that until I accepted Power's resignation he still remained a Minister. We agreed that we would announce it was correct that he had resigned, but I would say that I wished to consider the matter further. This I did when the House met at 3. He seemed a bit hesitant. He doubted if he would go back to practice in Quebec. Says he might open a practice of law in Montreal." The Prime Minister asked Ian Mackenzie to "see Power who I think might be perhaps prepared to stay on to see the war out. I think, however, there are two things weighing with him. One is he has made a great name through the Air Training. From now on there will be the appalling difficulties of demobilization. The second thing is that Ralston had given him a free hand and like Angus Macdonald, [he] feels especially drawn to Ralston. His letter of resignation makes clear his feeling in that direction. Power's case is a tragic one. He has a great popular way with him with men in the House."

The Prime Minister stayed in the House throughout the afternoon and commented that "the tone was quite different. The badgering was over. The Tories had evidently seen they had made a mistake. McNaughton was not so tired and really handled himself extremely well. I had engineered things to have the proceedings brought to a close at 6. Members I think were glad to get off for the week-end."

After the House rose, Mackenzie King went to see the Governor-General and told him why the Cabinet had passed the order. The Prime Minister referred to "the deep cut" they could see "had been made in Canadian unity; that Quebec Members would be in the House what Irish Members

General de Gaulle at the National War Memorial, Ottawa, July 11, 1944, with the Hon. J. L. Ralston and the Governor-General, the Earl of Athlone

Left: General de Gaulle speaking to the crowd assembled on Parliament Hill. Princess Alice is to the right of the Governor-General and the Prime Minister

The crowd on Parliament Hill. Members of the Cabinet may be seen in the front row

Mackenzie King examines the scroll presented to him at the banquet August 7, 1944, marking his 25th anniversary as leader of the Liberal party. It had been signed by all Liberal senators and members of the House of Commons. Also presented on this occasion were a bronze bust of the Prime Minister, a silver statuette of him with his dog "Pat," and a silver salver with the signatures of delegates from Waterloo and York constituencies who were present at the 1919 convention which chose Mr. King as leader

Above: The Hon. J. L. Ralston congratulating Mackenzie King after proposing a toast at the anniversary dinner

Right: Mr. George Hopper of Merrivale, Ont., shakes hands with the Prime Minister at a reception on the occasion of the anniversary dinner

The Cabinet, September 7, 1944: (*front row, left to right*) Angus Macdonald, J. E. Michaud, C. G. Power, T. A. Crerar, Mackenzie King, J. L. Ralston, J. L. Ilsley, C. D. Howe, L. S. St. Laurent; (*back row*) E. Bertrand, H. Mitchell, W. P. Mulock, N. A. McLarty, Ian Mackenzie, J. H. King, J. G. Gardiner, J. A. MacKinnon, C. Gibson, A. Fournier, L. R. LaFlèche

The Cabinet, June 19, 1945: (*front row, left to right*) L. S. St. Laurent, J. A. MacKinnon, C. D. Howe, Ian Mackenzie, Mackenzie King, J. L. Ilsley, J. G. Gardiner, C. Gibson, H. Mitchell; (*back row*) J. J. McCann, Paul Martin, Joseph Jean, J. A. Glen, Brooke Claxton, A. Fournier, E. Bertrand, A. G. L. McNaughton, L. Chevrier, D. C. Abbott, D. L. MacLaren

Second Quebec Conference, September 1944. Mr. Churchill, accompanied by Mrs. Churchill and Mackenzie King, leaves his private car to greet President Roosevelt

Below: The Prime Minister has a conversation with Mrs. Churchill

Below: The Governor-General, President Roosevelt, Mr. Churchill, and Mackenzie King on the terrace of the Citadel

British and Canadian leaders confer at the Quebec Conference: (*left to right*) General Pope; General Murchie; Vice Admiral Jones; C. G. Power (*hidden*); Louis St. Laurent; T. A. Crerar; Norman Robertson; the Prime Minister; A. D. P. Heeney; J. L. Ralston; Angus Macdonald; Humphrey Mitchell; C. D. Howe; J. L. Ilsley; Malcolm MacDonald; Lord Leathers; Mr. Churchill; Field Marshal Alan Brooke; Admiral Cunningham; Air Marshal Portal; Sir John Dill; General Ismay; Air Marshal Leckie

Mrs. Roosevelt is escorted by Mackenzie King to the Prime Minister's reception at the Chateau Frontenac, Quebec

General McNaughton, making his first public appearance as Minister of National Defence, at a parade in Arnprior, November 4, 1944

Below: General Crerar arrives with the Prime Minister on Parliament Hill to receive an official welcome on his return from Europe, August 7, 1944

v.j. Day on Parliament Hill, August 15, 1945.
The Prime Minister with the Soviet Ambassador,
His Excellency George Zaroubin, and Mrs. Zaroubin,
and the Chinese Ambassador, Dr. Liu Shih Shun

Mackenzie King and Louis St. Laurent broadcast to Canada from San Francisco, v.e. Day, May 8, 1945

v.j. Day celebrations on Parliament Hill, with the Canadian ensign flying.

Below: The Canadian group at the San Francisco Conference: (*left to right*) C. S. Ritchie, P. E. Renaud, Elizabeth MacCallum, Senator Moraud, Escott Reid, W. F. Chipman, L. B. Pearson, Senator J. H. King, Louis St. Laurent, Mackenzie King, Gordon Graydon, M. J. Coldwell, Mrs. Casselman, Jean Désy, Hume Wrong, Louis Rasminsky, Dana Wilgress, General Pope, R. Chaput

Dominion-Provincial Conference, Ottawa, August 6, 1945:
(*left to right*) Hon. E. C. Manning; Hon. J. W. Jones; Hon. S. S. Garson;
Hon. A. S. MacMillan; Hon. G. A. Drew; Mackenzie King; Hon. M. L. Duplessis;
Hon. J. B. McNair; Hon. J. Hart; Hon. T. C. Douglas

had been in the British House, through great difficulty in handling the great problems of reconstruction and on the international side. There will be a cleavage that may go very far. Power had said that he thought the Liberal party would cease to be any force in Quebec for a time. Extremists would hold everything. Later there would be a revolt of a section of the community against the lower clergy in their interference and a new party would be born in that way. Much as was the case in the coming into being of the present party under Laurier."

He went on to tell the Governor-General "about the action of the Chiefs of Staff and the Army Council in presenting McNaughton with the advice that they did and which he had secured in the form of a written memorandum, to the effect that voluntary enlistment would no longer be able to supply the men. How McNaughton had been left at the mercy of his military advisers. That if I did not accept that advice he would be able to get nowhere with the army and might be confronted with a sort of palace revolution. Evidence of what they would do was seen in the Winnipeg Commander tendering his resignation, which had been quickly accepted. Also in the action of the men in B.C. before they had had talks with Pearkes. I said that was my real reason for suddenly agreeing to a measure of conscription. That I had found not only the military advisers had so advised, but considering the position we were in as a civil power I was immediately confronted with the possibility of chaos in Canada, a complete collapse of authority of the Government and our country being left without any administration at this time. No one prepared to take hold and no military power in the country of a character which would keep order. The situation was desperate. The only way it could be saved was by myself being prepared to be crucified between those on one side who would be resigning for one reason and those on the other who would resign for an opposite reason. I told him how I had striven to keep unity as far as we could."

He added that he felt he "had taken the only right course, though practically all were against me at this time. The Governor asked me the question: Who would take hold, who is there? I said to him if I had resigned there was no one who would be prepared to take on. I would not be able to continue after having resigned, and spoke of Bracken not being even in the House. Said that Graydon would not take on and certainly not Coldwell or Blackmore and that even so far as our own men were concerned there was not one of them, Ralston or the others, who would. I was sure that Ilsley could not do anything at this time. The Governor said he could not see who there was."

The final paragraph in the day's diary reads: "At luncheon yesterday, I saw for the first time the framed address signed by all the Liberal Members and Senators which was presented to me on my 25th anniversary. . . . I looked at it and read it again. Thought of how quickly a man's position changes from the top of everything one month, and in a few months, at the bottom of everything."

The next morning (Saturday, November 25) Mackenzie King telephoned Ian Mackenzie and spoke to him about Power. Mackenzie "said he had talked to him last night. He was very friendly but was quite adamant about not continuing. He doubted the wisdom of saying much more to him. I told Mackenzie that I would prepare a reply [to Power's letter of resignation] but would not table it until the adjournment on Monday night."

The Prime Minister learned that there were meetings of Liberals being held in Quebec and it was suggested he should telephone Godbout. Mackenzie King "got him at his home. He spoke in a quiet sensible way and began by expressing his sympathy for me in the very trying position I was in. I referred to his position being similar to my own and appreciating it. I made no mention of having heard that any declaration was being issued or that they were contemplating issuing any statement but spoke along the following lines. Asked him if he could do anything to steady the situation until I had spoken in the House on Monday and said I thought this would help very much. Said I intended to have a talk with the Quebec men by themselves just as soon as the speech was over. I would tell them some things there that I had not been able to say to anybody as to the situation that would have been created if my actions had not been taken. Said that my speech in the House would make very clear how inevitable it was for me to take this step. There was bigger significance than the question relating to overseas reinforcements. I said the whole thing comes down to whether at the moment there is to be any Government in Canada at all. That I did not mean just a Liberal Government, but any Government, Conservative or C.C.F., in Canada. Said I would make very clear on Monday that I imagined there would be chaos in Canada if we had no Government in Canada in time of war. If my resignation was in as it may yet be then there would be the job of forming a Government and I did not think any Government would be formed in any way, except maybe after some days. In the meantime word would go out while this war was on and our men fighting at the front and that government had given place to anarchy in Canada. Anything that could be done to steady the situation would be helpful. Men voting against me was quite secondary. Sometimes men had to be driven to where they will be crucified to save the State. I felt that Friday was my day of crucifixion. Having men on each side of me taking opposite positions. If one group left the Government was gone, if the other group left the Government was gone, but if they would only stay with me until I made my speech and see what the motions are I feel that this way we should be able to carry the situation. But if anything happened to add flame to the fire chaos might instantly follow."

According to Mackenzie King, Godbout said he "was anxious to be helpful and that he hoped I would realize how his party and colleagues were pressing him to come out with a statement at once. He said he would do his best to hold back any statement until Monday." Godbout also "spoke about the attitude that he had taken in 1942 and also in his campaign which made it really difficult for him to do other than take a certain stand. I said I realized his difficulty in that regard, but the thing to do was to hold everything until after the speech. I mentioned that the matter was above anything about party victory, that it was affecting all parts of Canada. The real issue was whether there would be any Government at all. He seemed to appreciate the solemnity of this and said he would do everything possible he could. It would look as though we had come literally to the point of King or chaos.

"I thought everything Godbout said was very fine. He revealed a truly noble spirit, particularly when I realized what he is faced with so far as Duplessis and his own colleagues are concerned. He too is very much in the same terrible position I am in. In conclusion he assured me again he would do all he could to withhold the statement until Monday. As to the time of the vote, he assumed it would be Tuesday. I said it might be that the Members would be ready to vote after hearing the leaders, but that others might wish to speak and I could not be sure. I think he was anxious to try to hold things until the vote took place."

In the event Godbout did make a critical statement but there is no doubt this conversation with the Prime Minister helped to moderate his attitude.

That morning's newspapers, Mackenzie King noted, had carried a report of "1000 troops staging a protest parade in B.C. with signs 'down with conscription.' Fortunately these were not French Canadian troops. I have heard nothing serious since."

Pickersgill came to Laurier House that evening and Mackenzie King and he "spent until half past ten talking together in front of the fire of matters which I had referred to the special committee in the morning on the exact meaning of the conscription order in council and the position of N.R.M.A. men. Also on points to be brought out in speech. He gave me a splendid paragraph which Pope had secured from a speech of Sir John Macdonald at the time of Confederation."

On Sunday, November 26, Mackenzie King wrote in his diary that the night before he had difficulty getting to sleep and "got on to the idea of perhaps finding it would be advisable to resign before the campaign in the New Year.

"I have no doubt about the Government being defeated at this time. I have, however, considerable concern about attempting to go through an election and, particularly, as I certainly will not be able to think of taking up in the new Parliament the problems that are ahead of us. Before the year is out I will be over 70. I thought I might have a convention of the party at the time fixed for Parliament re-assembling, at which time I would be probably proroguing Parliament; then have the party select a new Leader. I could keep on in the office of Prime Minister, watching the war, while the campaign is on, letting the new Leader give his time to the campaign, or if desired have him installed in office, which would be better, and work steadily at his side, say as Minister of External Affairs, either with or without participating in the campaign. This got me a little roused. I tried to banish the thoughts."

Mackenzie King spent the morning of Monday, November 27, quietly going over alone the material he had assembled for his speech. He had just time to glance over his notes before going into the House.

"I had first of all to deal with Power's resignation, which I presented in a quiet way. After the letters were read—I think the way they were written made a good impression—Power made a speech in reply which he had written out and which I thought was exceedingly good. It said things that needed to be said but which only a man who had been in the war could well have said as, for example, being critical of the general plan of campaign which by the way he really disclosed to the enemy by saying that Eisenhower's plan was to go straight ahead. It is true that Eisenhower has said pretty much the same thing himself, but [Power pointed out] that the size of the army should be reduced and that the men should be taken out of the line. Power's speech gave me a splendid opening as it made clear in the House of Commons just as his speech and Gardiner's remarks have made clear in Caucus how I was between opposing forces trying to hold irreconcilable elements together. Power referred to having resigned for an opposite reason to that of Ralston. This gave me a splendid opening for what I had to say when the time came. I feel that I spoke well, having opened quietly and not referring much to notes, finding no difficulty in expressing myself and indeed being able to do so forcibly and adequately by not being tied to any manuscript. The one distressing part of the speech which spoiled its proportions and made it too long and was a genuine blur were the long quotations in regard to what was stated in 1942." He noted that "the quotation from Sir John Macdonald helped to focus not only the attention of the House but the attention of the country on how tremendously critical the situation is. It helped to force it right to the fore."

Quotations in his speech from Laurier and Lapointe, he felt, "gave me just what was needed to round off what I had to say. But not having had the chance to more than read them, I was unable to give them the setting that they should have had. This I could have done if I had not been so tired from the long reading of the other extracts. One quotation from Sir Wilfrid as to his aims and purposes was one that I was able to repeat verbatim as for myself. This was particularly fortunate. I was glad to be able to link my life so closely with his in the great purpose that each of us have had as the central one of our political lives. Altogether I felt at ease throughout speaking, and then was given a real ovation by the Members at the close."

At the conclusion of his speech, and after a direct and dramatic appeal to the Liberal rank and file, he moved a motion of confidence in the government, "That this House will aid the government in its policy of maintaining a vigorous war effort."

The next morning, Tuesday, November 28, the Prime Minister attended a caucus of the Liberal Members from Quebec. He reported that "all were exceedingly friendly. I shook hands with everyone. There was not an ill-natured remark or look on the face of any one. General McNaughton accompanied me. Dr. Thauvette [the caucus chairman] made a little speech in French and then called on me to speak. Here again I sought to bring home to the Members that the real question of the moment was not so much that of conscripting a limited number of men for overseas as it was the question of whether we would have any government at all. I made it very plain to them that I would not continue as Leader unless I got a good support from my own party. I let them know the care I had to take of my health to carry on without a break, to let them realize that the reaction from the present strain might even later on make it difficult for me to do more than see, at the time of the elections, if I would still be in shape to lead the party. I think they really began to see how vast was the issue, how very serious and critical and certainly realized that there had been no deception on my part, but circumstances had forced the situation as it is. I could see they were distressed as to how they could get their constituents to understand the position.

"Bertrand handed me a little note to speak to them about their electors. I told them to explain to their electors how it had come about that we had to take the action we did to save the Government and myself from having to resign, and if there had been no Government the almost certain result that the conscriptionist people of this country would get control of the Government and would then be for all-out conscription. Heaven knows what would happen to the country meanwhile. I explained to them that behind all this lay the desire of the financial interests to destroy our social legislation. They had never liked the family allowances and some other measures and had blamed me for catering to Quebec and certainly if they came into power that part of our policy would be sure to be wiped out.

"I spoke to them of the seriousness of not giving the men at the front all the support that was needed. I let them know that they did not have to take responsibility for the decision reached by the Cabinet, that that was something the Cabinet itself had taken and it was passed. What they were really responsible for was to say whether they would support the Government in the administration of its war policies. McNaughton then made a fine speech. They gave him a very warm reception. In fact they gave him an ovation when he began and at the conclusion of his speech. He told them of the position of the French Canadian regiments. Of his having given orders to have the French regiments and the others all brought back [on overseas leave] to the province to which they belonged. This they cheered very much. He also spoke of the response that had already come and dealt sympathetically with the whole position, making clear however how critical it was regarding the French regiments and how necessary to have them quickly reinforced. He announced that Hugues Lapointe had been made a Colonel which caused them all to cheer. It is a hard day for him as this is the anniversary of his father's death. I told McNaughton how much Lapointe was in my thoughts."

Before he went to the House that afternoon (November 28) Mackenzie King had received word from Hanson that Gordon Graydon was ill and that Hanson would be acting House Leader. "Said he was not going to make trouble himself, but some of his own party might be objecting to a secret session. We both went into the Chamber. The Speaker was waiting for Graydon before Prayers. I told him Graydon was not coming and when Prayers were over I spoke of understanding last night that we would meet in a Secret Session. There was some discussion about the rules, resolution not being necessary, etc.

"I read to them [the House] extracts of what had been said at Westminster and told them we decided to follow the practice there. The Speaker finally announced that he intended to declare a Secret Session. Harris [J. H. Harris, Conservative M.P. for Toronto Danforth] made a very strong protest which he followed up by walking out of the House. I rather admired the way Hanson made it clear himself in advance that he did not intend to offer any objections; would leave those that felt they had to speak out to say so. I am afraid poor Graydon is sick as a consequence of the division in his own party and the arrogance of some of the men he has to contend with.

"The session turned out to be really very worthwhile. McNaughton was able to give very full particulars of the situation; also figures as to casualties, etc. He indicated how the present crisis had arisen and others that showed the absolute necessity of getting troops overseas and having necessary reinforcements.

"Ralston I thought showed up in a poor light. He had to admit that it was not until after his return from Europe, at the meeting of the Cabinet on October 23, that he had seen for the first time a communication which General Crerar had sent to Stuart saying he was concerned about reinforcements." Ralston "had denied what had appeared in the Financial Post. Gave Gillis a wholly erroneous impression."

In fact on the previous Thursday (Hansard, Nov. 23, pp. 6553–4) Gillis, the C.C.F. Member for Cape Breton South, had read in the House the following extract from the *Financial Post* of November 18: "It appears that the start of the crisis was a telegram from England to Canada early in August. This telegram expressed alarm at the shortage of infantry and urged that further steps be taken to increase the flow of trained infantry reinforcements to the European theatre. Early in 1943 and again in the spring of 1944 increases had been made in the proportion of infantry troops to total army manpower. Instead of being acted upon apparently the telegram was pigeon-holed. Not only was no action taken by the military, but what is now considered much more serious, the situation was not brought to the attention of the Minister or the War Cabinet. Presumably the cabinet staff officers were figuring on an early end to the war and ignored the overseas request. Only when Colonel Ralston arrived overseas in October did he learn about the matter. By that time nearly two and a half months had passed. Had the matter been dealt with in early August and a large number of men diverted into the infantry pool at that time the present crisis might never have arisen." Gillis had then asked whether the Minister (McNaughton) had "any knowledge of the truth or otherwise of that statement." Ralston had intervened at once and said: "I do not imagine the Minister would have any knowledge of it. That would have to do with my own administration. I know of no telegram that was sent from overseas with regard to a matter of that kind which was not brought to the attention of the Minister. Any important wire on a matter of that kind would be brought to the attention of the Minister."

In his diary for November 28, Mackenzie King continued: "I was shocked at the time, but thought it inadvisable to say anything. But today, after he [Ralston] had spoken, Paul Martin came to me with the Hansard ... showing how completely different his statement was today and asking if he should not be exposed. I told Martin not to do so; there would be time enough in the debate. Members would see matters themselves and not to make it any more difficult and impossible.

"What was brought out very clearly was that we had had no real information in the Cabinet with respect to casualties and what was the real significance and need for reinforcements until, at the very earliest, September, before Ralston was going abroad, and then only a statement that there had been heavy casualties in Infantry. But he [Ralston] had made no recommendations at that time of the need for reinforcements and Members I think felt very strongly that first of all Ralston had not himself got the information he should have got from Stuart. Mentioned for example the telegram from Crerar and that he [Ralston] had not given the Cabinet any real information until his recommendation came before us. This was in answer to Sinclair's question that he could not understand why the Cabinet should have got the shock it did when he returned.

"Hanson sought to have it appear that we had knowledge of 'these casualties' before Ralston left. But I at once pointed out we had nothing of the sort. That the estimate was for over-all casualties which had not been reached and that the most we could have had was general mention of Infantry casualties being high but nothing of a character or nature of a recommendation at that time.

"Macdonald later made it clear he thought Stuart and officers overseas knowing the policy of the Government were doing their best to remuster in the hopes that they would get through all right, which undoubtedly is true. But Ralston admitted that until he was in Italy he was not fully apprised of the reinforcement situation."

McNaughton, in the Prime Minister's judgment, handled himself "extremely well in the secret session," and "the sitting on the whole was conducted in an orderly and for the most part sober and solemn way, though it was clear Hanson and one or two of his men were seeking to score politically. I felt very strongly that as a result of this afternoon's secret session our men would be greatly incensed at Ralston and that the feeling would turn heavily against him for having been really responsible for the Cabinet not having been informed as we should have been informed—not first of all getting information himself from his staff, secondly, not informing the Cabinet as he should have done, and thirdly, being responsible for leaving the whole matter so late and having precipitated this crisis in so short a time. I think too the Members must have come to feel it was pretty fortunate that I had steered the whole question as I have, and particularly that the Government and country were most fortunate in having McNaughton as Minister of Defence. He makes an excellent impression, giving a sense of real knowledge of the situation and complete understanding of what is to be done in addition to appealing to French Members by his known desire to have matters carried out on a voluntary basis. I shall be surprised if there are not some pretty strong statements made by some of our Members of the way in which the Defence Department has handled itself in the war and allowing this situation to develop at this time. I am sure too that all will feel it was a mighty fortunate thing that Parliament was brought together when it was.

"We had not completed the sitting at 6 and there was no objection to our continuing in the evening which made it clear that the Members felt they were getting real information, information that was most important and which could be given only in Secret Session."

The Secret Session continued from 8.00 till 11.00 P.M. Mackenzie King reported that "McNaughton did remarkably well and we got out a mass of information which I was glad indeed for our men to have. Ralston did not take much part but when he did he kept following the line that he did in Council—protesting that sending extra men to Italy meant nothing in the manpower situation. He tried to make out that he had told Council of the need for reinforcements one day when I was not there. I was able, however, on what Stuart said had taken place on August 4th and of no reference being made at Quebec, to state emphatically that it was not until after Ralston came back from Italy that any recommendation was made for reinforcements. I think the House generally was amazed at the situation. I am sure I am right. On all sides there is a feeling that it was a mighty fortunate thing for Canada that Ralston had been replaced by McNaughton. Ralston's management of the Department of Defence had permitted things to go far too far as regards the size of the army, the numbers of the men kept in the army in general service, but not in combatant service, but in other ways."

In the course of the secret sitting McNaughton was asked a question about disturbances in western Canada. He handed Mackenzie King a report he had just received. "He said he thought he should say nothing. I told him not to. He replied he was there to answer questions on the general situation but had not had a chance to discuss anything else with his officials. The report he handed me was as follows:

'From: The General Officer Commanding, Pacific Command

'The situation at Terrace can now only be considered as mutiny—approximately 1600 men affected in Fusiliers de St. Laurent, Prince

Edward Islanders and Prince Albert Volunteers paraded as a demonstration without disorder yesterday. About 25% of garrison controlling the remainder by intimidation, occupying well organized positions with six-pounders mounted. Have asked Attorney-General to close liquor stores and prevent movement of liquor into it. Brigadier Roy and Lt.-Col. L'Heureux now endeavouring to regain control of French units.'

We got through the evening without having to say a word on this phase."

After the sitting, Mackenzie King, McNaughton, and St. Laurent met to discuss the explosive situation at the camp at Terrace, B.C. "I have seldom seen a look of greater concern on anyone's face than that which came over St. Laurent's face as he thought of the situation as it might develop. The gravity of the situation was apparent the moment McNaughton told us what he had said in Council might happen. That if the troops began to resist he had not the soldiers or the men to enforce law and order. He added that what he could do was to call out the Militia in aid of the civil power but its men were for the most part employed in munitions and the like and that would mean cutting down supplies of ammunition and create other difficulties as well. He thought they could be trusted to do their entire duty, but it was a matter of trust. He added that in the Defence Department there had been nothing prepared in the way of plans to meet a possible situation of the kind. They had evidently taken it for granted that all that had to be done was to say the men would be conscripted and they would be. He had been kept in the House all day, unable to work out any plans with his officials and unable therefore to give much attention to this immediate situation, but would begin doing so tonight. Here was exactly what McNaughton had told the Cabinet would happen if we had to resort to conscription. The officers had lied by saying that the men were ready to go and were anxious to go but wanted to be ordered by the Government. Ministers who repeated the statements were completely in error. Also the radio has since said that the men were resisting because not liking a 'phony' conscription. This again was Tory inspiration and entirely wrong."

Sketchy accounts of the disturbances in the British Columbia N.R.M.A. camps had appeared in the press and, worried about the repercussions, General McNaughton "had called in the press and asked them to be careful about being over sensational in reports. Apparently they have not helped as they should. I asked McNaughton whether great care would not have to be taken as these men, armed, were moved into the province of Quebec and particularly when they were given their leave before going abroad, and about the situation that might be created as a result of their being in their homes and the opposition that would be offered there. His reply was: We could only trust to the people themselves; there was really nothing else. He was hopeful that knowing how serious the situation is, wise counsels would prevail. But the facts simply are that we have not the needed protection, either through the army or the police, to keep law and order if the situation gets out of hand. Here indeed would be a state of anarchy, not merely in the philosophical sense of no government existing, but as well in the actual sense of civil strife. One can only pray to God that we may be spared anything of the kind. I believe we will, but if we are it will be because of the belief that the people of Quebec still have in myself and now also in McNaughton. It makes very clear that had I not taken the course I did, and the Government passed into the hands of conscriptionists, that a measure of civil war would have been inevitable."

The next morning (November 29) the situation at Terrace was discussed in the Cabinet. Mackenzie King told the Cabinet "what had taken place last night. McNaughton had handed me the despatch from the West that spoke of mutiny. Referred to the conversation that he, St. Laurent and I had after the Council was over. I read to Cabinet the communication itself letting them hear every word of it. I then said this puts the seriousness of the situation clearly before us. I then added what McNaughton said about having no troops to maintain law and order and necessity of calling men out of factories if the militia had to be called out, and generally reviewed the situation as the three of us had seen it last night. I pointed out that I thought I might say that Members of Council would realize just wherein the General and myself were justified in drawing attention to this aspect of the situation when all-out conscription was proposed originally and what might have been expected had those who were in favour of conscription got control of the situation and had tried to enforce all-out conscription. I pointed out that the statement that the men were ready to go but were waiting to be commanded was a lie. The officers had lied on that. Equally the statement that it was a 'phony' conscription was a lie. I thought immediate steps should be taken to censor the press; also to see that the radio did not add fuel to the flames by making additional unnecessary sensational reports which had been the case up to the present. This led to some discussion as to how the matter could be controlled. McNaughton then received [in Cabinet] a communication which was to the effect that an officer in the West had tried to have the press not sensationalize the story but Purcell, head of the Canadian Press, had taken the view that the Defence Department had no right to interfere with the press, and that there was a possibility of a statement appearing today that the Government had come into conflict with the press over efforts to suppress news. This was a worse situation than ever. I took the bull by the horns to prevent further delays."

The Prime Minister then sent for Wilfrid Eggleston, the Chief Press Censor, and Augustin Frigon, General Manager of the C.B.C. When they came into the Cabinet, Mackenzie King "told them in the presence of my colleagues the situation as we had been reviewing it, mentioning about the use of the word 'mutiny' having got into the press, also spoke about the other reports and the absolute necessity of censors using the same methods and judgment in regard to the situation in Canada as they were using in regard to news affecting movement of troops and sensational incidents in connection with the effect on the war effort in relation to overseas. I made it clear to them this was not a matter of politics, it was a matter of patriotism. If once shots were fired and blood began to flow, no one could say where the whole condition of things would end, and we as a Government were helpless in avoiding a situation without co-operation of the press and radio. I suggested the heads of the press service should be brought to Ottawa at once and the situation explained fully to them.

"Eggleston said, if the Defence Department would give directions as to certain things which should not be published, they would follow them out. Up to the present all of that had been done voluntarily. It was thought on the whole it would be best to hold to the voluntary side. McNaughton agreed and said his Department would deal with this. I asked whether, while waiting for an order to be specially given, they would not take the direction from the Minister himself, at this moment, with regard to the question of any conflict between the press and the Government. That the matter would then be worked out further in detail.

"It was 2 o'clock when they [Eggleston and Frigon] left to talk over the situation, and try to get it under way. Charpentier [also a press censor] was with the others. All three were most willing and co-operative. Earlier it had been agreed that I would meet with the leaders of the House and explain the situation as reported in the communication received last night so that there might be some restraint in the debate. Also Macdonald pointed out the importance of having the debate over as soon as possible. Suggested to try tonight. I pointed out that this was impossible, as the public had had nothing yesterday [the session had been secret], and it was only on Monday that my motion had been put on. I did say I hoped we might get through by tomorrow night [Thursday, November 30]. However, that is dubious and if the situation did not develop too badly it would be better in many ways to have the discussion continued. Macdonald's point of course is that as long as it is unsettled whether this Government is going to carry on, it will be unsettled all through Canada."

In the House on November 29 there was a question by Hanson in which he spoke of "mutiny of soldiers in the West." The Prime Minister "gave assurances in the name of the Minister of National Defence that every-thing was properly controlled; also gave a word of warning to the House. Hanson termed it a lecture."

Later in the afternoon, Mackenzie King was horrified when "Angus Macdonald showed me a letter from Air Marshal Leckie, of the Air Force, to him, which was to the effect that General Pearkes, Officer Commanding the Pacific Command, had ordered the Air Force to make a demonstration flight over the camps.

"I was terribly alarmed when I saw this. I told Angus I thought he should see McNaughton at once about it. While he went to see McNaugh-ton, I left the Chamber and got in touch with McNaughton ahead of him. When I told the General what had happened, he instantly said: that was terrible; that these men must be crazy. He then said he must stop this at once. He had always been against using the Air Force in any way for a demonstration in connection with strikes and trouble. It was one of the worst things that could possibly have happened. For a moment it made him almost despair. We did not wait to discuss matters further. McNaughton went at once to his office and instantly sent word that this should be stopped, though from what Macdonald had told me we were both afraid it was already too late and the damage done. After he had been away for a little time, he came back to reassure me that things were quiet; that the flight had been made this afternoon, but fortunately word had been sent out a little earlier to the camp that there was to be a flight that afternoon; that the airmen were not carrying arms and that it was in the nature of a manoeuvre. Had this report not got ahead of the demonstration no one could say what might have happened. The men had fortunately been told that the aircraft were our own and unarmed. Otherwise, on seeing them approach, they might have fired on the aircraft, all having guns in their possession. The whole thing might have been the most appall-ing incident that could have happened. McNaughton had at once tele-phoned to the West. He gave instructions that on no account was this kind of thing ever to happen again. He spoke of that question having come up when he was Chief of Staff and said he had always been against using the Air Force for purposes of maintaining civil order. Fortunately the incident was over."

At six o'clock, Mackenzie King invited the leaders of other parties to his office. In attendance were Hanson and Grote Stirling, Angus McInnis of the C.C.F., and Blackmore. "Both Graydon and Coldwell were away from the House. I had St. Laurent and later McNaughton with me. I told them that the meeting was called to consider the serious situation which had arisen. I had asked them to come that they might understand how very serious the situation was becoming if the press and the radio were to be allowed to send sensational reports and to disclose movements of troops, trains, and the like. I spoke too of the use of such terms as 'mutiny' being terribly harmful; that these things went from one camp to another. If the men would see there was mutiny in one camp every camp might mutiny. I then pointed out we had no police to maintain law and order. That calling out the Active Militia meant men leaving factories and it was questionable if it would be possible to get the necessary force to control resistance and what would be in the nature of rebellion. To my great surprise Hanson said if he had known in advance he would not have used the word 'mutiny' and said it was his neighbour, and pointed directly to Stirling who was seated beside him who had been the one to tell him to do so. Stirling coloured up a good deal. I confess I was amazed as I thought he was one man who having been Minister of Defence would have recognized what the situation would mean. It shows how bitter the Tories have become. I am perfectly sure that someone, either the official himself or someone else connected with him, who sent the despatch to headquarters referring to the situation which might be considered as 'mutiny' must have sent this word also to Stirling and that Hanson had used it on the score that it was something that could be authenticated. That is a pretty bad business and shows how near we have come to an outbreak which might not possibly have been controlled. It is a crime that French Canadian regiments have been kept out in British Columbia under command of a man like Pearkes, and the group he is heading there. Ralston has been wrong, terribly wrong in all of this.

"When McNaughton came in I asked him to tell the others what we had gone through today. He told them about the despatches nearly going out to say that the press and the Government were at loggerheads which would have been a terrible thing. Then also read the communication which had just been stopped in time and which all present recognized would also have been appalling. I told them what we had done in regard to ordering strict censorship on matters within Canada in relation to our movements of troops, etc., and sensational reports. On all fours with what we have been doing all along in relation to movements of men and sensational stories overseas. They all agreed that this was the right course to take.

"In speaking to me, Blackmore said it was simply common sense. McInnis made it clear he felt it would be very risky. Said it ought to be done and both Hanson and Stirling also agreed."

By the following day, the situation at Terrace was under control.

During the afternoon of November 29, the Prime Minister was relieved to learn from St. Laurent that Alphonse Fournier had decided to stay in the government. "It was a great relief to me," he wrote, "to know that Fournier would stay on, keeping the Government's ranks as intact as possible, not losing a French Canadian from the list. It is a wonderful achievement. It would not have been possible except for letting time play its part."

Ralston began his major speech in the debate when the House resumed its sitting that evening. According to the diary, "Ralston began by saying he would wish to have more than his ordinary time. I at once stated I felt the House would be only too ready to give him all the time he wished. . . .

"It was plain from the way he spoke that Ralston carried a good deal of resentment, intensified I think by the attitudes of both Macdonald and Ilsley. Ilsley particularly has been very annoyed at my reference to the attitude of Ministers in Council, in which he is perhaps justified. On the other hand, it became necessary in the light of what Ralston was disclosing in regard to his own resignation.

"Ralston's statements gave me a chance in one or two corrections to get out more clearly than would otherwise have been possible to our men the point to which I had come in the Cabinet, namely that of being ready to tender my resignation if anyone would agree to take over. All this will help our French Quebec supporters to see that there has been no duplicity on my part. That I had gone to the limit in everything. I thought Ralston spoke much too long. He went far too much into detail. He had his material written out in a meticulous way and made it apparent to the House the kind of a colleague he was, namely one who would bend in nothing and rather boasted of this attitude himself." Mackenzie King added that he had never had any doubt that Ralston "would support the resolution. I was not surprised that he gave as a reason that it would be unfair to certain of his colleagues if he did not do so. That was a reflection on others. Altogether, as he was speaking I could see that our men were getting more resentful of his attitude. When he was through it really was a sad and humiliating spectacle to see him still at his desk shaking hands with Tories who came across to congratulate him. Not a man from our own side that I could see anywhere around joined in the congratulations. Before adjournment in the lobbies the men were indignant. They felt he had gone too far."

During the morning of November 30 Mackenzie King talked to St. Laurent about the kind of speech he might make in the debate; St. Laurent "indicated the line he would follow. I told him I thought it would be well for him to wait until perhaps the beginning of next week; for him to pour all the oil he could on the troubled waters. He might say it might have been better if we had no Canadians sent to Italy but would add that it meant much for Canadians to have relieved Rome. I said to be careful not to single out Rome, but to speak of Paris and France as well as Rome and Italy. He spoke of Dieppe, and of the Canadians being the first to invade the Continent. All of that I told him I thought was good. Then he would say that he had come to the conclusion that we had to have this measure of conscription for reinforcements."

One of the speeches that day particularly impressed the Prime Minister. "[Walter] Harris, of Grey-Bruce, who has been overseas, made a fine speech" in support of the motion. "Delivered without notes in a manner which shows he is capable of thinking on his feet. Has calm judgment." However, the event of the day for Mackenzie King was Cardin's speech announcing his intention of voting against the motion. "It really was splendidly expressed and delivered. I could not take exception to anything that he said. He came out for out and out independence which might well be expected from him. In a world like the present, it is necessary, I think, in Canada's interests that we keep in the family of British nations as a nation on equal status with all the other parts but not seek an isolated position in the world. Cardin looked very much older. He seemed to be realizing it would be one of his last speeches and a very significant speech coming from him as the oldest Member of the House of Commons at the end of his career. Such indeed it was. After speaking, he had gone to the opposite side of the House to have a word with one or two of the men who had interrupted him. I saw at a glance he was quite exhausted; face was filled with pain. I congratulated him on the manner of his speech. He regretted having to say what he said. I told him I noticed that he had been careful to say nothing against myself, and also [that] his friends in Quebec [should] remember their friends in other provinces, which I thought was intended in a friendly way, and I thanked him for it. I spoke of the part of the speech which referred to Ralston. He was very strong in that. It was quite clear Ralston's speech was a condemnation of his whole departmental administration. He was very strong in the way he spoke of the men who had forced my hand as it had been forced. They should have been made to stand up, and their names should be kept up to the fore. They were the men that were to be blamed for the whole situation which is perfectly true. I felt in talking with him that he was anything but bitter toward myself and indeed most friendly and understanding. We talked for quite a little while. No doubt Cardin's speech will be unsettling for some of the Members from Quebec. They have been coming more and more into complete desire to support the Government. This may make it a little more difficult for some.

However Cardin by maintaining he is a Liberal and not crossing the floor has stopped extreme action in that direction."

To Mackenzie King, it was "really little short of a miracle that not a French Canadian Member of the Cabinet should have left it in this crisis. This must never be forgotten." That same day, Mackenzie King had a talk with Gardiner. It was Gardiner's birthday. The Prime Minister had been concerned because Dr. King had been persuaded that Gardiner was "seeking to get into line with the Quebec end and tonight it was evident he had come in to sort of prepare the way for action at some moment that might prove to be quite embarrassing. He said he was wondering whether he could any longer be any help to me. Whether it would not be better if he were out, and resigned. I said at once: My dear Gardiner, you must not leave me on any account. We must continue to work together. I could not quite understand what he was saying. He did not make it clear; whether it was over difficulties in Council, getting his way on the livestock question or what it was, he mentioned nothing in particular. I rather sensed that he felt that Tucker's attitude [W. A. Tucker, Liberal M.P. for Rosthern, Saskatchewan] in dealing with the minorities in the West had given him, Tucker, an inside running, and that it really represented, as I believe it does, the point of view of the Liberals in Saskatchewan, but it was different when there was question of the existence of the Government at all and of Liberalism collapsing completely at this time. I pointed out to Gardiner that we must not let the Government pass into the hands of out and out conscriptionists. These were difficult days but we would get past them. Once the war was over, we would restore the situation. I noticed that his eyes filled with tears as he was talking to me. He was holding on only to the thread that I really wanted him. I think unless I had shown the utmost sympathy and understanding all along of late, he would almost certainly have left us or would be leaving us now. I talked with him about our getting a seat for McNaughton at once. He expressed his readiness to do that and left I think feeling still ready to stay on. I had counselled him against getting feelings stirred up at the moment in the Cabinet by saying things that would antagonize either Ilsley or Macdonald."

The Prime Minister also had a talk with Colonel Hugues Lapointe, Ernest Lapointe's son, who, he thought, was wavering in his attitude on the motion of confidence. The talk was "very pleasant," Mackenzie King felt. "He is measuring up in fine shape." As they talked, Lapointe told the Prime Minister something of the fighting overseas. "His Company had been the first to go forward after landing. He had lost half of the Company. He then spoke of the pace at which they had to fight, continuous fighting for 35 days; not sufficient rest. That the men were magnificent fighters, but they simply would collapse from the strain at the end of several days patrolling, etc. He spoke of how our men at Falaise and Dieppe had fought with a couple of brigades, whereas the British had fought with divisions in similar tasks. He felt that our men were unfairly pressed forward and had been given more than their share. Of course he could say nothing of it but that was his real conviction. He felt that the army was too large and they ought to lessen its size, but he recognized that, as Prime Minister, I could make no suggestion of interference with military plans. I am glad he is going to be in Canada for some little time before going overseas. He will be a helpful influence in Quebec with the men there."

At the Cabinet meeting the next day, Friday, December 1, "McNaughton made a good report on movements of men, maintenance of order; also on enlistments and conversions. Figures higher than they have been at any time. Ilsley, Howe and Macdonald and McNaughton were not in Council when it met. They had been having an important discussion with Keynes on financial matters." J. M. Keynes was in Ottawa with a British mission to discuss further mutual aid to the United Kingdom. The Prime Minister took advantage of the absence of the four Ministers "to impress on other Members of the Cabinet importance of avoiding further heated debates in the Cabinet or of bringing up any subjects of the past that could be kept down at this time. Just after the Ministers mentioned returned to the Cabinet I asked Ilsley to make a report on the discussion they had had in the morning. The matters referred to were of colossal proportions, relating to alternative plans of assistance to Britain to carry on the war against Japan and to help to hold her own in arrangements with the U.S. in working out terms of peace. The whole business comes to an additional billion dollars, over and above all we have thus far contemplated. It is bound up with questions of possible cancellation of indebtedness against Britain for what we have done in the care of prisoners of war from the beginning; paying for ships that we have been building for Britain; loaning them to her later; going to Parliament for a very large appropriation for further mutual aid which will increase our budget vastly; making an agreement with Britain for taking our cattle and to give priority to the purchase thereof until the end of the fiscal year 1945–46. This, however, subject to financial arrangements to be made in payment thereof which may mean when the time comes that payment will be accepted at ½ percent interest or no interest at all over a period of years.

"Ilsley stated that, strange as it may sound, he would be favourable to the cattle agreement with Britain and this has been the most difficult question between Gardiner and Ilsley. It was an immense relief to my mind when I found that Gardiner and Ilsley were prepared to meet each other on this matter. It removes what probably is the worst of all situations which remain to be dealt with, and which were liable to provoke further resignations.

"After my talk with Gardiner last night he must have felt tremendously relieved to know that he would be able to let the farmers of Canada see what he had done towards securing a sure market for them at this time when, with winter setting in, the farmers are having a desperate time marketing their cattle and when their choice had to be between having them go to the American market or to Britain, and that very soon to prevent what would be an appalling situation for the farming communities throughout Canada."

When the Minister of Finance had finished Mackenzie King posed three questions:

"1. What would the plan suggested mean in the way of providing employment in Canada for those making munitions . . . which would ensure continuous employment on a full scale.

"I asked the question in relation to how the money would be raised by loan, etc. It was felt by Ilsley that with full employment we would be able to raise what was needed. That was a very vital consideration. Ilsley also pointed out that by taking this course our military effort would be lessened. We would be taking a proportionate part in the war to that which Britain was taking, but which was much less than what the U.S. would be taking. It would mean, however, that more of our effort would go into materials and supplies than to actual contributions by the defence services.

"2. I next asked on what grounds the requests being made by the British were supported. It was reported that it was looked upon as part of one war effort; that Britain had come through with vast expenditures she had had to make at the beginning in Egypt and elsewhere. That we had all shared in the results of being saved through such expenditures. There was also the necessity of helping to meet the present situation in Britain where industry had got to the point where too much pressure was put on everyone—men and women could not keep up with the effort in the factories. It was looking at the war as just one effort and our being important in these ways to the whole. The arrangements the U.S. had made with Britain were also a factor. Of course, from our point of view, the whole business relates back to making sure of our holding a place in the British market. That Britain will be turning her orders elsewhere if, right now, we did not secure the market, e.g.: Danish cattle might come in, and others.

"3. The third thing I spoke of was the reported trade agreement with the United States, which Churchill spoke of a day or two ago in the House. It was explained that this was not a trade agreement. It was an arrangement regarding mutual aid under which Britain could not pass on any material received from the U.S. to help her own export trade. It had wrongly been named as a trade agreement. Ilsley made a marvellously clear exposition of what had been discussed. There was very little comment in Council.

"I asked how long these negotiations would take. Howe said it would not be well to give them a final answer until around Christmas. In the circumstances I thought we ought to let the Ministers who had been negotiating these matters have a chance to think further over them and make recommendations at their convenience. Gardiner said the cattle matter could be regarded as being settled at once.

"Ilsley agreed that had been a tremendous problem. It might well have broken things up anew, but was concluded in a moment of complete quiet."

Mackenzie King reported that the incident of most interest in the House that day (December 1) "was a motion which Jean [Joseph Jean, Liberal M.P. for Montreal Mercier and Parliamentary Assistant to St. Laurent] drafted to offset Cardin's speech of last night and to give the French Members a chance to vote against the Government on the score that our war effort having been overdone on the military side, thereby failed in making a success of the voluntary system and needing the introduction of conscription. Jean worked this out himself and I confess he surprised me in his astuteness and also manliness in taking the course he did, for one also saw that there could be no question about his acting on his own and his sincerity. It meant opposing the Government in his motion, tendering his resignation as Parliamentary Assistant and taking all chances and consequences. I know it meant something to him to lose even the small amounts of the honorarium attached. He made a good little speech of his own. Graydon raised the point about his resignation. Fortunately . . . I had gone to my room and found his [Jean's] letter there and drafted a reply to it before going back into the House. It was being typed while Graydon just before adjournment raised the points he did. I think Jean has something there which will be helpful." In his diary that day, he also referred to a short talk with St. Laurent and added that "The more I see of St. Laurent the nobler soul I believe him to be. One of God's gentlemen if there ever was one."

Reflecting on Sunday, December 3, on the preceding weeks, Mackenzie King wrote: "I have never abandoned what I said in Parliament as to 'Not necessarily conscription but conscription if necessary.' It did not become either until the morning of McNaughton 'phoning and coming to me regarding the representations made to him by the army council. From that moment it became both and this has been amply proven by what has since taken place."

On December 4, the Prime Minister had another talk with St. Laurent who had seen Godbout in Montreal during the weekend and who told him that "Godbout had come to the conclusion we have done the only thing we could do, regretting he issued the statement he did, but goes back to the days of Lapointe and myself when we told him he could be as strong as he liked against conscription. He does not recognize that the plebiscite altered that. He felt, however, that if he had not made the declaration he did, other Members of the former Government and the party would have issued a declaration much stronger. St. Laurent spoke to him of the dangerous nature of the situation we were facing and what might have happened had we not taken the course we did with a militia of only a certain size in Canada against much larger numbers armed and ready possibly to resist. He [St. Laurent] was not anxious to speak but is prepared to do so. He wished to make clear that what he had said about the people feeling they were deceived, had not meant that he so believed himself but was speaking as a lawyer, objectively, as to the attitude which many persons would naturally take."

At the Cabinet meeting, Mackenzie King urged very strongly that the session should be brought to a close as quickly as possible. "I thought it was advisable to reduce the number of speakers all we possibly could. If men spoke either inside or outside the Cabinet, they might say things which would either be resented by Ralston's friends—some who felt strongly of Ralston's point of view; or by others who felt strongly in regard to my point of view. We should leave to the adjudication of the future what should be said on that score. I also stressed the importance from a military point of view of having the country kept as free from further discussions as possible and desirability of troops and others knowing whether or not the present administration has the support of the House of Commons in their war policies. I referred to St. Laurent's talk and my own. Said I knew LaFlèche was anxious to speak and also spoke of Fournier who was immediately opposite but said I thought much could be said after Parliament was away; there would be time enough to make further explanations that were needed. Fournier said there would be need for many explanations. LaFlèche said nothing but what I said met with general approval of the Cabinet.

"McNaughton showed me a letter marked 'Secret' from Hanson taking strong exception to the movement of French troops from the West to Quebec. In effect it was that they would be prodded, etc. in the camps there [in Quebec] and he greatly feared movement might lead to civil war.

McNaughton was writing privately letting him know that every aspect has been carefully considered. That his officials are very strongly of the view that the course taken is the only one it would be wise to take. Also that the camps are not consolidated. They would not all be in one camp but largely scattered."

In the early evening Mackenzie King read with great approval what St. Laurent proposed to say in the debate. He noted that "later in the evening Sinclair [James Sinclair, Liberal Member for Vancouver North] spoke and made one of the best speeches I have heard in the House. Very clear, revealing an understanding of the whole military situation. From that side, quite all right. The speech lacks, however, the vision of the larger requirements for Canadian unity. He has a fine parliamentary style."

On Tuesday, December 5, Mackenzie King noted: "Tonight, Hugues Lapointe made a speech, parts of which were exceedingly fine. He spoke as a soldier who had served gallantly in battle. It was doubly effective and very telling in that he himself explained he had heard nothing about the need for reinforcements until he came back to Canada a few months ago. He also took a stand against even a limited measure of conscription as not being necessary and not likely to do any good. It was an entirely sincere speech and a very brave and courageous one. I confess, however, that I was amazed, that after saying all he did he found it necessary to say that he could not support the Government in the final motion of confidence. He admitted that the people wanted no one for Prime Minister but myself, but he himself took the line that he could not forgive a broken pledge; that it would mean the loss of faith in public men. It seemed impossible for him to have any regard for the pledge I had given in 1942 to support a limited measure of conscription if it became necessary and advisable so to do, as it certainly has. His attitude, if generally taken by the Quebec Members, would mean that he would hand over the Government of the country to a conscriptionist gang for the rest of the war, including the war against Japan, simply because I had not held to the statements made at the time of the elections in 1940, when in 1942 the same country released me wholly from those obligations in the light of the changing situation of the war throughout the world. I confess that what Lapointe has said has hurt me more than anything in the debate. It will do more to unsettle our own members in the House . . . and will do more harm to the Liberal party in the Province of Quebec than anything else.

"I never dreamt he would go the length of voting against assisting the Government in a vigorous prosecution of the war. It is a strange attitude for a soldier to take as well as for one who knows what the circumstances are that have made it necessary for me to take the stand I have. However,

I know what a searching of soul his speech had cost him. The preparation of it came between the third anniversary of his father's death and his burial. Undoubtedly he has felt that his father would never have altered the position he took on conscription and has regarded my action as a violation of my pledged word as given at that time. I can understand his position and I would be the last not to make every allowance for it. I am sorry he made his remarks in the connection he did about faith in public men quite so directly pointed at myself.

". . . I gather from what St. Laurent tells me that practically all his supporters whom he saw in a hotel in Montreal on Sunday said they wanted him to back me. However, the position [of Lapointe] is, as I say, understandable. All the circumstances of his life, feelings, etc., being considered.

"I have been debating whether I should not say something at the close of the debate in reference to broken pledges and faith in public men. I am a little overtired and may find it difficult to think out just what should be said but will be guided by how matters develop. My thought up to the time of Lapointe's speech was that I would simply say that the country was anxious to know whether, the most important thing of all, the Government was being supported in its war policies and say that I had nothing to add or subtract to what was said when I opened the debate and let things go at that."

That same day (December 5), the Prime Minister referred to a matter that "might be one very far-reaching and of grave concern were it known, it was a letter which came to me by hand from the Governor General at 5 o'clock, telling me of a tribute by the King to our army. In a letter received by His Excellency it stated that the King had seen the Canadian army both in Italy and Holland and that they are magnificently trained troops and have fought very well. But, the letter goes on to say, that the King wonders what they will think of the men who do not go overseas to join them. It refers to how difficult it is for the people to realize what is going on in Europe just at the moment when every able bodied man is needed to do his best at the right place and at the right time. The King says he feels it [the army] should be in northwestern Europe. It is there where the Germans will be beaten and the sooner the better. His Excellency adds in his letter that it might be of interest to my colleagues to hear this. I wrote at once to the Governor General by hand acknowledging his letter, referring only to the words of the King as to the army and saying I would let my colleagues know in Council tomorrow of it. There would however be an outburst if it were known by them that the King was telling Canadians, through the Governor General, what they should or should not do in the matter of any part of their people in the present war. The Governor General's comment that my colleagues would be pleased to hear this letter shows how very little he really understands Canadian mentality. I confess when I opened the letter, I began to feel that everyone was getting to be more or less crazy in what they were thinking or saying at this time. If I wished to make trouble, nothing more would be needed than to carry out the Governor General's wish to let my colleagues know what he has written. It is, however, my duty to protect both him and the King and I shall do this by not disclosing except in part what the King has said or what the Governor General has suggested I should bring to the attention of my colleagues. While I am doing this, I suppose the Tory party and others will be saying that I am doing my best to break up the British connection, etc. Indeed after listening to all that has been said today, unless one were very objective in one's attitude and had strong faith in the right of the course pursued, one might feel one was in a mad-house instead of at the head of a deliberative assembly."

There had been some apprehension in the Cabinet about having St. Laurent speak, but, on the morning of December 6, Mackenzie King decided that "Lapointe's speech of last night makes it necessary, I think, that some Minister from Quebec should speak. At Council I will seek to have it understood that at the right moment St. Laurent will do so."

At the Cabinet meeting Mackenzie King referred again to Lapointe's speech which was threatening to unsettle the Quebec Liberal Members. "I said it made me think anew of the course we should pursue in the matter of speaking. I had referred before to St. Laurent being ready to speak, but of being indifferent. I had now come to the conclusion it was necessary for him to speak. We could not afford to allow the French Members who are wishing to support the Government not to have before them the ground stated by one of their own Ministers on which it should be supported. Otherwise, we were letting Lapointe become the voice of Quebec in voting against the administration. MacKinnon, who is usually level-headed and who was sitting opposite me, shook his head in a negative way. Mackenzie came out boldly saying that notwithstanding the great respect he had for Mr. St. Laurent, he did not think he should speak. Mulock and Mackenzie had both been in my office earlier to advise me not to let him speak. I had mentioned yesterday that I might ask him to. Other Members of Council looked equally dubious. I then said that I felt both for the present and the future of Quebec it was imperative that the senior Member of the province should speak and give the grounds on which the Government's war policy should be supported.

"I then added that Mr. St. Laurent had been kind enough to let me see what he had in mind saying and I felt it would be wholly helpful and all to the good. But again others were shaking their heads. I then said perhaps Mr. St. Laurent would not mind reading to Council what he had prepared. That I thought if the Members of Council heard what he had written they would be deeply impressed. He thereupon, in a very nice way, opened his portfolio and took out what he had drafted and read it. As he read it I noticed the faces of the Ministers changing. Ilsley, who was following him anxiously, looked quite relieved. Macdonald who had had his hands over his face in a very negative attitude began to look a little more relieved. Before St. Laurent had concluded there was a chorus of general approval, Mackenzie being the first to congratulate him and others joining in. Crerar had suggested the omission of the words *partial* conscription, which Howe also suggested might be modified. This was done. There was some other phrase which was altered a little in emphasis.

"When I left Council I met Claxton talking with St. Laurent. Claxton wanted him to take out the passage in which he said he was there to do a war job and he should not quit. I suggested he might put it in a positive way: that he felt more than ever he should carry on as the reference to quitting might be looked on as a reflection on Ralston and Power.

"There was some discussion as to when he should speak. Bertrand thought it ought to come at once; not wait until after Jean's motion. I said I thought in view of Lapointe's speech it was desirable to bring St. Laurent on at once and have him speak this afternoon. This was finally agreed to."

To the Prime Minister "the feature of this afternoon's debate was St. Laurent's magnificent speech. Magnificent in the sense that it was forthright, honest, sincere, straightforward and true. His decision to stand or fall with me was tremendously applauded in the House. It was doubly significant in that he was representing the constituency which was represented first by Sir Wilfrid and then by Lapointe. Also he being Lapointe's successor in the office of Minister of Justice. He is indeed a sterling character. The House gave his utterance a great reception. There was not an interruption while he was speaking."

When the House resumed its sitting the next afternoon (Thursday, December 7) "Roy [Independent Conservative Member for Gaspé] having, before lunch, drawn attention to the statement in Borden's Memoirs that I would have been willing to go into the Union Government, I took advantage of the chance on a question of privilege to make clear that Borden had no authority for making any such statement. Also to put on record in Hansard that I had been approached to enter the Union Government (Clifford Sifton who was working on the Union Government having spoken to me about becoming Minister of Soldiers' Civil Re-Establishment). I am glad indeed to have had this chance officially to deny Borden's statement."

This was the last day of the debate. Mackenzie King did not spend much time in the House during the afternoon because he "wanted to revise what I had written out this morning for possible use in the debate on the main motion. It was well I did this as I could not possibly have got that part into final shape, had I not completed it in the afternoon.

"I walked into the House just after Cardin had spoken on the amendment against any conscription. In time to be there for the calling of the amendment moved by Jean. It was negatived 168 to 43.

"Graydon's amendment later for all-out conscription was negatived 170 to 44. These were large majorities and disclosed how difficult my position in being fired at from both sides was. It also makes pretty clear what the situation would have been if, on the one hand, we had refused to take any action under Bill 80, or on the other hand, had gone in for total conscription."

During the evening, Mackenzie King "became a bit concerned about our not getting through tonight. However, throughout the debate, I have not allowed myself to be irritated by delays feeling that everything would work out for the best in the end. If such were ever true, it was true tonight beyond what one could have hoped for or expected. In the first place, I got the unanimous consent of the House at 5 to 11 (both hands together) to continue the sitting so as to get through some time during the night.

"A moment came when Coldwell realizing the embarrassment it would cause his party to vote against the main motion suggested an amendment to strike out the words 'its policy of' before 'maintaining a vigorous war effort.' I saw in an instant as did St. Laurent and Mackenzie who were close at hand that if we accepted the amendment, the C.C.F. would have to vote with us on the motion as amended. Coldwell's speech had made that plain. Also the speech by Knowles. I am sure the C.C.F. believed that we would not accept the amendment and that they were hoping we would not, as not to have accepted it would have justified them in their contention that we were really seeking something through these words which could be construed to our benefit. To me, the taking out of the words did not mean a bit of difference. Indeed I have wondered once or twice in looking at the resolution how they came to be there. However my records will show that. I at once said that I would accept the amendment.

"During the next short time, our Members were in a state of confusion, none of them seemed to know just what this would mean. I confess I had one bad moment when I was told by Mackenzie through McLarty that Ralston was taking voluminous notes, likely to speak and that he might construe the taking out of these words as removing what he regarded as most essential of all—the conscription side. I heard too that Macdonald wanted to adjourn the House. Did not want to sit after 11 so as to give chance to confer about the effect of accepting the amendment. Then St. Laurent asked me if I had spoken to Ilsley about it. I had not. As he was nearby, I did say to him I hoped he saw that nothing had been changed which was material. That I would make quite clear that I was standing by all that was meant in the original motion. He was not in any way responsive, said he supposed it was all right but was not in the least co-operative. I assured him I would make the position very clear when I spoke. Gardiner suggested we should adjourn at 11 and have a Caucus in the morning as our men were getting unsettled by the amendment and perhaps they could be made to see whereby it really afforded a chance for the Quebec men to get in behind us. Mackenzie did not think a Caucus wise. I told him I had really been very patient but that my patience was getting exhausted. They would have to decide either to follow my lead or take the consequences if their vote should go against me. We were then leading up to the time that I had to put the motion for continuing after 11. I had been told that it would not be accepted. That the men in a corner, Bloc Populaire, Pouliot or others would object. It had to have unanimous consent. To my great relief, the motion carried unanimously and I saw then the way opened to a conclusion tonight; also I felt instantly that we would get a difference of 20 or more on a division by my having accepted the amendment. It was as though I saw forces from Beyond influencing the situation at this end. I am certain in my own mind such was the case. It gave me great heart.

"Graydon like a school-boy and with the worst judgment possible, made a speech all on the line of petty politics—one might say peanut politics— in which he talked of C.C.F. and Liberals combining against the Tories by using the old simile of Liberals and C.C.F. becoming curious bed-fellows in an effort to divide the Tories. Not a word on the significance of the resolution in reference to the war and the maintaining of forces overseas. I felt by accepting Coldwell's motion in good faith, he and his following would have to support me though their intention had been otherwise.

"Blackmore came along in splendid fashion. Touched the crux of the whole situation in speaking of what the vote would signify to the outside world, the enemy included.

"As I saw it was rapidly coming to my time to speak, I wrote out a sentence by which I hoped to raise the whole debate to a different level to bring the significance of the motion in its proper light before the House. I was concerned lest I might through weariness of the mind, find it difficult to speak. In a moment, I saw where I could say something as to the attitude of each of the Leaders of the 3 parties opposite and get our men lined up with me as far as that was possible. I was given a great ovation by our men when I got up to speak. Indeed it was some little time before by indicating to the men that they had applauded enough, I could get a chance for the Speaker to make clear that if I spoke, I would be concluding the debate. A word by Dan McIvor had really served to end discussion and give me a chance to go ahead.

"What I was most anxious about was to reach the point where I would have the last word without anyone having a chance to follow as was my right, having moved the main motion. To my delight, that moment came. From subsequent reference in the press, it came a little after 12.30 when the hands of the clock would be in a perfectly straight line though I, myself, had not glanced at the clock when I got up to speak. I had nothing in my mind except the first sentence that I had written out and what I had typed earlier to conclude with, and which had been prepared quite independently of what came up during the evening.

"After I had covered the first sentence, I went ahead giving expression extemporaneously to the thoughts that came into my mind and which I felt were appropriate. . . . I had to use quick and careful judgment in speaking not to overdo in any direction. I was able in a few words to associate C.C.F., Social Credit with our own men in approving a vigorous war effort. At the same time, bringing strong condemnation on the head of Graydon and his following for their decision not to support the motion. I thereby helped to give, before the world, greater assurance of the determination of the House of Commons to further Canada's war effort."

When the vote came, the Conservatives "found themselves in the oddest of all situations," Mackenzie King wrote. "Opposing a measure of support for a vigorous war effort and associated with them, the extreme isolationists from Quebec and the number of Quebec representatives who are not prepared to support the Government on the main motion. Tory Ontario and the anti-war Quebec groups tied with each other. I don't think men were ever more discomfited or political opponents, both foes and friends, more completely confounded, than were the official opposition and those of our own party who did not support the main motion."

Mackenzie King "was really amazed when the vote was counted, to find that it was 143 to 70. It took me some little time after to realize that I had had ⅔ of the House with me. I had been expecting 30 of a majority—some had said we might have 40. Gordon Ross [Liberal M.P. for Moose Jaw] at one stage had said to me he would not be surprised if we went as high as 50. I never believed that. I never thought beyond 30 or in the 30's. To have a majority of 73, I could think only in terms of manifestation of spiritual powers that were making all things work together in accordance with the will of God and in answer to prayer, and the law of God with respect to the power of faith. The result was really a miracle. There has been nothing like it I believe at any time in the political discussions of our Parliament. There was a tremendous applause from the House when the result was known."

When he "rose to thank the House for the confidence it expressed in the Government's undertaking to maintain a vigorous war policy, I was given a tremendous ovation. Never before have I received such applause from the House of Commons nor do I believe any other Leader has received anything greater. I expressed thanks in a word and moved immediately the adjournment of the House. This caused Graydon to ask a question which I have wondered had not been asked before and which I am immensely pleased and relieved should have been asked before adjournment. It was as to whether when the House meets on January 31, the new session will commence on the following day. I said quite openly that I could not answer that question and made it clear that I would be governed by circumstances at the time as to what it was best to do. . . . It had been amusing to me to see how little Members of the House have suspected that we might not have another session at which we can be tortured to the limit."

Mackenzie King felt particular pride that the numbers of "Members from Quebec who gave me their support were as large as they were [19 Members including the five Ministers]. I shall never forget the last hours of the sitting. The intense silence of the House while I was speaking. The power that I was able to put into my utterances and the readiness with which words came. The ovation and the greetings at the close, all of this on top of having been obliged to take a course which was quite the opposite of what I had believed would be necessary up until the moment the officers of the Department of Defence made it pretty clear that the military machine might disintegrate entirely and the Government itself dissolve unless I took the step I did. It was a tremendous triumph in the faith of men in their Leader and of their readiness to follow him at great sacrifice to themselves. But I am sure the right course has been taken and that it is the right course because each step itself was the right one."

The following morning (Friday, December 8) Mackenzie King concluded that "Certainly I shall never have another task comparable to the one of the past 6 weeks. Over and over again, I have thought of what I said to Ludwig that some day the world will know some of the things that I have prevented. I doubt if they will ever know what has been prevented at this time. I must make increasingly clear to the world that prevention of wrong courses of evil and the like means more than all else that man can accomplish. That lesson surely should be the one that comes out of the war."

After Parliament adjourned on December 7, the rest of the month was relatively quiet. On Saturday, December 9, Glen, the Speaker of the House, came to Laurier House for a talk. The Prime Minister reported that "he was most enthusiastic about the whole debate particularly the last night. Said many of our Members had flocked into his apartments after and were delighted beyond words. He wanted to know about possibilities of another session. I drew his attention to what I had said in the House. Told him I felt we should prorogue for some little time or from time to time, not having another session. It would be simply folly to do so, and at a convenient date in relation to the war, bring on the election which according to this plan will come likely some time in the spring after the worst of the winter roads had cleared up.

"The House having sat as late as December 7, we would have good reason for not bringing it together again until March or April. We could fix the elections from that date. I begged him to keep the matter wholly secret."

They had some talk about Glen's political future, but there was no suggestion at that time that he should succeed T. A. Crerar as the Manitoba representative in the government. Apparently Glen "thought Garson [Premier of Manitoba] would be the best man to come into the Government if he could be persuaded to do so." Mackenzie King told him "to see Garson and let him know I would like very much to have him come in. He promised to do so." Mackenzie King also noted Glen's statement that "Cardin had been in and talking with him and had told him he intended to remain a Liberal, stay with the party. Get a following, if he could, from Quebec and would not cross over. Did not want the extremists. Felt he could bring a large number with him. Indicated his friendliness toward myself and readiness to join with me in what might be necessary in the formation of a Government after the elections. I told Glen that I had known this right along but I felt it was important that any Government of which I should be the head, should not be dependent on any group in the House to sway the situation at a critical time.

"I was really relieved and pleased at Glen's genuine enthusiasm and certainty in his mind as to both the impression the debate had made on all our followers and as to the situation as he believed it might develop through the country."

That day Mackenzie King received a message from Winston Churchill dated the 9th: " 'Without venturing to enter in any way into Canadian politics, I feel I may now say what relief and pleasure it has given me to find you still so effectively at the helm.' This is a fine message. Churchill has the marvellous gift of expression using the right word at the right place. It is a comforting message. A fine word to receive from the Prime Minister of Great Britain."

There was one important meeting of the War Committee during the period, on December 13. The Prime Minister described it as one of the most satisfactory meetings they had had and noted: "I find General Mc-Naughton, as all members do, exceedingly helpful. He thinks so clearly and understands so well the problems he presents." The Committee "agreed to extra radar equipment for ships in the Navy, this because of it being now quite apparent that U-boat menace is greater than it was and also nearer our own shores. The most serious matter was one that Mc-Naughton brought up which indicated how very short our own men may be of ammunition. He rather hesitated sending any communication to Crerar to make sure that our men did not get into action without adequate ammunition. As he said, he did not want to interfere in any way with Montgomery's plans. I pointed out that the lives of our men were our responsibility and that I thought we could not allow a message such as he had received that morning, asking that the last scrap of ammunition should be sent over, to stand in the way of an enquiry which would give us exact information. Council agreed with this and McNaughton decided to use the message he had received in the morning as a basis for a reasonable enquiry. There is no doubt that there has been a great shortage of ammunition on the Western front generally. Fortunately Howe and his people were wiser than the British. They went ahead manufacturing even when Britain was cancelling orders. Of course, it is a very difficult situation to foresee.

"After the meeting, I talked with St. Laurent and McNaughton about making Gibson Minister of Air, Chevrier, Minister of National Revenue, and Harris, Parliamentary Assistant to McNaughton. I do not like leaving the Air Department without a Minister. St. Laurent thought the country generally wanted the three Departments consolidated into one again as quickly as possible. They had felt there had been competition between them and great waste, as a consequence, which is true. McNaughton thought it best not to appoint a Minister for the present at least. Mac-donald was handling things well. [Macdonald had become Acting Minister after Power's resignation.] He also wanted to get the army end straightened out first.

"He said the decisions in the Cabinet against seconding officers and men [for civilian duties] would help in getting rid of large numbers who are just being kept on the pay roll for extra benefits, etc. Also the decision to have the men in the Air Force who are not absolutely needed, dropped out, will be most helpful. This will give extra men to Howe and save the Treasury considerable sums.

"McNaughton, too, was most helpful in pointing out that he thought our forestry corps men should come back to Canada and help with the manpower problem here instead of being sent on to the continent of Europe, where they would become an additional commitment, and where people in the countries themselves should be found to cut what timber was necessary. In matters of this kind, he takes an almost diametrically opposite view to Ralston who was always ready to concede every request that came with very little enquiry. McNaughton said the country is littered with men who are holding posts which should be abolished or who should be out of the posts altogether.

"Spoke to McNaughton about the by-election. Gave him a few pointers though I know of no man who needs less in the way of guidance. St. Laurent, I find, is becoming quite pleased with the stand that he and his French colleagues have taken. There can be no doubt that it has done more for the unity of Canada than anything else, for a long while past. He found the Cardinal quite pleased with the way matters have worked out. Also adverse opinion much less than he had anticipated and many beginning to see that the situation had been well handled."

The following day Mackenzie King had an interesting conversation with Premier Douglas of Saskatchewan, who had been confined to the Civic Hospital for a month with phlebitis. "We had a very pleasant talk together during which he was quite apologetic about the reference he had made to me after having been elected to the premiership. It was in reply to questions over the telephone of which the reporter made the most. I gave him some particulars of the recent crisis. From what he told me, the C.C.F. were all pretty deeply concerned. All believed that Ralston had been remiss or his Department remiss in the way they had handled matters. He stated that the C.C.F. could not have formed a government. The only kind of government that could have been formed would have been one with Ralston at the head and conscriptionists from different parties. He said he doubted if they could have carried on. I said I doubted if they really could have gotten together a government that could have lasted any time. Also that they certainly could not have moved the troops. He told me that Coldwell and he had discussed Coldwell's amendment striking out the words 'its policy of' at the hospital together. That Coldwell doubted if I would accept it. He, Douglas, thought I would, especially if I had listened to Bracken's broadcast in which he kept talking about *its* policy—attaching significance to the word 'its.' I told him I did not even listen to Bracken. I thought he was not a factor at all.

"In speaking of Hepburn, I said I had not had anything to do with the Ontario situation at all. [A few days before Hepburn had become House leader of the Ontario Liberals.] Had left it entirely to themselves. I told him the great problem of the future was going to be to get men of the right stamp in public life. He, himself, referred to Houde being the Mayor of Montreal. I remarked that in some ways I was not sorry I was 70 and that my day's work was along as far as it was. I thought the problems that were coming to the fore would be almost incapable of solution for a considerable time to come. I felt a deep concern for the future and those who have to deal with its affairs. The condition in Greece today shows what lies ahead in many countries. Douglas said Coldwell thought my speech at the opening of the debate was quite marvellous, both in content and delivery. He, Douglas, said he wished he could believe that at 70, he would be able to speak for 2½ hours."

They had some discussion about the proposed Dominion-Provincial Conference. The Prime Minister reported that "Douglas himself said he and Garson had been working together and both of them working on Manning of Alberta, toward getting agreement among themselves for the Dominion-Provincial conference. He said the difficult person was Hart, of B.C. In reply to his question as to whether a conference could be held before the elections, I told him it could if men had a will to try and get agreement but with anyone taking the attitude that Drew would take, it would be folly to have a meeting. He, himself, added: Duplessis."

December 16 was a very satisfying day for the Prime Minister. It was the eve of his seventieth birthday and he felt "in better shape physically today than I was a year ago. Intellectually, I am keener, and spiritually, I have gained by the refining processes through which I have passed in the course of the year. It has been a very great year when one recalls what was accomplished in the legislative programme, in the meeting of Prime Ministers overseas, with the broadcast to the world from the Houses of Parliament at Westminster; the 25th anniversary of my leadership and the recognition accorded at the time by Members of the Government and the Party, and very widely by the press and the people of Canada generally.

"Then, most important of all, the saving of the Government of Canada itself in the course of the recent crisis; the forging of a new link in the unity of the provinces of Canada, and tonight, as a crowning event, a complimentary dinner by the members of the Press Gallery at the Chateau. This and much more has made the year a memorable one. What perhaps

I am most grateful for of all is the feeling of renewed strength of mind and heart and body which I seem to possess. Yesterday I felt like a young man, full of vigour, and really happy through every hour of the day, being continuously so active and alert. Today there is a little reaction. I may have overdone and feel a little tired and depressed. That again I think was due to heavy sleep. I never dreamt that I should live to be 70 years of age and to find myself after more than 25 years of leadership of the party still in the office of Prime Minister having held that office on into my 18th year. In many ways, I would greatly welcome today some regulation which would have made retirement from politics compulsory at the age of 70."

The Ministers who were in Ottawa came to Laurier House at 12.30 to make a presentation. Mackenzie King reported that "Crerar made a nice little speech, speaking of my 70th year and of the wish of the Members of the Cabinet to make a presentation to me on the occasion of it. He then presented me with a silver framed picture of the Governor General, Churchill, Roosevelt and myself taken at Quebec at the time of the Conference, the frame carrying with it the autograph of the present Members of the Cabinet. In expressing thanks I reminded the Ministers that I had asked both McLarty and Mackenzie to see that this birthday was allowed to pass without a further expression of the generosity of my colleagues. That more than enough had been expressed at the time of the 25th anniversary. However, I did deeply appreciate their kindness in calling and their good wishes and the gift which they had presented to me and which had associations that were most deeply valued. I told them my thoughts had naturally been much of the recent past. That I missed very much the presence of Ralston and Power. Felt deeply the break that had come in the Cabinet. I had been thinking it over and had come to feel that perhaps it had been inevitable—when one considered the opposing forces of opinion there were in the country and how they had focussed up in the manner they had. That strange as it may seem sacrifice seemed to be a part of the law of progress, and it may be that it was necessary for two of our number to be lost from our circle. That a greater national unity might be secured. I thanked them all for the way in which each had joined with others in coming to a common centre where we could continue to hold together. In this connection I said I did not think we could ever thank our French colleagues in the Cabinet. To realize that not one of them had left when the issue was conscription, and that we had maintained a united front. That this would mean more, I believed, to the future of Canadian unity than anything else. I spoke of how, all having been members of a government that had had the greatest responsibility of any government in

Canada, we had served in the greatest of all the periods in history. And that this was something which nothing would take from us.

"I then told them that when one reached 70 one had to realize one was at the place of new departure. That I could not but feel that, assembled as we were, together this morning, it would be scarcely possible that after another general election, sometime in the New Year, we could expect to be together a year hence, be the results what they might. That I felt that when a man was 70 at a time such as the present and with the problems what they are, it was neither fair to the country nor to oneself not to have other and younger men take hold. That I could wish there were a law which made retirement from the office of Prime Minister compulsory at the age of 70. That I would be the happiest man today, were there such a law. However, none of us could shape our own lives. I would be wholly content with whatever might come and would continue to serve as best I could. That the future lay with Providence and beyond oneself and one's ken. I did say that I felt stronger in body, mind and heart than I had felt in years and this I said was due to the fact that those who had been around me in the Cabinet had shouldered my problems and helped me to carry them."

That evening the Prime Minister attended a special dinner of the Parliamentary Press Gallery at the Chateau Laurier, an enjoyable and somewhat emotional occasion which he recorded in his diary at great length. What gave him particular pleasure was the presentation of an honorary life membership in the Gallery which was to him the "crowning feature on the last night of this very strenuous year and on the eve of my 70th birthday."

CHAPTER EIGHT

Grey North and the Aftermath of Conscription

THREE ISSUES successively occupied Mackenzie King's mind during the period between the adjournment of Parliament in December 1944 and the dissolution in mid-April. First, there was the North Grey by-election, which was held on February 5; then came the question of whether to hold a session of Parliament in the New Year or call an early election; and, when this question was finally resolved in favour of a session at the beginning of March, there was the session itself. In the background was the uncertainty as to when the war in Europe would end, the necessity of organizing Canadian participation in the war against Japan, and deciding what Canada's part would be in the conference to draft the Charter of the United Nations.

By the end of 1944 Mackenzie King was already seriously worried about the probable outcome of the North Grey by-election on which the government had originally embarked in the expectation of an acclamation for the Minister of Defence, General McNaughton. It had been decided early in December that W. P. Telford, the Liberal M.P. for North Grey, would resign so McNaughton could be a candidate in the riding. During the afternoon of December 8, the day after the adjournment, Mackenzie King "took up over the phone matters pertaining to securing a seat for McNaughton at Owen Sound. He will doubtless be elected there; if by acclamation, he may attend the ceremony of prorogation, but I do not think except for that limited time, he will likely sit in the present Parliament as I am quite certain we shall have no further session. We can carry on as a government until the right time for a dissolution."

Final arrangements for Telford's resignation were made on December 9; "offering of the nomination to McNaughton tomorrow, his promise to accept it though he still has in mind running in Qu'Appelle constituency where Moosomin is, when the general elections come. Moosomin is where he was born and lived as a boy. The more I see of McNaughton the finer character I find him to be."

Two days later Mackenzie King was surprised "to see that the Conservatives were likely to oppose McNaughton in a by-election, possibly also C.C.F. This is the way in which they aid the Government in a vigorous war effort considering that the purpose is to allow McNaughton to have a seat in the House in the event of one more session or a portion of a session. Should McNaughton be defeated, it will give me the best reason with the public for not holding another session. It should not prevent him from continuing to carry on and running in a seat in the general election in the West."

On December 16 the Prime Minister heard further rumours of Progressive Conservative opposition to McNaughton but could not "conceive of the Tories really deciding on a by-election though I am told that Meighen and McCullagh are determined to have it and really wanted to run Bracken against McNaughton. That surely is allowing personal hate and ambition to over-ride all thought of country at a time of war. Bracken, on the other hand . . . has planned to go to England and we have arranged his passage and that of his secretary and one or two others by plane. I wonder what his party will think of his getting out of the country when this by-election is on, staying out of Parliament himself while Members of his party are trying to keep the Minister of Defence out of the House of Commons. I really believe if the Tories go ahead with this, it will be their finish."

In his conversation with Premier Douglas earlier in the month, Mackenzie King had been told that M. J. Coldwell was urging the local C.C.F. organization not to oppose General McNaughton in the by-election. But on December 21 the Prime Minister was upset to see a newspaper report that the C.C.F. had decided to run a candidate in Grey North. "I cannot understand this in the light of their supporting the Government in the House on the resolution to aid in maintaining the war effort. All of this is playing havoc with our war effort. It shows the lust for power is stronger in the minds of both the C.C.F. and the Conservatives. If McNaughton is defeated, we will have no sitting of the House. Instead the contest in Grey North is one of the strongest reasons for not hastening the session."

On December 12 the Mayor of Owen Sound, W. Garfield Case, had been chosen as the Progressive Conservative candidate in the by-election and Air Vice Marshal A. E. Godfrey some days later had declared his intention to seek the C.C.F. nomination. Godfrey, a wealthy Gananoque manufacturer, was formally chosen as the candidate on January 8. Mr. King was somewhat reassured by McNaughton's report on December 22 that he had "no concern . . . over the entry of C.C.F. as well as Conservative candidates; he says the C.C.F. candidate is some Air Force man with a personal grievance. What it is, he does not know. He says he himself would rather welcome a fight. Personally I do not relish the thought of a by-election contest with the conflict overseas what it is at the moment. Also because of its possible effects on a general election." On December 29 the Prime Minister "took some time in writing Ontario Ministers regarding by-election in Grey North. This is all being left pretty much to chance. No Cabinet ever had a more indifferent lot of Ministers when it comes to matters of organization. If I find, as we approach election day, that the result is at all doubtful, I have made up my mind to dissolve Parliament in advance of that date. It will never do to encounter the defeat of a Minister on the eve of an election and he the Minister of Defence. None of our Ministers seem to be at all alive to the necessity for the most complete organization."

Mackenzie King's anxiety over the by-election increased steadily in the New Year. On January 3 he talked about it to Coldwell whom he had asked to come to his office. He argued that "it was more serious than he [Coldwell] may have realized to have C.C.F. and Liberals competing, and the possibility of letting a Conservative in. The Tories were at the bottom of everything today. This would put them on top of the earth if they were to succeed.

"I pointed out how Bracken, who is in Europe, has never come into the House. Tories were taking the position they could not let the Minister come in. His party promised support for war effort and yet would be making war effort impossible if the Minister had to go and fight in an election. I told Coldwell I had nothing to ask him but felt I should point this out to him. He said he had been talking on those lines himself. In fact, when Regina had been thought of, he had suggested neither the Tories nor the C.C.F. should run there and felt the same way about North Grey but he said these local committees were a law unto themselves. He said he did not want reactionaries elected. I said the day might come when he and I might have occasion to work together. I thought it would be well were we not to let our people become too antagonistic, apart from everything else. He was on the whole quite friendly and non-committal. I told him the talk was entirely between ourselves."

Later that day, in the Cabinet, most of the discussion concerned the by-election. Mackenzie King reported that the "Ontario Ministers met yesterday with Gardiner and presented a report today. I felt incensed when I read it. It began by suggesting I should speak in the constituency or make a couple of records. McN. should spend a couple of weeks in the constituency. Hepburn should be called in to help a little later on. Nothing about what Ontario Ministers would do. I spoke very strongly and said the report indicated in what bad shape we were in the matter of organization. This one constituency alone would be a test of all general elections. I thought it would be a mistake for me to go into a by-election. Tories wanted to make the fight one of simply destroying King and McNaughton. I thought we ought to make the issue entirely one of war effort, the government wishing to carry on war effort, and that McNaughton's presence and mine were both required here for that purpose; let the others do the fighting. I pointed out Churchill did not participate in by-elections except by a communication. When I asked the line of campaign, they indicated it referred to getting a seat for the Minister of Defence. When it came to speaking of material for speakers, it appeared they were sending a lot of stuff on other subjects. The truth is nobody has taken the job in earnest though McNaughton is trying to do his best. . . . I told the Cabinet quite frankly if there was possibility of defeat of McNaughton, I would have a dissolution before the defeat took place. If he was defeated unexpectedly, we would have the election immediately after. I would not hold on in any consideration. They might as well get prepared for the election now, regardless of war conditions."

The tone of the campaign in Grey North was set on January 4 with a speech in Owen Sound, under the auspices of the Canadian Protestant League, by Dr. T. T. Shields, a prominent Baptist minister in Toronto, an ardent conscriptionist, and an emotional anti-Catholic who could not resist a reference to the fact that Mrs. McNaughton was a Roman Catholic. Reading newspaper accounts of Shields' speech the next day, Mackenzie King was incensed that he had raised "in the most crude and cruel fashion, a religious cry. It made me definitely determined to see that there will be a dissolution of Parliament before the election in North Grey takes place. I mentioned this to the Governor last night as probable if any opposition were offered McNaughton. The whole attitude of the Tories is the most unpatriotic thing I have known in my experience in public life, encouraging class hatred, race hatred, religious hatred—everything that can make for intolerance and this while we are in the midst of war and men are sacrificing their lives to save the freedom of the world. I must get out and speak to the Canadian people fearlessly on the significance of all this."

On January 8, Mackenzie King got up in the morning "determined that I would enter today on the 1945 campaign by beginning the preparation of an address to the electors of Grey North, making clear the circumstances which have occasioned the by-election and placing on the Conservatives and the C.C.F. the onus of embarrassing the government in its war effort for bringing on the election at a time of war. I am sure that in their action, they have played into our hands though I can see that when I do dissolve after having let the election run on for some time, there will be a great cry to the effect that I had been afraid of the outcome. However, the really serious thing is the election itself while men are fighting at the front, if that can be avoided. I believe it is beyond question that by their opposition to McNaughton's entry into Parliament, they have made it impossible for the government to do other than to dissolve, without attempting further sittings of another session. I am quite sure that were we to begin another session, there would be turmoil and strife from the outset, embarrassing motions of want of confidence, questions, etc.—obstruction on everything. We will have gone to the limit of the constitutional term excepting all but a month or two. To wait that period out would mean I think pretty certain defeat of the government."

By January 10, the Prime Minister had decided to address two "open letters" to the electors of North Grey in support of General McNaughton's candidacy. "The first," he wrote, "relating solely to General McNaughton, to the sole purpose of the by-election, namely to gain a seat for General McNaughton in the House of Commons so as to permit of his being present at another session if one is to be held. That statement to be issued for publication on Saturday of this week—the 13th. Then a second statement to be issued a week later which will make clear that the controversy to which the by-election has given rise may prevent the holding of a special session and necessitate an earlier dissolution of Parliament while the war was on. If on nomination day, candidates are put into opposition to Mc-Naughton, we will then, the day following . . . dissolve. Some weeks later, announce the date of the general election and arrange for it taking place before the time for the Victory Loan Campaign—May 7."

In Cabinet the next day, Mackenzie King read the draft of his first open letter. "There was," he reported, "a profound silence while I read the letter through. All of them realized it was the preliminary to a general election. I made quite plain that this letter would be followed by another a week later, pointing out how the Conservatives and C.C.F. were making impossible the holding of another session and thereby forcing on a general election. Ilsley seemed concerned as to why the date of the election should not be announced at the time of prorogation. I made pretty clear that the 7th of May was the date I had in mind for the election which means that the loan will have to be postponed two weeks. I do not think we should let ourselves in for an earlier date, largely for reasons of the season itself.

"I looked over final revision of letter between 6 and 7. Had it sent off with a covering letter to the President of the Grey North Association. The whole business was impressive as being the beginning of the 1945 campaign, one of great significance for the future of Canada."

On January 16, the Prime Minister received a confidential estimate of "the probable course of the campaign in Europe which will mean our men getting into action to a limited extent in the first couple of weeks of February and from then on till the end of March in the thick of intense fighting. Some 6 weeks of intense fighting. This has a very great bearing on the wisdom of avoiding another campaign on conscription between now and the time that this fighting is over. We have all the reinforcements that are needed. If Parliament were sitting at the time, there would be discussion from day to day there which would be most embarrassing. A campaign such as was started before the special sittings were held. Indeed the campaign might well take the shape of Parliament having to dissolve with the issue being carried to the country which is what the Tories want and no doubt accounts for their anxiety to have an election brought on soon rather than delayed. There is no doubt they have inside information from the army telling them of the plans. If Parliament is dissolved, there will, of course, be an effort to have the campaign made one of conscription but if as is wholly probable the result of the six weeks' fighting during the latter part of February and the month of March results in victories for the allies by the end of that time, and the date of the election is still some 5 or 6 weeks away, the force will have gone out of the conscription issue before the time for election comes or, for that matter, the day of nomination which is a month earlier and the real problem of the electors, namely, peace negotiations, post-war problems, and our social legislation will come more clearly before the electorate before the vote is taken.

"Had there been no opposition in Grey North, we might well have had a session which would have expired on April 17, 1945, and then have been able to fix the date of election toward the end of June which would have made the probability of the war being over before the election stronger than ever. The election, however, has made it certain that the session would be one of political controversy of an extreme kind, embarrassing to the govt. and with a likelihood of nothing being accomplished while the Victory Loan campaign makes inevitable elections either before or after that campaign. To leave them until after the victory loan campaign, with no session in the interval, would be to govern too long without either a parliament or an election, particularly when it will take all of a month after the elections to have Parliament reassemble and begin on work. There is an old saying 'Whom the gods wish to destroy, they first make mad.' I believe that will be again proved in the action of the Tories and the C.C.F. They have wanted power above all else and that at the earliest moment possible. They have chosen and taken the course that is obviously unpatriotic, in seeking to keep McNaughton out of the House of Commons and to force an early election. All of this will react against them."

Despite his desire to be free of the by-election, Mackenzie King feared the reinforcement question would be the main issue in a general election unless the war was over before the vote was taken. As early as January 2, he had noted that "the casualties during the last two months instead of being 16,000 over all as estimated when Ralston was pressing for reinforcements, have not come to 6,000 in all. In other words, we are 10,000 to the good on casualties alone and 5,000 additional is what he was asking for at the time. There is in addition the several thousands which have been found among G.S. men. It was all political. The whole thing was as McNaughton said a 'mare's nest' and was political."

But, on the other side, an awkward situation concerning the conscripts had emerged. On January 5 Mackenzie King discovered that "some 2,000 of the N.R.M.A. men out of 5,000 who should be leaving for Europe by now have not reported after having been given leave. No doubt one reason is the Christmas, New Year's and Epiphany holidays all coming pretty much together at this time. Some are turning up from day to day. Others will be gathered in later. The interesting fact is that practically all of those who are missing are from regiments other than French-Canadian. However we are already in Europe far ahead of all requirements needed for reinforcements." The Cabinet on January 17, Mackenzie King reported, "discussed at some length the matter of publicity regarding men who have left without leave. The numbers are very large—out of 6,000 about 2,000. They are beginning to come in not too rapidly. The press are aware of what has taken place. The Globe and Mail and Gazette are getting ready to open up another real conscription campaign. LaFlèche said he learned that the day after the nomination, they intended to publish by regiments the numbers of the N.R.M.A. men who have skipped out; not so much attacking Quebec as showing how large the numbers are in the different regiments, etc. That seems to me to make it more advisable than ever that before the day of nomination, I should make clear the possibility of no session and also on the day of nomination itself, I should announce dissolution before reports begin to be made the subject of an immediate campaign."

Meanwhile, the Prime Minister had been drafting his second letter to North Grey, hinting at an early election. At the Cabinet meeting on January 18, a statement McNaughton might issue regarding absenteeism among N.R.M.A. men was discussed. "Fortunately in the disclosures the press will make on the matter the Ontario regiments will be among the first named. The numbers are large but it would have been difficult to treat the situation other than by granting to these men the same leave as others are entitled to. Some are coming back, others are being apprehended. What is important is that the full quota of reinforcements required have gone over and are now in England. Future quotas will be definitely assured. This thing will undoubtedly become a big issue in the campaign in Grey North. The Tories no doubt will have it appear that we do not wish a further session because of the discussion upon it in the House. It will become an issue for a time in the elections, but before they are over its course will be spent. There is of course in reality no blame to be attached to the government in this. It only helps to disclose how very difficult would have been the handling of the N.R.M.A. men had compulsion been used to a greater degree than it has been. I read what I had written for Grey North, second letter, including reference to what I said about the recent crisis, etc. Ilsley was present, also Gibson and Howe. I think practically all the others were men who would have stood by me to the end. There was no one who took exception to a line. They were all favourable to the elections."

For several days, Mackenzie King kept working on his second letter. On January 21, he noted in his diary that, before getting out of bed in the morning, "suddenly something seemed to suggest for me that there was no need to have an immediate dissolution. That instead of announcing anything of the kind immediately after nomination in Grey North if Conservatives and C.C.F. put candidates in the field, I could simply announce that the Government had decided not to hold another session and by Order-in-Council cancel the by-election. When prorogation comes, the House could be prorogued to a date late in February. Parliament would still be kept in being and could be kept in being up until the day we decided to fix the date of the session itself. In the letter I have made it pretty clear . . . that if the election is contested there will not be another session. This procedure means that we will have got over successfully all the dangers of pitfalls and trials of another brief session, but will have time free to prepare further for a campaign—to attend to the war effort and to come nearer to having the campaign itself when the war is over. I do believe that this is something we shall accomplish. If we do it it will be a tremendous triumph. I should like to be in office until the war in Europe is over and I am less concerned [about] having anything to do with either the making of the peace or postwar problems. If I can see Canada safely through the war—having put the interests of our fighting men first throughout—I shall be content regardless of what comes hereafter. With Parliament in being we could wait until

March 31st before dissolving but not having supply for the next fiscal year, we would have to dissolve before the 31st. We could fix the date for the election two, three or four months thereafter, which would bring it to May or June as we might think best. By that time there is the strongest probability that the war will be over. So far as the Tories and C.C.F. are concerned, they will never be able to get over the chagrin of having themselves been responsible for freeing the government of another session of Parliament which is the one thing they should have thought above all else to compel us to have."

He added that he was "anxious to clear the decks of all issues other than the new order of things for the peace table business—conscription in particular—before the campaign comes on. With these thoughts in mind, after reading, I went through all the material I had on the Grey North election, studying the sequence, looking for phrases etc. then going through for the last time the letter and making two or three significant changes. There was one clause which spoke of if we were not to have another session an early election would be necessary. I was able to change that to make clear that another session would have brought more within bounds the possibility of the end of the war before an election, but thereby left my hand free to have the election late rather than early, if I so desired. I believe that the country will come to recognize a certain generalship that is worth while in what I have done to carry Parliament to the last moment. At any rate we are now in a position where it cannot be said we are responsible for a wartime election, but that our opponents have made it inevitable."

For a day or two the idea of postponing the by-election by order in council continued to appeal to the Prime Minister. On January 25, however, he was advised by the Minister of Justice that the by-election could be neither cancelled nor postponed by order in council. "This brings us back," he wrote, "to the first position—namely the necessity of having a dissolution. Another course, however, has been suggested to me which would keep Parliament in being. It was one about which St. Laurent spoke yesterday—namely not to have McNaughton file any nomination papers. Simply state we were not going to have another session of Parliament. Unless something very critical arose we will be having a fairly early election. Then allow the contest to proceed with the two other candidates if they wished to proceed. The danger of this is that it will be interpreted as our being afraid of McNaughton not being elected. A dissolution, however, would be equally so interpreted, but the former course would have the advantage of keeping Parliament in being until the fixing of the date of the election itself. It would put the other candidates in a farcical position, fighting each other. One will have to consider carefully what the effect would be on the one defeating the other. C.C.F. showing themselves stronger than the Tories, or the Tories themselves stronger than the C.C.F. I attach great importance to keeping Parliament in being so as not to bring an election on sooner than can be helped with men fighting at the front. The present weather in Canada shows where we would have been in a general election at this time. The fighting overseas shows how distracted the people here would be and how terribly distracted the army would also be if we had been fighting elections all through December and January. I shudder to think of what would have been said of the Government that had brought on elections under these conditions this year." That same day, Mackenzie King decided McNaughton was needed in Ottawa and asked him to return from North Grey as soon as possible.

During the Cabinet meeting on January 25, the question of an early election was again canvassed. The Cabinet were "united in the view that, if possible, another session should be avoided and the elections held without much further delay. The question that came up was whether, first of all, the public might on Monday next, after nomination, be informed of dissolution—dissolution itself to take place on Thursday—thereby avoiding continuing of contest in Grey North. The general feeling was that we should not pull McNaughton out of the contest but allow it to go on until day of dissolution, but to dissolve on Thursday, February 1st. There was some feeling that it might be as well to let the contest run on until Monday [February 5]. I pointed out that if we did and McNaughton won we would have to have another session which Ilsley was very much against and which the Cabinet as a whole does not want, because of terrible pressure there will be before and during the session on government members, etc. On the other hand, were McNaughton to be defeated it would be a considerable blow to the prestige of the government and an election would be necessary immediately, and we would be starting into the campaign with a very great handicap. However, the fact that there were three candidates might help the electors to see the dangers of election of members for the next parliament by a minority of votes. We all agreed that McNaughton would probably not like to be pulled out of the campaign before dissolution. He personally would probably prefer to go through to the end. The situation has changed considerably and Mulock now reports that his chances are very good." W. P. Mulock, the Postmaster General, was supervising the McNaughton campaign in the constituency.

The next morning, Mackenzie King informed McNaughton and the local committee that the government would go on with the contest in North Grey and that nothing was to be said about a dissolution. McNaughton's nomination papers were to be filed at once. "Mulock reported that the chances were looking very good. He believed we would win. He said the Committee would be pleased at the decision to go on with the fight. Mc-Naughton was meeting with encouragement wherever he spoke and was much enjoying the campaign. Having decided to go on with the campaign through the week has made it necessary for me to turn over in my mind anew what it may be best to do about dissolution."

The date of a general election was considerably complicated by the necessity of having another Victory Loan campaign in the spring. Mackenzie King discussed this question with Ilsley and the Governor of the Bank of Canada on January 27. They told him that the campaign could not be put off until after May 7 so an election could be held on that date. Mackenzie King "pointed out if that was the case we might have to plan things to go over until June and have the election in June which would mean that if McNaughton won, we would have to call Parliament and table the estimates and war appropriations, and get as far as we could in getting enough passed to help us over the period of the election without Governor General's warrants. Ilsley was terribly distressed at this prospect. He said I was afraid it would come to that in the end. He pointed out that there would be terrible pressure on him and on all the Ministers to make more expenditures, that it would become so great that it could hardly be resisted, and touched on other well-known truths, adding too that he thought the government's chances were much better if we had the election while the war was still on than after it was over."

General McNaughton returned from North Grey that Saturday afternoon reporting that "things were going well" in the constituency. "He was meeting with a good reception wherever he went and he felt that on no account should we dissolve until the by-election was over. He himself would not like it if we did. He would be credited with pulling out. He said the best informed members of the Committee were prepared to concede a majority of 900. He thought he ought to go back on Sunday to be in the constituency on Monday and to stay there through the entire week. He was sure he was making good headway wherever he went. He brought a letter from Mulock which stressed some points. I told him I had phoned Mulock Friday night, telling him to let it be known to him and others that the election would go on. That Mulock had made a public announcement of this on Saturday. He, McNaughton, had not received word from him before leaving the constituency, but I noticed by the morning paper he [Mulock] had said they would go on with the election. He [McNaughton] stressed the point that our own men would be terribly discouraged in the constituency if we did not go on this way in a fighting mood and believed they could win. I asked about the letter I had sent. He said it was felt it was

too long, which as an appeal to the electors I agree with. I explained that
it was written for a double purpose—one being to justify us in an early
appeal without another session of Parliament."

The Prime Minister issued his third and last appeal to the electors of
North Grey on Monday, January 29. It again urged support for McNaughton and indicated that there would be a dissolution of Parliament before
April 11. "My mind is now definitely set on an early dissolution of Parliament—win or lose in Grey North," Mackenzie King wrote on January 30.
"The action of the Opposition parties has made that course both 'necessary and advisable.' I believe McNaughton will win and win handsomely.
A good candidate is ⅔ of the battle. He is an excellent candidate. Already
the tide in North Grey has begun to swing strongly in our favour." However, on February 1 he was not very hopeful of the success of the campaign
in the general election because of the total lack of organization; also the
absence of persons with whom he could confidentially communicate and
from whom he could secure reliable information.

"The situation as I see it from the Atlantic to the Pacific is very haphaz-
ard," he wrote. "Against this, the Conservatives have been organizing on
a large scale in the last couple of years. Have no end of money. The C.C.F.
appear to have lots of money and to have been organizing even more in
detail for a couple of years past. We have no central organization that is
worthy of the name. In this North Grey election, I do not think they are
doing anything. They have made very little headway in the federal field.
First of all, there is no one man that can be entrusted or who has political
knowledge and skill to take charge of the organization. Lambert [Senator
Norman Lambert] who could do very much is really unfriendly, for what
reason except that he would like to have been in the government, I don't
know. So there it is. We have as a government the best of records. On top
of all, there is the division that has grown out of Ralston's action in pre-
cipitating what was a real crisis in the party and might have split it for
good. Altogether the whole business is little short of a tragedy for I fear it
may mean a situation at the end of the campaign where no party will have
a majority over all and where we may have a very floundering condition
at a time when the most difficult of all the problems will arise. The one
hope on the horizon is McNaughton. If he wins North Grey, it will gal-
vanize life into the whole party. He has the personality which would help
in binding the party together. I am afraid, however, that money will play a
large part in North Grey and that the Conservatives may buy up the constituency. They will stop at nothing in this fight. Nevertheless I shall be surprised if McNaughton does not win. Certainly the outlook federally for a
party in a general election but a few weeks away is anything but what a

leader could wish it to be. We have no real organizers anywhere. These impressions are forced on me more strongly than ever today as I talked with different members of the party this afternoon."

He was, however, quite optimistic about North Grey on February 3, when he noted that "Mulock, reporting on Grey North is decidedly hopeful. The poll of newspapermen in the constituency indicates McNaughton at the top. McNaughton, the most favoured, C.C.F. next, and Conservative last. I believe this will be the order. I also believe that McNaughton will have a substantial lead. I shall be greatly surprised if that is not so. His speeches have been, I think, excellent, particularly what he said in this last broadcast about certain newspapers and control by a reactionary, very wealthy small group, who have a stranglehold on the Conservative leadership, differentiating from the old party led by Sir John and the present piratical gang. . . . He has immensely strengthened his stature in the Dominion. The fight will help us I am sure in the general campaign."

Entering the campaign with a speech at Meaford on February 1, the Progressive Conservative leader, unaccustomedly hard-hitting in his style, charged that a number of the N.R.M.A. conscripts had thrown their rifles and ammunition overboard while on troopships bound for England. The charge was angrily denied by General McNaughton who pointed out that only one soldier had jettisoned his equipment as he boarded ship. But the damage had been done. However, on February 4 the Prime Minister remained confident that McNaughton would win. "Bracken I think has hurt himself in the charges he made about N.R.M.A. men throwing their kits and guns into the sea—wholly unsubstantiated. His language too has been unworthy of public men. I doubt if Coldwell has made much impression either way. I still look to see the Tories at the bottom of the poll. Reading the different papers, it is apparent that members of the press have come pretty well to the conclusion that no good purpose would be served by another session, and that a general election in the immediate future is inevitable. I feel too that decisive battles in Europe will be fought this month. In the month of March, at the latest. I shall be greatly surprised if the war is not over before April. If that should be the case, I shall have few, if any, regrets as to what may follow so far as my future in political life is concerned."

On election day, February 5, the Prime Minister showed much less confidence. "All day," he wrote, "I have been much less certain than I was a few days ago. My main concern has been with the C.C.F., feeling that the young people may take the bit in their teeth. That has been perhaps my greatest concern. So far as the Tories go, I have been fearful of the Orange complexion of the constituency and the use that may be made of the Orange crusade against the French and the Catholics. The fact that Mrs. McNaughton is a Catholic would be used for all it was worth among Orangemen and what I equally fear is the power of money in the constituency—the buying up of votes. The Tories will spend no end of money for that purpose. I have not, however, had any fear that Case would win. My thought has been that he will come 3rd."

"I have thought particularly," he added, "of the heavy responsibilities on myself, should we lose. Everyone will blame me for having opened the constituency. Also the equally heavy responsibility for the decision, if we win, not to have Parliament resumed. That, however, is the least of all the cares. The election has shown beyond words the unwisdom of carrying the strife of the constituency into Parliament."

As the returns came in and the votes for the Progressive Conservative and C.C.F. candidates steadily outstripped that for McNaughton, Mackenzie King blamed "the effect of money and the Orange vote." After speaking to General McNaughton and others who had participated in the campaign, the Prime Minister issued a statement to the press in which he brought "forward the thought that the election certainly put an end to any further thought of another session of parliament and also the thought that it would make inevitable a general election, possibly at the time when fighting might be at its worst. I still feel we should have the election before the Victory Loan, but that we should try to have it before the end of the first week in May, taking a little time for the effects of the present by-election to blow over and to get our party properly united for the campaign. How I wish I were not so fatigued. Anything is better than another session of Parliament. . . .

"I am naturally disappointed at the result of the election. The first impulse of the party generally will be to blame me for having brought on the campaign in North Grey. However, as I see it at the moment, the result in North Grey should help us very much in Quebec, also in the West. The C.C.F. were more to be feared than the Tories. This result should keep some of our own party lined up with ourselves, rather than deserting to the C.C.F. When we launch our real program, which has not been discussed in the by-election, it will give a wholly different complexion to the campaign. Personally I would find more satisfaction in opposing the Tories than in opposing the C.C.F. I greatly fear however that with three parties in the contest the Tories will gain many seats which they otherwise would not have. What effect this may have on the troops overseas, I find it difficult to say. The most important factor of all, however, will be the progress of the war; should decisive battles be fought and victory assured, as I believe will be the case, before the campaign is over, the Tories' campaign on conscription will have lost its whole force.

"Whether the benefits will go to the C.C.F. or to ourselves is, however, doubtful. This is part of the inevitable fruits of Ralston's precipitation of the conscription issue. Everything considered, I think McNaughton has done wonderfully well. To have been faced in the course of the campaign with N.R.M.A. absentee problem, to have had so little time in the constituency and to have come to it a complete stranger, shows how truly remarkable is the impression which his personality made upon the electorate."

Final returns in the by-election showed an impressive victory for the Conservative candidate. Case received 7,333 votes; McNaughton 6,097; and Godfrey, the C.C.F. candidate, 3,118.

During the period of the by-election, there had been little other important activity. The early weeks of January were filled with diplomatic dinners and other social activities, on a much greater scale than at any previous time during the war, and the Prime Minister soon began to weary of them. L. B. Pearson had been appointed Ambassador to the United States on January 1 and the next day Mackenzie King had him to lunch and reported "a very pleasant talk with him about matters generally. He has a very quick intelligence and a most pleasant manner. Will make a fine representative. He spoke particularly of what it meant to the staff [Pearson was the first career officer to become an Ambassador], and said in a quite sincere way he was pleased indeed that the appointment had come from me. It is an interesting fact that I have had to do with all our legations and embassies."

On January 9 Mackenzie King had a lengthy and discursive conversation with Grant Dexter, the Ottawa correspondent for the *Winnipeg Free Press*, which indicated his growing concern about the attitude of several of his colleagues in the Cabinet. "Speaking of the recent crisis, he [Dexter] said that Sifton [the publisher of the *Free Press*] had become quite excited when the question of conscription came to the fore. Was all for it, going out any length. I told him that was natural as his father had been the one responsible for Borden's policy—for the Union Government's policy, though utterly opposed to it at the start. Dexter said in going through Dafoe's papers, they were finding material which indicated Sifton had been holding up the government over the Georgian Bay Canal which he did not think was right. I agreed with that. He said Victor would not do that sort of thing. He said the Free Press had taken a hard crack at me on the Ralston correspondence but to forget about that. I do not recall having seen what it was.

"He then spoke of the crisis itself and said the right thing had been done but it was truly marvellous how it had been achieved. He spoke of Crerar. Seemed most anxious that he should be appointed to the Senate. Said he [Crerar] was worrying a good deal. . . . Now was afraid that because of his recent attitude, he might not receive the appointment. I told Dexter what most of our friends had said is that he should not. I added that he had been extremely difficult. Spoke of the letters he had written. His remarks about Ralston having been asked to resign, etc. Dexter let me know that Crerar had been in touch with the Free Press right along which, of course, I had known but he, Dexter, knew about the letters, etc. I had always felt that pressure was coming from that source. I spoke about Crerar being upset over my appointing Ralston, leader in my absence, of his pride, etc. Dexter agreed he had no influence but . . . had been a helpful colleague over many years. Dexter told me that he knew that the Ministers were, one after the other, getting ready to go out. I explained how I had stopped that by calling Parliament, but he told me what I had not known before, that on the afternoon that Parliament assembled, there was a ganging up on the part of several of them and that Ilsley had agreed to form a government, that Howe along with Crerar and the others, Macdonald, Ralston, etc. had all agreed to go in with him. He thought Ilsley had been greatly concerned. Held out for some time but that he was very ambitious and evidently felt his chance had come. I, of course, had known that Howe could go anywhere. . . . This makes clearer than ever that the hand of Providence was in the success I had in that meeting, and my intention to hold off until the night and what took place in the Cabinet meeting there.

"Dexter told me that he did not think Macdonald should be in the administration anyway. He [Macdonald] was terribly disappointed; he had thought N.S. would allow him to succeed as Premier. They had told him distinctly they would not, so he has been left high and dry. The more I think of it, the more I feel I did exactly what was right at the time I did. Dexter seems concerned about Gardiner's loyalty, as Dr. King does, feeling that Gardiner is also most ambitious. Would like to play in with Quebec. He thinks if we had to have a second order in council to send more men overseas, Gardiner would try to carry the West along with Quebec against any move of the kind; I told him Gardiner had stuck well.

"Dexter says that there is no doubt I could have carried the House with me on the maintaining of the voluntary system as Western members were all with me and were hopping mad when I made the change. I told him then what had occasioned this in the attitude of the Defence Department, that we nearly came to having no government at all and later to having something in the nature of armed revolution. What he wanted to speak of particularly was the course from now on. I let him give his own views first. He said he could see no way out of the present situation short of a general election; that he thought there ought to be a general election rather than another session. That the course the Tories, C.C.F. had taken in Grey North was giving the government a wonderful chance to put on them the onus of having an election in war-time. He believed we would do better in an election in war-time than waiting until the war was over. The people would not want to change the government while we were crossing a stream. He could not understand why the Tories were so keen on having an election. Of course it is that they think they can force the conscription issue and get families of men overseas to vote with them.

"I then drew from my folder portfolio the manuscript of what I had written as an Open Letter to the Electors of Grey North and told him to be on the lookout for publication. I told him confidentially what was in my mind which he seemed to appreciate very much and with which he was in entire accord. It seemed to give him a great thrill. He was most friendly in every way."

On January 22 Mackenzie King had a talk with Premier Stuart Garson about the political situation in Manitoba. He found "Garson quite interesting, keen and alert. Got his opinion on the best men for the ministry to represent Manitoba in my reconstructed ministry. He thinks Crerar's day is past. Thought Glen [the Speaker of the House of Commons] would be the best person, everything considered, until I suggested Donald Mackenzie [former Minister of Agriculture of Manitoba; then Chief Commissioner of the Board of Grain Commissioners]. He then stated that Mackenzie without question would be in every way the best. Thinks he will accept. Personally I am afraid that is a little doubtful. If he does not I am inclined to centre on Glen as being more the cabinet type than others that are possibilities."

The 5th session of the 19th Parliament was due to prorogue on January 31 and, as the day approached, the Prime Minister gave some attention to the closing Speech from the Throne which was to set out the government's record of legislative achievement. On Monday, January 29, he had the Cabinet called for 4.00 P.M. and went over the Speech paragraph by paragraph, asking for comments. "The speech is already 7 pages, while 5 has been considered very long. The Cabinet wanted every paragraph retained though speech not yet concluded. Had slight discussion on some of the clauses. . . . I told Council that now that we were at the end of January we were able to see there had been no need whatever to have said we would be short of reinforcements at this time. Ralston had said we would be all right after January but the need would come in the interval. I pointed out that we had reason to know that in the interval, our men would not be fighting and that it was now clear that the whole situation might have been averted. There was not one present who said a word. They were like a lot of mice."

The following day Mackenzie King "wrote out by hand the concluding paragraph of the speech in the nature of a prayer, making mention of the dead, wounded, prisoners, etc.," and remarked to one of his secretaries that "the press would be a bit surprised that instead of getting something on the election in the prorogation speech they would receive a prayer instead. . . . Personally, I am sure that the press will attack me on the length of the speech. It is, however, a magnificent record of achievement in dealing with postwar problems. It sets forth in considerable measure the grounds on which the forthcoming general election will be fought. The press will claim it is an election document. The answer to that is that every line of it is true."

The Prime Minister, when the Speech was delivered in the Senate Chamber on January 31, "could notice intense curiosity to see what was coming in the conclusion of the speech; also some look of surprise when the prorogation was fixed for February the 28th. There will be lots of surmises about this date. I was interested in observing how keenly Ilsley followed the proceedings and that he was the last of the Commons members to leave the Bar of the House. He seemed quite concerned about something at the end, perhaps it was the date fixed for prorogation. He clearly is very keen on becoming leader of the party some day. Has certainly worked very hard."

The day before (January 30) Mr. King had approached Premier McNair of New Brunswick about succeeding Michaud in the federal Cabinet but, he reported, McNair indicated that he was not interested. They canvassed the whole political situation in the province but reached no conclusions.

After McNaughton's defeat in Grey North on February 5, Mackenzie King's first inclination was to avoid another session by dissolving Parliament at the earliest opportunity. At the Cabinet meeting on February 6 he told "the Ministers not to be discouraged by the results which had advantages in some respects as well as disadvantages. It certainly freed us of another session of the House. It would be time to consider the date of the

elections after the General and Mulock came down and we had an opportunity in Council to consider all sides. I thought we should not be in too
great haste in making a decision."

He found Angus Macdonald "more concerned about not having elections until the war was over than anything else. He thought the life of
Parliament ought to be extended. I told him I did not favour extension of
Parliament but we could fix the date at whatever time we thought best.
Personally I would wish above all else to be in till the war was over but
we would have to consider the course that would be best in the light of
existing circumstances and long delays might be prejudicial.

"I had thought the 7th of May would be the best. The way he spoke
seemed to indicate he was fully counting on staying on. Nothing was said
about giving up his portfolio. Having in mind the talk with St. Laurent
that it would be well to keep him on, I said nothing. Had in mind the
possibility of appointing Kinley of Nova Scotia [M.P. for Lunenberg] to
the Senate. He [Macdonald] could run in N.S. and win easily there. With
two Ministers from Nova Scotia, I could for the present forego Prince
Edward Island Minister."

Mackenzie King then talked with St. Laurent who apparently felt that
the result in North Grey would help the party in Quebec. "I could see that
he has very little knowledge as to what is best to do in way of organization.
Is really lost there.

"I told him of my talks with Picard and Lapointe. He believes they have
dropped the idea of any separate wing though holding to idea of independent Liberal."

The Prime Minister also talked with Howe about the National Liberal
Federation office. "He can think of no one better than Gordon Fogo [later
appointed National organizer of the Liberal party]. Admits the organization is of little help in most of the provinces but thinks Ontario pretty well
organized. I pointed out there was really no one to help in planning a big
campaign. He asked me if I was going to reorganize the government before
elections, seeming to expect that I would not. I told him I certainly would
to some extent. He is very anxious to have the election soon. Feels the
election of a Tory in Grey North will make it more difficult to get funds for
our campaign and may incline many to support the Tories who ordinarily
would not. Men like Howe do not see how much more important the cause
is than money though certainly there is need for the latter for proper
organization."

Mackenzie King's hesitation about dissolving Parliament at once was
no doubt strengthened by a letter he had received from Senator J. J.
Stevenson that morning. He noted that "it was about the situation in

Prince Albert and made clear there was not a chance in 100 that I could be elected there. C.C.F. control the whole constituency and Tories are likely to assist the C.C.F. in order to defeat me." Mackenzie King was relieved to be told by Norman McLarty that same day that his health would not permit him to stay in the government through an election, information "that cleared the slate of one problem."

The next morning, February 7, Mackenzie King recorded that the first thing he opened in the morning mail "was a telegram from Mayhew [Liberal M.P. for Victoria] which has impressed me very much. He suggests that on no account should I dissolve until the order to cease firing is given. Then having made the record of having won the war take up the question of who should make the peace. There is a lot of sound sense in what Mayhew proposes but I can see difficulty ahead with the Cabinet. Also with the problem of managing meanwhile. However I, too, feel we must watch the progress of the war a little before reaching a definite decision on the date of the elections. This I can state in a communication to the people. I shall have to give out something fairly soon. I must try to get rest before reaching a final decision as to the last campaign," he added. "Must give it careful thought. The result in North Grey shows my original idea when mind was very clear, to take the bold course of dissolving when our opponents put in their candidates on nomination, would have been the wise and right one. I recognize that I allowed my mind to be changed through being a little weary and less certain of things at that moment than I should have been. Of course a main factor was what was owing to McNaughton himself and the North Grey people, but it is apparent that a dissolution then with the campaign on now would have been telling in its effect. However the knock the C.C.F. got will be all to the good in the end."

General McNaughton arrived at 11.00 A.M. looking "very cheerful. Not a bit tired and was in good form generally. I congratulated [him] on the splendid showing he had made against the kind of conditions I knew he had to contend with. He began by saying there were some things that must be dealt with, first of all this destruction of discipline in the Army must be stopped. It would not do to begin with the smaller ones but Bracken ought to be the first. He should be proceeded against either by his dept. or by the Dept. of Justice. Would talk to St. Laurent about it. Connie Smythe, he thought, should be court martialled and a couple of men who came and interrupted one of the meetings, for what they had said, etc. He spoke of Bracken having been completely untrue in his statements, reckless, etc. Showed me the speech which he understood had been written by Drew. Also the extent to which it had been changed. Our own reporters had noted the changes in speaking. As written first, the tenses were all positive, for example 'are' had been changed to 'appear.' Other sections were left out. Some of them referring to myself. Altogether it was plain the document had just been put into Bracken's hands.

"McNaughton then began to tell me of the nature of the campaign. On Friday night, Homuth, Rowe, and other men all came to the constituency and disappeared. Quantities of liquor had been distributed that night and the following day, and money had been spent freely in the purchase of votes.

"McNaughton believes it can be proved that thousands of dollars were spent in that way. He described how the meetings had been interrupted by people that were paid: soldiers telling untruths, etc. The article which was attributed to L'Action Catholique describing my new Liberal program, ending up with independence and separation from Britain, etc. had been broadcast over the radio at 8.00 A.M. Monday morning from the Globe— the different Orange Lodges being told, and the Tory scrutineers, to listen in to get their cue to influence the people as they went to the polls. McNaughton said the Lodges were simply bought out brazenly, and ordered by others to change against McNaughton. One of our own Liberals had been asked what price he would be prepared to accept to pull out of the campaign. McNaughton seems convinced it was money and liquor and the appeal to prejudice, saying his wife was a Roman Catholic, and that sort of thing, which had influenced the vote at the time. He said organization is in fine fighting shape; that we will win the next time. . . . He said the Globe had sent up people to circulate stories—all kinds of stories about the reasons he had resigned; his connection with the Army had been broken off, etc. He said it may force him to come out and tell all the facts. He is ready to do this but it will reflect pretty seriously on Ralston if he does, he said. He then told me he had the actual documents, one of them from Eisenhower protesting against taking part of the Canadian Army to Italy, and Ralston's contention before the Army officers that if they were not taken, the whole fighting might be over without our having any casualties. In other words, the position of Ralston and Stuart had all been directed to fighting even against the will at the time of the British authorities as well as Eisenhower, the head of the American command. He spoke of the documents being very serious. They would involve Montgomery's determination to get control of the army in Europe. He gave me other information which he had cabled to Canada at the time of taking away the Canadian forces which I know never came before the War Committee.

"I recall quite well Ralston saying repeatedly Canada would have no real voice in peace if we did not do more fighting. I kept telling him the Chiefs of Staff knew what they were about, were holding the Canadian army intact for the best of reasons. Now we have received word the Canadians are being brought back from Italy to join other forces; that will save, so McNaughton said, many thousands of men in meeting any reinforcement situation.

"The whole situation has been created by the necessity of keeping up the lines of supply and communication that were never anticipated. I have no doubt that McNaughton has been completely vindicated on the stand he took.

"When he was through speaking, I counselled him against making a martyr of Bracken. That there would be difficulty in getting convictions against him but to seek some way of having him put in the position where it would become clear before the public that he made the statement he did without any authority. Also I told him to hold back anything about Ralston, Montgomery and others while the men were fighting at the front. He would be all the stronger in the end. As for other things, I was for following them up as rapidly and completely as possible."

Later that day at a Cabinet meeting, Mackenzie King reported that McNaughton "made a first rate report on manpower. Says he has no longer any concern. We have many more men than we need overseas assured. He reported that one of the ships with N.R.M.A. men aboard was almost torpedoed getting into the harbour yesterday. Macdonald took exception to N.R.M.A. men being called volunteers when they volunteered at the last moment. I stated the policy was that of rejoicing in the Kingdom of Heaven over the last sinner, etc. McNaughton made plain that the effect of morale on men coming to be classed with G.S. was very great. Made them more helpful in fighting and would have far reaching effect when the war was over. I said that I felt lots of people would prefer to persecute these men; would be happier if they were destroyed, . . . notwithstanding they were offering their lives on the battlefield.

"After Council, McNaughton, St. Laurent and I had a talk in my office about the course to be taken against Bracken. St. Laurent spoke as I had this morning of difficulties we had had in proceeding against Drew and, though we had the strongest case, there was the difficulty of getting a conviction from a Toronto judge."

Mackenzie King complained that "the papers are full of Tory interpretation of McNaughton's defeat as if the whole thing were a victory for Conservatives against the government on its conscription policy. Their abuse of McNaughton is very great and attitude toward myself much the same. The Tory press has always been this way getting their messages inspired from different sources.

"I have felt today quite relieved and more or less happy about the future for I do feel pretty certain that before the day of voting comes, the war in Europe will be over in which event Tories' talk and cry on conscription will be knocked endways. Meanwhile everything possible is being done to poison minds of troops, etc. I think Council now will see the wisdom of what I had proposed of dissolving on the day that our opponents put in their official nomination. McNaughton feels it would have done him a permanent injury for there is no doubt the constituency would have been disappointed and the whole business misinterpreted. If our men show where there has been corruption in the campaign, though this is always difficult, the result of the situation might not be too bad. There is no doubt the result has cost us heavily for the time being. I shall have to begin soon to prepare a statement for the press which will make clear determination not to have another session and, at the same time, to seek to hold to the position of the war being over before the date of polling."

The following day, February 8, the Prime Minister continued to be preoccupied with the coming campaign. His first thoughts "were of Prince Albert constituency and the wisdom of reconsidering what it might be best to do there. Stevenson's report that there is no hope of winning the constituency seems to make it inadvisable for me deliberately to court defeat and when the campaign is on, have the country continually told that the Prime Minister is going to be badly defeated. Also placing me in a position where my influence would pretty well be gone in dealing with any matters requiring readjustment after the election and also in relation to my post-war future. The Tories are so unfair in representing the significance of a defeat that it might be doing myself and the entire party a great injury to court it. I have been indifferent so far as I, myself, am concerned and would welcome an honourable exit from public life which defeat in the constituency might be so regarded, but if it helped to prejudice the position of the party in the contest, would not prove such.

"There are strong reasons which have come up since I stated I would run in Saskatchewan which would justify me in seeking another constituency. The most important of all is the coming of General McNaughton into the government." In his view, "with McNaughton running in Saskatchewan there would be three Ministers running in that one C.C.F. province. It would be reasonable that this should not take place. It would be better that I should run in some other constituency. I thought once of P.E.I. which province at present has no Minister, and was the constituency which opened its doors for me to go into Parliament. However that means a fight in a constituency that I could see little or nothing of myself though I believe I could be elected there.

"I could run in North Waterloo where I was first elected as a Member. However practically all of those with whom I was associated are either very far advanced in years or have passed away. It would be a heartbreak to be among another generation who neither know me or our family before me and most of whom I do not know myself. Besides it is a constituency that is so largely German.

"The constituency which I think would be best of all would be Russell county. It is nearby and I could put in appearances there through the campaign. I would not be much worried by the constituency after an election.

"Ottawa itself might be considered but that would make it very difficult for me to both administer affairs at headquarters, and conduct a general campaign while elections were on. There may be other fairly safe seats but I imagine Russell would be as secure as any. It can hardly be said that I am going back on my friends in Prince Albert seeing that they have kept up no organization. It could be made plain that I was taking Russell because of it being near the Capital and thereby not occupying much of my time.

"The outside world might never understand my being beaten by thousands possibly in Prince Albert and Bracken elected by a correspondingly large majority or a considerable majority and all other leaders elected as well. It would hardly be a fitting close to my career, or a deserved close knowing what the forces are that would be operating. I know the Party would much prefer that I should have a safe seat. It might come to look too much in the course of a campaign like seeking a way out and it might be interpreted that I had no faith in the party's win in any event. I might even come to be blamed for the party's defeat if I deliberately courted disaster. Stevenson's letter to me received on Tuesday the 6th (Mother's birthday) makes it wholly apparent that that is what I would be doing. . . .

"I come now to the general elections themselves. I have been giving much thought to this question and my present feeling which I believe will be the ultimate decision is very clear in my mind this morning. I have said all along I did not want an election in war-time and would do my utmost to prevent it short of extending the term of Parliament. I have made it clear that an announcement would be made not later than April 17.

"The outcome of the election in Grey North has changed the whole picture," Mackenzie King continued. "It has made wholly clear the inadvisability of holding an election while the war is on. The argument that the people will trust the present administration rather than any other to carry on the war would be partly offset by Tory propaganda that Grey North meant that the people wanted conscription but even more offset by the strong probability that the war would be over in any event before the election itself was over. The underlying purpose of an early election was to avoid the necessity of another session of Parliament with all the disadvantages that would have. We are now completely justified in not holding another session. That has been made apparent. The press generally has come to acknowledge that. With the time ahead clear of another session there is nothing to prevent us choosing any date we please between now and July the 1st. We must not run beyond June for the reason among others that the family allowances measure comes into operation on July 1. Besides it would be postponing to too late a date the re-assembling of Parliament with the public business that has to be attended to. Most important of all is the fact that any election being fought before the war is over, if it is possible to prevent that, will mean that the Tory party will capitalize Grey North to the limit; will make the contest one in relation to conscription, and the government will be having to spend all its time explaining and defending the conscription situation and we will have no chance of putting over our programme of social reform. It would be the emotional kind of campaign which was witnessed in Grey North.

"We have now very strong evidence that the war may be over by the middle of April. My own feeling is that the end will come before that. Once the war is over, it will be possible for the government to claim that we have carried the nation successfully through the war, also to expose the whole reinforcement business, making clear that the necessary men were in reality available but that the kind of campaign waged had made it necessary to guard against possibilities. We would then have the field perfectly clear for the party that was to govern in the next five years. The Tories would have lost the one thing around which their whole campaign has been built, namely, the conscription issue. Anti-conscriptionists would remember our stand, for there is still the war against Japan, but what I feel most important of all from the point of view of the people, and what the Liberal party stands for, is that we would then give our full time to putting across our programme of social reform." There was also the question, the Prime Minister felt, "of who was to represent Canada at the peace. My strength in the Dominion lies in what I have stood for, for the masses, in the way of social reform, and what my present position in international affairs means to the future of Canada. We would, in my opinion, be throwing away our two strongest arguments for the party's return—to not have the public in a position where they could concentrate their minds on these aspects. The argument that the C.C.F. would be able to apply in all sorts of directions—put forth all sorts of claims—would not, I think, be any different after the war than during the war, whereas by waiting until after the war we could begin to get back that portion of the Conservative vote which, at the moment, is likely to head back into the Tory camp. In other words, we would once again be about where we were before Ralston's action led to a change of the whole position."

"If we can hold off the campaign until victory," he added, "the people generally will admit that I have done a great piece of work in carrying through the whole war without an election in war time and still conserving to the people their rights to a general election. The Tory press can hardly seek to urge an immediate election while the fighting is on without getting into a wrong position. . . ."

However the question of timing was important. "The Victory Loan has always stuck up like a sore thumb in the way of either compelling an election to come almost immediately or making it necessary to postpone until June. The public will be quick to recognize that we cannot have the two campaigns going on at once. It can be explained that the victory loan people demand the 23rd of April to begin their campaign and will want three weeks in advance for preparation which would mean that if the victory loan is not to be prejudiced there should be an election before April 1st, which is now of course no longer possible. Were the victory loan to be on the 23rd, it would be over by the 14th of May. We could fix a date in the early part or the middle of June which would give time for men to rest up before the campaign and a breathing spell between the two. Not to prejudice the success of the victory loan would be patriotic in itself.

"We would then, too, be all over the question of roads; April admittedly is the worst month for electioneering; June has always been regarded as the best month for a campaign. If, meanwhile, the war was over, and victory achieved, the feeling of the people toward the Administration would be wholly different. By waiting before announcing the date, we could govern ourselves as to the matter of the best day for the election itself in the light of changes that will come in Europe. We could take any Monday in June—the 4th, the 11th, the 18th or the 25th—as circumstances might seem to render most advisable.

"One other thing: we must strengthen our organization, we must arrange somehow to have our candidates schooled on the line they are to take in the campaign. They should be brought to Ottawa and the whole situation outlined and presented to them; also careful directions should be prepared in writing. The later date would give more time for organization. True, it will give it to the others as well, but the C.C.F. have had a bad crack which will increase their problems. Our position vis-a-vis the

C.C.F. will be improved, and vis-a-vis the Tory position that will be gone altogether if the war ends before the campaign actually begins. They have nothing to offer for the period of reconstruction. It can be made apparent that if the country is left in their hands nothing need be expected but the control by financial and industrial interests. Meanwhile, the agitation of the C.C.F. toward that end will be assisting us. We will be in the best of positions to make clear that we are the one party that is capable of forming a government that is truly national. Practically all of the arguments urged in the last campaign can be urged in the one for this year, substituting the 'winning of the peace' for 'winning of the war.' I am convinced in my mind that what is here outlined is the best course."

The attitude of the Cabinet was also important. "I shall be able to count on McNaughton, St. Laurent and Angus Macdonald, to support this position," Mackenzie King wrote. "Ilsley and Howe will be against it. I think the other Ontario ministers will be for it. Where Gardiner will be I do not know—probably for an early election. On the whole I believe the result in Grey North will cause the great majority to favour delay until June. We went into Grey North with the highest and best of intentions—to permit of another session of parliament before an election, so as to avoid an election in war time, especially in the interests of the men overseas and in accordance with the wishes of their families and friends at home. Instead of co-operation, in carrying on until the war is over, we have reached the climax of obstruction from Tories and C.C.F. alike. From looking upon Grey North as a defeat, we can make it the corner stone of victory. That, I believe, we can do."

At the Cabinet meeting on February 9 McNaughton "brought forward a letter he had intended sending Bracken stating the truth as officially disclosed regarding the men and their rifles re the charges that rifles were thrown overboard asking if Bracken accepted it or whether he preferred an investigation. The wisdom of collective discussion was shown in the decision first, not to add the reference to investigation as he would be certain to say yes to everything regarding reinforcements, etc. which the press would make great use of. Then later, not to send a letter to him but to issue an official statement from the Department once all the facts were obtained and let the matter rest there. Bracken will then have to either accept the official statement or be in the position of one who was prepared to make reckless charges and cares nothing about their effect on the reputation of the country and the Army. We were also wise in not having him continue with Connie Smythe on a very small end of something he did or said in the campaign and to limit the court martial to the case of one officer who clearly violated the law. The other is mentally deficient and would be excused on that account. The Government is terribly handicapped in these matters, as anything done would be put down to political motives."

The effect in Ontario of the North Grey by-election was brought into sharp relief for Mackenzie King by a telephone call from Joseph Atkinson of the *Toronto Star* on February 10. Mackenzie King reported that he shuddered when he was told Atkinson was calling. "It was pretty much what I expected, only worse," he wrote. "He began by asking me if the Governor-in-Council could not pass some additional order which will make it clear that we had a general all-out conscription. He went on to say that the Telegram and other papers were pointing out what I had said in November that what we have is not all-out conscription and that unless we had this he saw no chance at all for the party in the Province of Ontario. That the defeat in North Grey was clearly due to that. He went on to say he had never tried to influence the Government in its policy but corrected that saying he had once or twice spoken of a social program. He went on to say that he thought perhaps our French colleagues would be prepared now to go the full length. He kept enlarging on this and the necessity if the government was to be saved at all of going the full length. I tried to tell him as best I could that the reinforcement situation was in every way satisfactory. That to alter anything now would be to unsettle conditions further in Canada. That I was perfectly sure we could hold off the election until the war in Europe was over. That it would be seen there had been no need for anything further in the way of conscription and that we would be able to have the election fought on our social program. I told him my latest information made me sure of this. He said Oh well, that is some reassurance, I am glad to have that. But then he began to go over the ground again and seemed rather to indicate that the Star had done its best to give us support. Then he would stop and say nothing further. But came back to I would know he was only advising for what was the good of the government, which, of course, I understood. He then went on to say that the measure we had taken was a compromise and was needed to keep the government together. He thought that was a justification for what we had done. He also admitted that if we could not go all out conscription at present without the government splitting that would be a justification but it would not help to save the government. I can see that, as I expected, once the heavy fighting began this conscription business will come along in a more terrific form than ever. It means that I will have to stand up to a desperate situation until the war itself is over. Happily I have enough information to cause me to feel that I will be justified in the end by holding out. The tragic thing is that while endeavouring to hold on to my supporters in Quebec and elsewhere, many of them will be hesitating to back me as they should and in an outright way. Brais [a former member of Godbout's government] told me last night that the provincial party had had a caucus at which Godbout and others were present. A few were very outspoken about having nothing to do with anyone who had the least to do with conscription, as the government had dealt with it at the last session. However, the vast majority were very decidedly of the view that the one thing for the party in Quebec was myself as leader and to back me solidly. I believe that is true.

"What Atkinson may do I cannot say but I again greatly fear the Winnipeg Free Press and possibly the Montreal Star may begin to press for some further all-out conscription, though I pray they will not. I certainly will not yield to anything that will be so disastrous to Canadian unity. The one thing I feel I must do is to clear the slate of everything excepting the work of the campaign from now on, keeping an eye of course on the war and giving my time over wholly to what will achieve results."

That evening, February 10, McNaughton came to Laurier House "to show me a statement to give to the press tomorrow, giving assurances that there are ample reinforcements and that the army is up to strength. This is very necessary as the country will be tremendously stirred up with the word of our men fighting as they will be doing from now on. There will be a tremendous pressure on me to do something in the way of calling Parliament together. With the Minister of Defence out of the House, I think the Government is justified in holding to the stand it has taken. If the fighting takes longer than I at present anticipate and the country gets greatly roused, it might become necessary to have the House assemble and notwithstanding all I have said, arrange to prolong its life. That would be yielding to public opinion as I did in the case of conscription, the opinion being so overwhelmingly one way and desirability so obvious in the light of everything. That is a reason for keeping Parliament in being. In these times, one can only take a step at a time. It must be apparent to everyone that it was fortunate we agreed to act in accordance with the 1942 understanding when we did seeing that the pressure methods adopted to create the scare regarding reinforcements were as powerful as they were, and impossible to cope with the situation in any other way in the light of Ralston's action. If the Cabinet had broken up at the time and elections were being completed now, there is not much difficulty in seeing what a hideous election we would have had. The troops not helped in the interval and the Liberal party in all probability swept out of existence. Especially if the elections, as in all probability would have been the case, would not have been over as yet. It would have taken all of 2 months and some days after Parliament adjourned before the day of polling. I wonder too what the votes of the men overseas would have been.

"The General and I had a pleasant short talk in front of the fire. When I spoke about it being fortunate he was here—better perhaps for him that he was—he said in a wistful way: but it is a great disappointment. He has all along hoped he might be leading forces now being led by Crerar. He feels bitter toward Montgomery whom he thinks deliberately sought to usurp his position. I am inclined to think it was more the High Command. They were anxious to get Montgomery into the post he is now in. . . . He told me he was having trouble with Ralston who keeps on writing asking for information as, for example, the split up figures showing this and that by provinces. He says he does not intend to give him this information at present, not thinking it is in the interests of the public to have it used in ways that Ralston would use it. I told him he could remind Ralston that while it was desirable that the War Committee should have certain information, he Ralston himself would realize wherein part of the information should not be given outside of the Committee, to any persons other than those who were members of the Committee. That there was much information that did not go even to other members of the Cabinet. He [McNaughton] must be the judge of this."

Returning to consideration of possible Cabinet reconstruction on February 12, the Prime Minister spoke to Speaker Glen about coming into the Cabinet as T. A. Crerar's successor, "saying I was making no commitment but wondered what his own chances would be of election. Glen did not enthuse particularly. I could see from his manner that he realizes he has neglected the constituency. He may have in the back of his mind an unwillingness to incur expense of the campaign. He is more or less set upon getting some diplomatic post later. I told him when he returned [to his riding] to be as friendly as he could with his executive. Go at things as though he meant to be a candidate again. See how far they responded. He asked me if he could speak confidentially with them by way of asking what they thought he should do if by any chance I should be considering him for the Ministry. I told him he could do that very quietly but not in any way to indicate that I had made a remote undertaking; simply that he knew I might be considering it."

Also on February 12 Mackenzie King, who had been reading the report of the Yalta conference, noted that "the mention in this report of a Conference on world organization at San Francisco on April 25th raises at once the question of who will represent Canada there. Canada will have to be represented and I imagine on Ministerial level. That means that I will have to go there." This, he felt, "gives an added reason why the election should not be on at the time that the conference is being held. What, however, seems to me most significant is that it is hardly probable that date would have been selected were it not expected that the war would be over by that time. I rather imagine that Churchill himself may have in mind being present and going on from San Francisco to Australia. Also the date has relation to the conclusion of the Treaty of Neutrality between Russia and Japan. I think this means Russia will join with the Allies at that time to get the Japanese out of business. Altogether that makes it more fortunate than ever that Parliament is still in being and that no date has yet been fixed for the elections. No matter what comes, we must shape matters so as to have the election after the war when the reinforcement and conscription issue cannot further be raised. The fight would be on our postwar programme."

On February 13, Mackenzie King had a talk with Alfred Goulet, the M.P. for Russell, to whom he "mentioned that since McNaughton's defeat in Grey North there had been some mention of my not risking defeat in Prince Albert but running elsewhere. Goulet said at once none of the party wants you to run in Prince Albert. You could have Russell any minute and would be sure of election there. He went on to say that while 75 percent of the constituency was French; the English part, mostly Conservative; the priests, he thought, were all favourable to me, as they were to him. The leading priest had spoken of his great admiration for me. All took the view that regardless of their attitude on conscription, there was no one else to lead but myself. Goulet had voted for conscription and found there was no feeling against him on that account. . . . I remarked that the Journal and the Citizen would both be against me and would be piling stuff into the riding. He mentioned that Le Droit was the French paper, also La Presse, and said he felt quite sure that the constituency could be carried. I told him to say nothing of the idea, and that I had only spoken of it to him because others had spoken to me, and that while I was indifferent myself I had to consider the interests of the party." Later in the day, he spoke to Gardiner about Prince Albert and read him Senator Stevenson's letter. "I could see his face flush a little as I read the letter. He has always tried to have me feel he himself was looking after the constituency. He could see from Stevenson having written me that others were in contact with him. He agreed that Stevenson was also looking after his own riding. He agreed that three ministers were rather too much in Saskatchewan, but thought while I might not be elected myself they would carry more seats in Saskatchewan if I were running in Prince Albert. Later, he said he thought

I could carry Prince Albert if they once got the campaign under way. He felt that quite an attack was being made on his own seat. The truth is Gardiner has lost a certain hold on Saskatchewan."

Mackenzie King sought the views of the Minister from Alberta, Mac-Kinnon, on February 15 and also "told him of Stevenson's letter. He seems to feel no such letter should have been sent to me. I told him I felt quite the opposite. It was an honest letter, which gave me just what I needed to know. I could see, from what MacKinnon said, that he, no doubt like others, took it rather for granted that I might be defeated in Prince Albert, but would find a constituency elsewhere immediately after. I told him on no consideration would I seek a seat elsewhere if I were defeated; that would mark the completion of my life in Parliament. He then began to think it would perhaps be wise if the ministers got together and arranged for some other seat. I made clear to him the alteration of the situation in view of McNaughton's defeat in Grey North, through being unable to give time to the constituency, and there being now three Liberal ministers booked for the constituencies in the one province of Saskatchewan. Mac-Kinnon is the most thoughtful and generous of men but our talk together made it clear to me that he, like all others, is thinking mostly of himself with an unwillingness to really get in and help in matters of organization. I gave him a broad hint that he might be able to do something by lending a hand at the central organization. It was apparent, however, he has not that much in mind."

Two days later Senator Stevenson dined with Mackenzie King. "The Senator," he wrote, "gave me an account of the hopeless condition in which he found things on arriving recently in Prince Albert but says that he has got the leaders at work in different parts of the constituency and cited an example or two which indicated that the people are already beginning to find dissatisfaction with the C.C.F. in some of their moves. He believes, however, the Tories would combine with them to defeat me and I could see little in what he said that would lead me to believe that the constituency could be won except his own professed faith that matters have begun to 'roll' my way and he believed the constituency could be won. However he felt that Russell would be a much safer seat, especially if the French would stand by me notwithstanding the conscription issue. He knows Russell well having resided there several years. He is going to see one or two of the leading persons himself. He feels I should not risk being defeated for the party's sake no less than my own. Believes it would be a disappointment to our friends in Saskatchewan but that they will acquiesce especially if Dr. Humphries [a prominent Liberal in Prince Albert] should come here for some meeting and be spoken to by the Ministers. He realizes that it will not be possible for me to give time to the constituency." There the matter of the Prime Minister's constituency in the next election rested for some weeks.

In mid-February Mackenzie King became quite concerned about increasing tension between Angus Macdonald and General McNaughton. On February 13 he "was greatly distressed listening to the (evening) news over the radio that Macdonald had stated that McNaughton was quite wrong in what he said about sinkings at sea—of the Atlantic being full of U-boats. He could easily have made a general reference which would have served the purpose but what he has said almost amounts to an open defiance of the wing of the government to which McNaughton belongs and may have something quite serious behind it. It is apparent that the conscription group intend to keep up their fight. No doubt there is the closest kind of relationship between Ralston and Macdonald still. I can only pray that this shameful act of Macdonald toward a colleague does not result in something again very serious."

The next morning, he was still worried. To Mackenzie King, Macdonald's statement looked "like an effort to undermine McNaughton and indicative of some continuance of vindictiveness between Macdonald, Ralston and company. In other words, the conscriptionist group and McNaughton." Later in the day he had a talk with the Minister of Defence and "advised him to ignore what Macdonald had said though he felt pretty bitter saying that what Macdonald had said was equivalent to calling him a liar. It was apparent to him, McNaughton, that the factions opposed to him were trying to make out that his word could not be trusted. I said when he had been as long in politics as I had, he would learn to pay no attention to these things at all. Also was for going after Bracken for his latest statement [again charging ineptitude in the government's army manpower policy]. I advised against that too, saying to hold back everything until time of general elections. . . ."

On February 20 the Prime Minister noted that McNaughton had been ill with influenza which he thought was "in part reaction from North Grey campaign and attacks upon him which are most unfair. Also trouble he is having with Pearkes and some of the senior officials of his staff. Have no doubt that a set of the Army are distinctly opposed to him and will continue to make all the trouble they can. He is brave and courageous. I, myself, am influenced by attacks on him. The selection of Grey North for the by-election was really most unfortunate. All a part of having no real organization to depend upon for elections. . . ."

Pressure on McNaughton from the anti-conscriptionist wing of the Cabinet, particularly from the irrepressible Minister of Agriculture, was also strong. Gardiner had issued a statement attacking General Pearkes for some critical statements he had made about the government's reinforcement policy and, on February 21, McNaughton informed Mackenzie King that he was "having great difficulty with Pearkes, who threatens to bring action against Gardiner for libel in the statement which he made the other day. McNaughton says Gardiner's statement was most indiscreet and spoke of thinking of writing me about it with a view to having Gardiner retract. He says all of this is having serious effects on discipline in the army. I tried to have him see that there were some things in politics that had to be dealt with by public opinion rather than by legal action, discipline, etc. I was anxious to save getting into a battle between Gardiner and McNaughton. No doubt Gardiner was wholly wrong going as far as he did. After all it was much on par with some other statements that had been made. These things are best dealt with as gingerly as possible. McNaughton at the moment is smarting under his defeat and is apt to be a little more aggressive than he would otherwise be. He naturally wishes to deal with the many things as they would be dealt with in the Army. Difficulties cannot be met that way in civil affairs."

Although the forthcoming San Francisco conference was the main international preoccupation at this time, the future of world trade also concerned the Prime Minister. On February 14 the main question discussed in Cabinet "was one related to postwar trade, developments that are now taking place, and which will be continued in the transitional period, whereby there is a danger of restrictions being hardened into barriers between Britain and the countries in the sterling area versus Canada, the U.S., and other hard currency countries. This might even lead to a movement for annexation with the States and would certainly have the effect of bringing a terrible depression to Canada in the course of four–five years were we to lose British markets as, apparently, we are risking doing today. What we agreed to was to continue giving Britain mutual aid and help her from getting into a state of bankruptcy, but asking her to recognize what was owing to the future of the British Commonwealth if it was to be maintained; try to protect her against herself in the preservation of the Empire as such. Really the British attitude is a terribly selfish one. Again, if the Empire is to continue, it will be because Canada has through her policies helped to save the day."

On February 16 Mackenzie King returned to domestic political problems in a conversation with St. Laurent about the political situation in the Quebec City ridings. The anti-conscription Liberals, while anxious to remain within the party, also wished to establish some measure of independence from the government's reinforcement policy. Mackenzie King and St. Laurent "agreed that it would be all right for the Liberals of Quebec to designate themselves as Independent Liberals if they wished to, but not to be members of a separate organization. If they wanted assistance they would have to be part of the Liberal party. It would not be fair to the Liberals of the province who had stood by us.

"St. Laurent seemed to feel that the men in the province felt he had been honest in his attitude but did not represent the Quebec view on conscription, and would prefer not to follow him at all. He said he was quite ready to get out if I wished that. I told him I would not stay in the government if he was not a member of it. We must try and work out a formula. He spoke of Power coming at the weekend. I nearly caved in when he said that. I was so tired. I told him I had a broadcast to prepare and Power would have to wait until after that time. He agreed to phone him. He knows nothing and professes to know nothing of the Montreal end of the organization. Really, our whole party is like sheep without a shepherd, so far as Quebec province is concerned. Very disheartening. We talked of the world organization and of the bearing of what the conscription issue here might mean on getting support for world organization in another parliament.

"St. Laurent said that the feeling in Quebec was against the United Kingdom, but that there would not be the same feeling towards a world organization under which Britain herself might be held in check against adopting an aggressive attitude. We had been discussing world trade, memos prepared by Robertson and others. He [St. Laurent] had made suggestions for amendments. Here again he thought that in anything in which the U.S. took a strong stand we would be able to get support from Quebec and this both as regards world trade and collective security. I said to him the situation looked to me, if these trading blocks developed, there might be a terrible depression in Canada a few years hence with inevitable movement toward annexation and continental union. He agreed entirely with this. Hoped the U.S. might be able to favour the world trade idea.

"I pointed out that the President, from appearances, could not last long and would have little power to press anything new on. Mr. Hull was the strong man in world trade, but he too was pretty much out of the picture. I did not know how Stettinius might be, but the attitude of the U.S. might change considerably very soon. St. Laurent felt I should certainly go to the world conference at San Francisco. He agreed also that the elections should not come until the war was at an end and that we might expect the whole political situation in Canada to change once the war was over and the issue was on our postwar policies."

Mackenzie King talked with both St. Laurent and Power on February 20. To him it appeared that "Power was anxious to create a certain wing which he himself would control. Also that he was anxious to justify his own action in resigning by labelling me as a conscriptionist and making himself a leader of anti-conscription. This with a view also to get St. Laurent labelled as a conscriptionist. An effort, in other words, to try to wrest leadership from St. Laurent to himself. I do not think the members, Lapointe, Picard, and others are anxious to make the difference as marked as Power would have them. Also I think his desire not to be identified or to have them identified with the regular Liberal organization is partly a matter of personal pride. One thing to have an office at the Chateau, having been an ex-Cabinet Minister, and not to be brought down to the level of a political organizer using offices of the organization for himself. This I can understand. St. Laurent tactfully suggested that the main thing was to get men nominated anyway. After the nomination the question of what particular auspices they should run under, regular Liberal auspices or Liberal independent wing, etc., could be settled. I took quick exception to Power's statement that I could be regarded as a conscriptionist and having betrayed the party when what I had done was to save the party by meeting a desperate situation that would have spelt ruin alike to Canada's war effort at home and overseas. He said that this was his own personal expression and rather backed away from it."

It was not until February 22 that Mackenzie King's plans for the session, the San Francisco conference, and the election really began to crystallize. He wrote: "I am beginning to feel the wise course re San Francisco would be to take Graydon and possibly Coldwell with me though it seems to me Blackmore is equally deserving, if not more so than Coldwell, as he has been co-operative. On the other hand, Blackmore is certain to raise exception to anything that looks like substituting sovereignty of Council for Dominion sovereignty. I certainly will not take Bracken. He should be fully ignored having nothing to do with Parliament. This and the meeting of the House will have to be decided soon."

Mackenzie King had arranged on February 21 to have a proclamation issued extending the prorogation until March 31, 1945, and the following day he told the Deputy Minister of Finance that "it would be necessary for us to have a brief session. . . . Spoke of having estimates and war appropriation ready."

Later in the day, Mackenzie King discussed the San Francisco conference with Norman Robertson. He noted that Robertson "spoke of Wrong going with me. I said I would of course want himself as well. It is characteristically modest of him to suggest Wrong.

"We talked of the delegation. I had previously thought if the U.S., U.K. and Australia have members of other parties, it would be wise for Canada also to do the same, not to repeat Wilson's error of seeking to monopolize international matters of the kind for one political party. I am quite agreeable to Graydon and Coldwell. Would like to have Blackmore but he would be difficult. I am altogether opposed to Bracken.

"Robertson made a rather odd suggestion of Cardin as representative of other groups in the House. I said, of course, the Minister of Justice would be with me. Robertson has already engaged accommodation on the train. I am glad he prefers the train journey. I may be able to arrange with the U.S. to have my car go through.

"In conversation, Robertson said that I might be asked to preside at the conference. My reaction at once was on no account would I wish this. That I am so tired, not sharp in regard to names, points of order, etc. and might find difficulty with many nations represented. Also only English speaking. He said the first thought had been to have Mr. Hull but he was not well enough."

The next day Mackenzie King expressed the opinion that it was embarrassing to keep secret the government's plans for the San Francisco Conference and the session, but expressed the belief that "the Victory Loan, the San Francisco Conference and the termination of the war will all raise in the mind of the electorate great mountains between the last weeks of the election and all that has gone before. Meanwhile the country will be spared more bitterness, contention, wrangling while our fighting men are undergoing their severest strain."

Before deciding definitely on a session, the Prime Minister had a talk with Malcolm MacDonald on February 24. He noted that MacDonald "had no definite word about the date of the termination of the war, but agreed that it would hardly run beyond the period of the San Francisco conference. He thought there might be some advantage in Eden being where he could be in touch with Roosevelt, when the end came, which might be immediately before or during the Conference. He agreed with me that there was a possibility of the Americans finishing off the Japanese by themselves, and told me privately that there was some possibility of a certain very secret weapon being used by the Americans against the Japanese. We discussed this particular weapon and what the mere possession of it is likely to mean in perpetuating dread among the nations through years to come once its existence and powers are known. It could mean the destruction of civilization."

During this period, Mackenzie King spent part of each day working on a radio broadcast to explain the government's plans for the session and the San Francisco conference. On February 26 he felt "strongly that a broadcast is desirable to let the people hear my voice and to be brought again in immediate touch with them. That, however, means a broadcast devoid of anything controversial and in the nature of a bare statement. That may be best. I had thought once of a political broadcast but that again would be running counter to the position I have taken since the beginning of the war, of not personally provoking controversy.

"P. [Pickersgill] favours a bald statement to the press on the meeting of Parliament and leaving the question of the date of election over for the present. I think the public would prefer a clear statement which would remove further uncertainty about the time of the election, save the exact time. There are advantages also in this, in that it enables me to give the best of reasons for having postponed the election till June. The papers are all getting very impatient about my ignoring Parliament and giving no clue as to the date of the election and a good deal of bitter feeling is being aroused against me on the score that I am treating Parliament and the people with contempt. That was inevitable once Parliament was not in session for some time, however, the situation will change again once announcement is made that Parliament is to be called, though I will be blamed for permitting so short a time but all will be again changed once Germany begins to collapse. Everything else that has gone before will be forgotten. Meanwhile I am avoiding, by holding the fort in this way, the House of Commons being made into a sort of bear garden and also helping to hold off a general election until the war in Europe is over. I cannot see how the collapse of Germany is not certain to come before the San Francisco Conference."

The next day, February 27, he told the Cabinet "of what I had in mind about the summoning of Parliament on the 19th and having the election sometime in June. I went over, in a way, much of what I intend to bring out in the broadcast, and advised them of my intention to broadcast. Council were in entire agreement about the reassembling of the House with a view to getting interim supply for the period of March 31st until elections are over. Also in entire agreement as to elections in June, and as to a delegation to the San Francisco Conference. I spoke of not having decided on the delegation, but asked them to consider the question of the possibility of taking leaders of the opposition parties along. I could see the first reaction was strongly against that, but I pointed out that I myself did not wish to make the mistake that Wilson had made in the formation of the League of Nations in ignoring representatives of other parties. I would have, however, to be sure of their loyalty and of agreement on policy in advance, which might be very difficult to obtain.

"I had talked with Clark previously about what should be prepared. I was glad to learn from him that Ilsley was quite agreeable to having Parliament called to vote a portion of the supply needed to carry on during the election. Ilsley himself has been at the point of another breakdown and has been resting at the Seigniory Club, Montebello. I said we would have to face the possibility of much contention and embarrassment. If it went too far we would be justified in dissolving and the onus for the use of Governor General's warrants would be on the opposition.

"I had given to the press word of my intention to broadcast and had Turnbull make enquiries as to possibility for Thursday night."

On March 2, Mackenzie King placed before the Cabinet an order calling Parliament for March 19 and read the text of his proposed broadcast. "Ilsley raised a question about inserting the date of the Victory Loan. He wanted to have Towers' authority given first. Also he raised the question about tying down the period of a month between nomination and elections. He seemed anxious elections should come early in June—even if nominations came while the Victory Loan was on. Other members of Council immediately protested that it was rushing the pace too hard. Macdonald and Crerar raised the question as to the insertion of the paragraph dealing with no extension of the life of Parliament. Macdonald wanted the way kept open for an extension. Crerar stressed that Parliament should be kept in being while the San Francisco Conference was on. This apparently was something from the Free Press. He had spoken to Pickersgill earlier about it. I pointed out that if we delayed beyond that time we would have to reveal the extent of all legislation; amounts for mutual aid etc., would be very large and many new questions would be raised. Also it was important to have elections over before July 1st, as family allowances were coming into force at that date. I recall what I have said in Parliament about fixing July 1st so as to prevent issuing of cheques before the election itself. Ilsley seemed perturbed about difficulties arising in connection with the income tax, etc. Council indicated some way will have to be found to meet that. Gardiner stated he thought I was stressing too strongly a truce to political strife. I had myself thought of giving the speech that title. He pointed out, however, we would probably be the only ones who would observe it and our opponents would protest against any steps we ourselves might take in putting forward a platform, holding conventions, etc. He referred to what he might wish to say at his own convention. Also what McNaughton might wish to say. I saw at once that he was right in this. Indeed I had this in mind myself. I said quite frankly I thought he was right and would modify what I had in that regard. Excepting these comments there was no other question raised concerning the broadcast. In the revisions made later in the afternoon I took account of all that had been said in Council."

Mackenzie King also referred, in his diary for March 2, to reports in the papers for the previous evening and that morning of "a statement from Hepburn in addressing some gathering at which he said he was probably wrong in making the personal attacks he did on me. I had waited long for this confession but he has found he has had to make it in the hope of getting back into a strong position in the party. I have never asked for anything from him.

"In the morning paper I also read that the Quebec Legislature passed yesterday Chalout's resolution [an Independent Nationalist Member of the Quebec Legislature] which stated that Mr. King had broken his most solemn promises. There were only five votes against the resolution, Godbout and other Liberals supporting it. I confess that this hurt me a good deal, knowing as I do what I have done to help to save the whole situation for the Liberals of Quebec. There were no broken promises but a complete release from promises in advance. This is the line that Hugues Lapointe, Picard and Power have all been taking. I know their difficulties but it shows how weak men are when it comes to taking a courageous stand. What all should have done was to have compelled a change in this wording, which would have made clear the position in which I had been placed and the purpose of my actions. As sure as I am dictating these words men who have supported the resolution will come greatly to regret it. I have been as true to Quebec as Laurier himself, and Ernest Lapointe. When one thinks of the position of the war and where we would be today had I not taken the course I did I have nothing to regret in the stand I have taken. It is all a part of what Christ himself had to endure from the friends who were with him until the moment came for crucifixion.

"This causes me to record today what I have been glad again to come to feel. That the whole course of events have now so shaped themselves that once again I may become the instrument to make clear to the country that God's will and purpose have been behind what my life has stood for in these times in the accomplishment of things which could only be accounted for by His purpose working out its aim. Just as General Dobbie and Malta will stand out in history as evidencing God's restraining hand helping to save the countries fighting for freedom, so I believe the development that has led to the present situation which I have set forth in today's broadcast will make it clear that all has been so ordained as to show that what has been accomplished could only have come about through God's help and in answer to prayer. In other words, I believe the present government will yet carry through to the end of the war and I may yet be the one chosen to at least make the beginning in the winning of the peace in relation to world organization for the preservation of the peace."

"Another session much as we may have reason to dread it with the turn events have now taken which throws the San Francisco conference into foreground may give me in the eyes of the people the greatest opportunity of leadership I have thus far had. It will change the whole trend of the campaign from the conscription issue in a general election to leadership in peace in the post-war world. I cannot but believe that the end of the war in Europe will come in a fashion which will make this possible."

After he had completed his broadcast, Mackenzie King saw W. P. Mulock to discuss the political situation in Ontario. There had been many signs that Mitchell Hepburn, restored to grace in the Ontario Liberal party, was anxious for a reconciliation with Mackenzie King and, indeed, might be interested in a return to federal politics. Mulock told Mackenzie King that "Hepburn had come to see him and they had had half an hour's talk together. He said he hoped I would not mind his having said to Hepburn he did not assume I would be wishing to stay on indefinitely in the leadership of the party and thereby leaving Hepburn to believe he might have a chance to come into the successorship. I told him the main thing to be aimed at was to have all of us working together to get the government returned. That that was what I was concerned in. I gave no indication of what I felt of any overtures that have been made to Hepburn though I can see, however, stronger men of our party will not quickly pass by Ilsley, Gardiner and possibly others for Hepburn. Indeed if Claxton had a better style of address, of speaking, etc., he would, in some ways, be the best of all to take on in the post-war period. However, meanwhile the thing is to get everyone to work."

Mulock also told Mackenzie King that "Hepburn thought he could defeat Drew at this session. That even arrangements could be made with the C.C.F. to divide some of the seats to make certain of this. He [Hepburn] did not wish to take any steps without my approval. I said to Mulock I really did not know enough about the situation to say whether he would be sure to win. That in the circumstances, I could not venture myself to advise either for or against. I might have added that after my speech of tonight on truce to party strife at this serious moment of the war, I could hardly support the idea of bringing on a provincial election in Ontario at this time."

The next morning (March 3) the Prime Minister made several revisions in the text of his broadcast for possible publication. He restored "the paragraphs re not extending the life of Parliament which I had in my original text but struck out without sufficient consideration after Crerar and Macdonald had raised the questions they did about it in Council yesterday. They are not the best advisers. I feel I am right in holding very firmly to the basis on which I have, from the start, planned elections, namely that this right secured by the Constitution should not be taken from the people. I have asserted it over and over again in Parliament but wanted it recorded in the final address." He felt considerable relief in "having a definite programme ahead, and an end thereby put to some at least of the criticism that has been so violent since the Grey North by-election."

On the morning of March 6, Mackenzie King began to feel that "it might be wise to try and get Power back into the Ministry before Parliament re-assembles. He could handle the Air end very well, and could be acting Minister of Defence. Whether he would come or not, I cannot say but I rather believe he would welcome the chance. It would be a splendid way of bringing the Province of Quebec back into line. The only difficulty will be the Ralston situation again. I might be able to persuade Power that by his coming in now, we might before an election work out other difficulties. I think he has had enough of being out of office to know what that is like. I am sure he is a good enough Liberal to want to help the Liberal cause and I think he would welcome being in the administration at the end of the war which is now so near at hand. It would give him a chance to figure permanently that way. I agree with Robertson that we miss him in the War Committee. While he has great failings, his political judgment is good. I see no reason why he should not come back at once if invited. Politics is not a matter of the ideal thing but of doing what is best to meet circumstances and difficulties that present themselves from day to day. A new session and the problems it opens up make it, it seems to me, very advisable to secure him at once if that is possible. I shall talk with St. Laurent about it at once."

Later in the day he did talk to St. Laurent who doubted the wisdom of the proposal. "First of all he might decline, which would make the situation more difficult. He might take the position that he could not countenance conscription as still existing, particularly if McNaughton might have to bring forward another order-in-council, and he would have to leave the government anew. St. Laurent himself spoke of my having mentioned that in the province they might be shown the errors of their ways and an explanation given of the government's position. He is so disinterested himself that I do not think he felt that Power would then become leader of the province and that his own, St. Laurent's, influence would be less. I think his point of view is right: that we had better hold consistently to the line we had taken. Also with Power coming back might concentrate agitation on the need for Ralston being taken back."

The Prime Minister was relieved to learn from McNaughton on March 6 that a second order in council conscripting additional N.R.M.A. personnel would not be necessary at that time. "Doubted if the necessity would arise before well on in April, but he thought he and I should keep this to ourselves. Neither say a word for or against the need for a further order. He tells me he got some 4,000 men from among G.S. men in England who have just been sitting around there and really should be in active service. He was speaking on the report that Walford [Adjutant-General] had made since his return. McNaughton says the fact that units are beginning to surrender as a whole is the one sure sign of what may lead to a sudden collapse in Germany. He does not think the war can go on much longer. Today Cologne has passed into the hands of the Americans. The British and our armies are now all past the Siegfried line and the banks of the Rhine. Churchill has been three days in Europe and with the armies at the front. Says that one strong heave will win the war. This can hardly mean another three months, though it may be another month. I spoke to McNaughton about a parliamentary assistant being taken on for him. I suggested Abbott, whom he would be prepared to accept if Ilsley can part with him."

The next day (March 7) the Prime Minister discussed this proposal with the Deputy Minister of Finance. Clark "thought Ilsley would agree," Mackenzie King reported, "and that there would be advantages in having Abbott handling the war estimates with his knowledge of the financial side. . . . Later I saw Ilsley who agreed to part with Abbott for the time being. We discussed war appropriations a little. Spoke about the terrible pressure on him to yield this and yield that for different purposes but that he had to stand firm. When I asked him about himself, he walked up and down the floor telling me that the trouble he had was that he began to think of little things; that perhaps he had been too generous in a settlement, for example, and could not get his mind off it. Also some other thing which was small and which was past would worry him in the same way. The doctor told him last year he would have to get more exercise; have some hobby, and try to get more sleep. He spoke of sometimes wishing he could go to a river and row a boat but had resisted that altogether. Mentioned all this kind of thing was starting again and worried him a good deal. Said he felt very well after coming back from California last year. That was an absence of a month. However he thought he would get along all right. I could see there is quite a risk as far as he is concerned, of a break. His being so rigid largely accounts for this. I advised him to take in an occasional movie; also to take a little exercise.

"I then rang up Abbott. He was very nice. Offered to do whatever I wished. Said he did not know the dept. at all; would have quite a job to master it and would do whatever he could. He said he would be in Ottawa tonight and would see McNaughton in the morning. I closed definitely with him on that line. This was an immense relief."

Later that day Mackenzie King again talked with McNaughton, with St. Laurent present. McNaughton was planning a speech for his nominating convention in Saskatchewan the following week in which he proposed "to pitch into Bracken and tear him to pieces. I advised him not to do this; to be very restrained in that regard. To hold to the dignified attitude he had taken in Grey North. St. Laurent joined in this. I told him we would compel the Tories to ask for him to come into the House if Abbott could not give enough information. Otherwise would try to avoid his having to come in.

"McNaughton gave a splendid account to the War Cabinet of the number of men available for reinforcements. They have got some additional 10,000 above the numbers that were given us when he took charge—he said there were 6,000 in England who were trained and should be fighting, holding down easy jobs. Another 4,000 G.S. men here in Canada. I spoke to him about a further order-in-council. He did not think any would be necessary until well on in April anyway and probably would not be necessary then. Best to say nothing either for or against."

For some time, the Prime Minister had been planning a trip to Washington to see President Roosevelt and be briefed on the Yalta conference and the American position on the United Nations. On March 3 he learned that Roosevelt would be expecting him to stay at the White House during his visit the following week. Two days earlier he had listened to the President's address to Congress and commented to one of his secretaries that Roosevelt was "a brave fellow but he is breaking up." On March 6 Mackenzie King decided that it would be well "to tell the press before I go to Washington of my intended visit there. Also to secure authority from the President to give out the announcement before leaving. I feel that I should decide at once about taking a delegation from the opposition to San Francisco, and perhaps tell the press of this before I leave for Washington. My idea would be to take Graydon and Coldwell as representing the opposition, not as representing groups. I received a letter from Graydon last night asking about business. This morning's paper mentions Coldwell saying he will co-operate in the business of the session. Taking both of them will help I think to ease matters there. If the Tories become too violent and nasty such action may prove a boomerang. The coming session may be made the means of getting our party united again. More depends than aught else on Ralston's attitude."

Mackenzie King had a talk with Gordon Graydon on March 7. He noted that Graydon "evidently felt he would enjoy it. Went out [and] got his pipe. Sat down and stayed for ¾ of an hour. Began talking about the last Parliament and said I had been put into a very difficult position. I told him a little of the inside. He agreed it would have been a terrible thing if I had let go. There might have been a state of anarchy. He thought Ralston had been let down by some of his officers. I told him Ralston should have dealt with Connie Smythe at once. Could have got along in the crisis if there had not been determination on the part of some to force conscription. He said he felt sorry for McNaughton. Thought he had done extremely well in North Grey. I told him I thought the whole business was very unfair, unparliamentary, etc. He said he himself was as I knew not his own master; very difficult position. Could not control his own people in Parliament. Would lend what help he could for the session. Might not be able to hold his own men at bay. I explained to him session was only for the appropriation of supply and resolution re the San Francisco conference. He seemed surprised at 5 months [supply]. When I explained, two of the months might be to serve him or Coldwell, he saw the thing in a different perspective. He could not say how long we might have to sit. I gather his people want to extend the time into April. Anxious to know about the debate on the Address. Felt it could be left over till other matters dealt with. He thought that would be wise all right.

"When I spoke of San Francisco saying I intended to take him and probably Coldwell, he was obviously greatly pleased. He said he would like to go to San Francisco. I told him I would take representatives of the Opposition who were in the House. On no account would I take Bracken. This seemed to satisfy him all right. He said he had intended mentioning to me that Bracken was going to advocate taking other parties tonight [in a radio broadcast]. It was not his business but he thought I would be wise to raise the thing above party politics. Seemed greatly pleased. I spoke of a resolution that all the House could vote for. He said that definitely would be very helpful.

"He asked about extension of Parliament. I told him I had not thought of it. Preferred to have elections held in June. Much depended on the war. Also within a reasonable time after, have another session.

"I am sure he will be helpful. He said he wished the people knew me better. Spoke about my kindness to his daughter and her friend when they were down, and the pleasure it gave them and him. He thought it was a pity I was not able to get out among the people."

On March 8, the Prime Minister had a talk with Senator Norman Lambert about helping with the Liberal organization for the election. They had some discussion about their past personal relations and Mackenzie King concluded that he had "cleared up the whole situation pretty well with him. He is ready to help as a sort of counsellor but not to take real charge."

Mackenzie King also talked with M. J. Coldwell. "Told him much of what I had told Graydon. He was most friendly and co-operative; said he and Angus McInnis had thought we would ask between 3 and 5 months' supply. He thought five was quite reasonable. Would be prepared to vote for a proportion.

"In regard to representation at San Francisco he was very pleased when I suggested his going. Thought that was wise. I spoke of his being present as a member of the delegation. He said: or as one of the advisers. Seemed to have more in mind going as adviser. I told him I would think that over. He said whatever we thought best. I told him what was planned in regard to the Speech from the Throne. He seemed a little surprised though I think he saw it was reasonable. Once they [the Tories] got started, there would be no stopping. The most satisfactory thing was himself suggesting we might be through by the 29th—10 days. I said that was what I was aiming at. Would be grateful if he would help. It was not fair I should have to go to San Francisco with no time to prepare and attend to other matters. He said he had heard Bracken's speech and thought it was most unfair. Has a strong feeling against him. Agreed he should not be asked to go to San Francisco."

Mackenzie King arranged to appoint Ilsley as Acting Prime Minister and St. Laurent as Acting Secretary of State for External Affairs while he was in Washington. After he had told the Cabinet of the various arrangements, including the appointment of Colin Gibson as Minister of National Defence for Air and Douglas Abbott as Parliamentary Assistant to McNaughton, he added that he "might be away till Wednesday or Thursday. Did not say any more. All were perfectly silent when I passed the orders. I mentioned I had to see the Governor-General and the press and said good-bye wishing all well. They all stood up as I left the room. One or two remarked they hoped I would have a pleasant journey. I let them see just where they would be without me for a time. I do not know how Angus Macdonald feels on not acting for McNaughton. I have no doubt that he and Crerar will get together to grouse. I doubt if they would raise another conscription issue. Ilsley after all never did say he would go with the others, though I think he was ready to do so. He at least tried to prevent a breakup.

"I then went down to see the Governor General and put the different orders before him. Told him of my leaving for Washington. He had just had the French Minister and his family for luncheon. Had invited me but understood my not being present.

"I had to hurry back. Met the press at 20 to 4. Large room full of reporters. All the Gallery present. Pleased I had decided to give them personal interview rather than issue statement.

"I told them of my intended visit to Washington and changes in the Ministry. Made comment on Bracken's speech of last night. Said I thought that was a curious statement for a man to make when he had been afraid to go in the House, to contest a seat, in the 2½ years he was leader. Told them of the representation at the conference in San Francisco. Intended to be opposition representatives in the House; persons taking responsibility of the opposition. Said I thought of following the British practice as regards government and opposition—not groups. Referred to the British Parliamentary system not having every Tom, Dick and Harry being given recognition by the government as leaders unless they were in Parliament. I said that all which had been done for Bracken had been done as a matter of courtesy—not as a matter of right. This was the first time I really opened out on him. It was the least I could have said after his speech of last night. The press seemed genuinely pleased at the conference. All shook hands after in a very friendly way."

CHAPTER NINE

Political Preparations

LATE IN THE AFTERNOON of March 9, 1945, the Prime Minister arrived at the White House experiencing the excitement and pleasure he always felt at the prospect of seeing and talking with Franklin Roosevelt. In Mackenzie King's judgment, their relationship was unusually close and intimate; Roosevelt invariably made him feel welcome and trusted as a personal friend. On this occasion, the Prime Minister's pleasure was mixed with concern about the American President's deteriorating health. Eleanor Roosevelt met him, as the President was detained, and they had a cup of tea while waiting. "Mrs. Roosevelt mentioned that the President had been pretty tired after his journey" to Yalta, he wrote. "I could see from her manner that she felt anxious about him. Spoke about his being pretty thin. Also about the unpleasant side of politics; how ungrateful people were, terrible pressure, etc. She herself looks a bit older and more worn."

When the President arrived, Mackenzie King was shocked by his appearance. "When I saw him, I felt a deep compassion for him. He looked much older; face very much thinner, particularly the lower part. . . . When I went over and shook hands with him, I bent over and kissed him on his cheek. He turned it toward me for the purpose. He then got from his chair on to the sofa and asked me to sit beside him on the sofa. Mrs. Roosevelt was on the other side.

"A little later, Norman Armour [a prewar American Minister to Canada] came in to tea and we all talked together. The President spent time telling us of his trip, particularly his meeting with the King of Arabia and his talk with Haile Selassie and his impressions of Sebastopol. I asked him about Stalin. He mentioned that Churchill had done about 90% of the talking at the Conference. He said Stalin was very friendly with him, Roosevelt, and friendly with Churchill though he, the President, felt that Stalin perhaps was more friendly with him himself. He said Churchill had been in good form. Seemed to be very well. Said Stalin had a good deal of humour; that he, the President, liked him. Found him very direct. Later he told me he did not think there was anything to fear particularly from

Stalin in the future. He had a big programme himself to deal with. He also told me very privately at night that Stalin would likely break off with the Japanese later but wished to be sure to be able to have his divisions up to the front near Manchuria before taking that formal step but he would also give the Allies bases [in Siberia] to operate from. He mentioned at tea that he was thinking of going to England in June.

"Mrs. Roosevelt was stressing Hyde Park as a good place for Cabinet meetings through the summer. The President's first remark had been he would be very well if he just were out of office and had his time free. He did not use those words but that was the meaning of it. I could see he was quite weary. To me his eyes looked very tired. On the whole, I found more strength in him than I had expected. In fact, felt less concerned about him than I had at the beginning. He looked a little firmer. Dieting has had its effect on his appearance for a while but now he is consolidating into a man of different size and shape, looking more like President Wilson. His front features thinner in the lower part of the face."

After dinner that evening, the President and the Prime Minister went into the circular room, where they "talked steadily from 8.30 until 20 past 11, when I looked at the clock. I thought it was about 10. The President said he was not tired; was enjoying the talk. We talked then until a quarter of an hour of midnight.

"The President gave me a pretty full account of what happened at the Crimea Conference. Spoke of Churchill doing 80% of the talking. Said Stalin had quite a sense of humour. That once when Churchill was making a long speech, Stalin put up his hand to the side of his face, turned to the President and winked one of his eyes as much as to say: there he is talking again. He said Stalin's relations and Churchill's are much friendlier in every way than they were. They were quite friendly this time. I asked him about what he thought about the duration of the war. He said he has not ventured to make any statement but said: of course we knew what had been fixed as the time for planning but he, himself, felt that before the end of April, as far as Europe was concerned, it should be over. He thought once Europe was over, Japan would collapse very soon thereafter. Spoke of possibly 3 months. When I asked him about certain weapons that might be used, he said he thought that would be in shape by August; that the main difficulty was knowing just how to have the material used over the country itself.

"In answer to a question, he said he thought the Russians had been experimenting and knew something about what was being done. He thought the time had come to tell them how far the developments had gone. Churchill was opposed to doing this. Churchill is considering the possible commercial use later. I said it seemed to me that if the Russians discovered later that some things had been held back from them, it would be unfortunate. I asked about the assistance that Russia would give [against Japan]. He thought they would want to be sure of having a number of divisions which they could use before actually breaking off all relations; that they would give the U.S. what was needed in the way of bases to use against Japan. He said great progress was being made at present.

"I spoke to him about the return of our troops. That I hoped when the matter of shipping came up, he would see, if possible, that our men who had been there for 5 years or 4 years or for a longer time than others got a reasonable share of allotments on the ships returning. The President replied he had already gone into this; would arrange to see that priorities were steadily followed. . . . When it came to their men and ours, for the same time, they should share. I told him I was very grateful for this. Thought it was wise having regard to the future relations of the countries. There would be much feeling if our men were delayed while other troops were coming back. I told him it would be helpful if this could be brought out—helpful to me later in the campaign to have it known that he and I had discussed the matter together. He said the best thing would be to have the question referred to the Joint Defence Board. I asked who would see that it was referred. He told me he would take the matter up with La-Guardia and we could have it discussed later. . . .

"Speaking of the San Francisco Conference, he thought it might last a month. That it would be a mistake if it lasted longer. Work would be done by half a dozen main committees. Some things might be left over. He himself would go to the conference to open it but would not stay. I asked if Churchill was likely to come over. He thought not. He said he himself would be going over to England later. I told him what I had said in the broadcast about the war probably being over before the conference was over. He said he did not think it could have been expressed better than that. I asked about the rule of the Big Five. They would take over, I understood, the control of Germany and be responsible for order in Germany and Japan for a number of years before they became admitted to the world security council. He thought that probably ten years would be required and maybe a longer time. There would, of course, be a division in the occupational areas. He told me nothing had been decided yet about the partitioning of Germany. Stalin wants to have reparations made in the way of machinery, lost equipment, etc. also to have German prisoners of war work in Russia—making the repairs for a period of possibly ten years. He specified the numbers—100,000—that would have to serve to rebuild Russia.

"He doubted if Mr. Hull would be able to go to San Francisco. Suggested sending Stettinius to Ottawa to talk over the situation as it had developed, the probable conference procedure at San Francisco. He said they would form an organization to carry on the Conference. There will probably be half a dozen main committees which would report to the entire group. They would follow the Dumbarton Oaks procedure as far as possible. He said he had in mind regarding the Council that it should meet at different places, away from the press altogether, possibly in the Azores for European affairs, in Canada for North American Affairs and the Hawaiian Islands for Pacific affairs. I pointed out that there might be considerable difficulty. That the permanent staff will be larger, etc. and it would be difficult to move about, but particularly in relation to the Assembly. He thought of the Assembly meeting in one country, then in another and said Geneva had not a good name. I pointed out to him that it would take very large staffs for records, etc. and there would be entertaining. Proper hotel accommodation would be very difficult, unless some one place became more or less settled. I also suggested that they do not try to settle on any permanent place at once but to name the next place for a time.

"The President said he would welcome some outbreak between a couple of countries with a view of just testing out the machinery of use of force. Let them see how it works before making too many treaties as to military undertakings. I asked if it would have to be referred to Parliaments in the first instance. He said that, of course, would be the case."

The next day, Mackenzie King had lunch with Roosevelt and his daughter, followed by another long talk, during which the President "referred to his mention last night of his going to England. He said he had heard that the King was disappointed he had not been in England and referred to the King's visit. Said he would probably go over in June. That what he would like to do would be to go from the ship to Buckingham Palace and stay there, and then to drive with the King through the streets of London and at the week-end, spend time with Churchill at Chequers. Also give an address before the Houses of Parliament and get the freedom of the city of London. He would probably visit their men on the battlefields; that he would also like to pay a visit to Queen Wilhelmina in Holland, stay at The Hague. From there, he would perhaps pay a visit to Paris but would not say anything about that till the moment came. It is clear to me from this that he and Churchill have worked out plans quite clearly contemplating that the war will be over before June. That this would follow in the month of June. A sort of triumphal close to the war itself. This in some ways is the most important information he has given me thus far. He did not propose himself to sign the foundational charter.

"Another thing I spoke to him of was seeing that Canada and other countries should be recognized in connection with any unconditional surrender in Germany. That what thus far had been received seemed to take account only of the Big Five signing. I said I thought care should be taken to see that all nations that had contributed armies should be included. He said he would communicate with Churchill about that. That that was right. That the statement should say that Germany had surrendered unconditionally and that the following countries who had participated, had contributed, etc. The surrender would be made he thought to a military council and then there would be recognition by the civil authorities.

"When we were talking of newspapers, he said: three years from now when I am through here, I am thinking of getting out a newspaper which will be about the size of four pages of foolscap—something like what is used for daily news on board ship. Have no editorials; just give the main news truthfully. By means of radio photography, have it distributed in every city and town of America and sold for one cent. What interested me was his remark which implied confidence in being able to go on with some new features at the end of another three years. I confess he seemed to be in better shape physically than I had thought when I saw him yesterday but it is clear his mind is mostly occupied with what is going on on the surface. I find that he repeats himself a great deal, for example he told me at luncheon over again the long story about his friend Byrnes having married a Presbyterian girl and singing in the choir, having left the R.C. church. Said if he had run as a candidate, it would have cost him a million or two votes on the score that he was a renegade. This he had told me last night at dinner. Last night he told about Winston being down at Miami and going in for a swim defying the waves to roll him over, being determined he would get the better of it; eventually having to clothe and come back. Tonight he repeated the same story without apparently recollecting that he had told it last night. I noticed that Mrs. R. and his daughter and son-in-law seemed a little embarrassed but no one said anything. There have been several of these occurrences. Indeed some of the stories he is telling he has told me on previous occasions. This of course is a sign of failing memory. I noticed in looking at his eyes very closely, that one eye has a clear, direct look—that is the left eye as he faces one. The right one is not quite on the square with the left one but has a little sort of stigmata appearance in the centre. A tendency to credit himself with the initiation in many things is another weakness. That is one of the terrible dangers of a situation like the present where 2 or 3 men do so much in directing the affairs of the world. . . .

"The President spoke to me about doing something with my papers and belongings similar to what he has done at Hyde Park. He said he will now have to add two more wings for a library to contain papers. He believes money can be raised without difficulty for that purpose. He was quite interested in what I told him about Hepburn's repentance. His remark to me was is he still in with those power interests in New York. I remember the President telling me years ago they were the worst possible crowd in the U.S. and most corrupt, dangerous in some ways.

"I talked with him about the location of the Assembly remarking that Geneva had the surroundings, buildings, etc. He seemed to modify a little on that. Thought the I.L.O. should perhaps stay there. Said that the Agricultural body used to meet in Italy and it should be somewhere else. Did not press too strongly his idea of moving the security organization about too much. He told me tonight that his idea was to have the first meeting of the Security Organization in July or August. That they would then elect their President and officials, etc. He had hoped that Mr. Hull might be well enough to be the first President but he was not too sure that he would be able to do more than be at a meeting. He said he would not be able to attend the meeting at San Francisco at present."

Mackenzie King went to the Naval Hospital to see Cordell Hull after his talk with the President. The previous day was the first time Hull had been out of bed for five months. "When I came over and shook hands with him," Mackenzie King wrote, "his eyes filled with tears. He spoke of how glad he was to see me. He was sitting there in a dressing gown with a dark brown undergarment. Had a leather-like appearance. First he wanted to know about happenings in Canada which he said he had been following closely. I then asked him about himself and he began telling me of how when the elections came on, the pressure became too great from every side. He had been working hard on the preparation of Dumbarton Oaks matters. Had been suffering from diabetes. Years ago he had had trouble in his lung but the scar was there and healed over. However with the pressure, the lung trouble flamed up anew and the one operated on the other. He was quite exhausted and could not hold on any longer. He said the President had done the best he could to have him stay but he had to come out to the Hospital. He had written the President that he could not possibly stay on. He referred to the problems that arose in connection with the campaign; how he could not leave for fear that it would be said by some that he had had some difference with the President and yet he was not able to work. It was a very difficult situation.

"He had been in hospital now five months. Was not sure that he could go to San Francisco, but would like to have a directing hand from this end. The President had asked me to give him his love and to say that he would be out to see him soon.

"He spoke nicely of the President. Told me that I knew of some of the problems that he had had to contend with in the State Department. He then began to speak of the period prior to war, around 1933, and thereabouts, when he sought to impress everyone with the way the world was going to wrack and ruin through lower standards in public life, indifference to public morality, unpreparedness, and determination to fight, etc. I told him I recalled all that he had said about the danger that was ahead. Those were the days when we negotiated the trade agreements.

"He next said that before the outbreak of the Japanese war the correspondence that had taken place showed how everyone was getting ready to blame himself and the President for it all, that they had been slow, etc. He then said that he had decided to publish the papers at once, which otherwise would not have been published for fifty years. He got out his official book, which showed how carefully everything had been prepared in advance. He then spoke of his going to Moscow and preparing the way for the Teheran Conference. In this connection he said he had told me what only the President and Churchill knew as to the word he had got direct from Stalin at that time. He had spoken of the suspicion there had been on Stalin's part of the President and of Churchill, and what he had done to remove that suspicion. How he had prepared the ground for the Teheran conference and had worked on from there on the Dumbarton Oaks. He has really been the founder of the World Security Organization.

"When I came away, he pressed my hand very firmly and told me to take care of my health. As I came out of the door, the old gentleman broke down, and Mrs. Hull went back to him for a minute. Spoke about how deeply touched he was and how great is the affection of both of them for me. I told him all the world was under an obligation to him for what he had done and was seeking to do to develop international goodwill."

Mackenzie King dined with the Roosevelts and later went to the train to go to Williamsburg. Reflecting on the visit, he wrote: "The visit has left the impression on me that the President has distinctly failed, but that he is not quite as bad or in as poor a shape as he appeared from photographs. He has lost a certain merriment, looks older and wearier, but has a certain firmness, which might carry him along for some time. His memory, however, is certainly failing. . . . He is fond of talking continuously. He does listen and takes in points quite keenly, but links everything too much to a personal point. The point is no human mortal was ever meant to possess the kind of power that these three men have come to have today. I feel that their thoughts are very largely of the world that they believe they themselves are shaping and where they will be seen in history. In God's sight, however, I think there is a profounder reality—much profounder, and that publicity tends to destroy this. I found my own feeling of health and strength greater at the White House this time than at any time I have been there previously. This gave me a feeling of hope and confidence, but I am concerned at not beginning to know the things I ought to know in meeting Parliament in the coming weeks and being prepared for the San Francisco conference. The latter will be so vast and so many nations and individuals will be represented that I think it may be possible to get through on the whole with a certain measure of enjoyment and interest and probably profit in a political campaign. I am very glad to have had the day with the President and to be seeing him again on Tuesday. All this will be helpful in reviving in Canada the close relationship I have had with him and Churchill during the war."

Mackenzie King was back at the White House briefly on March 13 and left that night for New York. He had "a very nice talk" with the President before a press conference in the late afternoon. "During this talk he told me a matter of very great interest, that the German army in Italy had made proposals for what amounted to peace between themselves and the Americans. That the military authorities were agreeable to having a meeting in Switzerland and to arrange for surrender. The President was agreeable to having this done in a way which would see that the army surrendered and were properly treated and that Kesselring might himself have his men saved. If this were done, he believed it would help to speedily end the war. He had cabled Churchill about it, but Churchill without communicating back with him, had communicated with Russia to ask if Russia was agreeable. Russia took the position that she wanted three Generals present. The President said Russia really had nothing to do with the Italian campaign. He was afraid Winston had acted too suddenly and they had made the situation very difficult. He had cabled Churchill this morning, pointing out there was no objection to the Russian Generals coming as observers, but that this should be between the British and the Americans and the Germans in Italy. He says he is actually waiting further word from Churchill, but feels quite anxious about the situation lest this chance may have been lost. Alexander, he said, was agreeable to it, but it was a matter entirely for the military and should be kept as such. This is interesting indeed.

"In speaking about San Francisco, the President said he was still undecided as to whether he should go to the opening and welcome every one or come along near the close. He thought a month should end the conference. . . . I asked if he would not put in a word for our having a representative on the Steering Committee. He said one from each nation would be on the Steering Committee, and that this committee would meet twice a week. There would be a half dozen on special subjects. The Executive would meet in secret. The assembly and the voting would be in public.

"He rather indicated that Stettinius would preside or would have the main direction of affairs. He repeated what he told me about Russia having three votes, Stalin having agreed to that. One for the U.S.S.R., one for White Russia, and the other for the Ukraine. The U.S. in the circumstances to have also three votes. That had been agreed to. The British Commonwealth to have six. He was not sure whether the conference would agree to give Russia 3. This was all before the press conference.

"After the conference, I showed him the draft resolution which I had for our House. When he read it, he quoted the words 'Purposes and Principles.' Thought that was very good. When he had finished he said he thought the whole resolution was excellent. I pointed out that anyone could vote for that. I drew attention to the fact that we would ask that the charter should be approved by Parliament before being ratified. He asked me when I would announce our delegation. I told him in Parliament. I asked him his opinion as to having delegates and associate delegates. He seemed to think it would be better to have the one delegation but to keep the majority control on it. He said that he had talked this morning with their delegation. Had suggested if they would like to go to San Francisco in advance to look over things to feel free to do so. He said he thought they would all go along with the government. That this was something to be very much desired. He said he thought I would be able to keep the delegation pretty much my way. I then spoke to him of the need of including the secondary allied countries in any statement about the surrender of Germany and watching carefully to see that their contribution was recognized in postwar matters, etc. I gave him the memorandum that I had typed at Williamsburg. He asked me if he could keep it. Said he would like to take it up at once. I told him that was what I had drafted it for.

"I then showed him the other memorandum on what I thought were the weaknesses of the proposals of Dumbarton Oaks, memorandum also copied out at Williamsburg. He read it over twice. Remarked on it being very good. He said he would take up the memorandum with Stettinius at once. He thought the suggestion of making known in advance what the Great Powers were doing with Germany was a wise one. He also commented favourably on two or three of the other suggestions. Said nothing adverse. I spoke to him about Pearson's food and agricultural committee which 18 countries have approved. Asked if the U.S. were going to approve. He said he had sent the matter to the Congress to be ratified. I pointed out if the U.S. were on that organization, it would be linked up with the other organizations."

At the press conference, Mackenzie King reported, the President "spoke very nicely of our friendship over many years and of the way in which by personal relations as well as official ones we were able to settle matters between our two countries. That Canada and the U.S. were an example to the world in these particulars. He referred to the Ogdensburg Agreement and Hyde Park Agreement being among matters that we had settled, and then read the press release which had been cleared, enlarging on it as well; ending up by saying that he might go over many matters much further. He spoke as if I had been at the White House right along, saying I had been with him for some days.

"He did not refer specifically to whether I was not to speak, though I had asked him previously to protect me if there were questions. The questions that were asked the President were mostly related to domestic measures, most of which he answered evasively and some of which he answered directly. There were a few questions with which he said he was not familiar enough to answer. It is a curious sort of business—a press conference—with very large numbers of men and women, crowded up just in front of the President's desk. It is covered with a lot of trinkets."

Mackenzie King's impression was that Mr. Roosevelt "seemed very tired. He also seemed to enjoy talking on with me—seemed to be in no hurry about sending for his letters to be signed or other things. . . . He is a very tired man. He is kindly, gentle and humorous, but I can see is hardly in shape to cope with problems. He wisely lets himself be guided by others and has everything brought carefully before him." The dinner that evening was strictly a family affair which the Prime Minister "greatly enjoyed." He wrote that "before coming away, I thanked the President for what he had said in the afternoon at the conference. He said if there was any way he could help me in my election he would wish to do it. To come and see him at the White House, Warm Springs or at Hyde Park. That I would always be welcome. . . . I told the President I fully expected not to win. I also said that I might have to change my constituency. He said I think you will win. . . . When he spoke of our meeting soon again at San Francisco I said I hoped the war would be over at that time. He said I would say to-night that I think there is a very good chance. I do not know that I would have felt sure enough to say so with such assurance until today. I think he had in mind the word that had come from Kesselring."

Mackenzie King left the White House about 9.30 P.M., never to see Roosevelt again.

The next day in New York, the Prime Minister "was surprised to read in the New York Times and in the New York Herald a despatch on the President's talk with the Press yesterday in which both papers mentioned that

I was being thought of to preside at the San Francisco conference. Apparently there has been much circulation of that possibility. I could not, of course, think of anything of the kind. The papers both made it clear that the President had sort of given me a leg up in what he said about our friendship and the relations between Canada and the United States. It was really a very fine tribute. I am glad the last word I had with the President last night was to thank him warmly for it." He also learned in New York that the American edition of his book *Canada and the Fight for Freedom* had been put on sale the previous day.

The Prime Minister was back in Ottawa on March 15. The next day he "was greatly surprised and shocked on looking at the paper this morning to read that McNaughton, at his nomination meeting yesterday, had opened up the question of reasons he had resigned his command in Britain and had made references to the discussions which arose at that time. It is most unfortunate for it will mean a battle in the House and is certain to mean that this session will centre around the difficulties between Ralston and himself, with what consequences no one can say. He should have followed the advice St. Laurent and I gave him, to be very moderate in any statements he might make at his nomination meetings. He also allowed his personal feelings to get the better of his judgment."

On Sunday, March 18, Mackenzie King had a short talk on the telephone with McNaughton whom he reported as "most cheerful and quite oblivious of having made any breaks. I told him I felt he had been mistaken about the reference to his reasons for resigning from the presidency of the Research Council. He thought that perhaps things had been mixed up in the press. He said he has had further word from [General] Sansom confirming strongly the position we are in in the matter of reinforcements. Everything is in splendid shape in that regard.

"I spoke to him about securing as soon as possible for my use in Parliament a statement as to both Army Corps being together in Holland and Germany. Security reasons may require holding the statement for a few days longer. It is an important announcement."

On Monday, March 19, the final session of the wartime Parliament opened. On his return from the Senate to the House of Commons, Mackenzie King was surprised "to see all the galleries really overflowing. I was given a warm reception by the members as I took my seat. It all seemed as though it had been but a few days since the House adjourned. Indeed that feeling was persistent throughout for I was struck by the fact that I, myself, did not find myself turning around to greet any of the members and similarly when the proceedings were over in the Commons and it was almost 6, but a very few of the members came up to shake hands. The only one to cross over was Grote Stirling. Graydon did come over during the proceedings.

"The Opposition, as was to have been expected, did begin by raising objections, Hanson having been chosen for this particular role. He did practically all the talking. However by being tactful and not antagonistic, I was able to get the entire programme worked through as I had hoped might be possible. The tributes, the various motions for the proceedings through the session; the setting up of the committees of supply and ways and means; the resolution on the San Francisco conference with the support of the Commons which is proceeding tomorrow. The debate on the Address moved, seconded and adjourned. Ilsley got his financial resolution introduced. His estimates tabled. All the Ministers got their reports tabled. Altogether we covered as much ground this afternoon before 6 as normally would have taken at least a month of an ordinary session. Such obstruction as there was was just sufficient to make clear that the Tory Opposition intends to be troublesome and to insist on getting a vote, if possible, on confidence at some stage before supply is voted. We, however, outmanoeuvred them by getting so much through today and also by getting under way at once the resolution regarding San Francisco before proceeding with contentious measures. It was plain from what Graydon said that the tactics of the Opposition are to try and wear me down with questioning on External Affairs matters. Here again I hope to be able to outmanoeuvre them with the assistance of the rules of the House which will compel the debate to proceed without questioning. I made clear that I would require careful thought before replying to questions that would be quoted, along with the replies, in all parts of the world. I also made clear that I hoped and expected the House would regard the San Francisco matter as above politics and that it was something on which I expected all members of the House would agree. I had enough material in readiness to counter objections that were raised on the score of cutting out the debate on the Address. On the whole, the day went much better than I had had reason to expect it would. Indeed had I not been so tired, I would have enjoyed the proceedings."

The next day, the Prime Minister introduced the draft resolution seeking approval of the United Nations Charter. He reported that "Graydon and others quite clearly were not ready to go on. Also were anxious to have it appear we were forcing them ahead and anxious as well to have me subjected to a sort of cross-examination as another means of creating embarrassment. However I was able to work out of the situation and Coldwell helped very much and scored completely for his own party as he was the one ready to immediately follow the government.

"I was given a very attentive hearing during the reading of the speech. Members remained in the House. There were very few who left. Leaving out quoted letters, etc., I was able to compress what I said into an hour. I thought the speech read very well. Hanson referred to it as a noble speech. Coldwell was distinctly helpful in his remarks. Endorsed all that I had said and did not cover much new ground."

A Liberal caucus was held on March 21 and Mackenzie King reported that he "referred to this being the first day of spring, with winter behind, and paraphrased Shakespeare by saying 'Now is the winter of our discontent made a glorious summer by the San Francisco Conference.' I pointed out how tactics had been based on avoiding a general election in war time; gave reasons for running McNaughton in Grey North. I then said something of the tactics there; of the significance of the election as making clear that conscription had not carried; also that it afforded us a picture of what the general election would have been like on that issue. . . . Also, now I thought we were going to reach the time when the war would be over before the San Francisco conference was over, and the election would then be fought on the question of the conference and the peace. Also on our social programme as set out in the Speeches from the Throne. I said only one thing could now prevent us from winning the election and that was that we might become divided again among ourselves; that we should seek now every way to get a united front; that Providence had been on our side in bringing the San Francisco conference into being at the time it will. I then explained that the campaign would be fought on the peace issues and the social issues. I spoke of Sir Wilfrid's attitude on conscription, and made clear that I thought everyone was entitled to vote as he thought best on that issue. It was not a thing that was permanent. It was now past. I asked them to imagine what position the government would have been in during the winter months of fighting if there had been any question in the mind of the people of the adequacy of reinforcements. All that was splendidly settled and we could go right on with outlook of the future forgetting the differences of the past and uniting to win the election.

"Dan McIvor [M.P. for Fort William] raised the question as to the position the party would be in, if I were absent in San Francisco. I told caucus I had to face that question realistically. It was a matter of indifference to me whether I went or stayed. My own feeling was that I should adopt toward the conference the same attitude I had adopted toward the war, which was to make consideration of national welfare as a whole rise above any party interests; that my attitude was directly opposite to that of Bracken who for a couple of years had been a political organizer of the party, keeping out of parliament. I had kept to the ship and had trusted to the understanding of the people in not giving my time over to party politics. I said it would be the same with regard to the San Francisco conference. If I went, I would have to be there from the beginning and stay to the close. I could not be flying back and forth. It would be a difficult situation to face there. There would be a strenuous struggle for different points of view. I felt, however, that the people would expect me to be there, and that the party in the end would gain by my having made it evident that I was more interested in the nation's future than even in the political fortunes of my own party. I dropped a hint, and then corrected myself, that I would probably lose my own constituency having to be absent. I said I nevertheless felt it was my duty to meet the present situation and trust the people as to the future. No expression of view gained more applause from the caucus.

"I then told them they would have to get busy on the preparation of the campaign themselves and would have to work out a way of handling it in advance of my leaving, but pointed out how little time there would be before leaving; also what little time there would be left for the campaign after coming back, watching the war at the same time. I said I was sometimes doubtful as to whether I would be able to or whether it would be wise to attempt such an aggregation of things, but I had learned that strength was given one for the task if one had faith. I said I believed it would prove so in this case."

The Prime Minister "was agreeably surprised at caucus itself. It was well attended though I noticed that neither Picard nor Hugues Lapointe was present. They are probably preparing their speeches. Neither Power nor Ralston was present. These were the significant absentees.

"The discussion turned on a number of matters: the embargo on hay; the destruction of surplus war materials; and the Japanese situation, and other questions. Many complimentary references to myself as the only person who could lead through the campaign or carry on after. Indeed the whole spirit was very different from that of last Caucus. Members tell me they find it so in the House. I stressed the importance of voting on the present resolution regarding San Francisco and sticking together in any amendment that might be moved on going into Committee of Supply. It would be want of confidence in the government which would mean want of confidence in the party. Equivalent to want of confidence in themselves. I felt no matter what came, we could stand united there and if we did, we would have a fine finish before the elections."

That evening he had another discussion with Senator Stevenson and Dr. Humphries about Prince Albert. Mackenzie King told them he "was quite prepared to run in Prince Albert, but had to recognize McNaughton's defeat [in Grey North] through not being in the riding, and his running as a third minister in Saskatchewan, were both factors that had come up. I had made my public statement. Also, there was the fact that I now would have to go to San Francisco and would be absent for a month. This meant I might not even be able to go to the constituency for nomination and certainly could not make more than one speech in the campaign. He [Stevenson] himself comes back as others do that if I could spend a few days in the riding they would feel very sure. That, however, is now out of the question. I said members of the Cabinet were urging me to change. It might be that the party itself would press very strongly. That, so far as I was concerned, it was up to them to arrange these matters. That whatever the outcome either way I would be content. One thing, however, I was determined on, if defeated in the general election, I would not continue longer in public life."

It was not until April 6 that the final decision was made about Prince Albert. Meanwhile there was a good deal of backing and filling. On March 23, Mackenzie King noted that "Dr. Humphries' visit to Ottawa has enabled me to bring things to a show-down in regard to where the party stands in seeing that my interests are taken care of in the general campaign." He added that "as Humphries was seeing Howe this morning I telephoned Howe and reminded him of his view so forcibly expressed that I should not run in Prince Albert and suggested he might perhaps talk with Humphries about the situation there.

"I phoned Dr. King and said I would not go to council this morning, which would afford him and the Cabinet an opportunity to discuss the whole situation and to do what they thought best. I later phoned Mac-Kinnon and told him the same. I made the suggestion that if any step were taken by the Cabinet a committee might be appointed to see Humphries while he was here. Also I thought later with members here it might be well for them to have a caucus and have their opinions stated, at which time, if Russell county were to move in the interval, their invitation might be made known to Prince Albert and the whole position made perfectly clear. Since my declaration that I would run again in Saskatchewan I have been prevented from making a tour of the West and spending the days in the riding I had hoped to spend last autumn. . . .

"Finally the report is certain to be spread that I cannot win in Prince Albert. That might affect the whole campaign by allowing opponents to say that I would not be in Parliament and would therefore not be available for representation at a peace conference. There is, of course, on top of all this, a question of how much I can continue to carry before I can begin to meet any of the demands of the campaign. I have made it perfectly clear that if defeated in the elections, I shall not seek re-election to Parliament. If returned and the party were defeated, I doubt if I would think of acting as leader of the Opposition, certainly not for longer than to get matters straightened away. I believe, however, should that emergency arise, I would be wise to call a convention and have a new leader appointed at that time. In all this powers quite beyond my control have been working together so as to solve the situation in regard to Prince Albert and to ensure my election despite myself and my wish not to continue longer in public life. From now on I take the position that I told Claxton among others this morning that the party will have to organize its own campaign and cease to look to me for anything more than what my life and its record in the time that I have been in public life stands for as a party asset and what as an individual leading a government I stand for. They can play that up if they like. If they don't I am wholly indifferent. They might as well learn now that I have gone as far as I can go short of rendering myself incapable for future public service by attempting to do more."

Later that day Mackenzie King reported that colleagues had told him the Cabinet was unanimous that he should not run in Prince Albert. "Later," he added, "Howe, MacKinnon and Dr. King saw Dr. Humphries and gave him the Cabinet point of view. Apparently the interview was most satisfactory. The next move now is to secure Russell as a seat and possibly a party Caucus to advise acceptance."

When Mackenzie King entered caucus on April 5 the members "had been discussing for some time the question of my seeking another seat. A resolution was before them which had been moved relating to the advisability of that course being adopted. I asked that the discussion should continue. Different speeches were made. . . .

"After listening for a little over half an hour, I rose to speak, and was given a great ovation. I told the members that it was the most complimentary caucus I had ever attended. I said quite frankly I had been concerned about the question we had been discussing. That, as they knew, the matter had been discussed among my colleagues and they felt I should not take the risk of being defeated, having regard to what the future might mean. . . . I said that when I had discussed the matter with my colleagues I had suggested that the matter should be taken up in caucus and the will of the members there would have to be canvassed. I said I was glad it had come up at this time. I pointed out that nearly all of them in speaking had assumed that even if I were defeated I could get another seat in plenty of time and would therefore remain at the head of the party. I pointed out that that assumed beyond a doubt that the party itself was going to be returned. I said I did not wish to commit myself any further than I could on anything. . . . I pointed out that the matter of real concern to me was the situation which might develop after the election when no one party was strong enough to command a majority. If I myself were defeated as Prime Minister, I would be handicapped in tendering advice to the Governor General to the effect that I thought our party should still carry on. That that was a vital consideration because it might mean either the Conservatives or the C.C.F. would have the arrangements of affairs which would possibly determine the parliament of the next five years and the complexion of it. I told them I wanted them to see that point clearly. . . . All I wanted to do was to do just what would ensure the return of the party. . . .

"I then spoke about the question of members running as Independent Liberals if they wished. I said every Liberal was independent. I was independent myself in many things, and I thought the name Liberal was the one to run under. The thing to do was to get elected. If it meant, in some constituencies, some extra adjective was needed, all right, but what I was anxious to see was that everybody was returned. I then spoke about the problems I would have to contend with. I said I would like to make every member of the caucus a senator. I even went so far as to say that I would like to make of everyone a minister, but said clearly I could not do that. There would be disappointments. That we were all part of one family and would try to work out situations together. I suggested that no matter what came they should try to see situations as best they can and we would try to help each other later on.

"In reverting to Prince Albert, I pointed out . . . I would find it very difficult to change my mind in regard to standing by the constituency which I had represented for nearly 19 years. I said I would consider what they were asking in the resolution but advised against passing any resolution at all. . . .

"Before I began to speak, I said to Dr. King that I thought I ought to stick by Prince Albert. I said the same to St. Laurent. When I had finished speaking, and we were walking out, I met the press at the door and told them the party had been discussing the question of the seat but that there had been no decision."

Mackenzie King noted that "I felt after the morning Caucus that it would not be wise to delay announcing my intention to run in Prince Albert, so at 6 o'clock I rang up Dr. Humphries. Was surprised to find he was still in Toronto. I told him of my decision. He expressed himself as greatly pleased." Dr. Humphries felt the Conservatives would "doubtless tell their people to all vote C.C.F. in order to defeat me. This Humphries feels is the greatest danger of all. I, myself, am not so fearful of that. I cannot believe that business men in Prince Albert who are Conservatives will willingly, in a secret ballot, support a C.C.F. as against the Prime Minister of Canada.

"I then got to work to try and draft a statement for the press. Here again unless some Power from Beyond had been guiding me, I could not have composed what I said in a couple of sentences. Just the right thing, it seemed to me, when I had concluded it. My mind felt tremendously at rest, to get this thing settled. I am sure it is the right thing and here is the value of a daily record. It will be interesting to discover what were the influences —whether it was a period of depression which caused me to yield to the possibility of running in Russell. The purpose of this diary is mainly that of a study of the circumstances which occasion certain results and how best to determine the right course of action.

"I had not been in Caucus for 10 minutes before I felt that the wise thing was to run in Prince Albert. I felt thoroughly happy in getting up to speak without disclosing what I intended to do but getting a chance to lay the situation before the party. Now no matter what comes, I have given the party a chance to settle what should be done and left it up entirely to Prince Albert to say what they wish to have done. They know that I can get any number of seats and perfectly safe seats. It ought to put the mettle into the men who will be responsible for my running in Prince Albert. . . .

"Now after going to San Francisco, I can come back and a little refreshed I hope and then speak without notes in different places. Also this meeting will justify me in taking 3 or 4 days in the constituency. That, I shall do regardless of the campaign as a whole. I believe my readiness to run in Saskatchewan will help the party tremendously and certainly the public will appreciate it. If I am defeated, there will be pretty much a complete understanding of the reasons and a tremendous revulsion of feeling against defeating a Prime Minister who has been as faithful to his task and carried the country through the war as I have these last 5 or 6 years.

"Altogether today has been a marvellous day."

Meanwhile good progress had been made in Parliament. On March 22, Mackenzie King commented that one thing about the San Francisco debate was "significant." That was "the fact that the present debate has kept up through the week and will wait over through the next week which gives me the week-end to rest and prepare reply. More than that however, it has completely changed the tone of the House and I find the debate itself is helping to consolidate our members who will all vote together, especially those in Quebec. The only opposition will be the Quebec nationalists who are putting themselves in a terribly false position—opposing an organization for the maintenance of peace. It will do irreparable harm to their province through years to come. The tactics in bringing on this resolution, not yielding to the Opposition in giving time in the beginning to bring up other matters, has worked out perfectly."

He commented that Howard Green "made a very good speech today from the Tory point of view. So good that it will help us in Quebec, and indeed in all parts of Canada, reverting as it does to a centralized point of view which Borden and Rowell had to combat at the time of the last war. The longer this debate continues the less time will be given for riotous discussion over Grey-North by-election, etc."

The next day Mackenzie King "followed the debate part of the afternoon. Diefenbaker made a fairly good speech from the Tory point of view —one voice—Empire business. He spoke nicely in reference to the report that I might be chosen as chairman of the conference. There was general applause from the House. This rumour has spread widely and has become a factor which, however, will probably be used against me when someone else is appointed. With a general election on hand, there will be good reason for not accepting it, if offered. Stettinius certainly will be chairman."

On Wednesday, March 28, Mackenzie King spoke for two hours in the House in closing the debate on the San Francisco Conference resolution. He "found it very easy to speak at the outset but had not got far under way before I realized that I was tired and was using more words than were necessary. I always find when I come to any reference about myself that I am apt to become a bit confused because of the misinterpretations that are certain to be placed upon it from what I say.

"I thought it well to make clear at once that there was no planning of my being made Chairman of the San Francisco Conference. I know only too well that if this had been allowed to pass and someone else was appointed, as would certainly be the case later on, the Tories would have sought to use this circumstance against me. I did not express at all well what I wanted to say about absence during the period of the elections but I did deliberately put on record the position with regard to Prince Albert so as to put the matter straight up to the Party. . . .

"I did not handle the part relating to the Empire representation at San Francisco or the question related to sanctions, etc. at all to my liking. I get so annoyed at the deliberate perversion and misrepresentation of statements by the Tories that I find it difficult to make to them the kind of replies I feel should be made or indeed to reply at all. I was perhaps a little too petulant in the way I spoke but, on the whole, it pleases our men to have something said in the way of criticism of Tory methods. I think on the whole the impression in that regard will not be adverse. I did feel that what

I was saying was much too long; also that I had more in the way of quotation than was necessary but the speech was a comprehensive reply to points raised. I was glad I decided to attack the so-called independent members from Quebec at the outset. I think those 5 gentlemen have been put where they belong and where they can be defeated in their own constituencies. They are neither willing to fight nor willing to support peace. The trouble there again is we have no leader in Quebec to take this situation in hand."

Later that day he wrote: "In every way the outcome of the session up to the present is beyond anything I could have come to hope. There is now a chance through the Easter recess to get prepared for the next two weeks and to look beyond at what will be necessary for San Francisco and still later for the general elections. Meanwhile the country's mind is being absorbed in the change of situation in Europe and directed toward peace and reconstruction, before the campaign comes on. It really looks as though the Tory party has been completely out-manoeuvred and will be bankrupt in its appeal to the people when the time for the appeal comes."

In late March the political situation was complicated by the defeat of the Drew government in the Ontario Legislature. Under the energetic, if erratic, leadership of Mitchell Hepburn, the fifteen Liberals in the legislature joined with the C.C.F. and two Labour Progressive members late in the evening of March 22 to defeat the government on a C.C.F.-sponsored non-confidence motion. Mackenzie King wrote: "During the afternoon Senator Bench came to tell me he had been on the phone with Hepburn who said that the Government would be sure to be defeated today. Hepburn was undecided whether he should withdraw either on the Liberal sub-amendment or on the C.C.F. amendment to the address [in reply to] the Speech from the Throne. Bench was wondering whether it would be better to have the Liberal amendment withdrawn and the Government defeated on the C.C.F. amendment or to have the Government defeated on the Liberal amendment. I told him I had no opinion to offer. That I did not know enough about the Ontario situation to advise anyone one way or the other. I thought it was better for me to keep completely out of the Ontario situation. Bench made it clear he was simply letting me know the situation and not seeking to get an opinion from me. I asked whether there was not a danger of the Liberals and the C.C.F. defeating themselves if the Government were defeated, but Bench would not express a view on that one way or the other."

"Personally I feel that Hepburn has been too impetuous," the Prime Minister commented the next day. "He has not yet got the following in the Province needed to let him get to the head of the Government again. The fact that the motion which carried was won by the C.C.F. which the

Liberals had to support and the Liberal sub-amendment was not carried would seem to make it clear to the public that the C.C.F. have got the lead. That they are the people who have really thrown Drew out of office. I am afraid that the C.C.F. and the Liberals will cut each other's throats and that Drew will come back with a larger majority. Many of his candidates may be returned by a minority vote. This may serve as a warning to Liberals and C.C.F. alike in the federal field. The chances are that the numbers of the C.C.F. will be much larger than those of the Liberals. Indeed the Liberals may lose even the small numbers they have at present. I, of course, hope they may do otherwise but fear greatly the consequences so far as the province is concerned.

"Coming to the effect on the federal field I am not at all sure that an election in Ontario between now and our own election may not be all to the good so far as we are concerned. It will certainly take the mind of the people off the issue of conscription. It will sicken them of endless elections, such as North Grey by-election, forced by the Tories. This [Ontario] general election was forced by Liberals and C.C.F. and may cause them to feel that I have given sounder leadership in carrying the country through the entire period of war without a general election. It will show the power of leadership in keeping the country united and on an even keel. At the moment it will weaken the position of the Conservatives at Ottawa in taking any step which might seek to precipitate a federal election here, until the Ontario election is over. It justifies me if I need to in taking a longer time before bringing on the federal election. It is now another factor which enters into fixing the date of polling in the federal arena. An Ontario election will probably come while the San Francisco Conference is on. There again it will be all to the good to our people if they are busily organized for the federal fight meanwhile and come on with our post-war policies immediately after. However, there will be much of confusion for some time to come. Should the war end while the provincial election is on the Tories will hardly be able to claim that they have won the victory if our Government continues to remain as it will in office. I feel deeply concerned about the future of government in Canada—provincial and federal alike. We have not the men entering public life capable of dealing with questions of the magnitude with which the country is faced at this time and will be increasingly faced in the next few years."

The War Committee tackled the controversial question of Canadian participation in the war against Japan again on March 29. The Prime Minister read a draft statement which raised the question of conscription again. "Macdonald in particular maintained that we must have conscription on principle. Ilsley also stated strongly that he was indifferent. Either the government should have conscription of N.R.M.A. men for Japan as well as volunteers from general service or else have avowedly an indefinite statement as to numbers, but an avowed statement as to no conscription for the Japanese war. I mentioned to Council anew what we knew from Churchill at first hand that the British had to force their way into having a place for their armed forces in the Pacific—as he described it—getting a box seat, and what Churchill had said about Canada now coming along and wishing to get in and Churchill promising to use his good offices with the President to try to secure a place for us.

"I spoke of my talk with the President, in which he spoke of our navy possibly controlling the Kuriles and our soldiers helping to drive the Japanese out of Manchuria and other parts of China, and how I had felt indignant at his even proposing anything of the kind. Michaud also reminded others of what was said at Quebec. I was able to tell Council that I knew of my own knowledge from a very high source that Russia [was] going to assist the Allies at a certain time. This of itself might greatly change the whole picture. Also that I had it from the President that his belief was that the war in Japan would be over in a very few months after the European war was over. I took strongly the position that to create a conscription issue over Japan before a general election would be just suicidal and absolutely wrong. St. Laurent was quite outspoken about saying some people would like to have another war just to have conscription. Crerar was really helpful in pointing out that he did not think there was any need for an army, but if we did he would favour as he had, if the need existed, getting men by conscription, but that in this case he saw no need.

"McNaughton was quite agreeable, though he felt it would be wiser not to have conscription. He did not think there was need for it. At the same time he had been quite prepared to state there should be no conscription but concluded it would be perhaps just as well not to have the question raised at all for the present. That the situation would probably clear up rapidly of itself. He read a report on the reinforcement situation overseas, which is extremely good, based on Sansom's observation. He stated emphatically that we should include mention that no one would be sent overseas until after their return to Canada and a month's vacation here. I pointed out that [at] the earliest, according to plans thus far considered, it would be September or October before the troops could leave to go to China and by that time the Japanese war might be over. I pointed out it would be for the government which followed after the election to decide what might be necessary in the way of numbers, etc., to be worked in with the British and Americans. It was apparent that the British themselves do not know yet what contribution they are going to make or are concealing it, or that Americans are ready to let us do what we wish. They will not make any demands. I pointed out that the mere desire of having token contribution for prestige purposes was not sufficient reason for raising the conscription issue or indeed needlessly sacrificing lives.

"It was finally decided to have Pope, Heeney, and the Chiefs of Staff revise the memorandum in the light of the discussion, making clear that whatever was done for the Japanese war would be on a voluntary basis, thereby avoiding the question of conscription of N.R.M.A. men, or voluntary enlistment, or any pressure on general service men for voluntary enlistment. It was suggested that the army contribution might be made up of men who would wish to be permanently in the army.

"I am coming to feel that if the worst comes to the worst, rather than have the issue of conscription raised in the election, I would cut out any contribution from the army, especially as we would be retaining one or two divisions for a couple of years in Europe. It was really distressing to have the whole conscription issue brought up anew today but it was apparent that this time Crerar, St. Laurent, Howe, Michaud and McNaughton were against it. Ilsley, while prepared to accept conscription, was equally prepared to have a policy of voluntary enlistment. Macdonald was left by himself in arguing for conscription. He made the statement he would only be in the government for a short time longer in any event. I felt anew the need of having a government which is of one mind. Certainly there will be no conscription for the Far East in any government of which I may be the head."

McNaughton spent part of Good Friday (March 30) at Kingsmere with the Prime Minister where they had a talk "on the shaping up of something in the way of policy regarding the army and in connection with the Japanese war. Also I went over with the General very carefully some of his remarks in the West and what he had in mind. He made clearer to me today than I have seen before just what is the cause of his strong feeling against Ralston. It began with that he feels Ralston–Stuart worked in with Sir Alan Brooke and Montgomery to change altogether the plans on which the Army had been built up with a view to its part in the invasion of Northern Europe. He has a statement from Ralston in which Ralston says that unless there were casualties of a certain amount, we would have no voice in the peace. That, I can vouch for, is something very similar to what he said in Council and to which I took exception—that it was necessary for us to be fighting in Italy, otherwise the war might end soon, and Canada would not have done her part. The General says he also has a telegram from Eisenhower to him with words something to the effect not to break up the army in Britain but to keep it intact for invasion purposes. He, the General, was quite favourable to allowing officers to go to Italy for battle training but saw no need for moving the troops, except for one task, an operation such as the taking of Greece, which gave them practice in amphibious warfare. He said, however, there was no justification for our men going on in to Italy. He feels an effort was being made to have them possibly used to go through the Balkans—all kinds of efforts were made in those directions. I know, from what Churchill showed me on the map, that he had that possible route in mind. The Americans of course were always against it. McNaughton feels that having the two divisions go to Italy meant extra lines of supply with a demand for very large numbers of additional men, reduced the effectiveness in the long run of the invasion and really was accountable for the shortage that came later on the continent. I think events show that he is right."

The full Cabinet considered the draft statement of policy on the Japanese war on April 3. Mackenzie King reported that he "tried to speak very quietly and to outline briefly what I felt should go into the statement, mentioning that we had discussed the matter at different times in the War Committee. I said that Council would recall that when we were deciding on a question of war policy generally and particularly in reference to the Japanese war at the time of the Quebec Conference, it had been agreed in the Cabinet that there should be no conscription for the army to go to Japan.

"Angus Macdonald questioned this. He said he did not recall it, but every member at the Council table agreed excepting him that that had been the understanding.

"Crerar spoke very strongly against any army going to Japan. He was taken up sharply by Mackenzie, who said that would be ruinous on the Pacific Coast. I pointed out that Mackenzie had misunderstood Crerar, that what he was arguing was not against our making a real contribution as between the different forces but the wisdom of an army force of a size which would necessitate conscription or which would not be needed for the effort against Japan. Crerar kept insisting that we should give up any thought of an army contribution. I contended, however, that as Macdonald had used the word, there should be a statement as to some contribution by the different services but that the numbers were to be indefinite. I made reference to any army having to be organized in Canada; if men from overseas enlisted, they should have at least a month's vacation here after returning. Ilsley again spoke of the necessity of Council definitely deciding on whether the general service men were to be considered as having enlisted for Japan or whether they would have to re-volunteer to go into the war against Japan. I said it was desirable, if possible, to keep out of the statement either the word conscription or the word volunteer. . . .

"It was getting on after 2 and I had still a statement to prepare on San Francisco Conference, so I finally said to the Cabinet: Are not all at this table agreed that there shall not be conscription for the Japanese war? There was a nodding of heads affirmatively but complete silence, then I said this is definitely understood. It was either there or earlier that Mac-donald used the term that the contribution would have to be indefinite. . . . I then emphasized again the indefiniteness of the extent of the contribution and pointed out that it would have to be determined after the war in Europe was over, and still in relation with our Allies, the U.K. and the U.S. I pointed out that it was not our business to give away either strategy or any more information than we could to the enemy as to either the ships we should use, the numbers of fighting men, and where we should fight.

"It was an immense relief to me when this decision had been reached."

Also that day the Minister of Finance made his statement asking the House to grant 5/12 of the proposed war appropriations. Mackenzie King "thought it was an excellent statement and some of the language he used as to the new Parliament having responsibility for further conduct of war, financial programmes, etc., gave me just what I needed for my statement. I asked him to let me have his manuscript. I copied off what I felt would effectively seal up the situation so far as both he and Angus Macdonald were concerned. The same language used by myself in the first instance would have met with a quite different reception in the House. His statement was in no way criticized.

"When Graydon followed, he made a very moderate speech. To my surprise and relief, he stated that the Opposition intended to help us get the needed monies for carrying on the war. At a single stroke, this caused to vanish the necessity of my having a dissolution and making use of Governor General's warrants. It was rather amusing that a few minutes before, Mackenzie had sent me a note saying he thought I should by all means dissolve the House a week from Friday. Tell the opposition that I intended to do this thereby showing leadership. This is a common failing with many men that leadership consists in showing that one has power rather than in getting one's end by means that lead to agreement on the part of all. Only the latter to my mind is a true kind of leadership. I personally feel that by letting Parliament run out by efflux of time would make clear to the public and to the soldiers that I have waited until the last possible moment before dissolving the House so as to avoid an election, so far as it was within my power, before decisive battles had been fought and victory achieved in Europe. I decided after Graydon spoke, to say nothing. His criticism that Parliament should have been called earlier, etc. I felt would pass unnoticed if I said nothing. Also when Case spoke. He was very guarded in his language. As Gordon Ross [M.P. for Moose Jaw] said to me: you cannot kick a lamb in the face, so there was no need for our men to start a row in the House. I am still a little nonplussed to note just how this change in tactics on the part of the Tories had come about. It looks to me as if the effect of the vote we had on the San Francisco conference has been considerable, and that my having agreed to have all parties represented on Canada's delegation has caused the Tory High Command to tell them all to softpedal as far as I myself am concerned. Also the obvious rapid successes of the allied armies in Europe and our own army in particular is making it impossible for them to continue to make much of the reinforcement issue.

"I took advantage of the way the debate was going to call in Graydon first and later Coldwell, offering formally to each of them a place on Canada's delegation to San Francisco. They were both obviously quite pleased and said so frankly. Graydon said he hoped I would understand if he had to say that he would want to consult with John Bracken before accepting or something to that effect. I told him he could say what he liked and I would understand. He suggested to me it might be as well if I did not make any comment that would antagonize his people so far as Bracken is concerned. He had in mind in this connection helping me to get through the session before the very last day. I said I thought we should be through by Thursday, if possible, of next week. He suggested Saturday and spoke of the difficulties of closing up the House. I said I would not sit on Saturday or in the mornings on any account. There was no need for it at this session. That I might say to the House if I found it necessary to sit on the following Monday, that I might find it impossible to be at San Francisco at the opening of the conference. I thought if I said this the public would have a certain understanding and sympathy with my so doing."

In the House's consideration of the war appropriations, the navy estimates were taken first and were largely non-controversial. Mackenzie King decided it was wiser not to rush in with his statement on the Japanese war at that stage. Indeed he was still working on the statement on April 4. "I got to work alone," he wrote, "on the final writing out of the statement as I thought it should be given out to the House. Heeney had given me a memo. taking rather strong exception to suggestions that Mc-

Naughton had made. I told him at the time that I had asked McNaughton to write a memo. along lines to which he, Heeney, was taking exception. That I thought this was the right kind of background to give. I had not seen McNaughton's statement at the time. When I began to read it, it was again as though an Unseen Hand had placed it before me just at the moment that it was most opportune to have it. It really set out the whole background as I felt it should be set out. Instead of narrowing the picture to the Japanese war, it read naturally out of the present situation in Europe into the possible activities of the future. By very little revision, I was able to incorporate practically all that he had written. This with what had been prepared before re Japan, deleting considerable parts and keeping in mind the discussion of yesterday and the last few days and above all the agreement reached yesterday, I was able to put into a very clear, correct statement, concise, yet comprehensive, covering all the really difficult points. First: no conscription, for any of the forces; second: Army force being made up in Canada, and men having a month's vacation here. 3rd: No detailing from general service but all to elect for service in Japan. The size of the contribution, indefinite and all still to be determined on further consultation with the U.K. and the U.S. Implied no compulsion at all re men serving in Europe. No compulsion to send N.R.M.A. men before others. Finally a pretty well implied possibility of no army force going at all because of the scarcity of ships and the great need if men abroad are to get home, that they shall have transportation for the purpose. Were the troops needed against Japan or even wanted, the situation would be different but there is no justification for incurring, for reasons of prestige or above all to suit the army's pleasure and desire to increase its own importance, further sacrifices of life and enormous unnecessary expenditures.

"I was able to bring in to good effect statements by Ilsley and to conclude with a paragraph which I felt at the time of writing to be a direct inspiration, namely, something to the effect that the next Parliament would be free to do as it pleased but what I was giving was the policy we intended to follow if again given the confidence of the people. This means that those who want no conscription will certainly be drawn in our direction and I am sure they are, so far as Japan is concerned, by far the greater majority.

"Secondly, it means that our opponents will have to bring forth conscription themselves as a policy and fight on that ground, if that issue is to be introduced. It is one thing to say that we ought to have conscription for reinforcements and another to advocate it for the war against Japan.

"In the 3rd place, I think our statement will be warmly welcomed by the overseas men. I doubt if any of them want conscription against Japan and by making it clear they may re-elect, we are considering how they can get home in largest numbers and at the earliest time, it is altogether probable that there will be a big swing toward ourselves on the part of the troops now serving abroad. What there are of N.R.M.A. men should feel that they cannot at least vote for the Tories. They may vote for the C.C.F.

After completing the draft, Mackenzie King went to Cabinet and had Abbott come in while he read it. "I read the statement slowly and carefully," he wrote. "It was received without an interruption and with general approval at the close. Some remarked they thought it was a splendid statement. There was one reference to the Navy—about leave of naval men which I thought superfluous. I asked Macdonald if he wanted it. He thought it would be as well out, so I took it out." The necessary pages were retyped and it was nearly 3.00 P.M. when Mackenzie King left Cabinet for the House of Commons.

"When the orders of the day were called, I rose and asked permission to make a general statement applicable to all the forces which I thought might assist in the discussion. This was granted and I read the statement. It was received with pretty much of a dead silence and an attentiveness I have seldom witnessed, or which I have witnessed only at a time of great expectancy. I could feel that the House was receiving it well and that there was a tendency to applaud the latter portion of it but I saw equally clearly that the Conservatives were in a quandary as to what they should say when I had concluded. The two or three questions asked made it apparent they were not prepared to raise the issue of conscription at once themselves but were rather seeking to still create the impression that men who had borne the burden and heat of the day were going to have to carry on against Japan. We have cut the ground completely from under their feet on that score. I think today's statement is perhaps the most effective thing that has been said this year and will go further than all else to win us the next general election. It should bring our Quebec friends completely into line. If they don't fall into line, it will be through the jealousy of factions but I think it makes certain that the majority will be with us in the next House on our war policies. If government means anything, it means government by the will of the majority. In this case, I feel that the justice of the whole situation is entirely on our side. Our men have fought for 2½ years before the Americans were in the war at all. There is no reason on earth why we should be sending large additional numbers to the Pacific."

The next day (April 5) the Prime Minister read a short statement at the opening of the House taking "exception to an editorial in the [Montreal] Gazette which was deliberately misleading as to Canada's part in the war against Japan. What is most interesting of all was that at this morning's

Caucus, there was not a word said against the no conscription policy for war against Japan. I have not heard a soul in the buildings taking exception to that policy. Many have spoken to me about all that it signifies and how helpful it should prove.

"Here I want to record what I feel about the Hand of Providence. Mackenzie in talking said he thought it was a miracle that I had the entire Cabinet agree to that statement. All the 20 of us were in the room and there was no exception."

The Army estimates were taken up that day by Abbott, who, Mackenzie King noted, "had a splendidly prepared statement—overwhelming in what it disclosed." The Prime Minister stayed out of the House the rest of that day and for most of the next day to avoid having questions directed to him. "I was amazed when 6 o'clock came [on April 6] to find there had been no unpleasantness. It was agreed the debate would run on tonight but apparently up to now—half past nine—all has gone remarkably well. In the House, the Tories were determined apparently to carry over the debate until Monday. They will then have a chance with their High Command to plan their battle for next week."

The Prime Minister entered the House late in the evening and "learned that all had gone well, although there was exception taken by Green and Dr. Bruce to not having N.R.M.A. men compelled to go to Japan to fight before allowing men who are in G.S. to elect to go. The Tories however were very quiet, their numbers in the House pretty thin. The truth is they see they are completely outmanoeuvred. . . .

"I confess that I was more surprised at the way this week has passed than anything that has happened since the beginning of the war. I fully expected a storm and a difficult time, particularly over McNaughton's speech in the West. Thus far nothing has been said of this and we are now well through the war estimates, and indeed have gained by having a chance to put before the country the statements we have re the future etc. Abbott has done exceedingly well. Very wisely has had no officials in the House. He has been able to take his time to answer questions—give the information a little later on. I understand the Opposition want to go on with the Army estimates on Monday but are likely to conclude them at 6. They may take the entire day. Between now and then I shall prepare a statement myself re winding up of Parliament."

In fact, debate on the defence estimates was not concluded until Tuesday, April 10. Mackenzie King was "immensely relieved" that the estimates had "gone through without any issue between McNaughton and Ralston being raised. This is a miracle of miracles. That whole business has been like a fearful apparition making me feel that I did not want to be near the H. of C. when anything rancorous came up and I was almost certain that a very rowdy time would be experienced. I am still at a loss to understand the complete lack of fight in Conservatives. The little they have said about Parliament not being called earlier, no boasting of North Grey, Bracken and his rifles settled that. Altogether a very weak and indifferent performance. It must be that they see they have been completely outmanoeuvred. That we have gauged events aright and that they are all telling for us and against the Tories. That the war is obviously drawing to its close—victory after victory. San Francisco Conference coming on and the almost certainty that the war would be over and therefore bring post-war programme to the fore when the time comes for us to go to the people. We have led the country from the beginning to the close through the greatest epoch in the history of the world, without a scandal in our whole war effort and with an achievement on the part of Canada greater than anything that could possibly have been anticipated. It is a marvellous record on which to go to the people. Also we have carried it to the last hour thereby doing all in our power to make sure that the men who had fought would have the chance to decide to cast their votes under most favourable conditions in the campaign."

Buoyed up by this success in the House, the Prime Minister turned his attention to the pre-election reorganization of the Cabinet. On April 6 he talked about Quebec representation with St. Laurent who "frankly admits he does not know in what direction to turn. Thinks it would be inadvisable for Power to come into the government at least until calling up of men is over. I am doubtful about it too until the election is over. He agrees LaFlèche is useless. No one would miss him. He thinks very highly of Abbott. I told him if Macdonald gave up the Navy, I would appoint Abbott at once as Minister of Naval Affairs.

"I would like to get Chevrier in probably as Minister of National Revenue. The Speaker in the place of Crerar. I will have to get someone for Secretary of State. That will be Dr. McCann or Joseph Jean or possibly Wilfrid Gagnon if it should be wise to select him."

Four days later (April 11) Mackenzie King saw LaFlèche, who, though disappointed, accepted the news graciously. He talked with Premier McNair of New Brunswick who was quite agreeable to Michaud's appointment to the Bench. McNair thought Murray MacLaren's nephew (D. L. MacLaren, subsequently Minister of National Revenue) "would be the best man to choose as Minister from New Brunswick. He is a Liberal in all his outlook though a son of a strong Conservative. Thinks possibly Veniot [M.P. for Gloucester] might be all right for a French Senate vacancy.

Would like to have one of his own Ministers appointed to the Senate—Pirie, I think his name is. He said he and Michaud were in agreement. I told him to discuss matters further with Michaud."

Later in the day, Mackenzie King had a talk with Angus Macdonald. "He knew what was in my mind. I said to him that I had come now to the point where I had to consider between now and leaving for San Francisco what arrangements may have to be made with regard to the elections, Ministry, etc. I asked him if he was still decided that he would not run again. He said: yes, that he had felt quite firmly on that. That to run again would be to incur another commitment for another five years which would be too long a time. I then said to him in those circumstances I would have to think over at once the arrangements that I should make whereupon he said he would send me a letter stating that he intended to resign. Later he said he would include in it reference to the fact that he had indicated this a year ago.

"He then said that he would be glad to stay on and assist in any way until such time as I might think it best to make the change of Minister. I told him I thought changes ought to be made at once immediately after dissolution. This seemed to surprise him a little for he said that he naturally would like to have stayed on until the end of the war. However that the service had now reached its peak. He stated that a little earlier in reference to feeling he should drop out at this time. That obviously he could not hope to improve on the point now reached. He felt that was a completion of a certain work. (I think his attitude and Power's are not dissimilar. They each realize things have got to a summit and that there would be anti-climax from there on. However Macdonald has made it clear to me that what kept him on last fall was just that thought of wanting to be in at the end, at the peace. Of course, Ralston had expressed the same natural view.) I then said to him I would like to thank him for the help he had been in the years he had been in the government. That I regretted the trying situation that had developed last autumn but that was one of the inevitable happenings in public life where there were differences of view. That I would like to say I appreciated his staying on at that time and not leaving the Ministry then. He said nothing by way of appreciation of the thanks that I had expressed. Said something as we were going out of the room that experience over the five years had been valuable.

"When we came to the corridor, I spoke to him about my conversation with LaFlèche. Asked him if he knew anything about his financial circumstances but he did not. He made no reference himself to desiring any position nor did he make any reference to MacMillan [Premier of Nova Scotia] who, Ilsley tells me, though now 73 years wants to be made a Senator. I don't think that can be done. I must say that I have been deeply disappointed with Macdonald. First of all, as a Liberal, because he has proved anything but such in his views, and secondly, to use an expression St. Laurent used this afternoon, of his intolerance. I thought he had a sunnier and more wholesome nature but I can see he is very vain, very selfish. Vanity is the besetting sin with many public men. I noticed he kept taking notes as Sansom's report was being discussed, all undoubtedly with the intention of passing on information to Ralston. He has been for a long time past simply a pipe from the Cabinet with some of its opponents outside. I will feel a great relief in having him out of the government altogether."

That afternoon in the House of Commons, Mackenzie King noted, to his surprise, "Graydon rose to speak of the business of Parliament. With nothing prepared except what had been in my thoughts at different times, I began to speak in reply along the opening which he gave me and went much further than I had ever expected to go this session. I was able to get on record what I wanted most to say about the session: the significance of election in North Grey; the position of the Tory party toward our parliamentary institution through Bracken's attitude at the time that he was chosen leader. Altogether it was a strong political speech. I confess I was amazed at the way the Tories took it all lying down. I had expected them to begin a barrage at once but the House listened in almost complete silence. I was particularly glad to be able to bring out how true the party and myself had been to the trust imposed in us from the time of the last general elections and having run our course, in accordance with the mandate given us. Also to give a final knock-out blow to any thought that we should have been a National Government. I was surprised at the ease with which I spoke and the absence of any fatigue either at the time or after."

He added: "Now I feel I see the end of the present session carried out with dignity and in a manner which lets the country see that I have been able to master the situation up to the last moment. For a last session of a last Parliament before an election, the situation is truly miraculous. We have not only scored strongly for the San Francisco Conference but equally on our whole war record and indeed have explained in a manner that will be satisfactory, all the points that our opponents hoped to win on. Each day the Tories have seen their opportunity vanish with the war drawing to its close and victory becoming daily nearer. All that I have worked for in the last couple of years is coming out now just exactly as I had hoped and prayed it might. It will become apparent to the men who have fought overseas, if not today, at least in the future that I have kept their interests to the fore to the very end."

Later in the day the Prime Minister met Power in the corridor and asked him for his assessment of the situation in Quebec. "Chubby began to go into the larger question of the future of Liberalism. He said that he thought from that point of view, things were very dark. That our party was more and more becoming Tory. Spoke of Ilsley having begun as a Liberal, now being completely Tory in his outlook. Spoke of Howe, being the same, etc. He then told me, what perhaps he should not have, what he thought I would like to know and would understand, which was that in some of the Liberal circles, particularly Montreal, etc. and in the mind of Cardin and his associates, I was thinking of possibly not running again or at most, if I did, only staying in for a short time. Consequently they were centring their efforts on having Howe become the leader of the party. I said at once that Howe was in no way fitted for the job. That he would go to pieces under it in no time. Power said: no. That he was perfectly indifferent to anything that was said to him. He would just go ahead and do what he likes. I said: you cannot run a government in that way. I said to Power: you [Power] could tackle the job of leader of a government. Have people pester you from every side and let them all go away with a laugh and not be worried. That he knew the inside of politics, etc. but Howe never could. I saw this made a visible change in Chubby's expression and also, his manner. It unquestionably has been the ambition of his life. He opened out a little more on the Quebec situation by saying that what he was now trying to do in the little Quebec group, was to drop the word 'independent' and call them Liberal Canadiens—Canadian Liberals. I told him that was better but better still was 'Liberal.' He said he was drawing a plan of fundamental principles the Liberal party stood for and they could make that their platform. He said there had been some effort to have him and Cardin come together but that Cardin was undecided. He agreed, however, it would be well for me to talk with Cardin."

Power also "doubted if any of the Ministers who had supported me on conscription would get a hearing in constituencies other than their own in the province of Quebec. I can see that what he is seeking to do is to be a political boss with a following. To have others like Cardin and certain interests also to be political bosses but to have nothing done really in the large statesmanlike way in leadership in ideas, etc. It comes down pretty much to patronage and control of government later on. It really is a tragic situation. He doubts if St. Laurent can be elected. He said he [St. Laurent] should not be speaking elsewhere than in his own seat. I begged of him to do all he could to help St. Laurent. He admitted St. Laurent was the ablest man we had in the government. The best person I could have found but he thinks his influence is gone for not standing out against conscription.

"As a matter of fact, Power ought to take leadership in a true way and help to educate the province. What I did not like in the attitude he continues to maintain is that I should be condemned for having countenanced conscription in any form instead of saying that what I had done was the best in a difficult situation. This I think is carrying things too far. Power later said he might himself not run. He said he had been offered a large retainer in connection with some business, and was beginning to feel better now that he was out of the stress of politics. He indicated that he might perhaps ask me to appoint him to the Senate. I doubted if he would ever be out of politics. It was too much in his blood. I told him at any rate not to make any hasty decisions. The interview I think was most opportune and most helpful. It can do no harm."

On April 12, Mackenzie King was told by a secretary that Premier Drew had just announced a provincial election for June 11. He noted that the secretary "seemed rather disconsolate and discouraged, realizing that this would in all probability give Drew a chance to get the Ontario elections over before ours, in which event should the Liberals run second or last in Ontario—last seems in every way most probable—the effect on the federal campaign which would come later would be disastrous—indeed not only in Ontario, a defeat which might hurt us in all the provinces. . . .

"When I went into the Cabinet the ministers were discussing some Orders in Council which were before the Cabinet. I interrupted the discussion to tell them that I had just received word that Drew had fixed June 11th for the election. I then began to secure the views of the different ministers. What I had been planning for up to that time was an election on June 25th. Claxton had written me a strong letter pointing out that St. Jean Baptiste Day was on June 24th and there would be processions which would be a great day for the nationalists. He stated in his letter that they would have parades in Montreal which would take three hours and keep people away from the polls. Claxton has since ascertained that the procession would be on Sunday. We spoke of the following week which would mean that the elections would have to come on July 3, as July 2 was the day fixed for observing Dominion Day, and the elections would have to come a day later. This meant that the Tories would have Sunday and Monday to get in their iniquitous type of campaigning. That made it out of the question. A week later got well into the month of July which meant if the crops were bad that would all be known at that time and would discourage the farmers. As Ilsley pointed out other situations would be getting worse and worse, for example, need for additional housing and the like. Also the questions that would come up on demobilization, etc. Howe, too, was fearful of what might happen in the transition period of unemployment. Gardiner seemed to think that we ought at least to take two weeks after the 11th to enable time to elapse to wipe off the ill effects of reverses in Ontario to be able to explain the situation. A week he did not think would be long enough. Howe said why not go on the 11th—the same day. That seemed to me very sudden. I said that it might be held against us in some quarters if we were responsible for the two elections coming on in the same day with the confusion that might create, etc. In this Angus Macdonald strongly concurred. Ilsley was very strong for June 11. He thought that would be best of all and the sooner we had the elections the better. In my mind there was naturally the question of success of the election on June 11, and how long it would be possible to remain at San Francisco. Also it seemed to knock out altogether the possibility of spending a couple of days in the riding of Prince Albert which was my last hope and last straw for success there. I said that almost certainly it would mean that I could not be elected in Prince Albert, but however the fortunes of the party were what should be first considered. This recalls to mind that the first letter I opened this morning was one from T. H. Wood of Regina, giving a careful survey of the situation in Prince Albert and pointing out that after a careful survey made by one of his travellers he felt there was no chance for me either in the urban or rural areas. Conditions were worse in both packing plants which were all C.C.F. in Prince Albert. He said that I would stand no chance at all and strongly advised against running in the constituency. That was not the most cheering pronouncement with which to begin the day. The discussion continued in Council for some little time. I then said I would turn the matter over in my mind and we would discuss it again. Advised Council to say nothing to anyone of the discussion that had taken place."

During the afternoon he discussed the election date with several of the members and was particularly impressed by Arthur Roebuck's opinion that it should be June 11. He also found out from the Chief Electoral Officer that an election could be held on June 11 if the announcement was made on April 13.

Consideration of political matters was abruptly interrupted during the late afternoon while Mackenzie King was receiving a treatment from his osteopath, Dr. Parsons, who told him he had heard a "rumour about President Roosevelt. I said what is the rumour. He replied that he had died. I said there are apt to be all kinds of rumours at any time. He said nothing more but the telephone rang and when he came back he said that Turnbull wished to speak to me, would they hold the line, or would I like to go at once to the phone. I said, oh no I realize what that means. He replied that he thought it was correct that the President had passed away. I told him I would speak to Turnbull after he had finished the treatment. I confess that I was not at all surprised, though from the letter that I had received from Leighton McCarthy the morning before yesterday, it emphasized how very weak he was but seemed to indicate some improvement. I seemed too exhausted and fatigued to feel any strong emotion. It all seemed like part of the day's heavy work. Just one more in fact. I was almost too tired to think of what, in the circumstances, I would be called upon to do. I thought of letting the [Governor-General] know but that thought seemed to open my mind and it turned on the necessity of having something prepared to say in the House at 8 o'clock. When I was through dressing I spoke to Turnbull. Oddly enough neither of us mentioned the President's name or any mention of his death. I simply said to him: Well, Turnbull, I knew what your message was about. Please see that P. [Pickersgill] and G. [Gibson] come up to Laurier House, as soon as possible. He said P. had been waiting there."

Mackenzie King's "first action on arrival at Laurier House was to pick up the 'phone and ask for Murphy, Deputy Minister of Public Works. I said I wished to give him a direct message. He had not heard of the President's death. I told him to have the flag put at half mast on the Parliament Buildings. This was followed later by a message I gave H. [Handy] tonight to have Public Works first thing in the morning request that flags should be at half mast on all Public Works buildings throughout Canada.

"I next wrote a message by hand quite personal to Mrs. Roosevelt at the White House making mention of Mrs. Boettiger [the President's daughter] in particular and other members of the family. I then began on the statement for the House of Commons at 8. I learned that Howe had been speaking in the House when the word came to him from the press and that he had made the announcement of the President's death.

"As I was writing out different lines suggesting thoughts, P. and G. helped me in the phrasing. Time seemed to pass very quickly and I had to make brief what I said. While that was being typed, I had just a bite, etc. for dinner and then went at once to the H. of C. I had not even time to read the typed manuscript through. The bell had rung. I spoke immediately from what I had written out. Had thought of having the House rise as a token of respect, on completing what I had to say. The little verse from Matthew Arnold I thought of while writing, copied it from my father's Essays in University days. I would have given much to have been rested when this word came and to have been able to express really as I should have liked the tribute I would have wished to pay to so dear a friend. However I could not do more than what I did. In my heart, I felt a great gratitude for having been privileged to know the President so well and particularly for the last happy days we had together and to have had the last word from him through Leighton McCarthy saying he would like to have extended an invitation to me to accompany him on his train to S.F. but Eden and others would be here and I would understand. Nothing could have been more friendly than such a word. I felt happy that he had passed away at Warm Springs in the quiet little cottage there; also that he would be buried at Hyde Park which was dearest of all places to his heart."

"When the House rose," he wrote, "I sat in my seat and talked to some of the other Ministers who were nearby; many of the members came up and extended expressions of sympathy in a very sincere and heartfelt way. Indeed I was surprised to find how many of them realized that I had lost a very great friend and that this loss would mean much to me.

"After sitting there for some little time, I asked St. Laurent, Mackenzie, Howe and Gardiner to come to Room 212. I also telephoned to Government House to say that I would be down to see H.E. Curiously enough, it did not occur to me at the time that there would be messages to be sent by him, etc."

Before going to Government House, Mackenzie King talked to the four Ministers about having the election on June 11. "Howe," he recorded, "had expressed himself strongly for it. Gardiner mentioned what I had said about the Ontario government claiming I would be cutting into their plans. That I was making their campaign difficult deliberately. I said I had thought of that, but had come to feel that after all they had been seeking to destroy us by having their campaign first and had planned notwithstanding their inability to get soldiers' votes at the time suggested. I could now see the whole scheme of the Opposition for the past week which was not to create opposition lest I should dissolve Parliament before efflux of time and go to the country at an earlier date than they would find it desirable to go. They had evidently been figuring on seeing we remained in session until it was too late to have writs issued on Monday. They would probably keep us here until the end. . . . I said they would have great difficulty in putting Drew and Bracken across at the same time. Also I felt very strongly if we came 3rd in Ontario or even second, it would be very harmful to us in Ontario and the other provinces thereafter. Also if Drew won, the whole Tory forces would be turned on us for the next week or two. This seemed in every way the fairest thing to the public to get an unprejudiced verdict. Also our forces would be able to work together. It would unite the Liberal party, etc. I was surprised to hear Howe say he would not bother a bit about Hepburn; spoke of the way he had been behaving of late; had been drinking, etc. Howe spoke of him as a mental case. Would not even support him in his own constituency. It was Howe who along with Bench encouraged Hepburn to come back. I was shocked when I heard he had been drinking again. He may go to pieces in the campaign and the party in the province may be left without any head."

Ian Mackenzie apparently agreed that the 11th would be wise. "He brought up my own seat in the West. Thought now that I should make sure of an Eastern seat as also did Howe. I told him it was too late. The matter was definitely decided that I would run in Prince Albert. Gardiner came around to feeling that perhaps June the 11th would be best and St. Laurent agreed. Got over any difficulty of St. Jean Baptiste's Day which comes at a later period. The more we discussed the matter the more I felt convinced in my mind that the right decision was being made. That it was absolutely necessary to take June the 11th and that indeed behind it all lay unseen forces and the guiding hand of Providence helping to assure us of triumph over the sinister methods and efforts being resorted to for the defeat of the Federal Government. I said to each of the Ministers to say nothing to a soul and that we would discuss the matter later in the Cabinet."

At Government House, the Governor-General spoke of seeking the King's approval for his own attendance at the funeral in Washington. The Prime Minister approved and indicated he would try to go to Hyde Park. He also told the Governor-General about having the election on June 11 and found him quite agreeable. Later he got in touch with Leighton McCarthy and asked him to consult Mrs. Roosevelt about going to Hyde Park.

Mackenzie King worked all morning on April 13 on a statement to be made in the House to announce the election on June 11. He secured the Governor-General's authority to announce the plans and saw the Chief Electoral Officer personally to make sure all arrangements could be made in time. He called a special Cabinet meeting for 2.45. "It was," he reported, "about 10 to 3 when I got to the room. The ministers were on all four sides of it. Seemed to be occupying all the space there was. Every Minister I think was present. I did not take time to look about but had the manuscript in my hand and told them I had here a statement which, if thought advisable, I proposed to read to the House at 3. I said that I had given much consideration to the question of the date of the elections and would read them what I thought of saying. I then read the statement without looking around. At one stage I did look over in the direction of my grandfather's bust, having him in my thoughts as I was reading. Angus Macdonald was sitting a little below. I thought his face carried the expression of acute disappointment and dismay. It had a darkened look which to me was full of disappointment. Instinctively I wished he were nowhere near the bust of my grandfather. I naturally had in mind the letter which he wrote me and which I had opened this morning and which showed clearly that he cherished a bitterness toward myself. It was apparent by his reference to colleagues but no specific reference to myself—natural expression of egotism—that when he had been invited to come he intended it only as a war job. Now that the Navy was brought to highest pitch he would leave his resignation in my hand to be used any time."

When he finished reading the statement, the Prime Minister asked for comments. "Nobody said a word of disapproval, some said they thought it was the right thing to do. I then said that I thought if we were all agreed —emphasizing the all—that there was not a word or expression by anyone —that this would make a great difference in the elections. The Tories would find they would have a hard job putting Drew and Bracken across together. Also indicated how tables had been completely turned on them and their seeking to get in ahead of us. Touched on other features, which all received with gratification. They had been pretty disappointed when the word came yesterday that Drew had decided on a date which they thought would naturally be the one we would select. I asked that no one should say a word of what I had in mind until I made the statement in the House. I said I had also something to read and read them the message I was sending to Truman.

"We all came downstairs together. Prayers were under way before it was time to go into the House. On the orders of the day which came quickly I tabled some orders in council, then read the telegram to Truman. While on my feet I followed with the statement of the business of the House reading the statement slowly and distinctly. It was interesting to watch the opposite side, when I came to the last paragraph. I looked across to Graydon and the others the moment I gave the date June 11. Our men sent up a great cheer and began pounding their desks, which was the first intimation they had. I did not see a soul on the official opposition applauding or pounding his desk. I drew Crerar's attention to it and also St. Laurent's. The Tories looked thoroughly knocked out. The other parties were applauding but their side was a blank as far as movement of any kind was concerned. When they saw I was noticing them one or two began to applaud a little. . . . It was clear that the decision had pleased our men immensely. Graydon made a speech which was like a schoolboy's effort— cheap, no dignity, etc. as though the whole business was just one of a game of who will be sitting on one side or the other. I thought he showed particularly bad taste in speaking about John Bracken being in and my being out in the seat which I was contesting. Grote Stirling asked a question which gave away the whole hand of the party. It made clear they have been figuring on days and hours which would make it too late for us to get on to the election before the Tories [in Ontario] were on with theirs. I learned later in the afternoon that while they had the Order-in-Council prepared fixing the day they had not yet fixed any writs. There is some talk that they might try to issue writs a little earlier but that would be impossible as far as recording of soldiers' votes are concerned."

The proceedings of the House were concluded that evening at 11 o'clock, though the prorogation did not take place until Monday, April 16.

In his diary for April 13, Mackenzie King wrote that the thought that came over him "above all others was how completely different the session had been from what I had thought it would be. Instead of demonstrations that were difficult to meet, confusion and the rest of it, there was not a point on which the government did not seem to have scored. The splendid showing on the resolution re San Francisco, then the quiet debates, the Opposition fearful I might dissolve, the whipping I gave them, getting on record what I most wanted to say about North Grey, no mention at all of difficulties between McNaughton and Ralston, all of that pretty well straightened out. The policy toward Japan explained and by the way, when I was speaking to our colleagues in my room upstairs, I pointed out how the no-conscription end had won the debate. This for Macdonald's benefit. What was really most significant of all was that after the 3rd reading of the Bills, I was able to move to have special order called and address of the Speech from the Throne carried unanimously. If ever a man in this world was guided from beginning to close in shaping the whole course of a session, I am that person. It has been the clearest evidence to me of guidance from Beyond that anyone could possibly have. What had seemed impossible, God has made not only possible but actually joyous and triumphant. Now it may come to be the same with the election itself, notwithstanding all that will have to be gone through between the present and the 11th of June."

Mackenzie King discussed Cabinet changes for Ontario with Arthur Roebuck that evening (April 13). "He thought it would be a great mistake to take Paul Martin in preference to McCann as representative of English-speaking Catholics. Martin was preferable as a man but we could not pass over that large section of the country. I said my feeling was the same—it was very strongly sincere feeling as well."

The next day, before leaving for Hyde Park, Mackenzie King had a talk with C. D. Howe about going to Prince Albert. He noted that Howe "Spoke of making a tour of the West. I said I hoped he would. There is little doubt that Howe has evidently in mind being possibly considered as a successor to myself. There are groups around him who are grooming him for that post. They would be the business groups but he will never be chosen by the party nor would he be able to sit in the Prime Minister's saddle for any length of time. He is too impatient. Has very little political judgment or sense."

The Prime Minister telephoned Hepburn and "thanked him for the message he had sent me last night letting him know I had been trying to reach him last night. I was agreeably surprised by the calm of his voice and the way in which he spoke generally, most respectfully, saying that he was solidly behind me. He said he had been at a political meeting last night—one of the finest held in Toronto. I told him I had told our men in Caucus to help him all we could. We would all work together. I also told him why it had not been possible to send him any word in advance of the announcement as to the date. He said they were at first dumbfounded when they received the word that we had set the same date. On turning the matter over, had concluded it was for the best. There were no references to the past but everything related to the future; in the best of spirit.

"P. and H. were in the room while I was telephoning. I am far from being sure about what Hepburn can do and whether he will last throughout the campaign. I am quite certain he has not the balance of a leader for any length of time but it would certainly be helpful to have his forces and my own working together against a common enemy."

In completing his diary for April 14, while on the train going to Hyde Park, the Prime Minister's thoughts were of the late American President. "Roosevelt's greatness was his love of his fellowmen. Love of the oppressed classes and the gallant fight he made for them regardless of classes and the bitterest kind of enmity and hatreds. It is truly amazing that in his four elections—having been elected to the office of President four successive terms—he escaped in this period of time both accident and assassination and that he was spared as long as he was. He certainly fought to the very end.

"As I go to Hyde Park for his burial, it seems really almost like going to see him again. Most of my trips to the States, if not practically all, have been for that purpose ever since the war began."

Mackenzie King derived great consolation from being at Hyde Park and described the simple ceremonies in minute detail. When he returned to the Library at Laurier House that night he "knelt down and thanked God for the great friend he had given me in the President. I asked for Strength to carry on his work along with Stettinius and others. That was my word with Stimson and others that we must now all work together harder than ever to carry on President Roosevelt's work."

Next morning while working on the final draft of the Speech from the Throne proroguing the session, Mackenzie King learned that Premier Drew had advanced the date of his election to June 4. When he received this information he added a clause in the speech "to the effect that ample provision had been made for the taking of the votes of our soldiers overseas. I cannot understand Drew's action, if he has the slightest regard for the rights of the soldiers as citizens of Canada. It is a form of highway robbery to seek to get into power by destroying right constitutional procedure. However this did not occasion me concern as I can see that our forces will be working hard with the Ontario Liberals. All will be welded into one and even if our men do get the worst of it provincially, they will be perhaps keen to get even federally."

Mackenzie King was quite concerned to receive word that W. P. Mulock might not be well enough to contest the election. "His dropping out," he wrote, "would leave us weaker than we are in men of ministerial calibre in Ontario." Most of the day was taken up with the prorogation, but he found time to talk to several members about the situation in Quebec. He told one of them that "if individual leaders in the party and members were afraid to stand up for me and others were going to oppose me I might decide to go and speak in Quebec myself. I would find out if at the end of 25 years of leadership of the party and all I had done to keep the country united this was all I had gained of confidence and would like to find out where the province stood. I had really come to the conclusion to wait until elections were over and see how things had gone but said that I certainly was not going to barter with anyone for their support. I was doing all I could in undertaking to stay on.

"Mackenzie told me the same thing as Power about the group around Cardin seeking to build up Howe as a possible P.M. when I dropped out. I said I did not think Howe would lend himself consciously to that and that I was indifferent to what they did in a way. This is the only attitude I will take. I will stand by those who stood by me. And when others gain preferment it will be because of the stand that they have been prepared to take at the time for me.

"I felt much better in my own mind after I had seen this aspect of the situation so clearly and decided, come what will, to show these men that it was they who had to come to me and not me to them. The one handicap is that I have not the use of the French language; also that I have so little time for the campaign. The fact that the time is short is bringing these men face to face with these realities."

At the end of the afternoon, Mackenzie King "had a talk with St. Laurent. He agreed with me that it was well to stand solidly by those who were loyal to us. He had seen Godbout lately and Godbout had quite changed his tone. Had come to the conclusion they should all support me very strongly. Said he would come and speak for St. Laurent in Quebec. Would come as a straight Liberal. I think I have only to stand firm to have a good many of them discover this is the only course to pursue. The people can be better trusted than the few men who want to control patronage. St. Laurent's counsel is very wise. He suggested taking Jean in at once as solicitor general. Jean is weak but it might be as well to let the province see that I was standing by the men who had stood by me. This will be clear by taking in Jean. St. Laurent has come to the conclusion that taking any strong person—anyone like Gagnon—would be to antagonize an opposite group. In that I think he is right."

During the evening, Mackenzie King made final arrangements for La-Flèche's resignation and more or less decided he should go to Argentina as Ambassador. In fact, LaFlèche was appointed Ambassador to Greece on June 9.

Later the Prime Minister saw C. D. Howe and discussed the proposed Cabinet changes. Howe "thought Jean would be pretty weak but I told him there again was the question of loyalty. He pressed a little for Chubby, but I pointed out if I had taken Ralston there would have been trouble one way, now if I took Chubby there would be trouble in another way. I said there was nothing to do but to let friends see one could not tolerate that openly when he was leader. Howe said you are entirely right, I agree with that.

"He himself was for MacLaren of New Brunswick. He seemed a little surprised when I mentioned Chevrier. I suppose he does not like the thought of losing him before the Parliamentary stage is over."

Still later the Prime Minister had Abbott call at Laurier House. He noted that they "had a little talk in front of the fire which I had put in the library. I repeated to him how splendidly he had done—how pleased everyone was. He said he had enjoyed it when he got in and saw what a fine record we had. I then turned to him and said "Abbott, to come to the point, I would like to have you come into the Government. I will probably ask you tomorrow. He at once said that was a very great honour. He thanked me for it. Said he did not know whether he should be in politics, but that he liked public life. I said I thought he had a very fine career ahead of him. He spoke also of his riding being difficult. I told him I had been sorry at the time that I took Claxton in to have passed over him. But I was glad now that I could see my way to bring him in. I said I would bring Chevrier to keep the balance of the French and English proportions in the Cabinet.

"We talked a little of Ralston. He said Ralston was in very good shape now. Seemed to be quite determined to get back to his practice. He had been a little stirred up when McNaughton spoke against him in the West but was in a better frame of mind now. He said he was a fine fellow and honourable. But also said quite frankly that it was Ralston who got us all in this mess. I said I did not like Ralston having made the statement he did when he landed in Canada on his return from England, when he said he would get conscription or leave the government, and that Power himself had said he could not agree to that. Abbott said he should not have taken that stand. I told him about the palace rebellion aspect. He thinks McNaughton is a splendid fellow but a little more the army commander than the civilian type of administrator. He does not think he is too good politically. He says he has got good men around him and has really got things in great shape. I then said to Abbott that I wanted him to become Minister of Defence for Naval Affairs. He could bring one of his gunboats to Montreal. I told him that Macdonald a year ago had said to me he was going to get out and had said so at different times since, long before the Ralston incident and of course since had been referring to his intention to leave. About Ralston I said there would be time later on when a post could be considered for him of a judicial character. He [Abbott] said that he would be very proud to be in the government and in an administration of which I was the head even if he was in for only a short time."

April 17 was another day of consultation about the Cabinet shuffle. Mr. King went to see Mulock at the hospital and urged him "not to think of dropping out but just of resting even if it meant doing so over the entire election." For a time, it looked "as if I could not take Paul Martin in if I had Chevrier who is, in many ways, the more attractive personality of the two and would be very helpful in Quebec, as well as in Ontario. Martin, on the other hand, very good with Labour—somewhat ponderous but forward looking with ideas. Taking them both in adds to the number of Catholics in the Province but the same numbers over the entire Dominion —Chevrier would offset Michaud, and Martin would offset LaFlèche.

"I had a long talk with Michaud who said all were practically agreed on MacLaren whom he thinks is a sure winner in Saint John, N.B., and will help very much with the entire province. He apparently is a man of considerable means and has given his time continuously since the last war, in the public service; lost one of his legs in the war. Has been head of movement for Victory Loan campaigns; has served on boards, commissions, etc. I am told his wife is a very charming person. While Michaud was there, I tried to get in touch with him by 'phone. He was then between Fredericton and Saint John. Michaud arranged to get him up by 'plane tomorrow. I got him on the 'phone tonight at 9.15. Told him over the 'phone that I hoped to have him come into the administration. That I found all were united on him. He was very nice in the way he spoke. Expressed warm appreciation of the honour. Said he would put his best effort into it. Do all he possibly could. I arranged to see him in the morning. He hopes to arrive about noon. My mind feels immensely relieved at this appointment."

The Prime Minister then telephoned Howe who had just arrived in Washington with Gardiner. "I told Howe about MacLaren, the choice being Transport or National Revenue. I spoke of Chevrier for Transport and MacLaren for National Revenue. He thought perhaps MacLaren would be better in Transport. It was a heavy dept. but he agreed National Revenue needed to have someone with strength there and was quite agreeable to my deciding on whichever portfolio I thought best of the two. He saw much to commend MacLaren for National Revenue at present. I told him of thinking of Jean for Solicitor General and said that I might take Martin in because I needed a Minister in Western Ontario as well as Chevrier. He thought this was the wise thing to do."

Mackenzie King later had a talk with Brooke Claxton who "asked me if I had made up my mind between Chevrier and Paul Martin. When I stated that I did not see how I could take Martin in as well as Chevrier, he spoke of Martin's value with labour.

"In talking with St. Laurent later in the afternoon, he suggested that I might as well appoint Jean Solicitor General and let him act as Minister of Justice in his, St. Laurent's absence. That would please the average run of the members in the House. They were inclined to feel they had no chance. That men came along like Claxton and Abbott and were taken in, and that there would be no hope for the others as long as I picked only the most brilliant men. Jean is honourable; also he helped to save the day when Ralston nearly broke the government. He gave up his parliamentary assistant position and deserves to be remembered. It will let the province of Quebec see that I am remembering those that were loyal and were not afraid to stand by me, by making it plain to everyone that in both ministerial and Senate appointments, I do not intend to give preference to those who left the government or who did not support it outright, above those who stayed with us, simply because they think they may have greater political power. Also I am making plain that I do not intend to have at my side as an adviser and counsellor and future law maker, etc., any one who up to this moment has not found it possible to say that he was prepared to stand at my side in the open and defend the position that I took, in the light of my 25 years of leadership."

Mackenzie King added that "during the evening, I 'phoned Paul Martin. Told him I was going to see him tomorrow. Believed I might have something to say that would be helpful. He spoke, appreciating very much my thought of him.

"I also 'phoned Dr. McCann a little earlier. Asked him to be on hand tomorrow. He will be, but his manner was anything but the kind of manner I like. Unfortunately he is really the only Irish Catholic sufficiently outstanding to bring into the government. Paul Martin would be regarded as a French rather than an English-speaking representative. He could offset in the Cabinet the loss that Catholics will receive through Michaud.

"Later in the evening, I had a talk with Godbout so as to have him feel friendly before I left. Let him see that I had only the friendliest feelings toward himself despite the stand that he and others had taken in Quebec. I let him know what I felt about taking others into the government at this time. He thinks there is nothing to be gained by trying to meet Cardin in any way; that so far as Power is concerned, he has lost much of his power but could be of help in organizing. Would be harmful if he tried to join with Cardin or to make a direct attack on the government but I have my doubts if he will do this.

"I doubted too very much if Cardin has the strength to lead a party. I have made all the approaches I intend to make. Godbout said he thought things looked very well in Quebec. The people were behind me. That is what he had told St. Laurent. St. Laurent has been splendid."

The Cabinet shuffle actually took place on April 18. The Prime Minister went to the office fairly early in the morning and sent for Paul Martin. "Told him of my intention to bring him in as Secretary of State. Paul seemed deeply moved. Spoke quite earnestly about how he had followed my career over many years and had sought to fashion his own in some measure upon it. I had not known until he told me that he had been at Harvard and that when he had gone there, the first thing he had done was to look up and see where I had lived as a student. He mentioned later that he and Mike Pearson (the present Ambassador), who had been one of his instructors at Toronto, had come up to L.H. together to wait to see me come out. Referred to other incidents which showed that he had been really interested in my life and work and had been influenced by it. He said that if application and work could help for success in the new position, he would do all that anyone could to that effect."

Lionel Chevrier came in next. "His eyes filled with tears and he could say nothing when I told him that I was delighted to be able to invite him into the Ministry. It was something I had hoped to be able to do for a long time and was glad to have him as a colleague. He spoke very earnestly and nicely. Thanked me in a very sincere way. Said he would do all he possibly could. I told him that there would have to be readjustments of portfolios later but that I was debating between National Revenue and Transport. He was quite prepared to tackle either but said he doubted if he would be as good in National Revenue as he might be in the other field. When I 'phoned Howe yesterday, he was not too sure whether MacLaren should be in Transport or in National Revenue. Finally he had agreed with me that National Revenue might be best for MacLaren because of need of having matters pressed along a little more rapidly there."

Mackenzie King's next visitor was Dr. McCann who, he wrote, "has not the pleasantest manner; is a bit dour. Not too gracious but he naturally was pleased. When I mentioned [National] War Services, I spoke of it having to do with radio which he had been concerned about; also Red Cross and war drives and the like—that there would have to be changes later on, and that the Dept. itself might have to disappear but other adjustments would come. He asked me one or two questions as to what was included. I said for the present the main thing was to meet certain classes of problems that came with re-adjustment, etc. I referred to what he had said in one of the Caucus meetings about the need of Irish Catholic representation. Told him I was bringing him in in that connection. As a matter of fact I had worried quite a little about having both Chevrier and McCann from Eastern Ontario. Mitchell, Mulock and Gibson are all from central Ontario and no one from Western Ontario. I saw no escape from bringing Martin in from Western Ontario. This means three Catholics. However, with Michaud dropping out and adding another Protestant in the person of Abbott of Montreal, the balance seemed to adjust properly. However I felt it was absolutely necessary to have Irish Catholic representation.

"The last one I sent for was Jean. A very quiet, nice, pleasant fellow; most unassuming. Told him I had appreciated his action at the time of the crisis last December and always remembered the way he had helped that situation. That I was going to revive the portfolio of Solicitor General and also take him into the Ministry. That I might even have him act as Minister of Justice while Mr. St. Laurent was away."

The scene at the Cabinet was described by Mackenzie King in his diary. "It was," he wrote, "just 12 when I got up from my seat in my office to go to the Cabinet Council. Ministers were all seated around the table. I spoke of the duty at the moment not being an easy one to perform. It meant giving up some associations that had lasted over the years. I said that as they were aware, I was making the necessary reconstruction of the Cabinet. That I would like to read the letters of resignation received from the different Ministers. I said I had not had time to prepare replies; that if the chance came before I reached San Francisco, I might find it possible to do so but they would understand if I did not." The first letter he read was "Crerar's—which was nicely expressed and for which I thanked him in the presence of others. Next, Michaud's—which I also thanked him for and then Macdonald's. I made a slight acknowledgment. Obviously not as personal as that of the others as his letter had no personal reference to myself. I think he must have felt ashamed to have it read out—all about himself.

"Then a letter from McLarty for which I thanked him, and the letter from LaFlèche which he had got across quite early in the morning.

"I then signed the orders accepting the resignations of those who were retiring from the government. Mentioned to Council that it had been understood for some time that Crerar would be appointed to the Senate. Also that Michaud would be going to the Bench as Chief Justice of one of the divisions of the High Court in New Brunswick. I made no promises about other colleagues but expressed my appreciation to all for the assistance they had been and for their part in the government.

"I then mentioned the names of the new Ministers in the order in which they have since appeared.

"After speaking of Jean, Mackenzie raised the question as to whether the office had not been abolished. I turned to St. Laurent and asked him to explain what he had looked up and I stated also that I had Varcoe's opinion which I read. I said I thought it was desirable to have Jean act in the absence of Mr. St. Laurent. They had been associated together for so long, he was familiar with the Department.

"I then asked if Claxton should act in my absence in External Affairs. After passing all the orders-in-council appointing new Privy Councillors and Ministers, after I had gone through the list, Mackenzie said that as the senior Privy Councillor, he would like to say how sorry we were to part with any Ministers. It was pleasing to see there was no unpleasantness or recrimination of any kind and he extended wishes to them all. . . .

"I said to Mackenzie that he had given expression to what I had in mind saying as a parting word. I wished again to thank all for the help they had given in the work of the government over the years that we had been together. I then said: God bless you all—and left the table. Went to my own office to meet the press."

The reshuffled Cabinet met later in the afternoon to appoint a number of judges and senators. Among these was the appointment of Crerar as a Senator and Michaud as Chief Justice of the Supreme Court of New Brunswick, King's Bench Division. In welcoming the new members of the Cabinet the Prime Minister commented "that it felt like spring to be sitting there with young men around. I sensed the difference in the atmosphere in a moment. Was particularly glad to be free of Angus Macdonald."

The following day, April 19, the Prime Minister left for San Francisco after some busy hours. He met D. L. MacLaren at the station and drove him at once to Government House to be sworn in as Minister of National Revenue. This was probably the only time Mackenzie King accepted a colleague he could not remember having met. His first impression was "of a very positive type—perhaps a little too much of the forceful executive but quite obviously a character and many qualities of leadership. We shook hands at the Chateau. I thanked him for coming into the Ministry and he at once expressed appreciation of having been invited." Later Mackenzie King added that, when he took MacLaren into the Cabinet "it was quite apparent he felt no sense of awe; no feeling of awe in coming into the Cabinet Council. Recognized a good many of the Ministers. Went around and shook hands quite freely."

The Prime Minister also telephoned Ralston to speak to him about the appointment of a Senator from Prince Edward Island. He reported that Ralston "spoke very nicely. . . . Ralston told me he thought he was working hard in Ottawa but seemed to be working harder than ever now. Everything was going well. I told him I was looking forward to seeing him again before long. Sorry not to have had a talk during the Session. He could not have been pleasanter."

At the Cabinet meeting, "questions were raised as to relations with Hepburn—re arrangements, plans of campaign, etc. I said I thought each of us had better arrange our own campaign. Make pleasant references on the platform but not work out joint meetings, etc. though each one to do what was best." The Cabinet also took an historic decision at this meeting, a decision which indicated how quickly the war in Europe was coming to an end. The War Committee was abolished and it was decided that the Cabinet as a whole would devote one day a week to War Committee business.

In his diary for April 19, the Prime Minister repeated that he "found Council very much pleasanter with the younger men around the table. They must have thought I was much more dictatorial and determined than they had believed. I had not meant to speak out as much as I did. I felt before going away the occasion necessitated it. There is only one way of dealing with men who are not willing to co-operate and seek to force opposition, and that is to let them see that one will not be held up in that way. The idea that Power and Cardin should hold the Liberal party at bay after the treatment they have received, both of them having left the Cabinet of their own will, is simply preposterous. . . .

"I have been thinking seriously of appointing McGeer to the Senate to shake up the dry bones of the Upper Chamber, specially the influence of money in that quarter, banking interests, etc."

On this belligerent note the Prime Minister left for San Francisco to make the peace. The train left at 3.00 P.M. on April 19 and Mackenzie King and his party arrived in San Francisco on the morning of April 23.

CHAPTER TEN

San Francisco and the Election

AT THE SAN FRANCISCO CONFERENCE, which met from April 25 to June 26, 1945, and included representatives of fifty nations, the 1944 Dumbarton Oaks proposals formed the basis of the discussion which finally led to the drafting of the Charter of the United Nations. The Canadian delegation included Mackenzie King; Louis St. Laurent; Senator J. H. King, the Leader of the Government in the Senate; Senator Lucien Moraud; Gordon Graydon; M. J. Coldwell; and Mrs. C. T. Casselman, M.P. Assisting the delegation was an impressive battery of senior government officials including Norman Robertson; H. H. Wrong, Associate Under-Secretary of State for External Affairs; L. B. Pearson, Canadian Ambassador to the United States; Dana Wilgress, Canadian Ambassador to the Soviet Union; W. F. Chipman, Canadian Ambassador to Chile; Jean Désy, Canadian Ambassador to Brazil; and Major-General M. A. Pope, the Prime Minister's Military Staff Officer. James Gibson and J. W. Pickersgill, from the Prime Minister's office, also attended the conference.

In the early stages of his stay in San Francisco, Mackenzie King did not contribute very actively to the work of the Conference. One reason was his unwillingness to compete with Herbert Evatt of Australia as the vociferous champion of the middle-sized nations against the great powers. In addition, he was allergic to the San Francisco climate, had a frightful cold, and was obsessed for days with the necessity of making an effective radio broadcast on V-E day. When that effort was over, the Prime Minister became increasingly concerned about the forthcoming election. However, as the time for his departure grew nearer, it became obvious that his talents in reconciling differences could be exceedingly useful and in his last few days in San Francisco his contribution was effective and, perhaps, decisive.

Mackenzie King's fundamental attitude to the central problem of international security is well put in a brief diary entry for April 25, two days after his arrival. Lord Cranborne, the Secretary of State for the Dominions, called and they talked for well over an hour. "I stressed to him the difficult position we were in in Canada with regard to immediate commitments for sending men overseas. How impossible it would be for us to make any commitments as to military contribution for overseas and necessity of Parliament approving whatever contributions are to be made.

"I spoke of seeking to work out something in the nature of investigation [of threats to peace], leaving to public opinion the findings of the members of the Security Council as a last step before any attempt to consider the application of force. He said he thought well of the idea and would speak with Eden concerning it."

That afternoon Mackenzie King met Anthony Eden who had just arrived from Mexico. Eden presided at a meeting of heads of Commonwealth delegations and they had some discussion of procedure at the Conference. But, according to Mackenzie King, "the great feature of the afternoon was Eden reading to those of us who were present, a message that he had received this morning from Churchill and which really is the most significant that has, thus far, happened. In a word, it was to the effect that Himmler was now the real person in control. That he had approached the British through the Swedish diplomats for a complete surrender of all the Western front. Allegedly to enable the armies to fall into the hands of the British first. Himmler was told that this could not be considered. That any surrender would have to be to all. He was also told later that surrender would have to include Poland, Denmark and Norway.

"Here is the most remarkable bit of news of all. Himmler said that Hitler, if not dead now, will be dead tomorrow. That he had a cerebral haemorrhage and could not possibly live any time. It was this that had left Himmler in control. Hitler from now on meant nothing. He was completely gone. Eden proposed tonight to show to Molotov the wires that had come."

At a meeting of the chiefs of delegations in the morning of April 26, Mackenzie King made a useful contribution. "In the early discussions," he wrote, "where the use of language came up, I was able by citing our practice in the Canadian Commons, to have French as well as English made a working language. Speeches to be delivered in English or French in the Plenary Session. Both to be translated on the record of the following day. In Committees, French to be used as well as English as a working language. This suggestion was referred to as 'Mr. Mackenzie King's motion' and was accepted by the gathering, much to the satisfaction of Mr. Bidault, the French Minister, who had been much concerned about the language question, and to the satisfaction of most of the delegates. The intention had been to have only English used for working purposes. That would have been a great mistake."

The Prime Minister had difficulty in preparing what he wanted to say at the Plenary Session but finally, in the early afternoon of April 27, he made "an important revision" which brought out "our main point as to proper recognition of lesser powers." He "was very tired when the time came for me to speak at about a quarter past five. I also was perspiring very freely. My throat was not in good shape. I managed however to speak with considerable vigour and with only a slip at one or two places."

When Mackenzie King returned to his hotel from a luncheon with Eden on Saturday, April 28, he found most of the members of his staff listening to a broadcast stating the war was over and about to be so declared officially by President Truman at any moment. He was told something was being prepared for him to broadcast to Canada. When he was shown the material, he noted, it gave him a feeling of indignation to think this was "suggested as the expression of the Canadian people to her fighting forces at the moment of victory." "I would be damned forever in the eyes of the army and the Canadian people," he added, "if I let anything of the kind go as an expression of what Canada feels at this time.

"I was too tired when we came in to attempt any writing so decided to get a rest. First of all I went to bed for an hour and then got up and began to draft something for a broadcast to Canada. All the while I was told that at any moment the President would announce the end of the war.

"After being at work for about an hour, locating meanwhile a few very helpful phrases in some of my other speeches, I found myself far too fatigued to do any really constructive thought."

"After we had been at work for an hour word came that the report was a bit premature which fortunately eased one's mind very much. It means however that tomorrow, Sunday, may have to be given over to preparing the speech to be delivered. All of this work however is work which every member of the staff has been brought along to perform. I thank God I have enough soul in me left to desire at all costs to say the right things. I pray now above all for strength and vision to be able tomorrow to complete the task in a way worthy of the great moment to which it will have reference. I am certain at least of one thing, which is that I am right in putting emphasis on the thanks to God for His Mercy as revealed in the deliverance which has come at last from the evil forces of Nazi Germany."

Unhappily for all concerned, the task was not completed the next day and the agony of preparation and revision complicated by the Prime Minister's dissatisfaction, continued right up to the last moment. On Sunday (April 29) Mackenzie King worked all morning on the broadcast. After lunch he recorded: "I felt tremendously the need of some out-of-doors in the sun. First tried to have Mr. St. Laurent come for a drive along with Dr. King and Senator Moraud, but as St. Laurent had promised to join Graydon and Diefenbaker at lunch—why Diefenbaker is here I cannot think—I got Dr. King to come with H. and me." He enjoyed the drive and went right to bed after dinner.

The Prime Minister, on April 30, expressed interest and even satisfaction at the death of Mussolini. Later in the day he reflected: "If it be true that both Hitler and Mussolini are dead, it will now be true that of all who were leaders of governments when the war commenced and who were participants in the war, up to the time that Germany attacked Russia, I am the only one who remains the leader of his country. Indeed that is true also of the United States. Apart from Stalin, I would be the only original left on either side. I have, of course, led my party longer than Stalin has his." He also was encouraged that day by reports from Canada that the Liberal party's prospects were improving but added that "what causes me concern is how I shall ever get together the topics needed for speeches" in the campaign.

Part of May 1 was again devoted to the broadcast but he found "it difficult through weariness and noise to make much headway. What I did was at least my own—more in accord with what I felt was worthy of the events one was seeking to chronicle for one's country. It makes me really a little sad to see how little the men around me realize what they might be writing of lines that could become a part of Canada's literature, dealing with the greatest moment in her history. They all have youth on their side and should be more vigorous in mind." The following day he revised the entire broadcast "writing much of it anew" and then went over it with his secretaries. The revision apparently "was a trying business at the outset as criticism of much of the material which had been passed before, seemed to be carried unduly far." However, it was worth all the strain once the entire broadcast was completed.

"No one had thought of arranging to give the broadcast to the C.B.C. or having a copy sent on to Ottawa for release, until I spoke of it myself, nor did anyone think of preparations of a record in advance in case when the moment of broadcasting comes, it might be impossible to either reach the broadcasting station or have the use of the wires, once that end was achieved. Having brought up the matter, arrangements were subsequently made to get off transcript to Ottawa tonight; have translation made; also microphone installed in the dining room adjoining my sitting room, and everything in readiness for making of a record in the morning.

"Should the defeat of Germany be declared tomorrow, I will be ready to go on immediately following the address by the King. It has, however, been a back-breaking business and I have had to give up meeting with other delegates of the conference."

Once the broadcast text was finally settled and the recording made on May 3, Mackenzie King began to give increasing thought to the election campaign. He was very disturbed that W. P. Mulock had not been nominated in North York and tried, unsuccessfully, to get the decision reversed even after another candidate had been nominated.

On May 4, he decided to leave San Francisco on May 12 and have the first election meeting in Vancouver on Monday, the 14th. He planned to be in Prince Albert from the 17th to the 20th. "This, I believe, will help to ensure my election," he wrote. The next day (May 5) he was further encouraged. "From what I read in the papers and particularly from a letter shown me by St. Laurent from Bertrand, and what I gather from other sources, the party's fortunes are beginning to look much brighter in Canada. I have felt today for the first time that I might win in Prince Albert and there is much to make one believe that Quebec will come again pretty much my way." On May 6, he went over the speech material which had been prepared for Vancouver and Edmonton. "Alas," he wrote, "it was like all the other material—wholly inadequate. Not what is needed for a great political campaign. I am afraid that I cannot keep the Liberal standard at the height it should be at with no chance to prepare in advance. I shall have to have a little quiet to think out what I am to do and the role I am to play. One thing is certain. I do not intend to be hauled about from pillar to post but I can see there is a big strain ahead."

The entry in Mackenzie King's diary for May 7 begins: "I slept on the whole fairly well last night. At 7 o'clock precisely, Nicol came into my bedroom and asked if I were awake. He said Mr. Robertson was going to call me at 4 but did not like to ring the telephone in my room at that hour. He had an important message to give to me. It was that the war in Europe was over. I said to Nicol: that is good news, Thank God. I then turned on my side and uttered a prayer of thanksgiving and of rededication to the service of my fellow-men."

The first message he received that morning was the official telegram from London announcing that the surrender had taken place at 01.41 hours, but indicating that the announcement was not to be made until May 8. Mr. King's thoughts at this time were much of "Skelton and Rogers. A little later of Ernest Lapointe." The morning paper in San Francisco, however, had banner headlines announcing that the end of the war was official. A little later in the morning, Wrong came to tell Mackenzie King that he had been talking to Arnold Heeney in Ottawa who had reported "that the Cabinet had been meeting and thought no matter what happened, tomorrow should be declared a holiday. That already the news was everywhere on the streets in Ottawa and in Toronto.

"Gibson had come in a moment earlier with a message mostly concerned about the flying of the Canadian flag. I thought matters over very carefully recalling discussions and decisions in the Cabinet. Then dictated a telegram to the effect that I thought the moment Churchill broadcast the announcement, the Union Jack should be flown as usual from the top of the Peace Tower. That it should continue flying there until after the King had made his broadcast. Then when I followed with the broadcast to the Canadian people, the Canadian red ensign should be hoisted to the top of the mast and should continue flying throughout the remainder of the day and over the day of the national holiday. That this should be done as a tribute to the important part which Canada's armed forces had taken in the winning of the war in Europe. That when the holiday was over, the Union Jack should continue to fly as usual, my thought being that the question of having a Canadian national flag as the recognized flag at all times was one which Parliament itself should decide."

Mackenzie King then got Arnold Heeney on the telephone and agreed to designating May 8 a public holiday. "The unfortunate part is the uncertainty still of the time at which Churchill is to broadcast and the King to broadcast. What I made clear is that my broadcast to the people should not come until after the King himself had broadcast unless the King were to let a day elapse in between."

This uncertainty continued throughout the morning and between 11 and 12, Mackenzie King sent word to Lord Cranborne suggesting he would not go to the luncheon to which he had been invited, because it might be necessary for him to stay at his hotel to broadcast. Word came back to ask him to come anyway, if possible. He finally went to the luncheon and later to the Committee on the Security Council where he stayed from 3 to 6.

Mackenzie King noted that "Robertson spoke in the afternoon about the flag. He also raised the question as to whether once the Red Ensign was flying it should not be kept up. I pointed out that a resolution from Parliament was the proper course to take to settle that question.

"I felt annoyed when on coming downstairs, after having asked G. to prepare a paragraph to add to my speech regarding the flag, he used the expression 'the Canadian flag.' He must have known that we have no Canadian flag; that is the whole source of controversy. It would be putting the Prime Minister in an appalling position to raise a flag issue of the kind at this moment. I am protecting the government and myself by making it clear that the Canadian Red Ensign is being hoisted for V-E Day and until sunset on Thanksgiving Day as a tribute to the men in the fighting forces who have used that flag on the battlefields of Europe. Having the Canadian Red Ensign fly in this way for an entire week, there is little doubt that once the soldiers begin returning with that flag, it will be accepted as the flag of Canada.

"I also felt a little indignant and hurt at the way in which Pickersgill shot at me that I would not think of taking down the flag once it had been up. Really a piece of impertinence for any member of a staff to speak in that way to a Prime Minister. I let him know pretty directly that the government had a certain responsibility to Parliament, and that I intend to see that it would be by a resolution of Parliament, not by an arbitrary act of a Prime Minister or a government without previous authority, that the question of the national flag of Canada would be settled. I cannot imagine anything that would provoke more bitter controversy and feeling at this moment than an endeavour to seize this occasion to force a flag on the Canadian people.

"I had sent telegrams earlier in the day but I found on returning to the hotel that Heeney had 'phoned to say that having made arrangements in accordance with the first message which was to hoist the flag after my speech, the Cabinet did not think the arrangements should be changed, but that the flag should be kept flying until Sunday. I seized at once upon the latter suggestion but decided to ring up Heeney at once and tell him to notify the Public Works to hoist the Canadian Red Ensign at sunrise to-morrow morning and to keep it flying until sunset on the night of the day of thanksgiving. To state that this was being done at my request, and as a tribute to the men of the armed forces who had used the Red Ensign in fighting their battles in Europe. I am sure I have got matters in such shape by this message that no exception can be taken to flying our own flag at this time, and that this step will lead to the Red Ensign becoming the national flag of the Dominion. During the campaign, I will advocate our having a national flag of our own."

After seeing to these arrangements, Mackenzie King drafted a number of messages about the end of the war and then began to worry about the campaign. "I began to see," he wrote, "it would be impossible to hope to speak in Vancouver on Monday night, so telegraphed Vancouver, Edmonton and Prince Albert of my intention to alter the schedule. I am convinced the only thing to do is to remain here till I have the speeches ready for delivery at these points. I will have no chance to prepare once I leave this hotel. I now am planning to leave about perhaps Tuesday or Wednesday of next week which will give me part of Saturday and Sunday to do some work. I believe I am gaining more political capital by participating actively in work here in San Francisco than I would be making by speeding back and forth across Canada, speaking at meetings, being badly prepared, etc.

"I got off a message to Prince Albert constituency agreeing to accept nomination if offered at the meeting which I understand is to be held on Friday of this week. No one has sent me specific word about it. I have only seen the announcement of the meeting in a newspaper item. Tonight, I believe I shall win that constituency. This victory in Europe is going to help immensely in the campaign. I am entitled to some credit for the timing." He was cheered later in the evening by word that Cardin was giving up his attempt to start a separate political movement.

On May 8 Mackenzie King got up before six o'clock in the morning and began listening to the radio. He listened to "President Truman's broadcast formally announcing the end of the war and later re-broadcast of Churchill's speech of which I think we only got a part. His voice sounded natural and vigorous. I was glad to hear him on this particular day. What he said was mostly in the nature of a record of aspects of the surrender. . . .

"When I turned the radio off about 7, I slept very soundly till half past eight and then breakfast and reading. Was particularly impressed by the little verse for today: 'This is the day which the Lord hath made; we will rejoice and be glad in it.' Could anything be quite as appropriate for V-E day!

"I did not attend meeting with members of the Canadian delegation. There is really nothing to be discussed there. The whole purpose is to keep the group in good humour.

"Had a short talk with Ian Mackenzie about Vancouver meeting, arrangements of which he had pretty well underway for Monday next. He accepted quite readily suggestion of change to Wednesday. This is a great relief to me. I am sure I am right in making certain that broadcast and outline of speeches for coming week are all completed before I leave San Francisco. I should at least be able to work on them most of Saturday and Sunday. Also advisable to be a little longer at the Conference here.

"I attended the meeting, this morning, of the Executive of the Conference. Mr. Stettinius, Chairman, and other members, were delayed over half an hour. They had been stuck in an elevator in the Fairmont Hotel for nearly that period of time. The elevators in the hotels here are much too small and always overcrowded.

"The morning's proceedings were given over to taking photos; discussing procedure, methods of voting etc. Most of the discussion of a trivial nature. There was one minute given to standing in silent dedication in appreciation of the day.

"I got back from the meeting a little before time to get the King's speech over the radio. I thought it was delivered with less hesitation than any I have heard thus far. It was a good speech. Eden had wanted me to join other delegations from the Commonwealth at his hotel. Word came later that they would like to send a message to the King. The idea had been to have all the Commonwealth delegations listen to the speech together and have Eden send a message to the King in the name of all, immediately thereafter. Robertson suggested it would be better for me to send a message on behalf of our own delegation, members of staff who had listened to the broadcast at the Hotel. This I did. It made possible getting through some work and saving more time than standing about, climbing hills, etc. Eden, Smuts and others made short broadcasts in connection with B.B.C. broadcast.

"I went on the air at about 17 past 12. Was followed by St. Laurent. We each spoke with a good deal of vigour. I am told the broadcast had the largest coverage of any the C.B.C. has thus far given to anyone. It included the entire Canadian network, U.S. national network and short-wave to Britain, also to sailors and soldiers. It was supposed to have gone to all the battlefronts."

From a political point of view, Mackenzie King felt, "a broadcast of the kind is worth more than two weeks' campaigning on party matters. Certainly all things are working together for good so far as the campaign itself is concerned. The Vancouver papers report today that Cardin has dropped his movement though he is running himself in Sorel.

"A wonderful message came from Churchill on Canada's contribution to victory. I have read nothing equal to it. I am sure Churchill had in mind not only feelings of gratitude which he entertains but, in this way, lending a hand in the present campaign."

In the afternoon of May 10 the Prime Minister attended a meeting of the Committee on the Security Council which was discussing "the means of securing consultation and representation on Security Council by smaller countries before they were asked to further the enforcement of sanctions, etc. The speech by a New Zealand delegate gave me a chance to get Canada's case before the Committee. I was tremendously relieved to have this opportunity. I was sorry to read the statement I had but it would be all the better for the record. I now feel that having stated Canada's position so clearly my leaving here early next week does not matter so much. I moved an amendment which Wrong had drafted hurriedly to the speech by the New Zealand representative, which went, I thought, a little too far in that it meant that the Assembly might weaken the power of the Security Council. . . . When I concluded it was suggested we leave over discussion of the matter till tomorrow morning."

He reported that "Smuts tonight wanted me to confer with him, New Zealand and Australia in the morning at 9. I had to put that off because of the meeting with our delegation. This reminds me that a couple of days ago Smuts said to me that the King was anxious to recognize Churchill in some way. Hoped he would accept the Garter, but that he did not wish to take any action if he, Smuts, and I would have any objection to it. I said that the question of the Garter for Churchill was purely a United Kingdom matter. Personally I felt nothing was too good for Churchill—anything that he might want or that the King might wish to confer, well and good. . . . He had the highest honour that a nation could pay in the confidence they had shown in him. He would in my opinion be much wiser if he were to drop out altogether, now that the war in Europe is over, though he might stay to finish up the war with Japan. Eden told me confidentially this morning that he would probably have to leave at the end of the week. Churchill was plastering him with wires, about wishing him to come back and to be present for important decisions. I said I was sure Churchill would not wish to delay the elections now that victory had been achieved. I thought he would bring on the elections soon. Indeed, he had told me once that such was his intention. My own view is that he will bring them on just as soon as he can be sure of having Eden, Attlee and others back in Britain.

"Eden told me he had heard things were going much better for me in Canada. He was glad this was so. Certainly, at the present time, the opinion seems to be coming in from different sides that the Liberal Administration would be returned. Turnbull told me that Coldwell had mentioned that the stock of the Liberal Party was going steadily up. I think there is no doubt that Bracken's stock has gone steadily down. Also that the C.C.F. is not what it was. Without question the victory and the broadcast from here will have helped very materially."

The next day (May 11) Mackenzie King met Eden at lunch, who told him "he was leaving either tomorrow early or Sunday. He rather hinted that Churchill was anxious to make a real decision; that they were debating whether with conditions in Europe what they are, coalition should try to hold together longer or have the campaign at once. He said he was anxious to get it over with. I told him I thought Churchill would certainly be anxious for an immediate campaign and that I thought he would be wise in not letting too long a time slip by after victory.

"I asked him to tell Churchill how much I appreciated the message from him. That there was nothing left unthought of or unsaid. That I recognized behind it all a desire to help all in the campaign."

At the end of the diary for the day, Mackenzie King reported that "Eden told me confidentially at the meeting last night that he was, at that moment, drafting a wire to Churchill strongly advising him to bring on his campaign at once. That a situation might develop in the next month or two which would make the position of the British Government much more difficult. He thought the sooner the campaign could be brought on, the better. This,

I am sure, accords with Churchill's own views, and I would not be surprised to see him fix the campaign for before the end of June."

On May 11 Mackenzie King went to General Smuts's apartment at the Fairmont Hotel and met with the Australian Minister of External Affairs, Herbert Evatt; the Prime Minister of New Zealand, Peter Fraser; and Frank Forde, the Australian High Commissioner to Canada.

"Smuts seemed to feel in a sort of casual way that to give interested countries a chance to be on the council for consultation would be enough without sitting as temporary members with voting powers. I said I would tell them my position in a word or two and gave them the lowdown that when Ralston had returned from Europe and insisted on conscription, I pointed out that he was taking a step which would help to make exceedingly difficult what lay nearest to the heart of the President and Churchill, namely, the United Nations World Security Organization. I said had we gone through the war without conscription, I could have had the Canadian House of Commons agree to any step almost which might have been proposed in connection with the organization. Now I did not see how it was possible to agree to a step which meant conscription of a nation's forces at the instance of four or five outside great powers. I doubted if such a charter with such a provision would ever be accepted by our Parliament. I said I thought what the Great Powers should be interested in should be in having as many countries as possible in the organization and as quickly as possible. That we were in a special position in that we, of the Dominions, claimed to have a friend in the United Kingdom on the Council which could defend our position with its veto, but there were other nations such as Turkey, Holland, Belgium, etc., which were differently situated. I doubted if they could get ratification for a charter which took the step that was being proposed. I spoke of how difficult it had been for us to come to concede the veto of the five Great Powers. We had worked ourselves into the view of granting it. Members of Parliament and certainly the country did not grasp the significance of that step as yet. It would come to them as a shock. I referred to how reciprocity was defeated between the United States and Canada after our Government had worked on this problem for two years and felt we had a sure thing.

"Smuts saw this very quickly. I think he was impressed by what I said.

"It was then suggested by Fraser and others we should all meet with Eden tonight and discuss with him before he leaves, matters we had been discussing today. This was subsequently arranged for 11 o'clock tonight."

He attended the meeting with Eden in Lord Cranborne's apartment from 11 P.M. until nearly 1 A.M. "The question of trusteeship was discussed," he wrote. "I took little part in that. Then question of position of countries not on the Security Council and desirability of their having opportunity for discussion and vote, where security enforcement action is expected of them. There were present all heads of delegations from the British Commonwealth and advisers. Cranborne seemed pretty well tired out and I felt sorry for Eden being kept up to that hour.

"It was hard to do much in the way of clear thinking. The discussion may have done some good but I doubt if it did much good."

Apparently it did more good than Mackenzie King realized at the time. The day he left San Francisco (May 14) he went at 11 A.M. to see Stettinius by appointment. Hickerson [of the U.S. State Department] was present. "The interview," he felt, "was a most important one. Mr. Stettinius began by asking me how I thought things were going. I replied it necessarily took a little time to get everything sorted out. I did not see serious difficulties ahead except with regard to smaller powers being represented on the Security Council when matters affecting sanctions and their own interests were being considered. I stated that I thought in drafting the Dumbarton Oaks proposals and what had been done since, those working on the revisions had more in mind a plan which could be followed once the organization was formed but little in mind what was necessary to get approval of the charter in the first instance. I thought it was very essential to get into the charter itself something that would be reassuring to the smaller powers, when approval of the charter was being worked out. I said Mr. Churchill must have had a real reason for saying what he had yesterday, namely, that care must be taken to see that the United Nations organization was not made a shield for the strong and a mockery for the weak. That this was really the position as it now stood in reference to enforcement of sanctions. I enlarged on the process and both Hickerson and Mr. Stettinius agreed that they could not hope to get approval of Congress if they were placed in a like position to Canada under the provisions as they stand. Hickerson then said that he would make a suggestion just as an individual himself which was that when we were undertaking a quota or setting forth what we would be prepared to do in the way of supplying forces, we might make it a provision before the forces themselves would actually be employed, that Parliament would have to approve. I at once said that would not do at all. In the first place, we did not want to get out of doing our just share. All that we wanted to do was to be able to assure our people of the fairness of what we were being asked to do. Were I to take the line suggested even tentatively by Hickerson, it would at once be said in our country that I was doing so to appease those who were not anxious to fight and that the country would become divided on the issue. Hickerson mentioned that the situation was a serious one for me as I had an election on.

"I replied that if the question became an issue in any election and the Government were defeated, it would certainly prejudice the chances of ratification of the charter in other countries. Mr. Stettinius said that the difficulty of meeting our position was that it would mean so many powers being represented on the Security Council particularly if the provision was to apply to countries providing facilities as, for example, allowing troops to pass through their territories, etc.

"I said I saw no difficulty on that score. That it seemed to me the proper procedure was for the Security Council on the basis of advice of military advisers to determine and decide that certain forces were necessary. The next step was organization of forces. When that step was being taken, if it was proposed to take a division say from Canada, Canada should be asked to come and sit on the Security Council as a member and vote in the Security Council. If there were other countries that felt they were affected or were being called, they would not sit on the Security Council at the same time but could come in when their turn came. In other words, if the Council was composed of 11, there would be only an addition of one when voting took place. If the Council could not get a majority in those circumstances, there would be grounds for believing something really was wrong. I pointed out it might be helpful for the Council itself knowing of reasons whether a certain step was appropriate or not appropriate. Something they might not have thought of, for example, differences between South American Republics. The United States might not wish to use its own forces. We might prefer to have Canada's forces used rather than those from some European countries. However if they were to be used against certain countries that were largely French, it might be a mistake to have Canadian troops sent in. These were only possibilities but they helped to illustrate what I had in mind. On the other hand, Canada being represented as a nation on the Security Council, to present its case there would enable its representatives to return to their own country and explain why forces of that particular country were being requested and could state if he had had a vote, that he had been over-ruled and that the majority rule must carry.

"Hickerson and Stettinius both seemed much relieved at this suggestion. They said at once it seemed to afford a way out. They asked me if Robertson had prepared anything in words. I said I did not know that he had but that we had been discussing the matter at our delegation meeting this morning and all had approved of the idea as I had expressed it.

"Hickerson said he would get in touch with Robertson and would get the position reduced to writing. I left with the distinct impression that the matter was settled so far as their agreeing to this step was concerned."

In the Prime Minister's opinion "the British have been talking with Stettinius since my meeting with Eden and Cranborne and Smuts and this appointment by Stettinius was to bring matters to a conclusion. I kept emphasizing that the absence of anything of the kind from the charter which could be pointed to when the measure was before the House, would be a very serious handicap. There was great advantage in having something to point to that would be reassuring.

"Stettinius asked me if I could think of any way of hastening the proceedings [of the Conference]. I told him I would allow a certain time for speeches at the Plenary Session, say five minutes or ten minutes, and then if there was more to be said, have it handed in in writing. Indeed this could be done with Committees. What delegates were interested in was letting their people know what they had said. Hickerson said same step might be taken as was done with Congressional Record. This seemed to be a helpful suggestion.

"I then said to Stettinius I had another suggestion which was that the signing of the charter should be in duplicate in case one copy should be lost. I asked if it would not be possible to have one copy at Washington which could be signed there instead of delegates having to come all the way to San Francisco for the purpose. I said I regarded it of first importance to have Molotov's signature on the charter; also Eden's, even if the charter had to be taken to Russia and Britain for the purpose. Those were the names that would count for the future. Mr. Stettinius said they had been considering the matter of signature. He thought the idea of making sure of Molotov's signature a good one. He then said: we must have your signature. I said I would like to sign but it was going to be very difficult for me to find the time to come back. He then asked me what I had in mind. I told him of the tour from Vancouver to Halifax; making several broadcasts—about ten or fifteen speeches in all.

"He then said: now may I speak of something very confidential. This is between the three of us. If I could get President Truman to come and close the Conference, would you come and be here with him? We would have the two heads of Government together. You would be photographed together and would become the central feature of the signing. We would do anything to get you here. I would supply a plane. Do you not think that that would mean even more to you politically than by staying in the country campaigning? I said at once I thought I well might do this. That one of the greatest assets I had in the public life of Canada had been my friendship with President Roosevelt. It would be very helpful to me to have the public see that I was carrying on that friendship with President Truman. Stettinius pressed the point very strongly as being something he thought would mean very much both to the Conference, the charter and myself in the campaign. I said to him that sitting here, it was easy to say I might be able to arrange it. In the last week or so of the campaign, I might find it almost impossible to get away.

"He then said: we must be through here by the end of May so that it would not be the last week. He continued to urge me very strongly and said he would not ask me to come unless President Truman were also coming to close the Conference. As he spoke, I had in mind what Roosevelt had said to me at one time, he did not know whether he should come to open the Conference or to close it. I had told him I thought the opening was the important thing. He said: You could come only for an hour or so. Could come by 'plane. Flying is very fatiguing. To fly from Ottawa to San Francisco is a greater distance than across to England. To do that both ways in the campaign would be a very heavy strain and tax. It might nevertheless be the most important step I could take in the campaign to win popular approval and to have the nation realize the influence that I have and the position in which I am held by the Government of the United States which is undoubtedly the most powerful Government in the world today. So there is that ahead."

Mackenzie King felt that the talk with Stettinius "had done no end of good. It has really meant victory for the smaller nations in the fight that was being made for their recognition on the Security Council. My part has been done quietly, unobtrusively but effectively behind the scenes. . . .

"I said on coming away that I regretted not having been able to be of much help. That I was pretty tired out when I came. He told me I had been of the greatest help and thanked me warmly for it. I have noticed that all the time I have been at San Francisco, Americans have paid me very special attention. There is no courtesy they have not extended."

Mackenzie King had been greatly touched on May 12 to receive a letter from Sidney Smith, then Principal of University College at the University of Toronto; it contained these paragraphs which were copied into the diary: 'We of University College rejoice in the celebration of the 50th anniversary of your graduation. You have brought the highest honours to your College and University. Your outstanding public service will serve as an example to future generations in this Institution. . . .

" 'It may well be that having regard to the election, you will be unable to be with us [at the Annual Dinner on June the 8th]. We trust that such will not be the case. If it is, your old classmates and all of us of University College, nevertheless, will be felicitating the most distinguished graduate of the Institution.'

"I almost broke down when I read the words of the last sentence, thinking first of the joy these words would have brought to my father but even more how little truth, in reality, there was in them, whatever there might be to appearances because of position. I have not measured up to my job as I should have and would have, had I gone about it more in earnest from the start."

On May 12 and again on May 13, Mackenzie King tried to settle down to work on his Vancouver speech which was to be the national broadcast opening the campaign. After three hours' writing by hand on Sunday, the 13th, he noted: "I see my way now if I get an early start in the morning or any time to myself during the day to get material sufficiently under way to be sure of having the broadcast in readiness by the time that we reach Vancouver. No one will ever know what a relief this is to my mind. I have been almost beside myself at the thought of having a great message to give the people but without the time to prepare it or the mental vigour to throw it into shape. I can only account for the progress made today as an answer to prayer and the efficacy of prayer."

He left San Francisco by train without getting any more work done on the speech. In his diary on the day of departure (May 14) he wrote: "In one way, I am naturally sorry not to be here for another fortnight and seeing the Conference through. I would have enjoyed it immensely, had there been no special demands on my time in Canada. On the other hand, I am far from sorry to leave San Francisco and the Conference; in the condition of fatigue which I am in, I find the whole business very trying. I dislike the City intensely because of it having no boulevard or parks; the way in which human beings are housed in every square inch of space along streets, on either side of a hard pavement. No place for children to play, no sign of verdure of any kind. Then the noise from the out-of-doors, cable cars, horns and the like. The weather, most uncertain. I am glad I will not have to participate in debate further. Have stayed long enough to get my position thoroughly understood and stated. It has been wise to wait until today—wise from the point of view of the Conference and point of view of elections. Nominations were today. I understand we have candidates in practically all the seats. Also I was pleased to learn that the Victory Loan had been a success."

The Prime Minister and his party arrived in Vancouver after midnight on May 15. The whole of the next day was devoted to the preparation of the broadcast with "only a cup of tea and a slice of chicken at 2." Although he took out three pages of his text it still proved to be too long and the concluding paragraphs were not broadcast.

Mackenzie King spoke in the large ballroom in the Hotel Vancouver, which was crowded with people. When he entered, he was given a tremendous ovation. To him it was "a moment of elation. When I began to broadcast I found it very easy, indeed a real pleasure to broadcast for such a splendid audience. The audience listened very attentively to introductory remarks and applauded quite enthusiastically practically all of the points as I went along.

"At the conclusion, another splendid ovation. I confess in writing the broadcast and in delivering it, I myself was surprised how the years have passed and what my own record of public service has really been."

He was particularly glad "to get through without having to touch upon problems of the Japanese war. That point was not mentioned to me in the course of my whole visit."

After calling on the Governor-General and Princess Alice in their private car at the C.P.R. Station, Mackenzie King drove with Gerry McGeer to his house. "Greatly enjoying the beauty of the scenery en route. Vancouver is a lovely city. A tremendous contrast to San Francisco. McGeer has a lovely home. A magnificent dogwood tree all in white." During this visit McGeer made a delicate reference to the Senate vacancy for British Columbia.

On Friday evening, the Prime Minister spoke in Edmonton at a dinner in the Macdonald Hotel. The first half hour was prepared and broadcast and he spoke for another half hour extemporaneously "really enjoying the pleasure of talking in a free and off hand manner."

While he was in Edmonton he spent some time with Arnold Heeney who had flown from Ottawa to consult the Prime Minister about a "statement regarding the forces going to Japan. . . . He read over to me the statement which had been approved by Council. I did not even wait to re-read it myself. Approved it at once. Later Arnold talked with Mc-Naughton over the 'phone about it. McNaughton had been sent a copy by wire. He approved it all adding just a few words 'and armour.' He told Arnold to tell me he thought things were going well and that at [his campaign] meetings, there were about 200 present and 30 or 40 at meetings of his opponents. Like all men who are new in politics, McNaughton may be judging too much by appearances, not realizing that many of those who were attending meetings were doing so because of his name and fame but would stick to the old Tory organization in the end. Heeney thinks he intends to stay in the campaign till the end of it. I thought of having him speak in different parts of the country but it may be as well for him to be kept out of the centre of controversy during the campaign.

"Arnold brought some other information, including telegram sent from President Truman inviting me to pay a visit to the White House before June 11, indicating he was anxious to have the same close relations with myself as President Roosevelt had had. This means either paying a visit to Washington or a visit to San Francisco before our elections are over. I am sure a visit would help politically but I regret not having a chance to make further direct appeals to the people of Canada. I think the meetings I am holding and the broadcasting are really effective. If the people I talked to have matters sized up rightly, an upward swing for the party would appear to be setting in. Some said to me it began with my speech in San Francisco on V-E Day. That speech seems to have created a great impression."

On May 19 Mackenzie King reached Prince Albert by train. He was very tired after the week's travelling and meetings and had no prepared text. "After dinner," he wrote, "went through material to prepare a sort of outline for the evening address. Unfortunately I never got to where I could arrange my thoughts in a consecutive order. Dr. Humphries took me over to the Armouries. I found myself tired out. When I saw the size of the audience which pretty well filled the Armouries, I recognized that it was going to be a great effort to speak.

"At about 20 to 9, Dr. Humphries introduced me. What he said was fine in itself and received repeated applause but was not well delivered. When I got up to speak, I found the minute I opened my lips, that I was done out and that it was going to be an effort from beginning to close. I found it difficult to follow what I had in my mind to say and indeed made a poor fist of the opening part of the speech. Found it necessary to put on my glasses and throughout felt at every turn, I was making a very special effort. There were no light touches. I had no joy in what I was saying. Took up the time with my record on labour matters. Did this deliberately as I thought the vote to be influenced in Prince Albert was the Labour vote.

"Nothing could have been finer than the audience, in numbers, appearance, attentiveness, etc. There was not a single interruption and very considerable applause. I felt, however, that I was not giving to the different things I said the kind of right and intimate touch which I had been able to give in addresses at Vancouver and Edmonton. Indeed I realized that I had made the mistake I had been seeking to guard against, not having time for rest and being overcrowded. From now on, at all events, I must avoid being jammed up against so much and without adequate rest. I should have made a very memorable and appealing speech tonight but disappointed myself, and I am sure fell far short of the impression that should have been created on this occasion. At the same time, I think the meeting has done good and I really feel from what I have seen and heard, that I am going to carry the constituency. The fact that there are three opponents, none too strong, also that some leading Conservatives have already indicated their intention to support me, and that our own party is getting pretty well lined up, and that the C.C.F. have been losing ground, causes me to feel that all may be well. I find, too, that the people have been following my work and career with interest and they have in mind the service that I have rendered during the period of the war. Indeed there has been nothing seen or heard today which makes me feel that there is not a decidedly friendly feeling toward myself, and a certain sense of pride in my representation of the constituency. All of this makes me terribly sorry at not being equal to a really first class address tonight which I could easily have delivered had I not been quite tired out after the reception."

On Sunday (May 20), Mackenzie King went to church in the morning and afterwards visited the Victoria Hospital with his campaign manager, Dr. Humphries. "I was a bit surprised and taken aback when he told me that Coldwell had arranged a meeting here for the 8th—for some day near the end of the campaign; almost at the close of it. He asked me if I would approve of the Committee having Hepburn speak one night. He, the Doctor, had already spoken to Hepburn in the East, and Hepburn had said he would be glad to come. I told him that on no account did I wish Hepburn to speak. That I doubted very much if he would improve his position in Ontario. Even if he did, I did not want him in my campaign, in my own seat. The Doctor then spoke of McGeer. I said I would welcome McGeer wholeheartedly. He would be better able to answer Coldwell than anyone else, but not to have Hepburn on any account. He says the Committee are in doubt as to what to do about a meeting. They don't want a poor affair. Coldwell should be important but they think it necessary to answer Coldwell if that can be done by the right person.

"I agreed to have no meeting at all unless they had a really good speaker. I do pray that things do not get badly mixed up in the constituency between now and the end of the campaign. The most delicate of all features is that there are two different groups of Liberals—an old group whom the Doctor is inclined to ignore, and those whom the Doctor has gathered around himself. He is pretty strong willed and determined, but Stevenson, Duncan and others are helping as conciliators and I believe are getting things under way."

The next two days were spent in the constituency and Mackenzie King was well received everywhere. He was particularly pleased by the meeting at Shellbrook on May 21. On May 22, he felt that "Altogether the visit to Prince Albert constituency was a great pleasure. Much more so than any previous visit. One more day would, I believe, make pretty nearly certain the final result. I hope very much all may go well. I really love being with the people, especially these simple, direct, humble, honest and genuine folk."

On the train on May 23, the Prime Minister worked on his speech for Winnipeg where the first big meeting of the campaign was to be held the next day. He "thought out a few ideas for tomorrow being Victoria Day— Canada's place in the Empire. A good chance to speak of the flag, of citizenship, etc. I see the outline of what I have to say more or less in nebulous form. While it will be a heavy job getting things finalized in type-written form for half hour's broadcast, if I get a good rest tonight, and have the day thoroughly secure, I believe we shall get through all right. That will mean that the election is half over tomorrow, that is to say so far as my part in actual campaigning is concerned."

The next morning he settled down in earnest to prepare the speech which was being broadcast. He "brought in many thoughts of my own; also sought to point up the material prepared. Finally got in a reference to Canadian citizenship and to the establishment of a distinctive Canadian flag. I had to work under tremendous pressure and at almost fever heat throughout the time I was at this task. It kept me at work steadily till about a quarter to 3. I had ordered lunch but did not take any until after having a rest of half an hour which I took between a quarter to 3 and 25 minutes after. I did not get to sleep but nearly dozed off. After dressing, I still have to look over part of manuscript and make a few additions. Most important of all, a reference to continuing to honour the Union Jack as a symbol of the British Empire and Commonwealth. I thought, too, of inserting words with reference to use of Canadian Ensign at conferences and by our troops when serving with the Americans in the war against Japan. There were a few moments in which I was deeply concerned as I could not find the material I had put aside for use in the broadcast.

"Pickersgill had prepared some wholly new material based on state-ments recently made by Bracken disclosing the alliance between Tory 'Independents' in Quebec and Bracken and his party. This I revised in considerable part dealing among other things with the crisis of last year pointing out it was to the French-speaking colleagues in the Cabinet that we owed avoiding a condition of chaos at a very critical time for our soldiers at the front.

"I would have given very much for a chance to have gone over this part more carefully. Indeed I never had a chance to read the speech through, save for the last page or two of revisions—any of the copy from beginning to close. Had to trust to typewriting, content, etc., being correct through-out. It was a long chance but in the delivery, it went all right. It was 10 to 4 —hands in a straight line when I joined the Committee outside my door to go to the Auditorium. A huge building which, on arrival, we found had been packed to the doors and further admissions denied."

Mackenzie King "began by speaking without any notes, thanking the audience for being present in such numbers and for the welcome extended. Also a word about the candidates, the new Senators, Glen as a new colleague. Then started in before the microphone with the typed part of the material. I had just got underway when some man in the Gallery began to interrupt making some reference to sixteen years. I took him up at once and referred to my years in office, years of leadership, years in the House of Commons, and expressed the hope that having addressed many meetings in that period of time, I would not encounter the first interruption on coming to Winnipeg. The audience soon took the man in hand and all became quiet. When Glen's remarks were a little too laudatory, I just heard a murmur of booing but made no reference to this. The audience itself was overwhelmingly friendly. I went through the speech in about an hour of which it took me about ten minutes by way of introductory remarks without notes and then balance of time on the written speech."

Mackenzie King felt that the part of the speech which brought the most applause was the section referring to "national unity and the treating of enemies of mankind, those who seek to raise racial, religious and sectional prejudice. I came out pretty strongly against those who seek to set province against province, against Bracken in his effort to ride two horses. To repeat the unholy alliance of 1911 between the Tories in Ontario and the nationalists of Quebec. I shall have another go at that in Ontario. The people also applauded very loudly the reference to having Canadian citizenship properly defined. I personally was not altogether surprised that my reference to a distinctive Canadian flag did not meet with too ready a response. I have all along felt that this question would be better left alone until Parliament meets. On the other hand, P., G., T., and H. have all been pressing so strongly for my coming out for a distinctive Canadian flag that I felt perhaps this was the time to do it. I did not wish to make any statement on that in Quebec. What I said today will meet with strong response there and also in the Canadian West but I should not be surprised if it caused a good many Conservatives who may have been thinking of giving us their support to refrain from doing so on June the 11th. On the other hand, it may cause some who would otherwise support the C.C.F. to give us their support. I was very glad that while taking a rest, I thought of the importance of inserting a sentence about our intention to, of course, continue to honour the Union Jack as a symbol of the British Commonwealth and Empire. That statement brought forth much more applause than the reference to a distinctive Canadian flag. What I said near the end about national unity, what I had observed in Prince Albert of the different races, classes, creeds, etc., uniting to make a nation, particularly the pride of the children in being Canadians brought forth a fine round of applause. I was given a great ovation at the close—an ovation which lasted for some time. A hearty response to the cheers proposed for myself. I proposed the usual cheers for the King.

"The audience was an interesting study. They were remarkably attentive and I could see they were serious minded. The impression I formed is that the tide has set in distinctly our way. That unless some very foolish mistakes are made in the next few weeks, we [will] have a considerable sweep except for constituencies we may lose because of feuds between our own candidates, selfishness of not a few of them."

The next evening (May 25) while on the train to Ottawa, Mackenzie King surveyed his impressions of the campaign. "My feeling at the end of the tour from Vancouver to Ottawa," he wrote, "is that the party's prospects are much better than I had believed they were when Parliament dissolved. Better than I thought they were when we arrived at Vancouver. Unless some unforeseen situation develops, I believe we will have an over-all majority and that I, myself, will be returned for Prince Albert unless the soldiers' vote, which may be against the Government, should make a difference either to the party or myself. That is pretty much an unknown quantity but I rather gather it will help the C.C.F. more than ourselves."

After several days of rest in Ottawa, Mackenzie King made his next speech in London, Ontario, on May 30. This was a national broadcast and a policy speech of some importance. Like all the Prime Minister's speeches during the campaign, it was a mixture of gentle nationalism, attachment to King and Crown, rejection of "special interests," pleas for national unity, hints of new social welfare programmes, and pride in the government's wartime record. The message was clear, trust the Liberal party with the consolidation of peace and postwar reconstruction. Mr. King worked all that afternoon on the revision of his text. At first he found it much easier to work alone because "there were some things I wanted to get into the speech which I could only put in myself. I had a good deal of difficulty, finding writing very hard. I began to find easier expression for my thoughts. I was sure I was being helped in what I was writing out.

"After half past four, I began revision with Pickersgill. Plunged ahead cutting out much of what he had previously prepared, and much of what I had prepared. Kept at this task until it was 7. I then felt that come what may, I must have a rest before the evening. Went to bed for half an hour and then had a boiled egg and cup of tea. Read over the speech as typed, taking out a couple more paragraphs, having reduced what had been written originally—about twenty-two pages—to fifteen pages in all. I held tenaciously to the parts that I felt were important. Was satisfied that in this I was right.

"It was after 8 when I left the Hotel having made a final revision. The only chance I had of reading the speech."

The meeting was held at the London Arena and Mackenzie King "found no difficulty to broadcast. Spoke with considerable vigour and was delighted to see the way in which the audience responded to the points to which I referred. Many of them were more in what was implied than what was actually said. It was this that the audience caught so well. Points like the provision the Government had made for soldiers' vote overseas; intention to vote in the Provincial election in support of Liberal principles and policies. Reference to the position as a leader in the war, etc. Also the Tory criticism being political dust to obscure their own limitations, etc.

"At the end of the broadcast, I was given a tremendous ovation, all of which, I understand, was in time to be recorded with the speech itself. It was a nation-wide broadcast, and, as such, I believe, will be effective." After the broadcast, Mackenzie King continued on extemporaneously for about forty minutes.

In Toronto the next morning the Prime Minister went to see Mulock. "I was delighted," he wrote, "to find him looking so well. He is still in bed. Looks rested. Indeed better than I have seen him in appearance for a year or more. He told me of how he had over-exerted himself in the North Grey campaign, sitting up till 4 in the morning, etc. It is easy to understand how his sickness came about. Smith [the Liberal candidate], he says, will win North York but I doubt it. I thanked him for his letter with the legacy [from Sir William Mulock] enclosed. Talked about his own resignation which I told him I was indeed sorry to have to accept. Would probably do so shortly after my return to Ottawa."

On June 1, Mackenzie King received through the American Ambassador an invitation from President Truman to pay him a visit at Washington. "The invitation is worded in an exceedingly kind way. It mentions that there would not be opportunity of talking over various matters of mutual interest at San Francisco, and that the President wonders if I would care to go to Washington in the near future. He goes on to say: 'If so, it would be a very great pleasure to welcome you at the White House which you know so well and to continue the informal talks which in the past have done so much toward creating the warm friendship and close understanding between our two countries.' It concludes: 'May I suggest June 3, 4, or 2 as possible dates for your arrival.' This it will not be possible for me to accept but I shall seek to get permission to have word of the invitation made public."

Next morning he communicated with the White House through the Canadian Embassy in Washington and got back word at once that "the President had said they recently had had an election in the States themselves and he fully understood the situation. Also that I was at liberty to publish his letter and my reply."

The Prime Minister had a meeting in Montreal that evening (June 2). He again had difficulty preparing what he wanted to say and after dinner on his private car he "went over once or twice a paragraph or two in French and then had literally to rush off to the meeting with Bertrand. We got to the Forum almost to the minute of the time I was expected to appear on the platform.

"I was on the platform before I really knew I was in the building. I was amazed at the size of the audience. Every seat of the vast building filled. The entire audience stood and I was given a tremendous reception. On the platform were Ministers, candidates, Senators and others. The programme had been well planned. A young Liberal made a fine, aggressive speech. Fournier also made a splendid speech in French. Madame Vautelet made a good speech. Senator David presented me. I was given a great ovation. Spoke a few words before the radio came on which were loudly applauded and when the radio came on, I began with a few words in French. Was given a tremendous ovation. As I went through the English broadcast, I had a feeling it lacked proportion. Lacked fire except in parts here and there. Was really far from what it should have been. Perhaps some of my feeling was fatigue but at any rate, I felt about the meeting very much as I did about the Prince Albert meeting though not quite so badly. It was really a shame that for this particular meeting, there had not been time for adequate preparation; also that I should not have been more rested before attempting addressing so vast a gathering. I do not recall ever having been greeted by a finer audience."

The impression Mackenzie King received was that the province of Quebec "is pretty solidly behind me. Bertrand says that men like Sarto Fournier are going to have a harder time in being elected than the men who supported me in the critical division. Sarto Fournier has now come around supporting me very strongly but people are saying he had voted against me. All our Ministers are enthusiastic about their stand."

On the afternoon of June 4, the day of the provincial election in Ontario, Mackenzie King left Ottawa by train for Saint John, N.B. His guess was "and it is wholly such with regard to Ontario elections, that Drew will probably have a majority over both the C.C.F. and the Liberals. That the C.C.F. will be second in the race. The Liberals not making much of a showing. I wish it might be otherwise but Hepburn has himself to blame.

The party is to blame as well for allowing him to go the lengths he did in bringing about its destruction. It has all been a great object lesson in the moral order which underlies all things and in the final analysis, turns them in terms of punishment or reward."

When the train reached Sherbrooke, Mackenzie King "got particulars about the Ontario elections. Found that Drew had made all but a complete sweep of the Province. Hepburn and Joliffe had each lost their own seats. I was not surprised that Drew had won. I have felt all along he would. Was disappointed that so very few Liberals were returned.

"It looks as if the C.C.F. were at the bottom of the poll which is not so bad. Both P. and T. seemed much disappointed and depressed. They had been hoping for a stalemate. Personally while I truly dislike Drew, I think results show the people were sick of tactics and the like of Joliffe and Hepburn. First of all, in bringing on the election when they did. Secondly, conducting the kind of fool campaign—talk of secret police and the like. Most indignant tomfoolery sort of procedure—no statesmanship of any sort. I am hoping now that the cry Drew in the Province and Mackenzie King in the Federal field, may still hold good. I believe it will. Not as largely as if both votes had taken place simultaneously. On the other hand, the result in Ontario should, I think, ensure us the elections in the Federal field. It has demonstrated that the C.C.F. have lost their power in Ontario which was where they gained it from Hepburn, in a previous election which led to Saskatchewan winning as it did. Of course Liberals have lost as well. But everyone knows that Hepburn represented a different kind of Liberalism than myself. We know that many of our own Liberals will not vote for him. The effect will be that in Vancouver the Tories will be strengthened. In Alberta, the Social Credit will lose some seats, and we will gain some. In Saskatchewan the C.C.F. will lose some seats and we will gain some. We should do better than was anticipated. I fear somewhat for McNaughton against Perley and also for our seat in Regina. I think my own seat will be safe. At any rate on the prairies a Tory victory in Ontario will not help the Tories much. It may help them a little in Manitoba. They will win where the C.C.F. will lose. In Ontario, the Tories will be strengthened and the C.C.F. will be less. We will lose a dozen seats. The Tories winning in Ontario should help us; give us pretty nearly a solid Quebec. I cannot see that a Tory victory in Ontario will help the Tories in the Maritimes. We shall hold our own there. Indeed do better in N.B. as well as in N.S. May lose a seat or two in P.E.I. though this not by any means certain. I shall indeed be greatly surprised if a week from tonight, the Liberals have not carried in the Dominion an over-all majority of at least twenty and possibly forty seats."

Final returns in Ontario gave the Conservatives sixty-six seats, the Liberals eleven, and the C.C.F. eight. The next day Mackenzie King continued to feel that the Ontario results would be a blow to the C.C.F. in the federal field. He wrote that "the fight for the Liberals has been, I think, made a little more difficult in New Brunswick by the Ontario results. I wish I had gone over that aspect of things more fully tonight. I am afraid the Tories will not hold to their idea of voting Drew for the Provincial and King in the Federal. They will now think they have a chance of winning both. However, the C.C.F., I think, will come our way. There is no doubt, however, the Ontario election being the great sweep it was, will have a prejudicial effect on our final result.

"The Tories have a fine organization and are using every means to make it effective. I shall have in my broadcast to stress more than ever: the question is not who is going to win as what is going to be done by whoever wins."

Mackenzie King was quite pleased by the meeting for MacLaren in Saint John where he spoke for an hour and twenty minutes. He "took the usual line of thanking the audience for their contribution to the war, speaking of returned men; what was owing to them, regretting inability to visit all parts of the Maritimes. I spoke on the things that remain to be done; let the war record speak for itself, and then launched out on to the Government's programme for full employment showing how they planned to keep money in circulation. Dealt with social security end particularly and closed with reference to permanent peace based on good relations at home, good neighbourly relations with all nations. I touched on results in Ontario pointing out they were a great object lesson showing the folly of advanced parties allowing the common enemy to get power by a minority of votes.

"I asked if another Government could carry on as well as our Government. A heckler called out: sure. I took him up at once and told him to come along to the platform and tell us how they could do it. The crowd caught the reply instantly and applauded very loudly. It was a real help. I was given a perfect hearing from start to close; from interruptions earlier, while concluding speaking, it was clear there were some there to make trouble. I was given a real ovation from the time of beginning to close, and considerable applause throughout."

As he turned back westwards that night, he expressed sorrow at missing Halifax and Charlottetown but added: "Surely Ilsley's Province will send its proper majority."

On the train journey to Quebec on June 6, Mackenzie King reached Rivière-du-Loup at one o'clock and found "that Pouliot had brought half of the community down to the station to extend a welcome; had arranged microphones, loud speakers, etc. He introduced me in the friendliest way to his executive and leading citizens. Had his little son Jean-François beside him. He told him what to say in reply to one or two questions I asked him. I was given a great reception by the crowd.

"At the station, when it came to addressing the gathering, Pouliot made a pleasant introduction; referred to me as his friend and also P.M., etc. I spoke mostly of the family allowances; Pouliot made a nice reply and then presented me and other members of the party with maple sugar and extended best of wishes. In speaking, he mentioned he was going to Hull to speak for Fournier, thereby making clear his support on the 11th. The election of Drew in Ontario has had and will have a profound effect in Quebec. This Province has no use for him. The fact that Pouliot found it necessary to identify himself so strongly with me after having taken his seat in the Opposition is a pretty good sign of what the people are thinking in the Province. I really believe we shall get out of Quebec at least 50 seats on which we can count."

When the train reached Lévis, Mackenzie King was met by St. Laurent who drove him to the Chateau Frontenac in Quebec City. Shortly after reaching the hotel Mackenzie King was preparing to take a rest "when Chubby Power phoned to say he was in a room nearby and asked if he could come in to see me. Poor Chubby has been more or less under the weather for the last fortnight. They were not too sure that he would be in a condition to speak tonight. He came in, slapped me on the back and said: we were good friends. Told me he thought St. Laurent was safe. His estimate is that I will get back with 90 seats in all; certain to be returned as Prime Minister. I told him I thought we would do better than that. He spoke about the condition of things in 1925. Said it would be difficult to carry on in that situation. I said I would not do it on any account. He made the rather naive remark: do not expect me to do it because I would not undertake it. It was one of those sidelights which reveals what has been the ambition of his life and what he regards his own influence in the party to have been. Hepburn had the same kind of illusion. That he more than anyone else really contributed to the success of my victories. As a matter of fact, he did the most injury to the party in Ontario by his habits and was responsible more or less for our losses in Quebec Province, for our not being as strong as we should be today. However, one has to overlook these things in public life, and make the best of everything and everyone. Chubby then told me that he was going to introduce me at the meeting tonight. None of the Committee were too sure of what he might say but felt they could trust him."

When it was time to go to the meeting "Colonel Oscar Gilbert turned up with his car and drove St. Laurent and myself to the Palais Montcalm. A fine hall for speaking in. Might have been made a little larger. There were great crowds out of doors that could not gain admission. The theatre chairs were packed. A very fine audience.

"Fafard presided and made an introductory speech. He presented me to his new wife. A very splendid looking person. A little girl presented me with a rose for my buttonhole and after Fafard had spoken, another young lady, Miss Trudel, presented me with a beautiful bouquet of roses from the Liberal Women's Association. Read a very nice address, nicely worded, in both French and English. Bobby Lapointe and Picard also made speeches; both were well delivered; of the two, I thought Lapointe's the better.

"St. Laurent made a fine speech and got a good reception. He spoke for about half an hour. Godbout then spoke—very sincerely and splendidly. He also got a fine reception. Finally Power introduced me, speaking in English of the years of my leadership of the party, referring to myself as his friend, twenty-five years of association, my leadership of the party, etc. Altogether it was a fine eulogy after which he shook hands again with myself and was going to speak anew in French but decided to let the English introduction go. He did fairly well; was far from being in good shape. The audience, however, knew him so well, that they made every allowance. What was finest was his coming out openly and as one of those presiding, to introduce me to the audience. I was given a great reception when I got up to speak and again when I used a few words of introduction in French. I began by referring to the flowers that had been presented to me; referred to Sir Wilfrid and to Lady Laurier; mentioned I would take the little roses back to Laurier House. That thought had come to me during the early part of the evening.

"I then began to touch on the speeches of those who had spoken and worked at once into the difficult place we had all been through. Made it clear we were differing honestly but that I had not sought to influence anyone; that I had great pride in the men standing by what they thought was right. We had looked each other squarely in the face. Also differences, realizing they were sincere, but also realizing that beneath everything else, we were Canadians and putting the emphasis on what we had in common. I did not seek to apologize for my attitude or to explain. As a matter of fact, I came out openly and said I had not sought the position of leadership in the war. I took it because it was my duty. I made up my mind that as long as any man or woman went to the front, I would never fail to give them the support which they might be in need of. Not being a military man, I made it clear I had to act on the advice of my advisers who also had to act on the advice of their experts. I said I had always had in mind the test would be the outcome in the end; what there was in the way of preservation of national unity. Our contribution to the European war was a great success and the best evidence of national unity was the presence of those on the platform tonight.

"In opening, I said quite honestly that of all the interests I had in my public life, the compliment which was being paid by what was signified in the meeting at Quebec was perhaps the most remarkable tribute of confidence that I had received at any time. I then got into the social reform programme; my interest in industrial questions; family allowances and then the need for a Government to put these reforms through and to have the backing of a party that had the support of all the Provinces. I stated that I believed we would have numbers from every Province. Pointed out wherein no other party had a chance of forming a Government that would be representative of all. Spoke of the Ontario elections as being a blessing in disguise or in the open, as making clear that the people of Ontario had felt what was needed was a Government that would carry on. Not another condition of uncertainty which was the result of competing parties. I did not bring out as I should have, or did the night before, the fact that they were returned by a minority of votes. I spoke then on the problems to be solved in the international arena. Need to have St. Laurent with me, and the promise that if returned, the Government would seek to leave a record as good in the future as it had left in the past. I emphasized that the choice was for the next five years which brought us until 1950; also I personally would welcome peace and quiet but felt the opportunities today were so great I would like to throw myself heart and soul into the completion of a programme of social reform, leading to the establishment of a national minimum of health and social welfare for all.

"I was given a tremendous ovation at the close and in getting out of the meeting, was literally crowded upon from every side by men and women wishing to shake hands. Some of them were almost passionate in the way in which they spoke. After considerable difficulty, we got into Gilbert's car with St. Laurent, and the three of us drove to my car at the station."

When he reached Ottawa Mackenzie King attended a Cabinet meeting and made a last unsuccessful effort to get one or other of the Liberal candidates in Ottawa East, where there was a bitter intra-party dispute, to retire. He did not get started on his final national broadcast, which was to be delivered at a public meeting in Ottawa the next evening, until 7.00 P.M. that day. The atmosphere in the final days of the campaign had become more frenzied and heated and the Progressive Conservatives, firmly wedded to the policies of conscription and free enterprise, began to direct their fire in a more personal way against Mackenzie King and his "pandering" to Quebec.

After he finally began his speech, Mackenzie King wrote, he found "that I was tempted to get off on to a different track. I read a lengthy statement Pickersgill had sent up on Bracken's leadership which was quite an attack on him and on the Globe. Quite contrary to the kind of thing I had in my mind for a final speech and this rather upset me. I wish to avoid following the tactics of the enemy and finding fault with the leadership of others, resorting to personalities, etc. I found my head getting weary, so gave up. Had dinner."

After dinner, Mackenzie King "found again I was too tired and distracted to do anything so got to work on going through all the papers and getting things blocked out for morning. I asked Pickersgill to get a few pages ready on lines I gave him. Decided if the worst came to the worst that I would simply have to repeat what was said in other broadcasts but I would like to be able to give a certain form and content to what I am saying in this all important broadcast. I understand tonight McCullagh made a very bitter attack on myself; everything talked of in the past. Also Tory campaign generally has been one of vindictiveness towards myself. I think I will answer that in a single sentence or two, that my record over the years has not been what it was without the people having certain degree of confidence in my integrity and ability. I must not at any cost depart from the constructive line I have taken right through the several addresses."

Mackenzie King "felt very depressed and downhearted tonight. I have lost something of the spirit I have had all through the campaign from the moment which, in some ways, was the greatest triumph of all, last night [Quebec City]. I can only pray that with the rest tonight, I may wake up restored in my mind and soul as well as body." "This," he added, "has been a trying and a sad day. Have not been equal to its task but felt very distraught. I realize very bitter things are being said against me all over the country. Lies and all that is associated with that order of things. It is the darkest moment I have had since I left Ottawa seven weeks ago. I pray it is the darkness before the dawn. May God's peace be given me tonight and His guidance and inspiration tomorrow."

On the morning of June 8, the Prime Minister was up early and, before nine o'clock, "got down to revising the beginning of what I dictated yesterday and writing in additional material. As the Tory campaign has been so completely one built up of Bracken and detraction of myself, I came to the conclusion that after all, I should perhaps expose the tactics of the group that are behind Bracken and go the length of mentioning McCullagh by name. His broadcast of last night was, I am told, particularly venomous."

After lunch, he began working on the final revision with his secretaries. "We were," he wrote, "working against time, very much against time, all afternoon. I was really afraid that I would have to simply use whole extracts from other speeches to finish out the broadcast. As a matter of fact, I took no rest from 2.15 till 5 or 10 minutes of 9 P.M. Worked steadily all the while on the broadcast. We had about 5 or 6 pages too much which involved considerable time in making the necessary deletions."

He took a second look at his references to Bracken and "cut out the parts that seemed at all likely to produce any reaction. I also had written something against McCullagh mentioning him by name but thought it wiser just to keep to the public statement he had issued and the significance of his having taken any part in the broadcast. That fellow is a vindictive conceited upstart who, if I am not mistaken, will pay dearly before his day is over, for his enmity toward myself. On what grounds it would be based save jealousy and envy, I do not know. He is the vindictive type who wants to rule by destroying other men. If I am returned to power on Monday, and it will be my last Parliament, I shall be able to say some things without fear of their affecting the party's fortunes which up to the present I have not felt advisable to expose. First of all, I was to have been at the meeting when it opened at 9. It was arranged later that if I got there by 9.30, that would be time enough. . . .

"When I looked at my watch, as I was about to start off, the hands were in a straight line at 10 to 10 P.M. I got to the Auditorium shortly before 10. Immediately after, I was piped up on to the platform; I was given a tremendous ovation on coming in. The building was well filled but not completely so. The fact that the speech was known to be broadcast doubtless kept many at home; also the lateness of the hour but it was a fine audience and very sympathetic. There was a little booing but in a mild way.

"Fournier made a good speech in both English and French. When I was called on at 10.30, I got a tremendous ovation. Throughout the speech, there was much applause and by reading a little fast near the end, I got through exactly to the second of the time allotted to leave one minute beyond for the applause, to be heard at the other end of the broadcast. There was not time to say anything as the people remained standing when I had got through speaking. I felt it was wiser not to attempt anything on local affairs. Said just a word about their knowing my interests in the Civil Service and improvement of Ottawa and that I hoped they would be sure to send a Liberal candidate from both East Ottawa and West Ottawa. Expressed no preference for anyone as an official candidate."

Mackenzie King was told at the meeting by the Mayor of Ottawa that a group of veterans were returning to Ottawa and being given a reception at the Coliseum. He went from the meeting to the Coliseum with George McIlraith. "When we went in to the Coliseum," he wrote, "there were many soldiers there, their wives and children, also relatives of the returning men. I was given quite a cheer but there seemed to be a considerable amount of booing. All good natured. I confess, however, that it saddens me at heart to realize that the minds of the members of the forces have been poisoned so strongly against me. It has been deliberate poisoning because in truth there is no one in the country who had been as much their friend as I have. I know that nothing has been left undone which could be done to make perfectly sure of the protection of their lives in battle and future, and the future of the dependents of those who have gone than myself. What is so cruel is that I am quite sure that thousands and thousands of those who will vote against me will come to deeply regret it later on in their lives." With this meeting, Mackenzie King's campaign ended.

On June 9, the Prime Minister went to Government House for luncheon alone with the Governor-General and Princess Alice. After lunch, he talked to the Governor about the election. "I gathered from the way the Governor spoke," he wrote, "that he felt the C.C.F. might not do as well in Saskatchewan. That Glen's seat was doubtful; also Gibson's. He did not think much of Mulock having to drop out. Spoke of him as an 'also ran.' He seemed surprised when I said Mitchell thought he might be safe. When he asked me my impressions as to possible results, I told him that while on the surface, everything looked well, and I had found the whole campaign more pleasing with less evidence of concern on the part of members of our own party than any others, I myself felt that the lack of organization of our party was certain to cost us many seats. That I felt the Conservatives had no end of money and spared no effort during the past two and a half years to organize the campaign which they have organized. To be quite frank and confidential, I believed we were now in an era where great world enterprises were taking shape, where a few wealthy interests were combining together to seek to control these organizations. That I thought Beaverbrook was one who would not hesitate to put money into Canada to get control for his friends. I might have added: Sir James Dunn. I said I did not understand Bennett's present visit unless it related in some way to his concern in certain interests and what he might be able indirectly to do to help destroy me. McCullagh was the one around whom others were focussed in Canada.

"I did not mention Bassett's name but might have done so. I am quite sure that is the gang working with McTague, Borden and one or two others who have been on the inside." Mackenzie King told the Governor he "thought we ought to get about fifty seats out of Quebec including those that I could count on for support in the House. Twenty-eight or thirty in Ontario. We would carry seats in all the Provinces; might lose one or two in P.E.I.; perhaps one or two in N.B. I thought N.S. would remain Liberal. We might gain in Alberta. We would perhaps hold our own in Saskatchewan. I thought I would win my own seat and that Gardiner would win his. In Manitoba, we would probably lose a couple of seats. Really felt we should have a majority over all and would call the figure around 130. But if we lost a seat like East Ottawa, and much of that kind of thing in other places, we might suffer heavily."

After returning to Laurier House he telephoned Prince Albert constituency. "Jack Sanderson spoke hopefully but not too positively about the probabilities for Monday next. McGeer himself not too positive but said evidences pointed strongly in my favour. He said Coldwell's meeting last night had not been much of a success. Hall only partly filled. About 1,000 or more and not too much enthusiasm. McGeer thought we might get eight or twelve seats in B.C. but after his estimate that Hepburn would have the largest number of seats in Ontario, I do not take much stock in his judgment. I am inclined to think he speaks without real knowledge or too good a judgment.

"He said he thought we would get twelve seats in Saskatchewan but the last word was that McNaughton seemed safe. I hope this is true but I am very doubtful.

"We shall probably lose Regina and one or two other seats. I said to McGeer that I had been at Government House for lunch with the Governor and that he would be interested in a document signed today [McGeer's appointment to the Senate]. That I would ask him to say nothing about it to anyone and no word would be given out until Monday afternoon but I congratulated him and said it had given me much pleasure to do what I have for one who had been such a true friend."

In his diary for election day, June 11, Mackenzie King recorded: "I voted for Pinard [the official candidate in Ottawa East] because of his having been a loyal supporter through different sessions of Parliament and particularly at the time of crisis when other than loyalty on his part might have created some real embarrassment. My feelings were strongly for Richard as the better type of representative but I felt I owed this vote regardless of consequences to one who has been true in his relations in the House of Commons with the Government and myself." During the afternoon, he noted, he "had mostly on my mind the writing of a statement for tonight. I felt sufficient confidence about the Government winning not to hesitate to write out in advance what I thought would be suitable and not preparing an alternative.

"I then dictated to H. what I thought would be appropriate. I am glad I did not try to write by hand as I was very tired. Sent for Pickersgill about 4.30. He, Gibson and I went over the dictated material and something that Pickersgill himself had also prepared. It was just about 6 when the final revisions were run off."

His friends, the Pattesons, "arrived as planned at 6 and the [Toronto] *Star* photographers were also at the front door at that hour. About 5 past 6, I was photographed on the front steps with little Pat. On coming in, I received word that the first returns indicated that Gillis, C.C.F., was leading in his constituency in N.S. This is characteristic of C.P. returns, always something that leans away from the Liberal party rather than toward it. There came, however, soon after, the word of Liberal seats being won and then the word that MacLaren was behind in Saint John. The first word of a defeat was that of his failure to be elected. I 'phoned him as soon as I could reach him. He was very cheerful. Said there had been a very bitter fight against him. They stopped at nothing. He thought the province would make up for it. I said to him not to be discouraged. I would see that another seat was found. He seemed immensely pleased. He believed that could be secured. I told him not to be concerned, that I would keep him in the Ministry and would arrange accordingly. He spoke quite affectionately of the relationship formed between us as a result of my day's visit to Saint John. He said his boy was home with Mrs. MacLaren. Thanked me most warmly for the help I had given him and what the day had meant.

"It was about 20 after 6 when dinner was ready. T. joined J., G. and myself. We had a nice talk at dinner. None of us felt any real concern. Immediately after, on coming upstairs, the returns began coming in slowly from the Maritimes. It was apparent that both N.S. and N.B. were coming strongly our way. Then the Quebec returns came along, making it wholly apparent that Quebec was going to be nearly solid again. What delighted me particularly was the word of St. Laurent's election by a good majority. Later in the evening when he rang me up he told me that the majority was over 10,000. This was where Power, the wise organizer, had said he doubted if St. Laurent could be elected in his riding in Quebec East. St. Laurent said it showed what Quebec wanted of their representatives was to do what they thought was right, no matter what the immediate consequences, and explain to them later why a particular course had been taken. That was all they wanted to know and they would do themselves what was right. St. Laurent's victory has given me great delight. Madame St. Laurent spoke to me as well.

"I was deeply concerned, as I had been all day, about the results in Ottawa, both east and west. It was a great delight when the returns showed that Richard was really safe. I was tremendously pleased when I learned later that he had a majority of 3,000 over all the other candidates, who lost their deposits including Pinard. This speaks well for his organization and determination of the people to be represented by the type that they deem worthy. It is fortunate indeed that I did not name any official candidate. The record will show that I was very uncertain and of two minds, but that the decision I finally made before taking any action in the way of naming an official candidate was the right one. What influenced me most in that was Richard's statement that I had made it a point of not interfering in constituencies but having the constituencies decide their own affairs. . . .

"I was glad to get the word of Claxton's return by a large majority. I was anxious for a time with regard to Abbott, Mitchell, and Glen. I was delighted when I found that Abbott had a majority over all. I was very surprised and pleased when I found that Mitchell's majority was in the couple of thousands and surprised and delighted when I found that Glen had been returned. I was also pleased to learn that Mutch [L. A. Mutch, Liberal M.P. for Winnipeg South] as well as one or two others had been returned in Winnipeg. The Winnipeg Free Press rendered yeoman service in the fight there. I felt concerned about Gibson in Ontario. I was relieved when word came that he had been elected. He is more reactionary than others, and I do not forget he was one of the men ready to slip out with the others on the conscription issue.

"Martin rang up and I was glad to know he had a good majority. I was however very much surprised and deeply disappointed that Johnston of London [former Liberal M.P.] had not been returned. Also I was surprised that Elgin was lost by such a large number. It shows that Hepburn had ruined not only his own constituency but I am sure is greatly responsible for the defeat of Johnston and others in the district round about. I don't know anything that gave me more joy than late at night to learn that McTague had been defeated in Wellington. That was particularly good news. Also another thing that delighted me was the defeat of Houde by Fauteux in Montreal. That is almost the outstanding victory of the campaign. Another thing that pleased and surprised me was that Smith had carried North York. That was particularly good news. It must mean that Mulock as I had thought, without assisting the general campaign, had given real help in the work of organization in North York. It was apparent from the beginning that the tide was coming as we had expected very much our way, and that there never was a moment that I thought the Government would not be returned with a majority over all counting of course the so-called Liberal-Independents as Liberals. It was gratifying to find some of the Independents who had been supported by the Conservatives also defeated in Quebec. The Manitoba results as they kept coming in were enheartening. Ontario did not do badly, but there were several seats that we should not have lost which had formerly been held by our own men, like Fraser [former Liberal M.P.] in Northumberland, also Kingston, where Macdonald [Angus Macdonald] had been and a few others. The return of Macdonald in Brantford was by a good majority at an early hour. This was a good sign. The complete wiping out of the C.C.F. in Ontario was a splendid result. These fellows are so treacherous that I would rather see us get back to the old two-Party system."

When the returns from the West began to trickle in Mackenzie King "was greatly surprised to learn that seats in Saskatchewan were very doubtful. It looked as though McNaughton had not won. Gardiner seemed to be regarded as safe. Finally word came that the C.C.F. was leading in Prince Albert. I said at once, That means I am beaten in Prince Albert, and I then began to alter in some particulars what I had prepared to say over the radio and to write out that what really mattered was that the party should be returned and that the loss of two or three, myself included, did not matter in the light of the all-important fact that we had won so splendid a victory. I had begun to say something about having entered yesterday on my nineteenth year as Prime Minister and that I would welcome re-sponsibilities now being carried on my someone else. I thought Ilsley would probably be the choice. This I did not write out. I began in my mind seriously to think of readjustments that would need to be made. I felt I would like to be made a member of the International Joint Commission, so that I could keep in official relationship with the United States. Also to become Chairman of the Ottawa Federal District Commission. I felt the Government would probably want me to take part in Peace Conferences whether in the House or not, and that I would have time to get my own affairs into shape and to enjoy more in the way of contentment and happi-ness before the end of life. When I really felt I was defeated, I felt a little outbreak of perspiration for the moment, but that was hardly noticeable and soon passed away. It was like a tiny shock. I doubt if I would have felt that if my faith had been stronger. What I really was mostly concerned about was that my faith should not be shaken by the result. I was quite prepared to believe that everything would be wholly for the best.

"A little later, Dr. Humphries rang me up and I got from him a different impression. It was that I was leading by 365 in Prince Albert and holding my own in the rest of the constituency. This looked better but far from being a certainty. The Governor General rang up himself about 10 to ask me about the results and particularly about my own position in Prince Albert. He seemed greatly concerned about that. Also did not quite understand what was meant by leading in certain polls, nor could he get fully in mind how the returns are coming in at different hours from different parts. So far as he could be justified in speaking over the 'phone, he made it pretty clear what his feelings were. He was glad to see that the Government was safe. He asked me when I would get final word myself. I told him it might come by midnight, but that I would see him in the morning, if that was agreeable to him. Later, I had word 'phoned from the studio to Government House that at least the Canadian Press conceded that I was elected.

"After listening to the news, and hearing Blair Fraser's account, which brought us up practically to my seat, without mentioning it, I felt we were near enough the final result for me to broadcast without any reference to myself on the results of the election itself. At 11, left Laurier House to go to speak over the radio at 10 past. Here again were photographers taking pictures."

As he came out of the broadcasting studio, Mackenzie King quite unexpectedly met John Bracken. "He put out his hand to shake hands and extended his congratulations. I thanked him but said nothing more. He then said to me 'we shall be seeing more of each other soon.' I said in a quiet way I hoped it may be so. The words had slipped through politeness more than aught else, but were the truth, as I would rather see him in the House of Commons than anyone else. We have got him now where we want him. He is like a fly having buzzed around outside and caught with the glitter at the end into the spider's web. I am sure as I can be that it will not be too long before the Tory party will get rid of him as a leader and substitute someone else. He had a very strong grip. His hand was like that of some woodsman in its rough strength and his features were all contracted. His face is a mass of lines. He was anything but happy. . . . It is necessary for me to forget the past, and I am only too happy to forgive it, but I feel I do not need to sacrifice my self-respect by immediately treating the whole political scene as if it were part of some circus. The photographers took a snap of the two of us shaking hands. Asked if I would repeat shaking hands with Bracken. I did this reluctantly, but resisted very strongly the effort of the C.B.C. of having me come in to the studio with Bracken and have a movietone made. I told Turnbull I would not submit to anything of the kind."

"I went into a room to 'phone Government House, and then had a word with Fogo, whom I congratulated warmly on his part, and went with him to a room downstairs, where I met Senator Robertson . . . and the staff that Fogo had around him. I congratulated them very warmly. I made a short speech to them, thanking them for their part in the campaign. I told them to remember that they had had a part in the making of history. This campaign was such in reality. I then stressed that I hoped that on no account should the office be allowed to lessen its efforts in its work of organization and publicity."

After returning to Laurier House, Mackenzie King "got latest reports over the radio. I 'phoned Humphries to get the latest word from Prince Albert. He told me I was still some 300 votes ahead. There were about 14 more polls to come, some 8 of which were very far north, very few votes in them, but he thought there was a possibility that my position might even improve in these other polls. Of course there is the soldiers' vote which is considerable in Prince Albert. He said this caused the C.C.F. not to concede anything for the present. He felt, however, though not positive, that I could feel fairly well assured of having been returned. He said they had the wildest lot of men in town that night that he had seen for some time. Everyone had worked well; had done their very best, and that I would know the reason why. He meant it as a matter of personal interest and personal regard. Certainly the little visit was most helpful in getting the right spirit into the organization. I felt at the time that one day more might have cinched things pretty well. On the other hand, one more day would have made difficult the programme to other parts of Canada."

Because of the delay in counting the service vote, it was over a week before what had appeared to be a victory for Mackenzie King in Prince Albert was confirmed as a defeat.

Shortly after he got up on June 12, the Prime Minister telephoned General McNaughton who had been defeated in Qu'Appelle. McNaughton "congratulated me very warmly," Mackenzie King wrote. "The paper had given his interview which I thought was very good. He said he was not yet sure that the soldiers' vote might not yet change things. I told him not to be concerned. We would find him a seat somewhere else. This was his second baptism of fire. He seemed most appreciative of that. He added not to do anything that would embarrass me, but seemed grateful of the thought that he might yet get into the House of Commons. He said he was sure that my seat was all right. The account he gave me last night was truer than what the press had given.

"Later in the morning I had a 'phone call from Premier McNair of New Brunswick. He extended congratulations and went on to speak of Bridges' election [H. F. G. Bridges, elected in York-Sunbury]. He referred to Bridges as a young man of good Cabinet material. I told McNair that I felt I owed an obligation to MacLaren—to get him a seat if possible. That, as a colleague who had fought, I was anxious to have him stay on in the Ministry." It was some time before Mackenzie King could bring himself to accept the view that it was not wise to face by-elections either for General McNaughton or for MacLaren.

Final returns in the general election showed that the Mackenzie King government had been returned to power with 127 seats, a narrow majority. The C.C.F. won twenty-eight seats, up from eight in 1940, but all were in the prairie provinces or British Columbia with the exception of a single seat in Nova Scotia. The Progressive Conservatives increased their representation in the House to sixty-seven, a gain of twenty-seven seats, but forty-eight of these were in constituencies in Ontario. The Conservatives won only one seat in Quebec while the Liberals took fifty-six plus a few Independent Liberals. In the prairie provinces, where Bracken's appeal was thought to be strongest, the Progressive Conservatives won only five seats, a gain of two. To everyone's surprise, the Liberals won the largest share of the military vote, 118,537, with the C.C.F. a close second at 109,679 votes. The Progressive Conservatives trailed with 87,530 votes.

Mackenzie King continued to received congratulations throughout the day on June 12. On calling at Rideau Hall, he found the Governor-General "very pleased. He put out his hand and shook hands warmly. He said he was so glad that all had gone so well. He was anxious about changes in the Government and the questions that might come up if there was not a full majority. I told him there was no question about the Government being able to carry on and really having a majority over all. I said I had received wires from Independents who wanted to be known as Liberals, and explained all of that group and also the C.C.F. group would support the Administration against Tories in tight places. That there could be no question about the Government's position. I expressed regrets at the loss of MacLaren and McNaughton but said I would try to get them back in the Government. I spoke of how remarkable it was that all the Ministers should be returned with these exceptions. He asked about my seat. I said nothing had been conceded yet, but I was not concerned. Naturally I would prefer not to be defeated by the soldiers' vote or further polls. If I was, I would make arrangements that would be satisfactory.

"He spoke about Alberta and the Social Credit. I have come to the conclusion that Campbell who owns the paper in Edmonton is responsible for our losing some seats through his not being appointed a Senator. Also we have lost through Gershaw [former M.P., appointed to the Senate] not being a campaigner. Certainly MacKinnon was far out in his findings. Another thing it seems to me folly that the meeting I addressed should be only to our own workers. Arrangements should have been made for a broadcast throughout the Province. That is evidence of how little we had in the way of practical organization. . . . "

During the day Ian Mackenzie called to discuss the results in British Columbia. "He explained that the conscription feeling had been strong at the coast; said that accounted for the defeat [the Liberals lost five seats]. He doubted if the part about shipment of metal to Japan had had any effect. I was astonished at the word of Mayhew's defeat by Sir Henry Drayton. I was sorry about Pearkes' victory over Chambers. Was sorry for the defeat of O'Neill [of Kamloops] and one or two others. There are only five in B.C. Mackenzie, himself, had over a thousand majority. Tom Reid had a good majority; Sinclair and Cruickshank were others elected. He said that Gibson [J. L. Gibson, Comox-Alberni], who succeeds Neill, as an Independent, is a Member I can count on at all times. He said he was financed by our party. I was surprised to find that Mackenzie did not seem too keen on McGeer's appointment. I think he would rather have seen it go to Stan McKeen, who probably had most to do with the financing. We have lost Prince Rupert and also Peace River. I am sorry to find that Irvine [W. Irvine, C.C.F. in Cariboo] has got the better of Turgeon. We will have to get Turgeon some good post. Fortunately we are in a position to look after any good man of our party. I am terribly sorry about Mayhew, who was as fine a man as we have had in Parliament." As it turned out, the service vote in Victoria returned Mayhew to the House of Commons.

Also on June 12, the Prime Minister "was delighted with a charming message received from President Truman—a message which brings with it congratulations from the people of the United States as well as himself. That is something of which one may be proud. I am sorry to say that while the President of the United States has expressed his personal thanks time and again, nothing of the kind has come from my own Sovereign. Churchill is pretty much alone in having given any recognition in a personal way of what I have done for the British Crown, its people, and the Empire, throughout the years of my life. Is it any wonder that so many of our people feel much more in touch with the United States than with the United Kingdom and that it is so difficult to keep the two together? I thought of this particularly as I drafted a telegram to the King from my colleagues and myself on the celebration of his birthday in Canada on June 14th. Even the Governor General, while he has shown he was quite anxious I should be returned, since the victory itself has not written a letter as he might well have done and has said very little in the way of congratulations in my talk with him this morning. Princess Alice, who was in the garden, did not come in to extend her congratulations, as I would have thought they both would have, our relations being as close as they are. The trouble with those people is that their concern lies with what is going best to meet their own convenience. There are few if any wiser sayings than: 'Put not your faith in Princes.' I am beginning more and more to see that the upholding of monarchy is a form of idolatry."

The following day (June 13) Norman Robertson telephoned by arrangement from San Francisco. He told the Prime Minister "that it looked as if the signing at San Francisco would not take place until the 23rd of June. He hoped that I might find it possible to be present. Said General Smuts had expressed a similar hope and he knew that others there would feel the same way. When President Truman's letter came last night, before it was received, I felt I should meet its request whatever it was though I was relieved when I found it did not mean an immediate trip to San Francisco. Robertson said Mr. Hull was much better, able to go out a little, and really might be at San Francisco. If so, he had hoped very much I would also be there. It begins to look as if this journey might become part of an international obligation and an invaluable one at this time. While it could have no political significance in the party sense seeing that from now on, I shall not be a candidate in any General Election, nevertheless it is what would be expected of myself as one who clearly has a place in the world arena, and should be identified as much as possible with the great events of our day. I told Robertson much would depend on my not having to make speeches."

Before the Cabinet meeting on June 14 Mackenzie King received word from the Chief Electoral Officer that the service vote, apart from Britain, "indicated the C.C.F. were sufficiently ahead of the vote for myself to give them the lead in the constituency. The Tories had comparatively few. I confess I felt a little disappointed at the thought of having to go through a by-election. I felt I could not think of anything else in view of the vote through the country generally. Also sorry to lose the riding after nineteen years and the splendid fight that was made there. Of course there is still a chance."

He added that the service vote so far available "indicated on the whole that the vote is for the Liberal Party, C.C.F. coming in next and Tories trailing behind. I am pleased with this but it does seem cruel it should be my fate, at the end of the war, in which I have never failed the men overseas once, that I should be beaten by their vote and this, particularly, by a C.C.F. man whose party at the outbreak of war were unwilling to even have our men participate at all. This all shows what organization can do, but it also reveals a new trend in affairs. It is in these great services that socialistic developments take place and communistic trends also take place. This uncertainty has cast just a little cloud over the clear skies which I have been enjoying in the last day or two but I feel nevertheless that the battle has been won and that in the long run all will be for the best. I am sorry for the boys in Prince Albert and also for the party's sake, as I am sure they would have liked to have seen me carry that constituency personally, leading a victorious army. However, it all helps to emphasize the gallantry and chivalry of the choice made to contest the seat when there did not appear to be a chance to win. Running in Saskatchewan has of course helped the whole cause very much."

That evening Mackenzie King took St. Laurent to Kingsmere for dinner. He wrote that St. Laurent was "a most delightful companion. We talked over the whole Quebec situation very fully and other matters. He told me Ilsley was much put out at the appointment of McGeer. Thought it would be regarded by Clark [Deputy Minister of Finance] as a reflection on himself. I had never thought of this aspect, though I knew Ilsley would be opposed to McGeer. I pointed out to St. Laurent that unless there was some evidence of radicalism from our party in Western Canada we would lose the whole West. McGeer can be a real force there. He is one of the few Liberal forces that are left. St. Laurent is strong in saying that from now on I should insist that everything I have said in the campaign is made a part of Liberal policy. He said if Ilsley objected to exempting Members' indemnities from taxation and resigned he thought we should let him go. This led St. Laurent to say that he thought as time went on Abbott might well become increasingly prominent. He seemed to possess most of the qualities of leadership. I told St. Laurent that that had been my own thought. St. Laurent is uncertain as to whether we should not take Bridges into the Government rather than MacLaren, Bridges being the younger man, very promising. He is also a little doubtful about McNaughton. He fears that McNaughton still adheres too closely to men like Price Montague and some of the others who have not been loyal to our Government; also seems to feel there is a considerable feeling against McNaughton. I pointed out that this was quite wrong. McNaughton had helped to save the Government and really neither election gave him a fair chance. Discussed doing away with the Department of War Services altogether and filling the vacant Postmaster Generalship.

"We spoke of External Affairs. St. Laurent said the press had mentioned the possibility of his receiving that post. I told him I would not think of linking it with another portfolio and that there was no one else for Justice. I do not know just what he had in mind in mentioning the possibility. Brooke Claxton is the most promising one for that portfolio. I will wait and have a talk with Robertson."

The next day (June 15) Mackenzie King gave further consideration to going back to San Francisco. "The more I think matters over I feel this is something I should do; as Mr. St. Laurent said, should the U.N. organization prove successful it would go down through the ages as one of the great charters. He thought I should be there representing Canada. I told him I would wish to have him with me. As a matter of fact I rather feel the journey would be pleasant. To experience a bit of a vacation with the elections behind and very little in the way of speaking—perhaps at most one short address. There would be a chance too for a few days at the side of the ocean and perhaps a glimpse of other parts of California. The one disquieting feature is the uncertainty of Prince Albert count, and the certainty if defeated of having to run in a by-election. But even that I think can be worked out on a schedule that will enable me to get into Parliament when it opens. It looks now as if that will be about two months from today or a week later than that." That day he noted in his diary that "Clark, Deputy Minister of Finance, had an operation today. Fortunately it has been successful but I am afraid he will never be too strong. The Government and the country owe almost more to him than to any other man for the war effort, as he has had so much to do with many of its financial and economic aspects."

On June 16, Mackenzie King found it difficult to sleep because his "mind was mostly on the probable result in Prince Albert. I kept going over in my thoughts what I should say in a letter to the constituents. I also felt in my heart a sense of sadness that the relationship which had existed over 19 years should now be severed by so very few votes and particularly by votes from overseas service, the battle having been won in the constituency itself. Fortunately it has not been over the issue of conscription as the Tories are considerably behind the Liberals. It is the C.C.F. vote that has done the damage. That too is tragic inasmuch as no man in Parliament has been more sympathetic to the well-being of the people than I myself. The soldiers' vote having been largely polled before the civilian vote also made a difference. They have not had the benefit of what there was by way of education in the campaign. I seemed to have a feeling that in the end I would be behind, though felt there was still a possibility."

The figures that day showed Mackenzie King 50 votes behind but there were still some service votes to be counted. That afternoon he had General and Mrs. McNaughton to tea at Kingsmere. "Both the General and Mrs. McNaughton," he wrote, "seemed tired and did not hesitate to say they were genuinely disappointed and disillusioned, though both were very brave. Mrs. McNaughton did not hesitate to say they had counted much on the great reception which had been given the General when he visited his home town while still at the head of the forces. They did not realize that the present generation is one that did not know their parents or themselves.

"The General felt that nothing had been too unscrupulous. He had felt almost from the start that he was up against a hard core with both the C.C.F. and the Tories. My recollection is that in 'phoning he rather kept believing that he could win. I am inclined to think that his Scotch pride and a certain touch of vanity make it difficult for him to look either defeat or possibility of defeat in the face. He is wholly inexperienced in politics and feels that because in his own mind he ought to win he will win. Unfortunately that is not true, as one comes to know it in politics. Too much emphasis is put on meetings and the applause received there. He was against a very strong candidate in the person of the woman [Mrs. Gladys Strum of the C.C.F.] who defeated Perley and himself. When we talked together of the future he was very fine in saying that I must not be embarrassed in any way—to feel wholly free to do what I thought best. It is a very baffling situation for me. I would like McNaughton in the Government and feel that he is a real strength. I can see, however, that some of my colleagues may feel it would be inadvisable to risk a third election with him at least at present. My own probable defeat in Prince Albert may make it easier not to have too many by-elections at once. I shall have the same problem with MacLaren in New Brunswick. The people there evidently would welcome Bridges, who as a younger man would perhaps be the preferable choice at this time. Maybe I can get MacLaren to take some diplomatic post though I rather imagine he would be anxious to remain in the Ministry.

"It was very wet out-of-doors. I put on a little fire which made the room cheerful but I could not but feel very sad at heart for both the General and Mrs. McNaughton. They are fine people and have deserved better of the country. However, as I reminded McNaughton it was his own wish to go to Qu'Appelle and he rather took the bit in his own teeth in announcing that intention without sufficient in the way of consultation with myself and others. In this respect the misfortune is his own. I would certainly have secured a different seat for him. Being in Saskatchewan may have avoided the election taking too much of a turn on conscription."

The next day (June 17) some further returns were received from northern civilian polls in Prince Albert which put Mackenzie King ten votes ahead. This cheered him a little, though he had not much hope.

"A happening of today which gave me great pleasure", Mackenzie King noted, "was a telegram of congratulations from Churchill—the wording of which was quite unusual—much was left to be read between the lines. Message as follows:

" 'Personal and private—Although it is not proper for us to engage in reciprocal congratulations upon our various fortunes at the polls, I must say with what delight I learned that you had once again attained the position whence you can lead united Canada ever deeper into the union of the British Commonwealth and Empire. With every good wish.'

"What caused me great concern, however, was his message from Prime Minister to Prime Minister re the forthcoming meeting between Stalin, Truman and himself, which concluded as follows: 'This will be a difficult and fateful conference. The future of Europe and indeed the peace of the whole world may turn on the outcome of our discussions. I trust that we may be able to reach some good decisions.' This is a paragraph which causes one to have deep concern."

The additional returns on June 18 made defeat in Prince Albert virtually certain. Mackenzie King recorded that he had "been interested in watching the effect on myself of the reports as they indicated a likelihood of winning and then an equal likelihood of defeat. Undoubtedly the one brought a feeling of relief and of elation. The other, a little feeling of fatigue and disappointment but neither very much one way or the other. Were I really rested I think I would hardly be able to perceive the effect one way or the other of either result though, of course, to win would be a great triumph. It may be that the result in Prince Albert may help to disclose to the country the need for some other way of giving a certain degree of certainty and protection to one who holds the office Prime Minister."

On June 19 his defeat was finally confirmed. "So little did I care about the reference that was made to the defeat, that when some of the Ministers spoke to me about the defeat, I did not know to what they were referring. We were pleased at the group photo taken.

"I then suggested that McNaughton, MacLaren and I should be photographed as the Big Three, being the three who were defeated in the campaign. This took a little longer than I expected. It was arranged to have another photo taken on the lawn, out-of-doors. This was effected subsequently. It was a nice afternoon, and the group should be a good one."

CHAPTER ELEVEN

Election Postmortems and Peace

ON JUNE 19, at the first full Cabinet meeting after the Liberal victory, the Prime Minister expressed general satisfaction with the results across the nation. However, the election had created a number of problems which required quick solution. First, a safe seat had to be found for Mackenzie King and, second, the political future of the two defeated Ministers, McNaughton and MacLaren, had to be determined.

Not unexpectedly, Mackenzie King's immediate preoccupation was with the first problem. He told his colleagues that it was for them "to say whether I should stay on and where I should run. There was a chorus at once that I must certainly stay on and the seats spoken of were: Ottawa East—which I said I would not consider on any account; Russell, Glengarry were others mentioned. Ilsley spoke about a seat in N.S. which he said he was sure we could get by acclamation as we had a Senate vacancy there, but I mentioned I thought N.S. was too far away.

"I spoke myself of Prince County in P.E.I. but there was a feeling that it, too, was far away and it might be a hard fight now. Chevrier seemed to speak with greatest confidence. He felt that Russell could be opened, it was a safe seat and an acclamation. That Glengarry would be preferable, not having so large a French background but might occasion a fight, though I would be pretty sure of winning.

"I brought up the payment of family allowance cheques to fathers instead of mothers in Quebec. St. Laurent said now that elections were over, he was more or less indifferent and was quite agreeable to having cheques made payable to mothers though there might be some question of interference with the law of Quebec which would have to be worked out. I said I thought if paid to mothers in eight Provinces, it should be in the ninth. To make an exception in Quebec would be to single out Quebec against the rest of Canada in a Dominion-wide social measure that would do Quebec harm. Now was the time to take a definite stand. It was arranged that cheques would be made out for mothers instead of fathers. In the meantime, we would try to get further justification of that course. Council was practically unanimous on the matter."

The next morning (June 20) early, Mackenzie King received word that "Mr. Macdonald, President of the Eastern Ontario Liberal Association, along with two other gentlemen from Glengarry were on their way to Laurier House. One was the President of the Glengarry Association, Mr. Major, and the other was Mr. Macdonald, a son of Archie Macdonald, former Member for the Constituency.

"I invited them up to my library and began by speaking of the recent campaign and particularly of the campaign in Prince Albert. . . . How badly I felt for the workers and supporters and also at the severance of an association of so many years. I explained how I had been unable to visit the constituency during the war. Talked of the war obligations and then spoke of the present situation and indicated that I would be glad to retire gracefully at the moment having carried the party successfully through to victory. With the party successfully returned under my leadership, were I to consult my own personal feelings and interests, I would be prepared to retire and spend the next few years, if spared, doing many matters I have in mind; going over my private affairs, writing; explained the position with regard to making a will, etc. They said at once that I could not do that. That the country needed me at this time. I replied I believed that that was true and had told my colleagues that I would be quite prepared in the circumstances to carry on if they so desired. Would have to leave to them matters pertaining to the constituency, etc.

"Mr. Macdonald said: Would you not run in Glengarry? I paused for a moment and said it was most kind of him to even suggest anything of the kind. I mentioned that when I became leader, Mr. Bell had spoken to me of P.E.I. but also I had received from Glengarry a suggestion that I should run there. It was interesting that this suggestion should be made at this time. I spoke of what followed my association in P.E.I., etc. The other two members of the delegation then joined in to say that they thought Glengarry would be an ideal seat. That it was nearby; a compact constituency. That I would not be troubled with matters of patronage, largely agricultural, few industries; the cheese question was one that had been arranged. They felt pretty sure I could be elected by acclamation, certainly so far as the local forces were concerned. Asked if I knew what the high command of the Tory party could do. I said I did not know but I could not trust them in any way. If it were thought it would be best for me to run in Glengarry and it was agreeable to the constituency, I would not mind a fight excepting for the fatigue that it would involve and the added stress with all I have to give attention to. They stressed that if there was a fight, we would be certain to win; the organization was in splendid shape. They had won both the Provincial and the Federal seats and everything had been cleared up satisfactorily. There was the best of feeling and they were sure the local committees would work enthusiastically. They also stated that they thought we could roll up a majority of a couple of thousands. I said I would not wish to do anything that would in any way be other than pleasing to Dr. MacDiarmid. He had been a loyal supporter and I would not want any pressure put on him.

"Major said he had spoken with Dr. MacDiarmid last night or this morning and he knew the Doctor was only too ready to co-operate in every way. That he had so indicated. Also he was in town today and thought matters could be settled with him at once. I pointed out it was desirable to get matters settled quickly for wherever I ran, it would be desirable to have elections over in time to be in the House when it opened. I stressed the point that I could not give much time to the constituency. To that they replied there was really no patronage to look after. The riding was nearby but far enough away that I would not be troubled with requests for anything. They were all exceedingly pleasant and enthusiastic. Stressed the fact that they had come purposely to offer me the seat as representing the organization in the riding.

"I remarked this was a very significant and memorable morning and thanked them most warmly. I mentioned that I knew Macdonald was coming and had spoken to Chevrier about seeing him if he were coming to talk about political matters. They said they would go immediately to his office which they did. Before they left Laurier House, I showed them over the drawing room and dining room. They were anxious to get under way so did not delay longer. It was just about 11 when they left.

"At noon, I rang up Chevrier and ascertained from him that the delegation had made representations to him, identical to those which they had made to me. Chevrier added he had seen Dr. MacDiarmid earlier in the day and MacDiarmid himself had offered, without suggestion from Chevrier, to resign in my favour. I pointed out to Chevrier it would be necessary to give him some appointment. No matter what kind it might be. He could not resign himself except on accepting an office from the Crown. This was a surprise to Chevrier. I told him to consult the Justice Department and also the Secretary of State and make sure of this feature. When I said that personally I would be prepared to appoint him to the Senate, he mentioned he was over seventy and he, Chevrier, thought it was wiser not even to suggest that to him. He thought that something could be worked out which would be satisfactory and promised that he would take up the question of appointment with Mackenzie. I thought something in Health might be possible.

"Chevrier spoke about the possibility of a fight. I said offhand that I did not mind that. He then asked me if I had seen the Globe and Mail. I told him I never looked at it. His reply was it would be nothing short of a calamity if I were not in the next House, and that I should be returned by acclamation. While this was all right, I said I did not care one bit.

"He then said they might have a word with Bracken. I said I did not want to be under any obligation to Bracken. I ended up by telling him that I would be prepared to take Glengarry and, if opposition developed, and it was necessary, I would be glad to fight.

"Before Council this afternoon, I saw Howe and Chevrier. They told me they had arranged with Dr. MacDiarmid to resign, and he was quite willing to do so. He had told them that the Conservatives and others had suggested to him he should let me have his seat and that it would be a great honour to Glengarry to have the Prime Minister. (The Committee in the morning mentioned that Glengarry might be wiped out altogether in a redistribution, indicating that if I had it, as I did not intend to run again, it might help also in that respect.)

"There was a question about the resignation before the Speaker was appointed to the House.

"Claxton had arranged to give Dr. MacDiarmid a nominal temporary job worth about $50.00, to advise on some matters in his Department, so as to meet the technicality of the Act, and to get two elected Members to certify to his resignation. I suggested it might be best to arrange all this while I was at San Francisco. We could bring on the election as soon as I got back."

At 6.00 P.M. the Prime Minister sent for Dr. MacDiarmid. "I told him I had been informed that he was prepared to give me his seat. I said that I had mentioned to others that I would not consider taking it if it embarrassed him in any way and unless he was quite willing to resign. He told me he was only too ready to let me have his seat. He was now over 70 himself. Different friends had spoken to him about resigning and he was only too glad to help the party and myself in any way in his power. He knew that the Executive had been here and had offered the seat. He was quite agreeable to their action. I told Howe and Chevrier to get from the Executive and from the Doctor himself an invitation in writing to me to run. Have it ready on my return."

To Mackenzie King this was "another milestone in my career. It is indeed a source of profound satisfaction that a constituency such as Glengarry should come forward in the way in which it has to help to meet the situation in which, as leader of the party, I have been placed by the defeat in Prince Albert."

Before the delegation came from Glengarry, Mackenzie King had spoken on the telephone to Premier McNair of New Brunswick "about MacLaren's position. Told him I thought it would be best for me to leave matters to be worked out between him and MacLaren as he had practically worked out with MacLaren all arrangements regarding N.B. in the Federal campaign.

"McNair said the difficulty would be securing a seat for him here. He mentioned that Richard had telegraphed MacLaren offering him his seat but said that he should not have done this. That it was for the organization to settle these matters. Also that it was a French constituency and he did not think it would be wise for MacLaren to represent a French county.

"He then spoke of the Lieutenant-Governorship as a position which he thought MacLaren should fill. I said to him I had had the same thought in mind; told him I would be glad to see that he was carried on [as a Minister] but of course it would depend on his getting a seat in the Province. I could not impose my will on the constituencies. He said he could speak very frankly to MacLaren and would strongly advise his taking the Lieutenant-Governorship. He did not like (nor did I) the suggestion of the present Mayor for Lieutenant-Governor. That he had not always been friendly to him. Also MacLaren would make a much more dignified Governor. To me, this is the ideal thing. I mentioned that MacLaren might also be considered for some diplomatic post but stressed above everything we could take no chances on any possible defeat in a by-election." The Premier said he could talk "very frankly" to MacLaren.

The same day MacLaren came to Laurier House for lunch. Mackenzie King told him of his conversation with McNair on the day of his defeat and the conversation that morning over the telephone, suggested that he see McNair, and that it might be well to leave the whole matter pretty much between McNair and himself. Mackenzie King added "that McNair had been the one who had been anxious to have him appointed Minister; also we had accepted McNair's suggestion of Senators. I had also agreed to what he had suggested regarding the Lieutenant-Governor. . . .

"MacLaren said to me that there were two constituencies he thought he might be able to secure. He mentioned certain persons and big interest groups, like Nesbitt, etc., whom he thought should be seen. He also spoke of making some possible arrangements with the Conservatives to ensure his being returned if a seat were opened. I told him I had never made an arrangement with the Conservatives all the time I had been leader of the party. I did not trust them. I thought we should act independently of them. I said we would have to be perfectly sure that we could win. One seat was a French seat. I doubted the wisdom of his taking that seat in the light of all the factors to be considered. I told him I really felt the best way was to work out everything with McNair himself.

"When I mentioned about McNair having recommended Bridges, he said that McNair had been very much on the spot at the time. He said that Bridges had not always played fair with the Liberal party; admitted he had talents, and had won a good victory. I spoke of McNair having referred to the Lieutenant-Governorship. MacLaren said he knew that he had that in mind but he said 'is not a man through when he takes that position?' I said I did not think necessarily so. Mentioned that Bruce was in Parliament having been Lieutenant-Governor of Ontario at one time. I said much depended on the man himself. I said if there should be difficulty in working out a seat—some of the men unwilling to give up seats they had won—I would like him by all means to feel there were other posts he would be able to fill. I then spoke particularly of the Lieutenant-Governorship, which I thought would please the province, and also of some diplomatic post. I referred to the High Commissionership in India or in New Zealand, or possible Minister to some of the European or South American countries. He asked me about the ones that were left. As he himself was leaving Laurier House, he said he would get in touch with McNair at once; would probably meet him on Monday next; would talk over the situation with him, and return later. He would talk matters over with his wife, particularly as regards Government House, and some diplomatic post. His preference, of course, is to continue in the Ministry, if that can be arranged. I thought he fully appreciated my position, and he saw that it was something that had to be brought about within the province itself."

During the afternoon Mackenzie King had the senior Ministers come in for a talk about McNaughton and MacLaren. "Ilsley thought McNaughton was very helpful as a colleague and a good administrator. I [King] found him a very useful member of the Cabinet. Altogether Ministers were high in their praise but some did not think it would be advisable to run him again after he had had two defeats. There was of course the difficulty of a seat. MacKinnon was not favourable to his running again. Howe had spoken to me previously, saying that we would never cut down expenditures with all that he wanted to do. Mackenzie had written me against having him run. Mackenzie's communication suggests himself for Minister of Transport, and to have MacLaren come back into the Government. I am afraid that Mackenzie is breaking up altogether. Gardiner was strongly favourable to McNaughton being continued. He said he owes his own seat in Saskatchewan to speeches McNaughton had made on his behalf. Gibson said nothing. St. Laurent said a seat could easily be found in Quebec, but was not too sure it would be advisable to have him run there. As regards MacLaren, I told them of my talk with McNair. On the whole, they were favourable to MacLaren personally, but most of them seemed to feel there might be difficulty in arranging for a seat. Also if we could not find a seat for McNaughton, we should not arrange one for MacLaren. I told them to take the time that I would be away in San Francisco to talk matters over and when I came back we would see what should be done. It was a very difficult situation.

"I saw McNaughton later and I told him of the conversation. I let him know that the Ministers were friendly toward him, but the problem was one of a seat and not taking chances on a third defeat. He stressed again not to be embarrassed in the least; also that he was no quitter. It was the Cause that counted and not the Man. He was prepared to do any fighting —he would never let up with these men. He spoke again of the situation that we were faced with at the time. He was sure we had done the right thing. I told him I was equally sure—that neither election was a fair test, so far as he was concerned."

The Cabinet meeting that day (June 20) was also an important one. The Prime Minister suggested that he might "meet the press later and give out the announcement of the opening of the new session, the date of the Dominion-Provincial Conference, also about St. Laurent and myself going to San Francisco. All this was approved, including statement re shortening the hours of Civil Servants by half an hour.

"Howe brought up an important matter of our continuing to help Russia, though she is no longer fighting an enemy. He said he had reason to believe that Russia would come in against the Japs. They wanted some of the metals we had promised them, but they were put off when the war against Germany ended. I mentioned we were in the same position in this matter as we had been regarding metals to Japan. We had met Britain's wish in keeping her supplied with metals, though she became an enemy later. There were those who feared that Russia might become an enemy later. On the other hand, there was the need of cultivating friendships with Russia at present and with the war in Germany over, refusal might create enmity, where fulfilling an obligation might increase friendship. It was clearly the consensus of the Cabinet that we should carry out our obligation. Howe was strongly for this. McNaughton was particularly strong. Ilsley was agreeable.

"We also discussed the question of an Air contingent against Japan. Two squadrons for air and five for transportation. I read the communication from Churchill and my reply. Council agreed we should not commit ourselves to more than the two and the five. I brought up the desire of the Services themselves to add supplementary equipment, to make the organization itself self-contained, like hospitals, etc. I pointed out that we should be able to share in these things with the Americans and the British, not to try to extend our own service. Further I drew attention to how

Churchill's despatch made clear that Britain was doing only what the Americans allowed her and what she was trying to do was to develop an Imperial Air Force. The language of the message itself spoke of it as a Commonwealth Force, etc. I did not think we should raise an issue on it at the moment but felt we should take care to see that every step was taken to preserve our complete autonomy."

On Friday evening, June 22, the Prime Minister and St. Laurent left by air for San Francisco for the signing of the United Nations Charter. They arrived at noon on June 23. In the afternoon Mackenzie King went to a meeting of the Steering Committee which had been called "to approve the Charter. A substitute introductory page as to the purpose of the Charter had been put forward. It provoked considerable debate.

"Fernandez, of Chile, said he would not sign the Charter if it was substituted for the introduction previously agreed to. Smuts explained the nature of the changes, one being a substitution of the word 'worth' for 'value' in reference to men. Another correction of a grammatical mistake in a clause which was wrongly constructed.

"The main difficulty was substitution of the words 'law and pledged word' in a clause that contained reference to treaties and obligation arising out of treaties. There was a debate of an hour or more on the matter.

"On comparison of the pages, I saw where by changing the order of the words, mistakes had arisen in the last two clauses. I made a suggestion to Halifax as to what should be done. He told me by all means to speak. Thought I was right. Later sent me a note saying he hoped I would speak which I finally did.

"I was given a rousing reception when I got up—a real welcome. I pointed out that the drafting had indicated the purposes of the Charter in words which began with a significant verb but that in the second last clause, a transposition of a modifying sentence would bring its language into accord with the other and if this were done, the final clause could begin, as General Smuts had suggested, with a verb and all would be in order.

"I then pointed out that, as others had mentioned, the insertion of the words 'will and thought' and 'law and pledged word' more than covered 'Treaty.' That there might be advantage in inserting the word 'Treaty' and that these changes all together might be satisfactory. I suggested it might be referred back to co-ordinating committee to consider those changes. Stettinius put this forward as the motion of the Prime Minister of Canada. It was finally accepted with the addition which Lord Halifax had earlier proposed that the co-ordinating committee should make the changes without referring back to a steering committee. If anyone had told me yesterday afternoon that I would be speaking on the Charter within twenty-four hours of the time of leaving Ottawa—as late as 10 at night—and coming by 'plane, I would have said that the thing was impossible. It was a sort of destiny that seemed to bring it about that, as a matter of fact, I had almost the last word in the revision of the Charter as I had almost the first word in respect to the languages to be used in discussion and other matters at the preliminary meeting."

The next day (June 24) at 11.00 A.M. Mackenzie King left his hotel to call on Field Marshal Smuts. "We had an exceedingly pleasant talk in his suite at the Fairmont. He seemed genuinely enthusiastic about my victory in Canada. Spoke of it having an important effect on the British elections. Also of it being a strong vindication of my policies and really a remarkable achievement.

"In conversation, he said to me: King, the thing we must watch is this tendency among the Civil Service in London to try and bring about machinery for keeping the Empire together. He went on to speak of Curtin as not having had much experience and went on to stress the very points I had stressed so strongly in London and with which he agreed at the last Conference but quite the opposite to what I felt his views were in previous conferences. He spoke about what had taken place here. Said that Evatt and Fraser had talked so much and had been so difficult at times that a week ago they had had an evening with Halifax when Halifax who was a good Christian soul had begun to speak about the exhibition the Empire was making in the presence of Americans and other countries. He, Smuts, had felt it desirable to break into the conversation and said he really felt it had been on the whole very good. The other nations should see that each part of the Empire really managed [its own affairs] and we were not following just one particular course. At heart, when great issues arose, we were together but each was master in his own household or words to this effect. Smuts agreed that it had been a fine demonstration of the absurdity of talking about the Empire having one voice and likely to go the same way in international affairs.

"On the whole, he feels that a good charter has been prepared. He spoke about the need of getting back to Africa saying that, in these days, times of war, etc., a P.M. is really the government and it does not do to be away too long. He spoke about my having a large French minority to handle. His problem was a Dutch majority which was quite difficult."

That evening the Prime Minister dined with Lord Halifax, Senator Vandenberg, Smuts, and Lord Cranborne. "After dinner, we talked in the sitting room until about 20 to 11. I enjoyed the evening exceedingly. In the early part, the talk was mostly of the democratic trends and the great influence which Russia was likely to have, in the different countries in

Europe and on this continent. All were agreed that it was necessary that legislation should help to equalize the opportunities for the mass of the people. There was a good deal of discussion of the Dominion election and some lessons to be drawn therefrom. All present felt that it would have been a pretty serious thing for Churchill and his chances in England if I had lost in the campaign. There was general feeling that Canada was in a better position this year than the other countries. The one question that Smuts kept asking was whether we could keep up in times of peace what we were doing in financial ways in times of war. I stressed the point that so much depended on what happened in other countries. We could hold our own unless there was too much of a depression in the United States or Europe. There was a recognition that the problems ahead are really very serious. They will demand great care.

"In the course of the evening, a number of subjects were discussed; among others, Smuts gave an interesting account of the situation at the beginning of the war in South Africa when Hertzog was Prime Minister and Smuts, Deputy. The Cabinet had discussed matters as to whether they should go into the war and were divided—7 to 6. 7 for going in. Hertzog thought they could maintain neutrality, that they could win by 13 on a vote in the House. Unfortunately for him, said Smuts, he made a speech which was rather a pro-Hitler speech. Smuts was able to point out that England had been fair in self government to South Africa. They had no grievances. The proposal now was to leave those who were their friends, and lean toward the camp of the enemies. He pointed to the position S. Africa would be in if the Germans came in their direction. He won the division by 13. He became Prime Minister and within two days had declared for war. He said in his speech he had not come out for declaring war but rather for severing relations with Germany. He had been up-braided for that but it was a necessary step. I asked what would have happened at the time of Munich. He said he could not have persuaded S. Africa to go into the war then. They needed time to see the develop-ment. I spoke about Canada being divided too at that time and said we would have found it difficult to go into the war.

"Halifax agreed that Chamberlain had been wise at Munich, but that the blame was rather that he had not become active after Munich in the preparation for war. Smuts was strongly pro-Chamberlain. Some-one had mentioned that Roosevelt had cabled Chamberlain two words after Munich which were: Good man.

"We got on then to the question of how self-government was obtained in South Africa. First, Smuts told of how Churchill had, during the South African war, represented one of the English papers. When the leader was killed, he a young fellow then of 22, became leader of a group against the Boers. Was caught. Arrested and brought before Smuts for trial. Smuts was Attorney General then. He pointed out he had used arms, etc., and had him sent to a prisoners of war camp. Also he was a Times correspondent. Smuts then concluded he should perhaps revise his sentence of Churchill. Churchill had been very wrathy when he was sentenced. He had the papers all made out for releasing him when he found that Churchill had escaped from the camp. They did not meet again until six years after when Smuts went as representative of South Africa to England for self-government. He had come to the Secretary of State for the Colonies Department and was brought in touch with Churchill who was Under-Secretary. He did not talk with Lord Elgin. Churchill then asked him if it was not only six years before that the British had taken the country and now they were being asked to give it back. Smuts argued that they did not wish to have a second Ireland in South Africa. Tried to point out that the Boers would be good friends, etc. Churchill, however, was opposed. Campbell-Bannerman who was Prime Minister said later that Smuts had convinced him that South Africa should be given self-government. The next day, he brought the Cabinet together. Said it must be done. There was no opposition in the Cabinet and the measure carried. Churchill had then done splendid work in promoting the Bill through the House. I asked if Canada's influence was not a real one. Smuts said: indeed it was. Laurier had been very helpful. His letters to Botha were important. He spoke very highly of Botha. I recalled the evening at Buckingham Palace when King George V spoke of Desmond Fitzgerald having been imprisoned and sentenced to be hanged, and about my speaking about a proclamation on my grand-father's head."

Later, conversation turned to Winston Churchill and his work habits. "Of his plan of resting most of the afternoon. That he could not go through a whole day. Took the afternoon off and was wakened up then for the night, although sometimes he would go on talking both to the Cabinet and to individuals. Both Smuts and Halifax felt that he [Churchill] was not overworked. That he did not try to read many papers or reports. That he gathered things from his colleagues. Had a natural flair for politics and seeing things. He thought Eden [who had been ill] was getting better and would be able to tackle matters in another fortnight. Neither Halifax nor Cranborne were too sanguine about the results or what might come out of the elections.

"I found Vandenberg very pleasant. He has had a time fighting the C.I.O. in Michigan. He took a serious view about the situation ahead. . . . They all felt that Russia had been difficult in the conference here. Halifax had a better opinion of Gromyko than Smuts had. Vandenberg said he did not like the British Empire, the U.S., China, France, all sitting around having to be told by Russia what they were to do. He could not stand too much of that.

"The evening altogether was an extremely pleasant one and I found myself very much at ease and happy in talking with this particular group. I think it is the weight of uncertainty off my mind and the vindication of my policies against the perpetual detraction."

Next morning (June 25) the Prime Minister had an interview with Evatt "who spoke very strongly against the way in which the British had, as he expressed it, gone back on everything that had been agreed to by them at London. He said to me that I had been right all along in regard to desire to control things in London; that he was strongly opposed to anything of the kind. Curtin, the Prime Minister, had gone to London without understanding these questions and had made suggestions he [Curtin] now sees are quite wrong. I told him about Smuts having said: we must watch not to let them develop centralized machinery in London. Said he thought this was right but that Smuts had been a great disappointment to him. That he had trimmed in so many different directions. He [Evatt] had come just to say good-bye. Was returning to Australia at once. I was relieved to find he had not come to say he was coming to Canada for a few days."

Mackenzie King talked to Lord Cranborne about his forthcoming visit to Ottawa and also about a successor to the Governor-General. "When I spoke of Airlie, he said that Airlie was a cousin of his. Thought he would be very good but was not too sure that his wife would not be a little too retiring.

"I spoke of George Macaulay Trevelyan. He could think of no better name. Doubted if he would be available. Also felt he was a little old. Spoke very highly of Mrs. Trevelyan whom he knew, in association with crippled children work at Passmore Edwards Settlement.

"I spoke of General Alexander. He thought he would be excellent. A very pleasant man. A great soldier but also a great diplomat, one who would be fond of going about the country to explore the recesses of Canada. Would get on well with a lot of people. I spoke of the Queen's brothers. He thought either of them would be very good, particularly the older brother, Michael, who was a country gentleman, who was friendly with everyone. He would be first rate, better than the younger brother whom I know and like exceedingly."

In the afternoon the Prime Minister drove out to the airport to meet President Truman. Mackenzie King reported that "his appearance was exceedingly pleasant. Very fresh. His whole manner, active. I was amazed at the lightness and rapidity of his step. After preliminary ceremonies, he received the chief heads of delegations. Stettinius in presenting me mentioned that I had come back from Canada to be present at the ceremony. The President spoke of the pleasure of meeting me and that he was looking forward to my visit to Washington. Was sorry to have had to delay it. I thanked Mr. Truman very warmly for the telegram of congratulations he had sent me on the outcome of the elections. I said I was much looking forward to talks with him later on.

"After the presentations, there was a review of the troops and then a procession was formed in Hamilton Field in to the City and through the streets of San Francisco. As we drove along, the name of Canada on the car and the Canadian flag were recognized by the people. We received a fine reception by groups all along the way and in the City. One could hear people saying: There is Canada, and immediately they would begin to applaud. Several times I heard my own name mentioned. Anyone might have been proud of the welcome that was accorded Canada all the way in. The sight in the downtown part of the city was a memorable one. The parade was well organized and all passed off splendidly."

That evening a plenary session was held at which the Charter was accepted by all the delegations. The actual ceremony of signing the Charter was on June 26. Immediately after his morning reading, Mackenzie King "began to work on a brief statement to read after signing. We had been told that the signing might begin at 9 and it would possibly be around 10 before Canada would be sent for. Fortunately the postponements came every half hour. It was finally about 1 when we left the Hotel for the Veterans' Building where the signatures were placed. Meanwhile I had time to prepare something myself. I did not care for the statement which had been handed me and which I think had been prepared by Chipman. I felt I should bring in thoughts of my own from Industry and Humanity. After all, that book contains the foundational principles on which the whole work of the United Nations organization is based. It took me back in thoughts to the days when I was preparing the book and made me feel that today really was the consummation of a heart's desire and life effort to bring about peace between nations to the extent that it might be possible to make some contribution through one's researches and writings.

"I found in the pages of Industry and Humanity what I wanted; also a sentence or two in some of the speeches based on what had been written there. Having to reduce one's remarks to a minute and a few seconds necessitated cutting out two paragraphs that I would have welcomed inserting. However the little statement prepared touched, I believe, the right note and in the circumstances was of the right length. I managed to get a half hour's rest before leaving. This was most welcome.

"At the ceremony, St. Laurent and I, having full powers, signed on behalf of Canada. The arrangements were well worked out—a circular table in the centre of a stage; members of our party standing in a semi-circle immediately behind where we affixed our signatures. I used the pen with the Harvard shield with my initials on it—a gift, some years ago, from Joan, though purchased by myself at her request at the Harvard Club in New York. This link with Harvard gave me very great pleasure. There was something most fitting about using this particular pen on this occasion, linking Cambridge, Mass., with San Francisco, Calif.—a sort of wider circle outside the political one from Vancouver to Saint John. There is no doubt that a kind Providence has been watching over me today. I might easily have missed altogether having any satisfying statement. This would have been an unfortunate omission. As it was, I think all went off as well as could possibly have been expected."

There was some suggestion that day of a possible visit to Canada by General de Gaulle. Mackenzie King was not enthusiastic, doubting the reception he would get and also fearing the political effect of a visit. He reflected that "while the large majority we have from Quebec is something to be grateful for, in carrying on of government, it is a terrible handicap for the party politically in its relations with the rest of Canada. Anything relating to the French or to the Roman Catholic Church which Orangemen and others, similarly inclined, can twist to their advantage will be exploited to the limit from now on. I can see where the appointment of Vanier and his wife, to my mind, who are the ideal persons for Government House, might lead to any kind of consequences were that selection to be made at the present time. It is here where qualities of judgment, vision, and experience have to be exercised to the full. The maintenance of national unity must continue to be the guiding star of all policies."

That afternoon the final plenary session of the Conference was held in the Opera House. Mackenzie King and his party "came in just a minute or two before President Truman walked on to the stage with Mr. Stettinius. There is an alertness about Truman's steps and movements generally which impresses one. Also his very pleasant smile. Proceedings were fairly long, and as some of the addresses were delivered in foreign languages, a little tiring. However, on the whole, most interesting. Halifax, briefest of all, and perhaps one of the best in substance. Personally I thought Paul Boncour's [Foreign Minister of France] delivery of his address without notes, almost verbatim of the English translation, was a remarkable feat. Delivery quite impressive. . . . Mazaryk's appealing in its delivery. I was disappointed in Smuts' address. I got a bit of a shock as it had special mention of Australia, New Zealand and India in connection with British Colonial Empire, but no reference to Canada excepting under the head of the 'Dominions.' I am sure it was an oversight in preparation and nothing intentional. He, himself, told me that no persons had been more helpful than Robertson and Wrong. He evidently was trying to make up with Evatt and Fraser in relation to a part of the proceedings which were significant to South Africa but not to Canada. I felt sorry for Robertson who, though he said very little, seemed to feel quite deeply about the omission.

"What made it doubly unfair and unpleasant was that Evatt had been specially mentioned at the final Plenary Conference by a resolution from Peru. To me, it looked like a case where if men are nasty and rough enough, they get the credit and the decent people are left behind. It was an unpleasant and indeed painful omission. It was the one disappointing feature in the afternoon's proceedings.

"I thought Truman's speech very good. On the whole, well delivered with no pretension. Direct and outspoken. I like his modesty and absence of affectation."

Mackenzie King's plane left San Francisco at 11 P.M. for the return flight to Ottawa, where he and his party arrived at two o'clock on the afternoon of June 27.

The following day, June 28, the Cabinet again discussed Canada's contribution to the war against Japan. Mackenzie King protested against the size of the proposed air force contribution and was also much annoyed "over Mackenzie having left this morning for England without having got my consent and apparently without having Ilsley's assent when I was away. I told the Cabinet no Minister was to leave the country for other countries without advising me in advance of his intention and having my approval. I had allowed a certain freedom during the last few months, also during the elections, and the years of war but that I would have to take my responsibilities more seriously from now on.

"Also we had a warm time over the word that Grattan O'Leary was among three or four persons intending to cross to England tomorrow to speak to soldiers on Canada's rehabilitation programme. It seemed an outrage that he who had attacked McNaughton and myself so vigorously and viciously [in the press], should be chosen for this purpose. What was worse is he came under the Wartime Information Board which is under the President of the Council." The whole expedition was cancelled as a result of the Prime Minister's protest.

Smuts and Cranborne were both in Ottawa at the end of June. The former spoke to the Canadian Club on June 29. Mackenzie King noted that "Smuts read his address. Spoke very highly of Canada's war effort. Touched also on the work of the Canadian delegation at San Francisco but not as much as I thought he should have in view of my having drawn his attention to the speech at San Francisco which seemed to credit Australia and New Zealand unduly. He told me he had meant it only in regard to Trusteeship business. That on the things that really mattered, the critical and important things, that Canada's contribution, of course, had been the most important. His review of the Conference was good."

On June 29, Mackenzie King found time to speak to McNaughton about a seat in Parliament. He reported that McNaughton said "the main thing was for me to get a seat first. I spoke of Nova Scotia and being able to get a seat there, but he thought it would open at once the contention between Ralston and himself and also between Angus Macdonald and himself. I spoke of how Macdonald had taken up the question of loss of life when sinking ships, and McNaughton's statement regarding same. McNaughton said it was clear they wanted to destroy him. He did not think it would be wise to run in Nova Scotia." Mackenzie King also telephoned Donald Macdonald of Glengarry and arranged to attend a convention on July 17.

One of the questions Mackenzie King had to settle in July, 1945, was the succession at Government House. He noted in his diary that the Governor-General had telephoned him on July 6 about some prospective visits. "I think what he really wanted to know," Mackenzie King wrote, "was whether I had made a decision on my recommendation to the King. I told him that Council would be meeting on Tuesday after which I would hope to definitely settle the matter of his successor. That I held in my thought to the names I had mentioned to him. The more I think matters over, the more I have to come to feel that the appointment of Airlie would be the best of any, unless possibly General Alexander.

"It is I think important that whoever is appointed should be someone whom the King himself would wish to have come to Canada. I know his preference is for Lord Airlie."

The Athlones came to Kingsmere to tea on Sunday, July 8, and the Prime Minister talked to Athlone about his successor. "I told him I was rather favourable to Airlie on the whole; particularly as the King himself had spoken of him when he was in Canada. I thought I would submit three names: (1) Airlie; (2) General Alexander, and (3) Trevelyan. They asked me about the Wakehursts. I said I thought perhaps the others would be preferable. I doubted if coming after seven years in the States and Australia, they would be best for Canada. H.R.H . . . spoke again of the King and Queen being anxious about a trip for Princess Elizabeth. Wished they might have been here at the time of the Royal Visit.

"It was apparent from the conversation that there have been communications between the Governor General and the King looking toward the possibility of Airlie coming out. Princess Alice spoke of his being

Scotch and of that being a guarantee of certain type of character, also of Lady Airlie being a very fine person—not one who had been spending most of her time in London society but very friendly among all the people in her own community.

"They asked me if I had thought of Lord Burghley and his wife who are in Bermuda. He is youthful. They said I might have to train him up myself but thought they were both exceedingly nice; she is one of the Buccleuchs; a sister of Gloucester's wife. I doubt the wisdom of a too youthful Governor General in these times."

At the Cabinet on July 10, Mackenzie King raised the question of the succession at Government House. "Mentioned the names of Trevelyan, Airlie and Sir Harold Alexander. McNaughton said he knew Trevelyan well and endorsed him very strongly. Paul Martin also, who had been at Cambridge. There was unanimous approval of all names. I counselled strict secrecy." The next day (July 11) the Prime Minister drafted a letter to the King submitting the names of Trevelyan, Lord Airlie, and Field Marshal Alexander.

On July 14, Mackenzie King received a "reply from the King re the Governor General pointing out Trevelyan's age a little against him. Not quite sure if Alexander would be free to accept, stating Airlie would be admirable if Alexander does not accept. My own guess is that Airlie will be the one though it is clear the King's preference is now for Alexander with Airlie, second.

"I had Robertson send Massey a further wire to see Trevelyan at once and make clear to him that so far as we were concerned, we did not feel his years would be a disadvantage for the position. Indeed with his alert mind, years would not weigh so heavily. I have no doubt the Court prefers someone with a title and someone more in the social and Court circle. However, I am glad to be on record in pressing for Trevelyan and am glad to have submitted three names to the King." In the diary for July 20, Mackenzie King recorded having "received word from Lascelles day before yesterday that General Alexander would be available from the military point of view. Word today from Massey that he had seen Trevelyan who deeply appreciated the thought of his name being submitted but felt his years would not permit of this; also his duties. That leaves the choice to between Sir Harold Alexander and Lord Airlie. I suggested to Robertson to prepare a despatch allowing the King to express his preference and agreeing to take into consideration the preference he might wish to have.

"After all, it is his representative and as long as we retain the right of recommendation, allowing the King to decide between two is not lessening our right in any way or reverting to an order where the King himself makes a choice. I am glad to be getting this matter straightened out."

The succession was finally settled on July 24 when Mackenzie King received a message from Lascelles, "saying the King was much pleased at being given an opportunity to express preference re the Governor General and giving reasons why he thought Sir Harold Alexander would be preferable to Airlie. He spoke of Alexander in the highest terms, also of his wife, made a suitable reference to his great position as a world figure and as meriting so great a recognition.

"I should have noted a few days ago that on Saturday last a picture appeared in the Journal showing Sir Harold Alexander and his wife in the garden giving their little boy a swing. As soon as I saw that picture, it settled my mind at once as to his being the right person. I am really delighted that the matter has come out as it has. I have felt a certain obligation to Airlie, but that is wholly fulfilled by having submitted his name to the King and the King himself having expressed a preference for Alexander. The appointment will show I have not necessarily been prejudiced against appointing a military man simply because he belongs to the Army. Alexander has the qualities of a very wise diplomat. I am sure too the Canadian people will like the appointment, which is particularly appropriate at a time when the country will be filled with returned men, many of whom have served under Alexander, also in years when we are liable to have difficult situations to deal with in which returned men will be involved. I feel there will be a certain added security in having Alexander as the Governor General.

"As soon as I got this telegram, which was shortly after 3 this afternoon, I revised a reply that Robertson had prepared. I sent it to Lascelles to forward to Sir Harold, saying I would like to submit his name to the King and that it was unnecessary to mention the reasons why my colleagues and I hoped he would accept the appointment. I added I felt sure he would be warmly welcomed by the Canadians."

Another issue still outstanding, of course, was the seats for McNaughton and MacLaren. MacLaren's case was much simpler, since there was an obvious successor and much less obligation to him. In fact, the matter was virtually settled on July 5 when MacLaren dined with Mackenzie King. He told the Prime Minister of the canvass he had made of the situation in New Brunswick. He "had come to the conclusion that there was a chance in one of the constituencies, namely Kent, and that conditions there were by no means sure. He agreed that the population being largely French, it might do the party a certain injury for the English-speaking element in N.B. They might resent the party being again represented by someone who held a French constituency. He was very reasonable about the whole matter. Suggested having Leger [the member for Kent] come here for a conference on Tuesday at which time we could definitely settle the matter. He said he would be quite willing to take the Lieutenant-Governorship. Spoke also of having to do with taking over the Chairmanship of the Harbour Board at Saint John, if that position were likely to be at all permanent. I felt an immense relief when he gave me the assurance—when he, himself, volunteered his readiness to take on the Lieutenant-Governorship. He agreed with me that in the interests of the party, we should take no risk. I would like him immensely as a colleague but I am not sure that everything considered, it may not be better to have a choice made from one of those who have been elected and who, throughout their lives, have been identified with the Liberal party. MacLaren himself has been thought of more as a Conservative."

Leger came to see the Prime Minister on July 9 and said he was ready to resign his seat for MacLaren if the Prime Minister asked him to do so. Mackenzie King told Leger that he was "afraid the English-speaking people of N.B. would resent MacLaren representing what was really a French constituency and that we might be embarrassed federally in Western provinces if we built up our strength too exclusively on the backing of the French. He agreed that this was quite true."

The next day Mackenzie King had a further talk with MacLaren. "I told him that while Leger was prepared to give up his seat I did not feel that we should trust any Conservative promise of not offering opposition; that I felt Members of New Brunswick generally were not anxious to have a by-election and that I knew also the Premier, Senator Burchell and others were much opposed to it. There was a feeling against having the Minister represent a seat that was mostly Acadian, where it was understood there would be a change from one to the other. I told MacLaren that I felt, everything considered, it would be better to have him take the Lieutenant-Governorship.

"MacLaren will be going back to New Brunswick and will be coming here again on Wednesday of next week to have matters finally settled. I let him know that I had not discussed the situation with our other Ministers but would have a word with them, but left him definitely with the impression it was my wish he should accept the Lieutenant-Governorship. I rather intimated I felt Emmerson [MP for Westmoreland] was deserving of careful consideration. That, as regards Bridges, I thought that men should prove their ability first of all in the House. I talked this over with Pickersgill a little earlier. He himself thought that was perhaps best. Emmerson had a son killed in the war; has had several sons in the war. He was in the last war. While he is not brilliant I would think he might fill some position quite well. He would not want to run in another general election."

On July 17, Mackenzie King noted in his diary that he felt very concerned about McNaughton. "I told him we would have a talk together in the next day or two. I doubt if he realizes that it may not be possible to have him stay on longer." Two days later, the Prime Minister discussed the problem with St. Laurent. "There was no doubt in St. Laurent's mind that we should not open a seat in N.B. Coming to McNaughton, he said he would be perfectly prepared to open a seat in Quebec and felt sure we could elect McNaughton there. He thought the time had come that while it might look like defiance we ought to make it clear to all Canada that Quebec was as much a part of Canada as any other part. With this, I agreed. I pointed out, however, that what we ought to consider is not to handicap McNaughton himself in the Ministry and asked whether in his own interests, a hiatus at least for a while might not be all to the good.

"I spoke of his making a review of affairs of the Defence Department with a view to accounting for all the forces, equipment, etc., and means of reducing the size of our military forces. The danger there is that McNaughton himself has big ideas and might present a report that might be embarrassing. St. Laurent feels that the one question of the unwisdom of having him stay on is that we might never get the armed forces to the proportions they should be at. Howe feels this very strongly. We talked of other posts. I agreed that I would see McNaughton later this afternoon.

"Later, MacLaren came in. He had come back yesterday from the Maritimes, and evidently from the talks he had had in N.B., he felt it might embarrass the party if he stayed on. He had found that the men who had helped him in N.B. had felt they had fought a big battle, especially in York Sunbury, and other places, and that they were more or less decided to let the choice be made from men who had been elected. Also they felt Saint John should not have the Minister, meaning that Saint John had not elected MacLaren. I gathered from what he said they were hoping for Bridges' appointment. He said he did not know much about Emmerson. Just what help he would be, which caused me to feel that while Leger was against Bridges, he, MacLaren, was not going to say anything against him. I told him I thought he had the situation summed up right.

"I then spoke to him about taking the Lieutenant-Governorship. He expressed his readiness to do this. Anxious to have the appointment announced at the same time as his resignation. Also have it made for the 1st of September. I read him parts of letters to the Lieutenant-Governor. Said I thought there would be no difficulty in arranging this. I had called

McNair earlier. He answered while MacLaren was with me. I got him later. He told me that Clark was prepared to retire at the end of October. There were some events happening in Fredericton in the interval which, as a matter of pride and interest, he wished to be in office for, at that time. McNair agreed to see him at once personally. This other information had come through his son and he would 'phone again to let me have word. This he did about 3 P.M. telling me that he had seen Clark and was authorized to say to me for him that he would like to retire on the 31st of October. McNair thought he was anxious to stay until that day and it would be inadvisable to suggest an earlier date. I can arrange that with MacLaren to his satisfaction by making his appointment forthwith to take effect on October 31st. This is a considerable relief."

Later that day, after the Cabinet, Mackenzie King had a further talk with McNaughton. He told him he "was concerned about what it was best to do in his case, the difficulty being that of getting a seat that seemed to be secure. I noticed in conversation he somewhat changed the ground that he had been taking before which was not to let me be embarrassed in any way but to do exactly what I wished to do. This time it was rather that if he were an embarrassment to the Government in any way, particularly as regards its social programme going through, he of course would not wish to stay on. He wished to be sure that all Members of the Government wanted him to stay. I told him I thought they all were as friendly as could be but the real problem was getting a safe seat. He agreed that the choice lay between Ontario and Quebec. I pointed out the necessity of getting the party to back him in the campaign. Told him that MacLaren might drop out because he could not get the Province and the Government to help him in a fight or others to give up a seat. We would have to be very sure in his case. He agreed about the security. I could see he has rather become set in the hopes that he will be kept on though leaving it entirely to me and the party to arrange.

"I told him I had still to consult the Ministers but would do so at once as to a seat. He said whether in or out, he would continue to fight the gang that had opposed him as they were not the people who should get control in Canada. I said to him I thought it would be well to let some of the persecution of the present die down and come in a little later. In that connection, I asked if he would be interested in representing Canada on the United Nations Council and on the Board that will be appointed in another month to bring the United Nations organization into being. His answer was that he really was interested in Canada and the development of resources here. That he was not anxious to leave Canada. It was a difficult subject to discuss but I was quite frank about the situation and I think he realizes I have a difficult problem to deal with; personally I would miss him out of the Cabinet very much. Also I feel we owe everything to him for helping us over a crisis. I spoke of that to him but he said in regard to that he had done what he thought was right. Had served the purpose that was intended at the time and would always feel that of itself was the right thing done at the right time and that was the only thing that mattered."

Mackenzie King noted on July 20: "I hope that before the end of next week, McNaughton's position will be straightened out. I shall be happy if it can be arranged to have him run. That is my own feeling but one must make perfectly sure of victory. I feel the defeat in the first election may have been our fault in the choice of constituency. The second defeat was clearly McNaughton's own determination to run in the constituency in which Moosomin was located. I would never have allowed it only I knew he would be put out if he did not have that chance."

The Prime Minister recorded two important interviews on July 24, with St. Laurent and Howe, concerning McNaughton. "St. Laurent had had a meeting with the French Members. They had come to the conclusion that Chateauguay-Huntingdon would be the best riding. Had seen Black the Member who was ready to stand aside. His organization were canvassing the field. It was thought that this riding would correspond in Quebec with Glengarry on the Ontario side, being partly French and partly English. One or two other ridings were mentioned but they were more distinctly all French. St. Laurent also said Parent's riding in Quebec City we could be sure of winning. I pointed out that Chateauguay-Huntingdon had had very narrow margins over many years. That Robb's [J. A. Robb, a former Liberal Minister] popularity as an Englishman held there but that we had lost the riding once or twice. Also it was like Stanstead which had been held by Davidson, who, however, was beaten in a by-election when they decided to run a French candidate, against having an English candidate take the seat. I said almost certainly the Conservatives would arrange somehow to have a French Liberal to run and would back him and the election would then be on a race cry. It was agreed that wherever he ran it would be a general election fight, everyone piling in to win the constituency. As for Quebec West, this was a distinctly French riding and it would be a handicap to McNaughton himself in the Administration. It would also be a handicap to the party in the other Provinces.

"Howe had seen some of the Ontario men. They concluded the only seat they would be sure about was Farquhar's in Algoma. We agreed that Algoma would be a difficult seat to fight. An easy one for Tory party to corrupt. With a Tory Government in Ontario anything might happen. It was thought that perhaps it would be better to go right into Quebec where

McNaughton would be safe. The upshot of the conversation was that we all agreed it would be taking too great a risk to open any seat. It would be different if some seat opened of itself. Also we all felt that for McNaughton to stay on just now would mean that the first session of the new Parliament might get off to a very contentious start. It was better, seeing how narrow our margin was, to start quietly to capture a few seats as we went along. Approval was expressed on this score. St. Laurent expressed great fear at trying to have only one opposition recognized. Said it might force the C.C.F. and Social Creditors to really take a stand against us. It would be better for our sake to encourage them to divide against each other. I, of course, feel that with our majority so slender, it may be better to go easy for a time and not seek to hold to the two-party idea.

"After Council I had a talk with Abbott about McNaughton. He was very strong against the wisdom of running him. He thought it would be very difficult to elect him and it would certainly stir up strong feeling in some of the ridings. Felt it would be embarrassing to himself. Today's recount safely established Abbott by a small majority. Gardiner too has been secured by a small majority." In a conversation with Brooke Claxton, Mackenzie King discovered that he shared Abbott's opinion.

The Prime Minister later took McNaughton to dinner at the Country Club. They "discussed general matters at dinner. McNaughton spoke as though he was taking it for granted he would be continued on. However, just as soon as we had reached the coffee stage, he turned and said: Having in mind the talk we had last Thursday, he had written me a letter and had afterwards torn it up. He was saying in the letter what he had said before— that he did not wish to embarrass me or the Government in any way. Would fully understand if we thought it wiser for him not to attempt re-election for the present. I thought it significant that he should use these three words: 'for the present.' I then said to him that quite frankly I had been greatly distressed about what was advisable and possible.

"I then told him of the talk with both St. Laurent and Howe and of our all feeling it would be taking almost too great a risk to open a seat. I could see as he spoke that he had been thinking things over and had evidently felt this would be the decision we would reach. He said at once that just now it did not matter so much. He had got things in shape in the Defence Department where anyone else could carry on all right. Had accomplished most of what he had set out to do, and then gave me a reason which he had not spoken of before, but which I think is important. He said that the question of his health was something he thought perhaps he should consider before tackling anything. It would be wise for him to take a few months' rest. That the last six months had been the bitterest of his life. Very trying. He felt pretty tired.

"I then spoke to him about other lines of work. He came back to not being anxious to go overseas. When I spoke possibly of some of our schemes for the development of Canada, this seemed to appeal to him and he thought there might be something there. His mind is very much along the lines of further research. It might be that in connection with housing he might be useful. At any rate at the end of our talk together, I said I would get Howe and St. Laurent to discuss the matter with me on Thursday and we could then reach a final decision. While I know this is a great disappointment to him I think he sees there is a certain amount of controversy about his being kept on and this to the embarrassment of the party as well as making things difficult for himself. I tried to have him see that once he is out of the arena there may be a considerable change of opinion and feeling that he has not had fair treatment by the public.

"I felt tremendously relieved after the talk and indeed it was all an answer to prayer as I have been most anxious about this situation. I think politically it is wise, but to me personally it makes the load much heavier. There are only very few men in the Cabinet who are capable of taking long-range views."

On July 26, Mackenzie King had a talk with McNaughton, St. Laurent, and Howe about McNaughton's position. "When we were together," he reported, "I outlined before McNaughton what I had asked St. Laurent and Howe to do, and the report that they made to me, the conversations we had together, also the tentative conclusions we had reached. I had, to supplement this, a letter, which came yesterday from Mr. Gebbie of Chateauguay-Huntingdon, Secretary of the Association there, saying he would work for getting him elected, but felt they could not elect him. What I stressed was that it is dangerous going in anywhere with an opposition government in office in the Province. That what Stevenson had told me had cost most heavily in Prince Albert, was the provincial Government throwing everything into that fight against me in the last few days. I pointed out that the Government would do the same in Ontario and Duplessis would do the same in Quebec. Also in Quebec the real danger would be a race cry having some Independent Liberal put in and the people appealed to to hold the seat for the French. St. Laurent was particularly helpful in supplementing what I had said. Howe was helpful also. McNaughton himself was not in the least difficult. When I had finished speaking he said himself he thought that the conclusion that I had reached was entirely right. He said that it would not do to risk a defeat and also felt that there was a real danger. What I stressed was that he would be going into a seat an entire stranger; that seats like Chateauguay-Huntingdon were held by Robb and Black. They were held because they were both well known in the community. McNaughton said he appreciated all this and felt that the wise thing for him to do was to drop out for a time. I took up the words 'for a time' and said that that to my mind expressed the real position. This was not the moment to hope to get him back into the House but I stressed we were all anxious to have him in the Government for the country's sake and it would be better that we might be able to arrange this some time when an opening comes in the course of things rather than the Government opening the seat itself.

"I had asked Godbout about Quebec. He said the Quebec people liked McNaughton and would help him but he agreed that it was better not to open a seat but rather to take advantage of a seat opening to get him back into Parliament. I spoke of what McNaughton had said to me about his health. He spoke more particularly about his family and the attacks upon him, his wife and his son. Both Howe and St. Laurent were quick to see that a reaction would follow the minute he left the Ministry. The public will begin to say we had not treated McNaughton properly. That his genius ought to be kept for public service in Canada.

"When I spoke of the desirability of having matters cleared up before the Dominion-Provincial Conference, McNaughton quickly said he wanted to get over the return of General Crerar first. Clear up everything to that point. Also he was anxious that nothing should be said in the interval which would cause it to be known he was leaving the Government. I pointed out I would take the position that until August 6th I would not know whether I myself was elected or not and would not rearrange the Government until that time. McNaughton's remark indicated how little he really understands about Government and the political side of it—what has to be taken into account.

"The interview could not have been pleasanter though it was naturally embarrassing to all of us and trying, but the General made it quite easy by repeatedly saying he was of the same conclusion that this was right. We shook hands at the end of the interview. In the meantime we will proceed on lines of his leaving around the 6th of August."

The Prime Minister also had to find a seat for himself. He had agreed earlier to go to Alexandria on July 17 and to have his name submitted to a Liberal convention in Glengarry riding. He recorded his visit in great detail and revelled in all the Highland associations. He was greatly pleased by Lionel Chevrier's speech and noted that "the newspapers say I spoke for an hour and 25 minutes. I think it was an hour and 10 minutes. At any rate, it was about 20 minutes longer than I should have spoken. I felt I was speaking a bit too long having regard to the intense heat of the night in the Armouries. However, the audience listened attentively though sitting on boards.

"I was given tremendous applause on rising and was surprised at the applause at the close of my remarks." He did not go back to the constituency during the campaign, and though a "crank" candidate appeared to oppose him, he won an overwhelming majority on August 6.

Meanwhile he had been watching the British elections with keen interest. In his diary on July 4 he thought Churchill's party would "be returned with a majority over all, but with a formidable opposition. The Liberals are likely to make a poor showing; the Labour Party a good showing. I would not be surprised if Churchill found himself in much the same position vis-a-vis his opponents as I am in as a result of our elections."

In his diary for July 26, Mackenzie King wrote: "When I turned on the radio at 8 the first words that came were about the British elections. They indicated that Labour was sweeping the country. A little later in the morning it became apparent that Labour had a majority over all. The Liberals very few representatives. No wonder when some Liberals were supporting Churchill and other Liberals refusing to support him and running a separate party. How can Liberals be divided into two opposites and hope to hold their own? I confess the results were a surprise. My last reaction was that Churchill would win because of the part he had taken in saving Britain in the war but that there would be a very strong movement to the left. The results show that Labour has been thinking a lot of its own position during the war and has made up its mind that it will not longer tolerate conditions under which it has been forced to live and work. I think Beaverbrook and Bracken, as Churchill's campaign managers, have done him irreparable harm. The people will not be controlled by influences of the kind. I am personally very sorry for Churchill. I would like to have seen him continue his coalition until the Japanese war was over and then drop out altogether. I think he has made a mistake in running again."

"My own belief," he continued, "is that a man of Truman's stamp is much nearer giving the kind of example which the people want. Back of it all of course is the hatred of the mass of the people for Toryism and the knowledge that Churchill is a Tory at heart though he has broad Liberal sympathies in a way, but it is the old Whig style of Liberalism. Then, too, people do not like any man to become a god.The higher a man rises on all counts the more humble-minded he should become. Then, again, his son running in one constituency, and his son-in-law in another—that kind of thing people do not like. It was Lloyd George's mistake to bring his family into politics around him. I am not sure that while I myself feel he was justified in having Mary and others with him at different places, that there was not resentment there because of a sort of favouritism. I do feel that there has been far too much expenditure of public money on these great gatherings; too much emphasis on the sort of 'Big Three' business. In other words, the public do not like the building up of a man. The press in the States were against Roosevelt because he lent himself to drastic extravagances. His infirmity, though, kept him in touch with the people. What above everything else is at the back of this is the feeling of the people that if this war is to mean anything it has to mean a social revolution and that the great body of the people are going to have a larger share of their own lives. I am afraid this will be a greater blow to Churchill than he realizes. Had he not run again, he could have given the rest of his life with zeal to writing. This will help to paralyze his mind. I doubt if he will have the zest for much more. He will age very rapidly and with his nature I would not be surprised if a certain bitterness developed. Looking into the future I am not sure Labour winning as strongly as it has may not help the peace of the world. It is only as human brotherhood is established that new peace will come. The Conservatives do not rely on international friendships. They rely on force and power. Force and power bring force and power to oppose them. Under a Tory regime for the next few years it is difficult to say how far antagonism might not develop between Britain and Russia and also through Europe. Labour in all the countries will be quicker to recognize common rights and to come to share them in a way which will not place burdens on the people themselves to say nothing of costing their lives."

Mackenzie King was particularly glad that Anthony Eden was re-elected. "His release from office for a while may enable him to restore his health. He has been near the end of his tether. I am convinced this is an epochal moment. We shall very soon now witness the end of the war against Japan. I am inclined to think Truman had been working with Russia for a peace, and China also with Russia to the same end. Japan can see no real hope of gaining anything by continuing much longer. Between the use that will be made of the atomic bomb and the possible coming into the war of Russia, I shall be surprised if negotiations from now on do not relate primarily to the speediest methods of ending the Japanese war. I should not be surprised if this came before our Parliament reassembles. . . .

"To me it is a relief also in that at Imperial Conferences and Peace Conferences I know I will not have to be bucking centralized Imperialism again. My sympathies were much stronger with Labour and its point of view than with the Conservatives. I do confess that this morning when I heard the news there came over me at once a sense of greater responsibility which is now mine. I am the only one who really was intimate with both Churchill and Roosevelt throughout the war. My position, internationally, will be heightened as a consequence. Also the victory in Canada strengthens that position."

From time to time during July the Cabinet continued consideration of the Japanese war with Mackenzie King still objecting to the scale of air force planning. On July 15 he "stressed . . . the probability from information received (I had in mind re Russia coming into the war and confidential communications from Churchill as to the same and the more effective use of high explosives) that the war itself might be over very soon.

"I learned from Howe tonight very secretly that we might within a couple of weeks see the new weapon in use which would be terribly destructive. It appals me to think of what may be involved in even attempting its use."

On July 18, Mackenzie King had a talk with the President of the Canadian Legion, Walker, and three members. He reported that Walker, who had just returned from England, "spoke about the difficulty of getting volunteers for the Pacific. I told him that was nonsense. We had refused men; also stated that the Americans were not anxious to have us in the war. One member of the delegation kept speaking about 'We must hold up our end' 'Do our part,' etc. I reminded him of our having been in the war for 2 years before the Americans. Also that Canada was in a different position than the United States. We had no possessions overseas. Spoke also of the difficulties the British had had in getting into the Pacific War. Having to take second place to the Americans in so doing. It is amazing how ready men are to sacrifice human lives, if need be, just to make a 'show' though there is nothing to be gained therefrom."

On July 27, Mackenzie King listened with interest to a statement in the news broadcast "that Japan intended to decline the ultimatum sent to her by Britain, the U.S. and China, and to fight to the bitter end. The ultimatum without doubt has been to prepare the world even more than the Japanese for their certain doom in the immediate future. Within a few days at the latest the power of the atomic bomb will be disclosed and with it Japan will be faced with either immediate complete surrender or complete devastation within a very short time. It is well that the world itself is being prepared for the revelation which the knowledge of the existence of this new weapon will disclose. I feel that we are approaching a moment of terror to mankind, for it means that, under the stress of war, men have at last not only found but created the Frankenstein which conceivably could destroy the human race. It will rest with those in authority to decide how it can later be brought to serve instead of destroy mankind. This responsibility is one of the many that comes upon those who will from now on continue to exercise authority in government in the different nations. Personally I have faith that Truman's influence will be used in the right direction, also Attlee's and that with Russia a way will be found to end the Japanese war fairly soon. I believe, however, it will mean great gains to Russia in the way of concessions which will have to be made to her by Japan with the consent of China. Where all this is leading to it is impossible to say."

On August 4 Mackenzie King's diary concludes with the words: "I have been thinking a great deal of the moment for the dropping of the atomic bomb. Believe it will come immediately after the return of the President and Stimson. It makes one very sad at heart to think of the loss of life that it will occasion among innocent people as well as those that are guilty. It can only be justified through the knowledge that for one life destroyed, it may save hundreds of thousands and bring this terrible war quickly to a close."

Godbout and Fontaine came to Ottawa on July 26 to invite the Prime Minister to a picnic to be held on Godbout's farm in his honour on September 22. He agreed at once to go. He reported that "they wonder if Duplessis will break up the coming Dominion-Provincial Conference and make an issue of that. I said I did not think any government would try that. There might be differences but they could not succeed. I advised Godbout strongly to take the position that French-Canadians were Canadians, that they were not going to run things on a provincial scale, but make their voice increasingly felt in national policies, and take the larger ground which he had taken originally. He agreed that was right. He thinks they may have an election in Quebec. I said if they had he would be sure to win."

Since the Wartime Tax Agreements with the provinces had been acknowledged to be temporary expedients to meet an emergency situation, the federal government was faced at this time with the problem of formulating new proposals acceptable to the provinces and suitable to the needs of the postwar economy. The federal proposals, considerably broader in scope than the Rowell-Sirois recommendations and to be applicable for a three-year period, placed primary emphasis on the maintenance of a high and stable level of employment and income to be achieved through a combination of fiscal changes, public investment, and social security policies.

It was proposed that the provinces should withdraw from the personal income tax, corporation tax, and succession duty fields in return for annual rental payments from the federal government which would not fall below a guaranteed minimum and which would rise in step with population and increases in per capita gross national product. Under this scheme, provincial receipts would have been approximately 50 per cent higher than under the wartime agreements. Substantial expansion of federal outlays for natural resources development, conservation, and public works was also proposed together with increases in federal contributions to provincial services and capital projects through grants-in-aid or joint participation. In addition to the family allowance programme already in operation, the federal government promised more generous old age pensions, contributions to provincially administered health insurance schemes, unemployment assistance coverage, and more vocational training and other rehabilitation assistance.

On July 26 the Cabinet began to consider the proposals for the Dominion-Provincial Conference and it was arranged to have daily meetings starting Monday, July 30. That day (July 30) the Cabinet began going through the White Paper which Mackenzie King described as "A splendid document, but setting forth far too much, and inclining too completely to the private enterprise side of things. I pointed out that no indication had been given that government ownership had been considered in the Government's programme mentioned in the Speech from the Throne; also pointed out that what the brief contained re continuing the War Measures Act over the post-war period would almost certainly create a debate in Parliament and would bring about a test of the Government's strength, in which all opposition parties could unite against us. Mr. St. Laurent pointed out that Duplessis would seize on this. Other criticisms were made. I suggested, at one o'clock, that the report be gone over anew before three, and we could then try to analyze the sections from the beginning, so as to get it to the press." The examination in detail continued for several days and, at the same time, a speech was drafted for the Prime Minister to use in opening the Conference on August 6.

Mackenzie King gave most of Sunday, August 5, to the revision of his speech for the Conference and the preparation of a speech welcoming General Crerar on his return to Ottawa. He reported that after dinner that evening he read the Conference speech aloud. "I feel that it is worthy of the occasion but it is God's mercy indeed that the material has been brought together in time. Pickersgill had prepared the draft but most of what he had was from material that Towers of the Bank of Canada furnished. Really very good material. I would have enjoyed having two or three days on this one subject. It is very important. The Conference may well prove, with the material we have prepared, to be the instrument of completely changing the emphasis of administration and legislation on social problems from the Provinces to the Dominion.

"I was in terror about the speech for Crerar because of the knowledge of the Conference opening tomorrow morning and because I shall have no time to prepare."

On August 6, "after opening the [Conference] proceedings with a few words spoken extemporaneously, I read the prepared address which was prepared as an introduction, intended primarily to give a certain spirit to the proceedings and to remove the possibility of certain antagonisms before they arose. St. Laurent was to have followed me, explaining the intended procedure, but Drew arose immediately and spoke at considerable length. I thought he spoke very well but he went out of his way to have it appear that we were adopting the wrong procedure in having statements made before the Steering Committee was appointed. He would have been right in this had it not been [that] by an exchange of letters, relating to proceedings, the procedure we were adopting had been agreed upon. When Drew questioned this I placed on record his own letter which clearly agreed to the procedure. He got very red in the face as I placed the letter on record.

"Something wholly similar followed when Duplessis spoke. He, too, in line with Drew, was going to take exception to our case being presented in the manner of giving it publicity. When Duplessis said that he had written at different times and referred to a letter of his, I got the letter and placed it on record. It too was wholly contrary to what he was saying. I confess I felt disgusted with that sort of thing on the part of leaders of the two most important Provinces of Canada.

"After considerable discussion, which lasted through the morning and into the afternoon, it was finally decided that our own proposals should be read. I got St. Laurent to begin the reading and to act as Deputy Chairman and also got agreement on an evening session." At about noon, as he was presiding at the morning's proceedings of the Conference, the Prime Minister received a note from Howe saying an atomic bomb had been dropped and that he was giving a report to the press. "I had only, just immediately before, placed Drew's letter on record and received from Mackenzie a note saying 'good work.' When I read the reference to the bomb dropping I thought at first it had reference to my having shown up Drew by his own letter. Then I suddenly realized it was the atomic bomb in Japan. I felt that all present would be interested in the news but being fearful that the report might be premature, I sent word to Howe to say that I had thought of making a statement to the Conference and asking what he would suggest. He then sent me down a copy of his own statement which he had prepared. He later came into the Chamber himself.

"At about 12.30 I saw him getting cuttings from the ticker which he handed to Mackenzie to look at. I asked Mackenzie to let me have them. Saw that they were an account of Truman's statement, so waited until it came to one o'clock and then adjourned the proceedings. I told those present that I had a world-shaking announcement to make. I then mentioned in a word the dropping of the atomic bomb. Read Howe's statement and later the paragraph from the ticker. I mentioned that as there were no afternoon papers today, it being Civic Holiday, I felt all present would be especially interested in this news. The statement was listened to in dead silence. I mentioned having Mr. Churchill's statement in my possession and arranged to read it when the proceedings opened at three. The statement is a little long but I felt it was all of historic significance. Felt it was proper to read all the statements in full. Naturally this word created mixed feelings in my mind and heart. We were now within sight of the end of the war with Japan. In this connection I should note that yesterday in revising the speech for the Conference I struck out the words, 'in reference to the ending of the Japanese war,' substituted the word 'hope' for 'believe' before 'swiftly.' I had it in mind that there was no doubt that this would come very soon and that the atomic bomb would be used this week. Strangely enough it must have been about 10.30 when I read this to the Conference. The word of the use of the bomb came at 12. While I was speaking it had already descended. The whole business was referred to as the greatest achievement in science. I think it was an equally great achievement in secrecy—a tremendous secret to have kept over four years. It shows what control of publicity by a Government can effect.

"Howe had handed me on Friday, Churchill's statement which I had with me in the country and read on Sunday. I brought it with me Sunday night and it was in my library over the night. Almost itself like a secretive bomb. It is quite remarkable that it should have been given to me to be the first in Canada to inform my own colleagues and the Premiers of the several Provinces and their Ministers of this most amazing of all scientific discoveries and of what certainly presages the early close of the Japanese war. We now see what might have come to the British people had German scientists won the race. . . . I am a little concerned about how Russia may feel, not having been told anything of this invention or of what the British and the U.S. were doing in the way of exploring and perfecting the process."

The other great event of the day for Mackenzie King was his election to the House of Commons in the Glengarry by-election. "It was, of course, pretty much a foregone conclusion that I would be returned. But after what happened to Churchill in his own constituency where some ten thousand votes were cast for a crank who said he did not expect to win one could not tell what might have happened in Glengarry. However, the wisdom of the tactics of keeping out altogether was made apparent before Dr. Monahan had got very far in his campaign. He became a public nuisance and was a public annoyance. The first returns came in about ten past seven as I was sitting in the Prime Minister's office revising my speech on the address of welcome. It indicated from a limited number of polls the certainty of victory.

"Later, by 7.30, returns had come from all polls excepting three which indicated a majority of 4,087—the total vote being 4,410 to 323. While I was still at the office a telegram came from Dr. MacDiarmid worded: 'Congratulations and best of wishes.' The returns indicating larger majority were given to me by Chevrier over the 'phone. Others of the Executive came to the 'phone and spoke to me: Major, the President of the Association; Donald Macdonald of the Constituency; J. D. McRae, former Member and one or two others. I told Chevrier to let them know that I was prouder and more honoured than ever. Also that I regretted the inconvenience they had been put to but was most grateful to the Executive for their management of the campaign by themselves."

The next day General Crerar returned to Ottawa. It was, Mackenzie King noted, "the 26th anniversary of my election as Leader of the Liberal Party of Canada. It has fallen to my lot to have the honour of greeting the Commander of the Canadian Army, the first General of a Canadian army, on his return from the battles he has fought in Europe and to drive with him through the streets of the Capital; to make an address of welcome to him on Parliament Hill in the presence of all Members of the Government, Premiers of all the Provinces with their Ministers, and others; to preside at the Dominion-Provincial Conference; to preside also at a luncheon given at the Chateau in honour of General Crerar. To share with him on the drive accounts in detail of much that related to the war and to hear from his own lips that the army had been denied nothing that they needed. That he could think of nothing which had not been done by the Government in the course of the whole war.

"I told Crerar I had made up my mind that the men who were fighting at the front would never suffer for anything that the Government could do on their behalf.

"We spoke at luncheon of the anxious time I had last November. He told me it was a very anxious time for them as well. That everything had worked out splendidly. I said it might all so easily have gone in the opposite direction, and Canada would have been without any government at all."

Most of that day and the next were spent presiding at the Dominion-Provincial Conference or following its work. He noted, on August 8, that "someone said to me yesterday he believed this Conference might prove to be perhaps the greatest part of my career. It certainly is the culmination of what I have most sought for in my life. The securing of greater goodwill between all parts of Canada and the raising of the standards of the people in the establishment of a national minimum of social security and human well-being.

"Shortly after half past two I arrived at the main entrance of the Parliament Building as Ministers and others were gathering for the group photograph. We were all obliged to wait a considerable time as neither Duplessis nor Drew had turned up. I learned later they had both been lunching together at the Chateau. Drew followed Duplessis, the former did not let on they had been together, said he had been reading. Curiously enough a little later in the evening, Drew said he was sorry to have kept the Conference waiting but had really not noticed the passing of the time, while he had been reading some things. I don't think either was wholly truthful.

"Just a few minutes before Drew arrived I was handed by the press a cutting from the ticker as follows: Bulletin—Washington, August 8 BUP 'Soviet Russia has declared war on Japan, President Truman announced today.' It was just three o'clock when this word came to me. I cannot say I was wholly surprised, though naturally I was immensely pleased when I received the message. I then rose from the chair in which I was seated and stepping back a few paces looked at the Provincial Premiers and Federal Ministers and other officials and facing the Peace Tower at the entrance of the House of Commons I announced that Russia had declared war on Japan. There was a spontaneous cheer. We then all resumed our positions and Drew having arrived, group photos were taken. When the large photo was completed we moved to another part of the grounds where group photos of the Provincial Premiers and our own Cabinet were taken. While there the press asked me if I would say a word about the entry of Russia into the war. I immediately gave them a few words which appeared in the press later this evening. Referring to the announcement regarding the atomic bomb I said that this was the most important event since V-E Day. I stated that it meant the end of the war soon, or the complete destruction of Japan, . . . and that Canada would continue . . . bearing her part until the final word of peace came.

"While this photograph was being taken with the Provincial Premiers there was much joking about my victory in Glengarry.

"When I stated that the secret of happiness was to have no more elections ahead of one, and stated that there were several queries as to whether I really meant not to run again, Drew said something to me about not making that statement in earnest. I said most certainly it was true. I had had my last election."

The Prime Minister went to call on the Soviet Ambassador at 5 o'clock that afternoon. "When I came into the drawing room," he wrote, "the Ambassador offered me a seat. He drew up a chair to my right. Olga, the Secretary, sat to my left as interpreter. After beginning speaking of the satisfaction it was to know that Russia had come in, I read over the news that had come on the ticker. It contained Molotov's statement. Mr. Zaroubin said he had not had any word from his Government thus far and thanked me for giving him the particulars of Molotov's statement. He then began to speak in a more formal way and said that Russia was determined to do all she could to prevent further aggression in the world and to end Fascism. He then spoke about the U.S.S.R. desiring to have close bonds of friendship with Canada. Said he hoped that Canada would continue to help Russia in the war against Japan as she had in the war against Germany. I said to him I did not think the war would last long. He said Japan has a very strong army; very strong. I said an army cannot do much if its sources of supply are destroyed. He replied that it took some time to destroy all sources. I replied I thought the atomic bomb would have a devastating effect. He then said to me that he had been told that some 100,000 people had been killed at Hiroshima. Seemed to feel keenly what that number meant. He said this would bring Canada and Russia closer together than ever. He then added that he, of course, was speaking only personally. He had not had any official word. I told him I felt that would be the wish of all of us. I then said that I felt that the people of the U.S.S.R. who had so long been under tyranny, now that they had freedom, would really be glad to devote their time to enjoying freedom and sharing it with others. I looked forward to Russia playing that part."

At the government dinner for the provincial premiers that evening, Mackenzie King reported that when he got up, after the Governor-General had proposed the King, he "started off by saying I had no steering committee and would have to barge about as best I could myself. This remark related as it was to discussions of the Conference caught on immediately. I followed it by saying that there being no press present, there was no occasion to make a speech therefore I would not attempt anything but wished to say a word of welcome and then spoke of the significance of the gathering—in some respects, the most representative of all Canada which had been held at any time since Confederation. I then made light of the positions of Premiers, speaking of ourselves as statesmen or should I say politicians. Mentioned anyone looking on a short time ago would have heard us saying a lot of nasty things about each other. That after all, we were pretty much one at heart in our desire of public service. Said something about not seeing the need for antagonism. I then spoke about timing being an important matter in politics. I asked them if they could think of a better timing than this for the Conference in the light of all that happened in the last three days which included the Japanese bomb, the entry of Russia into the war, and the return of General Crerar. I then went on to speak of how perfect the timing had been in the matter of the abolition of restrictions on alcoholic beverages coming into effect just on the morning of the Conference meeting. I then turned to His Excellency as though by approval of the action he had been responsible for it though I had difficulty with my own colleagues in getting it approved.

"I spoke of my efforts to maintain temperance at a time of war which had not always been received with the enthusiasm I felt they should have for a great patriotic move of the kind. Then I came down to the serious side and spoke of the need for co-operation in the world of today between Provinces and Dominion and all parts of the British Commonwealth, all the United Nations, etc. Spoke of it being a privilege for those of us who are here to have the opportunity of shaping a happier Canada and also of the significance of the events at this time. That for years to come, we would be able to look back on the last three or four days and be able to say we had all been together at a moment which was most significant in the history of the world since A.D. 1. From now on, the world would either become better or worse. It was our responsibility so far as Canada was concerned, having to take one direction or the other.

"I then said that I did not agree that all men were born free and equal. That I felt they were born neither free nor equal. That it was our duty to give to them as much freedom and as much in the way of equality of opportunity as possible. The war was not a matter of fights between nations. It was really at the bottom a struggle to gain more freedom and greater opportunity for the mass of men. That could not be accomplished alone by any Government. It could only be by co-operation of all Governments.

"I spoke of San Francisco and the impression I got there of men of different races, different creeds, participating, but all having the one great aim—helping to bring about world peace and friendlier relations. I spoke of the days when political orators were talking about the brotherhood of men. Today there had grown up a worship of nationality and the like. We must now get back to the brotherhood idea or the world would be coming into a state of chaos. . . .

"There was great laughter when I turned to Lord Athlone and said that I supposed he had heard about my election in Glengarry; greatest majority ever given to any public man, etc. Went on from that to refer to the good-will which had been demonstrated on the part of members of political parties, etc.

"Drew followed speaking on behalf of the Premiers present. He spoke very nicely but found it impossible not to bring in his Tory point of view by saying that while we wanted to help those who were not so fortunate, etc., we must take care not to take away from those that were capable of bigger things themselves. He claimed that the race belonged to the strong and not to the weak. The whole emphasis was that of the old laissez-faire. His remarks on that score did not get any reception. However the reply was all in good part."

Mackenzie King was delighted with the speech he had made. "I really had to laugh myself," he wrote, "as I thought of some of the things that were said and the way in which they were received, all circumstances of the evening being considered. It gave me a particular happiness to have my own Ministers feel the satisfaction which I know they would at the way the whole business had been launched. All of the Premiers and Ministers who spoke were very nice in their references to the way in which I handled the Conference at the Opening, and to the way in which things were going. I am sure all will leave the city with a pleasant impression and carrying, more than they otherwise would, the note of co-operation. If they could only know that the thing that in itself is the best is the best politics, they would help to make Canada a much stronger nation. The kind of speaking I did tonight is the only thing that is really worthy of the name. What one needs is to have in one's mind a few thoughts—2 or 3 thoughts and develop them on one's feet, expressing one's mind fully and just being one's own self."

Mackenzie King's one regret on August 8 was "concerning McNaughton's departure from the Government and the great oversight during the afternoon in his not being present for the photo. It was the old story of his being preoccupied with his work and no secretary to tell him what his engagements were. . . . It is a little short of a tragedy not having him in this particular picture which relates to the Conference. Knowing of the letter which had been written and what is about to take place, my heart ached for him tonight. Both the General and Mrs. McNaughton have shown a wonderful spirit, great reserve and poise. I spoke to him at the end of the evening of having received his letter. He said he felt I would wish to have it. It bore out what I had talked over with him."

On August 10 as the Conference was about to adjourn with no firm conclusions reached, there were news reports that Japan was prepared to surrender unconditionally but wished to preserve the prerogatives of the Emperor. Mackenzie King noted that at the Cabinet meeting that day, it was decided, in view of the news from Japan, to postpone the opening of the parliamentary session until the 6th of September. The Cabinet also discussed the pros and cons of proclaiming V-J Day as a holiday. Mackenzie King wrote: "I really felt like breaking down when the programme that was put before us of suggestions left the main part of everything to myself. Another address to be delivered on Parliament Hill. I did not feel equal to it and along with the thought of telegrams which would have to be sent out, messages to the King, etc., recalled the terrible period at San Francisco. I just told the Cabinet I could not think of undertaking anything of the kind. I would do the best I could but it was impossible to attempt more."

The news of the actual surrender was expected from hour to hour on Saturday, August 11. About 9.30 that evening Mackenzie King received word at Kingsmere that President Truman had called a press conference for 8.30 Sunday morning. When this word came, he felt he ought to go into town quite early and "be on hand with a statement for Canada if anything finally developed." Later in the evening, he became convinced that it "would not do to wait until tomorrow morning to prepare anything so began immediately to write by hand. It was about 20 past 12 when I looked at the clock. Meanwhile I had prepared enough to be sure of what I should say in the broadcast if one had to be made early in the morning. To my great delight, the resolution to do this and to go in early in the morning foregoing the Sunday I had looked forward so much to at Kingsmere, seemed to give me an exceptional peace of mind and heart and I wrote quite easily, almost as if it were by inspiration. I kept thinking of the joy my father had had in working in the quiet of the night when there were no vibrations about disturbing his peace of mind."

The next morning (Sunday, August 12), the Prime Minister was at the Chateau Laurier studios of the C.B.C. at 8.20 A.M. "In the studio," he wrote, "we were met by Mr. Bushnell and Mr. Wright who were glad to have everything arranged for an immediate broadcast. I sat in the outer room re-writing the broadcast, availing myself of every minute. Pickersgill brought a stenographer from the office and we had the material re-typed, expecting at any moment to get the word that would make it necessary to go on the air. We arranged for translation; also for the Quebec network to take up the broadcast in French later.

"Spent the morning in studio rooms, part of the time in the broadcasting booth; all the while listening to whatever came over the radio in the way of music or the continual interruptions for statements from Washington, telling of nothing having been thus far received and describing the President's movements; announcements as to Attlee's movements, etc. My whole nature seemed to be deeply stirred and alive to each and every impression.

"Between 1 and 2 o'clock, Pickersgill and I began to feel pretty fatigued; also hungry. Pickersgill secured a room two or three doors from the studio. We had lunch together there—a good lunch which we both greatly enjoyed, after which I lay down on the bed with a radio near my head and rested until between 5 and 6."

"Late in the afternoon," he noted that "P. suggested it might be well for me to make a record and he had gone over my material and made revisions which would suit either for later in the night or the morning. Had discussed this with the Manager. I approved of the idea. I then went into the studio and made the record which we listened to subsequently. It was understood it would not be used until after President Truman had made a statement. Indeed I had begun to word it that President Truman had by proclamation said so and so. P. suggested striking out Proclamation as we did not know the exact wording, though we had learned. . . that something of the kind was being prepared. This had all been suggested by the radio.

"As we left the Studio, P. told me that it was definitely arranged that the use of the record would be checked over with him before the broadcast was given to the public."

Mackenzie King called at Government House and the Chinese Embassy after leaving the Chateau. He got back to Kingsmere after 8.00 P.M. After dinner Mackenzie King was talking to Mrs. Patteson when he suddenly said: "Let us listen to the radio, to see what the latest news may be. We had scarcely listened above a few minutes when the programme stopped and a flash came through and we heard the words: PRESIDENT TRUMAN HAS ANNOUNCED THE ACCEPTANCE OF THE SURRENDER TERMS BY JAPAN. This was repeated a couple of times. Then the radio continued with music which was being played. A lovely hymn and chorus. This suddenly stopped and then came the statement of the broadcast by myself as Prime Minister. When I heard it, I wondered why the station had not waited until after President Truman had spoken and made his broadcast. It made me feel embarrassed as others might feel I was seeking to get in ahead of everyone else. I had a moment's feeling that there might be something wrong but the flash had been so emphatic and repeated and nothing further said, that I felt the news must be true. I immediately thanked God on my knees for

the word that had come of the end of the war, prayed that I might be of
service in the days of peace. J. spoke of G. being alone and we both went
at once over, that we should all share the news together, so we went at
once to Shady Hill. When we came to the door, G. said he had tried to
reach me by 'phone to tell me that the American news had stated that the
whole report of the end of the Japanese war was false. He explained what
had been said on the radio in this regard. I felt naturally a little chagrined
though I confess it seemed to me but one more thing in the nature of misrepresentation of my attitude which I have had to endure all my life. I
realized that my opponents and the press would make the most of this,
blaming me for the whole business and indeed I felt they would be justified
in holding me responsible for having allowed anything in the nature of a
statement which could be regarded as official to go out from Canada without being perfectly sure. I rebuked myself for not having remained on in
the city and handled the whole business myself to the very end. My conscience, however, did not rebuke me to any extent realizing that my
purpose had been of the highest; also that the error in having the broadcast
made was that of the C.B.C. and not of my own making though for anything the C.B.C. did I would be held still responsible.

"I came back and had a word with P. over the 'phone. . . . P. suggested
giving to the press a word of explanation as to how the error had arisen.
The 10 o'clock news was just coming on so I left this until after hearing
the news. I then 'phoned him again and agreed to his telling the press what
had taken place. I was anxious to find out about whether the statement
had been short-waved. It took him some time to get this information. I was
immensely relieved when I found the broadcast had been confined to
Canada and had not been short-waved. Also relieved to find the flash had
led to demonstrations through the States, Britain and elsewhere which
would make it clear that it would have been sufficient in Canada to have
occasioned any such, though I recognize that the press would be certain
to put the whole thing on my shoulders. I was grateful that P. had thought
of making explanations. Otherwise I might myself have remained perfectly
silent. It was unfortunate, however, that so much time was lost in having
the explanation made. It must have been 20 after 11 before the press were
told. I waited to get the different reports from P. Read editorials in the
Saturday Night of the recent Conference, the Governor General, etc.,
while waiting. Then after a final word with P. went immediately to bed. As
a matter of fact, I did not allow the incident to weigh on my mind realizing
that there was nothing that could be done; also that my motive had been
right."

The next morning (August 13), after listening to the news broadcast,

Mackenzie King wrote: "On the whole I thought explanation of the broadcast given over C.B.C. was very fair and kindly worded. I am sure that the Tory press will make the most of it and was not surprised therefore later when the morning papers came out and I saw the wording of the Journal: 'No word from Japs on terms. Erroneous broadcast recording by P.M. sets off V.J. celebrations across Canada.' The same malicious spirit [which] has kept up throughout but which I was hoping after the Dominion-Provincial Conference and with the certain knowledge that I shall not be in another general election, might begin to ease up a little. The truth is, however, there is a personal hatred among the Tories of myself for having beaten them at every turn. For the rest of my days, and after I am gone, I shall not be surprised if they continue to harp on this premature announcement. However, I am determined not to allow the incident to cause me loss of either peace of mind or heart. In the long run, it will I believe be all for the best in that it will help members of my staff as well as myself to realize more fully the need of meticulous care to the smallest degree with regard to anything which affects my work as Prime Minister. I do not seem to have been able to get this ever fully appreciated. Too much is left to chance. There is always a getting away from duty rather than holding to it until things have been finally concluded." His handwritten diary shows that he suffered a good deal of mortification over this incident, but throughout he blamed himself more than others. At the Cabinet on Tuesday afternoon, after a minute or two of silence, he "said that since we had last met I had been making history, whether for them or not I could not say, but certainly for myself." He then explained what had happened and noted: "There was a smile on the faces of the Ministers. I was a little surprised that not one of them said a word which might have helped to relieve my embarrassment, but none did."

At seven o'clock that evening Mackenzie King listened in his office to Attlee's broadcast of the surrender of Japan. "I felt myself perspire a little on the arms as I listened to Attlee & thinking how my broadcast must have sounded, & what a contrast it would have been to be broadcasting myself at this hour,—but it was only for a moment. I felt all would yet be well. Heeney came in to bring O-in-C to sign & fill in for V.J. day holiday—and Royal Proclamation—I filled out dates in both with my own hand & signed (as agreed on in Council). Those present began to suggest I see the press. I agreed to this. Robertson came into my P.M. office & was the first I shook hands with—thanking him for all his help—Pickersgill later—I am not sure if I shook hands with Arnold,—but certainly exchanged greetings— I gave orders to the carilloneur to play at once & looked out to see about the flag—but it was after 7.

"When the press came in, its members were all very kindly in their attitude. I had prepared nothing to say—made an allusion to what I had intended to say having already been made public; merely pointed out that it began with words—President Truman had announced etc. saying, I would not like it to be thought that I would have aspired to precede either Attlee or Truman. I then spoke of what the day meant, speaking of it as the greatest in Canadian history—the history of the world since A.D.— Then of the 'great price at which victory had been secured'—Wished messages could be sent into every home that had been bereaved—Spoke of believing those who were killed were in God's care—or with God—wishing to comfort hearts & to openly profess my *belief* while holding the office of Prime Minister at the most significant hour. Spoke of men not having been born free or equal & need for a different attitude—with emphasis on the individual—the need for brotherhood etc. etc. (see press). Then drew their attention to copy of my intended broadcast, to use if they wished—I noticed they all took copies—finally I announced the National holiday, Parliament Hill Parade, etc. and the Sunday of Prayer & Thanksgiving. Answered a number of questions re govt's intended method of procedure etc.

"I should have recorded that on arriving at East Block at 3, I read a note from Robertson saying the Governor General had suggested a march past on the hill,—he & myself taking the salute. I thought the idea a splendid one (leaving out myself except to attend) & spoke of it in Council & after Council phoned to thank His Ex for it. He was out walking, left word of approval with Eastwood, & told him of Attlee broadcasting at 7. After the broadcast almost immediately His Ex phoned personally to extend congratulations on the day which I reciprocated to himself & Princess Alice— he spoke of her being with him on the hill, also chiefs of staff & Ministers, all a good suggestion approved, & word sent to McNaughton to arrange. I then began with Pickersgill to get off telegrams to the King, Govr. Genl., the forces, Attlee, Truman, Chiang Kai Shek, Stalin, De Gaulle, other allied countries & Dominions, finally one to Churchill & last of all one to Mrs. Roosevelt. The first two went before Pickersgill & I left to go to Laurier House for dinner—which Jean got for us. It was a delight to me as I went into the dining room to look in turn at the different paintings of the loved ones.

"On the way down, I enjoyed seeing the young people begin to turn out on the streets,—as we drove past the War Memorial & down O'Connor St. After dinner we returned by a longer route—a pretty sight to see the crowds, all looking so cheerful, girls without hats—all looking so young. On prlt hill some paraded past the office. Pickersgill & I kept at the telegrams till about 10 past 11 taking time off to listen to the broadcast. I began to see where I might have said much more & been prepared with something. It was God's mercy, I yielded to the wishes of Pickersgill & others to see the press. It all worked out marvellously, with the announcement of the holiday & day of Thanksgiving & Prayer.''

In his diary for V-J Day, Mackenzie King referred again to "the appalling blow which came on Sunday night with the knowledge that in every part of the world, in the minds of the people of all classes and stations of life, there would be adverse and bitter comment on my action in having made any announcement as to the end of the war. The world will never understand that the mistake was that of the C.B.C. The real mistake was that of the C.B.C. but with External Affairs as well, seeing that I was not adequately protected against any premature announcement. I had done my part in preparing the broadcast. I had to leave it to others to protect me. However, I shall always take the major blame to myself in that I did not stay myself to the end to make sure that there could be no slip; also it would have been better if from the start, I had planned to make a speech on Parlt. Hill on V-J Day, not attempted anything else meanwhile.''

At the Cabinet meeting on August 16, when the Ministers were discussing a resolution on the flag, the Prime Minister noted "it was apparent some of the Quebec Members may wish to hold out for an entirely new flag that will have a design related to the French regime. I am surprised that they are now taking this position. If we get into a discussion of the kind, it will block altogether a national flag. I am sure that the Canadian ensign is the only ensign we can get approved by Parlt.''

After the Cabinet that day, Mackenzie King had a talk with McNaughton during which he "told him I thought it might be well now that the Japanese war was over for me to announce he would be retiring at the end of the week. I gave the reasons that I did not want attacks to begin; did not want the press to begin making fresh attacks as to why he was being kept. He said that was quite agreeable to him. He mentioned there were two or three things he was anxious to clean up before leaving and was glad to have until Saturday to get them into final shape. He spoke very strongly about keeping the good-will of the army. Also keeping it to a considerable size. He believes we might have a good deal of trouble through the demobilization period and immediately after. I find all these military men have an obsession about the fear of civil strife. . . . He said to me he was perfectly satisfied that he had done the right thing all the way through. That we should never have had Canada's army sent in part to Italy. That campaign was absolutely wrong. That men returning were beginning to make that clear. He referred to Churchill's invitation to have him come into the [British] govt. which I recall. Also the offer of commands in different places which he said had all been made simply to make a prisoner of him.''

Mackenzie King also now felt that McNaughton was "much too strong in his suspicions and dislikes and hatreds. General Crerar remarked that to me when we were driving through the streets. McNaughton was not a good man in politics for that reason. Sir Wilfrid was right when he said that it does not do to cherish resentments in public life. McNaughton then said that he had done the work that he wanted to do when he came into the govt. It had been work for Canada. He was sure the course we had taken was right. We would have had dead bodies scattered throughout this country if any conscription had been enforced in the way they were trying to enforce it. I sought to have him feel that his being Minister of Defence at the surrender both in Europe and Asia which had come in the time he had been in the Government was a career in itself. I am sure Ralston must be feeling deeply that it was not given to him to have that honour. I imagine Angus Macdonald, the same; and Power. They were all very foolish. It was their combined bad judgment in overdoing the numbers that helped to lead them all to where they are at this time; they combined to go entirely beyond what should have been done.

"McNaughton's eyes filled with tears when he was about to leave. Shook hands with me. He had said a little earlier that it might have been Providence that had guided him but he felt sure that the course he had taken was right. I said both he and I shared fundamentally the same beliefs in Divine guidance. He has the feeling very strongly that all the opposition to himself has grown out of his endeavour to keep Canada as a nation to the foreground. He said that when the British found he was really standing for a Canada on its own, the antagonism started. It was only when he drove into HQ. with his little flag that they really found they had to take recognition of Canada as a separate entity controlling its own affairs. He spoke of our having worked very closely together and meaning every word he had put in the letter he had sent to me. I told him I have not answered it because I was waiting to see how the war developed. He then spoke of feeling it well to take a complete rest and change for a time. This I think is right.

"I was sorry not to be able to offer him anything further though he did not expect an offer. I said to him in conclusion I was sure he had still a great career ahead of him and that in due time, in all probability, he would be back in Parlt. again.

"Later, on thinking matters over, I felt it was better perhaps not to say anything about the possibility of his leaving but rather have the two of us see the press together on Monday. The Day of Thanksgiving and Prayer would then be over, the Japanese surrender signed and I could say something about his work to the press. I 'phoned him to that effect. He seemed quite surprised. Said it would be unfortunate if any impression got abroad that there had been any difference which occasioned his leaving. That would go like fire through the country and that the other would offset this entirely."

The press conference was not actually held until Tuesday, August 21, at 6 o'clock when Mackenzie King "met the press along with General McNaughton and Abbott. I had 'phoned Abbott to tell him that I wanted him to be Minister of Defence. Heeney had prepared orders in advance for McNaughton's resignation and Abbott's appointment. I let McNaughton see the letter I had written him before the press came in. Asked him if there was anything he would like me to add or to change. He said there was nothing he could think of. I could not be quite sure whether he felt the letter had gone far enough or not. I said to him I had not made mention of his services overseas as that was an earlier chapter and did not relate to Government. He said to me he would be glad if I would give him a letter which would place on record the offer that had been made to him after his return from England and prior to his accepting office in the Government. He did not want that for publication but wished to have it for his records which is quite natural. I told him I would send him a letter which would serve that end. I have no doubt that he feels keenly that having given up the possibility of that appointment, he should not have met with the very hard time he had encountered since.

"When the press came in, I sought in my words to make it clear that I had appreciated deeply the part he had taken in helping to meet a very difficult situation and the service he had rendered Canada and that I felt he had earned the nation's thanks. I recounted some of his services and made it quite clear that they had been of exceptional value to the Government and to the country. What I said was in the presence of McNaughton and Abbott. I think McNaughton was pleased. He naturally feels badly at leaving the Ministry. He could not have been pleasanter or more manly in his acceptance of the whole situation.

"I did not give the letters we had exchanged to the press but it was understood they might be used at any time this was thought desirable."

Mackenzie King added that "before the press came in, I asked Mc-Naughton if he would like to be Chairman of the Canadian Section of the Permanent Joint Board on Defence. He thought the matter over for a minute. I knew it would appeal to him and he accepted it. I have Biggar's resignation in my hands on account of his health. Indicated to the press that he would be appointed. Had quite forgotten that Biggar had not dropped out completely. Pickersgill 'phoned him to explain my reason for making the announcement at the moment I did. I wanted to make it clear that the Administration had confidence in McNaughton and were glad to avail ourselves of his services in so important a post. I told him it would serve to keep him in touch with the Government and with matters in which he was deeply interested."

On Sunday, August 19, Mackenzie King listened to the broadcast of the service at St. Paul's attended by the King and Queen. "I confess," he wrote, "that the account that came over the radio sounded to me much more like a Coronation celebration than an occasion for prayer and thanksgiving related to the loss of millions of lives. There was cheering in the streets, trumpets blowing, etc. Really I feel that fundamentally the occasion was not far akin from the worship of idols. We complain of the Japanese and their Emperor. They at least believe he is a descendant of God. We are fortunate indeed in having the King and Queen we have on the throne today. I find myself, however, in the light of the world's problems and the rights and true liberties of the people becoming increasingly opposed to the institution of monarchy as something which is foreign to true democracy. It is too much the worship of power and position. The singing of God Save the King will some day give place to an anthem which will ask God to save his people from all that makes for differences between them, be the differences what they may."

As one way of celebrating the end of all hostilities the Prime Minister telephoned Howe on August 20 and "asked him to set in motion improvements on the opposite side of the Ottawa river, to have a model community started there. I wanted to link up this portion of larger Ottawa with the period of surrender—the signing of the terms of surrender by the Japanese Government. The end of the war. The press has seen the significance of the orders in council extending the field of jurisdiction of the Federal District Commission. I am sure that no memorial could be more suitable than the one which would make of the Capital of Canada something of an inspiration to the citizens generally."

Two days later (August 22) he brought up in the Cabinet "the question of the time having come to decide what the Government should think of doing in the way of a national memorial related to the war. Spoke of feeling that what we should do was to extend our scheme of beautification of the Capital so as to take in the other side of the Ottawa river and plan all the environs. Arranging to have such buildings as are to go up on the opposite shore conform to the proper style and to fit in to the landscape; also making a model community of housing and departmental buildings in Hull.

"I suggested as a first step we send a cable to Greber [architect of the National Capital Plan] to have him come and develop plans. I mentioned that I had been interested in the original project. Recalled in Dr. King's presence what was done by the two of us in the way of initiating beginning of beautification by taking out five blocks between Elgin and the Post Office, etc. I said I thought now was the time to start on the other side of the river and plan with a view to having the Booth property and the Eddy property all removed in the course of time, etc.

"I said that there were just one or two things I would like to do before I dropped out. That the time could not be very long. This was one I would like to see under way. There was unanimous agreement around the table. Ilsley did not say anything. I said to him I could not imagine it would cost too much. Howe and Mackenzie spoke out quite strongly in favour. Other colleagues were obviously of the same mind."

On August 23, the Prime Minister spent the morning going over reconstruction of the Cabinet. "Had a talk with Mackenzie who himself said that he had changed his mind as to what he would like to do. He felt he would wish to consolidate the Acts relating to social insurance matters— all the orders in council that have been passed for war veterans. Stay in that Department until the end of this session and then retire. He said he would need some help in administering the Department. He had spoken of possibly [David] Croll as an Assistant Minister. I told him our thoughts were running on the same lines. I really felt it would be best for him to stay in the Department, to complete the work as he has said, but instead of Croll, I would suggest Bridges, making him a Minister without Portfolio and making him Parliamentary Assistant as well. Mackenzie said this was perfectly satisfactory to him. I spoke about his needing to get more help there so as to get things done. We discussed appointments to the House of Commons, seating arrangements, Speakership, etc. I also talked over some of the other portfolios. He cordially agreed with all I had in mind, particularly Glen for Secretary of State Department."

The discussions were carried on with various colleagues all day and a number of calls made to prospective appointees as Ministers, Parliamentary Assistants and to the Speakership and Deputy Speakership. One of these calls was to Major Bridges, the newly elected M.P. for York Sunbury, in New Brunswick. Mackenzie King said "I wanted to have a word with him quite privately. What I was saying was non-committal in any way. It was just to let him know the situation I was faced with. Told him we were naturally preparing for the session and that there would be some reorganization in some ways. In connection with the Government, I was very anxious, as all of my colleagues were, not to pass over fellows who were in a previous House for men who have not been in the House at all. Said it gave me a real problem as regards New Brunswick. Said what I was thinking of was this: If I did not make any other appointment to a portfolio at the moment, but were to appoint a Minister without Portfolio, and in order to bring in war veterans' association, would attach him to the war veterans' Department as a Parliamentary Assistant—would leave this arrangement for this session of Parliament and probably make some readjustments later on—would that appeal to him at all? Bridges said he would like to have a word with Premier McNair to whom he says he owes a great deal. He understood that I was suggesting there would be no other Minister from N.B. at present—he would be the only Minister in the Government but would be in without a portfolio. At the same time, he would be Parliamentary Assistant to the Minister of War Veterans. Said he himself would be ready to do anything—serve in any way, whether he served as private Member or otherwise. He wanted me to know that was his attitude but that he felt he owed it to McNair to have a word with him. Would let me know later on this evening, if not, then in the morning."

The next person he telephoned was James Sinclair in Vancouver, to let him know "That we were thinking of consolidating three Departments of Defence under one man, and associate with him two or three Parliamentary Assistants. I was wondering whether if I were to put forward his name, he would be interested in having me suggest him as Parliamentary Assistant for Air. Sinclair said he would be very honoured to act as a Parliamentary Assistant. Thanked me very much for having him in mind. He has been retired from the Air Force. Has visited his constituency and everything is in good shape. He would be very glad indeed to have any part. Seemed quite happy and pleased."

The next morning (August 24) Bridges telephoned "to say he had talked with McNair. That he, himself, was ready to do anything that was desired but he would like to come to Ottawa for a personal conversation before making any final settlement. I stated I was anxious to make announcement today regarding Ministry. Might have to do that apart from N.B. but understood his desire to have a talk first. He said he hoped I was not annoyed at his not accepting at once any suggestion. I told him not at all. I did see advantage to a conversation but would have to leave it until Monday. I might have to have him come out to Kingsmere."

That day Mackenzie King telephoned Wishart Robertson at Bedford and sounded him out about taking the leadership of the Government in the Senate. At the Cabinet meeting that afternoon Dr. King was appointed Speaker of the Senate, Robertson was appointed leader and several other appointments were made and announced.

The Cabinet changes and other appointments were not completed until August 29 when McCann went to National Revenue, Bertrand to the Post

Office and Bridges to Fisheries, a move to please Premier McNair. All the prospective Parliamentary Assistants who had been approached were appointed except Sinclair; his appointment was not made because, in the end, Mackenzie King retained Colin Gibson as a separate Air Minister.

At the end of August, General de Gaulle paid his second visit to Ottawa, a visit about which Mackenzie King had earlier been doubtful. He arrived by air on the evening of August 28. Mackenzie King found him "particularly friendly." They were photographed many times together at the airport. Bidault was with de Gaulle and Mackenzie King noted that "he kept very close to me throughout the evening."

At Government House, de Gaulle sought out Mackenzie King for a talk. "It was clear," he wrote, "from what de Gaulle said in conversation that he thought Churchill and the President had gone too far in what they had done for Russia at Potsdam. He thought they should have stood up a little more firmly against some of the pressure that the Russians were putting on and that they would have yielded. When I spoke of Churchill, he used the expression 'poor Churchill' as much as to say that he felt sorry for him in his defeat though he was not saying anything about him one way or the other. I was surprised too to find that he still seemed to have a little feeling against Roosevelt. I sought to dispel that but there is something in the U.S. relation to France that I do not yet comprehend. He spoke nicely about President Truman but did not seem to be enthusiastic about the States. He seemed to feel both the U.S. and Russia were too conscious of their power and determined to manage everything. He was more friendly toward Britain than toward either of the others. He talked about his elections coming in the autumn. Explained the changes in the Constitution that were being sought. Seemed to feel quite sure that the elections would go as he hoped they might. He spoke most appreciatively of Canada's help during the war. Spoke of the food being a serious situation and particularly the lack of coal. He is not too optimistic about conditions in Europe."

The following morning de Gaulle and Bidault came to the Library at Laurier House for a talk. Mackenzie King "asked de Gaulle if there were any matters he would like to speak of in particular. He then spoke about what Canada had done, thanking us very warmly. Spoke particularly about the great need for trucks and certain classes of equipment, machinery, etc., to enable them to get on their feet. He also spoke about conditions in the Ruhr. Felt that the right settlement had not been made about the coal. That the problem of fuel was going to be a very serious one.

"I referred to the loan we had given France. Of this he was most appreciative. He then repeated part of what he had said to me the night before about not being satisfied with what was done at Potsdam. Began speaking about the Council of Foreign Ministers and their meetings. This caused me to speak of my feeling that Canada should be represented on the Council as a nation. . . . Finally de Gaulle asked me if I had made any representation along the line of which I was speaking, to Britain. I told him that the night before, I had sent a telegram in which I made it quite clear that I did not think the post-war settlement should follow the pattern of what had been done during the war itself. I spoke of Canada having made a very great contribution and that I felt on any matters on which we were expected to assume responsibility, we should be given fullest powers, not merely consultation but of complete knowledge by being parties to the Conference. I spoke of Canada feeling now toward the big Five much as France had felt toward the big Four. I pointed out that we were not particularly interested in political developments, in the fixing of boundary lines, etc. in Europe but that we were interested in the economic questions. I did not want it to be understood that we wished to get involved in all European situations. Quite the contrary. That we should be present at Conferences and would indicate where we thought it was best to leave certain questions to others but make our own contributions as to a point of view. I drew attention to the Canadian flag which I had on the flag pole at Laurier House. Told him it was the first time I had flown the Red Ensign there since I had been Prime Minister. Also that we were flying the Red Ensign on the Parliament Buildings today in his honour, this being the flag our Canadian forces had fought under.

"I told de Gaulle he could regard that as a symbol of the feeling we had of the place Canada occupied as a nation among nations. That we intended to assert that position very strongly.

"In speaking about the Russians, de Gaulle spoke particularly about how enigmatical they were. Of their complete silence and impossibility of knowing what they were thinking. They would only make one statement and say nothing more.

"After we had been talking—the conversation took from 11 till about 12—de Gaulle said to me privately, he was in entire accord with all that I had said. He appreciated our point of view completely and understood it, was sympathetic toward it. I thought it well to have our position known to him so that he could perhaps be helpful in getting our side more fully recognized in further settlements.

"Bidault who had not heard what de Gaulle said to me privately, said to me afterward that he was sorry the President, as he called him, had not spoken out about understanding our point of view and agreeing with it. He, Bidault, said he approved it entirely. He thought de Gaulle did also. I told him of de Gaulle's word with me in private."

After de Gaulle left Ottawa, Mackenzie King attended a Cabinet meeting and then had a press conference where, in addition to indicating the Cabinet changes, he "announced the intention of the Government to disband the Pacific Force as soon as the terms of surrender of Japan were signed. Also that it was not the intention of the Government to have any of our forces employed in the occupation of Japan, though one or two naval units might be employed about the coast. I also gave out an announcement regarding plans for developing the Capital as a National Memorial. I was anxious to have this announcement made before the surrender and the signing of the terms. Also it seemed most appropriate to make it on the day of the visit of de Gaulle to Canada, especially as I secured from both him and Bidault permission for Greber to come to Canada at once to help in the development of plans for the far side of the Ottawa River and areas lying beyond."

On September 1 the Prime Minister had a visit from his old friend T. V. Soong, the Prime Minister of China. During the government dinner at the country club that evening, the whole party listened to the broadcast of the signing of the Japanese surrender terms and the speech by General McArthur.

On September 2, the great event of Mackenzie King's day occurred during a walk with Mrs. Patteson at Kingsmere just before dinner. "After we had gone a short distance," he wrote, "I suddenly saw rise up out of the grass some twenty yards away, a huge black bear with a brown nose. He put up his paws above his shoulders as though offering to surrender. Looked enormous. I could hardly believe my eyes but was filled with delight in seeing this animal on my own grounds. He then came down and ambled off slowly into the bushes. I shouted at Mrs. Patteson to look at him. She just saw him after he had begun to amble off. Later on the way back, she heard the Williamson family with some dog evidently discovering the bear was near their property. I waited and suddenly I saw him come across to the Farm. Mrs. Patteson saw him and went immediately to tell her husband. While she was gone, the bear ran across the field up to where the chicken houses are. From there, he ran across to the trees on the far side. Meanwhile Mr. Patteson had come out and they both were able to see him travelling across. To me, it was a glorious sight to see his leaps and the way in which he travelled."

While Mackenzie King was at dinner, word came that the bear was in the orchard. He "went out along with the servants. I walked down the road to within twenty feet of him and keeping on this side of the fence. The bear was eating apples, looking at me, and finally moved slowly about the orchard. We telephoned for Harry Dunn, the game warden, who was rather late in getting over. It had become quite dark when he arrived. I did not think he could have missed the bear but his shot did not hit it. Evidently he missed him and the bear got off into the woods. It was really a thrilling and exciting moment. Maria [one of the servants] was about as happy as I was. Thought I was very brave in going so near to him."

Mackenzie King's rural adventure seemed to symbolize the sense of relief, the sense of freedom, he and the Canadian people shared at the end of the war in Europe and Asia. Ahead were hard decisions about reconstruction and Canada's international responsibilities and, for Mackenzie King, personal decisions about his own role in the Liberal party and Canadian politics in the new postwar world.

Appendix

CHANGES, MACKENZIE KING MINISTRY
MAY 31, 1944 – AUGUST 31, 1945

October 12, 1944   Ian A. Mackenzie resigned from *Pensions and National Health* (abolition of the Department was authorized by law on June 30, 1944)

October 13, 1944   Ian A. Mackenzie appointed Minister of *Veterans Affairs* (creation of the Department authorized by law on June 30, 1944)

C. D. Howe appointed Minister of *Reconstruction* (creation of the Department authorized by law on June 30, 1944)

Brooke Claxton appointed Minister of *National Health and Welfare* (creation of the Department authorized by law on July 24, 1944)

November 1, 1944   J. L. Ralston resigned from *National Defence*

November 2, 1944   General A. G. L. McNaughton appointed Minister of *National Defence*

November 26, 1944   C. G. Power resigned as Minister of *National Defence for Air* and Associate Minister of National Defence (the latter office was not filled)

November 30, 1944   Angus L. Macdonald appointed *Acting Minister of National Defence for Air* (ceased to act on January 10, 1945)

January 11, 1945   Colin Gibson appointed *Acting Minister of National Defence for Air*

March 7, 1945   Colin Gibson resigned as Minister of *National Revenue* (J. A. MacKinnon appointed Acting Minister on March 8, 1945)

March 8, 1945   Colin Gibson appointed Minister of *National Defence for Air*

April 17, 1945   T. A. Crerar, J. E. Michaud, N. A. McLarty, Angus L. Macdonald and L. R. LaFlèche resigned from the ministry

April 18, 1945	J. A. Glen succeeded T. A. Crerar in *Mines and Resources*
	Joseph Jean appointed *Solicitor General* (this office had been vacant since October 23, 1935)
	Lionel Chevrier succeeded J. E. Michaud in *Transport*
	Paul Martin succeeded N. A. McLarty as *Secretary of State*
	D. C. Abbott succeeded A. L. Macdonald in *Naval Services*
	J. J. McCann succeeded L. R. LaFlèche in *National War Services*
	D. L. MacLaren appointed Minister of *National Revenue*
June 8, 1945	W. P. Mulock resigned as *Postmaster General*. Colin Gibson appointed Acting Minister on June 9
July 29, 1945	D. L. MacLaren resigned as Minister of *National Revenue*. J. A. MacKinnon appointed Acting Minister on July 30
August 20, 1945	General A. G. L. McNaughton resigned as Minister of *National Defence*
August 21, 1945	D. C. Abbott appointed to succeed McNaughton in *National Defence* and continued in *Naval Services*
August 23, 1945	J. H. King resigned as *Minister without Portfolio* and was appointed Speaker of the Senate
August 28, 1945	Ernest Bertrand resigned as *Minister of Fisheries*
August 29, 1945	Ernest Bertrand appointed *Postmaster General*
	J. J. McCann appointed Minister of *National Revenue* and continued in *War Services*
	H. F. G. Bridges succeeded Bertrand in *Fisheries*
	Wishart McL. Robertson appointed *Minister without Portfolio* and Leader of the Government in the Senate

THE MINISTRY, August 31, 1945

Prime Minister, President of the Privy Council and Secretary of State for External Affairs	W. L. Mackenzie King
Minister of Veterans Affairs	Ian A. Mackenzie
Minister of Finance and Receiver General	J. L. Ilsley
Minister of Munitions and Supply and Minister of Reconstruction	C. D. Howe
Minister of Agriculture	James G. Gardiner
Minister of Trade and Commerce	James A. MacKinnon

Minister of National Defence for Air	Colin W. G. Gibson
Minister of Justice and Attorney General	Louis S. St. Laurent
Minister of Labour	Humphrey Mitchell
Minister of Public Works	Alphonse Fournier
Postmaster General	Ernest Bertrand
Minister of National Health and Welfare	Brooke Claxton
Minister of Mines and Resources	James A. Glen
Solicitor General	Joseph Jean
Minister of Transport	Lionel Chevrier
Secretary of State of Canada	Paul Martin
Minister of National Defence and Minister of National Defence for Naval Service	Douglas C. Abbott
Minister of National Revenue and Minister of National War Services	J. J. McCann
Minister of Fisheries	H. F. G. Bridges
Minister without Portfolio and Leader of the Government in the Senate	Wishart McL. Robertson

Parliamentary Assistants (not of the Cabinet):

National Defence (Air)	Hon. Cyrus MacMillan, April 29, 1943 – March 15, 1945
Munitions and Supply	Lionel Chevrier, April 29, 1943 – April 16, 1945
Finance	D. C. Abbott, April 29, 1943 – March 7, 1945
National Defence	William C. Macdonald, April 29, 1943 – November 14, 1944
	D. C. Abbott, March 8, 1945 – April 16, 1945
Justice	Joseph Jean, May 6, 1943 – November 30, 1944
Privy Council	Brooke Claxton, May 6, 1943 – October 12, 1944
Labour	Paul Martin, May 7, 1943 – April 16, 1945

Index